The Second Skin

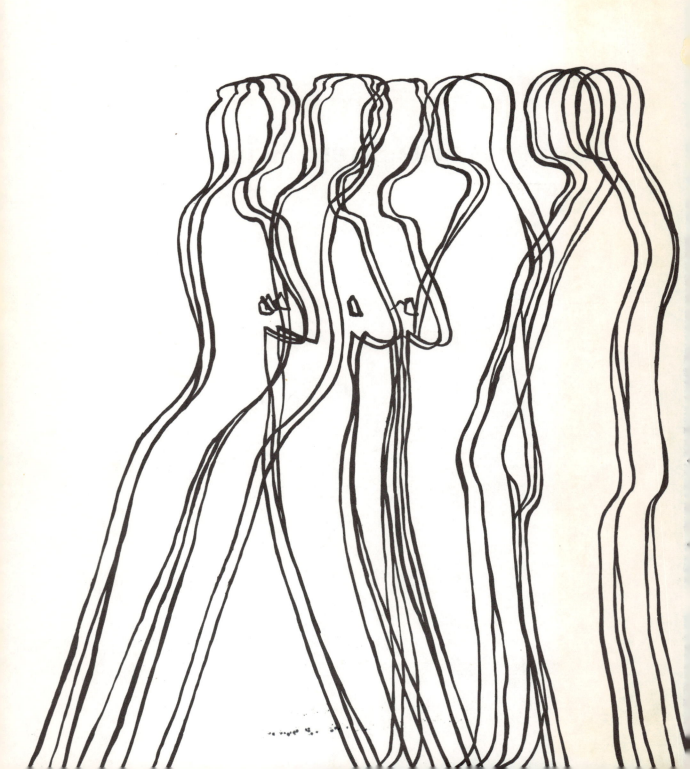

The Second Skin

AN INTERDISCIPLINARY STUDY OF CLOTHING

MARILYN J. HORN

University of Nevada

HOUGHTON MIFFLIN COMPANY / BOSTON

Atlanta

Dallas

Geneva, Illinois

Hopewell, New Jersey

Palo Alto

London

To the memory of my father

Library of Congress Catalog Card Number: 74–20115

ISBN: 0-395-18552-1

Preface

The rationale for the organization and content of *The Second Skin* is summarized in the subtitle: *An Interdisciplinary Study of Clothing*. It is based upon the philosophy that clothing decisions in real life are influenced by a multitude of factors, and rarely made on the basis of a segmented set of criteria. Clothing needs are not only complex, but they are often in conflict. It is the intent of this book to place the study of clothing within the comprehensive context of its cultural, social, psychological, physical, economic, and aesthetic relationships.

Any book that discusses contemporary dress is outdated before it goes to press. We live in an era of unprecedented fashion change, and nothing appears more ridiculous to the eye than the style which most recently faded into obsolescence. For this reason, many of the illustrations for this edition have been selected from historical or primitive sources. Unless some application is made, however, to current clothing practices, students are quick to assume that the theories are outdated and bear no relevance to life as it is lived today.

It is true that many theories relating to clothing have been very tentative in nature, and the findings of subsequent research and analysis have forced us to reject some of the early hypotheses and proceed along alternate paths. Advances in technology have also altered many of the concepts in textiles. For the most part, however, research is an extremely slow process, and it takes a long time to accumulate enough evidence to reject *or* confirm a whole body of theory.

A change in theory should not be confused with a change in emphasis. The relative importance attached to different aspects of dress shifts over time, and certain values take precedence over others. The earliest textbooks in clothing, for example, were published in the days when making garments in the home was the predominant if not the only way to provide the family with suitable attire. No wonder, then, that for the most part these were manuals on pattern-making and clothing construction. As the ready-to-wear industry developed, much of the early merchandise and workmanship was fairly shoddy, and textbooks began to include more information on consumer buying techniques to aid in the evaluation of garment quality. As goods became more plentiful, greater attention was given to the aesthetic values of dress, and chapters devoted to the application of art principles were gradually expanded.

It was in 1948 that George Hartmann,[1] speaking to a group of college teachers of textiles and clothing, asserted that the study of clothing

---

[1] See George W. Hartmann, "Clothing: Personal Problem and Social Issue," *Journal of Home Economics*, Vol. 41, No. 6 (June 1949), pp. 295–298.

behavior was a neglected but permanent and significant part of education. His admonition gave impetus to a growing concern and interest in the social and psychological aspects of dress. At first, attention centered around the importance of clothing in the personality development of the child. Little by little, as research tools improved, there evolved a body of empirical data which provided a sounder basis for the teaching of the impact of clothing on the social and psychological security of the adolescent and adult.

The body of subject matter, however, that gradually evolved into what we now call the socio-psychological aspects of clothing actually began with the early theories developed prior to 1930 by such writers as Veblen (1899), Flaccus (1906), Dearborn (1918), Kroeber (1919), Flügel (1930), and Hurlock (1929), among others. The economic depression of the thirties then suddenly forced a shift in our hierarchy of needs, and it was not until the period of growing prosperity that followed World War II that we could afford to refocus attention on the social values of clothing.

In the early 1970s, we witnessed a shift to an anti-aesthetic philosophy in which the bad was beautiful, and the beautiful was worthless. Teachers of clothing sheepishly changed the term "art principles" to "guidelines," (if, in fact, they mentioned them at all). Many were led to believe that the principles were no longer valid for judging design according to the current standard. Instead of rationalizing our judgments by rejecting the principles, let us recognize that we live in a period in which aesthetic values are unfashionable. It is not the first time in fashion history that this has occurred.

To be well informed on the subject of clothing, one needs the perspective of history as well as a continual source of new information. A textbook can give you the first, but not the second. Even a revision takes months of work by the author, followed by a year or more in production by the publisher, so that much of the material is old before you get it. Consequently, there is a tremendous need to supplement the text by keeping abreast with the times. I hope, therefore, that you will challenge, explore, test, analyze, and evaluate the theories presented in the chapters that follow within the framework of the most current information available.

I am indebted to my co-workers, Mildred Amis and Barbara Jean Margerum, for their help in gathering material for this revision; to Edmund R. Barmettler for his helpful and critical review of Part Five; and to Esther F. Rupel for her critique of the first edition.

MARILYN J. HORN

Contents

The Second Skin

1
Introduction

THROUGHOUT recorded history, clothing—along with food and shelter—has been recognized as one of the primary needs of mankind. The average person, however, is apt to interpret the significance of clothing solely in terms of physical or utilitarian needs, such as the need for protection against the weather. Often we forget that everyone has a variety of social and emotional needs that also must be met in some way.

Significance of clothing

There is probably no sphere of human activity in which our values and lifestyles are reflected more vividly than they are in the clothes that we choose to wear. The dress of an individual is a kind of "sign language" that communicates a complex set of information and is usually the basis on which immediate impressions are formed. Traditionally, a concern for clothes was considered to be a feminine preoccupation, while men took pride in the fact that they were completely lacking in clothes consciousness.

This stereotype of American culture is gradually changing as masculine attire takes on greater variety and color. Even as early as 1955, a research study in Michigan[1] revealed that men attached rather high importance to the value of clothing in daily life. White-collar workers in particular viewed dress as a symbol capable of manipulation, that could be used to impress or influence others, especially in the work situation. The white-collar worker was described as extremely concerned about the impression his clothing made on his superiors. Although blue-collar workers were less aware that they might be judged on the basis of their clothing, they recognized that any deviation from the accepted pattern of dress would draw ridicule from fellow workers.

---

[1]William H. Form and Gregory P. Stone, *The Social Significance of Clothing in Occupational Life*, Technical Bulletin 247, Michigan State College Agricultural Experiment Station, June 1955.

Since that time, of course, the norms have changed: the typical office worker may now be wearing the blue shirt, and the laborer a white shirt; but the importance of dress has not diminished. Other investigators in recent years have helped to establish its significance in the lives of individuals at various age levels and in different social and economic status groups.

Clothes also can be seen as an intimate part of the self. Hurlock once described this relationship as follows:

> We are apt to think of clothes as we do of our bodies, and so to appropriate them that they become perhaps more than any of our other possessions, a part of ourselves . . . in spite of the constant changes in clothing, it is still impossible to disassociate ourselves from this intimate part of our material possessions. We appropriate the admiration our clothes call forth, and this tends to enhance our own self-esteem. Indeed the Bohemian immigrant girl who, it is related, expressed her life philosophy in the short sentence: "After all, life is mostly what you wear," expressed the life philosophy of the majority of people who have inhabited this world, either in the past ages or in our modern twentieth century.[2]

Thus, on the basis of research done to date, as well as on the points of agreement found in some of the early writings concerning the interpretation of clothing behavior, we see that clothing is a symbol of crucial social and psychological importance to the individual. As such, it serves to communicate to others an impression of one's social status, occupation, role, self-confidence, and other personality characteristics.

Moreover, the ways in which individuals and families have fulfilled their clothing needs over the years provide ample evidence that the patterns of production, distribution, and consumption of clothing figure largely in the economic development of a country. In most cases, clothing behavior is influenced by the same forces—social, psychological, and economic—that affect other aspects of human activity. Even when this behavior manifests itself in fashion—a phenomenon that is often thought to be random and purposeless—there are fairly regular patterns which may be discerned. Not only do fashions follow a progressive and irreversible path from inception through acceptance to culmination and eventual decline, but they also tend to parallel to some extent the larger events of history.

In a detailed study of dress styles from the year 1788 to 1936, anthropologist Kroeber noted that the first forty-five years were marked by rather agitated fluctuations in design forms, while the modes in dress from 1835 to 1905 were relatively steady and tranquil. This was followed by another thirty years of comparative instability. He attributed the first period of agitation to the sociopolitical tensions that accompanied the French

---

[2]Elizabeth Hurlock, *The Psychology of Dress*, Ronald Press Company, New York, 1929, p. 44.

Revolution and the ensuing Napoleonic wars; while the seventy years of tranquility coincided exactly with the peaceful reign of Queen Victoria and concomitant industrial development. The second period of instability was accounted for in the mounting unrest that preceded and followed the first World War.[3]

In an earlier analysis, Kroeber presented the following observations in the comparison of long-term fashion swings and the growth in art styles:

> In painting, neoclassicism, romanticism, impressionism, expressionism, cubism, have each lasted no longer than some trends in Western dress; and the degree of change effected by them is no greater. The total form and effect of Occidental clothing in 1815, 1865, and 1915 seem about as different as canvases painted in the classic manner in 1790 are different from the romantic ones of 1840 and these from the impressionisms of 1890 and surrealisms of 1940. The main difference is that we like to think of picture-painting and art exhibitions as serious and dignified, and of clothes and fashion shows as frivolous. But the behavior manifestations of the two sets of phenomena are much alike, so that we are justified in assuming that the processes at work are similar. One might even suspect the genuineness of the greater formal or avowed respect accorded the painter's activity. Presumably for every ten people in our civilization really exercised about a change in the manner of paintings there are a thousand who participate personally in changes of dress style, and who would be intensely perturbed if poverty or a sumptuary law prohibited them from conforming.[4]

Thus, we see clothing as one of the most personal components of daily life, and at the same time as a manifestation of social activity deeply embedded in the cultural scheme of an era.

An interdisciplinary approach

A review of the literature related to clothing will indicate that the manifestations of clothing behavior have been interpreted from many points of view. Over the past fifty years there has been an exciting growth in the body of subject matter that constitutes this field of study. Many of the theories advanced by early writers are now being tested by anthropologists, historians, home economists, psychologists, and sociologists, many of whom are working together on problems of common interest. By its very nature, the study of clothing is rooted in a number of the natural and social sciences.

---

[3]A. L. Kroeber, *Style and Civilization*, Cornell University Press, Ithaca, N.Y., 1957, pp. 10–18.
[4]A. L. Kroeber, *Anthropology*, Harcourt, Brace and Company, New York, 1948, p. 392.

Anthropology

In order to gain even a limited understanding of the meaning of dress and adornment, we must explore some of the theories that explain why man chose to wear clothes in the first place. Much of our understanding of motivation in dress comes from anthropologists' cross-cultural comparisons of primitive societies. Anthropological studies enable us to conclude, for example, that clothing used as an expression of modesty is a function that is determined by the culture, learned by the individual, and not very likely instinctive in nature. People cover or decorate their bodies for a variety of reasons, "chief among which are status identification (symbolic advertising of social position), protection against inclemency of climate, real or imagined self-beautification or enhancement, and magico-religious requirements."[5]

History

Culture and society, although they exist in the present, derive from the past. The historian's methods make it possible for us to interpret current clothing phenomena against the perspective of time. By noting repeated regularities or fluctuations in dress over extended periods of time, we are better able to explain and predict the probable effects of social change on patterns of dress. Contemporary styles are not the unique and spontaneous creations of the era in which we now live. They evolved out of the past, and what they will be in the future depends to a great extent upon the conditions and influences that impinge upon them today.

Psychology

Much clothing behavior is psychological in nature. Psychology is the field of science that is concerned with how the individual organism responds to specific stimuli. It is centered around the basic concepts of motivation, learning, and perception. In many ways clothing is, in psychological terms, both a stimulus and a response. People perceive a clothing stimulus in different ways, and they interpret its meaning according to the associations they have learned to make with it over a long period of time. In addition, clothing is a tangible and observable phenomenon that is important to the concept of self and the development of personality. It is often a symptom of suppressed needs and desires, and the analysis of dress can lend insight to a number of hidden psychic processes.

Sociology

The sociologist, of course, is also concerned with human behavior, but in a collective sense. He focuses upon the regularities of human action that stem from society rather than upon that which is peculiar to the individual. Thus the normative aspects

---

[5]E. Adamson Hoebel, *Anthropology: The Study of Man*, McGraw-Hill Book Company, New York, 1966, p. 286.

of dress as seen through the rise and decline of fashions demonstrate one of the most basic social tendencies of man—the sharing of habits and ideals and conformity to a set of group expectations. The link between the individual and society as a whole is provided by the concepts of role and status. In this respect, clothing serves as a symbol of the role and status of the individual in society, and it obtains for the wearer the rewards of recognition, approval, and identification.

Art

The field of art usually is classified as one of the humanities rather than as a science, but it is nevertheless essential to a comprehensive study of clothing. One of man's most remarkable characteristics is his universal search for beauty and adornment. The standard for what is considered "beautiful" is subject to rather powerful cultural mutations, but any aspect of dress that provides perceptual pleasure can be considered a part of man's aesthetic experience. The ornamental potential of clothing is an important outlet for artistic drives and self-expression, as well as a source of tremendous sensuous satisfaction. Clothing also can be seen as an artifact that captures and reflects the whole spirit of an art movement that emanates from a particular set of social conditions.

Physics

The urge to beautify through dress and adornment is perhaps second only to the basic drives linked to biological survival. Clothing acts as a buffer between man and his environment, shielding him from the harmful elements of climate, infection, and trauma. In order to make the most effective use of clothing in the purely physical sense, one must understand the fundamental principles of heat exchange and have a supplementary knowledge of the physical properties of fibers, fabrics, and garments.

Physiology

Beyond this, there are a number of physiological adaptations to the environment made by the human organism which affect body comfort and alter the need for protective clothing. Conversely, a body covering can reduce the need for caloric intake and can influence other physiological processes as well.

Anatomy

The need for protection is closely allied with the desire for comfort. An understanding of the anatomical structure of the human body and its related movements is essential to the creation of functionally designed clothing that is comfortable, utilitarian, and convenient.

The economic significance of clothing is readily seen in relation to the individual and the family, yet its greatest impact lies in the contribution of the textile and apparel industries to the

Economics

American economy as a whole, and in their role in international trade. Through the study of clothing we are able to observe the factors of consumer demand, purchasing power, and market supply, and we can relate these to the production, distribution, and consumption of textile and clothing products at all levels—individual, local, national, and international.

Need for an integrated theory

Thus, it becomes clear that clothing is a product of a complex set of motives, all of which are interdependent and arise out of varied physical, psychological, and cultural conditions. It is obvious that an integrated theory is required to make an objective and satisfactory analysis of clothing needs and practices. Such is the plan of this book.

Plan of the book

Part One, Clothing and Culture, discusses clothing within the context of its anthropological and historical origins and relates it to the development of technology, folkways, mores, customs, laws, attitudes, and values. Part Two deals with the social and psychological aspects of dress, including its relevance to the self-concept and expression of personality, role, social status, and adherence to group expectations and normative social patterns.

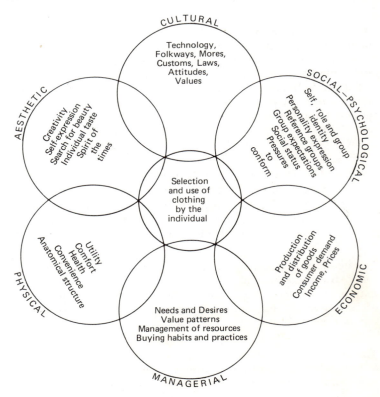

Figure 1-1. Schematic representation of the factors affecting clothing decisions.

INTRODUCTION

The related disciplines of art and philosophy are drawn upon in Part Three, Aesthetics and Dress. Clothing is analyzed as a medium for artistic perception, expression, and experience; as such, it is a parallel to other movements in the arts. Parts Four and Five emphasize the physical and economic aspects of clothing.

The final section of the book attempts to help the reader integrate his or her knowledge into a workable value pattern (which will by no means be the same for everyone). The student is asked to examine his own needs and desires, and to organize a system in the management of clothing resources that will minimize conflict and achieve the desired goal. The approach to clothing decisions from an interdisciplinary point of view seeks to avoid the distortion of values that may result from a fragmented study of selected aspects of dress.

The analysis of clothing behavior

In any field of inquiry, a scientific approach depends upon the organization of observations and experiences. In the ordering of our observations of clothing behavior, we seek to identify the common, regular, and repetitive elements in the action patterns of individuals and groups. Secondly, we attempt to account for such patterning by noting the relationships that exist with other phenomena in the environment. Obviously, those patterns which are followed by the greatest number of individuals, and which are repeated in many successive situations, offer a relatively high degree of predictability.

Scientific approach

The chief characteristic of scientific analysis is objectivity. Developing objectivity in the field of clothing is likely to be far more difficult than in other fields of study, because our clothes are so intimately involved with personal feelings; each person brings with him a set of preconceptions which potentially can lead to biased observations or distorted interpretations. Very often what we "see" in making clothing observations is what we expect to see or what we are looking for. In order to control for such biases, we must seek to establish a systematic scheme for testing hypotheses and theories, and to organize the resulting body of knowledge into some type of structure. An understanding of this "structuring" is necessary in order to view the present study of clothing in the proper perspective.

Need for objectivity

The first step toward understanding any field of study is the mastery of certain basic concepts. By **concepts** we mean words or descriptive terms that refer to an abstract idea. The most fundamental concept in the whole book, of course, is the term

Concepts

a

b

c

g

h

i

INTRODUCTION

d

e

f

Figure 1-2. Our consideration of bodily adornment includes any appearance modification made of the human form, such as tattooing, cicatrization, deformation, hirsuteness, hair plucking, ear piercing, and other forms of cosmetic surgery (**a**) Once a mark of manhood, the art of tattooing has spread to other fashionable applications. This young woman's chest is permanently stenciled with a colorful motif. (**b**) Scarification and (**c**) body deformation are indications of status in many cultures. (**d**) Shaving is as much of a modification as (**e**) the cut of the hair or the shape of the moustache (**f**) The trimming and arrangement of the hair is one of the most basic status representations in all cultures of the world. (**g**) Throughout history, the coiffure has been one of the most intense concerns. (**h**) The ear of this Masai girl is pierced with wire and sinew rings strung with beads. (**i**) Body painting is a less permanent form of decoration. (**j**) Body painting today.

j

clothing. This could be the abstract name or title assigned to anything that serves as a body covering. But there is much clothing that is not intended to cover the body at all, but rather to call attention to it. In the broadest sense therefore, the term clothing, or **dress** may be defined as any bodily adornment or appearance modification made of the human form. This definition would include such features as tattooing, cicatrization, cosmetic use, hair styles, hirsuteness, and so forth; it is the definition that we have accepted for use in this book.

Generalizations

Other examples of concepts related to clothing are words like *fashion, lifestyle, porosity, proportion, taste,* and others which constitute the building blocks of the field. Once the jargon or the language is understood, concepts then can be related to each other in the form of statements which explain how these concepts interact with each other. Depending upon their level of generalization, such statements may be called *hypotheses, propositions, postulates, principles,* or *laws.*

Theories

The ultimate goal, however, is the building of a body of logically interrelated generalizations known as **theory.** By theory, we mean a general summary of statements which explains the interrelationships among principles or propositions. Call it a conceptual framework, if you like, but the purpose of theory is to organize ideas into an integrated scheme. The goal is to move from narrow and specific observations to broader and more abstract applications.

The following chapters are designed to emphasize this kind of a structure. Each section is introduced by a presentation of some of the generally accepted theories related to the topic. This introduction is followed by specific illustrations which are used to (1) support the theory and (2) identify the common or uniform elements that will enable the student to generalize to a more abstract idea. Related research is cited whenever empirical data are available. The generalized statements which appear in the margin are intended to abstract the key idea in each unit of the chapter which is relevant to a wide range of observations. Rather than memorize such statements from the book, however, students should try to formulate their own statements of relationships. Finally, the summaries at the end of each section are more abstract formulations which tie the phenomena together in general terms. Essentially the summary is a restatement of the theory.

Predicting potential outcomes

Every field of study must proceed on the basis of an acceptable body of theory, even though much of that theory may not be subjected to scientific measurement for many years to come. The dynamic nature of clothing in itself forces us to reexamine clothing theories constantly in the light of changing social and technological conditions. Theories are essential to the analysis of clothing behavior, however, because they enable us to predict the possible consequences of particular clothing choices, not only in the lives of individuals, but to society as a whole. Thus, given a particular set of circumstances, the enlightened individual can make clothing decisions that will satisfy his personal needs, communicate to others the image he seeks to convey, and at the same time contribute to the best interests of others in the group.

The suggestion that clothes may be used to achieve certain goals is often looked upon with disdain by those who fear the connotations of manipulation. To "use" clothing, like the use of artifice, is to them like tampering with nature. But to employ no design in the utilization of our resources is to expect that the best will happen through a series of happy accidents. The aim of decision making in regard to clothing choices should be to secure, as Hartmann described it, the optimal value pattern — the choice that produces the maximum good.[6] This implies a conscious investigation and assessment of the functions of clothing as well as an ordering of one's clothing values. Those who see the "good" in clothing as the prestige that it affords, or as the comfort it provides, may still take their choice, but in full knowledge of the consequences.

Optimal value pattern

FOR FURTHER READING

Anspach, Karlyne. "Clothing Research in Home Economics, 1925–1958," *Journal of Home Economics* 51, November 1959, pp. 767–770.

Compton, N., and O. Hall, *Foundations of Home Economics Research: A Human Ecology Approach.* Minneapolis: Burgess Publishing Company, 1972. ("Textiles and Clothing," pp. 28–35.)

Harris, C., and M. Johnston. *Figleafing through History: The Dynamics of Dress.* New York: Atheneum, 1971. ("Before You Start — Why Should You?" pp. 3–10.)

Hartmann, George W. "Clothing: Personal Problem and Social Issue," *Journal of Home Economics* 41, June 1949, pp. 295–298.

Rosencranz, Mary Lou. "Social and Psychological Approaches to Clothing Research," *Journal of Home Economics* 57, January 1965, pp. 26–29.

---

[6]George Hartmann, "Clothing: Personal Problem and Social Issue," *Journal of Home Economics* 41, no. 6, June 1949, pp. 295–298.

Ryan, Mary S. *Clothing: A Study in Human Behavior*. New York: Holt, Rinehart & Winston, 1966. ("Introduction," pp. 2–7.)

Warning, Margaret. "Future Explorations in Clothing," *Journal of Home Economics* 52, October 1960, pp. 646–651.

DISCUSSION QUESTIONS

1. In what ways is the study of clothing based upon principles from the natural sciences? the social sciences? the humanities?

2. What is meant by a "scientific approach" to clothing decisions?

3. How has the emphasis on specialized aspects of clothing shifted over the years? What factors have influenced or contributed to this change?

PART ONE

Interrelationship of Clothing and Culture

2

Patterns of Culture

ALL OF MAN'S behavior stems from three basic sources: first, actions may result from *instinct*, appearing automatically without prior opportunity for learning; second, responses may develop through *trial and error*, a process that is conditioned by individual experience; and third, behavior may be *learned from other individuals*, either through imitation or direct tuition. It is the latter which by and large accounts for the distinction between human and animal behavior. This ability to transmit behavior patterns from one generation to another gives man an overwhelming advantage in the struggle for existence. Such learned behavior constitutes man's **culture,** or social heredity. Tylor's now-classic definition of culture is *that complex whole which includes knowledge, belief, art, morals, law, custom, and any other capabilities and habits acquired by man as a member of society.*[1] Without this accumulation and transmission of ideas and skills, the human race would never have progressed beyond the achievements of the Old Stone Age.

Our mode or manner of dress is a part of our social inheritance. The clothes that we wear are derived partly from the past, and partly from innovations that develop in our own lifetime. The evolution of certain forms of dress as the characteristic style of any era in Western civilization is the same evolutionary process that establishes the customs of dress for different tribal, geographical, social, and age groups. Clothing is an excellent example of the basic patterning that occurs within the context of particular technical, economic, moral, and aesthetic backgrounds. Yet, underlying the differences that result from varied cultural configurations, there are factors that appear to be common to all clothing and adornment, even within the vast span of time in which the arts of dress have developed.

It is our purpose here to examine the patterns of universality and variation in dress by means of a limited cross-cultural comparison. The term **pattern** is used to describe certain aspects of

---

[1]E. B. Tylor, *Primitive Culture*, John Murray Publishers, London, 1871.

clothing behavior that are consistent or repetitive (as opposed to those that are random). In making such a comparison, it will be seen that there are some common patterns of response in clothing that evolve in association with a given set of social and ecological circumstances. These common patterns are called **universalities**. As each society builds its culture, however, it makes a limited selection of patterns from all of those that are potentially available, and it rejects or ignores the others. It is this unique selection of patterns that makes every culture different in some respect from every other culture. A few such **variations** are described in the second section of this chapter.

To be able to discern the commonalities in clothing behavior is to understand a part at least of the orderliness and predictability of human action. At the same time, an analysis of cultural diversity helps us to see beyond the confines of our own habits and customs. Because our cultural conventions are so much a part of our own existence, we scarcely ever question their logic or rationality; they are "right" simply because they are familiar to us. If, on the other hand, we are aware that upon entering a place of worship the Jew puts on his hat, the Christian takes his off, while the Moslem removes his shoes, it becomes clear that one ritual of dress is no more "right" than the others, except within its own cultural setting. An acquaintance with other conventions should diminish ethnocentrism and lead toward a more rational pattern of clothing behavior.

Universalities in dress

Although the origins of dress and adornment remain obscure, there appear to be several universal motives underlying all clothing behavior. The earliest garments may have developed out of the necessity for protection from intense cold, but as soon as one's physical needs are provided for, any further creation or accumulation of items can only serve to gain greater prestige for the owner. A rich man may be able to wear more jewelry or clothing of finer quality, but the functional aspects of dress are the same for rich and poor alike. Man's natural acquisitive tendencies can be seen in his penchant for the accumulation of personal property, and because of the portable nature of clothing, it is highly probable that such items became one of the earliest indices of a man's wealth. The form that his clothing takes, however, is influenced by his physical environment, the resources that are available to him, and his technical skill in utilizing those resources. Man has found many diverse ways of fabricating and designing clothing, and yet from the technical standpoint, only three basic patterns of dress have evolved: the tailored garment, the draped garment, and a composite type which combines some of the characteristics of the other two.

Figure 2-1. Paleolithic tools: stone implements used to scrape the insides of animal skins to prepare them for cutting and needles made from bone and ivory.

Tailored garments, cut and sewn to the shape of the body, developed with the inventions of the sewing awl and the eyed needle.

The tailored garment

Man's concern and interest in his own appearance and comfort can be traced back as far as the Old Stone Age, when Neanderthal man inhabited the caves of Central Europe some twenty-five or fifty thousand years ago. Since man lived in and survived the years of glacial cold, it is logical to assume that he must have had some form of protective covering. He soon discovered, for example, that it was warmer inside the caves than it was outdoors:

> so, he smoked the bear out, killed and ate him with relish; then used the hide for the first form of human clothing. He had noticed that the bears did not freeze and, correctly, he attributed this to the fur, the uneatable outer layer of the bear. It was a racial emergency. If man could not connect in one plan of action such simple ideas, as bears, caves and furs, he was doomed.[2]

The simplest and probably the first article of clothing, then, was the untreated bear skin wrapped around the body like an enveloping cloak. Although actual garments do not survive in archeological deposits, indirect evidence is derived from the tools which were found among the remains. An untreated hide is stiff and board-like, but if the inside is thoroughly scraped of fat and flesh and then softened by beating, it becomes a flexible covering for the body. In order to do this, Neanderthal man fashioned crude stone skinning knives and bone scrapers. In the same caves and burials, pigments of red and yellow ochre have been found, indicating that even in this prehistoric period, man decorated his own body and perhaps the inner surface of his fur covering. The use of these colors gives us the first hint of adornment and the very beginnings of decorative art and design.

In the earliest stages, the animal skin was probably tied crudely about the waist and the neck with sinew thongs, but man soon realized that the warmth and comfort of his garment could be improved by shaping the skin to conform more closely to his body. In the later Paleolithic periods (including the Aurignacian, Solutrean, and Magdalenian cultures) there is evidence that man learned to cut the large skins into body-conforming shapes, first lacing the pieces together with thongs and later sewing them with needle and thread. The invention of the eyed needle was a product of the Magdalenian people who inhabited Europe about 14,000 to 8000 B.C. This simple yet brilliant device pierced the leather with its point and drew the binding thread through the hole all in one operation. Judging from the fineness of the needles found in the caves, we can assume that they were used for decorative stitching as well as for sewing the pieces of the costume together. In addition to the needles,

[2]M. D. C. Crawford, *Philosophy in Clothing*, The Brooklyn Museum, New York, 1940, p. 8.

Figure 2-2. Upper Paleolithic man wears a garment cut from animal skins and laced together.

Figure 2-3. Near the end of the Paleolithic period, clothing construction became an art. The Magdalenian woman on the right uses a needle to sew and to decorate her garments with geometric patterns.

other bone artifacts, such as buttons and toggles used to fasten the clothing, have been uncovered. Thus we see the evolution of the first tailor-made garment, cut from animal skins, shaped to fit the human body, and sewn together with needle and thread.

The draped garment

Clothing of the ancient Mediterranean civilizations, such as the early Egyptian, Greek, and Roman cultures, was not cut and fitted, but rather draped from a continuous length of cloth. The weaving of fabric was an outgrowth of two earlier developments—the cultivation of plants and the domestication of animals, neither of which appeared until Neolithic times. There is considerable evidence that man began farming about 6000 or 7000 B.C.; he gradually perfected the techniques that enabled him to take the wool from sheep and the fibrous material from plants and twist them into long continuous lengths of yarn. Remnants of actual cloth found in the Neolithic Swiss Lake dwellings attest to the use of flax fibers in the production of woven fabrics.

To be sure, people of the New Stone Age also had needles, but they seem to have used these implements largely for the decoration of cloth rather than for the construction of garments. Fabric woven on a primitive loom had the equivalent of a selvage on all four sides which would not fray out as long as the piece was kept intact. Weaving peoples were strongly disinclined to cut into loomed cloth, preferring instead to drape a rectangle of fabric around the body which was held in place by either its own folds or a band about the waist. In warm climates, the fabric was often nothing more than a small loin cloth, wrapped around the hips and tied with a cord or girdle.

Essentially, the *schenti* of the Egyptians, the *chiton* of the Greeks, the *toga* of the Romans, the *dhoti* and *sari* of the Indians, the *poncho* of South Americans, and the *sarong* of the

Figure 2-4. Tailored garments cut from the skins of animals are highly prized articles of clothing in the modern world.

Contemporary versions of the draped garment. **Figure 2-5.** Decorative toga from Ghana. **Figure 2-6.** Indian man wearing a wrapped skirt. **Figure 2-7.** Indian woman wears the draped sari, a long rectangle woven with decorative border along each selvage and across the end.

Draped garments, made from woven cloth which is never cut and seldom sewn, originated in Neolithic cultures having the invention of the loom.

Malayans, are all forms of the draped garment. Various cultures throughout history have decorated their fabrics by using dyes or prints, embroideries, or intricate weaves; also, an infinite number of design effects have been achieved by varying the size and shape of the piece as well as the method of draping. In most draped garments, the arrangement of folds is of equal importance to the decorative quality of the fabric.

The composite

Roughly 1500 years following the dawn of civilization in the Middle East, the Shang people in the Orient developed a culture that was almost contemporary with and fully comparable to the great civilizations of Mesopotamia and Egypt. It provided the foundation for the civilizations that later evolved in China, Japan, and other regions of the Far East. The Shang learned to cultivate the silkworm and wove its gossamer filaments into

Figure 2-8. Bronze Age costumes are early examples of the composite type. The material was woven from sheep's wool. The man's costume consisted of an undergarment which was wrapped around the body. The woman's dress was a waist-length, short-sleeved blouse with a slit at the neck for the head and a skirt which was draped around the lower part of the body.

beautiful fabrics. Although the traditional Oriental costume was tailored (i.e., cut and sewn), it also conveyed the effect of a draped garment through its straight-hanging lines and loose sleeves. While the ancient Chinese were a weaving people, their long contacts with the tailor-making needle-users resulted in a costume having some of the characteristics of both cultures. The pieces of the garment, rather than conforming to the shape of the body, were nearly rectangular in shape and usually were seamed on the straight grain of the cloth.

Modern clothing in the Western world is predominantly of the composite type, i.e., cut from woven cloth but shaped and sewn to conform to the contour of the body. Modified versions of the draped garment can be seen today, particularly in formal gowns, although they are rarely designed without seaming and stitching. Tailored garments of fur are still worn—not only by Eskimos—but by other people who live in suitably cold climates and have money enough to buy them.

As we study the early beginnings of clothing and trace the diffusion of the three basic patterns from one culture to another, it is the same story, as Crawford put it, told for convenience in separate chapters:

> No fundamentally new idea, either in costume or in fabric, in texture, design or color combination, has been evolved in the two hundred years which include the age of the machine. We are still working with the basic ideas evolved by craftsmen in different parts of the world and at different periods in the history of the world, brought together by the commerce of the world at various points of focus.[3]

A composite type of clothing, resulting from the early contact of skin sewing and weaving cultures, is the predominant type in use today.

Western dress predominates in much of the world today, yet many contemporary cultures still preserve the ancient traditions from which their costumes originally derived. These basic patterns of dress are visible expressions not only of the technical development of the peoples, but of their physical environment and their entire way of life.

The demise of basic patterns represents changes far more fundamental than a mere passing fashion, for the style of dress is linked to basic patterns of life and culture which are subject to the same forces of social change. The great diversity which now seems characteristic of our own form of dress reflects the intense geographic intermingling that occurs in the modern world.

Basic patterns of dress are expressions of the fundamental cultural patterning of different peoples.

SUMMARY *Universalities in dress*

The learned behavior that man transmits from generation to generation constitutes his social heredity or culture. The basic patterns of clothing and clothing behavior are part and parcel of the cultural configuration, and reflect the technical, economic, moral, and aesthetic backgrounds of a given society.

In spite of the varied patterns that have developed over the centuries, most of our clothing can be classified into three basic types: (1) the tailored garment, which probably originated in the regions of intense cold, was first cut and sewn from animal skins; (2) the draped garment, which developed in Neolithic cultures having the invention of the loom, was neither cut nor sewn; and (3) a composite type which resulted in a cut and sewn costume, made from woven cloth, either fitted or unfitted. The development of each basic pattern was closely linked to the cultural setting of the times.

---

[3]Crawford, *Philosophy in Clothing*, p. 19.

Diversity in clothing patterns

As we compare clothing patterns from society to society, we are struck by the infinite number of ways that human beings have found to utilize or fabricate materials, design and wear their clothing. What determines, for example, whether a man arises in the morning and dons a shirt and pair of trousers as he does in America, or wraps himself in a decorative toga as he does in Ghana? Several centuries before Christ, a young boy in the Aegean world might have described his attire as follows:

> On the feast day I woke at dawn. My old nurse dressed me in my best: my new doeskin drawers with braided borders, my red belt rolled upon rope and clasped with crystal, and my necklace of gold beads.[4]

A few thousand years later near the end of Queen Victoria's reign, a little ragamuffin, about the same age as the boy above, slipped into Windsor Castle only to be discovered by the scullery maid. After a thorough scrubbing by the Grenadier soldiers,

> . . . he was thrown a bundle from the housekeeper's charity bin. In this he found a boy's black trousers (patched) and stockings (heavily darned) which pretty well fitted him, a cambric shirt somewhat too large, a pair of shoes, battered but still serviceable and approximately the right size, a short jacket only slightly too long at the wrists, and an old cap. There was also a novel garment that delighted him. It was made of wool and had long arms and legs, and he had intended to put this on last as a sort of coverall, but the soldiers stopped him and made him put it on first. It felt pleasantly snug and warm, but it irritated his skin and he was not at all satisfied with the arrangement. But . . . he was thrilled with all these new clothes, the finest he had ever had in his life. . . .[5]

The time dimension which separated these two boys is not as significant as other differences we might note in cultural patterns. Effects of the natural environment can be seen as one factor which influences the diversity of clothing design; a lad clad only in a pair of leather shorts and necklace would hardly be comfortable in the cold dampness of Great Britain, nor would the snugly warm long wool underwear be a desirable garment in the sunny Mediterranean clime. The use of materials is markedly different, but we might suppose that this was due more to a difference in the supply of raw materials than to a wide discrepancy in technical skills; the Aegean culture had highly developed techniques for tanning leather, fashioning braid, working precious metals and stones. Nineteenth-century Englishmen possessed the same techniques but found it more economical to use a preponderance of wool. Perhaps the most

Figure 2-9. How the Aegean youth may have looked. (Painted stucco relief from the Palace at Knossos: "Prince with Plumed Headdress." 16th c. B.C.)

---

[4]Mary Renault, *The King Must Die,* Pantheon Books, New York, 1958, p. 5.
[5]Theodore Bonnet, *The Mudlark,* Doubleday & Company, Garden City, N.Y., 1949, p. 151 ff.

striking difference between the two cultures would be recognized in the aesthetic ideals expressed through dress: the bejeweled and decorated youth with his bright red belt and gold necklace stands out in strong contrast to the drab little Englishman in black suit and off-white shirt. Moreover, in Victorian society the idea of exposing one's chest and legs — even those of a small boy — would have been considered highly improper.

The second passage illustrates two additional culturally determined patterns. The patched trousers and the heavily darned stockings, even in the royal household, indicate the extreme frugality that was so characteristic of Victorian times. But more than that, a strict adherence to custom was demanded. Why was it necessary to wear a long wool garment next to the skin if it itched and scratched? Would it not have been just as warm and practical worn as a coverall instead of an underall as the boy originally supposed? Despite the logic of alternate patterns, however, the wearing of *under*wear as a permanent social habit precludes any possibility of wearing it as *outer*wear. Not only is there great variety from one culture to the next in regard to the kind and amount of body covering required, but within the same culture, standards for dress become modified with the passage of time.

Variation between cultures

At any given moment in human history, diverse patterns in dress serve to identify the cultural and often the geographic affiliation of groups and individuals. While striking differences still can be found in Far Eastern, Middle Eastern, and Western cultures, there are less striking but significant variations in nearly all cultures. In spite of the fact that the American heritage is so closely related to the British, for example, it is still fairly easy to spot an American in London, especially if he is over thirty. The U.S. version of the business suit is likely to be lighter in weight and more loosely cut than the Englishman's tailored tweeds. The Yank's softly finished wash-and-wear shirt is also in contrast to the more stiffly starched varieties worn by the British.

Even though the Savile Row tailors have been jolted by the Carnaby Street fashions, most of them continue to "speak in the tradition that accepts English tailoring as a symbol of English moral and political rectitude. A gentleman's attire, representing as it does a recognition of fashion but a denial of eccentricity, is an allegory of progress without revolution."[6] It was not until the latter part of the 1960's, for example, that the British gave up the five-button fly and accepted the zipper in the name of progress.

---

[6]John Canaday, "British Gentlemen's Tailor Advocates Zippers — In the Name of Progress," *The New York Times*, 19 December, 1966, p. 49.

Figure 2-10. A Frenchman wearing denim jeans, a *chemise cow-boy* (made in England), and tri-colored crepe-soled shoes. What cultural variations are apparent?

Figure 2-11. Proper British pickets wear their bowlers and polished shoes and carry rolled umbrellas. These insurance office employees were protesting working conditions at the Guardian Royal Exchange in London.

On the other hand, American travelers are regularly confronted by Britishers with offers to buy their authentic Levis and well-made shirts. While European ready-to-wear may have more flair in terms of fashion appeal, its quality and workmanship is decidedly inferior to what they call "American off-the-peg" clothing. Probably the only uniquely American fashion, Levis have become popular the world over. But even when worn with a Western shirt, subtle cultural differences are often apparent in accessories (see Figure 2-10).

To the French, the style of the true gentleman is still epitomized, however, by the London standard: closely fitted suit with vest, bowler hat, black polished shoes, and a rolled umbrella with wood handle.[7] Even though the London style is worn by few Frenchmen, it represents a cultural distinctiveness that is easily recognized.

Customs of dress vary not only in their social context but in terms of their religious significance as well. In New York, for instance, a religious Jew is easily recognized by the Hasidic overtones of his Western-style suit: the long, double-breasted black coat that buttons right over left instead of the usual masculine closing from left to right, and the large-brimmed black beaver hat. In many ways there is a strong resemblance between Hasidic and Amish dress, although the latter disdain buttons regardless of the direction of the closing. Many Moslem women still wear the enveloping veil in public, even though beneath it all they may have adopted a Western style of dress.

---

[7]"Est-il encore intéressant de s'habiller à Londres?" *Paris Match*, October 1972, pp. 32–33.

Morality is a close companion to religion, although standards for what is considered an acceptable degree of body exposure will vary from culture to culture. Many societies expose parts of the body which would be considered highly immoral in our own culture. An American male is expected to remove his hat in public, but certainly not his trousers—even though in most cases he would still be more adequately covered than he would be at the beach. A Chinese gentleman, on the other hand, may remove the outer layer of clothes without arousing anybody's indignation. The manifestations of morality in dress are discussed more thoroughly in Chapter 4, but it seems important to note here that dress as an expression of modesty is a cultural variation rather than being based in the universal laws of mankind.

It cannot be denied, however, that the jet age is rapidly supplanting these cultural variations with an international style of dress. Even today in the large cities of the world—Barcelona, Paris, Athens, Tel Aviv, Tokyo—there are more similarities than there are differences, especially among the youth. The disappearance of these distinctions in dress foreshadow the elimination of all other cultural differences as well.

The concrete facts of clothing behavior emanate from the culture and reflect a social inheritance of antecedent dress styles, customs, morals, and religion.

Variation within cultures

Thus far we have been discussing the widely diverse patterns of dress as they vary from culture to culture. But culture itself is never completely static or uniform; each age, each generation, each year, brings some modification of custom and accompanying clothing habits.

Probably nowhere in the world do fashions change more rapidly than they do along London's Kings Road. In sharp contrast to the traditions of fine English tailoring, the huge crop of boutiques put out a variety of fashions that change literally from week to week. The customers of these boutiques are usually young men from the working class. What they lack in the way of social position is counteracted by a monetary affluence. The far-out gear of these young Britons, however, has had a global impact on men's fashions in general. The fact that these styles gradually work up from the lower classes is some indication that Britain has moved toward a leveled society. "If style is a social expression, the jolt that Carnaby Street has given to English tailoring has its parallel in the jolt that the popular vote has given British government."[8]

Cultural change is always more rapid, and by the same token more obvious, when enforced through political disorganization or social upheaval. Radical changes in Western dress followed the French Revolution, and it is probably for this reason that

---

[8]Canaday, "British Gentlemen's Tailor," 1966.

INTERRELATIONSHIP OF CLOTHING AND CULTURE

Leopard-
trimmed
coats

Fringed
vests

Crepe-soled
shoes

Safari
suits

Striped jerseys
and canvas shoes

the costumes of the Directoire and the Empire periods are the favorite topics of fashion historians, for the events in France during those years influenced the costume of the entire Western world.

Oriental dress has undergone more radical changes in the last fifty to sixty years that at any other time in history. Under the Manchus, who ruled China from the seventeenth to the twentieth century, all Chinese males were ordered to wear their hair in Manchu style, i.e., shaved in front with the hair from the sides and crown braided into a long queue down the back. The traditional costume, which was completely indigenous to China, was the accepted form of dress for both ceremonial and everyday wear. Clothing symbols were prescribed rigidly according to rank and were enforced by law. Soon after 1900, the traditional patterns began to show subtle influences of alien designs, but the basic styles remained Manchu until the Revolution of 1911. It is significant, however, that these minor deviations in dress signaled the crumbling of the Manchu dynasty before the actual revolt.

The Revolution abruptly abolished the monarchy and began to demolish the entire structure of the former civilization. Sun Yat-sen introduced the military tunic with the high collar, worn with Western-style trousers. The elaborate costumes of the Imperial court were the first to be discarded, but the pageantry which had inspired all of the Chinese decorative arts and dress

Figure 2-12. A small sampling of the wide variety of styles that emanated from London's Kings Road in the early 1970's. Observers of the scene noted: "Somewhere in all this is the classic London pinstripe. There'll always be an England!"

Chinese official
c. 1850

Government official
late 19th Century

20th Century

Men's formal dress
1911–1949

Military dress
1936

Figure 2-13. Transition in Chinese men's dress. Today, Chou En-lai continues to wear a simplified version of the military uniform that symbolizes the Communist national spirit.

gradually disappeared as well. An edict was issued for men to cut off their long queues. Although many resisted, a Westernized haircut—formerly regarded as a suspiciously alien influence—suddenly became the symbol of nationalistic pride.

> The founding of the Republic in 1911 heralded deep-seated changes in China's political system and as a consequence her social structure. The everyday life of the people in the cities became subject to the increasing onslaught of outside influences and foreign methods which affected their manner of living, including their dress.[9]

A process of experimentation developed, and an intermingling of Western elements of dress with Eastern styles continued throughout the next few decades. After 1911, the most common Chinese men's costume consisted of the long gown worn with a soft felt fedora type hat and Western-style shoes.

---

[9]A. C. Scott, *Chinese Costume in Transition,* Theatre Arts Books, New York, 1960, p. 59.

For formal wear, men retained the Eastern style dress of a long blue gown worn with a short black silk tunic fashioned with wide sleeves and a mandarin collar.[10]

The increasing influence of Western dress was nourished further by the missionary schools and the fact that growing numbers of Chinese students went abroad to study in Europe and the United States. Chinese officials continued to wear their uniforms for most occasions, and this also contributed to the gradual disappearance of traditional dress. Although many men reverted to the gown or the loose tunic and trousers in the privacy of their homes, few wore anything but the typical Western business suit when out in public.

When the Communists came to power in 1949, they rejected the influence of both tradition and the West, turning instead to the examples set by Russia. Dress reforms were intended to symbolize the elimination of all class distinctions, and the entire nation—men and women alike—was cast into the drab, baggy uniform that marked the liberation of a new national spirit.

Still another example of cultural change is the gradual demise of the traditional *fez*, or *tarboosh*, in the Middle East. The dark red, brimless, cone-shaped hat was once the proud symbol of Arab manhood. Except for the servant classes in cities like Cairo and Beirut, the fez has now virtually disappeared from the scene. The first strike against the tarboosh came in Turkey, when Ataturk took over the Ottoman Empire in 1925. At first he tried to keep all government officials from wearing the fez by insidiously giving them a special allowance to buy new hats. When this failed, he banned the fez completely by forbidding any male citizen to wear it. Thus, the glory of the once proud symbol gradually waned in other parts of the Middle East as well, and as young Arab men took up the ways of Western culture, they discarded the fez entirely.

The same kinds of parallel changes in costume and culture occur in all societies, although they tend to be less noticeable when accomplished through evolutionary rather than revolutionary processes. Culture constantly is being modified by developments in the technical, political, social, and economic spheres of societies, and such changes are reflected visibly in the clothing of the people. The next three chapters deal specifically with the relationships between dress and the various cultural components that make for diversity in patterns of clothing behavior.

Figure 2-14. In China today, the loose tunic and baggy trousers comprise the uniform of the common man.

In all societies, standards of dress are modified by cultural changes that occur over a period of time.

---

[10]This appears to be a typical phenomenon in men's wear; traditional styles are relegated to formal dress before they are completely obliterated. In Western culture, the tailcoat, which started out as a riding habit, ended up as formal attire and is now virtually extinct.

SUMMARY   *Diversity in clothing patterns*

Man has found an infinite number of ways to satisfy his clothing needs. In different parts of the world and in different periods of history, people have utilized materials and designed
their garments in a multitude of patterns, each of which reflects
the unique combination of cultural elements that characterize
the society as a whole. Factors that influence the diversity of
costume design include the effects of the natural environment,
the supply of raw materials, the technical skills of the people,
moral standards and religious values, as well as aesthetic and
political ideals. As these cultural differences disappear, dress
styles also merge into more universal patterns.

FOR FURTHER READING

Beals, R. and H. Hoijer. *An Introduction to Anthropology*. New
York: Macmillan Publishing Company, 1965. (Chapter 13,
"Clothing, Shelter, and Transportation.")
Crawford, M. D. C. *Philosophy in Clothing*. New York: Brook-
lyn Museum, 1940.
Hoebel, E. Adamson. *Anthropology: The Study of Man*. New
York: McGraw-Hill Book Company, 1966. (Chapter 2, "Man,
Culture, and Society.")
LIFE, Editors of. *The Epic of Man*. New York: Time Incorpor-
ated, 1961.
Robertson, W. I. "The Stetson Story," *Nevada Highways and
Parks*, Spring 1973, pp. 26–31.

DISCUSSION QUESTIONS

1. What cultural conditions or circumstances gave rise to the
development of tailored garments? of draped garments?

2. How have the following factors influenced habits of dress or
adornment? Give at least one specific example of each:
(a) the natural environment, (b) moral standards, (c) religious values, (d) political ideals.

3. Compare British and American patterns of dress. How are
they similar? How do they differ? What factors may account
for such similarities and/or differences?

4. In what ways may clothing contribute to the stability or the
continuity of culture?

3

Relation to the Material Culture

CLOTHING IS but one of many elements that comprise the total culture of a group of people; yet it is one of the most visual expressions of the habits, thoughts, techniques, and conditions that characterize a society as a whole. A famous French philosopher, noting this close relationship between dress and culture, commented:

> If I were permitted to choose from the rubbish which will be published a hundred years after my death, do you know which I would take? . . . No, it is not a novel which I would pick in this library of the future, nor a work on history—when it offers something of interest it is only another novel. . . . I would take simply a fashion magazine in order to see how women will dress themselves a century after my death. And their fantasies would tell me more about future humanity than all the philosophers, the novelists, the preachers, or the scientists.[1]

Through the eyes of the anthropologist we are able to see how the design of a given costume is dependent upon the materials, the tools, and the techniques that are available to the maker of the garment. Also, by comparing clothing with other art forms, we observe that it reflects the typical mode of expression that characterizes the culture. In any given period, the style of painting, the design of a chair, the structure of a building, or the look of a woman are essentially the same.

As we shall see later, the development of certain styles in these **artifacts** of a culture reflect the less tangible **mentifacts**, i.e., the ideals and values, that are ascendant in that culture. Also, a study of the historical development of styles shows that changes in dress are conditioned by world events. The present

---

[1] The quotation by Anatole France is a translation by J. R. Hopkins, published in J. J. Brousson (ed.), *Anatole France Himself,* J. B. Lippincott Company, Philadelphia, 1925.

Figure 3-1. Probably the earliest garment was a hip covering made from the uncut skin of an animal.

chapter focuses on the relationship between the technical patterns of different societies and the resulting evolution of typical styles.

Technical patterns

There is no inviolate correlation between the amount of clothing worn and the natural habitat of a people, yet in general we can say that tailored garments of animal skins are usually found among aboriginals from the colder regions, while draped clothing is characteristic of those cultures which develop in warmer areas. Man has found numerous ways of utilizing the resources in his environment to fashion a body covering, and none of these techniques seem to be shared by all peoples of the world. Materials used for clothing, however, need to be fairly soft and pliable; relatively few are suitable in the natural state without some further processing to fit them for use. Consequently, man has had to devise methods and invent the tools necessary for the fabrication or manufacture of some form of textile.

Materials

Probably the first articles of clothing were made either from the uncut skin of a large animal or from leaves and grasses indigenous to the natural environment. The two familiar examples that come to mind are the fur hip coverings of Neanderthal man and the grass skirts of the Polynesians. Even in the modern world, animal and vegetable fibers still constitute the major source of supply for the textile industry on a global basis.[2] Animals still provide the pelts for fur coats and the hides for leather, although a more common method for utilizing animal products is to shear the hair or wool and process it as fiber. Although the wool from certain varieties of sheep is the most satisfactory fiber for cloth making, man has used the hair from camels, rabbits, horses, and numerous other animals in the manufacture of cloth.

Man has used the outer covering of birds as well. Feathers are particularly valued in the making of headdresses, but they have also been used for other articles such as capes and hip coverings.

Unprocessed vegetable materials in the form of leaves and grasses have extremely limited durability. Over the years man has perfected techniques for improving the serviceability and versatility of plant fibers. In the New World, cotton has been the most extensively used vegetable product, although flax, hemp, henequen, and pineapple fibers were also common. In

---

[2]Man-made fibers are gaining rapidly. See footnote 1, Chapter 17.

Figure 3-2. The most comfortable materials for clothing are those which are soft and pliable. However, people have had to make use of the materials available to them. The Indians, for example, gathered the long bark fibers from sagebrush to make fiber clothing. A Paiute Indian woman twines the sagebrush bark with a cordage of hemp into predetermined shapes. The resulting garments look like those on the right. The pants would be tied around the waist and legs with strips of buckskin.

primitive societies at least, the people who employ these fibers to make cloth must also cultivate the plant, so that the use of vegetable materials tends to be characteristic of agrarian rather than nomadic or hunting cultures. Sometimes the spongy bark of certain trees, such as the fig or mulberry, is stripped off in layers and pounded together to form a large sheet of cloth. Because of its paper-like qualities, bark cloth is not suitable for cutting and sewing and is therefore limited to use as a wrapped skirt or sarong.

The use of silk as a textile fiber harks back to 2600 B.C., when the legendary Empress Hsi-ling-shi dropped a cocoon into a bowl of warm water and discovered that the incredibly fine filament could be drawn out in a continuous length to form an unbroken thread. The Chinese kept the secret of the silkworm for over 2,000 years, until two monks hid some silkworm eggs in their hollow staffs of bamboo and carried them out of China. Other countries have attempted the tedious cultivation of the silkworm, but none have ever rivaled the Far East. Because the production and manufacture of silk requires not only the worm, but vast quantities of mulberry leaves to nourish it, sericulture

Figure 3-3. A worker stacks bundles of flax in preparation for the process of retting. The stalks are soaked in warm, soft water to loosen the linen fibers from the outer woody portions.

The raw materials available to man influence the design of his clothing.

Figure 3-4. Eskimos prepare the animal skins by chewing the hides until they are soft and pliable.

is limited to those areas having suitable climatic conditions. Today, the Japanese are the principal silk producers of the world.

Mention should be made of the materials used by man for protective clothing, or armor, since this area is the most conspicuously related to advances in technological developments. From the time of the Bronze Age which began about 2500 B.C., metal in various forms became a part of the warrior's costume. In the Greco-Roman period, a hinged cuirass of brass or bronze was molded to the shape of the chest and abdomen, and held in place with leather straps. Later the breastplate was made of iron, and then of small iron rings sewn closely together. This gradually evolved into the flexible coat of chain mail which became the typical garb of the knights of the Crusades. By the end of the fifteenth century the knight was encased in shining steel-plated armor, invulnerable from head to toe. Modern combat has become largely airborne and our attention is focused on flight suits and space suits. For these, we have the ever-expanding group of man-made fibers and synthetic materials, including aluminized fabrics, fiberglass, polyurethanes, and many others.

Man-made fibers also figure largely in civilian clothing consumption, and they are rapidly displacing the natural fibers as the predominant material used for clothing throughout the world.

Processes

Obviously few raw materials can be used in their natural state as wearable textiles without further processing of some kind. Animal skins must be thoroughly scraped and softened before they are suitable for clothing. Eskimos accomplish this by chewing the hides bit by bit until they are pliable. In other cultures, the skins are softened by mechanical methods, such as alternate beating and wetting and rubbing with oil. A more advanced technique is to treat the hide with tannic acid secured from the bark of certain trees, which keeps the leather soft and pliable even after repeated wettings. The true tanning process is known only in those cultures with a fairly well developed technology. In some areas where no large animals are available, several smaller skins must be joined together to make a complete garment. Skilled craftsmen can produce highly decorative patterns by combining different kinds of fur into one costume. Very often the most luxurious furs come from the smallest of mammals. Modern furriers utilize a technique known as the *letting-out process*, in which a small pelt is cut into narrow diagonal strips and sewn back together in such a way that one skin will extend the entire length of a coat. This greatly enhances the beauty of the peltry and also increases its pliability.

People that inhabit milder climates often completely remove the hair from the skin and cure or tan only the dermis to produce leather. American Indians favored the use of buckskin for much of their clothing, and many of the early American settlers adopted this durable leather for their own garments. The hair or the wool, minus the skin, could be used in still another way to fabricate a material suitable for clothing. The scaly structure and crimp of the fibers causes them to adhere together when agitated in a moist condition. Apparently these properties of wool were first discovered by an Asiatic people: they spread the fibers out in layers on a mat, moistened them with water, and then rolled the mat tightly back and forth from one end to the other for several hours until the fibers were firmly matted together. The resulting felt was commonly used for tents, saddlebags, boots, and rugs. Our modern use of felt as an apparel fabric is confined primarily to hats, since it is relatively thick and lacks strength.

The other principal methods of converting fibers into fabrics all require an intermediate step of spinning short lengths into long continuous yarns. The simplest method is to draw out the fibers, twist them together between the fingers, and wind the resulting thread onto a spindle. Many cultures used a distaff to hold the fibers, and weighted the end of the spindle so that it could be twirled and left hanging to provide a continuous and even tension to the drawn out strand.

Yarn is then made into cloth by weaving, knitting, braiding, or knotting. Of all the cloth making processes, weaving is by far the most common. The interlacing of yarns together at

Figure 3-5. In primitive societies, when hides from larger animals are difficult to obtain, the skins of smaller creatures are tied into ropes and woven into robes or blankets. After the pelts are stripped from the animals, they are scraped and linked together by tying the end of each skin through its own eyehole. The fur chain is then tied to a stick and twisted into a rope. The fur rope then is hung up to dry, and later the brittle ears are snapped off. It is then twined together with strings of hemp into the desired shape and size.

Figure 3-6. Modern furriers utilize a technique known as the "letting-out" process. The mink pelt is cut into small pieces and then resewn into a long, narrow strip.

The development and cultural diffusion of technical processes in the fabrication of clothing materials are key factors in the evolution of cultural patterns.

right angles was essentially the same technique employed to make baskets and grass mats, except that the soft, pliable yarns required some tensioning device at the ends to hold them in place. The prime implement in weaving, of course, is the loom — which consists of some sort of frame across which the warp yarns may be stretched and held in place as the filling yarns are inserted.

Even among nonliterate peoples, woven cloth was usually given some added treatment to improve its aesthetic qualities. Decorative patterns often were formed right in the weave by using different colored yarns, but if this was not done, the cloth would be taken from the loom and then dyed, painted, or embroidered. The technical skills and the characteristic styles developed by different peoples of the world in the decoration of cloth reveal many insights into their cultural habits. For example, design motifs are often symbolic in nature, and the source of an artist's inspiration is sometimes a clue to his beliefs and ideals.

Today, the development of new processes in the construction of clothing promises to change the character of our garments in the future. Tubular woven fabrics are already being pre-formed by steam-setting into a variety of seams, pleats, and gathers, a process which reduces the necessity for cutting and sewing operations.[3] Shapes can be set permanently into knitted fabrics made from thermoplastic fibers by pulling them over heated metal forms and then cooling them. The tube of fabric is subsequently cut at the neck and sleeves.[4] Other molding and fusing techniques rapidly are replacing the traditional methods of clothing construction. From the technical standpoint, once man has found a more efficient way to accomplish his task, he seldom goes back to the primitive method. This slow sharing of every progressive improvement from one culture to another is the process through which our modern technology has evolved.

Tools

Advances in technological processing depend on the invention or improvement of tools. Prehistoric implements discovered in archaeological diggings often provide the only evidence we have of man's early existence. In Paleolithic times, man had only stone scrapers to clean the animal hides and flint knives to cut the skins into garment-sized pieces.

The invention of shears did not come about until the ancients learned to work with metals. The earliest implement, probably devised to clip the wool from sheep, was forged from a single

[3]A. Sawhney, "Apparel Weaving — A New Concept," *Textile Industries*, December 1972, pp. 50–56.
[4]"Teijin 'Heat Sets' Dresses," *Women's Wear Daily*, 22 December, 1972.

bar of metal which then was bent until the blades came together. The first cross-bladed shears with a central pivot screw did not appear until centuries later. The art of tempering metals to a hard, sharp cutting edge developed slowly. It was not until the fourteenth century that the first steel scissors were made, and not until the invention of the famous Bessemer steel process in 1856—which sufficiently reduced the cost—that they came within the reach of those besides the very wealthy.

Today, electric cutters with blades mounted vertically in a maneuverable housing can slice with great speed and precision through many layers of cloth at a time. The laser beam is even more precise. The laser light, which is brighter than the sun, is aimed automatically at the cloth by mirrors and lenses. It can cut to a tolerance the width of a single thread, simultaneously annealing the edge of the fabric. The laser system also includes programmed cutting instructions, stored in a computer for repeated use.

Tools for sewing garments together came long after cutting tools but date back some 30,000 years. As we indicated in Chapter 2, the first implement was probably the awl, which pierced the animal hide for a sinew thread to be drawn through. Early needles, with the all-important eye, were made from polished bone, mammoth ivory and walrus tusks, wood, and drilled thorns. Later, the Mesopotamian cultures fashioned finer needles from copper, bronze, silver, and gold. Paralleling the development of shears, the first steel needles did not appear until the fourteenth century.

Attempts to mechanize the needle came as early as 1790, when an Englishman named Thomas Saint obtained a patent for a sewing machine to stitch leather. Some forty years later, Barthélmy Thimonnier in France produced a chain-stitch machine that used a needle resembling a crochet hook. By 1832, Walter Hunt, a New Yorker, had invented a lock-stitch machine that utilized two sets of threads and prevented the stitches from pulling out as they did in the older chain-stitch model. The invention of the modern sewing machine, however, is usually attributed to Elias Howe, who in 1846 patented a lock-stitch machine with a needle having the eye near the point rather than near the blunt end. A few years later, another machinist named Isaac Merritt Singer devised a machine with other improvements, and after negotiating with Howe, finally paid him $15,000 for the right to use his needle with the eyed point.[5] Since these inventions the needle trades expanded tremendously. Steam, water, and electric power have replaced the old treadle, and many industrial machines operate at speeds of more than 5,000 stitches per minute.

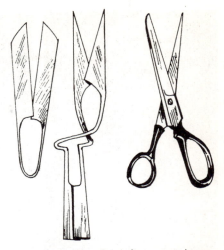

Figure 3-7. On the left are early versions of shears and scissors; right, a modern pair of shears.

Figure 3-8. Tools that were forerunners of the modern sewing machine. Tambour needle and frame showing the method of forming the chain-stitch, 1763.

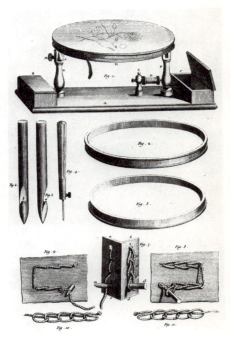

[5]Crawford, *Philosophy in Clothing*, p. 12.

Figure 3-9. Evolution of spinning processes. (**a**) Distaff and spindle (**b**) Early spinning wheel (**c**) Improved spinning wheel (**d**) Improved spinning jenny (**e**) Modern spinning frame.

INTERRELATIONSHIP OF CLOTHING AND CULTURE

Gradual improvements in the spinning of yarn over the years also were made possible through the invention of tools and machines. In Neolithic times, the distaff and spindle were used to twist wool, cotton, and linen fibers into continuous threads. The earliest spinning wheel was developed in India, but it was not introduced into England until the sixteenth century. Instead of twirling the spindle by hand, the spindle was attached to a driving belt and wheel which spun it rapidly. All spinning was done in the home until the latter part of the eighteenth century.

It was in 1764 that James Hargreaves devised a way to mount eight spindles vertically on a board so that one wheel could spin them all at the same time; by 1779, there were more than 20,000 "spinning jennies" in operation. Arkwright's spinning machine was an improvement over the spinning jenny, but it was so heavy that it had to be operated by water power. This gave rise to the establishment of a number of small factories that could provide the force necessary to run the large water frames, and it marked the transition of textile making from home production to the factory system. Modern spinning machines can whirl spindles at a rate of 10,000 times per minute. The newer man-made fibers undergo a process called chemical spinning in which the liquid is extruded through the tiny holes of a spinneret, solidified into continuous filaments, and twisted together to form a yarn.

Many forms of the primitive loom are still in operation among the non-literate societies of the world. Probably the earliest contrivance to weave cloth suspended the warp threads from a pole with the strands hanging free, but weavers soon discovered they could save much time by attaching alternate threads to a rod or stick that could be raised and lowered to form a space or "shed" for the filling thread to pass through. Also, a firmer cloth could be made by keeping the warp yarns under tension. This was first accomplished by constructing a rectangular frame the size of the finished piece of cloth. This system subsequently was improved by rolling the cloth onto a beam as the weaving progressed. Weaving remained a hand process until John Kay devised the flying shuttle in 1738, followed by Cartwright's heavy power loom. In 1801 a Frenchman named Jacquard designed an intricate loom that made it possible to control each individual warp yarn by a series of punched cards; it facilitated the weaving of elaborate floral patterns and figured damasks by a machine rather than a hand process. Modern automatic power looms and sewing machines have greatly increased the speed and efficiency of producing clothing. Even so, the needle and loom may one day give way to the mold.

The ancient processes of cloth and garment construction have been greatly accelerated through the development of improved tools and machinery.

SUMMARY *Technical patterns*

From a technical standpoint, it is clear that each method used by man to fashion a body covering for himself is influenced by

a

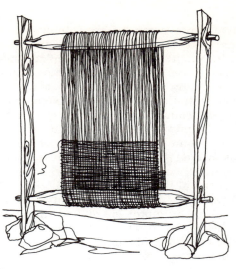

b

Figure 3-10. Evolution of the loom. (**a**) Earliest weaving apparatus (**b**) Simple primitive loom (**c**) Floor loom with pedals (**d**) Modern power (missile) loom.

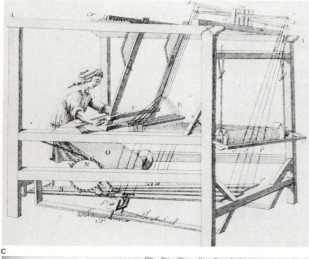

c

d

INTERRELATIONSHIP OF CLOTHING AND CULTURE

the availability of materials, the worker's skill and ingenuity in perfecting construction techniques, as well as the refinement and efficiency of his tools. In some cultures, people know how to tailor garments frm animal skins; some plait grasses or produce fringed skirts from leaves; others have the knowledge of the loom and weave cloth for their apparel. There are a few cultures which utilize more than one of these technical patterns, but it is rare—particularly in non-literate societies—that one pattern is not predominant. Even in our own technologically-advanced civilization, we still wear a preponderance of woven garments, cut and sewn into body-conforming shapes.

Evolution of styles

It is a fallacy to assume that because our modern scientific knowhow permits us to choose from all the technical patterns that man has thus far employed, our contemporary style of dress is therefore the most advanced order of apparel ever produced. In spite of all of our mechanical and chemical progress in the field of textiles, we have never been able to devise a garment that surpassed the efficiency of the Eskimo's garb in keeping out the cold. Yet, when the temperature drops below zero, we rarely see an American on his way to work in fur parka and mukluks. In all except a few primitive societies, there has always been an element of choice in the selection of one pattern over another.

Styles that are unique to a particular period or culture are of course limited by the technology. We might prefer a garment that is both warm in winter and cool in summer, lightweight, wrinkle-free, soil-proof, self-adjusting in size, and capable of changing its color and texture for the sake of variety—if we could figure out a way to make it. On the other hand, there are numerous techniques that reached the pinnacle of perfection in some bygone era but are unknown in the modern world.

In order to study the relation of clothing to the material aspects of the culture, we might sample from the thousands of years of man's history, comparing literate and non-literate societies, Oriental and Occidental, as well as ancient and modern styles of dress.

The Navajo

Perhaps more than any other aspect of the culture, costume reflects the historical experience of the Navajo people. If one knows nothing else about this southwestern tribe of American Indians, he knows at least that they weave rugs, which were made originally as wearing apparel. Like many other elements of their culture, however, rug weaving did not originate with the Navajos. Known as great culture-borrowers, the Navajos took over traits from nearly every group with which they came in contact. The culture of the modern Navajos, therefore, is quite different from that of their ancestors who migrated into the southwest from the northern regions of Canada.

Anthropologists believe that several hundred years ago these Indian people wore breech cloths and skirts made from yucca and grass fibers that were twisted and braided into a kind of cloth. Since they made their livelihood by hunting wild game, they probably also used buckskin for some of their clothing. About 1539, Spaniards began to invade the southwest, and the Spanish advances caused many Pueblo people to flee into Navajo territory. This contact with the Pueblos resulted in the development of weaving as a part of the local pattern of culture.

The earliest Navajo textiles were made in the natural colors of the wool—white, black, and various shades of brown or grey—and were used as robes by both men and women. They were warm and good protection against both wind and water. At first the only colors used with the neutral tones of the wool were a greenish-yellow derived from the flowers of rabbit-brush, blue obtained from boiling sumac with blue clay, and a deep dull red from the roots of mountain mahogany. Indigo blue was added to their weaving palette when the Navajos came in contact with Mexican traders.

The uniforms of the Spanish soldiers also had an influence on the designs of these woven blankets and belts:

> The bright red of the infantry and the yellow of the calvary were either bought or taken from the bodies of those killed—and *bayeta,* that rarest and most precious of blanket materials, was obtained by unravelling the fabric. This colored yarn was generally split and re-twisted and, spun fine and hard, was used to make Squaw Dresses or other show garments for men or women.[6]

The Spanish had still another influence on the clothing habits of the Navajo. Their tight-fitting leather knee-breeches and their leggings worn with hard-soled shoes were adopted by the Indian men. By the year 1750, most of the men wore buckskin shirts and short breeches and the hard-soled moccasin copied from the Spanish shoe. Occasionally they also wore the loose cotton pants of Spanish design that were slit along the outseam almost to the knee.

Women generally wore a leather moccasin with a wrapped top and a unique type of dress fashioned with red and blue designs on a black background:

> The dresses were made by sewing two woolen blankets together along the top edge and sides leaving a hole for the head and one at each side for the arms. . . . A woven sash was also worn. The dress

Figure 3-11. Navajo woman at the loom.

[6]Dane and Mary Roberts Coolidge, "Navajo Rugs," *Enjoy Your Museum,* Pasadena, Esto Publishing Company, 1933 (unpaged booklet).

may have been an adaptation of the Pueblo women's dress, or . . . a copy in woven material of the dress of buckskin worn by Plains Indian women. This costume was used by Navaho women until well into the American period.[7]

It is interesting to note how the Navajos took over certain aspects of the European technology and not others. They knew about the spinning wheel and probably could have traded for one, but they preferred to use the distaff and spindle to twist their woolen yarns. The Navajo loom also remained primitive, consisting of two cross-poles crudely attached to two uprights, with the warp stretched taut by the weight of rocks. Since the Navajos were essentially a nomadic tribe, they rarely accumulated more than could be packed onto a horse and moved elsewhere. A Colonial spinning wheel and permanently constructed loom was a bit too much to lash to the back of a horse.

The pigments used to dye the yarns came primarily from vegetable sources until about 1880, when aniline dyes were first introduced. The immediate result was such a violent combination of colors that the term "Indian blanket" soon became synonymous with any textile of garish design in loud discordant hues. Up until this time, American traders who travelled into Navajo country exchanged horses for blankets, and the blankets were eventually shipped to the east and to the west coast. But as the colors became more and more brilliant, the traders finally refused to buy them, so the weavers gradually went back to their natural colors and vegetable dyes, turning their creative instincts instead to greater variation in weave and pattern.

Navajo rugs are no longer used as items of apparel; their production today is primarily for commercial purposes. When he does wear a blanket, the modern Navajo goes to the trader for a soft Pendleton made from the fine Oregon wool which is more comfortable against the skin. The present-day dress of the men is a colorful variation of the cowboy's costume—wide-brimmed hats, colored shirts, blue jeans, and high-heeled boots, although many still wear moccasins at least a part of the time. Sometimes the shirts and the trousers show the early Pueblo and Spanish influences. Many men continue to wear the bowguard, ornamented with silver and set with turquoise. In times past, they were intended as protection against the bowstring, but today their function is purely ornamental.

For many years the dress styles of the Navajo women reflected the fashions worn by American army officers' wives of the mid-nineteenth century. Typical was the long and full, fluted calico skirt, worn with a bright velveteen blouse and intricately woven belt. Today traditional dress is seen only rarely,

Figure 3-12. The dress of this woman shows the mixture of styles characteristic of modern and traditional clothing.

---

[7]Malcolm Farmer, "The Growth of Navaho Culture," *The San Diego Museum Bulletin* 6, no. 1, San Diego, 1941, p. 15.

usually for ceremonial occasions. The fluted cotton skirt is more often combined with a ready-to-wear blouse. Although they would like to preserve their age-old crafts, few of the women are able to pass their skills on to their children. The young find more lucrative outlets for their labor out in the modern world. Like pottery making and basketry, weaving among the Navajos is becoming a vanishing art.

The clothing of the Navajos, however, clearly revealed their successive contacts with the Plains Indians, the Pueblos, the invading Spaniards, and finally the American traders and officers. In each case, they took over aspects of the material culture, reshaping them to their own needs in such a way that the products which emerged seemed typically Navajo. Their culture today is still characterized by a unique talent for absorbing alien ideas and American culture traits and making them seem consistent with the Navajo way of life.

Textiles and clothing, major elements of the Navajo's culture, reflected the influences of successive contacts with people of other cultures.

The classical world

Much of our knowledge of classical dress in ancient Greece comes to us through numerous vase paintings and pieces of sculpture. Greek artists must have studied anatomy as well as the techniques of weaving, carving, building, metalworking, and ceramics, for their work emphasized the play of garment folds against body contour and points of articulation of the human form. Like the Egyptians, the Greeks became expert weavers, and apparently each garment was woven in proportion to the size of the wearer, with a selvage on all sides. This eliminated the necessity for hemming and further enhanced the graceful folds of drapery that were so characteristic of all Greek clothing.

Flax and wool were the two principal fibers used, and the wealthier classes had garments made from extremely fine yarns. The fabric considered most luxurious was a very transparent linen that fell into soft narrow folds when draped on the body. A common method of weaving the flax in olive oil produced a silken effect and gave the fabric increased softness and drapability. It may be that the art of weaving a pattern into cloth was unknown to the early Greeks; most of their cloths were plain with decorative borders and surface designs applied by painting or embroidering after the fabric was woven. The spinning and weaving was usually done by the women of the household, and the distaffs and spindles of the ladies of high rank were often wrought in gold or ivory. The weaving of the plain fabric was generally the task of the female servants, while the lady and her handmaidens embroidered the material with beautiful decorative designs. Very often lengths of cloth would be sent to the goldsmith to be embellished further with fine threads of gold and silver.

Figure 3-13. Two forms of the male chiton.

The two principal garments of the Greeks were the *chiton* and the *himation*. Both were made from uncut lengths of material, draped and fastened around the body. The masculine chiton was a rectangular piece of linen or wool, reaching from the shoulder to just above the knees. It was fastened at the shoulders at points A and B (see Figure 3-13), girded about the waist and worn open down one side. Another form of the chiton was made in the shape of a double square. An opening for the head was left in the center of the piece during the weaving, and the selvages were then joined together below the armholes, with the arms emerging from the sides of the garment instead of from the top edge as they did in the first chiton. The himation (see Figure 3-14) was usually the sole garment of Greek philosophers, but it was sometimes worn as a voluminous cloak over the chiton. There were several methods of draping the himation, but it was common to fold it over the left arm, around the back of the body, under the right arm, and over the left shoulder

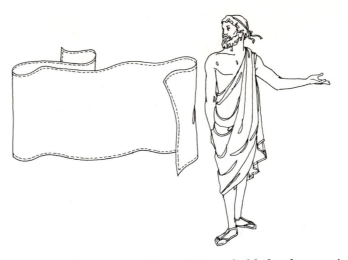

Figure 3-14. The Greek himation.

again. There were no fastenings to hold the drapery in place, and it required considerable practice and skill to arrange the cloth into graceful folds. The prestige of the wearer was judged by the precision of his drapery and only those who had time to devote to its careful arrangement could afford to wear it. Since all forms of manual labor were considered degrading by the aristocratic Athenian, his draped garment was a visual symbol of his lofty status.

The feminine chiton was based upon the same principle as the man's, but it was always full length. One version called the *Doric chiton* (see Figure 3-15) consisted of a length of cloth that exceeded the height of the wearer. The excess length was arranged in an overfold, and fastened together on the shoulders at points A and B so that the pin went through four thicknesses of fabric. Sometimes the overfold was long enough to be caught into the band at the waist, but since the Doric chiton was often made from wool, the upper edge usually hung loose for about twelve or fifteen inches over the chest and back without adding to the bulk at the waistline. The *Ionic chiton* was much fuller than the Doric, and made from a fine transparent linen. The width of the garment was equal to twice the distance from fingertip to fingertip with the arms outstretched (see Figure 3-16) and the front and back edges were fastened together at intervals along the shoulders and arms with a row of pins or buttons. A band that encircled the waist and crossed over the back and chest held the fabric to the body in graceful folds and gave the costume an illusion of having sleeves. Women also wore the himation as a cloak or mantle, or sometimes a narrower length of cloth draped over the arms like a shawl.

Both the Doric and the Ionic chitons were clearly designed to resemble their architectural counterparts. The Greek figure was treated in much the same way as a vertical column, and the

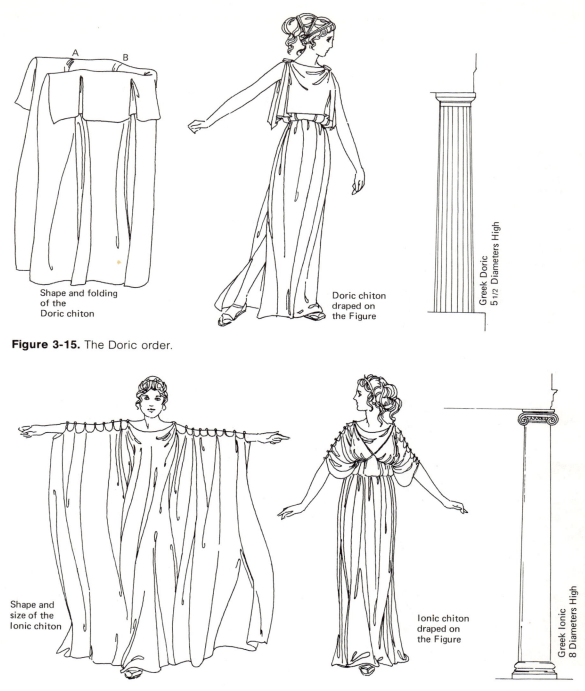

Shape and folding
of the
Doric chiton

Doric chiton
draped on
the Figure

Greek Doric
5 1/2 Diameters High

Figure 3-15. The Doric order.

Shape and
size of the
Ionic chiton

Ionic chiton
draped on
the Figure

Greek Ionic
8 Diameters High

Figure 3-16. The Ionic order.

RELATION TO THE MATERIAL CULTURE

two styles of dress exemplified the same feeling as the corresponding orders of architecture. The Doric column was thick and sturdy with wide flutings, and its capital ended in a flat, square member. In like manner, the Doric chiton, with its thick folds of wool drapery, gave the feminine form a solid appearance; the overfold gave the same effect as the square capital. The Ionic conception of form, on the other hand, was considerably lighter and more delicate. The column was taller and more slender, with narrower fluting, and its capital was a graceful double spiral derived from the curl of the nautilus shell. The folds of the sheer Ionic linen were lighter and more numerous than the heavier Doric, and the curve of its false sleeves repeated the curving scroll of the Ionic capital.

Ancient Greek dress was governed by the same sculptural and monumental principles that characterized Greek art and architecture.

Figure 3-17. A weaver works on an intricate pattern of silk brocade.

Oriental designs

From about the third century A.D. to the present, the cultivation of the silkworm and the weaving of elaborate silk fabrics has been a very important and a highly creative industry in Japan. The remarkable developments in fabric designs were achieved by the Japanese in many ways, but the most important technique was that of weaving the pattern into the cloth itself. Beautiful brocades were made of silk yarns, sometimes mixed with gold or silver threads, in which the pattern was superimposed by an independent weaving of the shuttle (see Figure 3-17). Elaborate damasks, woven in patterns of foliage and flowers, were solid in color, but the long float threads of the design reflected more light than the groundwork, giving the fabric a sculptured effect.

Some of the woven designs were embellished further with artistic embroidery, although many patterns were developed solely through the use of this technique. Decoration also was achieved by covering the design area with a wax similar to the Javanese batik, which resisted the color when the cloth was dyed. Another coloring technique was that of tie-dyeing, in which beautiful effects were obtained by wrapping tiny areas of cloth tightly with a fine thread before immersing in the dye bath. Besides this, there were block prints, hand-painted designs, cut-work and appliqué. The designs were usually conventionalized versions of the orchid, chrysanthemum, plum, bamboo, birds, or scenery. Not only the composition of the patterns, but also the beauty of their spacing on the cloth, made these textiles superb works of art.

No wonder then that the Japanese costume developed into a simple form that would display these beautiful fabrics to their best advantage. The cloth is not cut into tiny pieces and sewn into shapes that emphasize the curves of the body; nor is it draped into numerous and intricate folds as it was by the Greeks.

The Japanese *kimono* wraps the body like an artistic canvas, ignoring the breasts and the waistline, and drawing full attention to the beauty of the cloth.

The cut of the kimono is essentially the same for both sexes and all ages except that the *furisode* (with long sleeves) is worn only by young unmarried women. The variation and ornamental qualities are achieved solely through the decorative character of the textile, and the beauty of the garment depends upon the wearer's skill in choosing compatible fabrics for the kimono and contrasting *obi*.

The Middle Ages

The medieval age covered a period in history that extended roughly from the eleventh through the fifteenth centuries, reaching its height of brilliant color and pageantry in the later era known as Gothic. It was an age of heroism, chivalry, superstition, and a childlike enthusiasm for glittering stones, precious metals, and lavish ornamentation. The forces of Christianity and the art styles of barbarian Celts and Franks fused into a culture in which art was only decoration for their swords, shields, and churches. The opulence of the time was reflected nowhere more brilliantly than in the windows of the cathedrals and the dress of the wealthy. The Crusaders were back from the Near East with fabulous tales and souvenirs of Byzantine and Islamic art which contributed to a resurgent interest in goldwork, tapestry weaving, stained glass, and enamel work.

Two technical innovations, the pointed arch and the flying buttress, gave rise to the character of Gothic architecture. Crusaders had seen the pointed arch first in Mohammedan architecture, and the idea was gradually developed into extremes of great height. Stones set into thin, high ribs bore the weight of the entire vaulted ceiling, the ribs in turn being supported by buttresses which were anchored in the ground outside the building itself. Such construction techniques made possible the building of unbelievably high and narrow rooms in which all horizontal lines seemed to disappear.

This vertical conception of style governed clothing design as well. Pointed, elongated forms were considered the ideal, and Gothic costume went beyond the limitations of the body—the crown of the head and the soles of the feet—to give an illusion of slenderness to the figure and emphasis to vertical line. For men, this was achieved by the wearing of tall hats with sugarloaf crowns and shoes with exaggerated points that extended far beyond the natural length of the foot. The total effect was accented further by revealing the full length of the leg in long tight hose beneath a shortened doublet. The practice of dividing the body with a vertical line and making the right and left halves of the garment in two different colors was simply another manifestation of the Gothic predilection for the vertical.

The cut of the Japanese garment remains subordinate to the arts of weaving and dyeing the textile.

Figure 3-18. The simple cut of the kimono directs attention to the decorative quality of the textile.

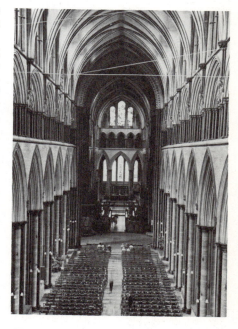

Figure 3-19. A Gothic interior showing the rib-vaulted ceiling and the high pointed arch.

Figure 3-20. Gothic costumes: the ladies are wearing the towering hennins, and their trailing skirts can be seen below the table; the men are wearing the short doublet, tight hose, and long, pointed shoes. **Figure 3-21.** A fifteenth-century painting by an unknown German artist that depicts medieval lovers, who symbolized their pledge by wearing identical left sleeves. The gentleman's pose is intended to display an elegant long-limbed figure to the best advantage. **Figure 3-22.** Detail from "The Hunt of the Unicorn," a medieval French tapestry.

But the supreme expression of this preoccupation with elongated forms was seen in that towering bit of fanciful eccentricity known as the *hennin*. It was a conical-shaped headdress which often extended several feet into the air, supporting a floating and transparent veil. At the opposite end, the woman's dress grew into a train which trailed along behind her, and her long tight sleeves added two more vertical forms to her total costume.

By the end of the fourteenth century, the art of weaving scenic picture-hangings had reached its highest degree of perfection. The weaving skills developed in tapestry-making carried over to the production of other luxurious fabrics that were rich in color and elaborate in design. Velvets, damasks, and gold brocades contributed to the lavish ornamentation of garments for both men and women. Because of the cold interiors, multiple layers of garments were found to be desirable, and many were lined with fur and trimmed extravagantly with ermine and sable.

Figure 3-23. Left, composite armor shows the last stage of the change from chain-mail to steel plate. Right, full-plated Gothic-style armor of the fifteenth century.

Probably at no other time in history did the knight's armor have a greater influence on fashion than it did in the Gothic period. The long, loose surcoat with deep armholes, eventually worn by both sexes, was originally intended to be worn over the chain-mail to reduce the glare of the sun. Gradually, sections of chain-mail were replaced with pieces of solid steel plate. By 1450, the metalsmiths had become so skillful that a fighting nobleman was solidly arrayed in meticulously jointed steel. The sharp edges of the metal required a thick padding against abrasion, and the male's doublet became expertly cut, padded, and quilted, "with sleeves so cleverly designed that the wearer could move his arms freely in a full circle—a highly desirable advantage in time of danger. The cut (was) surprisingly sophisticated. . . ."[8]

As the weapons of war increased in their destructive powers, knights used heavier and heavier armor, until eventually they became practically immobile. Finally, after centuries of use, armor was rendered obsolete by the invention of firearms.

Gothic dress was closely related to its architectural prototype just as it was in ancient classical times, yet it was the very antithesis of the classical conception of style. Greek garments, like Greek buildings, were in perfect harmony with the natural proportions of the human figure, while the Gothic predilection for exaggerated forms and over-ornamentation led to distortions of body and building that were flamboyant to say the least.

---

[8]Blanche Payne, *History of Costume,* Harper & Row Publishers, New York, 1965, p. 180.

Figure 3-24. A linked dress of polished aluminum applies a medieval technical process to a contemporary design.

The particular combination of technical patterns in Gothic times led to exaggerated design and garments intricate in both material and cut.

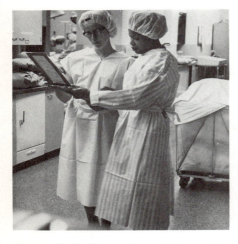

Figure 3-25. The notion of disposable clothing grew out of developments in paper towels, kleenex, and hospital gowns. With further technological improvements, inventive fashion applications may one day make clothing available in handy tear-off rolls.

Their textiles were every bit as intricate as the Japanese, and yet they lacked the restraint which coupled elegant fabric with simplicity of cut. The shaping of Gothic garments to body contour was perhaps the most precise technique ever developed in the history of costume. While these characteristics appear on the surface to reflect a difference in aesthetic values, their distinctive qualities of style are rooted at least in part in the evolving technical patterns of the age.

Contemporary dress

There are many aspects of our modern technology which have contributed to the evolution of styles that are distinctly contemporary. For one thing, the advent of central heating and closed cars initiated the ever-increasing trend toward lighter weight clothing. For another, the trend toward functionalism — again, a conception rooted in architectural form which began in the second decade of the century — has shortened a woman's skirts, put her into trousers, freed her from the corset, and given her the most practical wardrobe known to date.

The biggest story of the twentieth century, however, concerns the development of man-made fibers for the construction of clothing. For the thousands of years of man's existence, he had only the use of natural fibers—predominantly cotton, wool, linen and silk. Today new materials, like nylon, the polyesters, acrylics, polyurethanes, and spandex, provide unique combinations of properties that make possible many innovations in garment design. Elasticized and stretch fabrics, for example, permit body-conforming fit with give and flexibility. Shaping processes discussed earlier require fewer darts and seams. Other new fibers with amazingly high bulk and loft produce fur-like fabrics that are available within the price range of the most modest incomes. Leather also can be simulated with man-made materials so effectively that it is difficult to tell the difference from the natural product. In addition, the man-made fabrics are usually machine washable.

New fibers and finishes already have eliminated the need for ironing much of our clothing. The prospect of garments that are completely disposable eventually may eliminate the need for the washing machine. Non-woven webs of spun-bonded thermoplastics already are being used widely for hospital surgical gowns and throw-away underwear. Simple designs with a minimum of construction in easy-to-care-for materials are consistent with our speedy production methods and increased tempo of modern life.

New design forms continue to evolve out of modern innovations in materials, tools, and processes.

SUMMARY *Evolution of styles*

Many cultural factors influence the development of characteristic styles that are unique to a particular people or period. A strong relationship between design forms and the material aspects of any given culture may be demonstrated in literate and non-literate, Oriental and Occidental, as well as ancient and modern societies.

To some extent, there has always been an element of choice in the selection of one pattern over another. The Navajo Indian, for example, was aware of improved techniques for spinning but continued to use the distaff and spindle to prepare yarns for weaving. The ancient Greeks were expert weavers, but they preferred to fabricate plain cloths that would accentuate the graceful folds of their garments.

Among the Japanese the weaving of patterned brocades and damasks, painted, printed, and embroidered silks has always been a highly creative industry. Rather than arrange their fabrics in intricate folds, the Japanese use the simply cut, straight-hanging kimono to display their textile skills to best advantage. People of Gothic times had similar skills but combined them with highly developed techniques for cutting and tailoring pieces to conform to the shape of the body. This complex Gothic costume was dictated partly by concurrent technical innovations in architecture and armor. Just as the ancient Greek and the Gothic dress styles followed architectural prototypes, so our modern clothing reflects a predilection toward functionalism and streamlined design. Modern styles are further influenced by relatively recent developments in the area of man-made fibers, chemical finishes, and the bonding, molding, and fusing processes.

FOR FURTHER READING

American Craftsmen's Council. *Body Covering.* New York: Museum of Contemporary Crafts of the American Craftsmen's Council, 1968.

"Beauty of Kimono," a series of articles in *Japan Illustrated* 9, no. 2, 1971, p. 28–55.

Cunnington, C. W., and P. Cunnington. *Handbook of English Medieval Costume.* London: Faber and Faber, 1952.

Houston, Mary G. *Ancient Greek, Roman and Byzantine Costume and Decoration.* London: A. and C. Black, 1931.

Kluckhohn, Clyde. "The Navahos in the Machine Age," *The Technology Review* 44, no. 4, 1942, p. 178.

Wheat, Margaret M. *Survival Arts of the Primitive Paiutes.* Reno: University of Nevada Press, 1967.

DISCUSSION QUESTIONS

1. Why are agrarian and hunting cultures likely to differ in technical patterns with respect to the production of clothing?

2. How have concurrent technical innovations in other areas (such as architecture, engineering, and so forth) affected the design of clothes?

3. In what ways have the material conditions of the environment *limited* man's choice of raw materials?

4. In contrast to question 3, in what ways has man demonstrated an *element of choice* in the selection of one technical pattern over another? Answer this question by making one of the following comparisons: (a) a primitive with a literate society; (b) Oriental and Western societies; (c) an ancient and a modern society.

5. Explain how recent technical developments have altered our patterns of dress.

4
Folkways, Customs, Mores, and Laws

AS A HUMAN organism, every individual is motivated by a certain set of impulses or drives. Among these are the basic biological needs for food, air, elimination, temperature control, and sexual gratification. There are also social needs for prestige status and responsiveness from others — secondary drives which gain in importance once the basic needs are satisfied. All societies exert considerable control over the way in which such needs are met. The person who learns to gratify his urges according to the proscriptions of his cultural environment generally is regarded as a normal or well-adjusted individual.

The selection of customs that govern our need gratifications usually are based upon deep-seated assumptions about the "goodness" or "badness" of things or actions. It is on the basis of such postulates that every culture develops a fairly consistent system in which each custom bears a specific relationship to a total way of life. Thus, in every society there are certain accepted standards of dress that are considered "right," "proper," or "appropriate," while other forms of clothing behavior are regarded as "wrong," "improper," or "inappropriate." Social habits such as the norms which govern clothing behavior may be described more specifically by the terms *folkways, customs, convention, etiquette, fashion, mores,* or *laws.* Each of these terms has a slightly different connotation, although they are often used interchangeably and refer to the totality of behavior patterns that characterize a particular cultural group.

Most social scientists prefer to use the word **norms** to cover all types of social habits, defining each of the above terms in a more restricted sense. Although all are considered *social norms,* they are differentiated according to the degree of conformity required and the severity of the sanctions by which they are enforced.

Folkways generally are accepted as the conventional way of doing things, but they are not usually insisted upon. In certain

Folkways

social situations, a man who refuses to wear a tie chooses to ignore one of our folkways; he may be regarded as a bit gauche, but he is not necessarily excluded from the group.

Customs

Although the line between folkways and customs is hardly discernible, custom generally implies a social habit that is more deeply rooted in tradition. Many customs originate in association with magical or religious practices and thereby attain some measure of sanctity. The sanctions imposed against a man for failing to remove his hat in church are far more stringent than the sanctions imposed against him for failing to remove the same hat in the presence of a lady.

Mores

Social norms that carry the connotation of being morally or ethically "right" or "wrong" may be called mores. Clothing habits that are in some way associated with the control of sexual relationships in society are, by and large, part of the mores of a group. Violation of the standards of decency or modesty in dress usually is regarded as a threat to the welfare of society; therefore, violation of mores carries more severe sanctions than the violation of either customs or folkways.

Taboos are merely negative mores. A **mos** proscribes what *should* be worn; a taboo spells out what *shall not* be worn.

Laws

When social rules are enacted by those in political power and enforced through the machinery of the state, they become laws. Although sumptuary laws pertaining to clothing were quite common in bygone eras, there are relatively few rules of dress today that are prescribed by law. Many states, and most cities, however, maintain statutes against indecent exposure. The interpretation of what constitutes indecency in different parts of the country is an enlightening study in itself. Any regulation, however, which is enforced through some designated authority (such as a military uniform or a school dress code) may be considered a law.

All of these social habits are so overlapping that it becomes impossible to draw precise lines of distinction among them. Rather than a clear demarcation of categories, we have a continuum of conformity and enforcement that ranges all the way from approved behavior to obligatory behavior, from disapproved to forbidden. Precise definitions are complicated by the fact that we can always expect some departure from the code. The obligation felt by an individual within the group may vary all the way from complete nonconformity to elaborate overconformity.

Nevertheless, we are so inclined to take our own cultural habits for granted that we often assume our clothing behavior is natural and inherent. ("Of course men wear pants! What else would they wear?") An ethnocentric view of clothing customs in which the practices of one's own group become the standards by which all other patterns are judged merely serves to reinforce and strengthen the norms already extant in a given society.

Fashion innovation and acceptance are treated in more detail in other parts of this text, but it should be noted here that fashions are also a part of the normative system of society. Because they are more fleeting, less deeply imbedded in tradition, their changes may be observed more readily. But all social habits are subject to change over a period of time. Fundamental innovations in the environment often run counter to existing customs, and the custom gradually is modified in the direction of greater harmony with the spirit of the times. The factors that influence fashion change are the same forces that modify other folkways, customs, mores, and laws over a period of time. The only quality that distinguishes a fashion from other social norms relates to its tenure; customs and mores are more persistent, but they are no more rational, logical, or inevitable simply because they are durable. A social habit is "normal" for no other reason than that it is both learned and shared.

Folkways and customs

Both **folkways** and **customs** are manners or practices of dress that are transmitted from one generation to another. They are established through periods of relatively long usage. Nystrom differentiated between custom and fashion by explaining that in fashion, people imitate their contemporaries, whereas in custom they imitate their elders.[1] Folkways of dress are usually very persistent without ever being strongly sanctioned. On men's clothing, for example, buttons are always placed on the right side of the garment, whereas on women's clothing the buttons are always on the left. The logic of this habit has been explained by reasoning that a man could adjust his buttons with the left hand, leaving the right hand free to continue its work or fight with implement or sword, while the woman who habitually carries a child with the left arm, would have to use her right hand when buttoning or unbuttoning. Whatever its origin, the habit persists. But if an inept seamstress made the buttonholes on the wrong side of a blouse, it would probably be noticed only by the person who tried to wear it. Violation of

---

[1]Paul Nystrom, *Economics of Fashion*, Ronald Press Company, New York, 1928, p. 123.

Figure 4-1. Many traditional costumes for women include some type of bifurcated garment. Left, Turkish women in wide pants. Right, Indian woman in baggy trousers.

such a norm would hardly call forth group disapproval or subject the wearer to social sanctions.

Customs, like folkways, are slow to change, particularly with respect to activities that have rather strong emotional or spiritual content such as weddings, funerals, graduations, and other types of religious or ceremonial occasions. When such norms are violated, the reaction will range from mild to strong disapproval. The details of custom are spelled out in etiquette books, although such volumes rarely cover the wide variation that exists among different social classes and ethnic groups even within American society.

Probably more deeply ingrained than any other clothing customs are those habits which serve to distinguish between the sexes. For centuries, our code has decreed pants for men and skirts for women. The growing influences of sports and functionalism have resulted in an increasing relaxation of the code as far as women are concerned, but in American society at least, men have not yet taken to wearing skirts. This distinction, however, is far from universal. Many traditional costumes for women include some type of bifurcated garment, and many a vigorous male has been serenely proud of his skirts.

A distinguished visitor from a foreign country wearing a *dhoti* or *kilt* would attract many a curious stare on the streets of Middletown, U.S.A., but because his customs of dress are expected to be different, no further social sanctions would be imposed. A Middletown native, however, who dared to wear a

Figure 4-2. Many a vigorous male has been serenely proud of his skirts: a Scotsman, Greek Royal Guard, and Arabian men.

knee-length skirt on Main Street would cause his fellow citizens to (1) laugh or ridicule him, (2) question his sanity, (3) pretend not to know him, and/or (4) report him to the police.

Essentially this describes society's system for rewarding or punishing behavior. A slight infringement of the rules (such as the violation of a folkway) will tend to elicit only mild forms of response—an amused look or a chuckle or two. When departure from the norm is more blatant, group disapproval is correspondingly stronger. Questioning a person's sanity is making the assumption that he is not "normal," and therefore not to be trusted somehow. When this suspicion is strong enough, we no longer want to associate with the individual and either avoid him or bar him from group participation. If we report him to the police, we assume the infringement is severe enough to be covered by some type of law.

One of the most potent deterrents to the violation of customs, however, is not the external sanction from others. Rather, it is the internalized sanction produced by feelings of guilt, shame, embarrassment, or just being "out of it." The man who fails to wear a tie when everyone else is wearing one experiences only a minor form of discomfort, but a man who forgets his trousers suffers considerably more embarrassment.

In a cosmopolitan or international community the varied customs that derive from different cultures produce an atmosphere in which no one would be made to feel out of place no matter what he wore. In the smaller homogeneous society, customs tend to be stronger and more persistent because of their widespread use and acceptance.

Over the years, there probably has been no more universal custom of dress in Western culture than the traditional wedding gown. While the long white dress and transparent veil are not customary in all societies, special or distinctive garb for the bridal couple is a common characteristic of most cultures. White has been worn for centuries by English and Hebrew brides as a symbol of their innocence and purity. Actually the custom may be traced back to the days of the ancient Greeks, but it has not been in continuous practice since. The Romans added a red veil, and up until the time of the Renaissance, most European brides wore red. Red, a color which was thought to have the power of repelling demons, is still the traditional color in India.

Historically, the wedding veil is far more significant than the dress itself. Its origin has been attributed to diverse sources, but the fact is that the veil appears in China, Korea, Manchuria, Burma, Persia, Russia, Bulgaria, as well as in the majority of civilizations, both ancient and modern. The symbolism of the veil, however, has varied. Primitive peoples believed that it protected the woman from evil spirits; more widespread perhaps was the idea that the veil concealed the bride's face and form from all eyes save those of her husband.

The bridegroom, too, usually dons some special attire, although the male's "Sunday best" is often the common pattern. In many cultures the groom is treated like a kind of "king for a day" and garbed in the raiment of a chief, a prince, or a knight. Our own customs are really not too different; the common practice of renting formal attire for the groom is fair indication that he does not expect his exalted status to last very long.

Similarly, the raiment prescribed for other rites of passage, such as christenings, confirmations and bar mitzvahs, funerals, coronations, and ordinations, are also matters of custom. Ceremonial dress connected with religious observances, the opening of Parliament, and other governmental formalities, is almost always customary in nature.

Changing lifestyles more recently have challenged the validity of many of our traditions. In the early 1970's there was an outbreak of weddings in the most unlikely places—in treetops, on horseback, in cow pastures, and under the sea. Mothers and aunts nearly fainted, and fathers proclaimed that the whole social system was falling apart. In many ways it was. The deliberate violation of widely accepted custom is a symptom of basic changes in the structure of a society. New forms of wedding ceremonies are inevitable reflections of the changing role of women, attitudes toward premarital sex, communal living, and rising divorce rates.

BERRY'S WORLD

"Another tradition going by the boards—tennis whites! WHAT hath God wrought?"

Figure 4-3. Changing lifestyles have altered many of our traditions.

Abrupt change in custom is always more alarming than the gradual modifications that come about over a period of time. Until the 1950's, the accepted form of dress for Presidential inaugurations always included formal cutaway coat and high silk hat. President Eisenhower was the first to substitute the less formal Homburg. A decade later, President Kennedy landed another blow to custom when he abolished white tie and tails from the annual White House reception for foreign diplomats. The public reaction to this apparent disregard for tradition was reflected in newspaper editorials such as the following:

> The occasion will not be improved by this departure from the formal to the semicasual. A sense of occasion and the ability to dress properly for it are among the refinements of civilization.
> "Casual," a word whose meaning is much abused these days, too often means slack and slovenly. In this context it is a short step from a business suit to a sports jacket.[2]

These changes gradually paved the way for President Johnson to make his inauguration appearance in an oxford gray business suit and black fedora. A more conservative President Nixon restored a bit of tradition to the ceremony in 1973 by choosing semiformal daytime wear. It was clear by then that the life of the silk hat had expired.

Conformity to the folkways of dress is usually not considered essential to society; violation of clothing customs that are both strong and persistent is likely to incur more severe social sanctions.

Dress and morals

When customs are elevated to a higher level of concern for the welfare of society, they may be described as cultural **mores**. In all of the world's societies the regulation of sexual activity appears to be hedged by various taboos and restrictions, most of which are considered to be essential to the orderly functioning of the kinship system. The role played by clothing in stimulating or diminishing sexual interest therefore becomes a matter which is symbolic of the moral standards in any given culture. In general, the relationship between clothes and sex centers on the degree of exposure, concealment, or emphasis given particular parts of the body.

The casual observer is apt to think that the standards of decency and morality of his own culture are the only right ones. He will be able to see the bizarre aspects of clothing behavior in alien cultures but not in his own. Viewed in the historical and anthropological perspectives, however, we can appreciate our own pattern of morality as one of many variant configurations —a kind of local (rather than logical), temporary bias.

---

[2]Editorial, "JFK's 'No White Tie' Edict An Unhappy Fashion Note," *Nevada State Journal*, 10 June, 1962.

Figure 4-4. Men of the Tuareg tribe of Mali wearing caftans and veils.

Figure 4-5. Even at work, Moslem women in Pakistan keep their faces carefully covered.

In any discussion of decency in dress, one must consider the total range of possibilities, from complete nudity on the one hand to complete coverage on the other. One American made first-hand observations of several tribes inhabiting the interior of Africa, and followed this by a study of the people of the city of Khartoum, a center of Moslem culture. Among the primitives who habitually go naked, he noted a total lack of self-consciousness about the human body and concluded that a guiltless exposure of the anatomy was "the most normal, non-prurient, everyday thing in the world."[3] In contrast, the women of Khartoum were voluminously garbed and wore face veils which covered all of the features except the eyes. When one young girl accidentally unhooked her veil, she looked up in startled embarrassment and quickly fumbled for the corner of her veil to fasten it back into place. One might ask if the Moslem with the misplaced veil felt any more or less naked than the woman whose only body covering was a string of beads.

Even if we accept the theory that feelings of natural shame are universal in mankind, a number of illustrations could be

[3]Thomas Sterling, "On Being Naked," *Holiday*, August 1964, p. 8.

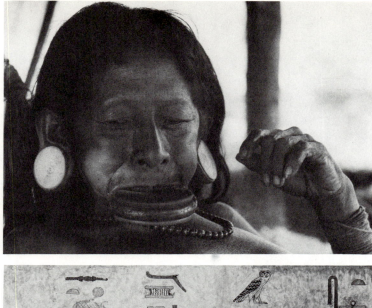

Figure 4-6. Above left. Lip disks and earplugs are indispensable to the Suyá Indians of Brazil.

Figure 4-7. Above. Minoan goddess wears the fashionable costume for high-born ladies of Crete, c. 1600 B.C.

Figure 4-8. Left. The typical costume of Egyptian woman of the Middle Kingdom, c. 2000 B.C. was a straight sheath dress with shoulder strap.

cited to disprove the assumption that such shame is necessarily associated with lack of clothes. Among the Suyá Indians of Brazil, for example, neither men nor women are the least bit embarrassed by their naked bodies, but are humiliated if caught without their lip disks. It is also an erroneous assumption that all "innocent nakedness" is confined to primitive societies, since it was prevalent in several early but highly developed civilizations. The honored bull dancers of ancient Crete performed in the arena with nothing except their arm-rings and necklaces, while the conventional feminine dress consisted of elaborate skirts in tiers and flounces with a short-sleeved bodice that left the breasts bare. Moreover, the tight lacing at the

Figure 4-9. A sense of modesty is completely lacking in small children.

Figure 4-10. Once the sight of the human body becomes commonplace, the importance attached to sexual differentiation soon disappears.

waistline encouraged an overly-erect posture, giving greater emphasis to the bosom which Cretan women exhibited with great pride. Well-bred Egyptian women of the Old and Middle Kingdoms wore straight sheath dresses extending from below the breasts to the ankles and hung from the shoulder by a strap or two. A young man in ancient Greece usually travelled in *chlamys* and *petasus* – a short rectangle of cloth fastened on one shoulder and a broad-brimmed hat.

Some writers contend that clothing is not the *result* of modesty, but the *cause* of modesty; that is, a child is not embarrassed by lack of clothes until he becomes accustomed to the wearing of clothes. Herein lies the paradox of clothing: that it is used not to cover, but to attract; that the removal of garments is far more erotic than going without them in the first place. In fact, one argument extolled by the nudists is that once the sight of the human body becomes commonplace, the importance attached to sex differentiation soon disappears.

Many authorities claim that this is precisely the reason that the wearing of clothes has become such a firmly established social habit. The fact that man, unlike other mammals, is not restricted to a mating season, has led to the development of sexual stimuli intended to maintain the mating instinct the

Figure 4-11. Body adornment that deliberately calls attention to sensual parts of the body.

Figure 4-12. Clothes that cover the body do not necessarily conceal it.

Figure 4-13. During the Renaissance, the male codpiece was an essential part of the costume. According to our present-day standards, it seems almost obscene.

year round. When clothing is the norm, "temporary nudity is the most violent negation possible of the clothed state."[4]

The exposure of almost every part of the human anatomy has been considered "indecent" or "immoral" in some period of fashion history. Even an area of the body which is not normally sex-connected (e.g., the arm, the ear, the foot) will become so if kept under wraps long enough.

Following the collapse of the Graeco-Roman civilization, Western culture was dominated largely by Christian doctrine, which conceived of the body as the source of man's temptation. In attempting to divert attention from the body, early Christians sought to hide it, and the loose, transparent classical garment was transformed into a heavy, enveloping costume that encased but dared not define the figure.

The Church inculcated strong feelings of guilt and shame in connection with the body, but it fought a losing battle against the forces of fashion. Many exaggerations in dress originated in a demand for modesty. For example, the tight hose that evolved during the Middle Ages were extremely revealing, to say the least. As the man's doublet grew shorter and shorter, the Church decreed the wearing of a codpiece to cover the front joining of

[4]Ernest Crawley, *Dress, Drinks, and Drums,* ed. T. Besterman, Methuen and Company, London, 1931, p. 111.

the breeches. Intended as concealment, the codpiece began as a small pouch, but gradually developed such fancy forms that it soon became the focal point of the entire costume.

For women, there was extremely limited décolletage in medieval times, but by the end of the sixteenth century, an exposed female bosom was regarded as a maidenly virtue and necklines were cut low and square. But at the same time, any exposure of the arms or legs would have been openly salacious. Arms were encased from shoulder to wrist, and like the skirts, sleeves were sufficiently widened so as not to reveal even the contour of the form beneath them.

The enormous crinoline that became the symbol of mid-nineteenth-century decorum reached its peak of popularity at the same time that Victorians exposed the bosom to such a degree that the look became known as the famous "Victorian valley." As if the crinoline were insufficient to hide that sacrosanct part of a woman, her legs, the proper maiden also wore pantalettes beneath her petticoats and high-topped shoes.

Hands, too, have been known to be areas of the body that must be kept covered at all times, indoors and out. At one time a lady was never to remove her gloves, except at meals when she changed to fingerless mittens. Reference has already been made to the Mohammedan's mortification at exposing the mouth in public. As late as 1930, Moslem women who dared to discard their face coverings were burned alive for blasphemy by outraged mobs.

Even today in many parts of the world, religious bans continue to impose restrictions on dress and appearance. Islamic law, for instance, forbids a woman to show her hair to a stranger, much less to allow a man to touch it. Consequently, females who visit beauty salons are considered sinners who face eternal damnation. Hairdressing is interpreted as "giving women an appearance other than that which God created,"[5] and along with hair dye and make-up, it is strictly taboo. At one time, a woman could be stoned to death for violating such a taboo; today the only sanction is the promise of a curse by God.

The changing standards of decency and morality may be observed easily within the span of a ten-year period. If, for example, someone suggested in 1915 that women would expose their knees in public, the idea would have been considered shocking. By 1921, however, the trend began to rear its ugly and obscene head, and a number of states enacted laws which prohibited the wearing of skirts shorter than a specified number of inches from the floor. Roaring and racy as the twenties may have been, women showed their legs, but not their backs or their bosoms! The backless evening gowns of the 1930's revealed a part of the anatomy that had not been revealed before.

[5]"Egyptian Women Defy Religious Hairdo Ban," Cairo UPI News release, 17 August, 1970.

Not only was the spinal column exposed to the waist, but for the first time in fashion history the bias-cut skirts suggested that the gluteus maximus consisted of two parts in place of the more modest mono-buttock. But then, people in the 1930's would never have believed that women would ever dare to expose their navels as they did when the bikini bathing suit was introduced, nor would people in 1950 ever have imagined that anything like the topless bathing suit would even be suggested in the 1960's.

Most people were outraged by the topless suit, and females who dared to wear one on the public beaches during the sixties were promptly arrested. By the early 1970's, however, we had been through a decade of see-through blouses, topless bars, and breast-revealing movies. A ban-the-bra movement became part of women's liberation. By 1972, the monokini made its debut on European beaches, and everyone casually ignored the phenomenon. The fashion spread to a few seasides in California and Florida, and although the reaction in the United States was somewhat more hostile, the police chose to "look the other way" rather than make arrests. Clearly the female breast had lost much of its seductive suggestiveness.

Fashion serves to maintain interest in the body by concealing parts of it long enough to build up its "erotic capital," as fashion historian Laver calls it. "You have to save up for quite a while to get any thrill out of seeing it," he said. The female bosom had not been exposed publicly since the end of the eighteenth century, so it had ample time to accumulate "capital." The leg had just as much capital in the early 1900's, and counterparts of the modern topless shows were called "leg shows" at the beginning of the twenties.

Does this mean then that there can be no immodesty in dress if practically every kind of a standard has been held as socially acceptable at one time or another in history? Quite the contrary, it means that as long as any state of dress is accepted as a permanent social habit, there will always be some costume, some style, that will be construed as immodest. Fashion is a part of the mores, and like the mores, it constitutes a kind of tacit agreement about what is right and what is wrong. Acceptance into the mores can transmute a salacious fashion into innocence, and vice versa.

Conflict over the question of decency in the modern world arises when standards are established independently by different cultural or subcultural groups.

During the 1960's, teenagers adopted the shortened hemline with alacrity, much to the dismay of school officials. It is probably a fair assumption to say that within the teenage culture itself, short skirts were no more suggestive of sexual impropriety than short socks. In the adult world, however, they *were* suggestive, and some high school students are more adult than

Figure 4-14. Rudi Gernreich's topless bathing suit of 1964. Many who wore it were arrested for indecent exposure even though it covered more of the anatomy than the monokini of the seventies.

others. If, in fact, "everybody's wearing it" (the teenager's ubiquitous explanation), then *not* wearing it would be the most attention-getting device possible. When only one girl in a school is sent home because her lack of underclothes is too revealing, it is fairly obvious that everybody has not forsaken underwear. Any girl who inspires a catcall should be aware that she is either doing or wearing something that is just beyond the pale of the accepted mores of the times. If, by chance, every girl in the school wore something suggestive enough to induce a catcall, one might imagine that the boys would be hoarse by noon. But obviously, this could never happen; by the time a once-suggestive style reaches mass acceptance, the taboo would be broken and the style would no longer be regarded as immodest.

The phenomenon can be explained simply enough: complete nudity in itself is not erotic. It becomes so only when preceded by or contrasted to a state of dress. In this very limited context then, all clothes become somewhat immoral, if we define immorality as inciting sexual interest. Habitual nakedness may indeed be capable of elevating man to a higher mental plane; but as one gentleman stated his dilemma, "I don't mind about the exposure, but won't it deaden the senses?"[6]

Although our consideration of modesty thus far has been largely theoretical, there have been several studies that have investigated modesty as a force in clothing behavior. Back in the thirties, Barr attempted to identify the underlying motives in women's choice of dress, and she discovered that of all the attitudes associated with clothes, modesty was probably the least important.[7] Creekmore analyzed the relationship between clothing behavior and the general values held by college women, concluding that the factor of modesty was significant only to the student who placed great emphasis on religious values, and only then when there was satisfaction of the physiological needs.[8] Similar kinds of associations between religious orthodoxy and measures of modesty have been found in other studies. In general, individuals who express a higher degree of commitment to religious tenets tend to be more conservative in their selection of clothing, particularly in regard to body exposure and tightness of fit.[9]

[6]Jessica Daves, "Can Fashion Be Immoral?" *Ladies' Home Journal,* January 1965, pp. 92g–92h.
[7]Estelle de Young Barr, "A Psychological Analysis of Fashion Motivation," *Archives of Psychology,* No. 171, 1934, p. 77.
[8]Anna M. Creekmore, "Clothing Behaviors and Their Relation to General Values and Basic Needs," Unpublished dissertation, Pennsylvania State University, 1963.
[9]See for example J. A. Huber, "A Comparison of Men's and Women's Dress and Some Background Factors Relating to Those Attitudes," Master's thesis, Ohio State University, 1962; J. K. Kleinline, "The Relationship of Mennonite Church Branch, Age, and Church Attendance and Participation to Attitudes Toward Conservativeness of Dress," Master's thesis, Ohio State University, 1967; and K. Christiansen and A. Kernaleguen, "Orthodoxy and Conservatism—Modesty in Clothing Selection," *Journal of Home Economics* 63, no. 4, April 1971, pp. 251–255.

Aside from the religious issue, however, the relationship between clothing and moral values has been demonstrated in other ways. A survey of a group of college men, for example, revealed that those who expressed lower moral values also held more liberal clothing attitudes. In 1971, these "liberal attitudes" were defined as favoring greater body exposure, going barefoot to class, sunbathing in the nude, men wearing beads, chains, and longer hair, and women wearing slack suits for most occasions.[10]

The "morality" or "immorality" of specific clothing practices can be evaluated only in terms of the behavior patterns that are considered "normal" for a given cultural group.

The wearing of clothing as an expression of modesty is not universal in mankind; it is a function determined by the culture, learned by the individual, and not very likely fundamental in nature.

Clothes and the law

Restrictions on dress that are enacted into laws and sanctioned through some type of legal enforcement are usually those that are regarded as necessary for the maintenance of social, political, or moral order. The issue of effective enforcement is always clouded by the difficulties encountered in drawing clear-cut lines of distinction between mores and the law, or between customs and the law.

Since dress is such a fundamental social habit, the public removal of garments generally comes under the regulation of law. In the United States as well as in most European countries, exposure of the person has for many years been considered a criminal offense. It seems somewhat paradoxical that such laws in Western culture are becoming increasingly lax and permissive at the same time that developing countries—where nakedness was once the norm—are enacting new statutes to regulate dress. In Uganda, for example, there is an official ban against miniskirts, hotpants, and maxis with a V-shaped slit down the front. The Ugandan President was quoted as saying, "These styles . . . are a disgrace to our culture. African women must wear decent dresses, so that they can get the respect they deserve."[11] The law makes no exceptions, however: foreign as well as African women are fined for having hemlines too far above the knee.

In similar fashion, the Masai citizens of Tanzania have been ordered to replace their loose shoulder cloaks with Western-style trousers, and Tanzanian office girls were forced to lower their hemlines in the name of African culture. The move was made to destroy the sartorial indecency that was "alien both to

---

[10]C. Mahla, "The Relationship of Selected Clothing Attitudes and Specific Moral Values for a Group of Undergraduate College Men," Unpublished Master's thesis, Stout State University, 1971.
[11]"East Africa's Hot Mini-Skirt War," Reuters news release, published in the *San Francisco Chronicle*, 29 May, 1972.

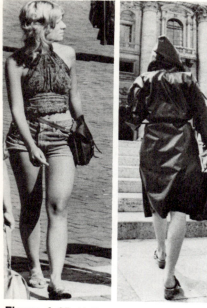

Figure 4-15. Vatican cover-up: Visitors to St. Peter's Basilica are required to cover "improper dress" with long black cloaks. The rule for women is that dresses cover the knee; for men, no shorts are allowed. Visitors who refuse to wear the cloaks are barred from entry.

Figure 4-16. The photograph above right was taken in Seoul, where the South Korean police arrested more than 9,000 youths in a nationwide crackdown on what authorities called "immoral and decadent elements." Young men were shorn of their long hair, and those who refused the free haircuts were sent to summary court.

African culture and to the socialist policies of the government."[12] The African republic of Malawi also maintains official restrictions against miniskirts and hotpants, and has deported foreign tourists for violating the code.

In Italy, Vatican guards will refuse admission to the Eternal City to anyone dressed in what the church regards as improper clothing, while in Singapore and Saudi Arabia, male visitors with long hair are turned back by airport police.

Although we discussed the phenomena of the topless bathing suit and the monokini as part of the mores of a culture, historically the propriety of the bathing suit has always been a subject for legal action. Early in the twentieth century, women were arrested for appearing on the beaches in bloomers. Such laws were not confined to beachwear, however. In 1895, Chicago passed a law requiring that "all cycle riders must wear baggy continuations. No knicker knee breeches or revealed stockings are permissible, but full and loose nether garments down to the heels." From time to time, lawmakers have attempted to legislate the length of women's skirts. In the beginning 1900's, two young ladies in Buffalo were arrested for raising their full-length skirts too high in the process of crossing a muddy street. Several years later, women were given jail sentences for appearing in split skirts, and during the twenties, several states attempted to pass laws that prohibited the wearing of any skirts which did not reach at least four inches below the knee.

These historical examples may lend some perspective to the widespread controversy over school dress codes that dominated

[12]Nicholas Moore, "Sartorial Strictures," Reuters news release, published in the *Chronicle Sunday Punch,* 21 March, 1971.

INTERRELATIONSHIP OF CLOTHING AND CULTURE

the educational scene in the late 1960's and early 1970's. The usual penalty for violating the school's code of proper dress was being sent home to change, but repeated offenses often drew permanent suspension. Early in the sixties, girls were sent home for outsized hairdos, and boys for wearing their trousers too tight. By the middle sixties, regulations were aimed at controlling the length of boys' hair, and the length of girls' skirts. The long hair issue continued well into the seventies, and numerous court battles were fought over the school's authority to regulate students' appearance. At the height of the controversy, a San Francisco newspaper polled its readers, who responded as follows:

	Per cent voting	
	Yes	No
1. Do you think schools are right to order boys to cut their hair short?	77	23
2. Do you think schools are right to forbid girls to wear clothing that school authorities regard as too revealing or otherwise unladylike?	89	11
3. Do you think schools are right to forbid girls to wear Bermuda shorts—as some high schools do?	87	13
4. Do you think schools are right to ban even the most modest fashion, such as "granny" dresses, merely because school authorities consider them ridiculous?	70	30
5. Which of these two alternatives would you favor in deciding such matters?		
a. These problems should be handled at home, and schools have no business interfering with parents' judgment.	21	
b. It is best that parents let school authorities have the final voice in how students cut their hair and what they wear to school.	72	
No opinion	7	

Results of Ballot No. 50 of the Chronicle Poll which appeared in the *San Francisco Chronicle*, 31 October, 1971.

In spite of the fact that public opinion overwhelmingly supported the school's prerogative to establish and enforce dress regulations, most school boards gradually relaxed their codes to conform to the current fashion.

Ordinances regarding the legal limitations of dress (or undress) also apply to performers. In many states, dancing in the nude is still considered "indecent exposure," although a strip artist usually can meet the requirements of the law with a pastie on each breast and a G-string. The exact requirements vary

Figure 4-17. A bottomless waiter serves lunch at a Honolulu nightclub. After serving their customers, waiters participate in a show.

Figure 4-18. Some people believe that police are overly suspicious of long-haired males.

with the state, sometimes the city. San Francisco police have recently tightened up surveillance of the city's topless shows, while Honolulu permits nude waiters.

Another category of regulations pertaining to dress involves those laws which attempt to protect society from the evils of misrepresentation. A person may be imprisoned, for example, for wearing a military or police uniform without the proper authority, while the death penalty is usually assigned to a wartime spy who is caught wearing the uniform of the enemy. Such laws also prohibit the impersonation of one sex by the other. It was Langner who posed the following question:

> The prohibition against men wearing women's clothing in public is far more strictly applied and is based on the belief that this would, if permitted, increase male homosexuality. Since many women are now habitually dressing in men's clothes, it is interesting to speculate whether or not this will also increase female homosexuality.[13]

City ordinances against transvestitism[14] are quite common, and any deliberate attempt on the part of a man to pass himself off as a woman (or a woman as a man) is regarded as immoral, improper, and, in some places, illegal.

It may well be that society's deeply rooted feelings of morality regarding an appropriate distinction between the sexes accounts, in part, for the open hostility encountered by many young men who adopted shoulder-length hair styles. In the early 1970's, sanctions against long hair led to suspension from

[13]Lawrence Langner, *The Importance of Wearing Clothes*, Hastings House Publishers, New York, 1959, p. 171 ff.
[14]Transvestitism is wearing the clothes of the opposite sex. It is not synonymous with homosexuality.

school for a number of boys. Several research studies have demonstrated that there is a relationship between a student's appropriateness of dress and his behavior in school. One study, however, found that students with records of discipline problems tended to epitomize the dress norms of the peer group, but their clothing differed significantly from the styles selected by teachers as appropriate.[15] This suggests that clothing does, in fact, single out individuals for disciplinary action.

Other laws intended to preserve the social order by restricting a person's dress to clothes that are indicative of his class, rank, or status, are known as sumptuary laws. In medieval times, the voice of the Church was supreme in dictating the social distinctions that were to be maintained between the nobles and gentlemen of lesser standing. Laver coined the phrase "Hierarchical Principle" to describe the use of dress in symbolizing one's position in society. Dressing to demonstrate the pride of one's wealth, he claims, is

> inevitably viewed with suspicion and distaste by our rulers, both ecclesiastical and civil. . . . Sooner or later the rich, rising man ventures to assume the fine clothes none-the-less, and consternation, not to say panic, ensues among the upper classes. Hastily a sumptuary law is drafted, and hastily passed. . . .[16]

Thus, the ancient Romans regulated the dress of each class and age by the strictest of sumptuary laws. During the reign of Charles IX in France, only ladies of high rank were permitted to wear dresses of silk and to carry fur muffs. The width of the farthingale and the amount of ornamentation was also prescribed according to the rank of the wearer. Edward III of England restricted the use of ermine and pearls to members of the royal family, and Henry VIII decreed that anyone below the rank of a countess was not entitled to wear a train. Queen Elizabeth attempted to regulate the size of her subjects' neck ruffs, the color and lavishness of their gowns, and the length of men's hair and beards! Her stringent clothing edicts engendered a good deal of resentment against the crown, and they were eventually repealed to avoid open rebellion.

Today, the lower classes still try to emulate the rich, and either through the use of synthetics or installment buying, they can almost accomplish their goal. There are fewer formal restrictions on dress, although codified regulations have not disappeared entirely. You can still tell a corporal from a colonel, and even in academic circles the ceremonial gown distinguishes the doctors from the masters, the masters from the bachelors, and the bachelors from those who have no degree at all.

Clothing practices considered necessary for the preservation of moral, political, or social order often are enacted into law and enforced through the machinery of the school or state.

---

[15]Thelma Leigh, "Discipline Problems as Related to School Dress Codes and Clothing Norms." Master's thesis, University of Nevada, 1971.
[16]James Laver quoted in "Laver's Law," *Women's Wear Daily*, 13 July, 1964, p. 5.

SUMMARY   *Folkways, customs, mores, and laws*

Habits of dress are a part of the folkways of a society. Like other social norms or habits, they may be differentiated by the degree of conformity required and the severity of the sanctions used to enforce them. Folkways, such as the wearing of a tie, the direction of a garment closing, or the hatband of a hat, represent conventional ways of dressing, but their violation is considered no particular threat to society. Clothing customs, on the other hand, have stronger emotional content and require a stricter adherence to prescribed form. The requirement of a hat for women in church, for instance, or the removal of the hat by men, are customs that are established through tradition and transmitted from one generation to another. In contrast, fashions are also a part of the normative system of dress, but they are habits of relatively short duration.

Clothing norms that carry the connotation of being morally right are included in the mores of society; taboos are considered morally wrong. Those aspects of dress which appear to be related to the regulation of sexual activity in society are usually subject to serious enforcement. We might expect clothes to promote greater sexual morality by covering those parts of the body that stimulate feelings of eroticism, but the fact is that any part of the body may become erotic if it is habitually covered by clothing. When a state of dress is the social norm, temporary nudity is sexually stimulating only because of its sharp contrast with the clothed state. Mores, like customs, change with the times. Fashions serve to maintain interest in the body by shifting the focal point from one area to another, revealing some parts and concealing others. Through this constant shifting, exposure of almost every part of the human anatomy has at some time in fashion history been regarded as indecent or immoral.

Clothing practices that are enforced through legal measures usually are construed as necessary for the maintenance of social, political, or moral order. Most societies have laws that regulate the degree of body exposure that is permissible in public. In some areas it is illegal to impersonate an officer or a member of the opposite sex by the unauthorized wearing of their garments. Still other laws, intended to maintain the social order by restricting an individual's costume to those articles of dress indicative of his position in society, are known as sumptuary laws.

Our own cultural habits of dress are usually taken so for granted that we are often inclined to believe that they are inevitable and logical; clothing norms are seldom rational, but they are almost always rationalized by the people who conform to them. Viewed within the perspectives of history and anthropology, we can see our contemporary patterns of dress as but one of many configurations on the clothing theme.

FOR FURTHER READING

Daves, Jessica. "Can Fashion Be Immoral?" *Ladies' Home Journal* 82, January 1965, pp. 92g–92h.

Flügel, J. C. *The Psychology of Clothes*. London: Hogarth Press, 1930. (Chapter 11, "The Evolution of Garments.")

Langner, Lawrence. *The Importance of Wearing Clothes*. New York: Hastings House Publishers, 1959. (Chapter 12, "Clothes and the Law.")

Laver, James, *Modesty in Dress*. Boston: Houghton Mifflin Company, 1969.

Rosencranz, Mary Lou. *Clothing Concepts*. New York: Macmillan Publishing Company, 1972. (Chapter 13, "Symbols of Sex Attraction.")

Rudofsky, Bernard. *The Unfashionable Human Body*. Garden City, N.Y.: Doubleday & Company, 1971. (Anatomy of Modesty, pp. 25–75.)

Sapir, Edward. "Custom," *Encyclopaedia of the Social Sciences* 4. New York: Macmillan Publishing Company, 1931, pp. 658–662.

DISCUSSION QUESTIONS

1. What is meant by "social sanctions"? How do they vary in degree or severity?

2. Compare the following norms in regard to their relative strength, duration, and type of sanction applied if violated. Give a specific example in dress or adornment for each: (a) folkway, (b) custom, (c) mos, (d) law.

3. In your own personal or family background, what types of clothing can you identify as "traditional" or "conventional"? How would your family react if you chose to ignore these conventions?

4. What is the principle underlying Laver's theory of the "shifting erogenous zone"? How does it differ from what he has termed the "Hierarchical Principle"?

5. If it can be shown that the wearing of clothes is not a universal expression of modesty, does this mean that there can be no immodesty in dress? Explain your answer.

6. Consider the role played by clothing in stimulating or diminishing sexual interest. What evidence can you cite that would support either a positive or negative answer to the statement that, "All fashion is basically immoral"?

5

Clothes, Attitudes, and Values

UP TO THIS point we have discussed clothing in relation to two major components of culture: the material artifacts that men create and use, and the institutions or normative patterns that constitute the rules which govern behavior. The third major element of culture involves ideas, i.e., the **mentifacts** of life. It encompasses the vast body of knowledge and beliefs that underlie or account for the particular choices and judgments made by man in following any of several alternate courses of action.

Values and goals are not directly observable, as are cultural artifacts, but they may be identified by noting the choices people make, the attention they give to some things and not to others, the things that they say are important or unimportant, and the kinds of behavior that they sanction or censure. In this context, clothing reflects the ideas people hold to be of value. As an oversimplified illustration, we might say that the ever-increasing tendency toward greater uniformity in dress is a tangible manifestation of one of our strongest political beliefs that all men are created equal, while the wide discrepancy in styles of dress between the nobles and the peasants in feudal times reflected their conviction that each man is born to a station in life, a place in the hierarchy of power and prestige.

Within its economic limitations, a family seeks to clothe its members in the type of dress it thinks they should wear. The words *should* and *ought* express values because they imply that some judgment of relative worth is being made. Consciously or unconsciously, every individual reflects, through the clothing choices he makes, a set of beliefs about himself that he wants others to believe about him too. In this sense, a set of beliefs and values provides a central motivating force in human action and clothing behavior. Belief in the Wesleyan translation of religious doctrine that "cleanliness is next to godliness," for example, prompts the daily bath, the weekly shampoo, a regular change of underwear, and a clean shirt every day. Expressed verbally, a person might say, "It really doesn't matter what you wear as long as it's neat and clean."

Obviously, for many Americans cleanliness does not take precedence over other crucial values, but takes its place within a hierarchy of dominant to subordinate values. Such variation complicates our study of values, but it does not preclude the possibility of identifying the typical patterning of beliefs and values that may characterize a culture, an era, a group, a family, or an individual.

The cultural setting

Like other aspects of culture, beliefs and values are not inherent, but are acquired in the process of living with others and sharing ideas. The dominant themes of a culture are reflected in those values which are most commonly shared, and the socialization of the individual always takes place within the value patterns that prevail in the larger cultural group. Even in the pluralistic United States—a nation that attempts to assimilate many diverse ethnic and religious groups—there develops a national character which, while unseen and unrecognized by the very people who display it, is identified immediately by those who are not subject to its uniformities. And although it is subject to the forces of continuous change, some basic aspects of this national character seem to persist from generation to generation.

While it is always hazardous to attempt to define a national "personality" or "type," there seems to be sufficient evidence of the difference in value patterns among various peoples and periods to note the existence of certain dominant themes. It is our purpose here to illustrate a few of the ways in which clothing relates to the ideas and values in different cultures and in different periods.

Women in China

Chinese men's dress was used in Chapter 2 to illustrate transitional variations in cultural patterns of dress. Chinese costume is a particularly apt example, not only because there have been such marked changes in ideologies, but also because the contemporary socialistic ideal represents a set of values that differs sharply from those that characterize a democracy. It was noted earlier that the revolution of 1911 in China marked the beginning of a corresponding revolution in dress in which the indigenous Oriental styles were gradually supplanted by Western designs.

Up to this time Chinese women were expected to live a secluded existence. The social restraints imposed upon women

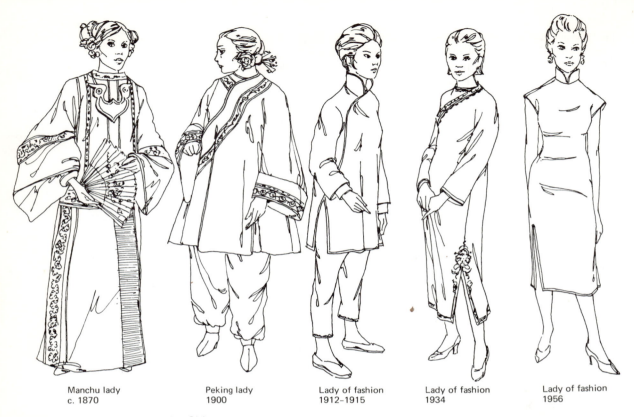

| Manchu lady c. 1870 | Peking lady 1900 | Lady of fashion 1912–1915 | Lady of fashion 1934 | Lady of fashion 1956 |

Figure 5-1. (a) Transition in Chinese women's dress. (b) At the Nixons' official reception in Peking in 1972, Chinese women wear similar versions of the nationalist uniform topped with black or navy coats.

were symbolized by their bound feet and cumbersome robes, both of which reflected a physical and mental withdrawal from the outside world. Little girls' feet were bound tightly from childhood on, producing a deformed little foot that resembled a tiny hoof. The distortion resulted in the mincing steps and teetering gait that characterized the traditional Chinese female. Among the reforms initiated by the revolution of 1911 was the abolition of this painful custom.

Reform in dress was the natural accompaniment to a reform in status. There followed a great confusion of styles—a mixing of Chinese elements, such as the short tunic, with long full skirts and Western shoes. Women were groping for a style of dress that would be compatible with the demands of their new emancipated status without departing too radically from the traditional styles. Some time between 1912 and 1915, there appeared a modernized version of the old tunic and trousers which, unlike the loose, cumbersome styles of the earlier period, allowed a freedom of movement and became an interim step toward a new national style.

It should be remembered that Chinese women were subjected to two further influences during this period. Like their

Western sisters, they began to participate more actively in the expanding world of sports; and second, the tubular, short-skirted fashions that evolved in Europe and America during the 1920's had their effect on Chinese styles. The whole purpose of Western dress seemed to be to display the leg and turn the body into a tube. Skirts above the knees, however, were considered altogether too immodest by the Chinese; but a very similar effect was achieved by lengthening the tunic and maintaining the slits up the sides. This one-piece dress became known as the *ch'i p'ao*. Chinese women had at last achieved a basic style that represented the important values of the period—a distinctive and recognizable national dress, a symbol of their active and progressive way of life, and a costume that was both fashionable and flattering to their racial characteristics.

When the Communists came to power in 1949, they brought with them a philosophy which recognized no distinction in rank or in sex. The drab tunic and trousers and soft peaked cap were worn alike by men and women. By 1950, the glamorous and feminine *ch'i p'ao* had disappeared entirely from the mainland, along with jewelry, cosmetics, and all other forms of decoration. The colorless uniform became an ideological symbol that expressed economic austerity, practical utility, and absolute classlessness. China was a worker state, and life was shorn of frivolity. The Communists, faced with the more pressing problems of economic shortages, regarded dress, adornment, and beauty as not only dispensable but even unpatriotic. Drabness became the national mode.

While all these changes were taking place in Chinese dress, the country people working in the fields continued to wear their simple and loosely-cut tunic and trousers. Their work, their status, and their values remained unchanged—and so did their dress. An interesting parallel existed in European folk costumes in which many styles were passed down intact from the Middle Ages. Because there was no shift in the dominant value patterns of the peasantry, there was relative stability in their national dress.

A hierarchy of values is represented by the particular forms of dress that become characteristic of a people; clothing thus presents a value model in shaping national attitudes.

Fashion in the nineteenth century

Change in the dominant ideals of a culture takes place slowly and is frequently a difference in emphasis rather than a complete departure from antecedent value patterns. The changes which appear to be so radical in times of revolutionary upheaval are expressions of feelings that had been smouldering for some time under the imposed cover of entrenched social and political institutions. Moreover, once the extremes of pent-up emotions have been spent, the relationship to the historical past becomes re-established.

Figure 5-2. Influence of the classical revival (c. 1799). Except for the bonnet, she could have been an ancient Greek.

The nineteenth century is no better example than any other century in history, except perhaps that it began in the aftermath of revolution. The preceding period was marked by an excessive lavishness of dress that symbolized an elegant and sophisticated way of life. It was Rousseau who expressed so eloquently the growing resentment against the blasé attitudes of the French aristocracy. Even before the outbreak of hostilities, the French intellectuals had already begun to admire the simplicity of the English country gentleman's costume. During the Revolution itself, it was unsafe to be caught in the streets wearing beautiful clothes, but it was not until the furor subsided that the people had time to express their reaction through dress.

The most extreme stand was taken by the *incroyables* (the incredibles) and the *merveilleuses* (their feminine counterparts), who registered their contempt through a deliberate and contrived disarray of their clothes. Their uncombed hair hung in slovenly fashion from beneath their beaver hats, and their tight trousers, clumsy boots, coats with huge lapels, wrinkled cravats, and heavy knotted walking sticks all suggested the antithesis of the sleek-groomed refinement of the earlier period. The mode was short-lived, however, and Frenchmen soon settled for the tastes of the English tailor, whose styles were simplified versions of the former court costume adapted to the rugged life of the outdoorsman.

Women's fashions, on the other hand, proved to be more malleable in reflecting the change in dominant ideals. The growing interest in classical forms, engendered by the discovery of the ancient cities of Pompeii and Herculaneum, culminated in a revival of the Greek and Roman styles of dress. Women did their best to look like an antique piece of statuary, draping their cashmere shawls to effect a classical pose. This neoclassicism in dress symbolized a corresponding return to the political ideals of the early Greek democracy and republican Rome.

When the Bourbons returned to power following the defeat of Napoleon, it seemed as if they thought they could restore the leisured and privileged days before the Revolution by reviving the styles of an earlier period in French history. Costume balls became the rage, and an odd mixture of period revivals characterized the contemporary styles of dress. Laver believes that the reappearance of the neck ruff helped to restore an element of prudery into the value pattern of society:

> After Waterloo the whole of French society was in conscious or unconscious reaction against the libertinage of the Revolutionary period and even of the Empire. Though Napoleon had done his best to introduce a more moral tone into his immediate circle, the example people remembered was that of Josephine, and Josephine had never been a prude. Gone were the days when ladies thought it permissible to bare their bosoms in the public street, to walk about

bare-throated even in winter. . . . Now dresses rose to the throat, and a frill of lace seemed their obvious finish.[1]

The end of the 1830's marked the beginning of Victorianism, an age in which prudery seemed to be carried to extremes. The nineteenth century was not an age that catered to a reigning aristocracy but rather to a new class of wealthy manufacturers who established their fortunes in the years following the Napoleonic wars. Such men were inclined to be hard-working and unpretentious, although somewhat puritanical and sanctimonious in outlook, and these attitudes set the dominant tone of society. This, coupled with the growth of the democratic idea that all men were social equals, resulted in the somber, unattractive apparel for men that continued to be the pattern for over a century.

The woman of this new class led the sheltered life of the gentlewoman. A lady had no responsibilities save her household duties, and a career was absolutely unthinkable. By far the most significant element in women's dress in the mid-1800's was the extended popularity of the crinoline. After the slender gowns of the Directoire, the silhouette was due for an increase in width, but the extreme dimensions of skirt fullness that prevailed throughout the 1850's and 1860's could have occurred only through the added impetus given by concomitant social influences. The number of garments worn, for example, seemed to symbolize the material prosperity of the wearer, or at least that of her husband, and the difficulty with which fashionable ladies passed through doorways, entered carriages, and squeezed into church pews was enough to discourage anyone from straying far beyond the immediate surroundings. The skirt, moreover, created a physical barrier that kept men at "a proper distance."

It was not until the end of the century that the idea of the "liberated" woman began to take shape. The rise of a new attitude toward woman and her place in society gradually came about as the result of two *fin de siècle* phenomena: education and sports. The passing of the Morrill Land Grant Act in 1862 gave impetus to the establishment of state universities throughout the nation, and the doors of higher education were at last opened to the daughters as well as to the sons of American families. No longer content to accept a life of dependency, women began to strike out for themselves, and by accepting positions in offices and in the professions, they entered into a competition with men that was a new and purely economic kind.[2]

At the same time, society saw the launching of a new invention called the bicycle. The enthusiastic acceptance of cycling

Figure 5-3. The crinoline helped maintain the moral standards of the Victorian period by keeping men at a proper distance.

[1] James Laver, *Taste and Fashion,* George G. Harrap & Company, London, 1945, p. 27.
[2] Laver, *Taste and Fashion,* p. 76.

CLOTHES, ATTITUDES, AND VALUES

Clothing has a reciprocal effect on social attitudes and values; it reflects the ideals already extant, but it also shapes ideas in the direction of change.

Figure 5-4. This caricature by John Held, Jr., epitomizes the famous flapper features: bobbed hair, painted lips, short skirts, rolled stockings, accent on legs.

Clothing is a tangible, visual symbol of the ideas and values that typify the times.

as a feminine sport created problems for the moralists that were not easily overcome. Which was worse: hiking up the skirts to reveal both ankle and calf, or enveloping the legs in bloomers? Obviously the bloomers won out and went on to set a precedent for the development of functional clothing in other areas of sports activities.

The body-revealing clothes that came about through the channel of sportswear conditioned the whole of society to a new set of values toward exposure of the female form, and in no small way contributed to the freeing of the modern woman from the conventionally circumscribed conduct of previous generations.

Fashions of the flapper

In probably no other period of history has the fashion image of the woman been more symbolic of the spirit of the times than it was during the Roaring Twenties. Although the emancipation of women had been in progress for several decades, the events of the war gave it the final push. Women were on their own, and they liked it. Gone was the old ideal of the loving wife and mother; far from being admired, motherhood was to be avoided as long as possible.

The emphasis was on youth—a kind of eternal adolescence that indulged itself in extremes of dress and behavior. The flapper drank and, even worse, she smoked; her skirts grew shorter and shorter, revealing more than calves and knees when she sat down. All of the attributes that were so long associated with the ideals of femininity were renounced: women cropped their "crowning glory" to a boyish bob; they all but abolished their breasts with a flattening brassière; and waists were completely obscured by a tubular silhouette that straightened out the natural female curves. If diet and exercise failed, women resorted to the corselet to achieve the hipless, bosomless, boyish figure that became the vogue. All attention was concentrated on the lower limbs, which, covered in flesh-colored stockings that were rolled to the knee, became the center of feminine seductiveness.

Feminine dress of the period was, moreover, a frank expression of the stark functionalism that became the working philosophy of furniture designers and architects. The exposure of arms and legs was prompted by the same kind of thinking that exposed the joints of the modernistic chair and the structural members of the contemporary house. The flapper so typified the ideals of the times that it is no wonder her name is synonymous with the age.

SUMMARY *The cultural setting*

Ideas and beliefs constitute a third major component of culture. While the mentifacts of life cannot be observed directly, they are reflected in the clothes that we wear and the fashions that are typical of any given culture or period. Consciously or unconsciously, the choices we make in clothing reveal many of the things we hold to be important: democracy, equality, beauty, practicality, economy, extravagance, tradition, maturity, progress, individuality, austerity—such are the values and beliefs that are motivating forces in clothing behavior.

Value patterns differ from one culture to another, and from one generation to the next. Dress in socialist China, for example, is characterized by widespread uniformity in contrast to the rapidly changing fashions and great variety of styles that dominate the democratic societies. Chinese dress, on the other hand, has been highly symbolic of the changing status of women over the years. This has also been true in the Western world, where education (followed by economic independence) and a concomitant participation in sports have been the natural precursors of liberating fashions and increased social status.

Group and individual values

Just as value patterns vary among cultures and between generations, so do they differ from one group to the next and from individual to individual. The chief agency through which the individual acquires his values is the family or kinship unit responsible for the socialization of the child in the early formative years. Children are quick to recognize those qualities that have high value and those which have none, behavior that brings reward or punishment, actions that are admired or disapproved.

Although the family experience in most cases is paramount in the transmission of cultural patterns, other agencies make a significant contribution to the formation of ideas and the ordering of values which eventually characterize the person as an adult. Like the family, the school also transmits attitudes and values as well as knowledge and skills, and at the same time provides a setting for the exchange of ideas that occurs within the peer group itself. Of increasing importance in today's society is the influence of mass media in shaping the standards by which the growing generation will seek to live. Movies, television, and all forms of mass communication are constantly presenting value models which either strengthen or dilute the teachings of the family and/or the school.

To the extent that the family is a dimension of the larger society, i.e., a unit which adheres to a similar system of values, beliefs, and sentiments, it may be expected that the child will develop in like manner. To state it another way, we may assume that values associated with clothing originate in the cultural milieu, are adopted by the family, and ultimately are transmitted to the child. In some cases, however, the views—either of the family or a subgroup with which the individual may identify—are in serious conflict with those of the general culture. As a child matures, the number of influences outside the family increases, and each of these exerts a varying degree of control over his thoughts and actions.

Theoretically at least, attitudes and values are significant because they represent a predisposition to act. It is a common observation, however, that what a person thinks or says he will do is not always consistent with what he actually does. It is for this reason that researchers have identified the subcomponents of values. One of these represents an individual's conscious values, that is, the ideas which he can express verbally. These are sometimes called **explicit values,** or what a person says he believes. He may believe, for example, that others judge him by what he wears, or that clothing is not a valid criterion of one's real worth, or that the time one has to spend on clothes detracts from other more important things in life.

The behavioral component is inferred from what the person actually does. These are referred to as **implicit values** and may not consciously be recognized by the individual. In actual fact, however, he may be observed to wear inconspicuous clothes or may refuse to participate in certain social activities because he lacks appropriate attire. Implicit values are assumed to be conditioned by a third component, and that is the way a person **feels** about a given object or entity. With respect to clothing, this could mean that an individual may be emotionally insecure or embarrassed about his appearance, constantly worried or frustrated in his attempts to achieve the look he desires.

Some of the research related to attitudes and values has been concerned with identifying the relationship among these three components—the cognitive, the behavioral, and the affective. Many studies have been limited to an assessment of attitudes held by particular groups or segments of the population. Still other researchers have concentrated on the larger value patterns into which individual attitudes are organized. It is this unique ordering of values that ultimately helps us understand how people can resolve their value conflicts.

Clothing values

Explicit values can be identified simply by asking people what factors influence their choice of clothes. Comments made by college women and collected over a period of several years have revealed attitudes similar to the following examples:[3]

> In general, I refrain from extremes. Standing out in a crowd does not appeal to me.

[3]Subjects were home economics students at the University of Nevada.

> I choose the conventional type of clothes that the majority of people are wearing.

> I value being properly dressed for the occasion. Nothing makes me feel more uncomfortable than showing up in the wrong clothes.

These kinds of comments, and others relative to being "appropriately" or "simply" dressed, reflect a desire to conform to the general pattern of group dress; in terms of frequency, they constituted the type of comment made most often. Attitudes expressed often, but less frequently than those illustrated above, pertained to a desire for self-expression:

> I like to stand out in a crowd and have people notice me. Some of the clothes I wear I'm sure other people wouldn't think of wearing, but I enjoy clothes that are in some way different.

> I'm continually searching for clothes that are new, different, and exciting. I make many of my own clothes because it gives me a sense of accomplishment, and more important, I don't see everybody else wearing the same thing.

Some researchers have defined this desire for self-expression as "individuality" or "distinctiveness" in dress. It is also akin to what some have termed the "exploratory" value in clothing, which refers to the use of clothing as a medium for experimentation.

Many statements showed a concern for beauty or becomingness, and these were categorized as aesthetic values:

> I seek clothes in bright and cheerful colors, clothes that are becoming and flattering to my figure.

> I feel that if a person has a few well-designed good-looking outfits that others will enjoy seeing her more than a person who wears a different costume every day.

Other comments referred to the prestige value of clothing:

> I like to make a good impression on others. I'd like others to be able to tell that I know fashion and observe its rules.

In some studies this is called a "political" value in the sense that clothing is viewed as a vehicle for gaining prestige, leadership, or influence.

Some attitudes were centered around the desire for social participation and/or sexual attraction. This "social" value is directed toward a concern for the opinions of others:

> Clothes are important to me in the way that others think about me; I believe I will have more social opportunities if I dress well.

> I love clothes that are feminine. I must admit that I dress for the opposite sex, but then, who doesn't?

Comments relating to the values of comfort and economy also were made, but they were by far in the minority:

> I consider first the economic and functional values. I don't feel I have to keep up with everybody else; I'd rather buy something a little less expensive and get more use out of it than waste money on clothes just because they're fashionable.

> In general I choose clothes that are comfortable and practical. I avoid frills because they are neither functional or serviceable, and they require too much upkeep.

Economic values are usually thought of as those which emphasize the conservation of time, energy, and/or money. The desire for comfort in dress is sometimes called a "sensory" value.

The dominant values reflected in these comments represent a very select segment of the population. They do, nevertheless, provide a framework for studying individual values as well as some basis for organizing them into broader value patterns.

Over the years, various measures have been devised to ascertain the relative importance of clothing in the lives of individuals. Several early studies seemed to indicate that women in general placed a higher value on clothes than men did. Silverman's work with adolescent girls, ranging in age from 12 to 18 years, revealed a particularly high degree of interest among teenagers; roughly 96 per cent of those in the study expressed a willingness to sacrifice other values for the sake of clothes.[4] In 1949, Rosencranz reported findings relative to adult women. Females under 25 were found to attach greater importance to clothing than women over age 30.[5] Baumgartner found that the amount of money expended for clothes by college freshmen was observed to be higher among women than among men, and higher for members of sororities and fraternities than for independents. Measures used to establish the importance ascribed to clothing showed similar responses.[6]

A number of investigations have been made dealing not only with relative values, but with specific attitudes associated with clothes. One of the earliest of these was carried out by Hurlock in 1929.[7] At that time, the most prevalent attitude that seemed to determine whether or not a person spent a disproportionate amount of money on clothes was the feeling that clothes helped to put up a "good front," and thereby contributed to one's professional advancement. At the conscious level at least, people

[4]Sylvia Silverman, *Clothing and Appearance; Their Psychological Implications for Teen-Age Girls*, Teachers College, Columbia University, New York, 1945.
[5]Mary Lou Rosencranz, "A Study of Women's Interest in Clothing," *Journal of Home Economics* 41, October 1949, pp. 460–462.
[6]Charlotte W. Baumgartner, "Factors Associated with Clothing Consumption Among College Freshmen," *Journal of Home Economics* 55, March 1963, p. 218.
[7]Elizabeth Hurlock, "Motivation in Fashion," *Archives of Psychology* 17, no. 111, 1929.

did not acknowledge that they used clothing as a status symbol, and men in general claimed that a regard for modesty dominated their selection of apparel. Nevertheless, all of the men studied believed that their estimate of a person was affected by the impression his clothes made, and almost 97 per cent of all subjects reported feelings of increased self-confidence when they were well dressed. About half of the women in the study indicated that they would deprive themselves of certain pleasures in life in order to be in fashion, and about a quarter of them would have foregone even necessities.

On the basis of the attitudes identified in Hurlock's survey, Barr went a step further in trying to determine the relative strength or importance of group attitudes toward clothing.[8] Results showed that the most fundamental attitudes associated with clothes were those related to the desire to conform, the desire for comfort and economy, the artistic impulse, and self-expression. These attitudes occurred so positively and so prevalently—cutting across differences in educational background, economic status, and other variable characteristics—that they were thought to be universal in nature. The desire to conform in matters of dress was the most widely diffused, varying only in intensity among the different groups studied. Warden's research, conducted almost a quarter of a century later, indicated that many of these same attitudes still persisted.[9] All of the college women who were surveyed expressed a desire for clothes that would attract attention some of the time, but which would conform or be similar to those owned by their friends. Although they regarded comfort and serviceability as important factors in clothing, they were not willing to sacrifice style or fashion for either one. It is interesting that Barr's analysis, made in the depression years of the early 1930's, perceived the "desire to appear prosperous" as being unimportant in the value patterns of her subjects. However, in the late 1950's, a period of economic prosperity, Warden's subjects wanted clothes to "be in large quantity" and to "look prosperous and expensive"—tangible evidence that attitudes and values are modified by changing conditions.

In 1958, Runbeck identified a number of different values held by college students in the selection of apparel, but most subjects believed that it was important to be fashionably dressed.[10]

A decade later, the interest in fashion appeared to subside, at least at the cognitive level. The young liberals were declaring that "fashion" was "out of fashion," and the values of "comfort" and "convenience" became the current catch words. To be

[8]Estelle Barr, "A Psychological Analysis of Fashion Motivation," *Archives of Psychology* 26, no. 171, 1934.
[9]Jessie Warden, "Some Desires and Goals for Clothing of College Women," *Journal of Home Economics* 49, December 1957, p. 795.
[10]Dorothy Runbeck (Stout) and Alpha Latzke, "Values College Women Consider in Clothing Selection," *Journal of Home Economics* 50, January 1958, pp. 43–44.

Figure 5-5. The Women's Liberation Movement has been, in part, responsible for a waning interest in fashion.

BERRY'S WORLD

"I, personally, resent their air of superiority because we're 'bums,' and they're 'street people'!"

Figure 5-6. Synthetic poverty is often not accepted by others as the most sincere statement of a person's true values.

lavishly dressed in the latest high fashion was even considered by the wives of political candidates in the 1972 election to be professionally hazardous.

> The selling of the candidates' wives, 1972, seems to have been inspired by what might be called "the Pat Nixon cloth coat syndrome." . . . The fur coats, or at least most of them, have been left home in the closet. The skirt lengths are neither too midi nor too mini. The dresses smack of Paris, Ill., rather than Paris, France.[11]

Some believed that this was due partly to the state of the economy and partly to the Women's Liberation Movement. In London, fashion was being hailed as a "capitalistic ploy" by British Communists who claimed that it was "merely a sales gimmick used by the clothing industry to persuade people to buy more clothes."[12] The feminists on the other hand, complained that fashion put women on display and made them out to be nothing more than fragile, decorative sex objects.

Values, of course, are reflected not only in what people say, but in what they do. Like Baumgartner, Walker used actual expenditures made for clothing as a behavioral index of the importance attached to dress. There were highly significant relationships between subjects' expressed interest and the amount of money they spent for clothes.[13] There have been other instances, however, in which actual behavior has contradicted professed values. One of the most blatant examples can be found in the anti-materialistic philosophy expressed by the youth culture. Many give lip service to the triviality of appearance and in fact look as though their entire wardrobe was picked up at the Goodwill. But

> if you check the label, you'll find the "surplus" jacket came off a rack at a hip little boutique just last week. The T-shirt is new, too; the tie-dyed version costs $2 more than the regular kind. The jeans are also brand new; you have to pay extra to get them all faded and tattered like that. As for the sandals, they're the new "tire-look" numbers. The knack of making them was picked up from impoverished South American Indians; you pay $10.[14]

This kind of inconsistency is bound to occur when a person adopts a set of synthetic values just to be "in" with the crowd. The process is often not a conscious one. How often do we parrot values that have been indoctrinated through public opinion and in fact do not reflect what we really consider to be important? In the matter of conforming to an accepted standard of

[11]"Fashion: The New Political Taboo," *New York Times* Service news release, published in the *San Francisco Chronicle*, 6 April, 1972.
[12]"The Left's Fight Over Fashion," Associated Press news release, published in the *San Francisco Chronicle*, 5 Feb. 1973.
[13]Norma Walker, "Clothing Expenditures as Related to Selected Values, Self-Actualization, and Buying Practices," Unpublished dissertation, Pennsylvania State University, 1968.
[14]Barry Newman, "Riches in Rags: Companies Find Profits in the 'Antimaterialism' of the Youth Culture," *The Wall Street Journal*, 27 April, 1971.

dress, for example, there is rather overwhelming evidence that even though people do not consciously acknowledge the value of conforming, their behavior indicates extremely strong tendencies in a conforming direction. College students in particular tend to express negative attitudes toward the notion of conformity in dress, men favoring nonconformity more than women. One study demonstrated, however, that when actual behavior was observed, both sexes actually conformed to a greater extent than they thought they did, and men were significantly more conforming in dress than women were.[15]

Even the early studies by Hurlock and Barr indicated very strong tendencies to prefer clothing that would be similar to or accepted by one's friends. Teenagers have been found to give greater weight to clothing as a means of gaining acceptance and approval than do mature persons. The latter group tends to place a higher value on the effects of physical enhancement.[16] The desire to conform to the norms of the peer group seems to be highest at about the eighth grade.[17] By the time students reach senior high school, dressing in a more individual manner and dressing to attract the opposite sex become important values.[18]

In most groups, values usually change with advancing age. Interest in clothing is generally higher among young people, decreasing as age increases.

Value patterns

Values held with respect to clothing, such as those which have just been described, are meaningful only when placed within the context of an individual's total value pattern. Several researchers have attempted to analyze attitudes and values associated with clothing against a background of other behavioral or descriptive characteristics. Lapitsky's work, for example, dealt with the relationship between clothing values and general values. As would be expected, positive correlations were found between the specific values held with respect to clothing and parallel general values, e.g., subjects who emphasized the aesthetic aspect of dress also scored high in terms of general aesthetic values.

More pertinent, perhaps, to the present discussion is the fact that aesthetic and economic interests were more important in the value configurations of the women studied than were any of

The importance of clothing as a means of achieving approval and acceptance is paramount in the value configurations of adolescents, but for those with greater maturity and/or self-confidence, it appears to decrease in favor of aesthetic or economic considerations.

"We have so much in common, Albert!"

Figure 5-7. An open desire to dress like others is often strongest during the teen years.

[15]L. Anne Swanson, "Male and Female Conformity in Dress: A Study in Perception and Behavior," Master's thesis, University of Nevada, 1971.
[16]Olive Alexander, "A Pilot Investigation of the Motives Underlying the Desire to Feel Well-Dressed at Various Levels," Master's thesis, Cornell University, 1961.
[17]Sandra Ehrman, "Clothing Attitudes and Peer Acceptance," Master's thesis, Colorado State University, 1971.
[18]Shirley Kopitzke, "Aspects of Dress of Teen-age Girls," Master's thesis, Colorado State University, 1971.

CLOTHES ATTITUDES, AND VALUES

Figure 5-8. With the growing threat to our natural resources, Americans are becoming increasingly concerned about "green grass and trees" and extinction of wildlife. These demonstrators are protesting the killing of animals for the production of fur fashions.

the other clothing values that were investigated. When these results are compared with the findings of earlier experiments, there are some interesting points of agreement. Lapitsky's subjects were adult women; other studies of adult women also indicate that beauty in dress is of primary importance. The more mature female regards the social aspects of dress (i.e., wanting clothes like others, desire for social approval) lower in her hierarchy of values than the desire for comfort and the conservation of time, energy, and money. Furthermore, when Lapitsky's subjects were divided on the basis of anxiety measures, the emotionally secure group scored significantly higher in aesthetic values, while those who were judged to be socially insecure placed greater emphasis on the social value of clothing.[19]

Creekmore also studied this relationship between general values and behavior.[20] Significant associations were found between certain types of clothing behavior and specific values. People who were strong in aesthetic values were shown to place a corresponding degree of emphasis on the tactual aspects of clothing as well as upon the symbolic meanings associated with particular styles of dress. Those whose economic values were high stressed the factors of cost, maintenance, and the general management aspects of clothing, while those who scored high in religious values tended to be concerned with modesty in dress.

The important point here is that values held in relation to dress and adornment do not exist in isolation. They are all interrelated with the other things we hold to be important, and they are based upon some deep-lying assumptions about what is "good" and what is "bad." The term **value pattern** refers to a whole configuration of values, all of which we hold to be important but which fit together in some kind of orderly hierarchy.

Many of the value orientations in America today are outgrowths of what is commonly known as the "Puritan ethic." First and foremost in the value configuration of the early Protestants was an undying faith in God. Thus undergirded by powerful religious sanctions, the drive toward hard work became a sign of grace. People oriented to the rewards of a life hereafter were also characterized by a willingness to "do without" in the present. Frugality and simplicity were natural accompaniments to their way of life, and comfort was merely incidental. Anything but a conservative mode of dress and ornamentation would be alien to such a value pattern.

For most Americans today, a growing affluence has lowered the value once placed upon hard work and saving money. With more and more comforts of the "good life" and increased leisure time, the emphasis has shifted to a desire for peace and

[19]Mary Lapitsky, "Clothing Values and Their Relation to General Values and to Social Security and Insecurity," Unpublished dissertation, Pennsylvania State University, 1961.
[20]Creekmore, "Clothing Behaviors," 1963.

security, and to getting along with others. In 1970, *Life* magazine surveyed a cross section of Americans on matters pertaining to goals and lifestyles. The poll asked people to choose the things most important to them. For the 4,047 respondents, the following percentages were reported:

Green grass and trees around me	95%
Neighbors with whom I feel comfortable	92%
A kitchen with all the modern conveniences	84%
To be at peace with yourself	82%
To be able to wear what I feel like wearing	82%
Having a full and relaxing time in leisure life	59%
Fixing up your house the way you want it	54%
Hard work and saving money	47%
Getting to the top in your work	38%

It was interesting that 78 per cent of the people perceived that "traditional values are being torn down, and that's bad," and more than half (54 per cent) thought that "new styles in hair and dress are a sure sign of moral decay in America."[21]

Value conflict

Conflict always arises whenever the total value system gets out of whack. You cannot change the bits and pieces without altering the whole hierarchy. This is the basic reason that many religious sects[22] view technological innovations with suspicion —because "progress," for whatever it's worth, is a threat to a total way of life.

Lifestyles in American society today are so diverse that conflict is inevitable. The variety of subcultures make it difficult to generalize about dominant value themes of the population as a whole, but we can at least look at the so-called "traditional values" in light of those that have been called "antiestablishment."

Perhaps one of the most widely known proponents of the values of the "new generation," Charles Reich summarized its dominant theme as a concern for "human values." His thesis is that the "new generation" people must reject the values of the present society and reassert a rational control over the encroachments of the industrial system and the corporate state. As an expression of such a philosophy, the clothes of the "new generation" become an important symbol which represents a "deliberate rejection of the neon colors and artificial, plastic-coated look of the affluent society. They are inexpensive to buy, inexpensive to maintain."[23] Such clothes, he says, are:

Values held in relation to clothing are integral parts of a total value configuration.

---

[21]Bayard Hooper, "The Real Change Has Just Begun," *Life*, 9 January 1970, pp. 102–106.
[22]Notably those of the Mennonite movement, such as the Amish, the Brethren, the Dunkers, and so forth.
[23]Charles Reich, *The Greening of America*, Random House, New York, 1970, p. 234.

Figure 5-9. Traditionally clad Amish of Indiana exchange curious glances with a long-haired Southern California surfer.

Primarily functional; people are not objects to be decorated.

Comfortable, expressive of freedom; expensive clothes enforce social constraints.

Machine-made, with no shame attached to mass-produced goods, no social points lost for wearing something that sells for $4.99 from coast to coast.

Profoundly democratic; there are no distinctions of wealth or status, no élitism, people are shorn of distinctions.

Not uniform, because they express the body inside them, and each body is unique.

For all these reasons, Reich claims, "the new clothes are worn with pride, as befits a statement of principles and basic values."

In essence, it sounds like a return to the Puritan ethic. The basic conflict lies in its incompatibility with our modern material culture. This is also a time in which people are concerned about exploding populations and the loss of individual identity. Rather than seeking the faceless anonymity of the new philosophy, the majority of people are searching for ways to achieve and maintain a semblance of individuality.

On an individual basis, problems often arise when two competing values lead to divergent courses of action. Value conflict appears to be particularly prevalent among youngsters of immigrant parents. When the value patterns of the family differ sharply from those of the larger culture, considerable tension may arise among the children who find it extremely difficult to maintain loyalties both to parents and to peers.

Even within the so-called typical American family, we have seen how values change at different age levels. We have only to observe the flood of problem letters in the advice columns to know that clothing is a continual source of conflict between parental and teenage values.

Picking up the bits and pieces of the "new philosophy" can only lead to value inconsistencies. The director of an exclusive

Figure 5-10. Scores of young people have retreated to wilderness areas seeking a return to nature and the ways of a quieter past. Value conflict can thus be reduced by withdrawing from the mainstream of the dominant society.

girls' school in the east noted that the widespread acceptance of jeans has had a strongly democratizing influence, but that "the labels on sweaters and blouses still mean something."

Still another example is the case of a young woman who, in seeking independence from her affluent family, turned to a career in prostitution. "I've always had a split personality about middle class things," she confessed. "If I had $100 right now to spend on clothes, I'd still go to Altman's and blow it on a skirt and sweater, rather than to Macy's and two skirts and two sweaters. See my shoes—they're Gucci," (green suede platforms, worn with blue jeans and an old burgundy sweater).[24]

Or, take the girl who would like to attract the admiring glances and attentions of the masculine guests by choosing a backless black satin gown for Saturday night's party; but the dress is really beyond her budget, its use would be limited, and her father would have a fit. In most cases the individual is able to order his values so that one takes precedence over the others. If it is difficult to accept one because it implies open rejection of the other, people usually find some socially acceptable reason for ignoring the one that they do. If the girl buys the backless black satin dress, she can save the needed money by skipping lunch for the next two months, and this will help her to lose a few pounds, which she ought to do anyway. Father will never know if she keeps the dress at school, and besides, his idea of suitable dress is strictly nineteenth-century.

Most conflict is resolved through the choice of one of several acceptable alternatives, but if no satisfactory solution to con-

"You don't see Thurgood Marshall dressing like that!"

Figure 5-11. Values conflict at different age levels. Drawing by D. Fradon; © 1969 The New Yorker Magazine, Inc.

[24]Judy Klemesrud. "Former Prostitute Finds Going Straight Difficult," *New York Times* News Service Special, 14 March 1973.

CLOTHES, ATTITUDES, AND VALUES

When two or more values lead to alternate courses of clothing behavior, the individual resolves the conflict through a unique ordering of alternate choices.

flicting values can be achieved by choosing one over the other, it is possible that the individual may follow a deviant course of action. A girl from a low-income family, for instance, strongly desiring the prestige and social recognition that new and expensive clothes will command but lacking the economic wherewithal, may sacrifice the value of integrity and develop a regular habit of shoplifting.

Value change

We have now seen how the value patterns of societies, groups, and individuals are subject to change as they come under the influence of new sets of experiences and circumstances. Adjustments that must be made to a persistent and widespread conflict in general values inevitably leads to social or cultural change.

In American society today, it is easy to exaggerate the extent of such change. One reason for this is that conflict, when it occurs, is widely publicized, and we tend to generalize about what we see in the news media. A 1971 survey of young Americans between the ages of fifteen and twenty-one revealed a set of values that the researchers described as "remarkably moderate, even conservative." In general the findings showed that the attitudes of the younger generation differed very little from those of their parents. "The majority of youth listens to the rhetoric of dissent, picks what it wants, then slowly weaves it into the dominant social pattern."[25]

In 1970, it was estimated that less than 7 per cent of the youth population could be considered "radical activists," that is, those whose views are deliberately counter to the mainstreams of the established society. About 20 per cent were described as "concerned liberals," and over half were found to be conservative, even reactionary.[26] Such statistics are supported by the fact that in the early 1970's, over 40 million families (60 per cent of all Americans) had annual incomes under $10,000. With respect to the potential appeal of an anti-materialistic ethic, one writer noted:

> Certainly, the 20 million family units with incomes of less than $5,000 would like nothing quite so much as to "make it" into the middle class and its traditional values. An equal number of family units, moreover, find their energies bound up in the struggle to get more of—or merely to hold on to—the middle-class amenities they have only recently attained. Indeed, most of the ten million family units earning between $5,000 and $7,500 a year and many of the ten million in the $7,500 to $10,000 bracket would be surprised to learn that they have much discretionary income at their disposal.

---

[25]Louis Harris, quoted in "Change, Yes—Upheaval, No," *Life*, 8 January 1971, p. 22.
[26]Walter Thomas, "Value Change and American Youth," *Penney's Forum*, Fall/Winter 1970, p. 7.

. . . Far from being sated with goods, most Americans would like to consume more, and are willing to work hard in order to do so.[27]

Apparently a majority of today's youth agrees. In answer to the question, "Do you believe that hard work leads to success and wealth?" 61 per cent answered yes. When asked if that kind of material success was worth striving for, 66 per cent answered yes.[28]

Reich was not the first to criticize our insatiable appetite for consumer goods. More than a decade ago, Vance Packard preached that "Americans must learn to live with their abundance without being forced to impoverish their spirit by being damned fools about it."[29] Among the suggestions that he made to "remedy" the wasteful spending engendered by fashion obsolescence were to (1) restore a pride in prudence, and (2) restore a pride in quality. However worthy such values may be, the simple fact is that vast numbers of Americans see no real purpose in prudence; why engage in self-denial when you can have what you want and enjoy it? Quality is nice, but why pay for quality that will outlast the fashion life of the garment?

We expect to discard garments before they are worn out; the skills of patching and mending are rapidly becoming lost arts. There is, moreover, a greater willingness to go into debt in order to have the clothes that go with the "good life." The widespread practice of buying on the installment plan is regarded as the normal state of affairs in a high percentage of American homes.

These are the popular values today, and they represent a significant change over the frugal ways of our forebears. In his day when grandfather bought a suit, he expected it to last, and he did not buy a new one until the old one wore out.

> "Why, it's durned near brand-new," he said, referring to the wedding suit that hung in the closet at home. "I looked at it the other day, and there ain't even a worn place on it. That's a good suit, you know. I paid an awful lot of money for it back when we got married, and there wasn't a better or a stronger suit in Reno."
>
> He did not have to remind us how strong it was. There was no denying the quality of the material that went into it. That was the trouble. It was like a suit of armor, and another thirty years would have as little effect on it as the first thirty had.
>
> "But, Pop," we argued, "don't you think it might be a little bit old-fashioned? Times have changed quite a bit since then, you know."
>
> "Bho!" he said, waving the objection aside with one hand. "A suit's a suit, and," he added, "it's durned near brand-new."[30]

[27]Charles Silberman, "'Identity Crisis' in the Consumer Markets," *Fortune*, March 1971, p. 94.
[28]"Change, Yes – Upheaval, No," *Life*, 8 January 1971.
[29]Vance Packard, *The Wastemakers*, David McKay Company, New York, 1960, p. 327.
[30]Robert Laxalt, *Sweet Promised Land*, Harper and Brothers, New York, 1957, pp. 40–41.

CLOTHES, ATTITUDES, AND VALUES

Persistent and widespread conflict in the general values related to clothing inevitably results in cultural change.

Values that were highly appropriate half a century ago cannot survive when other situational factors have changed. We can look back over time, see the gradual evolution of change in our value system, and wonder how long our present values will remain important. But if we know where we are, and where we have been, we can see the future more clearly. We cannot afford to ignore the voices of the activists for change, because even though they're few in number, society will never again be quite the same for all their shouting. They have contributed to the long-term shifts in values that will be taking place for many years to come.

SUMMARY *Group and individual values*

Clothing is an expression both of the dominant value-themes in American society and of those attitudes and values held to be important by various subcultural groups and by individuals. In most cases, the family derives its values from the larger society, and through the process of socialization transmits these values to the child. However, other agencies also make a significant contribution to the individual's value pattern: the school, movies, television, and all forms of mass communication.

Several studies have demonstrated the relative importance that different groups and individuals assign to clothing. In addition, investigations have shown that the attitudes most often associated with clothing relate to (1) a desire to conform, (2) a desire for self-expression, (3) a desire for aesthetic satisfaction, (4) prestige values, (5) the desire for social participation, (6) physical comfort, and (7) economy.

Decision making in regard to clothing choices is sometimes difficult because an individual often holds competing or conflicting values. Most conflict is resolved by placing one value above another, although in some cases, the individual may follow a deviant course of action. Because all personal values must be viewed against the general cultural setting, a change in other circumstances—such as economic conditions, technological advances, and the like—often leads to a changed attitude with respect to dress.

FOR FURTHER READING

Allport, G. W., P. E. Vernon, and G. Lindzey. *A Study of Values*. Boston: Houghton Mifflin Company, 1957.

Baldwin, DeWitt C. "The Generation Gap: A Question of Changing Values," *Penney's Forum*, Fall/Winter 1971, pp. 10–11.

"The Commune Comes to America," *Life* 67, 18 July 1969, pp. 16–23.

MacLeish, Archibald. "Rediscovering the Simple Life." *McCall's* April 1972, pp. 79–89.

Reich, Charles. *The Greening of America*. New York: Random House, 1970.

Ryan, Mary S. *Clothing: A Study in Human Behavior*. New York: Holt, Rinehart & Winston, 1966. (Pp. 57–63 and Chapter 5, "Individual Values, Interests, and Attitudes as Related to Clothing Behavior and Clothing Choices.")

DISCUSSION QUESTIONS

1. What values are held to be important in American society today? Give an example of how each of these values is expressed through clothing and appearance.

2. What aspects of the "Puritan ethic" have carried over into our present value system? How are these reflected in dress?

3. Evaluate the statement: "New styles in hair and dress are sure signs of moral decay in America."

4. What are your reactions to Charles Reich's thesis? Present your reasons for agreeing or disagreeing with his basic premises.

5. In light of the changes in our material environment discussed in Chapter 3, and the changing cultural habits discussed in Chapter 4, what are your predictions for value changes in the future?

6

Cultural Change and Fashion Change

IN THE PRECEDING chapters we saw how the customs or traditions of dress provide for the stability or continuity of a culture. In all cases, however, our social inheritance is modified by the changes that occur in the whole cultural climate, so that each historical period leaves its visual imprint stamped into the fashion of the times. It is for this reason that most items of apparel, by virtue of their style, material, and workmanship, can be dated at least within the decade of their origin.

To be garbed consistently in old-fashioned dress is a sign that the wearer is somehow out of step with the times. Yet this changing aspect of dress is the characteristic most often deplored by observers of the social scene. The necessity of discarding a garment—not because it has outlived its usefulness but because it has outlived the fashion—implies a senseless economic waste. In any age, there are some forces at work that tend to restrict or impede fashion change, while other factors serve to stimulate or accelerate such change. The rate of change in any given period of history is dependent upon the balance that exists between these two sets of forces. As we shall see, the factors that promote rapid changes are particularly ascendant in our own society and are responsible for the increased tempo of fashion obsolescence in the contemporary world.

Resistance to change

If we go back several hundred years in history, we are able to observe a time when the rate of fashion change was slow enough to be imperceptible within the span of an individual's life:

A land-owner of the fourteenth century, for instance, would dress in clothes very similar to those of a land-owner of the eleventh century. A cowherd of the fourteenth century might have inherited his garment from his great, great . . . grandfather (several times removed), in so far as the style and cut were concerned. Moreover, a cowherd in either century would no more have thought of dressing like a land-owner than a corporal in the army would think of dressing in a colonel's uniform: that is to say, he might well think of it, but would not dare to do it.[1]

The acceleration of changes in fashion had its beginnings in the Renaissance, when a rising class of wealthy merchants sought not only to emulate the knights and their ladies, but to outshine them in the sumptuousness of their dress.

Rigid class distinctions

A society in which a ruling class is able to maintain both wealth and power has little need for fashion-racing. The line of demarcation between the feudal lords of the Middle Ages and the poorer classes was strictly drawn; a serf had no possibility whatever of emulating the dress of his lord and master. When extreme differences in wealth exist and only a few are able to maintain a costly wardrobe, fashions tend to remain stationary for a longer period of time. In earlier days, moreover, clothing was so expensive that even the wealthy could not afford a frequent change of costume. Most of the finer fabrics had to be imported from the Far East, and the intricate cut of the garments necessitated such tedious and skilled workmanship that the cost of each item was prohibitively high. It is reported, for example, that the shoes worn by Richard II were worth $2,000 a pair, and his cloak, $90,000.[2] Even as late as 1850, when the voluminous gowns of the crinoline age were the vogue, the yardage required was so extensive that even if made in the cheapest of fabrics, a single dress was unbelievably costly. Few women could afford more than two or three dresses in their entire wardrobes, and one's "Sunday best" had to serve the wearer for many years. When the lower classes are thus prevented from copying the clothing of the privileged few, there is little necessity for the rich to change their style of dress in order to preserve their distinctiveness.

A rigidly defined class system, reinforced by an unequal distribution of wealth, retards fashion movement and gives rise to traditional forms of dress.

Sumptuary laws

When a ruling class finds itself unable to maintain its position of fashion supremacy through the control of wealth, it often restricts the consumption of the lesser citizens through the enactment of sumptuary laws. When the feudal lords, for example, found themselves outdone by the ostentatious extravagance of the newly rich merchant classes, they resorted to legal prohibitions for dress and personal decoration. In the

[1]James Laver, *Dress*, John Murray Publishers, London, 1950, p. 8.
[2]Hurlock, *"The Psychology of Dress,"* p. 78.

Sumptuary laws that restrict fashion imitation reduce the necessity for rapid change.

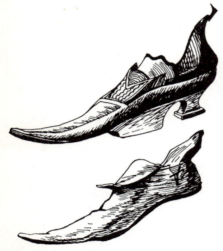

Figure 6-1. Fifteenth-century poulaines.

Traditional forms of dress that are deeply rooted in custom and habit tend to preserve the status quo.

Susceptibility to fashion change is greatly reduced by geographic isolation.

fifteenth century, the imitation of the long-toed hose and shoes known as *poulaines* led to a regulation on the number of inches that shoes were permitted to extend beyond the toe: 24 inches or more for a nobleman, 12 inches for a gentleman, and 6 inches for a commoner.

Although sumptuary laws for the civilian population are rare in modern society, they are found to be prevalent in almost every nation where class distinctions are recognized, and when the social structure has reached a stage of development where the national wealth is no longer in the hands of the nobility alone.[3] Such laws helped to curb senseless extravagances, but their primary function related to the preservation of class distinctions.

Custom

Laws and customs have both been discussed in greater detail in Chapter 4, but they must be recognized here as important factors in the retardation of fashion change. Traditions are perpetuated through the symbolic use of clothing, and a reverence for the past causes people to cling to the time-honored forms of dress that signify one's status, role, or position. National costumes such as the Japanese kimono, the Indian sari, the colorful provincial costumes of Brittany, Normandy, Yugoslavia, and many others, are fast giving way to the Western style of dress, but most people relinquish traditional garb with great reluctance. Bridal gowns, academic attire, judicial robes, church vestments, and various other forms of ceremonial dress remained relatively unchanged through centuries of use. Although there have been recent attempts to uproot many of these traditions, such elements of dress are slow to give way to newer modes of fashion.

Isolation

When people are out of touch with the world of fashion, their mode of dress falls into conventional patterns that usually derive from local custom or tradition. Such conditions of isolation formed the basis for much of the provincial attire that characterizes remote villages and communities. At one time, there were marked differences in our own country between the urban and rural populations, but today, because of improved communication and transportation, there are relatively few areas that do not have access to fashion information. In places like Hawaii, for example, it is far easier to hang onto the muumuus and the poi pounders than it would be if the islands were attached to the mainland. The geographic isolation of the islands imparts—even to the tourist—the tendency to abandon

[3]Hurlock, "*The Psychology of Dress*," p. 64 ff.

more civilized forms of dress for the comfortable garb that symbolizes the Hawaiian way of life.

Fear

Fear of the new and the unknown is another of the factors that heighten resistance to fashion change. A certain security is afforded by styles that are familiar, and most people refrain from buying anything which is startlingly new or daringly different for fear of being ridiculed. Primitive and uneducated peoples often attach a symbolic significance to particular designs or styles, and to discard the old is to risk the possible evils and misfortunes that may accompany the new and unproven. To depart from the sure and the safe way of doing things requires an adventurous spirit and *courage sans peur*.

Fear of the new inhibits fashion change.

Government restrictions

When the source of raw materials is limited, legal regulations are sometimes necessary to insure an equitable distribution of the supply that is available. In America, the L-85 restrictions during World War II retarded fashion changes by limiting the amount of fabric that could be used for specific articles of dress. In Britain, the wartime designs were known as CC41 styles, and they were rationed to consumers by a coupon system in which each person was issued 60 coupons for a period of 14 months. A man would exhaust his allowance if he bought one suit (26 coupons), a set of underwear (10), one shirt (5), a pair of shoes (7), and four pairs of socks (at three coupons a pair). Obviously, people "made do" with what they had and repaired old clothes rather than buy new. Even in peacetime there may be restrictions on the importation of goods from other countries. Excise taxes imposed on articles that are considered luxury items, such as furs and leather goods, restrict rather than promote their widespread use.

Shortages and/or restrictions imposed on the use of raw materials retard fashion changes.

Socialism

The many forms of socialistic or totalitarian societies are characterized by their attempts to do away with all class distinctions or inequalities in dress. In their early stages of development at least, this is accomplished by a uniform type of clothing. The Marxist-Lenin brand of communism produced the drab jackets, the ill-fitting trousers, the crude black boots that were so long a part of the image of the typical Russian citizen.

In previous chapters, we have discussed the effects of the communist revolution in China:

> Almost overnight as it seemed, the nation was garbed in a dress whose sexless regimentation of style and shapelessness symbolized the liberation of a new national spirit according to Marxist theory,

although to less politically perceptive eyes it appeared, however utilitarian, unnecessarily drab.[4]

In like manner, Castro's regime in Cuba produced the bearded, green-clad "Barbudos"; men and women dressed exactly alike; smart clothes were "unpatriotic" and inconsistent with the spirit of the times. Austerity in dress is like a badge of honor that symbolizes the leveling of classes.

This expression of classlessness through dress is by no means a twentieth-century phenomenon. Costume in England under the Commonwealth of Oliver Cromwell manifested the same drabness and uniformity of style, and our own Puritan ancestors went to great extremes to eliminate all forms of ornamentation in dress that would distinguish one colonist from another.

It is particularly interesting, however, to note the gradual renewal of interest in fashionable clothes once the major crisis has passed. As the colonists became more wealthy, new styles were adopted in America almost as quickly as they were in Europe. By 1957, GOUM department store in Moscow held fashion shows that promoted ivy-league suits for men and fashionable clothes for women. In the late 1950's communist China had its first fashion show in Peking, featuring modern versions of the tradional *ch'i p'ao*, the woman's long sheath gown with side slits.

The attempt to eliminate class distinctions by totalitarian regimes is manifest through the suppression of fashion and the adoption of austere forms of dress.

No population is content for long with drab, uniform-like clothes; a resurgence of status incentives and aesthetic drives is the inevitable outcome of an improved standard of living.

SUMMARY *Resistance to change*

The degree of change that occurs in any society in a given period is dependent upon the balance that exists between the forces that promote fashion obsolescence and those which impede progress. Factors that tend to work against fashion change include (1) rigid class distinctions, (2) sumptuary laws, (3) custom, (4) isolation from the fashion world, (5) fear of the new, (6) governmental regulations, and (7) totalitarianism.

Agents of change

The tremendous acceleration of fashion change that occurs in contemporary society has been the subject of much social criticism. The adversaries of planned obsolescence treat it as a kind of social disease for which we have not yet discovered an effective cure. In order to weigh the value of such commentaries on American life and times, we must examine the forces

---

[4]Scott, *Chinese Costume in Transition*, p. 92.

that increase the tempo of change and consider their possible alternatives.

An open class system

We have just seen that both rigid class distinction and its antithesis — the classless society — function in ways that limit the degree and speed of fashion change. Democracy, on the other hand, provides the ideal climate for fashion-racing. The constant push of the middle classes up the ladder of social mobility creates the impetus for an ever-changing shift in the design of clothes worn by the upper classes.

The foundations of fashion-racing were laid in the period of the Renaissance, which gave rise to a wealthy merchant class, and at the same time made available luxurious importations from all over the world. The Industrial Revolution then gave considerable momentum to the fashion movement by increasing the ease with which styles could be reproduced and distributed, and also by contributing to the elevation of the common man; the latter greatly increased the number of people who were both willing and able to be fashionable.

Fashion changes flourish in the open class system that characterizes American democracy.

Abundance

One of the most important factors in speeding up the process of fashion movement is a wide diffusion of wealth and an increase in the family income that exceeds the amount required for the bare necessities of life. The purchasing power of the average consumer in the United States has increased tremendously in the last quarter of a century. At the same time, commercial expansion and intense competition among the ready-to-wear manufacturers have greatly increased the range of fashion goods to which such purchasing power may be applied. Greater equality in the distribution of income has been further intensified by our system of taxation and the numerous social services that are provided at government expense. Many more people today are able to afford the amenities of middle-class life. Thus, an increasingly affluent society indulges in greater expenditures for luxury items, and as they do, wardrobes expand.

It is also significant that at the same time that Parisian couture houses find it difficult to stay in business,[5] the number of designer-owned firms is on the increase in the United States. Most of these houses retail at prices between $250 and $500. While there are fewer women who can afford to pay $1,500 for a St. Laurent, there is a growing number who buy Bill Blass at $350.

A diffusion of wealth in the mass society increases consumption and greatly accelerates fashion change.

[5]"Couture: Not what it was but still a power," *Women's Wear Daily,* 26 January 1973.

Leisure

The natural accompaniment to increasing affluence is a decreasing necessity for long hours of work:

> In the last century a drastic decline has occurred in the work week. In 1850 it is estimated to have averaged just under seventy hours, the equivalent of seven ten-hour days a week or roughly six at from six in the morning to six at night. A hundred years later the average was 40.0 hours or five eight-hour days.[6]

The spread of leisure to the reaches of the lower- and middle-class groups has the effect of intensifying the importance of fashion in the lives of individuals. Not only do people have more time to think about fashions, but leisure provides greater social opportunity to wear them. Even though their jobs may require work clothes or a uniform, few men today lack occasion to array themselves in a wide variety of dress for evening or weekend activities. Leisure time can also lead to boredom and a search for amusement and novelty, both of which find direct outlets in fashion change.

Increased leisure gives impetus to fashion.

Sports

Probably the most important single influence on fashion during the last sixty years has been the world of sports. In the early development of fashion, position and wealth were indicated largely by the elaboration of dress; but by the end of the eighteenth century, the English country gentleman's costume began to set the pace for all masculine attire. Enormous prestige was attached to the huntsman since the sport implied that he owned a vast acreage. The embroidered coat, the satin breeches, and the white silk stockings were hardly suitable for riding to the hounds, so the Englishman fashioned a "sports costume" consisting of a plain cutaway coat and riding boots, which soon became so popular that it was worn not only for hunting, but also for regular day dress. Gradually elements of the hunting costume crept into formal wear, and its influence was complete.

Nineteenth-century sports were confined mostly to hunting, archery, and lawn croquet. The costumes for these activities were decidedly nonfunctional from a modern point of view, but they slowly evolved in the direction of greater utility. It is important to realize that prior to the advent of sports, functional utility in clothes would have implied that they were intended for physical labor; hence no prestige value could be attached to comfortable garments. But to participate in sports meant that one had sufficient leisure to devote time to play activity, and modifications in dress that permitted strenuous movement

Figure 6-2. The English country gentleman's dress c. 1790.

[6]J. K. Galbraith, *The Affluent Society*, Houghton Mifflin Company, Boston, 1958, p. 334.

Figure 6-3. Participation in the world of sports revolutionized women's dress.

CULTURAL CHANGE AND FASHION CHANGE

became entirely acceptable as long as everyone knew that the physical exertion was all in fun.

Although bloomers actually made their appearance earlier, the acceptance of bifurcated garments for women became socially legitimized through the sport of cycling. But perhaps the most drastic changes in the female wardrobe originated on the tennis courts and bathing beaches. When Suzanne Lenglen walked onto the courts in 1920 wearing a pleated skirt shortened to midcalf, it may have shocked the spectators, but it paved the way for the gradual rise of skirt lengths in the ensuing five years. Gussie Moran's lace-trimmed bloomers still made news in the mid-twentieth century. The feats of serious swimmers like Annette Kellerman in the early 1900's were facilitated by streamlining the bathing suit. In 1910, the maillot was scandalous, but by 1924 it had been stripped down to essentials and given social approval. Thus, as people—and women in particular—began to lead more active lives, their clothing gave greater freedom to their limbs. Sports accustomed the eye to body exposure, which in turn had a lasting effect on all other categories of dress.

Sportsmen and sportswomen continue to enjoy widespread popularity and publicity, and their actions are followed as avidly as those of fashion leaders. Stretch ski pants may have been designed for the snow-covered slopes, but we find them in abundance on paved city streets. The functionalism of sports extends even into those areas where the functionalism is not needed.

Participation in active sports has had tremendous influence in the mutation of dress toward greater utility.

Education

Widespread education also accelerates fashion changes. It opens the door to new areas of experience, and it increases the interest in and desire for a more fashionable appearance. Entrance into what Galbraith has called the New Class of leisure is accomplished overwhelmingly through increased education. Education not only helps to increase earning power, but it extends consumer wants especially into those areas in which fashion plays a part. Moreover, knowledge helps to dissipate fear of the new and the unknown and frees people from the inhibitions that are rooted in custom. They become more aware of the choices and the possibilities that are open to them and more confident of their judgments in making clothing decisions.

Widespread education dissipates the fears that so often inhibit fashion change.

Culture contact

Just as geographic isolation tends to ossify patterns of dress, increased communication and contact with various cultures

Figure 6-4. A curious mixing of styles is evident in this blending of traditional Eskimo dress with modern ready-to-wear. **Figure 6-5.** In Japan today, the dress of both men and women is dominated by Western styles, but not everyone has abandoned the kimono. **Figure 6-6.** The impact of culture contact is often responsible for incongruities. These women in Gabon wear miniskirts but carry their babies in the tradition of their culture.

antithetically speeds up the rate of change. While the language of another country may be difficult to learn, the outward symbols of clothing are easily transmitted from one culture to another. The eagerness with which the once-isolated communities adopt Western ways can readily be seen, especially among the younger generation. Before the coming of the white man, for example, Eskimo clothing had always been made of animal skins; now nylon windbreakers replace the skin parkas, and rubber boots are worn instead of mukluks.

The intermingling of cultural elements in the modern world can be seen in almost every country. Even in the United States we have had adaptations of the Oriental cheongsam, the Indian sari, the African bournouse, native sarongs, primitive jewelry, Tyrolean hats, Spanish toreador pants, peasant blouses, Middle Eastern caftans, ad infinitum. Such cultural diffusion is facilitated, of course, through increased travel and improved communication, as well as through the inevitable exchange brought about by war. Vestiges of American G.I. uniforms can be seen in all parts of the world, and soldiers and sailors return home with souvenirs from the places of their encounters.

CULTURAL CHANGE AND FASHION CHANGE

Increased culture contact, made possible through improved transportation and communication, speeds up the rate of change in fashion movements.

In recent years air travel, movies, magazines, and television have greatly increased the dissemination of international fashions throughout the world. While such diffusion portends the ultimate disappearance of unique patterns of dress, it also functions in removing the barriers that separate one nation from another.

Youth

A way of life that emphasizes a reverence for custom, age, and tradition gives little vent to fashion changes; conversely, a society that places high value on youth tends to be oriented in the direction of change and progress. Retail clothiers are very much aware of the dollar value of the teenage market. With increased incomes and few family responsibilities, young people invest heavily in cars and clothes.

When fashions cater to youthful tastes, more radical changes are likely to be introduced.

The assumption of fashion leadership by the younger generation has led to the development of a male couture that all started when Carnaby Street overtook London's conservative Savile Row. The result was a revolution in men's finery that spread throughout the world. Pierre Cardin, a French couturier, began designing men's suits. American women's wear designers quickly followed: Bill Blass, Oleg Cassini, Geoffrey Beene, Oscar de la Renta, John Weitz, and many others all put out a men's line. Thus, in the decade from 1960 to 1970, expenditures for men's and boy's clothing went from $9.7 billion to $18.6 billion.[7]

Social agitation

A thorough study of the history of costume and the concurrent social events of each period will make it clear that fluctuations in fashions are indicative of the pace of social change that occurs within the society in general. In the Far Eastern civilizations that maintained rigidly structured and unchanging caste systems, little innovation in clothing styles could be observed from one century to the next. Conversely, the historical periods that are marked by social agitation, tension, and strain show intense variability in fashion departures from the basic pattern.[8]

The sociopolitical tensions that surround wars, revolutions, social upheavals, and struggles over the rights of man appear to cause fashion to violate the fundamental contour: normally wide skirts may become narrow or short, slender waists become thickened or dislocated in position.[9]

---

[7]Walter McQuade, "High Style Disrupts the Men's Wear Industry," *Fortune,* February 1971, p. 75.
[8]Jane Richardson and A. L. Kroeber, "Three Centuries of Women's Dress Fashions, A Quantitative Analysis," *Anthropological Records* 5, no. 2, University of California Press, Berkeley and Los Angeles, 1940, pp. 111–153.
[9]Kroeber, *Style and Civilization.*

Figure 6-7. Labor-saving devices freed women from responsibilities of the home. Here an emancipated wife reads a 1914 newspaper while an early version of the washing machine does clothes for her. Women's increasing involvement in other activities implemented fashion change.

Thus, the sensitivity of fashion to social problems provides a visible index of agitation and unrest. Drastic changes in clothing patterns are evidence of changes elsewhere. Back in 1963, Mandelbaum predicted that if women's evening dress should suddenly "take the form of tight trousers or should present standards of propriety in skin exposure be abandoned, sober observers of our society may well take it as a token of a truly major social upheaval."[10] Interestingly enough, when the counterculture demonstrations reached their peak in the days preceding the end of the Vietnam war, that is precisely what happened.

Emancipation of women

A radical change in the position of women in society has the same effect as other types of social upheaval. The accepted form of dress in those cultures which keep the female subservient to the male remains static for generations, sometimes for centuries. Conversely, in the periods in which women refuse to accept an insignificant status and seek to put themselves on an equal footing with men, feminine modes in dress are found to change more swiftly.

In the past fifty years, women have gained the right to vote; labor-saving devices have freed them from home responsibilities and moved them out into the working force; during World War II they took over the work of men in the factories and achieved further status as members of the armed forces; they have become increasingly involved in the political and economic affairs of the country; and their avid participation in sports has contributed greatly to their freedom — both physically and socially.

The rate of fashion change is related to the degree of social change that occurs in any given period.

---

[10]David Mandelbaum, "The Interplay of Conformity and Diversity," in S. Farber and R. Wilson (eds.) *Conflict and Creativity*, Part 2, McGraw-Hill Book Company, New York, 1963, p. 248.

Figure 6-8. When sexual equality is achieved, differences in male and female clothing become less distinct.

The wardrobe of the Victorian lady, for example, would have indicated clearly that she could not possibly have indulged in strenuous physical exercise of any sort, while the abundance of sportswear in the feminine wardrobe a hundred years later would prove the exact opposite. Cunnington claimed that if we had no other source of information save the typical clothing of the period, we could reconstruct much of the wearer's habits and outlook. We would know, for instance, that the early Victorian lady's

> . . . physique was poor, her chest compressed, her health delicate; that she took no real exercise and spent most of her time indoors; always cold, with bad circulation, in spite of hot rooms and shut windows. Her tiny hands would be fit only for "elegant accomplishments," at which by long practice she would excel. In this shut-in existence her mental outlook would be trivial and petty, sustained by daydreams of the Cinderella sort. We can picture her as a doll-like, ineffective, kittenish creature, innocent and picturesque. A Dora Copperfield, in fact, emerges simply from an analysis of the costume. This sort of woman was not only usual, but the ideal of the day.[11]

Feminine dress in the twentieth century has moved toward greater similarity to masculine attire. The increasing use of bifurcated garments by women is but one of the many indices of this trend. Women have of course worn shorts and slacks for several decades, but it was not until Norman Norell designed the trend-setting culotte suit in 1960 that divided garments made the transition from sportswear to sophisticated town wear. By 1964, even the French designers were decreeing more trousers for women. André Courrèges gave the trend another boost in the sixties when his tight-legged, hip-slung pants were shown in every fabric from flannel to lace. His stated philosophy is that he designs for the woman who is "active, moves fast, works, is usually young and modern enough to wear modern, intelligent clothes."[12]

[11]C. W. Cunnington, *Why Women Wear Clothes,* Faber and Faber, London, 1941, p. 28.
[12]"The Lord of the Space Ladies," *Life,* 21 May 1965, p. 54.

Women's independence from male domination is increasing economically as well as socially. Fashion historian James Laver notes that whenever women can afford to choose husbands who attract them as men rather than as providers, the clothing of both sexes becomes much alike. The corollary in modern men's wear is a trend toward higher fashion in masculine dress. Men have begun to take on gaily colored vests, shaped jackets, ruffled shirts, and fashionable shoes. Their use of jewelry and perfumed toiletries has increased threefold within the last decade.

We are forced to conclude that when the woman is confined to the more or less graceful bondage of the home, her contours become more softly rounded and her style of dress becomes relatively static; given freedom and status, the feminine mode moves much more swiftly and the differences between male and female clothing diminish.

> The rate of fashion change has a direct relationship to the degree of freedom and status assigned to women in society.

Technology

In Chapter 3 we discussed the impact of a changing technology on the evolution of styles. It is important to the present discussion, however, to point out how such progress in tools and machinery contributes to the acceleration of the fashion process. The invention of the sewing machine gave tremendous impetus to fashion, since it not only laid the foundation for the ready-to-wear industry, but increased the speed with which styles could be copied at home. As new machines were perfected, manufactured clothing was produced at lower and lower prices, making fashion goods available to more and more people. The introduction of the cutting knife replaced the tedious method of hand cutting a few layers of cloth at a time. The invention of the zipper—a gadget taken so for granted today—caused a minor revolution in garment construction. In modern industry, specialized machines for literally every aspect of the construction process operate at high speed to produce low-cost fashions.

In addition to mechanization, change has been hastened by the chemical revolution. Before the turn of the century, silk was a luxury commodity available only to the wealthy; but with the invention of artificial silk—later known as rayon—in 1892, garments with the appearance of silk became accessible to the masses. This was followed in rapid succession by the development of other man-made fibers and synthetic materials which not only simulated the qualities of costly status items but introduced a whole new field of fabrics that influenced the design of the finished product. So great was the impact of nylon on the women's hosiery industry that the common name for stockings was changed to "nylons." New fibers and chemical finishes have opened the world to minimum-care, wash-and-wear, and permanent-press. Fur fabrics have flooded the market, and developments in stretch fabric have produced radical changes

Figure 6-9. Modern electric cutters can rip through more than a hundred layers of cloth at a time, greatly speeding up the process by which ready-to-wear fashions can duplicate the changing modes.

Figure 6-10. Early automobile travel required special attire.

Fashion change is accelerated by contemporaneous advances in technology.

in garment design. As technology continues to alter the functional and aesthetic quality of clothes, fashion will continue to take advantage of its new and improved products.

In a less direct way, fashion also has been modified by technical advances in communication and travel. We have already seen how they function to increase culture contact, and when communication is slow, fashion change is also slow. When the first mass-produced automobile appeared on the market in 1908, fashion followed with dusters, caps, goggles, and motoring veils. Today, increased air travel has heightened the demand for light-weight, packable, and crease-resistant clothing, and heavy, bulky garments are passé. The movies and television also play a part in the acceleration of fashion change; since seeing is the first prerequisite for wanting to buy, the latest fashions worn by the popular idols of the day condition mass tastes and the resulting consumer demand.

Technical improvements in automatic heating and air conditioning have provided all-season environmental control. Gone is the long red flannel underwear; in its place are lighter-weight garments designed to be worn the year round. Labor-saving equipment, both in the home and in industry, has released people from long hours of toil and contributed to the country's mass leisure. Not only has this meant more time for relaxation and entertainment, but an increase in sports participation as well. It becomes obvious that all these factors are interdependent, each having an amplifying effect on the other to produce a total picture of rapid fashion change.

Planned reform

Whenever fashion reaches such an extreme that it appears either to endanger the health of the wearer or to threaten the moral standards of the day, some individual or group will attempt to initiate an organized reform movement. Such crusades have been made in the various names of health, hygiene, practicality, utility, comfort, decency, and beauty. Numerous references in the Bible denouncing the extravagances of fashion will indicate that open criticism of clothing practices is certainly not confined to the modern world. During the Middle Ages, the Church waged constant warfare against the evils in dress; the deeply cut armholes of the medieval surcote were named *fenêtres d'enfer* ("windows of hell"), and the Gothic *hennin* was regarded as a tool of the devil. In 1555, the Bishop of Frankfurt distributed inflammatory pamphlets against the masculine mode of *Pluderhose,* which he claimed were causing scandal and creating a bad example.

Other attempts at planned reform were progressive in outlook and advocated changes that were far in advance of their time.

110   INTERRELATIONSHIP OF CLOTHING AND CULTURE

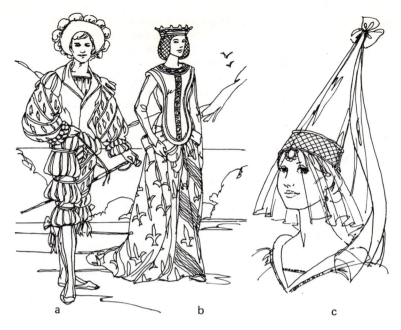

a   b   c

Figure 6-11. These medieval styles were subject to severe criticism from the Church. Left, (a) German Pluderhose with paned and slashed codpiece; (b) a surcote with large armholes worn over a long-sleeved tunic; (c) the Gothic hennin.

Figure 6-12. The Turkish trousers and tunic introduced by Mrs. Bloomer in the 1850's did not make much headway until the advent of cycling at the turn of the century.

Figure 6-13. The Aesthetic Movement of the late 1870's advocated knee breeches, velvet jackets, and loose-flowing ties for men as shown in this cartoon of Oscar Wilde.

Following the French Revolution, the painter David was commissioned to design a "republican costume" that would express the reaction against excesses of the old regime. The men never adopted his styles, which were based on the Greek and Roman models of antiquity; but the ensuing decade saw the development of neoclassical sentiments in the feminine dress of the period made famous by the fashionable Mésdames Tallien and Récamier. In 1851, an American, Amelia Jenks Bloomer, advocate of women's rights, urged the feminine readers of her paper to renounce the cumbersome dress of their day for a costume consisting of a knee-length tunic worn over Turkish trousers. But few ladies adopted the revolutionary style of the feminist reformer, and it was not until the turn of the century with the advent of cycling for women that "bloomers" came into their own. Sports, the great emancipator, achieved what Mrs. Bloomer and her followers could not fifty years earlier.

However rational the concept, attempts at dress reform that run too far ahead of the natural evolution of the times are rarely successful.

Men's dress, hoop skirts, short skirts, trailing skirts, corsets, low necklines, high heels, pointed shoes, and bathing suits all have been the subject at one time or another of crusades for change. Few, if any, made much headway in their day, although many were precursors of changes that evolved in later years as the spirit of the times gave vent to their expression. Many of the suggestions for the improvement of men's wear

Campaigns for change that predate or run counter to fashion have limited influence on contemporaneous clothing norms.

made by Wilde in 1870, by Jäger in 1890, and by Flügel in 1930 are just now beginning to take hold in a few limited categories of masculine dress. Feminine fashions appear to have progressed more rapidly; the stretch pants worn by many modern women make Amelia's bloomers—so scandalous in their day—look like something out of the Dark Ages. The leaders of revolts against fashion rarely achieve more than the kind of fame which comes through ridicule and abuse.

The alternatives to fashion

At this point perhaps we should consider the value of possible substitutions for fashion. Could the function of fashion in society today be replaced by more acceptable patterns of conformation?

The most obvious way to eliminate fashion from clothes would be to eliminate clothes altogether. People who are committed to the philosophy of nudism propose that this is a sure way to wipe out prejudice, snobbery, class and caste distinctions. They maintain that the disappearance of clothes would mark not a regressive "back to nature" movement but progress toward a higher culture than man has ever known. Its implications are that the individual would at last be secure in the acceptance and control of his own body, and that he had mastered the control of his environment to such a degree that clothing would no longer be necessary. But even if an advanced technology could provide us with satisfactory control over our physical environment, it is doubtful that the elimination of clothing would be acceptable from a social and psychological standpoint.

A second alternative to fashion would be the adoption of a kind of uniform. If we wished to maintain the status symbolism that clothing provides, we could adopt a system similar to military dress in which the garment clearly indicates not only the occupation of its wearer but his rank within the hierarchy. Uniforms could be produced with great efficiency, they could be worn until they wore out, and they would eliminate the effort of decision making. Most would agree, however, that the uniform—no matter how attractively designed—soon becomes monotonous, and the opportunity to express one's individuality is extremely limited.

Figure 6-14. Organized crusades against fashion have been aimed at everything from shoes and corsets to the level of the hemline. A militant group of mini-skirted girls, calling themselves GAMS (Girls Against More Skirt) outraged at the lowering of hemlines in 1970, took to the streets in behalf of their cause and picketed in New York. They claimed that longer skirts were uncomfortable and unflattering.

If we wished to abolish the signs of class and status along with fashion, we could adopt a more nondescript uniform such as the one described by Laver:

Prison clothes are sensible enough and by no means uncomfortable. They are completely free from all the excrescences and extravagances of fashion. They do not promote class consciousness; they lend themselves with difficulty to the purposes of seduction. And they hardly ever wear out. In fact they are all that clothes should be except that they do not glad the eye of the beholder nor promote the mental well-being of those that wear them.[13]

The uniform idea could be modified in another direction toward the traditional type of dress exemplified by the Indian sari or the Japanese kimono. Both of these garments rate high in aesthetic attributes, and both provide for variation through the use of color and fabric design. The obsolescence factor is minimal, and although initial cost is quite high, they last a long time. It is a curious thing, however, that in those countries that have perpetuated a traditional garb, progress in other spheres of activity, both cultural and technological, has been limited.

In his description of life in the utopian community of Walden Two, Skinner presented his conception of the ideal way of dressing, if one were free to reshape existing social institutions:

> We want to avoid the waste which is imposed by changing styles, but we don't want to be wholly out of fashion. So we simply change styles more slowly, just slowly enough so we needn't throw away clothing which is still in good condition. . . . We choose the kind of clothes which suffer the slowest change—suits, sweaters and skirts, or blouses and skirts, and so on.[14]

We must realize, however, that the accelerated change which takes place in fashion today is the direct result of the democratization of fashion. In our society, fashions are copied quickly into low-priced lines, and only a relative minority of the people are prevented from emulating the fashion through lack of economic wherewithal. A deceleration in fashion change, therefore, would require a restriction on upward mobility in the class system.

Fashion change in society usually parallels change and progress in other spheres of human activity.

SUMMARY *Agents of change*

The acceleration of fashion change in contemporary society has been explained in terms of the coexistent and interdependent factors of (1) an open class system, (2) abundance and diffusion of wealth, (3) increased leisure, (4) the growing influence of sports, (5) extended education, (6) greater culture contact, (7) the emphasis on youth, (8) concurrent social agitation, (9) the improved status of women, and (10) advances in technology. Various attempts at planned reform in dress, although seemingly futile at the time they are made, often have long-term effects as the precursors of change in the direction of greater utility and practicality.

Those who would eliminate fashion through the adoption of an enduring and constant style of life make the erroneous assumption that our clothing habits exist as independent

---

[13]James Laver, *Clothes*, Horizon Press, New York, 1953, p. 268.
[14]B. F. Skinner, *Walden Two*, Macmillan Publishing Company, New York, 1948, p. 35.

Figure 6-15. Puritan costumes of the seventeenth century. When religious values are ascendant, dress becomes austere.

Figure 6-16. A French court costume c. 1780. The eighteenth century was an age of extravagance and frivolity.

phenomena totally unrelated to the social setting from which they derive. One cannot stem the tide of fashion change without halting progress in other aspects of our daily lives as well.

Forces that shape fashion change

By definition, the concept of fashion implies continuous change. In the preceding sections we have discussed those forces that affect the rate of such change, that is, elements within the culture that may either retard fashion change or accelerate its obsolescence. Aside from the influences of sports (which we have seen to obtain toward greater utility), and the status of women (in which equality with men tends toward equality of dress), such factors do not explain the *character* of fashion change.

Two theories appear to be dominant in the analysis of fashion variation. One is that fashions follow an immutable and ordered pattern from one extreme to the other. The second is that fashion is attributable to a kind of cultural determinism, which defines fashion as a reflection of the political, economic, intellectual, and artistic events of the times. As we shall see, both theories are tenable within the perspective of costume history. We will get to the cyclical nature of fashion in Chapter 8, so we will focus here on the cultural determinants.

Dominant ideals

The variants possible within the typical style for any period are multifarious. A tubular silhouette, for example, may be one which reveals the form of the body beneath it through the use of diaphanous and supple materials, and combines a deep décolletage with an empire waist as it did in 1810. Or it may utilize heavy-bodied fabrics to cover a rigid frame with a neckline encased up to the ears in whalebone as it did in 1910. Even though many elements of a costume from a given period and culture may be revived in later eras, the total effect produced by the combined details creates a look that is unique and characteristic of no other time but the one in which it developed. Were this not true, the bustled gowns of the 1690's would hardly be distinguishable from the bustle-backed costumes of the 1790's and the 1880's; yet even the student with a superficial knowledge of fashion history finds no difficulty whatever in making the distinction. It is obvious, then, that the underlying features of the styles of the day are molded by specific kinds of cultural influences.

We can trace certain similarities of dress among the cultural periods in which similar social ideals were manifest. When religious values are dominant, dress tends to enshroud the

Figure 6-17. "Touch me not," said the crinoline. The Victorian notion of propriety was to keep a man at a safe distance.

THE SAFEST WAY OF TAKING A LADY DOWN TO DINNER.

Figure 6-18. Afro garb, a symbol of independence to black Americans, became popular at the peak of the Civil Rights Movement. Versions of the African styles are worn by both men and women.

figure in a relatively loose garment of simple design. The enveloping tunics, wimples, and head veils of the early Gothic period were perpetuated in the habits of Catholic nuns.

The rise of Puritanism in England during the early seventeenth century stripped clothing of its ornamentation and supplanted the sober, drab costume that spread to America in the garb of the early colonists. The same influence persists today in the dress of the Quakers and the Mennonites. Eighteenth-century costume, on the other hand, was a creation of the sophisticated, extravagant, and artificial world of the French nobility; it was elaborate and profusely decorated, the dress of idleness, frivolity, and pleasure.

Our discussion of value patterns in Chapter 5 has already demonstrated the relation between the mentifacts of culture and dress, and we have seen how ideals of patriotism, frugality, order, beauty, and youth all are expressed through clothing whenever such concepts become the dominating theme of a period. Because such ideals seldom exist in isolation, they blend with others which are also characteristic of the times. This unique synthesis produces the typical costume, which may indeed be imitated but never duplicated in succeeding periods of fashion history.

The dominant ideals which shape the thought and action of a cultural period also influence the character and direction of fashion movements.

Events

In addition to wars and revolutions, which appear to trigger more radical changes than would occur under ordinary circumstances,[15] there are other historical events which can often be seen to exert a strong influence upon the fashion image of a period. Some time before the French Revolution, for example,

_____

[15]During actual periods of conflict there is little time for fashion change; war activities usually make for more austere and functional clothes, with perhaps an emphasis on mannish or militaristic elements. The real change is effected in the aftermath of conflict.

CULTURAL CHANGE AND FASHION CHANGE

Important historic events trigger public interest and enthusiasm for fashion change.

Figure 6-19. Peace negotiations in Vietnam and the initiation of cultural relations with China in 1972 touched off renewed interest in Oriental styles.

Fashion adaptations of art forms and clothing of other nations reflect the political sentiments that are characteristic of the times.

the discovery of the ancient cities of Pompeii and Herculaneum created the initial resurgence of interest in classical antiquity. The style made itself felt in minor motifs until the sentiments which accompanied the revolt gave it full expression. In like manner, the publicity given the opening of Tut-Ankh-Amen's tomb in 1923 developed a sudden passion for all things Egyptian. The famed Garibaldi's Sicilian expedition in 1860 inspired a flood of Garibaldi jackets and Garibaldi shirts. The Panama Canal was opened in 1904, and American men adopted the custom of wearing Panama hats from the beginning of May until Labor Day each year. The Centennial Exhibition held in Philadelphia in 1876, the World's Fair in Chicago in 1893, and the 1925 International Exposition of Industrial and Decorative Arts in Paris all had profound influence on the shaping of public taste in their respective eras. Outstanding fairs and exhibits of recent years also have called attention to the major artistic and industrial movements which help to characterize the spirit of the times.

International relations

Political sentiments are also reflected in the phenomenon of fashion change. Strained relations with unfriendly countries automatically make their national styles and art forms extremely unpopular. Political approval or acceptance, on the other hand, is often accompanied by a revival of interest in the fashions derived from the folklore or national dress of friendly countries.

The recurrent appearance of Oriental elements of dress— the turban, mandarin coats, coolie hats, kimonos, Nehru jackets, Mao tunics—mirror our on-again-off-again attitudes of association with nations of the world. At various times throughout history, fashion has helped to foster U.S. relationships with South America, Russia, Mexico, India, China, Japan, as well as the countries of the Middle East.

Entertainment and the arts

The relationship of art and clothing is treated in Chapter 14, but it should be noted here as an important factor in determining the direction taken by specific fashion movements. The forces which give rise to the development of certain styles in painting are also operative in the field of fashion. Manifestations of the Bauhaus philosophy, abstractionism, nonobjective art, surrealism, pop art, and op art have all been observed in the fads and the fashions of contemporaneous dress.

One of the most outstanding influences stemming from the performing arts came out of Russia in 1909 in the form of the

Figure 6-20. Theda Bara personified the vamp look.

Figure 6-21. Movies like "Bonnie and Clyde" and "The Great Gatsby" inspired a revival of twenties and thirties styles.

Russian ballet, which introduced not only a new type of music and dance, but new costumes and scenery which gave enormous impetus to fashion. The organizing genius of Diaghilev, the superb dancing of Nijinsky and Pavlova, and the designs by Bakst took Paris by storm. The settings and costumes were of equal importance to the actual dancing, especially for *Schéhérazade*, the most memorable ballet of all. The voluptuous Oriental décor and costumes burst forth in brilliant colors of crimson, gold, and orange, in harem skirts, tunics, turbans, and veils. So lasting was its influence that the surge of Orientalism survived the First World War and was brought back to a boil by Rudolph Valentino who starred as "The Sheik" in the movies of the twenties. Ladies bedecked themselves in Persian pantaloons, turned-up toed slippers, and turbans garnished with egret and ostrich plumes. Theda Bara and Pola Negri, their eyes blackened with mascara, their bodies slinking in gold lamé, personified the look of the day. The era of the vamp was launched.

The overwhelming success of the musical hit, *My Fair Lady*, with its 1912 settings and costumes by Cecil Beaton, created the "Fair Lady Look" of the 1950's. The publicity surrounding Elizabeth Taylor's filming of *Cleopatra* in 1963 had everybody going Egyptian again. Albert Finney's smash hit in the British film, *Tom Jones*, gave rise to the long, white, and beruffled blouse that bore the same name.

To be successful, such fashion revivals must come at a time far enough removed from the original event that the styles appear new instead of old-fashioned. Moreover, the tastes of the times which cause people to respond enthusiastically to a particular type of painting, play, or music are the same tastes that give support to fashion movements. Another *My Fair Lady* produced in the twenties instead of the fifties may have

Fashion movements and revivals are given focus and impetus through the appeal of art and other forms of entertainment.

been a complete flop. The styles which succeed are those which are somehow in harmony with the spirit of the age.

As we look back over the fashions of the past, we can see that every era had its characteristic line and form, an extraordinary relevance to the *Zeitgeist*. Yet to define this in advance is quite a different task from viewing the relationship in retrospect; it is difficult indeed to pinpoint the essential elements in the varied and seemingly haphazard design of contemporary life.

SUMMARY *Forces that shape fashion*

In attempting to explain the nature of fashion movements, it can be seen that they are, by and large, determined by the same dominant forces which mold other aspects of the culture in any given period. Ideals such as equality, piety, modesty, frivolity, and so forth, all are expressed through the clothing of an era whenever such concepts are ascendant. Public sentiments and tastes are often shaped by important historical events as well as by national and international relationships. Further influences may be noted which stem from the arts, the theater, the movies, and other entertainment media. These function to give focus and impetus to the spirit of the times.

FOR FURTHER READING

Bell, Quentin. *On Human Finery*. London: Hogarth Press, 1947.

Johnston, Moira. "What Will Happen to the Gray Flannel Suit?" *Journal of Home Economics* 64, November 1972, pp. 5–12.

Laver, James. *Dress*. London: John Murray Publishers, 1950.

Men's Wear, (75th Anniversary Issue). A Fairchild Publication, 25 June 1965.

Viking Press and Vogue, comps., *The World in Vogue*. New York: Viking Press, 1963.

DISCUSSION QUESTIONS

1. Discuss the pros and cons of each of the following alternatives to fashion: (a) nudity, (b) traditional dress, (c) a uniform.

2. What are the disadvantages of fashion? What are its values?

3. Compare the "new generation clothes" (discussed in Chapter 5) with those of a totalitarian society. How are they alike? How are they different?

4. Why does a democracy provide the ideal climate for fashion racing?

PART TWO

Clothing and Human Behavior

119

7

Clothes and the Self-Concept

IT IS SOMEWHAT traditional for clothing courses and clothing textbooks to consider the topic of clothes in relation to personality. The general assumption usually made is that clothes may be used to reflect, to express, or to enhance one's personality. Of course, this phenomenon occurs whether we go about it consciously or not, but the intent of the lesson is to help the individual achieve some consistency between the tangible aspects of the self and the intangible aspects of the dress, both of which communicate impressions of the self to others in the social environment. Very often the extremes of personality characteristics are cast in the dichotomy of "yin" and "yang" types, which represent opposing traits of temperament, body structure, and other physical attributes.

Few psychologists can agree on an adequate definition of personality, but in general it denotes the sum total of behavior patterns of the individual. It is commonly accepted that many aspects of personality are not fixed and static throughout life, but undergo mutation through growth, development, and experiences in the social situation.

It may be more meaningful, therefore, to begin with one aspect of the personality complex and attempt to discuss clothing as it relates to the ideas and feelings one has about himself. The explanation of self made by Cooley many years ago has become known as the "looking-glass self":

> As we see our face, figure, and dress in the glass, and are interested in them because they are ours, and pleased or otherwise with them according as they do or do not answer to what we should like them to be; so in imagination we perceive in another's mind some thought of our appearance, manners, aims, deeds, character, friends, and so on, and are variously affected by it.
>
> A self-idea of this sort seems to have three principal elements: the imagination of our appearance to the other person; the imagination of his judgment of that appearance, and some sort of self-feeling, such as pride or mortification. The comparison with a looking-glass hardly suggests the second element, the imagined judgment, which is quite essential. The thing that moves us to pride

or shame is not the mere mechanical reflection of ourselves, but an imputed sentiment, the imagined effect of this reflection upon another's mind.[1]

The **self**, then, is the object to which we refer with the words "I," "me," "mine," "myself"; the **self-concept** is how I think and feel about "me" or "myself." Let us consider first how such ideas about self are likely to develop.

Development of the self-concept

Although we do not actually know, we can guess how the world must look to a new-born baby. At first the baby is able to make no distinction whatever between himself and the blur and confusion of the surrounding environment. But we are able to observe him as he "discovers" a hand or a toe, and he examines these parts of his own body much as he regards other objects which surround him—a rattle, a toy, or even a finger that belongs to somebody else. Gradually he is able to distinguish between the things that are "me" and the things which are "not me." If you ask a child of three, for example, who he is, he will probably reply with his name, "John." If you point to a table and ask, "Is this John?" he will say, "No." If you point to his sweater, he may answer yes or no; if you point to his leg, he may say, "No, that's my leg!" If you tease him about taking away his nose, he responds as if his nose were indeed an object that could be separated from his body. It is clear from such observations that the image of what constitutes the self must be learned.

Clothing and the boundaries of the self

It is common to assume that the locus of the self is contained within the body, and that the skin marks the distinction between the self and the environment. But in our society, almost from the moment of birth on, there is some form of clothing which separates the body from the surroundings. Dorothy Lee has described this relationship between clothes and the self:

The body is never naked, or perhaps, only when absolutely necessary. Mothers often arrange to bathe and change the baby without undressing it all at once. The new pediatric practices and the new books on child care demand immersion, but it is all a matter of hygiene; no joy of the naked body is mentioned anywhere. Conversely, dress, and particularly festive dress, "dress of splendor" and ornamentation, are of great importance, and in fact, are essential to complete the body. When beautiful girls are described, their clothing and their jewelry are given at least as much place as their bodily charms, and are not treated separately; and when a brave youth is mentioned, his trappings are part of the picture.

Figure 7-1. Development of one's self-concept begins in infancy when the baby "discovers" his fingers and toes.

Figure 7-2. The action of the dancer is not only extended but magnified by the movement of her costume.

[1]Charles H. Cooley, *Human Nature and the Social Order*, Charles Scribner's Sons, New York, 1902, p. 152.

Figure 7-3. The Edwardian woman was well defined by boned, stiff necks and straight-laced corseting. How could she relax her decorum when she could not even bend her waist?

Clothing, as a part of the body-image, acts as a "second skin" in establishing the physical boundaries of the self.

. . . And the lower world which holds no joy is a place where there are no ornamental trappings. The naked body, like the naked word, is stark and incomplete.[2]

Is it so surprising then, that a child should have difficulty in learning the distinction between himself and his clothing? Is it not logical that an extremity of the body, such as an arm or a leg, would appear to the child as belonging less to the self than an article of clothing which is somehow closer, and more functional in establishing who one is?

Throughout life, clothing functions as an extension of the bodily self. Whenever an object is brought into contact with the body, the conscious existence of the self is extended into the extremities of the object, thereby providing the individual with an increased sense of size, power, movement, rigidity— whatever the characteristic of the object.

Thus, the wearer of the corset takes on the straight-laced qualities of the garment, the graceful movement of floating chiffon lends increased motility to the dancer, and the knight assumes the steel-plated strength of his armor. The individual becomes taller in a high hat, more forceful in striking colors, less refined in coarse fabrics.

Research has shown that individuals vary in the degree to which they extend their self-feelings beyond the boundaries of their bodies.[3] Compton's work was done with psychotic patients, but her findings suggest that clothing does indeed function in the strengthening or weakening of the body-image boundary.[4]

Clothes, then, become a part of the body-image, and the same concerns that are attached to the body are often attached to clothing in like manner. Particularly at the age of puberty, adolescents become acutely aware of the changing dimensions of the body, and are often troubled if their growth does not parallel the growth of others of comparable age and status. This is also a time when youngsters seem to become obsessed with their clothing and appearance and spend a great deal of time and effort finding out what "they" are wearing, how "they" are cutting or styling the hair, in order that they may present the same or similar image as their peers.

Sex and role identities

At every stage of development, clothing helps to establish the identity of the individual to himself and to those with whom

[2]Dorothy Lee, *Freedom and Culture*, Prentice-Hall, Englewood Cliffs, N.J., 1959, p. 147.
[3]S. Fisher and S. Cleveland, "Body-Image Boundaries and Style of Life," *Journal of Abnormal and Social Psychology* 52, 1956, pp. 373–379.
[4]Norma H. Compton, "Body-Image Boundaries in Relation to Clothing Fabric and Design Preferences of a Group of Hospitalized Psychotic Women," *Journal of Home Economics* 56, 1964, pp. 40–45.

he interacts. By dressing the baby in blue, we signify to others that he is to be called and treated like a *boy*, and described as "handsome," "strong," "big," or "rugged." By dressing the baby in pink, we automatically invest her with femininity and call forth the responsive adjectives of "sweet," "beautiful," "dainty," "fragile," and everyone knows that she is a *girl*.

In the last decade, the growing feminist movement contributed to an erosion of the culturally defined symbols of sex differentiation in American society. Many child development specialists believed that this led to a confusion of sex role identity in the child. Long before women's lib, some parents—who may have been disappointed in the sex of a baby—imposed a masculine or feminine patterning on their child that was in conflict with the genitally defined sex. Such a practice has often been blamed for maladjustments later in life.

Everyone recalls the tired joke about one child asking another how he could be sure that the infant in the crib was a baby brother and not a baby sister. The response of pulling down the covers and saying, "See, blue booties!" is not at all unusual in light of the fact that small children are very apt to make distinctions in sex on the basis of clothing symbols rather than actual physical differences, even when appraising adults.

Thus, clothing helps the child very early in life to identify his sex. Further, clothing facilitates the enactment of roles that help the child to learn the appropriate patterns for male and female personality expression and performance as they are defined by the culture into which he is born.

The process may be observed most easily in the children's game of "playing house." The child dons the attire of the mother or the father, and in effect *becomes* the mother or father. Stone studied adult men and women in their recollections of childhood play, and at least 65 per cent of his respondents could remember "dressing up" in adult costumes when they were children. The play costume most frequently chosen was that of a parent of the same sex, that is, little girls dressed in mother's clothes, and little boys in daddy's.[5]

Gardner Murphy explains how the process of such identification involves the enacting of the other person's role:

> The child dresses up to *play* pirate, not just to *be* pirate; he wants daddy's hat and cane not merely to look like daddy, but to aid in immersing himself in the daddy round of activities. It is likely, indeed, that the psychology of clothing has too often been conceived in terms of a simple narcissistic delight in one's appearance; clothing is largely a means of making real the role that is to be played in life.[6]

BERRY'S WORLD

© 1969 by NEA, Inc.

"Ma! What's the difference between boys an' girls again? I forgot!"

Figure 7-4. Lack of differentiation in dress may lead to confusion of sex roles.

---

[5]Gregory P. Stone, "Appearance and the Self," in A. Rose (ed.), *Human Behavior and Social Processes*, Houghton Mifflin Company, Boston, 1962, p. 111.
[6]Gardner Murphy, *Personality: A Biosocial Approach to Origins and Structure*, Harper and Brothers, New York, 1947, p. 494.

CLOTHES AND THE SELF-CONCEPT

There are roles that cannot be assumed in life without the aid of the "props" of the costume. The role of the cowboy is much easier to play in boots and chaps, spurs and hat, but a three-year-old cannot play it at all without the modicum of guns and holster.

Thus, the self-concept is developed through the assumption of a series of social roles, and the individual learns the set of behavior patterns that other people expect of him in the performance of such roles.

Therefore, role identity is subject to constant modification, although as we shall see later, the individual tends to integrate his various role experiences into a unified pattern of responses: the woman who goes through life as "daddy's little girl" becomes the childlike, naive, dependent wife, and may present herself in most situations in frilly, fussy clothes in feminine colors and dainty detail.[7] It is highly unlikely that this same woman would be comfortable in casual, rough-textured clothes in strong or earthy colors, even though the latter may be appropriate for certain activities.

Gradually a person abstracts the commonalities from his experiences in different role categories, and he integrates these into a unified feeling toward the self. Clothing will function most purposefully if it is consistent with the individual's core of feelings about himself.

Person and group identification

An understanding of the process of **identification** is essential in analyzing the development of the self-concept. As we have seen, the child is likely to identify with the parent early in life. Through imitation, he takes on the appearance, behavior, and feelings of the parent, and in doing so he not only learns to play the role, but learns to see himself through the eyes of the parent. In acting out the role of mother, for example, the little girl demands for the child (in this case herself) the same standards of conduct which she thinks the parent holds for the child. By taking on the dress of the parent, the child can take on more easily the accompanying gestures, values and orientations of the parent as well as the attitudes held toward himself. Thus, in taking on the role of the other, the individual learns to evaluate his own appearance and behavior according to the norms and values held by the other.

As the child's social contacts expand, his choice of models also expands. The ideal person that the child chooses to imitate may be an older sibling, an aunt, an uncle, a friend—but usually a person who possesses something that the child

Clothing is a necessary "prop" in the establishment and maintenance of one's sex and role identities; it reflects what the individual thinks of himself.

----

[7]Alexandra Symonds, a New York psychiatrist, has described various clothing behavior patterns that emerge from one's unconscious state of mind. She has reported these in lectures and in syndicated columns.

wants, such as love, recognition, prestige, or power. Gradually the process of identification spreads from single persons to groups of people, and the individual learns to play a role by learning the group values and norms for appearance and behavior. The idea of the "other," as Mead calls it, involves an organization of attitudes held by everybody else on the team; the social group which gives to the individual his unity of self may be called the **generalized other.**[8] Thus, a whole pattern of responses may be determined by a particular reference group with which the individual identifies. Various writers have designated the reference group by such terms as "model," "referent," "generalized other," or "significant others."

While the process of identification is observed easily in the imitative play of children, it is probably displayed most prevalently and overtly in the years of adolescence. Vener and Hoffer attempted to demonstrate the kinds of persons or referent groups that adolescents aspired to emulate. Of the students who responded, almost 58 per cent indicated a peer or peer group as the model for emulation in patterns of dress. Typical responses cited in this category were: "There is a certain group of girls my age who are a clique. I like the way they dress." "If I could dress like any person I would like to dress like S. S. because I think she dresses nice." "D. B. because he always wears tight jeans and cat-shirts, so I'd like to wear that kind of clothes." "P. W. because he has nice clothes, not real flashy but they are nice and he also has a nice personality."[9] During adolescence, the peer group takes on added significance. The group chosen for emulation is usually one to which the individual aspires to belong. The person selected as a model is usually a peer or a near-peer who is slightly older, or more popular, better looking, more skilled, or possesses an attribute or power that the individual would like to possess himself.

A second group of referents reported in the same study were classified as "mass media celebrities." Almost a quarter of the boys and girls mentioned some Hollywood, television, or sports figure who had an influence on their pattern of dress. Less than 12 per cent indicated a relative or family member as their model, and about 7 per cent chose some person or group from the community. Even though the latter categories were mentioned less frequently, it gives some evidence of the extent of adolescents' identification.

"Significant others" may be defined in still another way, and this relates to the manner in which patterns of dress are evaluated. In the adolescent study just cited, respondents were asked

[8]George H. Mead, *Mind, Self and Society,* University of Chicago Press, Chicago, 1934, p. 154.
[9]A. M. Vener and C. R. Hoffer, *Adolescent Orientations to Clothing,* Technical Bulletin 270, Michigan State University Agricultural Experiment Station, 1959, p. 21.

Figure 7-5. A Cub Scout's uniform helps to strengthen a small boy's identification as a scout.

The imitation of clothing behavior is a direct and tangible means of identifying oneself with a model person or referent group; it not only facilitates the learning of new social roles, but also becomes an important process in the formation of the concept of self.

the question, "Whose opinion counts most when you are deciding what to wear?" Mothers and peers were designated as the most influential persons in determining how clothing behavior would be evaluated. It is significant that less than 4 per cent considered their fathers' opinions about clothes to be important. Acceptance of the mothers' opinions, however, was strongest among eighth graders, and diminished as the teenagers grew older. Older adolescents begin to see themselves in different social roles, and as new persons become significant to them, the old influences fade in importance. Such changing roles, along with the changes in body-image that occur during adolescence, usually produce a marked change in the concept of the self.

Identification with certain groups is often reflected in group membership, although this is not a prerequisite of identification. The wearing of a Boy Scout uniform, for example, strengthens a boy's identity as a scout. All uniforms, of course, are among the most obvious examples of overt identification, but there are many more subtle manifestations that illustrate the process more precisely. (The mere fact that a person wears a uniform may not mean that he *identifies* with the uniform.)

The manifestations of the process of identification through dress can be observed among members of both sexes, at all ages, and in every stratum of society. In the early 1960's, females from age seven to seventy emulated the fashions and style of Jacqueline Kennedy. Teenagers all over France, and many in America, imitated the appearance of Brigitte Bardot.

Dress and appearance also provide a vehicle for identifying with particular groups. One black coed, for example, explained: "I adopted the Afro [hairstyle] at about the same time I became involved with the Black Panthers in 1968 . . . it was an expression of black identity."[10]

In most instances, the model or the ideal possesses some qualities that are not only desirable but socially approved. It is not uncommon, however, for individuals to identify rather strongly with referents that are not acceptable to the general society. Delinquent gangs, for example, maintain their visual identities via the symbols provided by clothing such as black sweaters, leather zippered jackets, and tight pants. Such identification, though not socially approved, gives the individual power, importance, and approval of the referent group, which is, after all, the only group that he values.

The specific person or group that is chosen as the model is not so important to our study as the recognition that the imitator sees himself through the eyes of the referent group, and thus selects his clothing to meet the expectations of that group. If the group norm dictates that men should affect complete indifference to dress, it becomes extremely important for group

[10]Phyl Garland, "Is the Afro On Its Way Out?" *Ebony*, Feb. 1973, p. 130.

members to select clothing which gives the impression that they really do not care how they look. Thus, as the individual takes on *the attitude of the other,* as he appraises his appearance and behavior in relation to various role partners and groups, he forms a constellation of attitudes that represent his concept of self.

Figure 7-6. In the late sixties and early seventies, young blacks identified with leaders like Angela Davis by adopting the Afro hairstyle as a symbol of angry militancy and pride in their African ancestry. Later, blacks experimented with new ways to retain their cultural identity through such styles as the braided cornrow.

Physical constituents of the self

The emphasis thus far on the social nature of the self, however, is not intended to deny the existence of inborn physical differences among individuals that may have a direct relationship to personality. Precise measurement of the organic traits of individuals is yet to be achieved.[11] Attempts to relate personality traits to bodily constitution date as far back as the ancient Greeks, and at least two modern studies have identified significant linkages between body type and behavior.[12]

While many psychologists question the validity of "somatotyping," as it is called, the external appearance of the body is a relatively fixed aspect of the self, and certainly influences how the individual thinks of himself, and how others may respond to him. Physical characteristics are important factors in the process of stereotyping in which we are often apt to think of all fat people as jolly, all thin people as wiry and energetic, and all muscular types as athletic and outgoing. While stereotyping is usually fallacious in nature, it is quite possible that the chubby child who is treated as if he were expected to be jolly will grow up in the realization that he can evoke the most positive responses from others by being "jolly" in his disposition.

[11]For a more detailed explanation, see S. Fisher and S. E. Cleveland, *Body Image and Personality,* Dover Publications, New York, 1968.
[12]Kretschmer's classification of physical types and Sheldon's somatotypes; see W. H. Sheldon, *Atlas of Men: A Guide for Somatotyping the Adult Male at All Ages,* Harper & Row, New York, 1954.

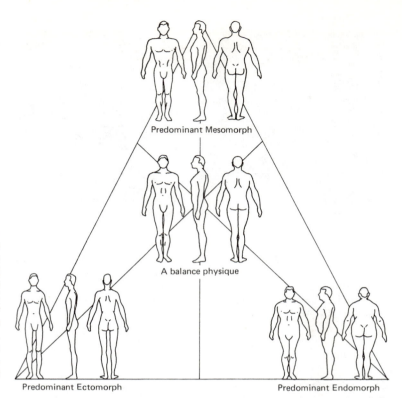

Predominant Mesomorph

A balance physique

Predominant Ectomorph   Predominant Endomorph

Figure 7-7. Sheldon's constitutional types: the *endomorph* is predominantly rotund in body contour with soft body tissue; the *ectomorph* is characterized by a long, slender shape with stringy muscles; the *mesomorph* is the typical "athletic type" with a hard muscular build. Every body type represents some combination of these three extremes. The center figure shows a physique with the three components in equal balance. Women, on the average, tend to be somewhat more endomorphic.

As we shall see in the last section of this chapter, the individual strives toward a consistent way of looking at himself, and this "style of life" must be at least compatible—if not in true harmony—with the set characteristics of the physical body type. It would be difficult, for example, for a predominant "endomorph" to reconcile his body type with aspirations of becoming the sophisticated fashion plate, just as the large-boned, muscular female will experience difficulty in effecting the role of a demure and dainty damsel. Realistic perception and appraisal of one's physical characteristics is basic to the attainment of congruity in the presentation of the self.

Even though the relationship between body type and personality is still somewhat nebulous, there is considerable evidence that body type affects the way we feel about ourselves. In our culture at least, most females want to be "taller" or "thinner" than they actually are, and most males desire to be "heavier" or more "muscular." Even among male children, the mesomorph is clearly the preferred type, and children as young as eight years of age appear to be able to report self-perceptions of their body-images quite accurately.[13] Among men, the large

[13]J. R. Staffieri, "A Study of Social Stereotype of Body Image in Children," *Journal of Personality and Social Psychology* 7, 1967, pp. 101–104.

mesomorphs tend to like their bodies better than other physical types, while tall, thin men put the lowest value on their bodies. Apparently potency and physical strength is associated not with height alone, but with height and bulk. Among women, those with ectomorphic body types are significantly more accepting of their self-images than are endomorphs.[14]

Body-cathexis (i.e., the degree of feeling of satisfaction or dissatisfaction with the body) has been shown to relate positively to feelings of self-acceptance and self-esteem.[15]

Individuals who express a high degree of satisfaction with the physical self tend to score high on measures of psychological security.[16] Other studies have demonstrated significant relationships between body build and preferences in clothing, but the analysis of physical characteristics in relation to suggested patterns of line and design will be made in Chapter 16. The emphasis of physical typology in the present context pertains to its relevance in establishing rather fixed and stable aspects of the self.

> Body type constitutes a relatively fixed aspect of the self and exerts a significant influence in the development of the self-concept.

SUMMARY *Development of the self-concept*

Although physical body type contributes to its development, an individual's self-concept is derived largely from the social situation. Because the self is rarely presented in the social situation without some form of clothing, the boundaries of the body often are extended to incorporate one's clothes into the body-image. At every stage of development, clothing helps to establish the identity of the individual to himself and to others with whom he interacts. It sets the stage for rehearsing the roles that one will be expected to play in life, and also assists him in portraying such roles more convincingly. Clothing contributes to the process of identification by which the individual takes on the attitudes and values of "the other," and his self-feeling is shaped by the imagined judgments of these significant other persons.

Clothing and evaluation of the self

We have seen how one's ideas about himself are socially derived. Thus far we have dealt primarily with the **cognitive** component of the self, that is, a recognition of "who and what I am." A nine- or ten-year-old child may respond with such answers as

---

[14]W. R. Alexander, "A Study of Body Types, Self-Image and Environmental Adjustment in Freshman College Females," Unpublished dissertation, Indiana University, 1967.
[15]P. Secord and S. Jourard, "The Appraisal of Body-Cathexis: Body-Cathexis and the Self," *Journal of Consulting Psychology* 17, 1953, pp. 343–347.
[16]D. Torreta, "Somesthetic Perception of Clothing Fabrics in Relation to Body Image and Psychological Security," Unpublished dissertation, Utah State University, 1968.

"I am a boy. I go to school. I have a mother, father and little sister. I'm not as tall as other kids my age. I like to wear jeans and T-shirts most of the time." Such responses may not be made verbally, but they establish the identity and characteristics of the individual. How the person *feels* about his identity and characteristics is usually referred to as the **affective** component of the self, that is, the person's estimation of his own worth.

Achieving unity

It is useful here to refer to the principle of operant conditioning in the explanation of how such feelings develop. In simple terms, this means that you do, or continue to do, those things for which you are rewarded, and refrain from doing those things for which you are punished or not rewarded. If a little girl, for example, examines herself in the mirror, smooths her skirt and adjusts her sash, and the family members who observe this behavior respond in a positive manner, openly enjoying the demonstration and calling attention to the child as they do so, such behavior is reinforced and likely to be repeated by the child. It is very probable that the same behavior on the part of a little boy would not be reinforced by the parent, particularly not by the father. On the other hand, the child who continually is criticized or ridiculed about his clothes or who feels his clothes are inadequate, soon becomes overly self-conscious about them.

According to Sullivan, the self is made up of a series of "reflected appraisals."[17] By the time the child is nine or ten, he has had many such experiences of noting the reactions of other people to his behavior, and he has a fairly good idea of the usual reaction he is able to elicit. The child who is reminded continually that he is a bad boy because he gets his clothes dirty comes to see himself as a bad boy. Thus, at age ten, the child is able to make a number of evaluative statements about himself: "I don't do what my mother says. I'm careless and sloppy about my clothes. I never put things away where they belong."

The problem of achieving a consistent way of looking at one's self would be relatively simple if the individual's social contacts did not extend beyond a limited number of people who tended to respond to him in a uniform manner. But as we discussed earlier, a person develops many different identities, and he perceives himself as being evaluated differently by different groups of "significant others." A girl from a small town, for example, may consider herself to be particularly well dressed because she perceives that other students in her high school think she is well dressed. If she attends a large university as a

[17]Harry Stack Sullivan, *Conceptions of Modern Psychiatry*, William Alanson White Psychiatric Foundation, Washington, 1947.

college freshman, she may find herself in a situation in which other students do not have the same high regard for her taste in clothes. What adjustment, if any, does the individual make in the concept of self?

Secord and Backman present a theory which suggests that the individual may employ any one of a number of techniques to maintain the established self-concept.[18] A person may simply *misperceive* how the others actually see him. In the case of the college freshman, she may see herself through rose-colored glasses, misperceive the judgment of the new college group, and continue to think that others regard her the same way she was regarded in high school. Or, she may *select to interact* only with those people who do consider her to be well dressed. A third possible response might be to *devaluate the opinions* of those who are at variance with her self-concept, and convince herself that their views are not important because none of them know how to dress anyway. Another possibility would be for the girl to *devaluate the importance* of being well dressed, and find more positive outlets in athletic achievement or scholastic performance. Or, she may make a more conscious effort to select her clothes with particular care in order to create the impression that she is well dressed; in other words, she is careful to *control the cues* that she presents to other people for evaluation.

This is very similar to Festinger's theory of **cognitive dissonance**,[19] which centers around the idea that a person will do a variety of things to achieve consistency in his psychological world. If two pieces of information do not "fit together," the individual will make certain alterations in the information which Festinger calls "dissonance-reducing changes." The person can restore consistency by (1) changing his opinion, (2) changing his behavior, (3) changing the information he has, or (4) distorting his perception. In most cases, he will resort to mechanisms that will not require him to change his original opinion or decision.

It is interesting to consider at what stage of development an individual is likely to achieve unity or stability in the self-concept. The very young child is apt to shift his identities in rapid succession, being a cowboy one minute, a fireman the next—a kind of trying on of roles before one decides who he is really going to be. In early adolescence, as we have seen, the patterns of identification tend to shift from parent to peer, gradually giving way to a more "generalized other." It is apparent, however, that many have not yet achieved a high degree of stability in the self-concept, even at college age. Ryan asked

[18]Paul F. Secord and Carl W. Backman, "Personality Theory and the Problem of Stability and Change in Individual Behavior," *Psychological Review* 68, 1961, pp. 21–32.
[19]Leon Festinger, "Cognitive Dissonance," *Scientific American*, October 1962, pp. 93–102.

Figure 7-8. In recent years there seems to have been an epidemic of putting together various kinds of antique clothes and old theatrical costumes in a half-joking, half-serious search for "individuality." Such fantasy clothes provide the wearer with an opportunity to try out a variety of new roles and deliberately alter his identity.

college women to describe the type of person they considered themselves to be, and the majority of respondents were unable to do so.[20] They described their clothing preferences in terms of the simple tailored clothing that represented the prevailing style on the campus. Even though their clothing preferences were manifested in terms of their likes and dislikes, they had not yet made conscious recognition of their most salient self-characteristics.

A similar kind of study was made of students enrolled in clothing courses at the University of Nevada. By and large, the majority of the students was unable to describe a core of feelings that represent the self in a distinctive way, and clothing preferences usually were stated in terms of the existing norm. About one-third expressed rather clear-cut impressions of themselves as "feminine and dainty," "classic," "wholesome," "original and different," "outdoorsy," and the like. About 10 per cent openly acknowledged fluctuations in the self-concept.

Such vacillations certainly are not uncommon, particularly at an age when new social roles must be assumed. Erikson describes this diffusion of the self as a common problem of adolescents, who have not quite given up the identities of childhood and have not yet mastered the identities of adulthood.[21] Lack

[20]Mary S. Ryan, "Report of Interviews with a Selected Sample of College Women," *Psychological Effects of Clothing, Part III*, Cornell University Agricultural Experiment Station Bulletin 900, August 1953.
[21]E. H. Erikson, "The Problem of Ego Identity," *Journal of the American Psychoanalytic Association* 4, 1956, pp. 56–121.

of a well-defined self-concept may also be due to the fact that in our culture introspective behavior is not generally encouraged. Given the opportunity to think about and to verbalize their self-feelings over a period of time, the college women described above were often able to evolve a more distinctive pattern of feelings about themselves. This clarification of the self was usually accompanied by a more consistent style of dress.

In a subsequent study by Ryan,[22] students' personality traits were compared with feelings of being well dressed. The findings indicated that girls who were high on the trait of "dominance" as measured by the personality inventory tended to rate themselves high on feelings of being well dressed. Girls who were submissive rated themselves lower in their clothing appearance. Another notable outcome of this study was that a high correlation existed among the ratings on the various scales. For example, if an individual rated herself high on feelings of being well dressed, she also rated herself high in her evaluation of physical characteristics, individuality in dress, and her own self-confidence. Moreover, the same kind of correlation was found in the group evaluation of a given individual, that is, if the group rated a girl high on appearance, the group also rated her high on physical characteristics, individuality, and self-confidence. This "halo" effect in the ratings gives some tangible evidence that a generalized impression of the self is gradually derived from one's experiences with other persons.

Rewards (or punishment) received in connection with clothing behavior tend to reinforce the generalized feeling toward the self. Clothing contributes to a stabilization of the self-concept.

Self-enhancement

Most theorists agree that people in general have a strong need for self-enhancement, and clothing as an instrument in the beautification of the self is so commonplace that it is usually taken for granted. Few aspects of the self call forth as much open admiration as one's clothes, since there are rare opportunities, for casual acquaintances at least, to comment on one's gestures, facial expression, posture, speech patterns, intellect, and other character traits, even though these, too, are all a part of the self.

Thus, because clothes are such a visual part of the self, they are often included in the conscious evaluation of self-characteristics. For most people, clothes are more often a source of positive feeling toward the self than of feelings which are negative. In a study of Negro and Caucasian adolescents, Lott discovered that teenagers of both races who possessed a high degree of confidence in their adornment behavior also had high self-concepts of their physical attributes.[23] Jersild's earlier

---

[22]Mary S. Ryan, "Perception of Self in Relation to Clothing" *Psychological Effects of Clothing*, Part IV, Cornell University Agricultural Experiment Station Bulletin 905, August 1954.

[23]Isabelle Lott, "Self-Concept and Related Adornment Behavior of Negro and White Adolescent Girls," Master's thesis, Michigan State University, 1966.

work also indicated that clothes were frequently mentioned in descriptions of what children and adolescents liked about themselves.[24]

For some people, however, clothing may be a source of embarrassment, discomfort, or deprecation, even though this is not the dominant or generalized pattern. There is considerable empirical evidence that feelings of clothing deprivation have a significant relationship to lack of social confidence and to low self-concepts.[25] Some of the students in Ryan's study who felt less well dressed than average also indicated that they were likely to feel self-conscious and try to keep from the center of group attention. In such cases, the individual reacts with negative feelings to the imagined judgments of the referent group and measures his self-esteem against the clothing expectations of "significant others," as he sees them. The greater the difference between the self-feelings and the imagined group-feelings, the more difficult it becomes for the individual to fill the social role which is required.

Clothing is also operant in the *restoration* of feelings of self-worth. Rather startling examples of this can be observed in the behavior of the mentally ill. During the last few years, doctors and other hospital personnel have taken increased recognition of the fact that personal appearance is one of the clues to mental health. **Fashion therapy** is the term usually used to designate programs geared to helping patients improve their physical appearance. One of the first projects of this type developed at a state hospital in California in 1959. With the help of the California Fashion Group, a dress was designed for each patient, and she was then helped to make it for herself. With renewed pride in their appearances, most patients began to improve, some responding to fashion therapy after all other attempts to reach them had failed. One such case was described by a member of the hospital staff:

> We took a very classic example of one patient who, no matter what you would put on her, was able to get her dress up to her mouth and start eating at the neckline and she would eat as many as sixteen or eighteen dresses a day. We tried putting leather around the neck. Somehow she would manage to get to the stitching between the leather and the material and was still able to eat her dresses. We took her in and talked to her and told her that we were going to dress her up in the nicest of things: silk stockings, shoes, and either nylon or cotton print dresses. This may sound fantastic, but this has

---

[24]Arthur Jersild, *In Search of Self*, Bureau of Publications, Teachers College, Columbia University, New York, 1952.

[25]See Vener and Hoffer, *Adolescent Orientations to Clothing*. Also, Mary Brawley, "Feelings of Clothing Deprivation As Related to Self-Concept and Peer Acceptance Among Black and White Fourth Grade Girls"; and Mary Edwards, "The Relationship Between Feelings of Clothing Deprivation, Self Concept, and Peer Acceptance Among Low and Middle Socioeconomic Status Fourth Grade White Male Students," both Master's theses, University of Tennessee, 1971.

been going on for three years now and she hasn't eaten one dress. She goes to the shows; she goes to the dances, and she is just one of the crowd.[26]

Again, this demonstrates the significance of clothing in the formation of attitudes and feelings toward the self.

Clothing is a significant force in the enhancement of the self, and when used positively, it contributes to one's feelings of self-acceptance, self-respect, and self-esteem.

In defense of the self

We have seen how one's self-concept is derived from the responses of significant others. The group's picture of a person's self, in turn, will determine their reaction to him. It is obvious that how a person *thinks* he looks is not always the same as how he looks to others or how he really is. People's evaluations of others often come out sounding like, "Boy, is she conceited!" or "He's terribly self-conscious." Obviously, such statements represent one person's idea of another person's self-concept. Since it is very difficult for someone to know exactly how the other person feels about himself, evaluation of another's self-concept is not always correct. It becomes important, therefore, to understand the meaning or impression that clothing conveys to others, and how others perceive such meanings.

Several research studies have provided some information in regard to the way clothing is perceived in various situations. In a study of white-collar and manual workers,[27] subjects were asked what they thought about people who spent a lot of time, money, and effort on clothes. More than two-fifths of the white-collar workers approved of people who were extremely clothes conscious, while most of the manual workers felt that it was "foolish and silly" to spend much time and money on clothes. It became quite clear that those who attach little importance to clothing themselves also expect others to attach little importance to it. These same two groups of men were asked if they thought they could determine a person's occupation by the clothes he wore. Two-thirds of the manual workers thought that they could, while only half of the white-collar workers thought they could. But when it came to the actual identification of people by their garb, the manual workers were able to identify fewer occupational categories than the office workers. In other words, clothing is perceived in relation to one's concept of what clothing should be, and what one perceives is not often consciously recognized.

Similar variations in group perception were noted in a study of women shoppers.[28] Women were asked if they thought the

[26]Reported by Robert H. Tuttle, Supervisor of Nursing Services, Mendocino State Hospital in Ukiah, California.
[27]Form and Stone, *Social Significance of Clothing*, pp. 14–16.
[28]G. Stone and W. Form, *The Local Community Clothing Market: A Study of the Social and Social Psychological Contexts* of *Shopping*, Technical Bulletin 262, Michigan State University Agricultural Experiment Station, 1957.

way they dressed made any difference in the service they received from salesclerks. Most of the women who "dressed up" to go shopping felt that there *was* a difference in the way they were treated, while the greatest proportion of negative responses to the question came from the women who wore housedresses or slacks. In effect, these women made their evaluations in terms of their expectations.

Probably the most pertinent piece of research in this regard is Ryan's study of the perception of self in relation to clothing.[29] Four scales were devised to yield estimates of an individual with respect to how well dressed she appeared, her physical appearance, individuality in dress, and self-confidence. Each subject rated herself on these four factors, and the group rated each individual in like manner. Subjects were then asked to make an estimate of how the group rated them. There was a highly significant relationship between the self-ratings and the group ratings, indicating that individuals in general tend to see themselves as others see them. It is interesting that self-ratings which were high were almost always higher than the group rating, while self-ratings that were low were usually lower than the group rating. As we might expect, the girl who rated herself high on a given scale also thought that the group rated her high on that scale. Those who rated themselves either high or low tended to over- or under-estimate the group rating, as was the case in the comparison of actual self-ratings with group ratings.

This same experiment was repeated for seven successive years among groups of students in clothing selection classes at the University of Nevada, and results were generally in agreement with the findings of the original study in the above respects. There are, however, always some individuals whose concept of self in regard to appearance and dress differs markedly from the group's concept of the individual. Although such discrepancies are not the dominant pattern, they are sufficiently common to indicate that positive conclusions about another's self-concept cannot be made solely on the basis of his physical appearance and overt behavior.

Earlier in this chapter we referred to a theory of cognitive dissonance which attempted to explain how people distort the objective world in order to reduce conflict or inconsistency. The drive to reduce dissonance is most powerful when one's self-esteem is threatened, and the individual often uses a variety of defense mechanisms to keep from acknowledging unpleasant truths about himself. One way to maintain self-respect is to have logical and socially acceptable reasons for doing the things that we do. The term **rationalization** is generally applied to the process of inventing excuses for your behavior when you do not have an excuse ample enough even to satisfy yourself.

---

[29]Ryan, "Perception of Self," 1954.

The woman who "simply cannot keep warm" in a cloth coat rationalizes her desire for the mink she saw on sale last week. The home economics student tells her father that she "must" have a new sweater to match the skirt she just made or she will receive a poor grade in her clothing class. By giving the self false excuses we may retain a higher self-concept than the group is apt to ascribe to us.

We have already discussed the process of **identification** as a positive mechanism in learning role behavior, but it may also be responsible for misjudgments with respect to one's self-concept. In copying the actions and attitudes of the other, an individual may also claim as his own the admirable traits of the model, which in reality he may not possess at all. Dressing up like Raquel Welch may impart to the self of the wearer a semblance of the sex appeal of the originator, but the observer may be unable to perceive any such transformation.

The mechanism of **projection** is just the reverse of identification. Instead of assuming the desirable traits of another, we assign our own attributes to other people. This provides the self with the assurance that others are equally or worse off than we are: in a world of sloppily dressed people, my own sloppiness will go unnoticed; if everyone else is too fat to be wearing shorts, it becomes acceptable for me to wear them because "If *she* can get away with it, so can I!" Projection is an indirect way of bolstering one's self-esteem, and may also account for discrepancies between the self and the group judgment.

Under ordinary circumstances, it is quite natural and desirable for people with deficiencies of one kind or another to compensate with superior performance in some other area or activity. Few people would refrain from covering up physical deficiencies with clothes: camouflaging hips that are too full, shoulders that are too narrow, arms that are too thin, or a waist that is too thick. These, of course, are all minor forms of compensation. A good job of camouflage obviously will influence the group judgment away from the reality of the self. In more extreme cases of frustration, an individual may **overcompensate** for his feelings of inadequacy. The person labeled by the group as being conceited—that is, one who holds an unwarranted high opinion of himself—is very apt to be covering up rather deep-seated feelings of inferiority. The woman who feels socially inferior may overcompensate by wearing conspicuously expensive clothes, or the salesman who lacks real skill on his job finds that he can gain acceptance and attention with flashy suits or unusual ties.

Some individuals find comfort and security in falling back to childish patterns of behavior. **Regression** is a reaction in which the individual returns to earlier habits that may have elicited positive responses from others at another time in life. The supposedly mature man who finds satisfaction in donning his old college sweater; the teenager who reverts to the messy habits of childhood when mother took care to see that his clothes were clean and well pressed; the middle-aged woman who subconsciously believes that her "baby doll" dresses will recapture the protective concerns of others that she enjoyed as a little girl—such are the manifestations of regressive behavior.

Another behavior pattern that may be adopted is commonly known as **repression.** Some writers define this as "motivated forgetting," a process in which one closes his eyes to reality. If an individual's early experiences with clothing caused him humiliation, embarrassment, or discomfort, he may put all thoughts about clothes out of his mind and pretend that they hardly exist at all. A person may have a strong desire for clothes that enhance his personal appearance, but if he lacks the requisite purchasing power or the "know-how" to achieve his goal, he may adopt the attitude that clothes are really very unimportant. Too wide a discrepancy between what one has and what one wants results in a situation that is intolerable.

A response that is similar to repression is called "goal substitution," or **sublimation** by the Freudians. Sublimation enables the individual to substitute socially acceptable patterns of behavior for desires that are considered taboo by society. Fundamental sex drives, for example, are restricted by well-established conventions that block overt satisfaction of sexual desires. Such drives are quite commonly rechannelled into clothing behavior. It is perfectly acceptable to be attractive by virtue of one's clothes, but very unacceptable to attract attention with one's body.

A type of reaction that becomes habitual with some people who are excessively shy is that of **insulation.** They are so insecure in their skills of social participation that they seek to withdraw from even the slightest bit of public attention. Inconspicuous clothing, of course, is a perfect shield for their seclusion. Clothes provide not only physical insulation from heat and cold, but they provide psychological insulation as well.

Although it is impossible to categorize all types of human responses to conflict and frustration, there is one final mechanism that should be mentioned in relation to clothing behavior. **Reaction formation** is a process that seriously interferes with the accuracy of group judgments of an individual, since it is an attempt to conceal one's real motives by displaying attitudes that are exactly the opposite. The person obsessed by obscene thoughts and desires may exhibit extreme prudishness in dress and protest the "indecency" of modern fashions. Or the individual who spends most of his money on clothes and most of his time deciding what to wear may claim that he has absolutely no interest in dress whatsoever, and that his appearance is purely "accidental."

In most cases, clothing provides a real clue to personality since it conveys an impression of what one is, what one does,

Clothing is a general reflection of how the individual thinks of himself, although the accuracy of such judgment may be altered by faulty perception, lack of knowledge, or the operation of defense mechanisms.

and what one believes. The majority of people tend to see themselves in much the same way that others perceive them. We must be cautious, however, in forming opinions about the underlying motives of behavior, since an individual may employ any one of several mechanisms that defend the self from detection. Moreover, the impression that one may wish to create through clothing may not be perceived in the same way that one would like it to be. This may be attributed in part to a person's ignorance of the cues that are communicated to others through dress, or it may be accounted for in the fact that people tend to see what they are looking for — that is, they perceive and evaluate the other's appearance in terms of their own expectations.

Thus, in terms of operant behavior, clothing is both a *stimulus* and a *response*. It provides stimulation to the wearer as well as to the beholder. It stimulates the social and the sexual appetite. It calls forth responses of admiration, approval, acceptance, rejection, condemnation, or ridicule. Clothing is also a response in that it registers conformity to group expectations, rebellion to parental control, and satisfaction of psychological needs.

SUMMARY   *Clothing and evaluation of the self*

The effects of operant conditioning in relation to clothing behavior have been discussed. Positive attitudes expressed toward one's clothes tend to reinforce a generalized positive feeling toward the self, while negative responses contribute to the deprecation of the self. A unified and consistent way of looking at oneself is gradually developed from the "reflected appraisals" of other persons, although vacillations in such feelings are common, particularly in the assumptions of new social roles. Clothing aids in the stabilization of a central identity.

For most people, clothing provides a positive means of satisfying the need for self-enhancement. It can beautify the appearance, make the physical self more desirable, increase acceptance by the group, and prevent rejection. It may be a source of overt admiration, resulting in increased self-esteem, self-respect, self-confidence, and security.

Clothing is a cue to personality in that it conveys to others an impression of what one is, does, and believes. The impression one wishes to create through clothing, however, is not always perceived in the same manner as one would like it to be, since others tend to perceive clothing in terms of their own self-concepts and expectations, and individuals may lack a knowledge of the meanings conveyed through clothes. Moreover, accurate judgment is impeded by the use of clothing in the manifestation of a wide variety of defense mechanisms, such as identification, projection, rationalization, overcompensation, regression, repression, sublimation, insulation, and reaction formation.

Clothes, self, and society

"Clothes make the man," the saying goes. What seems at first to be a flippant appraisal of the importance of dress takes on added depth of meaning as we analyze the close relationship between clothing and developmental processes. Hurlock explains how the careful selection of clothes for a young child can satisfy some of his important needs: autonomy, attention, individuality, as well as peer group and sex identification.[30] We have already discussed how patterns of behavior established in the early years of life are apt to carry over into adulthood. The continuing importance of dress even in later life is emphasized by Stone's contention that (1) every social transaction must be broken down into at least two analytic components or processes, appearance and discourse; (2) appearance is at least as important for the establishment and maintenance of the self as is discourse; (3) the study of appearance provides a powerful lever for the formulation of a conception of self; and (4) appearance is of major importance at every stage of development.[31]

Sub-identities

Stone's insistence that appearance is at least if not more important than language in communicating impressions of the self to other people is corroborated by studies which have shown that the initial or primary impression created by individuals is likely to be an important and lasting one.[32] First impressions are largely derived from outward appearances and established by nonverbal cues and symbols of the kind that clothing provides. The way in which a person is first perceived is particularly important in establishing the self in new social roles. Every individual maintains a series of such sub-identities which are defined and delimited by the boundaries of specific roles.

Thus, the identity established by the college freshman among juniors and seniors in a sorority house is apt to differ in many respects from the identity which that same student enjoys among old high school friends in her home town. Each of the two sub-identities may require conformity to a different set of clothing expectations, and the individual is likely to make a more conscious effort to control the clothing cues in the situation which is less familiar to her. The clothing requirements of a man's role as a department manager may differ only slightly from those required as a member of the executive board (men

Clothing requirements for various sub-identities are defined within the context of specific or segmented roles, and they contribute to the mutable nature of the self.

---

[30]Elizabeth E. Hurlock, *Child Development,* McGraw-Hill Book Company, 1972, pp. 406–408.
[31]Stone, "Appearance and Self," p. 87 ff.
[32]See, for example, S. E. Asch, "Forming Impressions of Personality," *Journal of Abnormal and Social Psychology* 41, 1946, pp. 258–290; and N. H. Anderson and A. A. Barrios, "Primacy Effects in Personality Impression Formation," *Journal of Abnormal and Social Psychology* 63, 1961, pp. 346–350.

usually pay more attention to their attire on "board meeting" days), but both sets of requirements are put aside when he gets home in the evening and changes to his "husband-and-father" clothes. Various sub-identities, then, contribute to the changing and flexible qualities of the self. The self gradually absorbs or accommodates the requirements prescribed by the social groupings in which membership is claimed or sought.

An emerging lifestyle

In spite of the fact that the self is developmental in nature, most individuals tend to respond with one generalized mode or pattern of behavior. Adler's phrase for this fixed expression of personality is "style of life."[33] The implication is that one type of response becomes dominant in an individual's life experiences, and a central, unified style emerges.

A "style of life" applied to patterns of clothing behavior will reveal that some men respond to almost all situations with attire that expresses a high degree of inconspicuous conformity — "he is the best-dressed whose dress no one observes." Other men (who are by far the minority in our society) exhibit a "style of life" through clothes which is built upon the philosophy of "fine feathers make fine birds."

The point is that one's preference for different styles is not just a vicarious adoption of a set of values. It is no accident, for example, that many black leaders are among the best-dressed politicians and athletes in the country. To black men, avant-garde dressing is rarely considered an affectation. Clothes are considered a symbol of pride — a legitimate masculine concern — and the source of personal compliments.

Athlete Nate Thurmond explained, "Different races put emphasis on different things. We put more emphasis on telling one another we're sharp. We invariably mention clothes."

One explanation for this emphasis on dressing is that for blacks who never had an opportunity to possess property, and never had enough money to save for anything really big, clothes were what they spent their money on. "Clothes were a way to say that we felt good about ourselves," said another prominent man. "We used to dress to get attention. But now it's what we call 'styling.' I'm styling now," he said, referring to his new beige suit with orange trim. "I style every day. It's not just to say 'look at me' — that's shallow. It's to say I am somebody."

Some of the men speculated that as blacks become more solidly entrenched in the Establishment, clothes will cease to be as important to them. But it hardly seems possible that these men, whose wardrobes are nothing short of splendid, will ever look ordinary.[34]

Figure 7-9. At professional boxing matches the spectators often become part of the action. Said one observer: "People who attend fights are beautiful people in beautiful clothes. They look great, and they know they look great."

[33]Heinz and Rowena Ansbacher, *The Individual Psychology of Alfred Adler*, Basic Books, New York, 1956.
[34]Beverly Stephen, "Why Do Black Men Dress With Such Flair?" *San Francisco Chronicle*, 20 Nov. 1972.

"I wish we had a life style."

Figure 7-10. For most people, the development of a lifestyle is an unconscious process. Drawing by Lorenz; © 1973. The New Yorker Magazine, Inc.

It is probably safe to say that the development of a lifestyle is an unconscious phenomenon and quite difficult for most people to discern in themselves. The messages broadcast by other people's attire are often easier for us to receive and to understand than are our own.

A number of unique patterns of clothing behavior have been identified by Symonds through her experience as a psychoanalyst. If you are like most people, she explains,

you have some clothes in your closet which you never wear, even though they're perfectly good. You also have some you're always wearing. That's because some clothes fit your inner picture of yourself, while others don't. Unconscious factors guide your choices of clothing as surely as though you were following a blueprint and you wear what satisfies your true feelings about yourself—whether you consciously know it or not. . . .

Your state of mind may change from day to day, or year to year, and your clothes will reflect it. This phenomenon has proved most helpful to me as a psychoanalyst in understanding the person I'm trying to help.[35]

This would seem to suggest that we often approach the problem of clothing selection from the wrong direction. Instead of trying to analyze one's personality (which is difficult with or without objective tests or devices), Symonds is proposing that we analyze one's clothes, which may in turn tell us more about the self than direct approaches to personality assessment.

[35]Alexandra Symonds, M.D., "A Psychoanalyst Reveals Why You Dress the Way You Do." *This Week*, 27 May 1962, pp. 18–22.

Clothing types are certainly easier to identify than personality types, and they can be scrutinized with considerably greater detachment and objectivity.

However it is achieved, understanding the self is a prerequisite to the development of a "style of life" that is consistent with one's recognized values and aspirations. For as Symonds concludes, it is only after you acknowledge what is really *you* and have accepted yourself, with your own particular idiosyncrasies, that change is possible.

Consistent patterns of clothing behavior emerge as a type of dominant response and gradually evolve into a "style of life."

SUMMARY *Clothes, self, and society*

We have seen that the *self* is a configuration of (1) the cognitive components, of intellect, character traits, and various sub-identities, (2) the affective aspects, of feelings and emotions about the self which are conditioned by the social environment, and (3) the somatic constituents, representing rather fixed physical characteristics. Clothing affects all of these aspects of the self and is a powerful medium through which the self is presented to and perceived by significant others in the social milieu. It is only as the self is analyzed, as one develops a vocabulary for expressing feelings about the self, and as one brings values and aspirations to the conscious level of recognition, that resulting patterns of clothing behavior can be modified or altered to a "style of life" that will achieve optimal satisfaction and reward.

FOR FURTHER READING

DeFleur, M. L., W. V. D'Antonio, and L. B. DeFleur. *Sociology: Man in Society*. Glenview, Ill.: Scott, Foresman & Company, 1971. (Chapter 4, "Personal Organization.")

Hall, C., and G. Lindzey. *Theories of Personality*. New York: John Wiley & Sons, 1970. ("Freud's Psychoanalytic Theory," pp. 29–77.)

Murphy, G. *Personality—A Biosocial Approach to Origins and Structure*. New York: Harper and Brothers, 1947. (Part 4, "The Self.")

Rosencranz, Mary Lou. *Clothing Concepts: A Social-Psychological Approach*. New York: Macmillan Publishing Company, 1972. (Chapter 2, "Awareness of Physical Attributes.")

Ryan, Mary S. *Clothing: A Study in Human Behavior*. New York: Holt, Rinehart & Winston, 1966. (Chapter 4, "Clothing and the Wearer—His Personality and Self-Concept.")

Stone, Gregory P. "Appearance and the Self," in A. Rose (ed.), *Human Behavior and Social Processes*. Boston: Houghton Mifflin Company, 1962.

DISCUSSION QUESTIONS

1. What is meant by the "self-concept" and how does it develop? Utilize Cooley's theory of "the looking-glass self," Sullivan's "reflected appraisals," and Mead's "generalized other" in formulating your answer. What role does clothing play in the development of the self-concept?

2. Differentiate the following terms: body type, body-image, body boundary, body-cathexis. How may clothing affect or relate to each of these concepts?

3. In what ways do people strive for consistency or congruence in the evaluation of the self? Give specific examples using hypothetical clothing illustrations.

4. Outline some of the theories that would (a) give support to the acceptance of one's outward appearance as a clue to personality; (b) explain how outward appearances may lead to inaccurate perceptions of one's personality by others.

5. Discuss the pros and cons of retaining clear-cut distinctions between masculine and feminine forms of dress. What impact is it likely to have on the individual's sex and role identity?

6. Review quickly the major points in Chapter 5 on value patterns. How are these similar to or different from Adler's theory of "style of life" as a fixed expression of personality?

7. In regard to the avant-garde dressing by black males, some people speculate that clothes will eventually cease to be important to them. Writer Stephen's reaction was: "But it hardly seems possible that these men, whose wardrobes are nothing short of splendid, will ever look ordinary." What do *you* think?

8

Conformity and Individuality in Dress

AS WE HAVE seen from our previous discussion, man seeks an identity and a sense of belongingness through conforming to a given set of norms, and yet at the same time, he strives to achieve some distinction from his fellow men:

> The personal dilemma rises from the fact that a person must be, and wants to be, a conforming member of some social groups and he wants to play a part as himself, as a distinctive individual. . . . The more benign aspect of diversity—at least in our usual parlance—includes creativity, originality, adaptability. The other range of meanings for diversity takes in abnormality, delinquency, chaos. One face of conformity is identification, loyalty, solidarity; another is monotony, totalitarianism, rigidity. The fact is that both conformity and diversity are inevitable in social and personal life and that one must always complement the other.[1]

Nowhere is this paradox of human nature reflected more visibly than it is in dress. These two social tendencies—conformity and individuality—form the basis for all fashion behavior. Simmel emphasized that both are essential to the establishment of fashion, and that "should one of these be absent, fashion will not be formed—its sway will abruptly end."[2]

Either one, carried to an extreme, is incompatible with human social existence; complete order and rigidity contradicts man's need for new experience, but complete freedom or normlessness leads us to a state of *anomie*. The basic question is how much freedom is desirable within what degree of conformity or control. In attempting an answer, this chapter will be concerned with the forces that motivate innovation, conformity, and deviation in clothing behavior.

---

[1]David Mandelbaum, "The Interplay of Conformity and Diversity," in S. Farber and R. Wilson (eds.), *Conflict and Creativity, Part 2,* McGraw-Hill Book Company, New York, 1963, p. 241 ff.
[2]Georg Simmel, "Fashion," *American Journal of Sociology* 62, May 1957, p. 546.

Norm formation

In Chapter 4 we discussed the process of norm formation in relation to folkways, customs, mores, and laws. Fads and fashions are also a part of the normative system, but they represent clothing practices that fall at the opposite end of the continuum in terms of strength, duration, and sanctions. It is this transitory nature of fashion, however, that makes it the ideal medium for the study of norm formation, norm replacement, conformity, and deviation. Our analysis of conformity versus individuality in dress will be facilitated if we begin by defining the terms used to describe various kinds of clothing phenomena.

Definition of terms

It would be appropriate to say that the wearing of trousers by men is a custom deeply embedded in the normative system of Western culture. It is also customary for men's trousers to be pressed into a lengthwise crease in front and in back. While many men may wear trousers in which the crease has almost disappeared, there are few who would wear trousers in which the crease had been pressed from side to side. We can, of course, cite a number of societies in which a bifurcated garment is *not* the "normal" or typical style of masculine dress. More important, perhaps, is the fact that trousers as we know them today have been in existence less than two hundred years. Viewed against the span of man's recorded history, they may some day be regarded as a "fleeting fashion of the times"—but certainly not as fleeting as "ivy-leagues," "bell-bottoms," or "baggies."

The point here is that our definitions of terms are relative rather than absolute. What may appear to be a dichotomy in the comparison of a fluctuating fashion with an enduring custom is in reality the comparison of two extreme cases selected from different points along the same continuum. As already defined, a **clothing norm** represents the typical or accepted manner of dressing manifested by a social group. By **conformity,** we mean acceptance of or adherence to a clothing norm, i.e., dressing in accordance with the norm of a specified group. With the exception of the term "style," all of the following may be considered clothing norms.

Style is a characteristic or distinctive form of dress; it is possessed of certain recognizable qualities or features which distinguish it from other forms. The popularity of a style will vary, but the style itself is unchanging. The bouffant skirt, for example, is one style of dress that was considered fashionable in the 1860's and the 1950's, but it was definitely *un*fashionable in the 1920's and 1930's. In general, the styling of a garment refers to its design or cut, a quality that can be described in terms of its line, form, or proportion. Thus, there are styles of coats (box, redingote, Balmacaan, Chesterfield, trench, wrap-around), styles of sleeves (bishop, dolman, kimono, raglan, leg-o'-mutton), styles of hats (Breton, bowler, fedora, cloche, Homburg), and styles of shoes (oxfords, sandals, pumps, boots, brogues).

Mode is a statistical expression that represents the most common form of clothing behavior among a given group of people, or, to say it another way, the greatest frequency of a style. If we were to observe the clothing behavior of a population, we could count the number of times each variation of dress was worn. Such a counting procedure would give us two kinds of measurements: (1) the range of variability in dress, and (2) the style of highest frequency (the mode).

Universals, *alternatives*, and *specialties* are terms that help us to describe the extent of a norm's applicability. A **universal** norm generally applies to every member of the society. Most societies, however, permit some degree of variation from the modal pattern. In a campus population, for example, Levis may be the mode among males, but bell-bottoms, baggies, and ivy-leagues are also acceptable **alternatives.** Each is a norm, but one does not exclude the other. **Specialties,** on the other hand, are norms that are restricted to a particular subgroup. In 1970, micro-mini skirts may have been the mode for young females between the ages of 13 and 25, but it was not the norm for all females.

Fashion represents the popular, accepted, prevailing style at any given time. In this sense, it is synonymous with the mode. However, fashion is further characterized by its cyclical nature, i.e., the gradual rise, culmination, and eventual decline in the popular acceptance of a style. On its way into popularity, a style is worn by the relatively few people who can afford to be different. As its popularity spreads, more and more people hop on the bandwagon until the style finally snowballs to the peak of acceptance, and no one can afford to be different. But once everyone has it, the attraction is past, and there is no place left for the style to go but to slip gradually into obsolescence. The forces that give vent to the rise and fall of fashion are identical with the tensions that exist between conformity and distinction in dress.

Classic, sometimes known as a "fashion Ford," is the term applied to an occasional fashion that becomes so universally accepted that it gradually crystallizes into a conventional norm of dress. Such styles remain popular for so long that they rest on the borderline between fashion and custom. Over the years, styles like the shirtwaist dress, skirt and sweater combinations, polo coats, and Chanel suits all have been known as classics.

High fashion is found only in the incipient stages of the normal fashion cycle. Because of its newness, costliness, and novelty, it is worn only by those people who have the attributes

Figure 8-1. Classics, like this tweed suit with pleated skirt, have a certain timeless quality. Actual vintage: 1969.

Figure 8-2. By 1970, the miniskirt had become a popular fashion.

Figure 8-3. When longer skirts were introduced in 1970, they were openly rejected as a replacement for the mini.

of fashion innovators. It has the snob appeal of exclusiveness; once it is no longer confined to restricted consumption, it loses its status as a high fashion. The rapid dissemination of high-fashion copies today shortens its life span considerably. The potential success of a high fashion, however, must be reasonably assured before manufacturers are willing to mass produce it.

Not all high fashions mature into full-blown fashions; some, because they depart too radically from the conventional patterns of dress, fade into oblivion before the bandwagon rolls by. Others, because of prohibitive cost or availability, continue in restricted use.

Fad is a term used to designate a kind of miniature fashion, usually more trivial or more bizarre than the normal fashion. It often reaches fewer people and is sometimes confined to a subculture. Fads have a sudden burst of popularity, enjoy a bandwagon plateau for several weeks or months, and then drop out of existence as quickly as they came in. Fads have included goldfish swallowing, telephone booth stuffing, the fifty-mile hike, and streaking. In clothing, there have been fads of plaid shoestrings, colored tennis shoes, decorated sweatshirts, beer jackets, rope beads, raccoon hats, striped blazers, shoe boots, hooded blouses, charm bracelets, elbow patches, ad infinitum. Fads sometimes cluster around a particular person, group, or event. The popularity of the Beatles gave rise to Beatle shirts, Beatle jackets, and Beatle haircuts. In a few rare instances fads survive the usual rapid decline into obsolescence and develop into enduring fashions (e.g., the bobbed hair of the 1920's,

Figure 8-4. Fads of the early seventies. Here today, gone tomorrow . . .

pearls worn with sweaters, white buck shoes), but the vast majority last little more than six months.

With the exception of style, each of these concepts is dependent upon varying degrees of conformity. The classic is widely accepted and worn over a long period of time. The fashion, usually initiated as a high fashion worn by a very select group of people, reaches its peak of mass acceptance and then gradually fades into obsolescence. A fashion represents the mass taste, what "everybody" wears; it becomes the property of a large and diverse group in the total society for a period of time. Fads usually reach fewer people and are very short in duration.

Specific types of clothing norms may be differentiated on the basis of their relative endurance and the magnitude of their acceptance.

The cyclical nature of fashion

The term **fashion cycle** refers specifically to the gradual rise, culmination, and decline in the popularity of a given style (see Figure 8-5). The theoretical representation of the stages in the fashion cycle shows symmetrical bell-shaped curves. Since actual observations always represent a sample of the total population, statistics obtained from fashion counts almost never produce the smooth curve of the prototype (Figure 8-6), although they yield a fairly accurate measure of the duration and magnitude of a style's acceptance.

If we were to make similar numerical tabulations on a regular basis and in different places, the fashion count would enable us to estimate the relative position of a style in terms of its anticipated cycle (Figure 8-7). Let us say, for example, that

CONFORMITY AND INDIVIDUALITY IN DRESS

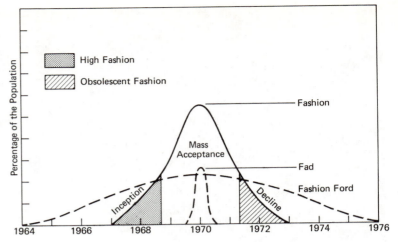

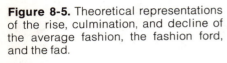

Figure 8-5. Theoretical representations of the rise, culmination, and decline of the average fashion, the fashion ford, and the fad.

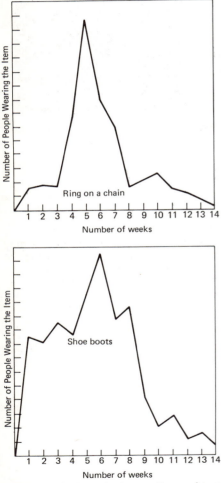

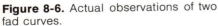

Figure 8-6. Actual observations of two fad curves.

we want to determine the acceptance of baggie-styled trousers for men. We can stand on the corner of Broadway and Main in Smalltown, U.S.A., and count the number of men wearing baggies. At the end of an hour or two, we may have observed that 6 men out of 150 turned out to be baggie wearers. This does not tell us very much, except that baggies have been adopted by roughly 4 per cent of the Smalltown males. If we stand on the same corner every Saturday afternoon for the ensuing six months, however, we get a picture of increasing or decreasing acceptance. Another dimension is added to this analysis were we to have scouts make similar tabulations during the same time intervals in several large cities such as San Francisco, Chicago, and New York. A third comparison could be made if we were in a position to count the number of men wearing baggies in the fashionably elite resorts. Figure 8-7 shows a theoretical representation of the fashion cycle at each of these levels.

It is entirely possible, of course, that a small but particularly fashion-conscious community might adopt high fashions before they are generally worn by large segments of the population in bigger cities. Fashion counts are useful in determining the degree to which this is so. There is an understandable time lag, however, between the introduction of the original high fashion and the availability of copied-down reproductions. In earlier days, it took almost two years for a high-fashion design to be worn universally by the average person on the street. Today, the ready-to-wear industry can turn out copies in a matter of months; with some items that are easy to reproduce, the time lag may be reduced to weeks.

From our theoretical model, we can see that if the percentage of people wearing a given item in high fashion circles exceeds the percentage at the local level, it is a fair indication that the

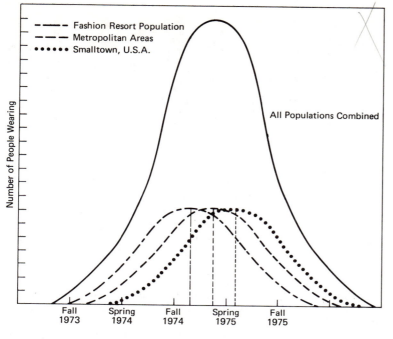

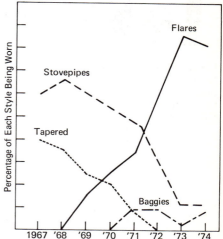

Figure 8-8. Observations of men's trousers, 1967–1974.

fashion has not yet reached its peak of popularity. On the other hand, if more men on Main Street are wearing baggies than they are on Fifth Avenue, chances are that baggies have begun their downhill trip into decline and obsolescence.

This kind of comparison also can be made by counting successive illustrations in magazines instead of actual people in various locations. Assume that you had been able to observe the type of trousers worn by male students on campus over a period of years (see Figure 8-8). Back in 1967, stovepipes and tapered slacks dominated the scene. Although stovepipes were still the predominant cut in 1971, they were losing ground to the flares, which gained rapid acceptance between 1969 and 1970. Full-cut trousers were just beginning to appear. Even though your observations do not furnish you with the complete fashion cycle for each of these styles, the trend lines enable you to predict where they might fall on the theoretical curve.

In order to determine the fashion followership of men on your campus, you could then plot the curve of the incoming fashion against comparable fashion counts made in popular and high-fashion magazines (Figure 8-9.). Again, if these three curves are compared with the theoretical model in Figure 8-7, it becomes evident that the style reached its saturation point between 1972 and 1973.

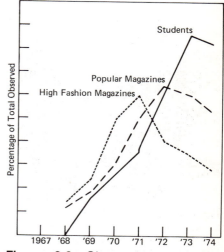

Figure 8-9. Observations of men's flared trousers, 1967–1974.

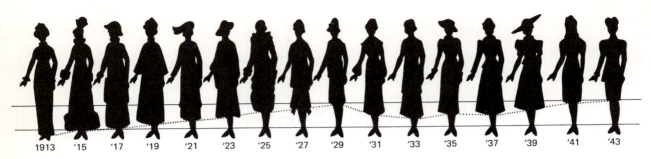

| 1913 | '15 | '17 | '19 | '21 | '23 | '25 | '27 | '29 | '31 | '33 | '35 | '37 | '39 | '41 | '43 |

Figure 8-10. The recurring cycle in skirt lengths. Try this with other aspects of dress, such as the width of men's trousers, shoulder width, shoe proportions, and the like.

Figure 8-11. How luxury items lose status. Just as soon as the currently popular status symbol is acquired by a large proportion of the population, it has no place to go but down.

The time required for a fashion cycle to run its course obviously varies with the type of norm that the fashion demonstrates. An evanescent fad may dissipate in a matter of weeks or months, while a classic may remain popular for fifteen or twenty years. The average fashion usually lasts from seven to nine years, from inception to its ultimate obsolescence. There is some evidence, however, that the duration of the fashion cycle is becoming progressively shorter, which is to be expected in times of rapid social change.

Aside from the fact that fashion counts provide valuable information in predicting the life span of a style, they are a means of producing graphic evidence of the degree of conformity that exists to local or national norms. Every fad or fashion can be traced from its inception, through its validation by fashion leaders, its growing influence, its mass acceptance and its decline, to final obsolescence. Fads are even more dramatic than fashions in this respect because the cycle is so short; they snowball rapidly and approach their peaks like mental epidemics from which no one is immune. Many have such severe attacks that all the symptoms become grossly exaggerated. If full skirts are the rage, one or two petticoats are good, but seven or eight are better; if narrow trousers are "in," one must be "in" even further with a pair several sizes too small and reaching halfway up the calf. This kind of frenzied enthusiasm results in the vulgar excesses that sound the death knell. When the people who imitate fashion are far removed from those who set the fashion, they often have a vague and incomplete understanding of the boundaries. In attempting to imitate, they overreach, and thereby nullify the fashion they seek to adopt.

Another dimension of the cyclical nature of fashion relates to the principle of **recurring cycles.** Independent studies of costume characteristics over the centuries indicate that certain styles or patterns of dress tend to recur at fairly regular intervals. The analysis by Richardson and Kroeber, for example, pointed out that the basic dimensions of feminine dress alternate between minimum and maximum measurements approximately every fifty years, taking a full century for the silhouette

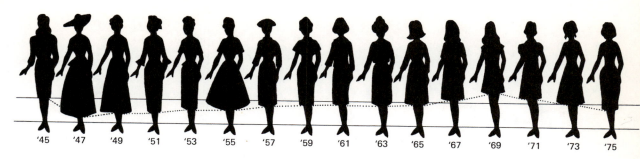

to complete the cycle from the wide to the narrow and back to wide again.[3] Thus, in terms of general contour, we are able to observe peaks of fullness at about 1570, 1660, 1750, 1860, and 1950, with silhouettes that gradually diminish to the slender tubular shape in the intervening years. Young maintained that the transition from the wide to the narrow always passed through a period of back fullness.[4] While the theory seems to hold true for fashions from 1760 through the early 1950's, it has not been borne out by the changes that have occurred within the last decade or two.

It is true, nevertheless, that the dominant elements of fashion (e.g., the length and fullness of the skirt, the size and placement of the waistline, the width of the sleeve) progress through waves of continuous evolution. The typical fashion must always be different from that of the preceding year, yet it rarely differs in any marked degree from its predecessor. Each year's fashion is built upon the past and can be seen as an outgrowth or modification of the previous style. In addition, the pendulum of fashion must swing from one extreme to the other.[5] Under normal circumstances, it cannot move from an extremely narrow sleeve to a moderately full one, then jerk back to a moderately narrow one before it continues its way to extreme fullness. Skirts of the 1860's became so full that at their peak it was almost impossible for the wearers to squeeze through a door. The silhouette then began its slow progression back toward narrowness until some fifty years later we see a skirt so tight about the knees and ankles that a lady could

"Bell bottoms are being with it. I'm with it."

Figure 8-12. Some people overreach and nullify the fashion they seek to adopt.

[3]Richardson and Kroeber, "Three Centuries of Fashions."
[4]Agnes Brooks Young, *Recurring Cycles of Fashion (1760–1937)*, Harper and Brothers, New York, 1937.
[5]The fact that both full and narrow skirts may be seen to exist during the same year does not contradict this basic assumption. Each season many new designs are introduced which undergo a period of experimentation before a trend is clearly discernible. This is the reason that current fashions are difficult to analyze with accuracy; one often needs the benefit of historical perspective to identify the typical or dominant theme of an era. Moreover, one can always observe deviations from the theme; the degree of variability from the ideal norm of any period is an important index of the stability or instability of the times.

CONFORMITY AND INDIVIDUALITY IN DRESS

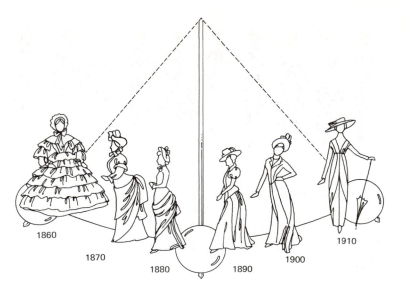

Figure 8-13. The pendulum of fashion swings from one extreme to the other. Shown here, the gradual change in the fashion silhouette.

1860
1870
1880
1890
1900
1910

Clothing norms are subject to continuous change; each year's fashion is different from the last but without any radical departure from it.

barely take a comfortable step. Many writers who are prone to interpret all bodily adornment in terms of its sexual significance see the hobble skirt of 1912 as a masculine attempt to dominate women by impeding their movements. In terms of the cyclical theory of fashion change, the famous hobble skirt was nothing more nor less than the logical conclusion to the diminishing amplitude of the preceding fifty years. The farther the pendulum begins from dead center, the farther it will swing in the opposite direction. The extremes of elongation observed in the late Gothic period in the form of tall hats and pointed shoes reached its antithesis in the extreme width of the fashions of the Renaissance.

Thus, the cyclical nature of fashion may be explained in terms of (1) the rise, culmination, and decline in the popularity of a style and (2) long-term cycles of recurrence.

Pressures toward conformity

No society in human history has ever been a "free society" in the sense that its members were free to do exactly as they pleased in all respects. There are some areas of activity in which society maintains rather rigid controls over human behavior; in others, conformity to or deviation from the accepted norm is a matter of choice left up to the individual; in still others, nonconformity may even be encouraged and rewarded. In the case of clothing behavior, there are few institutionalized controls, and considerable deviation from the norm is tolerated. Fashion leaders, however, are *expected* to depart from the established norm, and their status is increased when they do so. But within the broad range of human activity related to

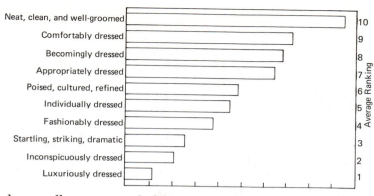

Neat, clean, and well-groomed	10
Comfortably dressed	9
Becomingly dressed	8
Appropriately dressed	7
Poised, cultured, refined	6
Individually dressed	5
Fashionably dressed	4
Startling, striking, dramatic	3
Inconspicuously dressed	2
Luxuriously dressed	1

Average Ranking

Figure 8-14. Student responses to phrases describing appearance values.

dress, adherence to clothing norms is largely voluntary. To what extent, then, do people actually conform in their clothing behavior, and what are the factors that encourage such conformity?

As children, all of us have played the game of "Follow-the-Leader." The child who is quick enough to be the first to shout "Leader!" is accorded the privilege of initiating the behavior that others must imitate. Obviously, if everyone insisted on being the leader, the game would fall apart; the whole fun of the action is seeing how many people can duplicate the innovator's maneuvers. Everyone but the leader, therefore, must agree to be a follower. The reader is invited to try an experiment in behavioral contagion: take a friend or two to the corner of the busiest street in town; stand in a conspicuous spot and look quizzically toward the sky or the top of a building. See how many passing strangers follow your glance skyward. Or, follow the sales in the bargain basement of the local department store, and watch the customers fight to reach the edge of the most crowded counter without even knowing what items are for sale behind the figures of the mob.

It is this same kind of contagious behavior that causes innovations in clothing norms to flourish into fads or fashions. The desire to conform—consciously or unconsciously—to the established norms of the group appears to be strongly reinforced in human behavior. Several groups of undergraduate students at the University of Nevada were asked to analyze their motives in clothing behavior by ranking a list of ten phrases describing the ways in which an individual might prefer to dress or wish to appear.[6] The weighted rankings of these students are represented in Figure 8-14. In first place, almost all students ranked "neatness" and "cleanliness," both of which are values that have long been held by Americans as second only to "godliness." "Appropriateness" can be interpreted only in terms of what is "fitting" or "proper," i.e., the acceptable form of dress. Being "luxuriously" dressed was the least valued of the pos-

[6]The phrases were adapted from McJimsey, *Art in Clothing Selection*, p. 5.

Figure 8-15. Behavior is contagious. People in all walks of life, at all ages, seek an identification with one another.

sible choices and the one which would have been most inconsistent with the norms of the group. It is significant that few students wished to be "inconspicuous," but neither did they want to be "striking" or "dramatic." Most students interpreted the term "fashionably dressed" to mean "in the height of fashion," i.e., synonymous with *high fashion* rather than *fashion* as the terms have been previously described. The combined rankings placed "individuality" in dress near the middle, although not a single student rated this value as her first choice.

All of these examples merely indicate that the phenomena of contagion and conformity are prevalent in most forms of clothing behavior. One might ask *why* these forces seem to be so deeply embedded in human response patterns, more so than drives toward creativity, individuality, or distinctiveness. Our discussion in the previous chapter pointed out that much of our social behavior is imitative. In the child's early life, the ability to discriminate among the many cues in his environment is limited, and he learns the appropriate responses by imitating the actions of parents and older siblings.

Beyond this, there is considerable evidence that people have a rather strong need to be "correct," and they look to others for the validation of their opinions and actions. Several experiments in social psychology have indicated that the tendency to follow the suggestions of others is particularly strong when the expectations are ambiguous, or if the individual has little confidence in his own opinions.[7] We might infer from this that

7See, for example, the series of experiments reported in Edward L. Walker and Roger W. Heyns, *An Anatomy for Conformity*, Prentice-Hall, Englewood Cliffs,

　　　　　CLOTHING AND HUMAN BEHAVIOR

"I feel like a damn fool."

if a person feels his understanding of the right form of dress is limited or incomplete, he is more apt to rely upon the judgment of others. "Independent thinking typically involves a deliberate exposing of oneself to the challenges and discomforts of uncertainty, of confusion, of alienation,"[8] while imitation of the clothing behavior of a high-status person gives a feeling of assured success.

Obviously, different subgroups of the population take their clothing cues from various categories of leaders. Young teenagers are apt to attach their patterns of emulation to the current idols of the entertainment or athletic worlds. Upper-middle-class women may choose the "ten best-dressed" as their source of fashion information, while the rest of the middle class may find more suitable models among the wives of prominent men who project the typical housewife-and-mother image.[9]

In an experimental study of junior high school girls, Traub tested the relative influence of peers and parents upon the subjects' opinions of "appropriate" dress. Regardless of the accuracy of the norm information given, peer group preferences were found to be far more important than parental opinions in

N.J., 1962. Although not specifically related to clothing behavior, the factors that make for a high degree of conformity in human behavior are clearly described.
[8]Richard Crutchfield, "Independent Thought in a Conformist World," in Farber and Wilson (eds.), *Conflict and Creativity*, Part 2, McGraw-Hill Book Company, New York, 1963, p. 210.
[9]Bernard Barber and Lyle Lobel, "Fashion in Women's Clothes and the American Social System," *Social Forces* 31, 1952, p. 129.

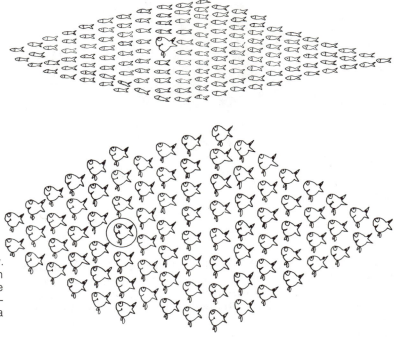

Figure 8-17. Conformity brings security. Lorenzo stuck out like a sore thumb in the school of sardines, but back home with his red-tailed family his belonging-ness was so complete that one needs a circle to find him.

Figure 8-18. A human "Lorenzo" in a sea of homburgs. Find the man without the hat.

CLOTHING AND HUMAN BEHAVIOR

shaping the clothing choices of the adolescents studied.[10] There are some popular leaders, however, who seem to possess a personal charisma that appeals to almost all age groups and class levels. Rudolph Valentino was such a person in the 1920's, Grace Kelly in the 1950's, President and Mrs. Kennedy in the 1960's. In any case, the clothing norm is derived from persons or groups who have high prestige and/or attract emulation.

Years ago, Riesman suggested that American society fostered the development of an increasing degree of "other-directedness," i.e., sensitivity to and concern for the opinions of others.[11] Centers attempted to compare the conforming behavior of "other-directed" and "inner-directed" persons by first informing them of the opinions of a number of well-known and important people, and then asking for their responses to a series of items. Other-directed persons were found to be more susceptible than the inner-directed group to social influences, as measured by the similarity of their responses to the opinions of well-known and important others.[12]

Rogers attempted to test Riesman's theory specifically in the context of clothing behavior. Other-directed individuals, when found to deviate from the norm, tended to deviate in the direction of fashion innovation. When inner-directed individuals failed to follow the norm, their deviations were more often described as obsolescent.[13]

Pressures toward conformity also are thought to be related to the need for maintaining harmonious relations with others. Taylor's research gave support to such a theory by demonstrating that interaction-oriented subjects emphasized the maintenance of harmonious group relationships over individualism,

Figure 8-20. Miniskirts did not reach their peak of popularity until 1969, but Jacqueline Kennedy legitimized above-the-knee hemlines as early as 1966. By the time everyone else was wearing minis, Mrs. Onassis had switched to the "longuette."

---

[10]Sue Traub, "Conformity of Junior High School Girls' Opinions of Appropriateness of Dress When Under Social Pressure from Peers or Parents," Master's thesis, Ohio State University, 1970.
[11]David Riesman, *The Lonely Crowd*, Yale University Press, New Haven, 1950.
[12]Richard Centers, "Social Character and Conformity: A Differential in Susceptibility to Social Influences," *Journal of Social Psychology* 60(2), 1963, pp. 343–349.
[13]Jean Rogers, "The Relationship of Conformity in Dress to Riesman's Theory of Social Character," Master's thesis, University of Nevada, 1967.

and that those who were high in interaction-orientation were also high in conformity in dress.[14]

Following the dictates of group opinion obviously has its rewards. There have been a number of studies that have identified a positive relationship between conformity to group standards of dress and peer acceptance.[15] Of the wide variety of individuals who have been tested, the vast majority desire to emulate the modal style of dress for their respective social groups. Thus, conformity appears to have certain positive social values. On the other side of the ledger, however, conformity has been associated with a variety of psychological and personality inadequacies. Crutchfield, for example, reported that individuals who were high in conformity-proneness displayed feelings of personal inferiority coupled with an intense concern for other people's suggestions and opinions.[16] Those who exhibit greater independence of thought tend to rely more upon their own judgments.

We have then, a picture of a clothing style being introduced and legitimized by persons of social status or prestige, with such endorsement spreading inevitably to the vast majority of the population. The imitation of clothing styles worn by the leaders has the function of helping individuals identify with prestige models, thus bridging the gap, psychologically at least, between themselves and the model.

The phenomenon of the fashion cycle thus can be explained in terms of social and psychological pressures toward conformity. When a new style is introduced, it is relatively easy to defend and maintain one's current tastes to one or two others, more difficult to stand up against eight or ten. But there comes a point at which it is no longer feasible to hold out against the tide of mass opinion. When fashion leaders adopt a new style, they are

> objects of interest and excitement. . . . A few more follow, impelled to be *a la mode* by the need to assert their difference from those less fashionable. The bandwagon is gradually on and soon it begins to roll. In the end no one can afford to be different. The final blow comes when the woman standing aside appears ridiculous even to herself. "They" are no longer odd; she herself is. Popular taste, even one's own, has changed.[17]

Thus, fashion can be seen as a form of collective behavior in which people feel compelled to yield to a mass norm enforced by an anonymous multitude.

BERRY'S WORLD

"I'm not making soup, dummy—I'm tie-dyeing my overcoat!"

Figure 8-21. In 1970, tie-dyeing was "in." Sooner or later, *everybody* gets on the bandwagon.

The compelling nature of fashion is beyond the control of any single individual; its power lies in the collective definition of the clothing norm.

---

[14]Lucy C. Taylor, "Conformity in Dress and Selected Color, Design, Texture and Personality Variables," Master's thesis, Utah State University, 1967.
[15]For examples, see B. Smucker and A. Creekmore, "Adolescents' Clothing Conformity, Awareness, and Peer Acceptance," *Home Economics Research Journal,* December 1972, pp. 92–97; and Shally VanDeWal, "A Study of the Relationship Between Clothing Conformity and Peer Acceptance Among Eighth Grade Girls," Master's thesis, Purdue University, 1968.
[16]Crutchfield, "Independent Thought," p. 225.
[17]Kurt Lang and Gladys Lang, *Collective Dynamics,* Thomas Y. Crowell Company, New York, 1968, p. 471.

SUMMARY *Norm formation*

Two social forces—conformity and individuality—form the basis for all fashion behavior. Conformity is both necessary and desirable to the extent that it provides for the transmission of functional normative patterns and gives the individual a sense of belonging. In the mass society, consumer demand for a style of dress often is enhanced by the mere fact that others are wearing it. This bandwagon effect may be demonstrated through a series of numerical tabulations called fashion counts, which not only help predict the life span of a fashion, but also provide evidence of the degree of conformity that exists, nationally or locally, to a given clothing norm. Most fads and fashions reach their peak of popularity accompanied by an overzealousness in which people carry an idea to extremes.

The validation of new clothing styles by people of high status or prestige ultimately spreads the norm throughout the population. Conformity in dress appears to be widespread, and the desire to be like others is strongly reinforced in human interaction. Many people continue to rely upon the judgment of others, particularly when their own understanding of the clothing norm is incomplete.

Fashion innovation

Just as clothing **fashions** provide an extraordinary opportunity to study contagion and conformity in mass behavior, so do they provide a medium for the observation of the processes of **innovation.** Essentially, fashion innovation is a departure from the established norm and the creation of a new one.

Sources of innovation

For centuries, armchair philosophers have debated the question of where the source of fashion power really lies. Does it lie in the hands of a small group of dictatorial designers who foist their styles upon the helpless public without regard for people's needs and desires? Is it in the hands of the socially elite, the "fashion arbiters" of the upper class whom the masses seek to emulate? Is the force controlled by the disseminators of fashion information, the publicists and editors of *Vogue, Harper's Bazaar, Mademoiselle, Women's Wear Daily,* and so forth who communicate, predict, and advise the public of the latest trends? Is the power restricted to the volume producer who chooses from the designers' work only those models which he cares to promote and make available for mass consumption and who deliberately plans the premature obsolescence of his products? Does the power lie in the hands of the ultimate consumer, the mass public, who in the end makes the decision to buy or not to buy, and whose changing tastes and craving for novelty

Figure 8-22. Fashions may originate in the showrooms of the designers, but not all of the designers' creations become fashions.

Figure 8-23. The introduction of a new "style" is not limited to professional designers, but unless the independent innovator is also a legitimizer, the style has little chance of becoming a fashion.

create a demand for newness every season? Or is changing fashion a spontaneous reflection of other changes taking place in society, the "influence of the *Zeitgeist,*" as Flügel calls it, the climate of opinion, a sign of the times?[18]

The answer is as complex as the question. Each of the above plays an important role in the phenomenon of fashion, and each is interdependent with the others.

Every style, of course, must have an origin, and the creation itself is the product of an innovator—an individual who designs for himself or a professional who designs for others. To be successful, a professional innovator must know exactly how far he can depart from the current mode in any given year. He will remain in business only as long as he is able to net a profit, so he must somehow divine what people will buy before the people themselves are aware of it. If his styles run counter to the *Zeitgeist,* they are doomed to failure.

A number of people mistakenly believe that designers get together each season and plan the major style changes for the coming year. The clothing business is one of the most highly competitive industries in existence, and every house guards its new collections with the utmost secrecy. How is it then that such a marked degree of similarity is seen from one designer's collection to the next? For one thing, they are all subject to the same influences of the *Zeitgeist:* "it is inevitable that living in the same milieu, witnessing the same sights, selecting from the same fabric collections, subjected to the same influences, reading the same press, and meeting the same people, should result in similarity."[19]

Moreover, a designer must have accurate information of the market. Each season a careful stock-taking reveals which styles sold the best, how many of each were purchased and by whom, which ideas seemed to "catch on," and which models appear to have reached their saturation point. Most fashions are the result of slow evolutionary changes, and an analysis of the fashion cycle yields additional clues to the styles likely to be popular in the future.

Fluctuations in the hem length of women's dresses may be used to illustrate the point. Skirts in the mid-1920's were the shortest they had ever been in costume history. From 1929 to 1932, skirts descended gradually, inch by inch, from knee level to bottom calf, and remained at a low-level plateau for the ensuing three or four years. (Refer to Figure 8-10, p. 152.) From 1936 to 1939, skirts inched their way back up to the knees. Three years later, when we might normally have expected another descent, Paris was under German occupation, and fashions in

---

[18]John C. Flügel, *Psychology of Clothes,* The Hogarth Press, London, 1930, reprinted 1950.
[19]Madge Garland, *Fashion,* Penguin Books, Ltd., Harmondsworth, Middlesex, 1962, p. 54.

both the United States and Great Britain were restricted by wartime fabric shortages. Fashion changes abruptly came to a halt, and the short narrow skirt remained the accepted style of dress for over seven years, long enough to pass from fashionable dress to conventional dress. The distinction here is important because it helps to explain the mass resistance that met the *New Look* in 1947.[20] If the normal current had not been interrupted, skirts probably would have made their evolutionary descent from 1942 to 1946, and a low hemline in 1947 would have been nothing at all unusual. Instead, having become so accustomed to their habitual short skirts, the people protested en masse—and then went out and bought a new wardrobe anyway.

From 1947 on through the fifties and sixties, hemlines crept almost imperceptibly back toward the knee—so slowly in fact, that the only noticeable change came when a woman put a new coat over an old dress and discovered that a half inch was visible beneath the coat hem. Then, an incident occurred which seemed to demonstrate that the *New Look* would never have been successful back in 1947 had the social climate not been ripe for a change. In 1963, skirts had been on the rise for fifteen years, and every good designer worth his salt knows that what goes up must come down. The trick, of course, is in knowing when the peak has been reached. At least one Paris designer felt the trend had been going on long enough, and Jacques Heim's fall collection that year came out in mid-calf lengths. He was the only one—just as Dior had been the only one in 1947—but this time the guess was wrong. The current was too strong to stem the tide, and skirts continued on their upward course.

By 1970 it seemed that hemlines had reached their peak (both literally and figuratively), and fashion publicists began to push "the longuette" (otherwise known as the midi). Radical departures from the current mode always elicit a preponderance of negative reaction, and protests against the mid-calf length were nationwide. True, the mini had reached its culmination, but the normal cycle had not been interrupted as it had been in the forties, and the drop was all too abrupt. Consumers wouldn't buy the midi—but neither did they buy more minis. The majority switched to bifurcates until the hemline made its orderly way down to the knee.

"Hems are going down all over the world, Bradley. I fear they shall not go up again in our time."

Figure 8-24. What goes up must come down. Drawing by Carl Rose; © 1970, The New Yorker Magazine, Inc.

---

[20]For those who are too young to remember, the *New Look* represented a revolutionary change from the broad-shouldered, straight-hipped wartime styles. It emphasized feminine curves, a tiny waist, a natural shoulder line, and most conspicuously, a long full skirt that reached ten to eleven inches from the floor. The *Look* was attributed largely to the work of one designer, Christian Dior, whose fame and business sky-rocketed as a result. Unfortunately, many writers use the *New Look* as the "classic example" of the way in which a designer superimposes his ideas on a railroaded public. In actual fact, such drastic changes in dress have not occurred more than two or three times in costume history, and have always been associated with other radical social or political change. The post-Revolutionary fashions in France and the *New Look* are the exceptions rather than the rule, although both were entirely consistent with the spirit of the times.

A radical innovation usually is required to change any style that has been firmly established for a long period of time. The cropped and "clean-cut" hairstyle for men had been a universal norm for two-thirds of a century. It took a few innovators with shoulder-length locks to shake the crewcut out of its rut. Extreme styles, however, rarely become the *fashion*. The innovation is nearly always modified before it is accepted by the masses.

In general, men's styles are more deeply entrenched and slower to change than women's, but the fashion cycle is there. Shoulders go from padded to unpadded, lapels progress from wide to narrow, trousers move from tapered to full.

Fashion leadership

We have seen that the **fashion innovator** plays an important role in the whole process of fashion change, in that he is responsible for the introduction of a new style. The innovator, however, rarely has the power to enforce mass acceptance of his creation. Any new idea must progress through an established pattern of legitimation before it becomes the popular norm.

If we go back again to the theoretical model of the fashion cycle (Figure 8-5, p. 150), we can see that different percentages of the population adopt a particular style at various stages of its cycle. If we were to take the statistical model literally, we would expect that not more than 15 per cent of a given population would be **early adopters,** that is, those who will buy a new style in its incipient stages before it is generally accepted by others.

The vast majority of the population (roughly two-thirds) are seen in this model as **fashion followers,** and constitute the people who are responsible for the mass acceptance of a style. It is obvious that some who fall into this category adopt a style before it reaches its peak, while others are among the last to take it on during its period of greatest popularity. Those who continue to wear a style long after its popularity has faded might be classified as **obsolescents.**

In several studies, observations of fashion innovations have supported this theory of diffusion and acceptance. ZoBell's investigation, for example, began with the introduction of midi-length skirts in the fall of 1970. In every group that she observed, there were a few who tried out the new long lengths, but the number never exceeded 5 per cent, even at the height of the midi's promotion in the current fashion media.[21] Thus, the midi did not succeed immediately as a norm replacement. Janney's study, on the other hand, gives us a more complete picture of fashion leadership and followership. The sample

Designers provide the inspiration for clothing norms, but the consuming public makes the fashion.

BERRY'S WORLD

© 1972 by NEA, Inc.

"I went back to narrow lapels as soon as I found out wide ones were 'in' again!"

Figure 8-25. Lapels progress from wide to narrow, trousers from tapered to baggy, hair from short to long.

---

[21]Toni ZoBell, "Fashion Diffusion: Influence of Mass Media and Prestigious Reference Groups," Master's thesis, University of Nevada, 1972.

consisted of 279 undergraduates in a women's college.[22] Within a two-year period, there were some sixty-seven clothing fads observed, most of which were initiated by a relatively small group of students who were members of a prestige-bearing clique. The **distingué faddists** were a group of seven girls who

Group	Students in the clique or group		Number of fads initiated
	(Number)	*(%)*	
Distingué Faddists	7	2.5	20*
Bizarre, Oscillating, or Egregious Faddists	20	7.2	47
Conforming Faddists	232	83.1	0
Obsolescents	20	7.2	0
Total	279	100	67

*True fads, in the sense that they were followed by others

received considerable masculine attention and whose counsel was greatly sought by other girls. This group initiated twenty fads that were usually variations of modish attire (e.g., pearl necklaces with Brooks sweaters), all of which were adopted by others. The **bizarre faddists** and the **oscillating faddists** initiated a total of thirty-two fads, most of which were worn by members of the clique only or followed by others when there were no men on campus. The three **egregious faddists** were not only unable to start a fad (they tried fifteen) — but they killed any going fad as soon as they took it up. Most significantly, the study showed that 83 per cent of the students were followers rather than initiators; that is, they *conformed* to the fads that the leaders had started.

Three-fourths of the total group waited until the fad had been going for two or three weeks before they got on the bandwagon. Twenty students never did join the crowd; the obsolescents never followed any of the fads, their clothes were generally ill-fitting and haphazardly selected, they received no masculine attention and were more or less social isolates.

The importance of this study lies in the fact that it clearly distinguishes between the initiators or early adopters and that small elite group of influentials who are truly the fashion leaders. The term **fashion leadership** is thus applied to the process of influencing others to accept a style innovation as a replacement for the currently accepted norm. It is the process of legitimation to which we have referred earlier.

[22] J. E. Janney, "Fad and Fashion Leadership Among Undergraduate Women," *Journal of Abnormal and Social Psychology* 36, 1941, pp. 275–278.

There have always been fashion leaders. Status gives impetus to fashions, and the notion that the "best" people are wearing them (however you define "best") constitutes an endorsement for acceptance. In primitive societies, the successful warrior set the pattern in feathers, paint, and other forms of ornamentation. Until the end of the eighteenth century, new forms of dress were legitimized largely within the court circles; the kings and other royalty were the supreme dictators of fashion change. Following the French Revolution, there were no ruling sovereigns with sufficient power or magnetism to exercise much influence, and the fashion leadership fell to the well-known "dandies." Most famous among these was George Bryan (Beau) Brummell, who had an eye for propriety and demanded perfection in fit and in workmanship.

This marked the transition of fashion leadership from the hands of the ruling class to a set of socially elite men and women having both wealth and influence. The important prerequisites were generally personal attractiveness, impeccable taste, and a social life that afforded the individual opportunities to be filmed and photographed. The last criterion was an important link in the whole communications network, because it kept the leader in the public eye and illustrated the styles that were to be given the seal of approval.

In the modern world, the vast majority still seek for a kind of **symbolic leader**—a person who sets the example. By emulating the style of the leader, the masses achieve an identification and share in the leader's prestige. In the wake of an antimaterialistic ethic, however, prestige has faded from the wealthy elite, and new mass-media models have replaced them.

There is also growing evidence that such emulation is not a direct process, but rather one which passes through the mediation of a reference group before it is taken on by the individual. Rogers[23] suggests that there are basically five steps in the process of adopting a new norm or practice: (1) the *awareness stage,* in which the individual is exposed to the new style; (2) the *interest stage,* in which he seeks additional information about it and listens to the opinions of others; (3) the *evaluation stage,* when he considers the possibility of trying it out himself; (4) the *trial stage* of testing out the innovation by wearing it on a limited basis; and (5) the *adoption stage,* at which he makes the decision to wear the new style on a broader basis.

Thus, there is an intermediate step in which the individual is influenced by certain key people in his environment. In other words, information about the new style (its "goodness" or "badness") is filtered first through the opinion leaders of the

---

[23]E. M. Rogers with F. Shoemaker, *Communication of Innovations,* Free Press, New York, 1971, p. 100. Rogers named the stages; the interpretations in relation to clothing have been added.

primary reference group and then relayed to the less active individuals. In effect, then, it is the opinion leader within the smaller reference group that exercises the greatest power in the adoption of a new norm, for it is the immediate social group that can offer the rewards for conformity or apply the sanctions to those who deviate.

In most cases, even the symbolic fashion leaders are not the very first to wear the new styles. They pick up somebody's innovative idea and give it status. Their departures from the going norm are regarded not as violations but as precedents for the proper and acceptable thing to do. Opinion leaders, like Janney's distingué faddists, always know how far they can go without appearing ridiculous. But unlike the innovators, they tend not to be highly creative themselves. It is not surprising, therefore, that the college women tested by Kernaleguen who scored high on fashion leadership also scored significantly low in creativity.[24] In another study, Schrank found fashion innovators to have a relatively high degree of psychological security; fashion leaders, on the other hand, tended to express more conforming attitudes toward clothing, and in general came from higher socioeconomic levels.[25]

There is considerable evidence that leaders are popular, so it follows that the popular thing to wear is what the leaders wear. Whether they are symbolic leaders or leaders within a

Figure 8-26. American presidents have been known to exert some fashion influence. Harry Truman gave the stamp of approval to loud sports shirts worn outside the trousers, and John Kennedy started the trend toward the "Harvard Look." Lyndon Johnson improved the hat business considerably with his penchant for the ten-gallon variety. A modified form, in five-gallon sizes, brought renewed interest in a broader-brimmed hat for men.

[24]Anne Kernaleguen, "Creativity Level, Perceptual Style, and Peer Perception of Attitudes Towards Clothing," Unpublished dissertation, Utah State University, 1968.
[25]Holly Schrank, "Fashion Innovativeness and Fashion Opinion Leadership as Related to Social Insecurity, Attitudes Toward Conformity, Clothing Interest and Socioeconomic Level," Unpublished dissertation, Ohio State University, 1970.

Figure 8-27. The socially elite, such as Mrs. Henry Ford II, have gradually been replaced by mass-media models like rock star Mick Jagger. The symbolic fashion leader usually has a coterie of admirers and followers who seek to identify with a prestige model by taking on his manner of dress.

primary subgroup, they appear to have certain qualifications in common. First of all, they must exemplify certain values, values that are held to be important by the individual himself. Second, they must be regarded as competent, i.e., having more expertise or knowledge about dress and appearance than anyone else (this was Beau Brummell's claim to fame). Lastly, they must be in a strategic social location that gives them high visibility, public exposure, and a wide range of contacts. There are many studies that have demonstrated a high degree of relationship between fashion leadership and participation in social activities.[26]

The crux of all fashion activity, however, lies in the complementary behavior of the leaders and the followers. Innovations in fashion are made by those who wish to set themselves apart from others in the mass society. Fashion leaders select from those innovations the styles to which they give their approval and thereby legitimize the style for the masses. The masses, in turn, seek to identify with the leaders' prestige and to emulate them. As the fashion becomes available to all, its symbolic value of distinction is lost to the person who started it in the first place. Thus, the first to accept the new styles are also the first to abandon them.

Taylor's study of fads at the high school level showed a relationship between fad adoption and status. Senior students were usually the first to take up a fad; by the time most of the

[26]One example is offered by Helen Allen, "Adolescent Fad and Fashion Leaders Compared with Fad and Fashion Non-Leaders on Selected Personality Factors and Social Participation," Master's thesis, University of Tennessee, 1971.

juniors hopped on the bandwagon, the fad had already lost its novelty for the seniors, and the latter group soon dropped it entirely.[27] This continual process of innovation, legitimation, and emulation marks the ever-present struggle on the part of some to attain exclusiveness, and the compelling desire on the part of others to be "in the swing" of things. "To look like nobody else is mortifying; to be mistaken for one of the rabble is worse."[28] The resulting product of this circular pattern is the phenomenon of the fashion cycle. High fashion has snob appeal to the leader, i.e., its attractiveness lies in the fact that few other people can afford it. The true fashion, however, is dependent upon the snowballing effect of the bandwagon; it is carried by the masses who cannot afford to be left out or to be different. Paradoxically, once everyone wears the fashion, it no longer offers distinction to anyone. As soon as it reaches its peak of saturation, everyone tires of the current fashion and it soon fades into oblivion. All fashions end in excess.

Diffusion of fashion

In order for an individual or a group to conform to a particular pattern of clothing behavior, information concerning the normative expectation must be disseminated.

As we have seen, all clothing innovations are not the exclusive prerogatives of professional designers, but for the bulk of the ready-to-wear industry the designer's showroom is the source of most of the new styles. Between the designer and the consumer, there are a number of mass media and interpersonal communications that take place, each of which exerts some influence in the adoption of styles that ultimately become popular fashions.

New styles are legitimized through the approval given them by people of prestige status; such referent individuals may be symbolic leaders or opinion leaders within a primary subgroup.

Journalists who write for the daily newspapers and fashion magazines reach an immense public. "The fashion editor . . . has two potent weapons: silence and space. She can ignore the collections she considers bad, and she can give the largest possible amount of space to those she thinks good, with priority in placing and the preference, if any, of colour reproductions."[29] Usually it is the fashion editor who gives the style a name (e.g., the A-line, the longuette, hotpants, etc.) which helps to identify the innovation in verbal communication. This initial filtering process has a tremendous influence on what the customer will be looking for in the shops the following season.

Fashion and trade publications

[27]Anne W. Taylor, "An Investigation of Some Aspects of Clothing Fads and Fashions in Junior and Senior High School," Master's thesis, Cornell University, 1964.
[28]William Hazlitt, "On Fashion," in P. P. Howe (ed.), *The Complete Works of William Hazlitt*, Vol. 17, J. M. Dent and Sons, London, 1933.
[29]Garland, *Fashion*, p. 105.

Volume manufacturers

Since it is only through the ready-to-wear market that a style can become a fashion, the choices made by apparel manufacturers are rather crucial decisions. No manufacturer can afford to embark on the large-scale production of a design unless he is reasonably sure that it will be widely accepted. In order to back up his choices, therefore, he immediately initiates advance publicity for his models to assure himself of a consumer demand.

Fashion consultants

There are the reporters and interpreters of the fashion scene on national, international, and local levels. They cover everything from charity balls to rock concerts. They observe what people are wearing; they keep abreast of social, artistic, and economic trends that have an impact on fashion. They scout the local scene in cities all over the world. From this wealth of data, they sort, assimilate, evaluate—and then send out to their clients a weekly report on fashion trends.

Central buying offices

Many retail stores utilize the services of resident buying offices that are located in the strategic market centers of the country. They make a daily check of the market and keep the retailers informed regarding national trends on fast-selling styles, daily and weekly price fluctuations, and supply conditions in general. In most instances, the buying offices do no direct buying but simply act as advisers, reporting on what is selling, looking for new items, placing reorders, and perhaps working on special promotions.

The retail buyer

The retailer of fashion merchandise is the person responsible for getting the kind of goods that the customer wants into the store at the time that the customer wants to buy them. Overall selections made by the retailer usually take into account both national and local fashion trends. His selections are certainly important in shaping the tastes of his customers, but he is guided, in turn, by his daily and weekly sales records.

It should be noted that communication within these mass-media channels is a two-way process. There are a variety of ways in which the consumer makes a feedback of information into the whole diffusion process. To be sure, an effective promotion and advertising campaign can contribute a great deal to the acceptance of a style, and within certain limitations the journalists, the manufacturers, and the retailers are in a position to manipulate the mass taste. However, the critical decision to adopt or to reject an innovation is still made by the majority on an interpersonal and individual basis.

If we go back to the five steps in the adoption process, it becomes obvious that the mass-media channels are particularly effective in creating an awareness of the innovation and in providing information about it to the potential adopter. There is some research evidence that the early adopters or fashion leaders are inclined to use mass media rather than interpersonal contacts as a source of fashion information.[30] But for the average person, some further legitimation of the style becomes necessary before he is willing to try it himself. The opinion leader within the immediate reference group thus becomes the key agent of influence in the step toward mass acceptance.[31] It is the reference group, moreover, that has the power to apply the sanctions for conforming or not conforming to the expected behavior.

Time is also an important factor in the fashion diffusion process. The time lag that exists from the introduction of a new idea to its widespread adoption is one of the measures that we use to differentiate among the various types of clothing norms. We also use the time variable to distinguish the fashion leaders from the fashion followers, and the followers from the obsolescents. Further, by analyzing the time that it takes for an incoming fashion to gain acceptance, we can estimate its entire life span with greater accuracy.

In the process of fashion diffusion, the mass tastes are influenced by publicists, producers, and retailers; but no style will ever become a fashion if it does not follow the general trend of consumer acceptance.

SUMMARY *Fashion innovation*

Fashion changes are caused by the substitution of new clothing norms for established ones. The process through which such substitution is made may originate with the designer, although all successful innovations are predicated on a thorough understanding of cyclical trends and consumer demand. Fashions become diffused through the work of fashion editors and reporters, photographers and illustrators, publicity campaigns of the volume producers, and retail store advertising. In this way, the average consumer is provided with the fashion information necessary regarding the potential norm replacement.

However, before a new style is accepted as a norm, it must progress through an established pattern of legitimation. The validation of new clothing norms takes place through the

---

[30]Margaret Grindereng, "Fashion Diffusion," *Journal of Home Economics*, March 1967, pp. 171–174.
[31]In distinguishing between opinion leaders and their followers, Rogers noted that opinion leaders in a group have greater exposure to mass media, demonstrate a higher degree of social participation, enjoy a higher social status, and tend to be more innovative than their followers (Rogers, *Communication of Innovations*).

process of fashion leadership, in which persons of high prestige or status give their stamp of approval to particular styles. Even in the case of superficial fads, most of which are initiated locally, the power to instigate is vested in those who have demonstrated opinion leadership. Fashion leaders depart from the established norm because they seek to set themselves apart from others in the mass society. As their styles are copied by the masses, the quality of distinctiveness is lost, so the first to adopt the new styles are also the first to abandon them.

Nonconformity

While the vast majority of people choose to dress as others are dressed, there are some members of society who strive to be different. Fashion innovation is one form of deviation from the established norm, but other types of nonconformity also may be observed. Some individuals are able to make clothing decisions that are completely independent of the fashion norm. Still others belong to marginal groups that seek to replace the mass norms with norms of their own creation.

Marginal groups

In preceding chapters, several examples were given of certain types of subcultural groups that tend to substitute counter norms for the norms of the larger society. Many minority groups find outlets for expression through their particular kind of deviation from clothing norms. Marginal groups are characterized by a degree of alienation from the general social structure, and consequently they are more prone to violate the conventional modes of dress. Groups that lack full acceptance often seek to achieve recognition through the establishment of their own group codes. Their antipathy toward society is reflected directly in their refusal to meet the standard clothing requirements.

Throughout history, there have always been groups that have considered themselves the symbols of nonconformity (the "incroyables" of the eighteenth century, the "aesthetes" in the 1880's, the "beatniks," the "hippies," ad infinitum). In any era, their style of dress will be the antithesis of the currently accepted mode. In other words, they demonstrate an acute sensitivity to the norms of society and adopt a style of dress that is deliberately counter to those norms. In the process they create norms of their own. As Crutchfield cautions, "the mere fact that the individual does sometimes express eccentric and deviant ideas is not necessarily proof of independent thinking in him. For one thing, this may simply reflect his conformity to the thinking of a socially deviant group. Or, for another thing, this may simply reflect his deliberate rejection of the majority

"WE'RE BECOMING SLAVES TO UNCONVENTIONALITY!"

Figure 8-28. Rather than being "nonconformists," those who adhere to the norms of a deviant group are more accurately described as "counterconformists."

group's ideas or the prevailing social norms."[32] It is all a matter of conforming to the clothing expectations of the group with which we identify.

Members of marginal groups are usually those who experience similar problems of adaptation to society and find mutual support in a collective solution to feelings of powerlessness and isolation. Adolescents are among those who are especially susceptible to status problems. Researchers who have studied discipline problems in the high school have reported a high degree of relationship between the way teenagers dress and their behavior in school. One high school principal predicted:

> If you see a boy come into your room with dyed hair, his pants at half-mast, skin tight and this far above his shoes, you can bet he will be into the counselor's office within a week. Out of the eleven boys who had three poor work notices at mid-term, ten had already been in my office for deviations in dress; of the nine who received four poor work notices, eight had been sent to the office to be checked on their appearance. The one boy who would've received five notices at mid-term had already been suspended for poor dress.[33]

---

[32]Crutchfield, "Independent Thought," p. 211.
[33]Quotations are adapted from the statements of teachers and school administrators during a panel discussion on "Clothing and Adolescent Problems," Western Regional Meeting of College Teachers of Clothing and Textiles, Logan, Utah, October 1964.

CONFORMITY AND INDIVIDUALITY IN DRESS

Other teachers and school administrators have attested to the fact that a student's attire and his actions are closely interdependent. A recognition of this relationship has caused some schools to adopt dress codes, but the basic question is whether enforced conformity to a set of dress regulations will eliminate the underlying insecurities that cause the deviation in the first place. At least one psychiatrist has explained that

> . . . the type that responds very positively when rules and regulations are made, is probably expressing a need for some interest, some restraint, and some involvement on the part of authority. Children and adolescents need to have limits set by authority; it expresses an interest, and the type of clothing they wear is a form of communication, asking to be restrained, whether they are aware of it or not. The indiscriminate and casual type of clothing that youngsters wear in high school shows a lack of interest on the part of the adults who are concerned with them.[34]

The theory has been given some support through empirical observations of clothing and behavior. In Kiebler's study of high school boys, there was a significant relationship between deviant dress and aggressive personality characteristics. Boys whose parents were separated or divorced tended to be more deviant in dress, and they also tended to be more aggressive. Subjects who were planning to attend college, on the other hand (and who were probably "better" students), were found to be more conforming in dress.[35] Still, there is some question as to whether the clothing is a manifestation of an underlying behavioral problem, or whether the clothing in itself is interpreted as the difficulty. The "problem" students in Wildes' study had a greater difference of opinion from faculty on what was considered appropriate clothing for school wear.[36] Leigh's subjects also conformed more closely to peer-established norms than to teachers' expectations, and it was suspected from this that deviant dress has the effect of marking the students who are singled out for disciplinary action.[37]

Coleman's analysis also seemed to indicate that clothing in itself may be responsible for much behavior. High school students were asked to respond to the two following questions: (1) "Of all the girls in your grade, who is the best dressed?" and (2) "If you could trade, would you be someone different?" Few of the girls who were rated most often by their classmates as "best-dressed" wanted to be someone different, while the girls who were not highly regarded for their dress tended to

[34]Dr. A. Symonds, participant in the foregoing discussion.
[35]Carolyn Kiebler, "Relationships Between Deviant Personality Traits and Clothing Behavior of Male Adolescents Attending Junction City High School," Master's thesis, Kansas State University, 1966.
[36]Dorothy Wildes, "Clothing in Relation to Adolescent Behavioral Problems." Master's thesis, Auburn University, 1968.
[37]Leigh, "Discipline Problems."

wish they were someone else. The security of being well dressed seemed to contribute to a healthy acceptance of one's status and role.[38]

It should be noted that conformity among teenagers is exceedingly high, particularly conformity to peer group norms. Those who try to be drastically different from other students either crave to be noticed or find that this is one way to defy the conventions of a society that has somehow discriminated against them. Many deviants have a very low self-esteem; they are misfits trying to be something other than what they really are. Klapp contends that this is not confined to the stage of adolescence, but that our whole society is currently undergoing what he calls "identity dislocation."[39] This has come about, he explains, as the result of a breakdown in status symbols, with a tendency for fashions to obscure classes in contemporary society rather than differentiate them. The blurring of lines between youth and age, between maleness and femaleness, between occupations, and all other types of social categories, produces a state of confusion in which people do not know *who* they are or *what* they are. In short, he says, we have become a society of "made-up" people masquerading on the streets in search of identity. The extremes in faddism and exhibitionism in dress are forms of ego-screaming that plead: "Look at me, look at me!"

Marginal groups, then, are both conformists and nonconformists. In the process of growing up, the adolescent moves away from parental influence and domination; he rebels. At the same time, he yields to the pressures of his peer group to which he clings for support, and thereby conforms.

Thus, marginal and subcultural groups tend to seek recognition by conforming to counter-codes of dress, and at the same time, refusing to conform to the norms of society. A rigidly structured class system that encourages extreme conventionality in dress only serves to increase the cohesiveness within the subgroup. Greater tolerance for the expression of deviant tendencies will obviously reduce the pressures toward conformity.

Marginal and subcultural groups are nonconformists in the sense that they violate the dress codes of the larger society; they are conformists in the sense that they meet the counter norms created by the deviant group.

Individuality

Fashion leaders are nonconformists in that they seek constantly to differentiate themselves from those who follow their actions. Like the counter-conformist, their behavior is based upon an awareness of the norm and a desire to set themselves apart from it. Neither one (fashion leader nor counter-conformist) can operate independently from mass behavior; the fashion

[38]J. S. Coleman, *The Adolescent Society*, Free Press, New York, 1961.
[39]Orrin Klapp, *Collective Search for Identity*, Holt, Rinehart & Winston, New York, 1969.

leader must be ahead of it, the counter-conformist against it.

The true individualist, on the other hand, is one who can make a decision that is independent of group action. Such behavior requires an independence of thought and action that stems from a set of strong and internalized standards, and is what Riesman describes as "inner-directed," i.e., characterized by individual conscience and self-imposed goals. The ability to resist group pressure requires a high degree of psychological security as well as extreme faith in one's personal convictions. The individualist is often regarded as something of an eccentric and consequently must have the strength to withstand the criticism or ridicule elicited by his deviations in dress.

Although research is limited, there is some evidence that the true nonconformist is more independent, more socially secure, more creative, and more intelligent than most conformists.[40] Conversely, there is also the suggestion that conformists tend to be more other-directed, more submissive, more conventional in values, less creative, and more dependent, with greater needs for social approval.

No one fits precisely and consistently into any one of these categories. Each of us finds that we conform to group standards in some situations and feel freer to express our individuality in others. Conformity tends to help people fit more easily into their social roles; individuality fosters creative expression and facilitates an intelligent, rational, and free choice among the available alternatives in the selection of clothing. The ascendance of either set of values, with their accompanying consequences, is dependent upon one's personal needs and desires.

Individuality in dress requires a strong sense of personal conviction and psychological security.

Figure 8-29. Liberace's red, white, and blue fringed and spangled hotpants, covered with beads and other jewels, were designed by the entertainer himself. No one (but *no one*) could call Liberace a conformist.

SUMMARY *Nonconformity*

Several types of nonconformity may be observed in the clothing behavior of individuals and groups in society. Subcultural and marginal groups tend to substitute counter-norms, which in turn, dictate the standards of dress followed by their members. Wide discrepancies in dress between the subgroup norms and the general norms are usually indicative of a commensurate degree of alienation from the larger society. Members of such groups are nonconformists only in the sense that they do not meet the standards of society in general; but they are conformists to subgroup deviations.

[40]A broad generalization, but look at the findings of such studies as: B. White and A. Kernaleguen, "Comparison of Selected Perceptual and Personality Variables Among College Women Deviant and Non-Deviant in Their Appearance," *Perceptual and Motor Skills* 32, 1971, pp. 87–92; Elva Heidle, "The Extent of Conformity to the Modal Pattern of Dress as Related to Selected Student Variables for University of Tennessee Women," Master's thesis, University of Tennessee, 1970; and Judith Herk, "Clothing Conformity-Nonconformity as Related to Social Security-Insecurity for a Group of College Women," Master's thesis, Pennsylvania State University, 1968.

Figure 8-30. On a hot day in New York, this shopper in striped shorts and pajama top attracted the curious stares of passersby. The individualist usually is regarded as something of an eccentric and must be possessed of a relatively high degree of psychological security to "carry it off."

Fashion leaders themselves are nonconformists in their striving to be different. Others, lacking the power to become leaders, openly defy the accepted standards of dress by assuming a contrary position that will insure their being noticed. Their action, however, is still dependent upon group opinion. The true individualist is guided by an independence of thought and action that neither relies on group opinion nor deliberately counteracts it. While conformity helps people to fit more easily into their social roles, individuality is necessary for a completely rational choice among available alternatives.

FOR FURTHER READING

Grindereng, Margaret. "Fashion Diffusion," *Journal of Home Economics,* March 1967, pp. 171–174.

Klapp, Orrin E. *Collective Search for Identity.* New York: Holt, Rinehart & Winston, 1969.

Lang, Kurt, and Gladys Lang. *Collective Dynamics.* New York: Thomas Y. Crowell Co., 1968. (Chapter 15, "Fashion: Identification and Differentiation in the Mass Society.")

Rogers, E. M., with F. F. Shoemaker. *Communication of Innovations.* New York: Free Press, 1971. (Chapter 5, "Adopter Categories.")

Rosencranz, Mary Lou. *Clothing Concepts.* New York: Macmillan Publishing Company, 1972. (Chapter 8, "Individuality and Conformity," and Chapter 9, "Custom and Fashion.")

Young, Agnes Brooks. *Recurring Cycles of Fashion (1760–1937).* New York: Harper and Brothers, 1937.

DISCUSSION QUESTIONS

1. Define each of the following clothing norms and differentiate them by giving a specific example of each: (a) fad, (b) fashion, (c) classic, (d) universal, (e) alternative, (f) specialty.

2. What is meant by "the cyclical nature of fashion," and how may it affect the adoption or rejection of new styles as norm replacements?

3. What factors help to explain the phenomenon of "behavioral contagion," and why is it so prevalent in human behavior?

4. What is the difference between a fashion innovator and a fashion leader? Which one is apt to have the greater influence in affecting a change in fashion? Why?

5. What other influence agents operate in the whole fashion diffusion process? In what way are they in a position to influence mass tastes?

6. Discuss the pros and cons of conforming to the norms or the fashions of a group with respect to its potential effect on (a) the individual himself, and (b) the society in general.

9

Clothing Symbolism

IT IS A COMMON experience in daily life that when we meet a person for the first time we form immediate impressions of his personality. A quick scanning of an individual's appearance has the effect of communicating to us a whole complex of information pertaining to the person's character, position, and status in life. Allport describes the process as follows: "With briefest visual perception, a complex mental process is aroused, resulting within a very short time, 30 seconds perhaps, in judgment of the sex, age, size, nationality, profession and social caste of the stranger, together with some estimate of his temperament, his ascendence, friendliness, neatness, and even his trustworthiness and integrity. With no further acquaintance many impressions may be erroneous, but they show the swift totalizing nature of our judgments."[1]

While first impressions are sometimes altered as we accumulate additional information about the person over a period of time, we can no more prevent the formation and rapid growth of these initial judgments "than we can avoid perceiving a given visual object or hearing a melody. We also know that this process, though often imperfect, is also at times extraordinarily sensitive."[2]

Clothing is a part of the "silent language" that is communicated through the use of visual but nonverbal symbols.[3] Goffman describes such symbols as "sign-vehicles" or "cues" which select the status that is to be imputed to an individual and define the way others are to treat him.[4] These short cuts to person perception enable us to categorize an individual—at least tentatively—and set the stage for further interaction.

---

[1]Gordon Allport, *Personality—A Psychological Interpretation*, Henry Holt & Company, New York, 1937, p. 500.
[2]S. E. Asch, "Forming Impressions of Personality," p. 258.
[3]Edward Hall, *The Silent Language*. Doubleday & Company, Garden City, N.Y., 1959.
[4]Erving Goffman, "Symbols of Class Status," *British Journal of Sociology* 2, no. 4, 1951, p. 294.

BERRY'S WORLD

"No, man—this isn't my wife and daughter—it's my husband and son!"

© 1965 by NEA, Inc.

Figure 9-1. An effective clothing symbol would make it possible for a stranger to determine the social category to which the wearer belongs, and thus avoid actions that would be considered social errors.

Therefore, it becomes important to understand the meanings that are conveyed through clothing symbols in order to present the self in such a way that the desired impression is achieved. In today's mobile and urbanized society, a great many of our person-to-person contacts are impersonal and ephemeral in nature; first impressions are often the only impressions that are formed, and for all practical purposes, clothing becomes an intimate and inseparable part of the perceptual field within which a person is located. Not only does clothing furnish clues to self, role, and status, but it also helps to define the situation within which a person is perceived.

We shall consider first the qualities of clothing which present stimulus information to the perceiver; second, some of the variables in the perception process that determine the accuracy or inaccuracy of the impressions formed; and third, the consequences of impression formation in the social interaction process.

Clothing cues

One always hesitates to accept the validity of judgments based on outward appearances in the knowledge that "you can't judge a book by its cover." The difficulty is that cultural stereotypes are both true and not true. They are true in the sense that a generalized composite represents a kind of statistical norm for particular roles and statuses. At a recent governor's conference, for example, the typical "head of state" was described as a white male, a Democrat, age 49, who has been a soldier, is an attorney, and a holder of some other public office. He would be married, the father of three children, recipient of a university degree, a Protestant, and have been born in the jurisdiction he serves.[5] There is probably no governor in the country with all twelve of those characteristics, but the description is more right than wrong.

Stereotypes are *not* true in the sense that they do not spell out the wide range of variability that occurs within a given role or status. They ignore the fact that every individual has a unique and complex set of characteristics, and the error of stereotyping is an error of oversimplification. There are several other problems also associated with the acceptance of clothing symbols as positive and accurate indices of self, role, and status. One is that the value of a symbol changes over time, thereby altering its meaning. Many people are now able to afford the symbols which have traditionally been associated with a particular social class, while others who may be bonafide

---

[5]"What Governors Are Made Of," *Nevada State Journal.* 5 June 1973, p. 14.

members of the upper social stratum may reject the symbol because it is no longer a mark of distinction. Moreover, the extended educational opportunities now available make it possible for all people to become knowledgeable in the manipulation of such symbols.[6]

On the other hand, a number of factors may be cited which restrict the use of symbols in fraudulent ways. First of all, there is the **intrinsic restriction** imposed by one's inability to attain the symbol; if a mink coat costs several thousand dollars, there are relatively few paths to the goal unless one really has several thousand dollars. But assuming that a woman has somehow acquired the money to purchase a mink coat—and she would in fact like to own a mink coat—she may still refrain from indulging her desires on the basis of some inner **moral restriction.** She shuns the possibility of being a "Mrs. Commonplace" trying to look like a "Mrs. Gotrocks" by a conscious recognition of her rightful place in society.

There are also the restrictions of **cultivation** and **socialization** which make it difficult for a person to acquire the social style and manners of a class to which she does not actually belong. Thus, the woman described above might, in fact, be recognized by others as out of place if her speech as well as her mannerisms and deportment were inconsistent with the role and status signified by the coat. Furthermore, if the accompanying details of her dress and grooming did not show a cultivation of taste commensurate with the quality of the coat, misuse of the symbol would be suspected. Such restrictions usually require considerable time and experience to overcome; this is particularly the case in understanding the subtleties of restraint in dress that are required to achieve a distinctively refined appearance.

Finally, there are **organic restrictions**[7]—such as the condition of the hands, the face, or the body—which betray one's life-long exposure to the elements, to diet, and/or to work. No beauty treatment can eliminate the lines, the calluses, and the muscles that develop over many years of manual work.

In other words, taking on the symbol without the accompanying patterns is revealing, and the inconsistencies that are detected between the clothing symbol and other characteristics of the stimulus person usually leave some doubt in the mind of the perceiver that the person is really what he pretends to be.

As another illustration, the cowboy's dress is part of a way of life that has been handed down to him for many generations. His clothes are designed to stand the stress of work in rough country, and most features have a practical purpose. The hat

Figure 9-2. The condition of the hands, face, or other parts of the body betrays one's life-long exposure to the elements.

Figure 9-3. To the experienced eye, a Westerner's hat tells a good deal about a man—its style, color, crease, angle, degree of dirtiness, and how it is doffed.

---

[6]This book, for example. Goffman refers to the organized teaching of symbol manipulation as "institutionalized sources of misrepresentation." See Goffman, "Symbols of Class Status," p. 303.

[7]The terminology used to label these restrictions was suggested by Goffman.

with its wide brim not only protects the cowhand's neck and head from rain, sleet, and sun, but it also serves as a good water bucket and a place to stash his portable belongings. Waved vigorously in the air, it will steer a cattle herd toward the rail-head, and tipped over the face during a midday snooze, it will keep off the bugs and provide the only shade for miles around. They say there are sure ways to tell a genuine cowboy from a dude. For one thing, the dude wears his pants short to show off his fancy boot tops; the authentic working type wears his long to protect himself from the brush. "And then notice whose hands have done a good day's work. It takes a pretty good man to flank a 300-pound calf."[8] He has no time for the fancy fringed shirt or the bright polished boots. His Stetson will have "accumulated fingerprints on a certain spot on the front of the brim. To the knowing, this marks him as a true cowhand. For he always takes his hat off with the same fingers in the same place. Dudes don't."[9] And once the hat is removed, there is always the telltale line between a white forehead and the sun-bronzed face beneath it.

In less obvious cases, clothes have been found to be fairly accurate indicators of the personalities and lifestyles of the people who wear them. In a study of university men, for example, Kness found that conservative dressers had a greater concern for clothes and attached more status symbolism to appearance than did hippie-type dressers. Those who were conservative in dress also tended to hold more conservative social and political beliefs than their hippie counterparts.[10]

Cues related to personality

In Chapter 7 we discussed clothing in relation to the development of a dominant response pattern or "style of life." Just as the individual develops a generalized mode of behavior, the perceiver in the situation is also apt to form a generalized impression of the stimulus person. Asch's experiments revealed that the perceiver tends to organize the various traits of an individual into a relatively consistent impression. In the process, some characteristics are determined to be central, while others are seen as peripheral. Numerous theories have been advanced in regard to the particular qualities of a costume that are judged to be indicative of the wearer's personality traits.

---

[8]Comments from a College of Agriculture graduate, *Sagebrush*, University of Nevada, 24 June 1969.
[9]"Where the Hat is the Man," *New York Times* Service news release, 27 May 1973.
[10]Darlene Kness, "The Clothing Attitudes and Social-Political Beliefs of University Men Identified as Conservative and Hippy Dressers," Master's thesis, Pennsylvania State University, 1971.

Many years ago, Northrup adapted the ancient Chinese concepts of **yang** and **yin** to dress and personality in the interpretation of congruent aspects between the two.[11] The terms represented extreme opposites, *yang* denoting the characteristics of strength, forcefulness, dignity, assurance, and the like, and *yin* indicating delicacy, gentleness, warmth, and submissiveness. Various writers have described the individual with a predominance of *yang* characteristics as tall, large-boned, large-featured, with strong or vivid coloring, erect posture, sleek hair, slightly coarse skin, and vigorous in movement and temperament, while the *yin* person is described as petite, small-boned, dainty-featured, with delicate coloring, graceful walk, softly curled hair, finely textured skin, and light in movement, pliant in temperament. Congruent styles of clothing exhibiting *yang* characteristics are described as having straight unbroken lines with few details, patterns that are large in scale, colors that are bold and in striking contrast, and textures that are heavy, rough, and stiff. Clothing representing *yin* qualities would be softly curved in silhouette, with broken lines that produce dainty, small details; patterns would be small in scale in closely related tones, colors light with limited contrast, and textures that are soft, pliable, or sheer. A number of intermediate types and variations of the *yin* and *yang* extremes have been described in considerable detail, accompanied by descriptions of dress that relate to the corresponding personality traits.[12]

Douty studied the influence of clothing in the formation of impressions of personality and used the dimensions of the *yang* and *yin* classifications. Four women were used as stimuli-persons and were presented to groups of subject-judges. Each appeared in a costume selected from her own wardrobe and then appeared a second time in a control costume consisting of a plain blue smock. The wardrobe costumes were also rated with the heads of the stimuli-persons blocked out. Findings indicated that the personalities of the four women were perceived quite differently when they wore costumes from their own wardrobes than when they wore the control smocks. Further, there was a strong positive relationship between the costume ratings and the ratings of the persons.[13]

A high score on the *yin-yang* continuum indicates that a person is perceived to be forceful, assertive, self-assured, and dignified in nature, while a low score indicates an impression

[11]Belle Northrup, "An Approach to the Problem of Costume and Personality," *Art Education Today,* Vol. 2, Teachers College, Columbia University, 1936, pp. 94–104.
[12]See for example, Harriet McJimsey, *Art and Fashion in Clothing Selection,* Iowa State University Press, Ames, Iowa, 1973, pp. 74–99; and Grace Morton, *The Arts of Costume and Personal Appearance,* John Wiley & Sons, New York, 1964, pp. 48–65.
[13]Helen Douty, "Influence of Clothing on Perception of Persons," *Journal of Home Economics* 55, no. 3, 1963, pp. 197–202.

of gentleness, receptivity, and submissiveness. On the assumption that warm colors have always been considered bold and advancing and cool colors quiet and receding, Mahannah combined the variables of costume color and personal coloring in a study of the influence of color on personality assessment. Four photographs of the same stimulus-person were shown to groups of subject-judges. In one, the model was photographed wearing a brunette wig and a bright red costume; in another, she was photographed in a blonde wig and a pale blue costume. The third and fourth pictures combined blonde wig and red costume, and brunette wig and blue costume. The results showed that impressions of *yinness* and *yangness* were greatly influenced by the interaction of wig and clothing colors: the brunette in the red costume was perceived to be significantly more *yang* than the other three combinations.[14]

So it is not costume alone that determines our impressions, but costume combined with specific physiognomic cues. Secord and Muthard reported that in the rating of women, a generally well-groomed appearance contributes to impressions of social acceptability, and narrowed eyes and full, relaxed lips were associated with sexual attractiveness. Bowed lips appeared to create the impression that a woman was conceited, demanding, immoral, and receptive to the attentions of men.[15] Berelson and Salter concluded that fair coloring and blonde hair usually were associated with the heroes of fiction stories, while dark hair and swarthiness were most often ascribed to the villains.[16] Another study revealed that the character traits of warm-heartedness, honesty, intelligence, responsibility, self-confidence, and refinement in men were perceived to be related to such facial features as bright, widened eyes that had a direct gaze, a straight nose of average width, well-groomed hair of average waviness, an up-turned mouth with lips of average fullness, eyebrows of moderate heaviness set against a smooth brow. Conversely, the less desirable character traits of ruthlessness, brutality, hostility, boorishness, and vulgarity were seen to be associated with close-set narrowed eyes in downward or averted gaze, either a wide or narrow nose with distended nostrils, slicked down or disheveled hair, thick or thin lips with the corners turned down, and heavy eyebrows set against a knitted, wrinkled brow.[17]

Again, these kinds of associations are the result of a form of cultural stereotyping, and cultural ideals are subject to change

[14]Lynn Mahannah, "Influence of Clothing Color on the Perception of Personality," Master's thesis, University of Nevada, 1968.

[15]P. F. Secord and J. E. Muthard, "Personalities in Faces: IV. A Descriptive Analysis of the Perception of Women's Faces and the Identification of some Physiognomic Determinants," *Journal of Psychology* 39, 1955, pp. 269–278.

[16]B. Berelson and P. Salter, "Majority and Minority Americans: An Analysis of Magazine Fiction," *Public Opinion Quarterly* 10, 1946, pp. 168–190.

[17]P. F. Secord, "Facial Features and Inference Processes in Interpersonal Perception," in R. Tagiuri and L. Petrullo (eds.), *Person Perception and Interpersonal Behavior*, Stanford University Press, Stanford, Calif., 1958, pp. 300–315.

over time. Public opinion in the 1960's was running strongly against the long-hairs. Hirsuteness among males was generally associated with uncleanliness, rebellious behavior, and a radical lifestyle. In 1973, an inquiring photographer for a San Francisco newspaper got the following answers to the question, "Do you distrust the clean-cut type?"[18]

> Yes. Short hair, like the crew cut, is from another era. And they're usually that way in their thinking, too.

> The clean-cut types are always very up-tight. Not open minded at all. They're not able to see anyone else's side. They're very conservative.

> I'd just think he was terribly old-fashioned. Outdated. When they have those real short hair cuts, they're always kind of straight. I'm not comfortable with them.

> Only squares have crew cuts.

> I just feel they're terribly boring people. Anyone with really short hair, the clean-cut type, is very conservative, very self-righteous. I don't care for them.

In another research study by Rosencranz, an attempt was made to assess the symbolic meanings attached to clothing through the use of a projective technique.[19] A modified Thematic Apperception Test was devised in which a series of seven drawings depicted incongruities between clothing and other aspects of the characters in the pictures. Subjects were asked to tell a dramatic story about each of the pictures. Without any initial reference to clothing in administering the test, most subjects referred to some clothing cue in analyzing the drawings. About one-fourth of the total comments made by the average subject related to dress, and for some informants the clothing comments ran as high as 50 per cent.

We can draw two basic conclusions from the clothing research to date. One is that judgments of an individual's personality traits are, in fact, influenced by the clothes that he wears. The second is that judges usually agree on the symbolic meanings that are conveyed through dress. Whether or not such judgments are accurate evaluations of the individual's character is another matter entirely. While some studies, such as the one by Kness, have demonstrated positive relationships between a person's beliefs or other aspects of lifestyle and the clothing he actually wears, results in general have been inconclusive. Knapper's research tested the relationship between personality and style of dress in a group of male subjects. Assessments of dress made by the wearer himself correlated significantly with many

[18]"O'Hara, the Question Man," *San Francisco Chronicle*, 11 May 1973.
[19]Mary Lou Rosencranz, "Clothing Symbolism," *Journal of Home Economics* 54, no. 1, 1962, pp. 18–22. Test items from the Clothing TAT are also reprinted and discussed in Rosencranz, *Clothing Concepts*, pp. 69–80.

of the personality dimensions, but there were relatively few correlations between personality traits and ratings of dress made by peers. Knapper concluded from this that the wearer's notion of how he dresses does not always agree with the way he is perceived by others, and that perceivers who use clothing as a cue to personality are apt to make inaccurate judgments.[20]

Such findings, however, are entirely consistent with the theories set forth by people like Symonds,[21] who suggest that the most direct approach to personality assessment is to ask the wearer himself to analyze his dress and the factors that guide his choice of clothing.

Clothing is an important cue in the formation of impressions of other persons, and it is particularly significant in limited contact situations.

Cues related to role and status

The term **role** is used here to designate the particular position or category of an individual in social relationships. It includes occupational roles (teacher, doctor, rancher, barber), family roles (mother, sister, uncle), and age-sex roles (a young man, a little boy, an old woman). The term **status** refers to the place of an individual on a scale or continuum of prestige, that is, the degree of social value attached to a given capacity. Thus, a person is perceived and evaluated on the basis of how well he fulfills the requirements of a specific role, and that role in turn is assigned a relative status position.

In the study of occupational clothing which was cited in previous chapters, it was observed that the main cues used to identify men in particular occupations were clothing symbols.[22] Manual workers were readily identified by their overalls, coveralls, aprons, or other work uniforms, while suits and sport clothes were mentioned in relation to the white-collar workers.

There were many other cues used to distinguish occupations, however, that were almost as important as the type of clothes that were worn. The condition of the fabric, for example, was often noted, such as paint, grease, or dust markings on the garments, and whether the clothes were clean or dirty. The expensiveness or quality of the fabric was generally used to identify office personnel. Men also detected differences in taste, garment upkeep, and the expressive quality of the clothes. Office workers tended to identify their own group as "conservative," "subdued," or "well-tailored" dressers, while clothes that were "flashy," "loud," or "frilled" were most often associated with the manual workers. Rather subtle differences were also noted in terms of being "well-dressed" or "dressed up," "neatly dressed" or "presentable." Additional cues included the cleanliness of the hands and the type of shoes worn.

[20]Christopher Knapper, "The Relationship Between Personality and Style of Dress," Unpublished dissertation, University of Saskatchewan, Canada, 1969.
[21]Refer to the discussion of "An Emerging Lifestyle" in Chapter 7, pp. 141–143.
[22]Form and Stone, *Social Significance of Clothing*, p. 18.

CLOTHING AND HUMAN BEHAVIOR

Un agent de la justice   Un gendarme   Un militaire de carrière   Un aviateur   Un marin   Un moniteur d'éducation physique

Un policier   L'administration de la France   Un chercheur   Un postier   Le président de la République   Le Parlement

Un écolier   Un lycéen   Un étudiant   Un invalide de guerre   Un économiquement faible   Un détenu   Un chomeur

Figure 9-4. These are clothing symbols that carry universal meanings for various role categories in the French society. How many of these would also be recognized in American society?

The shoe, by the way, appears to be a particularly expressive item in the identification of roles and statuses.[23] Pictures of men's feet wearing alligator shoes and loafers were presented to groups of students at the University of Nevada over a period of four years. Using a free response technique, students were asked to identify the role of the person wearing the shoes. The alligator shoes were associated with some type of business executive by 43 percent of the respondents; another 20 per cent identified the shoes as those of a salesman, while 15 per cent used such terms as "playboy," "gay blade," or "man about town." An additional 10 per cent assigned the wearer to a

---

[23]An interesting case of shoe symbolism appeared many years ago in *Life* magazine. On the assumption that people's feet reflect the faces to which they belong, photographer Burt Glinn presented a series of pictures of eleven men and three women detached from the pictures of their shoes which were arranged in random order. Readers were invited to test their skill in matching feet and faces. A number of readers experienced difficulty in making the correct choices, but several thought they could identify the person's occupation on the basis of his appearance. University of Nevada students consistently score 100 per cent in matching the feet of the three women with their faces; scores for the eleven men are considerably less accurate. See "Speaking of Pictures," *Life,* 4 December 1950, pp. 26–28, and subsequent letters to the editor in the 25 December 1950 issue. It would be intriguing to test the photographer's hypothesis.

CLOTHING SYMBOLISM

Figure 9-5. A model of the typical Englishman.

Figure 9-6. Fraudulent cues: Is she perhaps an eccentric dowager who operates an antique shop?

"wealthy" or "rich" category. The remaining 12 per cent responded in terms of idiosyncratic cues that were highly specialized, such as "diplomat," "lawyer," "sportswriter"—but none were inconsistent with a monied class of people.

Even greater agreement was found in the responses to loafers. Over 56 per cent of the respondents classified the wearer as a student, 28 per cent thought the shoes looked more like a young businessman, and 12 per cent identified them as belonging to a teacher or professor. Only 4 per cent of the responses in this case were single or idiosyncratic in nature.

In this same study, universal agreement was found in the responses to pictures of a rodeo rider, a nun, a policeman, and a bride. The rodeo rider was usually called a "cowboy" or "ranch hand," and the nun was sometimes called "a sister." And while all respondents designated the picture of the bride by that term, or "new wife," or "newlywed," not a single respondent recognized the same model when she appeared later in the series wearing a pair of pink stretch pants, sheer ruffled blouse, and mules. In this latter capacity she was classified as an artist's or photographer's model by 59 per cent of the subjects, and as some kind of actress, dancer, or entertainer by another 39 per cent.

The close range of responses to all of these illustrations emphasizes the similarity of meaning and the surprising agreement among those who perceive such symbols. The extent to which such cues are assigned true or erroneous meanings depends not only on the clothing variable itself, but upon the fidelity of the symbol. For example, the gentleman in Figure 9-5 is usually perceived as a high-status businessman or professional, and in almost half of the cases the words "English" or "British" are attached to the role description. The man is, in fact, a well-to-do Englishman. At the other extreme, most people see the character in Figure 9-6 as a wealthy old lady or grandmother, and not a single respondent has ever identified it as the familiar face of Alfred Hitchcock! The cues of wig and apparel (in this case, false) are so powerful that they obscure even the sex of the wearer—a role which is normally assumed to be not only fixed, but obvious.

In cases when the cues presented are either ambiguous or in conflict, the range of interpretations is much greater. Most perceivers detect the inconsistencies between details of dress and the total expressive quality of the costume. Statements such as, "She's trying to look like a lady of the upper crust, but she isn't really," or, "She's better dressed than she should be in this home," are based upon incongruities of dress with apparent status or surrounding environment.

Vance Packard once said that historically "clothing has been one of the most convenient, and visible, vehicles known for

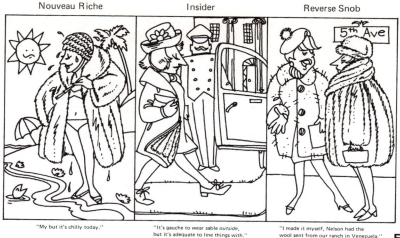

Nouveau Riche	Insider	Reverse Snob
"My but it's chilly today."	"It's gauche to wear sable *outside*, but it's adequate to line things with."	"I made it myself, Nelson had the wool sent from our ranch in Venezuela."

drawing class distinctions."[24] In 1961, Kittles asked a college population to identify specific apparel items that would be considered status symbols. Most often mentioned were such items as fur coats, fancy hats, expensive jewelry, and well-tailored suits. At that time, nearly all the status symbols mentioned proved significant in distinguishing between white and black women of comparable income levels, i.e., white women actually owned more of these status items than did the black women.[25]

The shifts in status during the 1960's are mirrored in Hunter's 1967 study. She found that black women owned greater numbers of all types of dresses than did white women. Too, the blacks thought clothes were more important and felt they were judged more often by clothing than white women did.[26]

The stimuli-persons in the Douty study mentioned earlier were rated on a status scale as well as on personality traits, and it was concluded that clothing was a strong influence in determining role and status impressions of unknown persons. Rosencranz's subjects also often used clothing cues in identifying status incongruities. All these studies point to the importance of clothing symbols in formation of role and status impressions.

Situational cues

Clothing provides stimulus information not only for the determination of personality, role, and status, but it also supplies a

Figure 9-7. Since many people now can afford the status symbols of the upper class, the symbolic meanings of things are adjusted accordingly.

Clothing is a significant factor in determining the role and status of unknown persons.

---

[24]Vance Packard, *The Status Seekers*, David McKay & Company, New York, 1959, p. 131.
[25]Emma Kittles, "The Importance of Clothing as a Status Symbol Among College Students," Unpublished dissertation, Ohio State University, 1961.
[26]Marilyn Hunter, "A Comparison of Clothing Between Negro and White Women of Low Socio-Economic Status," Master's thesis, University of Missouri, 1967.

Figure 9-8. Clothing symbols provide the situational cues in these pictures. Verbal descriptions are unnecessary to understand the events that are taking place.

Clothing is a means of defining the situation in which social interaction takes place.

definition of the social situation in which it appears. The adaptation and use of clothing to demonstrate situational change is explained by Stone and Form:

> Visible objects and gestures provide cues in defining situations, and clothing is one of the most crucial of these cues. Thus, for example, every change in a significant life situation—birth, entering school, graduation from school, getting a job, marriage, parenthood, and even death—requires a change of wardrobe. Even in the course of daily life, situation after situation requires a change of dress to facilitate and symbolize the situational changes.
>
> A change of dress indicates to others that a person's situation has changed, thereby assisting everyone (including the person) in defining the new situation. The soldier's change of uniform for the dress parade and the civilian's change of "uniform" for the dress ball provide extreme examples of these general observations.[27]

"Appropriateness" or "inappropriateness" in dress is determined primarily by cultural and situational factors. A costume that would be entirely acceptable on the beach would be considered "out of place" at an afternoon reception. Probably the most common cue presented by clothes relates to observed differences in degree of formality or informality: "You're all dressed up! Going some place?" The sole purpose of verbal cues such as "formal," "semiformal," or "informal" at the bottom of written invitations has been to inform guests how to dress for the occasion. Although the proscriptions attached to situational appropriateness have been greatly modified in recent years, dress still sets the stage for most social activity.

Missed signals or misinterpretations of situational cues often can cause considerable embarrassment. Differences in cultural patterns often make it difficult for Americans abroad to anticipate incongruities between dress and situational requirements. A State Department wife returned from an assignment in the Far East concerned about the image that Americans were creating by their casual dress in Oriental communities. "The Oriental believes that the more richly you dress, as a guest, the more honor you do your host. Silk is still their highest status fabric. You can see how these simple wool dresses seemed a direct insult, to them."[28]

In other words, we *expect* clothing to set the stage for the kind of social interaction that is to take place. Moreover, clothing is used in a myriad of ways to announce or describe an event or occasion. Witness the "widow's weeds" and mourning bands that symbolize in very exact terms the passing of a family member; the bridal gown which can be worn for no other event save

[27]Stone and Form, *Local Community Clothing Market*, p. 8.
[28]Karlyne Anspach, "The American in Casual Dress," *Journal of Home Economics* 55, no. 4, 1963, p. 256 ff.

the wearer's own wedding; the wearing of green on St. Patrick's Day; the Shriner's fez that lets everyone know of the convention in town; the formal riding habit that announces even to the fox that the hunt is about to begin.

SUMMARY   *Clothing cues*

Clothing is one of the significant nonverbal symbols which communicates and defines certain aspects of personality, role, status, and situation. Such cues may be true or erroneous expressions, depending upon the way in which they are used or manipulated. Fraudulent use of clothing symbols is limited by a number of restrictions that have been labeled as intrinsic, moral, socialization or cultivation, and organic. Lack of congruence in clothing cues usually creates suspicion or confusion in the mind of the perceiver.

Research has demonstrated that changes in clothing alter the impressions formed of an individual's personality traits. Several studies have shown that rather high agreement is found among judges in assigning persons to role and status categories on the basis of dress. In addition, clothing is an obvious key in the perception of situational factors which set the stage for subsequent social interaction.

Perceiver variables

The accuracy of judgments made on the basis of clothing cues or symbols depends not only upon the fidelity of the stimulus information presented, but upon a number of variables in the way such information is received and interpreted by the perceiver. The weighting of clothing cues as significant elements in forming impressions of other people is strongly influenced by the amount and kind of additional information about the person that is available to the perceiver or judge.

As we have seen, there is more universal agreement on some types of cues and more variation with others. Ambiguous cues are likely to be interpreted in ambiguous ways, but some of the ambiguity may be attributed to the idiosyncrasies of the perceiver.

Levels and modes of perception

Research has shown that individuals vary in their degree of sensitivity to stimulus information. Further, their responses appear to be differentiated in terms of concreteness and complexity. Let us compare the responses of different students to one of the pictures in the Clothing TAT (see Figure 9-10).[29]

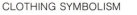

[29]These data were derived from administering the Clothing TAT to groups of University of Nevada students. They were not taken from the original study.

Figure 9-9. When asked to describe the situation taking place in this picture, most perceivers note the incongruity in dress between the two men.

Figure 9-10. One of the stimulus pictures from Rosencranz's Clothing TAT.

One student simply describes the characters in terms of their outward appearances: "The masculine female on the left is dressed in masculine clothes and has a boyish haircut. The feminine female on the right is dressed up, with hat and beads. These people are both women."

A second student perceives the difference between the two characters in terms of their deviation from a single or central trait: "Each girl is sloppy but in a different way. One needs her hair combed and needs to pay a little more attention to her appearance. The other one is over-dressed and overly made-up. It's a case of either too much or too little."

The response pattern of still another student seemed to conform to descriptions of personality that were congruous with the masculine or feminine traits suggested by the difference in clothing cues: "These two girls have just met and are conversing for the first time. The girl on the left is very plain; she likes tailored clothes, a short, simple hair-do, and never wears any make-up. The other girl always dresses nicely, takes a great deal of pride in her personal appearance, and enjoys wearing the latest fashions. Neither girl can quite understand the other, since their tastes are so widely divergent."

A fourth student was obviously able to resolve certain incongruities perceived in the picture and inferred that there was probably more involved in the situation than one could fathom from casual observation: "These two young people seem to be having a rather serious time together. Their eyes are sad and troubled. The hat on the girl makes her look much older than she really is; perhaps she wears it to attract the attention of the boy in hopes that he will think she is more sophisticated and grown up. Their whole appearance portrays an involvement far beyond their level of maturity."

These four responses demonstrate differences in the level or complexity of perceptual abilities, ranging from a very simple mode of perception to observations of a complex order.[30] It is probable that the degree of complexity with which one perceives the stimulus person is directly related to the intelligence and maturity of the perceiver, although this has not been tested empirically.

Another way to define such levels would be in terms of the degree of concreteness or abstraction that is represented. One person may perceive others in very concrete or specific ways, making extreme distinctions between what is good and what is bad, and refusing to accept any possible ambiguity. Such a person usually relies upon some external set of rules to guide his judgment rather than the powers of his own reasoning. Following is an example of such concreteness in reference to the same

---

[30]These levels of person perception have been outlined by Secord and Backman. See P. Secord and C. Backman, *Social Psychology*, McGraw-Hill Book Company, 1974, pp. 15–16.

picture: "The woman on the right is very well-dressed, and she is obviously giving the girl on the left some advice on how to dress like a young girl should. Apparently this girl is a tomboy and likes to wear mannish clothes, but underneath it all she really envies the woman who is pretty and feminine."

Greater abstractness in a person is characterized by increased tolerance of ambiguous situations. Such an individual sees many ramifications in particular clothing cues and tries to place himself in the role of the stimulus person in an attempt to evaluate several possible explanations: "One might almost suppose that the figure on the left were a male, except for the definition of the bustline, which is clearly discernible. She may be wearing a school uniform of some kind—perhaps as a member of the band or a team. Of course, she could simply like things that were plain and tailored. In any case, the two girls seem to have distinctly different tastes in dress."

Another factor relating to modes of perception was described previously in connection with the development of the self-concept as the "halo effect." This principle operates as a kind of bias in our perception of others, that is, we tend to see a person as a "package," and judge him in terms of a total impression of goodness or badness. For example, one student's interpretation of the figure on the right in the picture was as follows: "You can tell from the cut of her dress that she's a woman of ill repute. She's just returning home after being out all night, and her son is confronting her with the facts. She lies and tells him she had car trouble, but he knows better than to believe her."

Also mentioned previously were the effects of "primacy" or first impressions on the accuracy of person perception. The way in which a person is first perceived may have lasting consequences in regard to the way he is evaluated in later situations, even though more information about the stimulus person is then available.

Inferences made from clothing cues depend, at least to some extent, upon one's level or mode of perception.

Relevance of clothing symbols

If a person were to perceive all possible stimuli presented by another individual's appearance, he would be burdened by the overload of information. In actual practice, the observer selects certain aspects of the person which he considers to be particularly relevant. Berelson and Steiner explain this phenomenon in concise terms: "We look at some things, ignore others, and look away from still others ('selective exposure'). Beyond that, only a fraction of those stimuli that have gained effective entry to a receptor ever reach awareness ('selective awareness')."[31] This brings to mind immediately the "inconsiderate" male who

---

[31]Bernard Berelson and Gary Steiner, *Human Behavior—An Inventory of Scientific Findings*, Harcourt, Brace & World, New York, 1964, p. 100.

crushes the woman's spirits by failing to notice her new dress. Or, when the wife asks him what Mrs. Jones wore when she visited his store yesterday, the husband replies, "How should I know?"

The Clothing TAT was originally designed as a measure of clothing awareness, and significant differences were found among the respondents with respect to the number of clothing cues that were perceived. The degree of clothing awareness was statistically related to such factors as social class and all of its indices (occupation, income, education, organizational membership, and magazine readership) as well as verbal intelligence.[32]

Another simple measure of clothing awareness was designed by Rosencranz which consisted of twenty-five words having double or triple meanings. One of the meanings of each word had a clothing connotation, such as the word "alligator." The test is based on the assumption that people with a high clothing awareness will interpret the word in terms of its clothing implication. When the test list was administered to several hundred students, it was found that students majoring in the arts, humanities, and the social sciences had higher clothing awareness scores than those majoring in engineering and the physical sciences. As would be expected, women had significantly higher scores than men.[33] Other studies have been made that have demonstrated a high degree of relationship between awareness of dress and awareness of other aspects of the popular culture, such as painting, sculpture, music, movies, theater, and the like.[34] Research in general has shown that girls are more aware of clothing than boys are.[35] Over the years, children of various age levels have been tested, and it may be concluded that sensitivity to clothing is already well established by the time pupils reach the eighth grade. Data also reveal that boys and girls who are more "other-directed" (i.e., sensitive to the feelings and opinions of others) tend to be more conscious of factors related to dress.

The extent to which an individual uses clothing symbols in the formation of impressions of other people depends upon the relevance of clothing stimuli to the perceiver.

Furthermore, if previous feelings and cognitions in relation to clothing behavior have been positively reinforced in the perceiver's past experience, it may be assumed that clothing stimuli will have a fairly high degree of relevance.[36]

[32]Rosencranz, "Clothing Symbolism," p. 22.

[33]Rosencranz, *Clothing Concepts*, p. 62.

[34]See Judith Orkus, "Fashion Awareness of Men as Related to Aspects of the Popular Culture," Master's thesis, Pennsylvania State University, 1971; and Janice Patterson, "Fashion Awareness as Related to Aspects of the Popular Culture," Master's thesis, Pennsylvania State University, 1968.

[35]See Vener and Hoffer, *Adolescent Orientations to Clothing;* and Katherine Merrick, "Clothing Awareness: A Comparison of Fifth Grade Boys and Girls in a Middle School and an Elementary School," Master's thesis, Pennsylvania State University, 1970.

[36]For amplification of this theory, see A. Hastorf, S. Richardson, and S. Dornbusch, "The Problem of Relevance in the Study of Person Perception," in Tagiuri and Petrullo (eds.), *Person Perception*, pp. 54–62.

Perceiver characteristics

The fact that the same person is perceived in diverse ways by different individuals may be attributed not only to differences in level or complexity of perception and to the variation in clothing awareness, but also to certain aspects of the perceiver's own personality. In Chapter 7, for example, we discussed the evaluation of appearance in terms of one's own particular set of expectations: the manual workers who attached little importance to clothes expected others to attach little importance to clothes; the women who dressed up to go shopping held a different set of standards for judging other women shoppers than did those who shopped in semicasual dress. The manual workers in the first study were sensitized to the distinction between "clean" and "dirty" manual jobs, and consequently used the cue of clothing cleanliness more often in assessing social status than did the office workers.

Thus, we see that every perceiver has a particular set of standards and a particular pattern of past experiences that condition his impressions of other people. One person may stress cleanliness, neatness, simplicity, modesty, and constraint in dress, and will emphasize these criteria in sizing up the other person. Another individual may judge the stimulus person against such categories as smartness, sophistication, becomingness, distinctiveness, and suitability. Although there is not a great deal of empirical evidence to date, some preliminary research seems to indicate that (1) people tend to have a *core* or set of central consistent categories against which they measure other persons, (2) people use a rather limited number of such perceptual categories, and (3) there is a strong positive relationship between the categories that people use to describe others and the categories they use to describe themselves.

Some research suggests that personality traits of the perceiver are highly influential in the way clothing symbols are judged. Dickey found the personality syndromes of self-esteem and security to affect the way an individual evaluated pictures of clothed figures.[37] Individuals high in levels of self-actualization also have been found to be more analytical in their perceptions,[38] and those who have a high degree of self-insight (i.e., those who rate themselves as others rate them) also tend to judge other people more accurately. Whether the judgment is accurate or not, the fact remains that each perceiver views the other in light of his own idiosyncrasies.

Associations made with clothing cues depend to a fairly large extent upon the perceiver's unique frame of reference.

---

[37]Lois Dickey, "Projection of the Self Through Judgments of Clothed Figures and Its Relation to Self-Esteem, Security-Insecurity and to Selected Clothing Behaviors," Unpublished dissertation, Pennsylvania State University, 1967.
[38]Linda Boehme, "Persuasibility and Visual Perception of a Dress Design as Related to Selected Personality Characteristics," Unpublished dissertation, Pennsylvania State University, 1970.

"Here comes your knight in shining armor."

Figure 9-11. Drawing by Stan Hunt; © 1970 by The New Yorker Magazine, Inc.

"Well, if you aren't a sight for sore eyes!"

Figure 9-12. Drawing by Alan Dunn; © 1970 by The New Yorker Magazine, Inc.

SUMMARY *Perceiver variables*

It has been demonstrated that some clothing symbols elicit meanings that have more universal agreement than others. Clothing cues that are interpreted in a variety of different ways may lack fidelity or be incongruous with other cues presented, but such variation also may be accounted for in the personality of the perceiver.

Different individuals may describe stimulus persons at varying levels of complexity, ranging from a simple or concrete impression to a mode of perception that is highly complex or abstract. Furthermore, individuals tend to exercise the economizing processes of "selective awareness" in determining which of the many cues presented will be recognized. The third group of variables discussed relates to the personal characteristics of the perceiver. The way in which one perceives others depends upon one's own particular set of expectations and frame of reference.

Consequences for social interaction

Clothing symbols that are (1) true representations of the self, (2) presented in an explicit and perspicuous manner, and (3) consistent with other cues, are apt to be perceived fairly accurately. The more ambiguous the cue, on the other hand, the more the perceiver is called upon to interpret its meaning in light of his own idiosyncrasies. Individuals may utilize a number of processes in making inferences from limited stimulus information. These will be discussed in the following section as judgment processes. In addition, the perceiver's interpretation depends to some extent upon socially structured expectations, and upon the relationship that exists between the judge and the person who is judged.

Judgment processes

The influence of first impressions on sustained social interaction often may have lasting effects. A person who is first perceived to be slovenly and poorly dressed is often thought to have little concern for his own appearance and little regard for the opinions of others. Sometimes this appraisal is extended to associations with unfriendliness or even rudeness. Although subsequent contacts with the stimulus person may, in fact, contain perceptible elements of amity and courtesy, the judge has already been conditioned to look for the opposing characteristics. Studies in perception have shown that people tend to see things in terms of a "relevant direction," that is, as they want or need to see them. Thus, particular clothing cues may be linked to other characteristics which, to the perceiver at least, seem interdependent and logically related. These characteristics, in turn, may be regarded as enduring attributes.

An inference process is usually based upon some "logical" method of reasoning. For example, a person who wears glasses probably suffered from eye strain; eye strain is often caused from too much reading; a person who reads a lot is apt to be very intelligent; consequently, it is "logical" to assume that people who wear glasses are intelligent. Whether or not the association of such attributes is accurate and truly descriptive of the person being judged is not as significant as the fact that judges usually show rather marked agreement in the evaluation of such stimulus information.

Sometimes the association is made between two similar individuals rather than between or among analogous traits. A new acquaintance may remind us of someone else: "That fellow looks just like Joe Johnson!" And, consciously or unconsciously, we assign Joe Johnson's traits to Bob Smith. The transference of personality characteristics from one individual to another is a fairly common although involuntary process.

To categorize stimuli persons on the basis of selected criteria is known as **stereotyping**. A person is categorized and then assigned a whole set of characteristics that are typically associated with that role, status, or classification. We saw, for example, in the response of one student to Figure 9-10, that the feminine-looking figure was categorized as "a woman of ill repute"; not only do women of ill repute wear tight dresses and low-cut necklines, but they also stay out all night, and they lie about their activities, even to their own sons. The gaudy, bedecked American male is the Englishman's stereotype of the typical U.S. tourist. Responses to Figure 9-5 indicate that Americans also stereotype the Englishman; he wears a conservative suit, bowler, and carries a rolled umbrella. Even though, as we indicated before, all stereotypes are—at least partly—false, the image of the "typical" freshman, professor, athletic coach, spinster, or politician is always there to provide a basis for identification.

Relation of the judge to the judged

The average person is well aware of the fact that he is more likely to be judged on the basis of his appearance by people who do not know him intimately. There is less compulsion to be on our "best behavior" with life-long acquaintances than with those whose contacts have been more limited. Moreover, the value which we place on the other person's opinion affects the degree to which we find it necessary to control our clothing signals. Hurlock's early study of motivation in dress provided some data in this regard. In answer to the question "In which

Figure 9-13. We all make judgments on the basis of appearance. Drawing by Lorenz; © 1970 The New Yorker Magazine, Inc.

Individuals employ certain inference processes in the associations that are made with clothing symbols.

Figure 9-14. Some people find anonymity in strange places and wear garb they would never think of wearing on the main streets of their own home towns. Sculpture by Duane Hansen.

case do you care most about your appearance?" almost 56 per cent of the respondents indicated concern for their appearance was greatest when they were with friends; 43 per cent said it mattered most with strangers, and only one per cent thought it to be important with one's own family. None of the respondents deemed clothing to be of importance when one was alone.[39]

Thus, our families and our most intimate friends know us too well to judge us on the basis of clothing. Friends who know us less well are still forming their opinions about us, and since we value their opinions we find it important to dress for their approval. The opinions of strangers, on the other hand, may or may not be valued. Office workers in the occupational study cited earlier found it extremely important to dress up for strangers, especially if they were likely to be potential customers or high prestige people. Conversely, manual workers dressed more for the approval of their fellow workers, since strangers would have little influence over their success on the job. In like manner, some people who go to a different city may pay greater attention to their dress than they would if they were in their hometown. A woman going to shop in San Francisco, for example, may dress up in the belief that her appearance will affect the service she receives from the store clerks. Other people often experience a sense of anonymity in being far away from home, and find it possible to relax their standards of dress in places where they know no one will recognize them. The extremely casual dress worn by many Americans away from home has resulted in a rather unflattering stereotype of the typical U.S. tourist.

The consequences of judgment or inference processes have also been shown to be related to feelings of liking or disliking for other persons. Several studies have supported the theory that perceivers are inclined to like those whom they judge to be *similar* to themselves, and dislike persons whom they see as very *different* from themselves. Legal experts often claim that court judges are influenced by clothing in assigning penalties and criminal sentences. A study of misdemeanor cases in Detroit's Recorder's Court found that defendants who appeared in court in work clothes had a much greater chance of going to jail than did defendants wearing suits or sports coats and ties.[40]

There are those who believe that justice should indeed be blind. One man proposed that "every defendant should appear before the bar clothed in total anonymity accomplished by requiring each to be completely enshrouded in a litigant garment."[41]

[39]Hurlock, "Motivation in Fashion," p. 41.
[40]Glynn Mapes, "Unequal Justice: A Growing Disparity in Criminal Sentences Troubles Legal Experts," *Wall Street Journal*, 9 Sept. 1970.
[41]Burke Rummler, "Toward Justice," *Reno Evening Gazette*, 23 July 1969.

Moreover, the characteristics that bring recognition in one role may bring rejection in another. One high-school youth attracted considerable attention from his peers through extreme forms of dress, long hair, and a beard. Upon graduation, however, he found it difficult to find a job. When he checked back with personnel heads, they all told him that his qualifications were good but that his appearance was against him.

Obviously a number of problems arise from inaccurate associations between role or status categories and assigned traits. A receptionist in a large business office who failed to recognize an esteemed customer was taken to task by her boss. The writer of an advice column defended the secretary by writing: "Clergymen who insist on walking about in casual mufti cannot complain when they're herded like hoi polloi. The moral is, if the customer is so valued and esteemed, but dresses in a manner not associated with his august presence, he should be prepared to identify himself and not expect hard-working secretaries to discern his invisible 'Roman collar.'[42]

> Effective relations between the judge and the judged will be influenced by an understanding of the meanings that dress communicates to others.

The consequences of inaccuracies in judgment can be disappointing for both the judge and the judged.

SUMMARY *Consequences for social interaction*

Clothing cues that are clear, consistent, and accurate representations of the self are likely to be perceived more correctly than cues which are fraudulent or ambiguous. Individuals employ certain judgment processes in associating meanings with given clothing symbols; these include (1) the extension of clothing characteristics to other "logically related" personality traits, (2) the transference of personality characteristics from one individual to another, and (3) role and status stereotyping.

The relation of the judge to the judged determines not only how an individual is perceived, put how the individual seeks to present himself. Clothing symbols are deemed to be more important in those situations in which the individual (1) is recognized but not too well known, and (2) considers the perceiver's opinion to be of value. Relatives or friends who have intimate knowledge of an individual's personality are not apt to use clothing cues in judging the stimulus person.

FOR FURTHER READING

Douty, Helen I. "Influence of Clothing on Perception of Persons," *Journal of Home Economics* 55, no. 3, 1963, pp. 197–202.

Goffman, Erving. "Symbols of Class Status," *British Journal of Sociology* 2, no. 4, 1951, pp. 294–304.

---

[42]Abigail Van Buren, "Dear Abby," syndicated column, August 1972.

Hastorf, A. H., D. J. Schneider, and J. Polefka. *Person Perception*. Reading, Mass.: Addison-Wesley Publishing Company, 1970.

Rosencranz, Mary Lou. *Clothing Concepts*. New York: Macmillan Publishing Company, 1972. (Chapter 5, "Situational Awareness," and Chapter 6, "Awareness of Incongruities.")

Ryan, Mary S. *Clothing: A Study in Human Behavior*. New York: Holt, Rinehart & Winston, 1966. (Chapter 1, "First Impressions.")

Tagiuri, Renato and Luigi Petrullo. *Person Perception and Interpersonal Behavior*. Stanford, Calif.: Stanford University Press, 1958.

DISCUSSION QUESTIONS

1. How can a stereotype be both true and not true?

2. Describe an inference process. How may an inference process lead to faulty perceptions of clothing symbols?

3. Explain what is meant by a "limited contact situation." Are clothes more or less important in such a situation than they are with more intimate contacts? Why?

4. What kinds of clothing cues are apt to be interpreted accurately?

5. What limitations are there to the presentation of fraudulent clothing cues?

6. Examine the clothing symbols presented in Figure 9-4. How many of these can you identify correctly? (After you have tested your skill, have someone translate the subtitles for you.) Which ones did you miss? Describe the role symbols that one might expect of an American in a comparable position.

7. What relationship do you see between the theory of cognitive dissonance discussed in Chapter 7 and the judgment processes described in Chapter 9?

8. What is meant by a "status symbol"? What are some of today's symbols of luxury?

10

Clothes, Roles, and Status

IN THE PREVIOUS chapters, we discussed clothing as it relates to the learning of new social roles which function in the development of one's concept of self. In addition, we have seen how the clothes of an individual furnish significant cues to the perceiver in determining one's role and status. The present chapter is concerned primarily with an analysis of clothing expectations in regard to role and status requirements.

The term **role** has already been defined as a particular position or category occupied by an individual in social relationships, while **status** refers to the place of an individual on a scale of prestige.[1] As we shall see, each social role carries with it a set of behavioral expectations, many of which are manifest through the use of clothing. How an individual learns what is expected of him and whether or not he chooses to fulfill such role obligations are also matters of concern to us in the analysis of clothing behavior. Moreover, we shall consider clothing as it facilitates a change or transition in particular roles and statuses.

Clothing expectations

Implicit in the definition of **role** are the associated rules or norms of behavior to which the role occupant is expected to conform. The way in which such group norms are established has been discussed in general terms in Chapter 4. It is clear that no society can operate effectively without providing for its

---

[1] It should be noted that the terms "role" and "status" have been defined differently by different writers. Linton, for example, in *The Study of Man*, uses "*status*" to designate the position of an individual in each of the social systems, and does not restrict the definition to a prestige continuum. He describes the term "*role*" as the "sum total of the cultural patterns associated with a particular status," including the attitudes, values, and behavior ascribed by society to all occupants of that status. More recently, writers have used the term "*role*" to define both the position and its related behavioral expectations.

members some guide or consistent patterning that will insure the accomplishment of specific social tasks. Roles are, therefore, something like job descriptions, and group members usually share notions of what is desirable or appropriate behavior in any given situation. Specific expectations in regard to clothing are discussed below in relation to age and sex roles, occupational roles, and other social roles.

Age and sex roles

Differentiation in roles on the basis of sex is probably the most universal determinant of social behavior. All societies ascribe a different set of obligations and expectations to males and to females, and while such ascriptions are usually rationalized on the basis of physiological characteristics, the actual restrictions that evolve are almost entirely determined by the culture.[2] In practically every society the world over, there is a marked distinction in the typical garbs of men and women, and strict taboos are often maintained against the wearing of garments assigned to the opposite sex. "In our own society," Brown explains, "women may wear men's clothing but there is the strongest kind of feeling directed against the man who wears feminine attire."[3]

In Western civilization, the most predominant cultural norm with respect to sex differentiation in dress has been that the female is *supposed* to have an interest in dress, while the male is *supposed* to have little or none. The woman is expected to be soft, round, colorful, delicate, and decorative; the man should be hard, vigorous, strong, drab, and inconspicuous. Interestingly enough, such secondary sexual characteristics are by no means universal in nature. In the animal kingdom, it is the male of the species that usually inherits the decorative plumage, while the female is most often plain and subdued. Even in human life, the masculine member of most primitive tribes is more highly ornamented than his feminine counterpart.

As a matter of fact, this particular distinction between the sexes has not held even among the higher orders of civilization. Prior to the eighteenth century, for example, the most sumptuously dressed member of society was the knight, the priest, the prince, the lord, the dandy, or the macaroni, and their ribbons and laces were rarely associated with effeminate traits. Since the French and the industrial revolutions, however, we have gradually become accustomed to a world of "dingy men and bright women."[4]

The division of sex roles by means of clothing is so deeply embedded as a social norm that in some states it has become a

[2]Ralph Linton, *The Study of Man*, D. Appleton-Century Company, New York, 1936, p. 116.
[3]Ina C. Brown, *Understanding Other Cultures*, Prentice-Hall, Englewood Cliffs, N.J., 1963, p. 26.
[4]For an explanation of why this transition occurred, see Quentin Bell, *On Human Finery*, Hogarth Press, London, 1947, pp. 91–92.

part of the penal code. There are numerous city ordinances against transvestitism, some of which go so far as to prohibit impersonation of the opposite sex on the stage. The rules are usually applied more stringently in the case of men dressing like women, and to many it becomes a misdemeanor akin to sexual perversion.

Some writers contend that distinctions in dress were intended primarily to augment sexual characteristics. The corset, for example, not only reduces the circumference of the waist, but it also increases the size of the bust and hips. Further, the breathing activity is displaced upward, thereby rendering the breasts even more prominent. In masculine dress, tights, breeches, and trousers supposedly emphasize most effectively the male attribute of energy and activity as represented by the lower limbs, the organs of locomotion.[5] At least one researcher claims to have identified a positive correlation between tight trousers and western heroes and has concluded that, historically, tight pants have always been a badge of masculinity.[6]

Havelock Ellis maintained that "the extreme importance of clothes would disappear at once if the two sexes were to dress alike."[7] A case in point was the virtual loss of sex identity in post-revolutionary Russia. Women, having achieved full equality with men, adopted the same uniform-like jackets, shirts, and boots, and both sexes rejected all forms of dress that would in any way add to their physical attractiveness. Their shabby, drab, and "mildewed" suits became a badge of self-sacrifice to the state.[8] It was not until the late 1950's, as standards for the "classless society" became more relaxed and consumer goods more available, that a renewed interest in clothes began to develop. Western-style fashion shows were initiated in Moscow, and the Soviet woman gradually recaptured her desire to look feminine.

The close relationship between the status of women and the expression of sex role through dress can be demonstrated in almost every period of fashion history. Clothes that restrict or hamper the movements of the female have always been prevalent in cultures or periods in which the woman's position is inferior, and her sphere of activities confined largely to the home. In periods of greater freedom and emancipation, feminine dress tends to take on more of the characteristics of male attire. The wearing of bifurcated garments, for example,

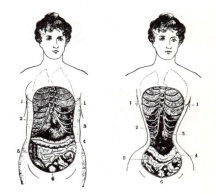

Figure 10-1. The ideal female form at the turn of the century could only be accomplished with the aid of a corset. Tight lacing compressed the waist (and internal organs as well!), rounded the hipline, and emphasized the bosom.

---

[5]Crawley, *Dress, Drinks, and Drums*, p. 129.
[6]Psychologist Murray Sherman reported a study of the Freudian aspects of male attire as part of a motivational research project. He concluded that the adult male in tight pants has never shed his childhood admiration of the cowboy, and "has a deep-seated unconscious desire to remain eternally young."
[7]Havelock Ellis, *Studies in the Psychology of Sex*, Vol. 4, Random House, New York, 1936, p. 209.
[8]John Gunther, *Inside Russia Today*, Harper and Brothers, New York, 1958, p. 41.

CLOTHES, ROLES, AND STATUS

Figure 10-2. A seventeenth-century gentleman. Men's clothes have not always been dull and dingy.

Figure 10-3. (Right) By the age of three, a child is indoctrinated with the fact that she is a girl (or that he is a boy), and appearance, becomes a vehicle through which sexual identity is reinforced.

Figure 10-4. A certain amount of tomboyishness in girls is reinforced through positive sanctions.

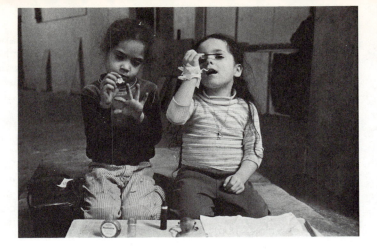

has increased steadily in America since the suffragette movement of the late-nineteenth century.[9]

As early as 1965, research showed that more than one-third of the average college girl's wardrobe consisted of bifurcated garments,[10] a trend that increased dramatically during the late sixties and early seventies.

Young children begin to learn the differences in sex roles very early, so that even by the age of two or three, distinctions in attitudes and interests may be noted. Much greater conformity in dress is usually demanded of men, and stronger social sanctions are enforced against males who wear feminine attire. Patterns in child rearing reveal that parents strongly influence such sex role ambiguity. Little girls today are often dressed for play in overalls or shorts, and a certain amount of tomboy behavior is regarded with amusement on the part of the parent. Little boys, however, have no corresponding freedom, and any tendency toward feminine behavior is given immediate disapproval. Pitcher noted that fathers especially tend to emphasize a kind of exclusive masculinity in their sons.[11]

Thus, the cultural definition of appropriate sex role behavior tends to be more ambiguous for females than it is for males. On the surface, this kind of role flexibility might seem to give women the advantage, but studies have shown that our culture gives greater priority to masculine qualities, and females are quick to perceive this. In an analysis of adolescents' self-concepts, Ehle discovered that girls more often than boys con-

---

[9]There are notable exceptions to the correlation between female status and the wearing of bifurcated garments, but in all such cases some other element of dress restricted mobility, e.g., Chinese ladies wore trousers, but their feet were bound and deformed.
[10]Betty L. Davis, "The Relationship Between Masculine-Feminine Personality Traits and the Feelings Associated with the Wearing of Bifurcated Garments," Master's thesis, Pennsylvania State University, 1965.
[11]Evelyn G. Pitcher, "Male and Female," *Atlantic*, March 1963, p. 87.

sidered their appearance to be less desirable than their peers', and they more often desired a change in the way they looked.[12]

There are, however, signs of diminishing differences in dress between the sexes. Despite the fact that women's lib has placed the emphasis on changes in the woman's role, the real change in recent years has been the cultural definition of masculinity. Women have always had the freedom to take on the male symbols of dress without much social ostracism. Women like Joan of Arc, George Sand, Lola Montez—all of whom were famous for their adoption of masculine attire—were admired more often than scorned. Today, the real breakthrough in dress has been a growing permissiveness in the standard for what is accepted as manly.

There are those like designer Rudi Gernreich who believe that unisex clothing is the thing of the future. In 1970, Gernreich designed miniskirts, leotards, and pant suits for men and women alike, eliminating all sexual variation in dress. There are others who maintain that whatever the age or the era, there will always be a necessity for children to learn appropriate sex roles, and that clothing provides strong support to one's sense of identity in being a girl or in being a boy. This point of view was expressed by Broderick, when he wrote: "Times change and cultural definitions of what is masculine and what is feminine change. What does not change is the need in each individual to feel secure in his own identity and that includes his sexual identity. However the symbols may evolve which reassure me and others that I am a man and my mate is a woman, there will be such symbols and they will matter."[13]

While clothing is not as distinguishable with respect to age as it is to sex, every society maintains some differentiation in clothing norms for each stage in the life cycle. Most often these are broadly defined in terms of dress that is considered appropriate for children, adults, or the aged. In our own complex system, we make age-grade distinctions (not only in size, but in style) for infants, toddlers, children, subteen, teen, junior, misses, and women's wear. The high value placed upon eternal youth in our culture prohibits the use of any commercial category that extends beyond clothes for the mature woman, although the growing proportion of elderly people in the U.S. population has given impetus to an increased study of the clothing needs of the aged.

Clothing expectations for various age categories are seldom enforced as rigidly as they are for sex roles, but we quickly identify the black velvet strapless as too sophisticated for the teenager's first formal dance; and the woman past forty who continues to wear gay bouffant styles and ribbons in her hair rarely escapes social criticism. Incongruities between

---

[12]Kathleen Ehle, "Adolescent Self Concept and Appearance," Master's thesis, University of Wisconsin, 1971.
[13]Carlfred Broderick, "The Importance of Being Ernest—or Evelyn," *Penney's Forum*, Spring/Summer 1973, p. 17.

Figure 10-5. The standard for what is "masculine" has changed over the years. Many little boys today are mistaken for little girls, and vice versa. Which of these children can you identify as male or female?

Figure 10-6. The diminishing differences in dress between the sexes requires a whole new cultural definition of what is masculine and what is feminine.

Figure 10-7. A woman of 40 will never look 30 dressing or acting like 20—because of the disparity in age-role expectations.

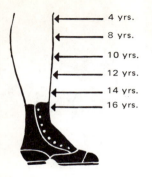

Figure 10-8. "The proper length for little girls' skirts at various ages." Like little boys' pants, the length of girls' dresses was precisely prescribed. This was the standard in the 1860's.

4 yrs.
8 yrs.
10 yrs.
12 yrs.
14 yrs.
16 yrs.

Age and sex roles are reflected in the clothing expectations held for all members of society; the more stable or clear-cut the role, the more explicit the requirements of dress.

age and dress are obvious, not only because they highlight the individual's physical disparities, but because they are essentially in violation of the normative expectation.

Not very many years ago, a boy's age had a direct relationship to the length of his pants. Boys under the age of six or seven were usually clothed in shorts; prepubescent boys wore knickers; and the first pair of long trousers really marked one's initiation into manhood. Bush and London have attempted to account for the disappearance of these age-role symbols by analyzing the fundamental changes that have taken place in the social role of the prepubescent boy.[14] Greater permissiveness in theories of child growth and development have gradually obscured the Victorian notions of a child's proper place in society. Today, he is permitted greater freedom; the fewer restrictions placed upon his activities, the less structured his role becomes. Fewer restrictions in age-role expectations lead to greater variability of acceptable forms and styles of clothing. Hence, the prepubescent boy is no longer restricted to the wearing of knickers.

A similar analysis could be made of the age-role expectations of women. Improved health and the widespread use of youth-preserving cosmetics have blurred the distinctions between adulthood and old age. Grandmothers are no longer confined to the image of Whistler's mother. It is highly probable that if age-roles were more specifically defined, corresponding clothing expectations would be more explicit.

In spite of the increased variability in role and clothing expectations in modern society, there are still discernible patterns associated with age-role and dress. In early adolescence, rigid conformity to the peer group is expected. A twelve-year-old girl is not content with a sweater similar to her friend's —it must be an exact duplicate. Among adult females, however, an exact duplicate of a costume in the same social set would mean disaster. Moreover, it is permissible for a young man in his twenties to engage in activities that will attract the attention of numerous members of the opposite sex. He spends a high proportion of his income on clothes, pays particular attention to the latest changes in fashion, and is accorded the privilege of wearing bright colors, fancy patterns, and extreme styles. A married man with three children, however, would be regarded with some suspicion if he continued such clothing behavior into middle age. A man in his forties is expected to be dressed in good taste and well groomed, but to flaunt in sartorial splendor like a peacock is obviously inviting trouble! Men in their seventies are expected to pay greater attention to their physical comforts in clothes, and their overall appearance is an-

[14]George Bush and Perry London, "On the Disappearance of Knickers: Hypotheses for the Functional Analysis of the Psychology of Clothing," *Journal of Social Psychology* 51, May 1960, pp. 359–366.

ticipated to be somewhat relaxed and subdued. An older man who prefers a more fashionable image than the norm allows runs the risk of being type-cast as a "lecherous old goat."

Age and sex roles are thus arbitrarily ascribed to individuals on a biological basis, and each is associated with a particular set of clothing expectations which are defined in varying degrees of specificity. Sex roles tend to be more clearly defined since they are determined immediately at birth and remain fixed throughout life. Age roles also begin at birth, but follow a pattern of constant change as the individual gradually progresses through a series of chronologically determined statuses.

Occupational roles

Clothing expectations for particular occupational roles have been discussed to some extent in Chapter 9 with respect to clothing symbolism. The study by Form and Stone of white-collar and manual workers revealed a rather clear-cut pattern of established clothing norms. The acceptable garb for office workers proved to be a business suit or a sports jacket worn over shirt and slacks, while manual workers wore uniforms, overalls, or various combinations of old clothes on the job. Office workers tended to evaluate their clothing in terms of a well-groomed appearance and canons of good taste, while the orientations of manual workers were structured in terms of the functional aspect of clothes, i.e., garments were supposed to be efficient and comfortable in order to facilitate maximum work performance and contribute to safety on the job.

Zweig noted similar standards in workers' ideas of dress. Manual workers did not believe in wearing heavy clothes and seldom wore hats or gloves. Men in positions of authority, however, such as foremen or supervisors, were expected to wear better clothes than the laborers, although nothing that would make the distinction too great. "Lack of ostentation is another characteristic of the workers' way of dressing," says Zweig. "Smartness is not valued highly by the majority of them; on the contrary it is treated with suspicion."[15]

Even though the white-collar workers admitted that they like to wear new clothes on the job, most of them felt more at ease if they were able to "break in" such items in a social situation first. Having the benefit of a positive group reaction to their new articles of dress gave them greater security in wearing the new clothes later on the job. Laborers had to wear new clothes first "to get the starch out" of them, so they would be comfortable at work.

Differences also were noted between these same groups of workers in their clothing expectations for the job interview

Figure 10-9. Career apparel has been "sold" on the basis that it gives a company a recognizable public identity, and suggests efficiency and stability. It also eliminates competitive dressing among employees and copes with the problem of extreme fashions that may distract from the professionalism of the job.

[15]Ferdynand Zweig, *The British Worker*, Penguin Books, Harmondsworth, Middlesex, 1952, pp. 157–165.

Figure 10-10. Military uniforms have always been a symbol of occupational role.

A particular set of clothing norms generally is associated with each occupational role; the sanctions used to enforce such norms vary with the status of the occupation.

and specific social situations. When applying for work, office personnel usually dressed up in their best suits, while the majority of manual workers appeared in overalls, work clothes, or trouser and shirt combinations. When asked what they would wear to church or to public meetings, many respondents in both groups suggested that a "best," "blue," "dress," or "conservative" suit would be appropriate. However, a much larger proportion of manual workers did not feel that the suit *had* to be "best," "blue," "dress," or "conservative," and almost a third of them considered sports outfits, trouser and shirt combinations, or simply clean and pressed garments to be acceptable attire for such occasions.[16]

There is considerable evidence that anticipated clothing behavior in many occupational situations has a close relationship to the statuses of the employees or workers. Roth's observations of protective clothing worn by the medical personnel of a state hospital is a case in point.[17] The investigator noted the percentage of doctors, nurses, and other staff wearing surgical caps, gowns, and masks in their contacts with victims of communicable disease. If the use of such garments is effective in preventing the spread of disease to others, it is logical to assume that no distinctions should be made in the category of individuals required to wear them. Fewer than 5 per cent of the doctors, however, wore the surgical garb in their contacts with patients. Roughly a quarter of the professional nurses and about half of the practical nurses were so attired when entering patients' rooms, while aides and student nurses were the only groups who wore the garments faithfully. Thus, the data showed an inverse relationship between the wearing of protective clothing and occupational status level: the lower the status of the employee, the more frequent use of protective clothes. One possible explanation, of course, is that the threat of criticism for not dressing properly increases progressively down the status scale. No one would enforce a sanction against a doctor, but every employee in a position superior to the aides and students could censure them for not protecting themselves.

It is possible to define most occupational positions, however, in terms of the general type of attire which is acceptable or anticipated. A policeman is supposed to wear a blue uniform, the salesman must keep his pants pressed and his shoes polished, and the lawyer must look prosperous enough to inspire confidence in his clients. Low-cut dresses, tight sweaters, and conspicuous jewelry generally are considered to be inappropriate for the secretary, while a college teacher finds that his image is enhanced if he dresses in a fashion that is consistent

[16]Form and Stone, *Social Significance of Clothing,* p. 28.
[17]Julius Roth, "Ritual and Magic in the Control of Contagion," *American Sociological Review* 22, June 1957, pp. 310–314.

CLOTHING AND HUMAN BEHAVIOR

with the role of a professor. At least one study has shown that people who look like professors are judged by others as being more successful in this role than those who fail to meet the appearance expectation.[18] Thus we see that an individual learns to be a doctor or a dressmaker, and in the process, learns the definition of the accompanying statuses and the behavior patterns appropriate to such statuses.

Social roles

All roles are social roles, including those that are *ascribed* on the basis of age and sex, and those that are *achieved* through occupational learning. There are numerous other activities, however, that do not fit into these precise categories, and although the distinction is rarely clear-cut, most people readily perceive a difference between a business situation and a social situation. In the realm of clothing behavior, appropriate or suitable dress is defined largely in terms of social activities, e.g., sportswear, dinner dress, formal attire, etc. Almost any book of etiquette will furnish adequate descriptions of masculine and feminine costumes that are considered "correct" for a wide variety of social functions. The majority of Americans, however, rarely consult the etiquette books unless they find themselves involved in an unfamiliar situation in which they want to create a favorable impression.

Writers of etiquette books would be the first to agree that regional customs and local patterns of behavior strongly influence what is considered proper in any given situation. Campus clothes for college women may be given a relatively abstract description in terms of jeans worn with sweatshirt or tanktop, which may in fact be the predominant norm in universities across the country. But each campus is apt to add its own bit of local color. Eastern colleges tend to differ from western colleges, and clothing norms on urban campuses in the center of a large city are apt to be quite different from those in a small college town.

Another factor that interferes with a predictable set of clothing expectations is the rapid and continuous change that occurs in the social patterns of any dynamic society. Since the end of World War II, America has experienced an increasing degree of informality in patterns of social behavior. The roots of such change lie in economic factors that bring a greatly improved standard of living and increased leisure time to large segments of the middle and lower classes. Upper-class living standards have been flaunted on the television screens, tempting the appetites of all those in lower statuses. At the same time, the speedy and relatively inexpensive reproduction of what once

[18]R. A. Ellis and T. C. Keedy, "Three Dimensions of Status: A Study of Academic Prestige," *Pacific Sociological Review* 3, 1960, pp. 23–28.

Figure 10-11. A professional panhandler projects an image of an honest man fallen on bad times—well-worn shoes and coat, with a touch of past elegance added by a hat to carry off the right combination of pride, poverty, and misfortune.

Figure 10-12. The differences between western and eastern riding costumes illustrate how regional customs determine what is considered proper attire in certain situations.

had been exclusive styles of dress now brings fashion within the reach of the majority. Thus, life in America has become characterized by an endless striving to obtain the material possessions of the next higher social status, while occupants of the upper class find that it is no longer smart to live lavishly.

In spite of the gradual merging of class lines in American society, there are still those inevitable distinctions that must be made between groups or individuals who are widely separated on the status continuum. Even the newer "common sense" books of etiquette are directed toward those who have some opportunity to give formal dinners, attend the opera, fox hunt, or travel abroad. Because such activities are still beyond the reach of those in the lower strata, any mannerisms adopted from the same social code would be considered "putting on airs."

Lack of consensus as to what constitutes the appropriate norm is obvious in the following statement of a woman who was, at the time, having an argument with her husband over the way she was dressed: "Why should I get all dressed up and put on a girdle just to go marketing in my own neighborhood? Lots of other women wear housedresses worse than mine to go shopping, and if anybody I know sees me dressed this way, they won't think anything of it!" One reason for the dispute was that the woman and her husband perceived the norm differently: he was more conscious of the well-dressed women shoppers, while she noticed the women who were dressed more casually than herself. In addition, the man and his wife were affected differently by the potential sanctions of enforcement: he was fearful of the disapproval of others as well as the reflection it might make on his own ability to marry and support an attractive woman; she saw little reward for her efforts to dress up, and her own desire for physical comfort outweighed the cost of any negative reaction. The people she might meet in the supermarket were perceived as exerting little influence over her behavior, and the strongest sanction they could enforce would be to overlook or ignore her appearance.

This kind of disagreement is not resolved by attempting to prove who is right or wrong, but it does illustrate the kinds of social problems that arise when norms are not clearly defined. Americans have been taught to place such a high value on individuality that they resist the idea of any fixed standards for social behavior. Yet the most embarrassing moments occur when an individual does not anticipate the group expectation accurately, or in some way fails to meet the expectation. Some clarification of the social code is necessary to avoid the confusions that stem from our diverse ethnic origins and class mobility. We are prone to pity members of a society who are restricted to prescribed statuses of class or caste, but because their lives are fixed and precisely arranged, they know exactly what is expected of them. "Membership in a rigidly organized society may deprive the individual of opportunities to exercise his particular gifts," Linton wrote, "but it gives him an emotional security which is almost unknown among ourselves."[19]

The fact that norms develop in virtually every aspect of human activity seems to indicate that people have a basic need to validate their opinions and behavior against the opinions and behavior of other individuals and groups in their social milieu. Knowing the ground rules of a society enables the individual to live more comfortably and operate more efficiently within it than he could without such rules to guide him. Social codes take time to learn, and require judgment in applying them to the many situational ramifications to be found in a diverse social system. Adolescents in particular find difficulty in learning the rules fast enough to keep pace with their changing status. Hence, they rely on absolute conformity to peer group behavior in order to protect themselves from social errors. A boy of 13 must have jeans of not only a particular size and color, but of a particular brand name and model, because only then can he be sure that they will meet the required expectation in every detail.

Clothing norms were studied by Wass and Eicher in relation to the role behavior of ninth-grade girls. In the particular school studied, students were free to select their own attire since there were no dress regulations enforced. When students were questioned, however, 83 per cent were under the impression that the school *did* have rules, and 80 per cent felt that all schools *should* have such rules. These teenage girls conformed closely to the norm, and although they indicated that a wider range of garments would be appropriate for each role, the range in garments actually worn was quite limited. Respondents thought that a student should dress more casually for a basketball game than for school, unless she happened to attend the game with a boy. Since she would then play the role of somebody's "date," they believed that dressier clothes would be required. Moreover, these ninth graders felt that certain roles were so specific in regard to dress requirements that they often did not participate in an activity because they lacked the appropriate costume. In many cases, the girls indicated that they had gone places when their dress was inappropriate and then wished that they had not gone. It was apparent from this study that clothing was chosen in relation to specific roles, often changed when the roles changed, and frequently influenced the behavior of the wearer. In addition, when there was no formal dress code in operation, the group established its own.[20]

An individual's security and success in any given social role are directly related to his accuracy in estimating the clothing expectations of the group.

[19]Linton, *The Study of Man*, p. 131.
[20]Betty Wass and Joanne Eicher, "Clothing as Related to Role Behavior of Teenage Girls," *Quarterly Bulletin* 47, no. 2, Michigan State University Agricultural Experiment Station, November 1964, pp. 206–213.

Common notions of appropriate dress for a variety of social situations help an individual learn the behavioral expectations for particular role categories. In our society, the most obvious distinctions in dress are made on the basis of ascribed age and sex roles. Virtually all societies assign a different set of clothing expectations to males and to females, and violation of the established norms by either sex may be met with negative sanctions, although the costs are usually greater for the male. Although clothing expectations for various age categories rarely are enforced as rigidly as they are for sex roles, society maintains some differentiation in clothing norms for each stage in the life cycle.

Most occupational roles may be defined in terms of the general type of attire which is considered appropriate for the position. Part of the training for an occupation or profession includes learning the clothing behavior that will project an accurate image. Suitable or proper attire is defined largely in terms of specific social activities, but the degree of consensus as to what constitutes the going norm will vary with the group. Factors that interfere with the establishment of predictable clothing expectations include (1) the influence of regional customs and local patterns, (2) the rapid and continuous social change in American society, (3) inevitable distinctions between classes of people widely separated on the status continuum, and (4) qualifying circumstances peculiar to the situation. In spite of the high value that many Americans place on individuality, most people instinctively desire to conform to the expectations of the group.

Role learning and portrayal

Costumes that are designed for the stage must reinforce the character to be played and help the audience visualize the dominant traits of the role. From early childhood on, the individual in society learns and rehearses the social roles he will enact in life, and his clothing is as essential to the successful performance of these roles as the costume is to the actor. Just as the costume designer must be able to identify the distinctive features of the part and translate these into visual symbols of dress, the individual must learn to identify his role and acquire the appropriate symbols of dress and behavior.

Role differentiation and identification

In the preceding unit we discussed sex role as one of the first categories to which an individual was assigned. One of the earliest distinctions that a child learns to make regarding himself and others is that some people are boys and others are girls, and clothing and dress are often the initial criteria used by children to make such differentiations.[21] Many preschool youngsters find it impossible to make sex distinctions in the absence of these symbols.

A number of investigations have been conducted which shed some light on the way in which children begin to discern specific role distinctions. Weese studied the preschool child's capacity to recognize the sex appropriateness of selected items of dress and appearance.[22] Data from the study indicated that both boys and girls were able to identify female articles (e.g., lady's blouse, brassiere, hosiery, etc.) more accurately than masculine articles (man's shirt, necktie, socks, and so forth). Girls were found to be more accurate than boys in the sex designation of such appearance items, while boys were more accurate in the sex designation of task items (egg beater, iron, wooden spoon; wrench, screw driver, pliers, and so forth). These findings suggest that the feminine role is more readily identified because preschool children spend most of their day in the female environment of the mother or nursery school teacher, while the father works away from home. This is coupled with the fact that American mothers often take on elements of masculine dress, while the reverse pattern is rarely true. Moreover, in the basic process of role learning, the child begins to think, feel, act, and become like the *significant other* person(s) in his environment; in most cases, this is the parent of the same sex. Through such identification, girls take on the attitudes and interests of the mother, and boys take on the identity of the father. Thus, it appears that by the age of three or four, girls have developed more of the mother's interest in clothes, while boys seem to be more aware of the symbols of work orientation.

An earlier study by Brown also indicated that children tend to develop relatively dichotomous sex role impressions early in life.[23] The investigator constructed a child-figure drawing that was sexless in appearance and used it in relation to pictures of various articles of clothing and other objects and activities commonly associated with masculine or feminine roles. Eighty-five per cent of the boys and 45 per cent of the girls assigned the "it" figure to a sex category that was consistent with their own. The tendency to show strong opposite-sex preference or mixed masculine-feminine preferences was more frequent in girls than in boys—that is, boys tended to show a more clear-cut preference for masculine roles than

Figure 10-13. Traditionally, clothing expectations for the male role in American society have been rigidly explicit. Compliance to such prescribed patterns of dress produced a picture of multiple carbon copies.

[21]H. Conn and L. Kanner, "Children's Awareness of Sex Differences," *Journal of Child Psychiatry* 1, 1947, pp. 3–57.
[22]Audray L'H. Weese, "Cultural Objects and Apparent Symbols as Sex Discernment Factors Among Preschool Children," Master's thesis, Michigan State University, 1964.
[23]Daniel G. Brown, "Sex-Role Preferences in Young Children," *Psychological Monographs* 70, no. 14, 1956, pp. 1–19.

CLOTHES, ROLES, AND STATUS

girls did for feminine roles. This is not surprising in view of our earlier discussion of child-rearing practices and parental sanctions involving the child's behavior. A little girl's tomboy activities are often rewarded as much as her lady-like behavior, while boys experience no such freedom in the assumption of ambiguous roles.

This also helps to explain why appropriate men's attire is defined in such specific minutia of detail. When punishment is consistently applied for not conforming to the appropriate type of role behavior, the expectations attached to a position or category become clarified. If an individual understands clearly what is expected of him, role learning is greatly facilitated. The female, on the other hand, has a more difficult time learning the behavior which is appropriate to her role because she is confronted with an ambiguous set of expectations. Her clothing, therefore, reflects a much wider range of acceptable patterns.

The expectations assigned to the age role of the adolescent is another case in point. His role behavior is ambiguously defined, and he finds himself treated like a child one minute and like an adult the next. His adoption of numerous bizarre fads in rapid succession reflects the instability of his role and the lack of consensus surrounding its expectations.

Thus, we see that "proper" attire can be more explicitly defined when role expectations are clear-cut. A sensible approach to the study of suitable or appropriate clothing requires the student to follow a logical pattern of reasoning. He must first be able to identify the role he wishes to play. (This is not often as simple as it sounds, for all people play a number of overlapping and sometimes conflicting roles.) Second, he must devise a method for determining the degree of consensus that exists regarding the norms associated with that role, and must be able to visualize such role requirements in terms of appropriate clothing symbols.

A high degree of consensus in the definition of role expectations results in fairly stable, limited, and prescribed patterns of appropriate dress; ambiguity or lack of clarity in role definition increases the variability of acceptable clothing styles.

Figure 10-14. The costume is the fastest way to declare a role.

Role enactment

It is not enough for an actor to identify his part in the play; he must somehow acquire the look, the mannerisms, the gestures, the skills, and the feelings of the character he is to portray. The performer learns a single role in a relatively short period of time. The individual in society often learns several roles simultaneously, and the process extends over a lifetime.

An actor's success in conveying the meaning of a role to the audience is greatly enhanced by skillful costuming. In describing his approach to the designs for Kate in Shakespeare's *The Taming of the Shrew*, a costumer explains how he focused on the dominant trait of the character. Her volatile temper was symbolized throughout the play by the repeated use of red, beginning with a rich cherry red velvet gown in the first scene. As the action of the play progressed, the tones of red for her successive costumes became more and more subdued:

> When the (final) curtain rises, we see Kate in a soft pink chiffon gown, the decolletage rounded and softened with pearl trim, her hair falls softly down her back. We feel reasonably sure that Petruchio, her husband, has finally tamed the shrew. . . . Petruchio quizzes her about her constancy, we see her chin tip up jauntily—then she turns quickly on her unsuspecting husband, and we see as she turns, a brilliant red petticoat peek from beneath the cloud of pink chiffon making the final statement, as Shakespeare does, that one never really tames a shrew.[24]

Role enactment, then, refers to the actual performance of the role which either validates or invalidates the expectations associated with it—in other words, the ability of the individual "to carry it off."

In the learning of new social roles, the neophyte usually identifies with an experienced occupant of the same position, and by copying the latter's actions, he soon acquires an understanding of the appropriate norms and values. A college freshman, for example, will usually look to the sophomore or upperclassman for cues that will guide his clothing behavior. In most cases, the more opportunity one has to familiarize himself with the norms and values of his particular group, the more apt he is to conform to them. It also follows that the greater his conformity to group expectations, the greater will be his acceptance by the group.

Role enactment also implies the interaction that takes place between the role and the self. We have already seen how the self develops out of a series of role-taking experiences in which the individual is placed in various counterpositions to significant others. The evaluation of the self is thus made in terms of how well he enacts a given role. In each new role, the neophyte sees himself through the eyes of his role partners, and in the process adds another dimension to his concept of self. For example, the fashion merchandising student gradually learns and takes on the clothing behavior of the fashion buyer. As she is recognized by others as a fashion buyer, she begins to see herself as a fashion buyer. If she is unable to develop the associated clothing behavior, few people recognize her role assignment, and her self-image is weakened.

The cogency of one's performance is dependent not only upon the person's ability to perceive the exact dimensions of the role, but upon his skill in projecting such perceptions into observable behavior.

Figure 10-15. The cogency of one's performance in a role is clothing-related. It would be difficult to accept a man in the attire pictured here in the role of a business executive.

One criterion used in the evaluation of a person's role performance is the skill with which he translates clothing expectations into congruent clothing behavior.

---

[24]Leon Brauner, "Character Portrayal Through Costume," speech given at Western Regional Clothing and Textiles Meeting, Logan, Utah, October 1964.

SUMMARY *Role learning and portrayal*

Clothing is an obvious and visual symbol by which an individual learns to identify and differentiate specific social roles. When a high degree of consensus exists regarding the definition of a role, the associated clothing expectations tend to be fairly explicit. Appropriate attire for men, therefore, is more narrowly prescribed than it is for women, because the masculine role is more consistently and rigidly defined. A study of what is considered suitable or proper dress may be approached through (1) the identification of the role, (2) a survey of the clothing norms associated with the role, and (3) the ascertainment of the degree of consensus surrounding such norms.

The cogency of one's performance in a given role depends upon the accurate perception of clothing *expectations* and their subsequent translation into observable and congruent clothing *behavior*. In the process of role enactment, the interaction which takes place between the *role* and the *self* causes the individual to evaluate himself through the eyes of his role partners, and the concept of self is altered accordingly.

Variation in role performance

Conflict often arises from the fact that an individual always occupies more than one role in society. Mrs. Smith, for example, is not only a woman; she is also a wife, a mother, a church worker, a part-time teacher, a sorority alumna, a PTA member, a musician, and a participant in numerous other activities in the community. Whenever the requirements for any two of these roles are conflicting or incompatible, problem situations develop. In the case of clothing behavior, such problems are usually resolved through compromise or deviation from the normative expectation.

Clothing compromises

One type of conflict that is often manifest in clothing behavior is incompatibility between certain role requirements and the self. Maryellen, for example, aspires to be a fashion coordinator. Fashion coordinators represent people who have a talent for combining costumes, colors, and accessories in new and unusual ways; their refinement of taste should be coupled with an inventiveness that one expects to see reflected in their own attire. Maryellen is considerably overweight; she refrains from buying new clothes because she vows to go on a diet and does not want to invest in dresses that will soon be too big for her. She never did like extreme styles because they only serve to call attention to her figure, and she prefers to be inconspicuous anyway. She knows she does not *look* like a fashion coordinator, but she argues that this should not interfere with her ability to do the work. The wide discrepancy between Maryellen and the expected image portends difficulty. Brophy's study of the self and role requirements led him to conclude "that congruence in the intrapersonal relationship between the self concept and the ideal self is one of the most fundamental conditions for both general happiness and for satisfaction in specific life areas."[25]

Another form of conflict may be observed when the requirements of one role are incompatible with the requirements of another role. Women are commonly subjected to conflicting expectations in their adult sex roles. A girl's family or teachers often exert pressures toward professional pursuits and expect her to utilize her capacities to their maximum. Her desire for male friends encourages a leaning toward the typical homemaker role, and she may even perceive scholastic achievement as a threat to her femininity. Such vacillation creates a desire for fussy, feminine clothes one day and the garb of a tomboy the next.

Fortunately, all roles do not have to be played simultaneously. When a man comes home from the office he usually sheds his business clothes and dons his "family clothes" — perhaps a comfortable pair of slacks, a sport shirt, and sweater. His role as a businessman becomes latent, and his family roles come into play. If it happens to be lodge night, he sets aside his family roles, puts on his fez, and becomes a Shriner for three hours. When conflicting roles are separated by a time interval, the individual is usually able to handle both successfully. The career woman can be efficient and detached sitting behind her desk in a smartly tailored suit, but after five o'clock she can slip into something sheer, lacy, and feminine, and be as sexy as she pleases.

In addition to this kind of role segregation, people play their roles with varying degrees of involvement that may range all the way from casual or minimal interaction to intense participation in the role. The woman in the supermarket, for example, performed her role as a shopper with a minimum of involvement; she was a shopper for less than an hour or two, she collected her groceries in automatic fashion, and she was not particularly concerned about the opinions of the people she might meet there. If it rained, or if a friend came to visit, she might even postpone her shopping role to another time. In her professional role, however, she is apt to be considerably more involved.

Thus, in almost all role enactment, the individual establishes priorities of importance and decides which role will take precedence over another. The teenager's pants style or hair style may

---

[25]Alfred L. Brophy, "Self, Role, and Satisfaction," *Genetic Psychology Monographs* 59, May 1959, p. 300.

If an individual is unable to segregate conflicting roles, he tends to meet the clothing requirements of the role that takes precedence in his hierarchy of values.

be frowned upon by parents, and school officials may even impose regulations against them, but the high-school boy will wear them anyway because he is more intensely involved with his social role in the peer group than he is as a student.

Deviation in role performance

Earlier in this chapter we indicated that considerable variation may exist in the clarity or consensus with which roles are defined. Certain roles and statuses expressed through clothing, such as those of the army captain or the Eagle Scout, are defined in highly specific terms. The role of a student, however, could be defined in terms of almost any individual between six and sixty. Since the category is so broad, it encompasses a wide range of acceptable clothing behavior.

Usually when there is a high degree of consensus concerning appropriate role behavior, even the slightest departure from the norm would be regarded as a deviation. As we saw in our previous discussions, however, deviance is a matter of social definition rather than a characteristic of behavior per se. The definition of what one "should" wear may be interpreted differently by different people. The mother of a high-school teenager nearly went into a state of shock when Jimmy arrived to pick up her daughter: he was wearing swimming trunks in an open convertible, in the middle of winter, and it was starting to snow. To the mother, Jimmy was a "naked imbecile," a deviant of the first order. To the daughter, Jimmy was merely conforming to the norms of the Polar Bear Club whose members take midwinter dips in Lake Michigan.

Most individuals make an honest effort to meet the role expectations of society. There are those groups of individuals who consider themselves "above" or "beneath" or "beyond" the dictates of fashion, such as the "underdressed snobs" described by Russell Lynes, who "wouldn't be caught dead at a cocktail party" in cocktail dresses.[26] It is all a matter of conforming to the clothing expectations of the group with which we identify. New social situations, however, present some problems to newcomers, who have not yet had the opportunity to clarify the roles they must play. It is far easier to conform to explicitly defined dress standards than it is to guess at the limitations of roles which are nebulously constituted.

In recent years, we have seen the limited adoption of what has been labeled "identity clothing," that is, a kind of unspecialized dress worn for all occasions. Charles Reich described such "new clothes" as expressing a "wholeness of self.

---

[26]For a humorous treatise on dress snobs, see Russell Lynes, *Snobs,* Harper and Brothers, New York, 1950. He maintains that everyone is a snob of one sort or another.

. . . There is not one set of clothes for the office, another for social life, a third for play. The same clothes can be used for every imaginable activity, and so they say that it is the same person doing all these things—not a set of different masks or dolls but one many-sided, *whole* individual."[27] By the same token, Reich claims, the individual is not limited to a single role, but can pick up "whatever new and spontaneous thing may come along."

According to the "new" philosophy, an individual may be a court jester one day, a cowboy the next, a sheik the next—whatever happens to suit his fancy. Psychologist Erik Erikson sees this constant thirst for novelty and newness as an identity crisis for the whole nation. The proliferation of changes in everyday lifestyles of dress and behavior, he says, "are in some circles on their way to becoming a matter of obsession, as if any more defined identity were only too much conformity, and only absolute choice were freedom."[28] He believes that this has greatly disturbed our sense of reality.

At the same time that some groups avidly seek a release from formalized role expectations, many more have found new ways to meet the social requirements of dress. The rental and sale of formalwear, for example—particularly men's wear—has expanded to nearly thirty times the volume of ten years ago.[29] Just the fact that the big chains like Sears, Roebuck and Montgomery Ward have entered the formalwear rental business in a big way is sufficient indication that the demand for such attire is growing among the mass consumers.

Everyone deviates from clothing norms to some extent, because one cannot always know precisely what is expected. Or, people may know what is expected, but because of the pressure of conflicting role requirements, they choose to deviate from one set of norms in order to conform to the requirements of the more valued role. The most obvious deviate, of course, is the person who knows the requirements and deliberately sets out to violate them. There is some research evidence that such individuals demonstrate a general disorientation to society. Even within a so-called normal population of college women, consistent clothing preferences were found to be highly related to social maturity and positive feelings toward society, while people who were socially ambivalent tended to fluctuate in their clothing behavior.[30] In another study of adolescent boys, nearly

Deviation in clothing behavior may be a manifestation of one's misunderstanding of the norm, strain between conflicting roles, or feelings of hostility toward society.

[27]Reich, *The Greening of America*, p. 235.
[28]Erik Erikson as quoted in "Truth is Newness in America," *Washington Post* Service news release, 13 June 1973.
[29]Les Gilbert, "Sears, Ward's to Expand Formalwear Rentals," *Daily News Record*, 4 May 1973.
[30]Donna Ditty, "Social-Psychological Aspects of Clothing Preferences of College Women," Unpublished dissertation, Ohio State University, 1962.

CLOTHES, ROLES, AND STATUS

"This daily metamorphosis never fails to amaze me. Around the house, I'm a perfect idiot. I come to court, put on a black robe, and, by God, I'm it!"

Figure 10-16. In each new role the neophyte sees himself through the eyes of his role partners. The "props" of costume can bolster one's self-image in the enactment of such roles—real or imaginary. Drawing by Handelsman; © 1971 The New Yorker Magazine, Inc.

one-third of those who deviated from the clothing norm were found to be social isolates.[31]

Transitions in role and status

Thus far, we have treated role and status as relatively stable elements in the social system, with variation attributable largely to the way in which individuals or subgroups meet the associated clothing expectations. Roles and statuses themselves, however, undergo certain changes. In addition to the daily shifts in role occupancy, there are transitions that occur as a person passes through the successive stages of the life cycle. Then there are the long-term social changes that alter the way in which roles and statuses are defined.

As we have seen, the role occupancy of an individual may shift several times during the day, as well as from day to day, and many of these shifts require a change of attire. In most cases, such change provides a welcome relief from monotony. Other shifts occur as the person passes successively from childhood to adolescence to adulthood and old age. In the case of adolescence, role requirements are redefined in terms of the peer group, and values attached to former patterns established within the context of the family no longer seem appropriate. As we mentioned earlier, the ambiguity with which adolescent roles are often defined, as well as the conflict between peer and family expectations, leads the teenager into confusion. On the other hand, clothing sometimes helps to clarify one's new status: the first dark suit for the boy's confirmation or bar mitzvah, the girl's first formal dress or the first pair of high heels—these are the badges of advanced status and greater privilege.

A larger wardrobe or a new fur coat may be the manifestations of changes in the economic status of the family. The increased upward mobility of large segments of the population necessitates the redefinition of many roles in terms of changing social statuses. A family may move from a rural area to the city, or from the city to the suburbs. Each of these changes results in a different set of clothing expectations.

Changing social patterns also affect gradual transitions in the attitudes and expectations associated with given roles. The deliberations of the Pope's Ecumenical Council in the 1960's resulted in a radical revision of Roman Catholic doctrine, and the impact will be felt for many years to come. A modernizing of the habits of various religious orders has taken place, and most nuns have returned to secular dress in the execution of their more worldly responsibilities.

Clothing once served to separate the aristocracy from the lower working classes; appropriate attire for a Negro slave, for

[31]Patricia Lee, "The Relation of Deviation from Clothing Norms of Eleventh Grade Male Students and Peer Acceptance," Master's thesis, University of Nevada, 1969. It should be noted that the "clothing deviants" in this study included fashion innovators and independents as well as counterconformists.

example, was fairly well established a century ago. Within the last decade, progress in the Civil Rights Movement, coupled with a rising standard of living for all classes of people, has greatly reduced the distinctions that formerly were made in clothing expectations.

Increased leisure time and the mass move to suburbia have produced a greater demand for casual, informal clothes, and at the same time have created an unprecedented participation in active sports. Woman's entrance into the field of sports as well as her increased acceptance in the business and political worlds have had tremendous influence in reshaping the clothing expectations of women's roles. The same kinds of social changes have produced concomitant alterations in men's dress.

SUMMARY *Variation in role performance*

People occupy a number of social roles, some of which may be incompatible in terms of their clothing requirements. If an individual is unable to segregate conflicting roles by a time interval, he tends to favor the requirements of the role in which he feels more intensely involved. Some roles may be inconsistent with one's self-concept; when this occurs, the person usually attempts to resolve the conflict by resorting to one or more of the ego defense mechanisms. Such role conflict often results in deviation from the expected norms of clothing behavior. Everyone deviates to some extent from clothing norms because many role requirements lack a clarity of definition; thus, people cannot always know precisely what is expected of them. In addition, norms are shared by different individuals and subgroups, so that the degree of consensus on normative behavior may vary widely. Those who know the rules of clothing behavior and deliberately set out to violate them demonstrate a negative response to social expectancies.

Role occupancy not only shifts from day to day, but it changes as the individual passes through successive stages of the life cycle. Role requirements are usually redefined in terms of a new reference group. Other shifts, such as class mobility or change in location, also result in a changing set of clothing expectations. Over the years, numerous transitions in social patterns have modified our conceptions of what constitutes proper dress.

FOR FURTHER READING

Laver, James. *Modesty in Dress.* Boston: Houghton Mifflin Company, 1969. (Chapter 13, "Male and Female Created He Them.")

Linton, Ralph. *The Study of Man.* New York: D. Appleton-Century Company, 1936. (Chapter 8, "Status and Role.")

Changes in the clothing of an individual are indicative of changes in his social roles and status.

Figure 10-17. Evolving social patterns affect transitions in clothing expectations associated with given roles. The traditional attire of the Irish Dominican Order, garb carried over from the thirteenth century, is shown at left. On the right, a member of the Mission Sisters of the Holy Ghost, whose order calls for habit-updating every five years.

Miller, Sister Mary C. and M. E. Roach. "Religious Garb: Significant or Sentimental," *Journal of Home Economics* 58, November 1966, pp. 731–734.

Rosencranz, Mary Lou. *Clothing Concepts.* New York: Macmillan Publishing Company, 1972. (Part Three, "Role.")

Secord, P., and C. Backman. *Social Psychology.* New York: McGraw-Hill Book Company, 1974. (Chapter 13, "Social Roles," and Chapter 14, "Role Strain and its Resolution.")

"The Surprising Story of Career Apparel," *American Fabrics,* Winter 1971, pp. 55–66.

DISCUSSION QUESTIONS

1. Specifically, what are some of the contemporary symbols of masculinity (or femininity) in dress and appearance? Do you agree with Gernreich that unisex clothing will be the inevitable outcome of the current trend toward sexual equality? Why or why not?

2. Explain how role learning takes place.

3. In the promotion of career apparel, use of the term "uniform" has been carefully avoided. How do you think most people react to this kind of symbolic identification of occupational role? Why? In what kinds of occupations would a uniform be essential?

4. What are "regional differences" in clothing expectations? Give one or two specific examples.

5. What are some of the factors that may account for an individual's failure to meet the clothing expectations for a particular role?

6. How do Erikson and Reich differ with respect to the concept of "role clothes"?

7. In a new social situation, how would you go about identifying the clothing expectations associated with a particular role?

8. Explain what is meant by the statement, "Deviance is a matter of social definition."

11

Differentiation in the Mass Society

MORE THAN HALF a century ago, George Dearborn observed that one's social movements are determined more by clothing than many have ever stopped to think or to realize.[1] He maintained that a person's raiment influenced how much one went out, both into the street and into society in general; where he went and with whom he associated; the job he was able to get and to hold; the job he missed or lost. Thorstein Veblen's observations of the relation between dress and social class were also made before the developing theories of social stratification found their base in empirical fact. While behavioral scientists still argue a good deal over the precise definitions of class and status, there is fairly general agreement that (1) all people in society are ranked in terms of a prestige hierarchy, and (2) one's style of life is a criterion commonly used to make such ranking.

Clothes are an important part of the material possessions and patterns of behavior that constitute one's lifestyle. In this chapter we shall consider some of the ways in which clothing both influences and reflects the caste and class distinctions that are observable in American society. We also shall be concerned with the function of dress as it relates to class consciousness, group identification, and social mobility.

Clothes and class distinctions

In terms of the democratic ideal, social class distinctions may seem inconsistent with the philosophical declaration that all men are created equal. Yet in every human society, some individuals stand higher than others in the community.

The earliest status symbols may be traced all the way back to Paleolithic times, when the hunter adorned himself with the antlers or the skins of animals he had killed as a badge of his achievement. The leader of any sect or tribe is usually accorded

[1]George Dearborn, "The Psychology of Clothing," *Psychological Monographs* 24, no. 1, 1918.

some mark of distinction in dress in order to signify his position. From these beginnings a complex set of status differentiations evolved. Some of these symbols are observed more easily than others, such as the crowns worn by kings and queens; the robes that distinguish the Pope, the cardinals, the bishops, and other officials in the ecclesiastical hierarchy; academic gowns that mark one's degree of scholastic attainment; uniforms of the general, the major, the sergeant, the private; and the myriad of other symbols that identify the policeman, the nun, the jurist, the nurse, the mailman, the pilot, the cook, and the doorman.

There are, however, more subtle forms of clothing status symbols. Veblen's theory has become a classic explanation of this function of clothes:

> Our dress, in order to serve its purpose effectually, should not only be expensive, but it should also make plain to all observers that the wearer is not engaged in any kind of productive labour. . . . The pleasing effect of neat and spotless garments is chiefly, if not altogether, due to their carrying the suggestion of leisure — exemption from personal contact with industrial processes of any kind. Much of the charm that invests the patent-leather shoe, the stainless linen, the lustrous cylindrical hat, and the walking stick, which so greatly enhance the native dignity of a gentleman, comes of their pointedly suggesting that the wearer cannot when so attired bear a hand in any employment that is directly and immediately of any human use. Elegant dress serves its purpose of elegance not only in that it is expensive, but also because it is the insignia of leisure.[2]

Modern writers have attacked Veblen's thesis on the grounds that our improved standard of living now makes leisure and patent leather shoes available to all. Nevertheless, any article or costume that will gain for the wearer a feeling of recognition, approval, or belonging may be considered a manifestation of the search for status. Evidence in support of status seeking as a paramount force in clothing behavior is furnished by a number of empirical studies. Evans' investigation of motives in the clothing behavior of adolescents revealed that in 50 per cent of the cases the desire to wear clothing which would win recognition from others was the most intense desire determining the clothing wearing behavior of both boys and girls.[3] In Ryan's study of college women, reasons given most often for the importance of being well dressed related to the social contribution made by clothing. This category of responses included statements such as, "it creates a better impression on people," "popularity has much to do with one's appearance," "to get anywhere we have to impress others," "people judge others by what they wear," and so forth.[4]

[2]Thorstein Veblen, *The Theory of the Leisure Class,* Modern Library, New York, reprinted 1931, pp. 170–171.
[3]S. E. Evans, "Motivations Underlying Clothing Selection and Wearing," *Journal of Home Economics* 56, 1964, p. 743.
[4]Mary S. Ryan, *Psychological Effects of Clothing, Part I,* Cornell University Agricultural Experiment Station Bulletin 882, 1952, p. 24.

The extent to which people themselves identify their own class association is indicated by their common references to "our kind of people." Members of the same social class, therefore, intermingle because they tend to share the same values and have a certain unity of outlook. In this way, groups set themselves apart from others and form that which we term a social **class,** i.e., a group of people of similar status or prestige in the community whose members have intimate access to one another. This type of social stratification differs markedly from that of the **caste** system, in which upward mobility is restricted and intermarriage between members of different castes is taboo. Caste distinctions usually are made more visible through such physical signs as skin color (in the case of the American Negro) or symbolic differentiation in dress.

> Caste membership is hereditary (by ascription), whereas class membership typically starts that way but is subject to shift through achievement. Actually classes exist within castes: for example, there is a quite elaborate class system among Negroes, based partly on wealth, occupation, and style of life, as in the parent system, but also including such characteristics as respectability and even degree of pigmentation.[5]

In any case, stratification is a reality in every community.

Indices of social status

People are stratified into classes on the basis of a number of different criteria. Each person acquires his initial status from the position of the family into which he is born; but in addition to this kinship relationship, other badges of class affiliation include one's wealth or income, authority, power, occupation, education, achievement, manners, tastes, appearance, clothes, and other possessions. The degree of value placed upon these various indices is a matter of local designation; classes are defined differently in Newport than they are in Newark; upbringing may be heavily weighted in Larchmont, but money talks in Las Vegas. In small communities where people are well known, the emphasis is likely to be placed on family background and personal attributes, but in large cities there is a tendency to rely more heavily on the common criterion of money and what it will buy. For the majority of Americans, however, prestige is closely tied to occupation. In almost all studies of status characteristics, occupational rankings prove to be important determinants of social class ascription. Moreover, there is fairly widespread agreement on which occupations rank high in status and which rank low.[6]

---

[5]Berelson and Steiner, *Human Behavior,* p. 460.
[6]R. W. Hodge, P. M. Siegel, and P. H. Rossi, "Occupational Prestige in the United States: 1925–1963," *American Journal of Sociology* 70, November 1964, pp. 286–302.

Although the economic significance of occupation makes it a most reliable single indicator of prestige, there are other manifestations of money that may, in the long run, be more important: "Even wealth and income are not in America the ultimate badges of belonging: they are currency to be converted in time into the 'right kind' of associations and thus into the 'right kind' of manners, clothes, behavior, in which each person shapes himself to the model of the class to which he aspires."[7]

One's style of life and accompanying patterns of consumption, therefore, are the more visible indices of status. Lynes agrees that class distinctions in the American social system are based not so much upon wealth as they are upon differences in cultural tastes. The "high-brows," he claims, are a class of elite intelligentsia who affect a shaggy indifference to dress in their comfortable (albeit not inexpensive) Harris tweed suits. The "low-brow," on the other hand, has no fashionable tastes whatever and would not recognize a Harris tweed if he saw it. By far the largest in number, the "middle-brow" conforms to all the conventional codes in his search for culture and a better life.[8]

Barber and Lobel's analysis of women's fashions from 1930 to 1950 gave some empirical support to such a theory of differentiation in dress among the social classes.[9] The investigators concluded that the women at the top of the American social class system — those from the "old money" families having an established position of status preeminence for several generations — had little need to demonstrate their superiority through conspicuously fashionable attire. Their tastes in dress were distinctly more British than French, with a preference for "well-bred" tweeds and classic woolens. Most of the high fashion was found in the social class just below the "old money" families. Paris originals provided these women with clothing symbols that were related to wealth and high living rather than to family connection. In the middle and lower classes, clothes were observed to be conservative but smart (where "smart" was interpreted to mean what everybody else was wearing). High styles were regarded with some distaste, and extreme or daring clothes were avoided. Similar findings were reported in a more recent study. In an analysis of three different groups of homemakers, Francl found that the group holding the lowest status position made the most conservative fashion choices.[10]

[7]Max Lerner, *America as a Civilization*, Vol. 2, Simon & Schuster, New York, 1957, p. 528.

[8]See "High-Brow, Low-Brow, Middle-Brow," *Life*, 11 April 1949, pp. 99–102; also Russell Lynes, *The Tastemakers*, Harper and Brothers, New York, 1954.

[9]Bernard Barber and Lyle Lobel, "Fashion in Women's Clothes and the American Social System," *Social Forces* 31, 1952, pp. 124–131.

[10]Janell Francl, "Fashion Choices Associated with Values of Homemakers," Master's thesis, Iowa State University, 1970.

Vener's findings also appear to be consistent with such observations. His data showed that clothing increased in importance to the individual as the person's social status increased, although clothing was given the highest importance by the medium-high status group, and was ranked as less important by the highest status group.[11] This same pattern was reported by Snow, who found that interest in clothing increased with education up to the level of college attendance, and then seemed to decline as more education was acquired. There was a relatively high degree of clothing interest among attorneys, salesmen, and school teachers, while factory workers attached the least importance to clothes.[12]

In addition, personal estimates of clothing importance have been found to be directly related to social participation, i.e., those who place a greater emphasis on clothes tend to be more socially active. A fairly early study of social stratification described the lower-status female as one whose activities were confined to the tasks of housekeeping and child rearing. Her wardrobe was correspondingly limited. Upper-class women, on the other hand, were absorbed in extended social affairs, and their personal costumes were "multiple in number."[13] Similar relationships between clothing and social participation have been found among males as well as females,[14] among the elderly[15] as well as among the young.[16]

On the surface, it would seem that the youth of the seventies openly rejected the use of clothing as a status symbol. "Minimal wardrobes of jeans and shirts, worn until they fell apart, were a sacrificial purge of parents' overstuffed closets. The young were wearing the cumulative guilt of a rich society like a hair shirt." "This," said Johnston, "was a direct and dishevelled challenge to the impeccable dress of the establishment."[17] To be sure, there has always been a small yet influential minority of young people whose parents had sufficient wealth for them to make a mockery of fine clothes. The "Pepsi Proletariat" costume consisted of "overalls, flannel shirt, and heavy work

Figure 11-1. Bib overalls, hard hats, and work boots were elevated to fashion status in the early 1970's.

[11]Arthur Vener, "Stratification Aspects of Clothing Importance," Master's thesis, Michigan State College, 1953.

[12]Janet Snow, "Clothing Interest in Relation to Specified Socio-Economic Factors of Men in Four Selected Occupations," Master's thesis, Texas Woman's University, 1969.

[13]J. Useem, P. Tangent, and R. Useem, "Stratification in a Prairie Town," *American Sociological Review* 7, 1942, pp. 331–342.

[14]Elizabeth Harrison, "Clothing Interest and Social Participation of College Men as Related to Clothing Selection and Buying Processes," Master's thesis, University of Tennessee, 1968.

[15]Marian Moore, "The Clothing Market of Older Women," Unpublished dissertation, Purdue University, 1968.

[16]Patricia Lindley, "The Relationship of Dress and Grooming to the Success of the Mexican-American Student in a Selected High School," Master's thesis, Texas Technological College, 1968.

[17]Moira Johnston, "What Will Happen to the Gray Flannel Suit?" *Journal of Home Economics* 64, November 1972, p. 6.

boots, the traditional accouterments of the working class."[18] The outfit could have been bought cheaply enough at the local Sears store, but, the wearers explained, "We buy all our clothes in New York. My work boots came from a groovy leather store, and we got our overalls at a hip boutique."

For the vast numbers of young people who subsequently followed the lead, however, the adoption of such clothing hardly represented an identification with the working classes. To them, bib overalls became the new status symbol of the upper classes.

The high and the mighty

Historically, the American aristocracy was built upon a monied class of people who amassed their fortunes through a peculiar combination of good luck, personal ingenuity, and plain hard work. The men who achieved great financial success in the nineteenth century—the miners, the manufacturers, the merchants, and the railroad builders—were a breed apart from the traditional European aristocracy who passed their inherited wealth along the blood lines of a ruling class. American society was thus based upon a strong philosophy of upward mobility.

There is, to be sure, a cluster of families in the United States who derive their prestige from a blood relationship to the "first families" of New England, New York, and Virginia. The third and fourth generations of the industrial and business magnates also received a family heritage that ultimately emphasized one's lineage and kinship connections in the admission requirements to high society. In addition, there have been numerous examples of American heiresses who earned their tickets to positions of prestige by marrying into the royal families of Europe. Today, there is hardly any royalty left, even for the royalty to marry. Consequently, in more recent years, many status positions have been turned over to the celebrities of the mass media. Despite this shift in character of the upper class, these are the people who are the tastemakers of American society. They have both the money and the social prestige to make their lifestyle one which the masses seek to emulate.

Certainly one of the most tangible measures of status and prestige as far as clothing is concerned, the annual "Best-Dressed List" publicly identified those individuals who had a significant influence on contemporary dress. Even to be considered for the BDL a woman had to spend between $20,000 and $100,000 a year on her clothes, exclusive of jewelry. It is reported that Jackie Onassis spent more than $1.2 million on clothes during the first year of her marriage to the Greek

Clothes are symbolic indicators of status, and as such they obtain recognition, approval, or identification for the individual.

"Do you have something a little more garish? We're nouveaux riches."

Figure 11-2. Drawing by D. Fradon; © 1969 by The New Yorker Magzine, Inc.

---

[18]Blair Sabol and Lucian Truscott, "The Politics of the Costume," *Esquire,* May 1971, p. 124.

228

tycoon. But money is not everything. Elizabeth Taylor, with all her jewels and furs, never made the list.

Among those who have achieved fashion "Hall of Fame" status through the years are Queen Elizabeth II, the Duchess of Windsor, Princess Grace of Monaco, Queen Sirikit of Thailand, Jacqueline Onassis (when she was Mrs. Kennedy), Gloria Guinness (wife of the British stout heir), Rose Kennedy, Mrs. William Paley, and Gloria Vanderbilt Cooper. Men who have been named to the list in recent years include former New York Mayor John Lindsay, film stars Robert Redford and Richard Roundtree, and film executive Robert Evans.

There are those who would consider it a dubious honor to be acclaimed for what might be called such conspicuous consumption. The members of the upper classes, however, are not the ones who are responsible for the BDL's falling into disfavor. The real culprits are the members of the not-quite-so-upper classes who work all their lives to acquire the status symbols of the class above them. When status symbols fail to maintain class distinctions, their value is zero. The mink coat is one example: today with cut-rate assembly-line methods and department store credit, almost anyone can come home swathed in fur. As one observer quipped: "No more will anyone mistake you for the wife of an office clerk. . . . They'll mistake you for the wife of a truck driver."

Ostentation in dress has rarely, if ever, been considered "in good taste." If an outfit looks like something that you have been waiting years to buy, chances are you really cannot afford it. Among the very rich who can afford just about anything, however, ostentation is difficult to achieve (although Liz Taylor did with her 69.4 carat diamond and $125,000 Kojah coat). The more typical response among the highest income groups is to seek that which may be costly but does not look it. As one Fifth Avenue furrier explained, his customers want mink that doesn't look like mink. So he offers, "for $2,500, a dyed variety that includes pink, yellow and blue-denim colored mink; shaved mink stenciled to look like tiger, cheetah and leopard; mink imprinted with assorted patterns; and even a rainbow coat made of vari-colored swatches sewn together like a patch-work quilt."[19]

Among the truly elite it is more fashionable *not* to be fashionable. One columnist noting Mrs. Nelson Rockefeller's unstylish mode of dress commented: "Mrs. Rockefeller . . . is in casual, tried-and-true good taste. She's from the good skirt, good sweater, good string of pearls school. . . . Her look is the look of the typical well-dressed Philadelphia Main Liner, which is exactly what she is."[20]

[19]"Sorry, New Canaan, but now they wear mink in the Bronx, too," *Wall Street Journal*, 11 March 1971.
[20]"'Happy' Rockefeller's Personal Campaign," *Cosmopolitan*, October 1963, pp. 58–59.

Figure 11-3. When ordinary mink lost its status, Elizabeth Taylor had hers tinted blue. Here, she arrives at a rainy airport in a full-length blue mink cape with Richard in brown mink jacket.

Figure 11-4. Status is never cheap. These travellers carry Vuitton satchels— "a half yard of plastic, a zipper and a couple of handles for $85." The famous brown luggage once bestowed instant good taste upon its proud owners, but now the exclusive bags are being bought up by "people who can't even pronounce the name (Vwee-tohn)." Will the rich and fashionable discard their favorite totes once they are carried by secretaries in the tourist class?

The relatively few people in the upper classes of American society are in a position to set a standard of dress that others seek to emulate; those whose social positions have been established for generations are less likely to use fashionable attire as a symbol of their preeminence.

Whether people qualify as "upper-upper," "lower-upper," or simply "upper," they become "the arbiters of the 'proper' use of money, physical appearance and dress, etiquette, language, and aesthetic taste."[21]

The great middle mass

Of the three broad strata in American society (upper, middle, and lower), only the middle class has increased steadily in proportion to the whole (see Table 19-6). The very rich are, relatively speaking, not as rich as they used to be. During the 1940's and 1950's, the incomes of the richest 5 per cent of all Americans were falling, while the share of middle-class families went up. During the 1960's, the poor were the big gainers, largely as the result of increases in social security and the increased demand for services which made the earnings of service workers rise rapidly.

The composition as well as the size of the middle class has changed from a group of independent farmers and small businessmen to larger and larger numbers of salaried professionals, salespeople, and office workers. As Mills explains, the "white-collar people's claims to prestige are expressed, as their label implies, by their style of appearance."[22] With changing fashions, the white-collar worker is now apt to wear a blue shirt, the blue-collar worker probably wears the white shirt, and the fellow in jeans and denim shirt is likely to be the boss' son.

Nevertheless, the desk-worker is clearly in a position to wear a different type of attire on the job than is the manual worker. This basic difference in clothing symbolism is probably the most important single criterion used to establish the line of demarcation between middle class and working class. Salary alone is no reliable index, for the hourly wage of many workers today may equal or exceed the salary of white-collar employees; but if we compare the clothing budgets of workers and white-collar people of similar income, we will find that a much higher percentage is spent on clothes by the latter group.

Thus, the middle class is the consuming class; the stress that is placed on clothes and appearance reflects the continual striving for upward social mobility and the search for higher and higher status. The middle classes are the eager emulators, the "crucial audience," as Lerner calls it, for the fashions set by the upper classes. The costly and original designs that the office girl sees in fashion magazines, movies, and newspapers, are quickly copied into less expensive imitations, and despite the differences in quality and workmanship, the

"Oh, Edith we're only going around the block, for God's sake!"

Figure 11-5. Drawing by Stan Hunt; © 1969 The New Yorker Magazine, Inc.

[21]Berelson and Steiner, *Human Behavior*, p. 488.
[22]C. Wright Mills, *White Collar: The American Middle Class*, Oxford University Press, New York, 1951, p. 63.

smartness and the look of a fashionable appearance may be had by all.

At times, the middle class seems to be obsessed with the search for the right way to act and the right thing to wear. The number of possessions—including clothes—becomes a significant expression of social position, and the middle class is far more status-conscious than either of the two groups above or below. Because of their strict observance of convention, people of this middle stratum are not likely to adopt a new or daring fashion until they are sure it has been accepted by the class above them. Yet for all their insecurities, America's middle classes are the carriers of the culture and the group largely responsible for the great productivity that characterizes the nation as a whole. It is the middle-class image that makes Americans the best-dressed people in the world.

Members of middle-class society constitute the bulk of fashion followers; their status is more dependent upon the symbols of appearance and dress than either of the other social classes.

What the well-dressed worker wears

The working class is most often defined in terms of its occupational characteristics to include those individuals and families in the semi-skilled, unskilled, farm laborer, and servant class positions. National polls taken as far back as the early 1940's show that well over three-fourths of the people in this category call themselves "middle class" rather than "lower class,"[23] although Centers' survey revealed that almost 52 per cent of the population identified with this stratum when the label was changed to "working class." In the broadest sense, these are the people who work for hourly wages (as distinct from a salaried position) and in the majority of cases wear some type of uniform or work clothes on the job.

The process of stratifying individuals into social categories is always complex, and few individuals conform in every respect to the total class configuration. There is in today's society the class-blurring effect of mass production, which makes the products of the ready-to-wear industry not only more available but at the same time less reliable as indicators of social class position. One has to look more closely for the subtle differences in cut, fabric, and workmanship that distinguish the hand-tailored suit from the mass-produced copy.

If we are to generalize anything at all from studies which indicate significant relationships between clothing behavior and social class position, it would be that clothing is decidedly more important to those who are upwardly mobile in their aspirations. Because the worker generally is more concerned about his economic security than he is about his social position,

---

[23]See "The People of the United States—A Self Portrait," *Fortune*, February 1940; and G. Gallup and S. Rae, *The Pulse of Democracy*, Simon & Schuster, New York, 1940.

Figure 11-6. A trip to the local laundromat does not exactly provide the social opportunity to wear fashionable attire.

Clothing tends to be regarded by the worker as having limited importance to his social position, although he now has access to clothing commodities that would symbolize a higher status.

he tends to place little value on clothing and probably could not care less about its symbolic interpretation.

In two separate investigations, both Delp[24] and Smith[25] found significant differences between children from advantaged homes and children from disadvantaged homes in their awareness of dress considered appropriate for different occasions. By the age of four or five, the child from the economically "advantaged" family has already been conditioned to the nuances of dress that would make one costume suitable for play and another costume suitable for parties. Children from the lower economic groups apparently have less opportunity to develop such sensitivity.

Similarly, the woman from the working class does not find it necessary to spend large amounts for a fashionable wardrobe. She has little social opportunity to be fashionably dressed, and she finds it more important to be "neat and clean" than "all dolled up with no place to go." Even within the context of a common activity such as shopping, class differences may be noted.[26] Tucker observed highly significant differences in the normative patterns of dress between women who shopped for clothing in the designers' salons of local stores and those who shopped in the fashion departments of discount houses.[27]

Thus we see that the importance of clothing appears to increase as one progresses up the social ladder until one finally reaches the top. Then, because there is no place left to go, the significance of clothing again diminishes.

Minorities and subcultures

Although great strides have been made in amalgamating the differences of diverse ethnic, racial, and religious groups in America, the preferred characteristics for many of the favored statuses and positions remain white, male, Anglo-Saxon, and Protestant. Among the Jews, Catholics, Negroes, Orientals, Indians, Mexicans, Italians, Poles, and so forth, there are ambivalent pressures toward the ultimate assimilation within the broader culture on the one hand, and toward a preservation of subcultural identities on the other. The more distinctly the marks of physical appearance separate the minority group from the larger society, the more difficult assimilation becomes, and concomitantly the stronger their status sensitivity develops.

[24]Janice Delp, "Awareness of Clothing Differences for Age and Sex: A Comparison of Four-Year-Old Children from Advantaged and Disadvantaged Homes," Master's thesis, Pennsylvania State University, 1970.
[25]Velda Smith, "Awareness of Appropriateness of Dress Among Four- and Five-Year-Old Children from Advantaged and Disadvantaged Homes," Master's thesis, Pennsylvania State University, 1968.
[26]Stone and Form, *Social Context of Shopping*, 1957.
[27]Susan Tucker, "The Relationship Between a Normative Pattern of Dress and Upward Social Mobility," Master's thesis, University of Nevada, 1969.

Myrdal observed, for example, that among the American Negroes, a penchant for flashy, bizarre, and ostentatious dress was supposedly a predominant characteristic.[28] Schwartz analyzes this pattern of clothing behavior by reasoning that "when the black is denied access to many status symbols, (he) is forced to use compensatory devices to raise self-esteem, aid status symbolization, and cushion the traumatic effects of a subordinate position. Clothing is one of these available devices, along with cars, furniture, and housing. Being a more portable and relatively less expensive object of conspicuous consumption, clothing is more easily exhibited than other status symbols."[29]

The study also indicated that at all income levels over $1,000, expenditures for clothing were significantly higher among blacks than among whites. In the comparison of consumption patterns for food, clothing, housing, and furnishings, clothing ranked as the second largest expenditure for blacks but ranked in fourth place for whites. It was also observed that the black male's orientation to dress emphasized the social importance of style and appearance, and minimized the physical aspects of fit and comfort. Even though the Negro foot is both larger and wider than that of Caucasians, the preferred shoe was usually a slim, sharply-pointed high-fashion model in delicate leather. Following Veblen's theory, the black uses such styles to communicate his dissociation from the laboring class and to affect an identity with the status symbolism of leisure activity. In short, the study demonstrated a fairly clear-cut use of clothing by the black to compensate for lack of status in other areas of activity.

An interesting parallel to the above analysis of men's clothing is provided in Kittles' study of women's dress which was cited earlier. Even though white women in general owned a greater number of high-status clothing items, black women in the lower-income levels owned more of these items than whites grouped in the same category. As the income level of the blacks went up, the ownership of high-status clothing decreased. The reverse was true for whites since the mechanism of compensation was not operant, and their pattern of clothing consumption followed a typical middle-class striving toward the style of life of the next higher class.

Other minority groups may use clothing to accentuate their subcultural characteristics and thereby perpetuate a style of life that might otherwise disintegrate within the larger society. Among the religious Jews of New York, a number of internal discriminations in status, exhibited through the visual symbols of dress, are employed to encourage stricter conformity to religious practices. Social stratification within the Jewish community is based entirely upon one's dedication to ritualistic

[28]Gunnar Myrdal, *An American Dilemma*, Harper and Brothers, New York, 1944, p. 962.
[29]Jack Schwartz, "Men's Clothing and the Negro," *Phylon* 24, 1963, p. 225.

observances. The common criteria of lineage, wealth, success, education, morals, and so forth have little to do with the prestige position to which an individual is assigned.[30] A variety of Hasidic garments serve to identify the relative position of each person in the hierarchy. The lowest class of *Yiden* (i.e., the least intense in their religious observance) are permitted to wear the dark, double-breasted, outmoded suits that button right over left; these are considered to be the very minimum of Hasidic status symbols. The next highest class is permitted a beard and sidelocks in addition to the double-breasted suit. The third stratum may add to this a large-brimmed, black beaver hat, while a still higher status is indicated by the wearing of a long black overcoat in place of a jacket. Near the very top of the hierarchy, a man may wear—in addition to the beard and the sidelocks—the hat, the long overcoat, and a long silk coat with rear pockets. Only the *Rebbes*, the top-ranking and most religious members of the community, may wear the slipper-like shoes and white knee socks into which the breeches are folded. Through these external symbols by which each person is identified with his appropriate social position, the group is able to maintain control over its members and extend its religiosity. Thus, through a system of visible rewards, the Hasidic community succeeds in stemming the forces that might otherwise lead to assimilation in the secular society.

Clothing symbols that distinguish minority groups from the larger society inhibit the process of assimilation and increase the possibility of discrimination.

SUMMARY *Clothes and class distinctions*

In every human society, individuals are ranked on some form of prestige continuum. Social stratification in America is based on an open-class system which permits fairly easy access from one level to another. Clothing is an important part of one's style of life, and it is one of the more visible indices used to identify an individual's class affiliation. The fashion leaders in American society tend to come from the upper class by virtue of the fact that they have both the money to buy high-fashion clothes and the social opportunity to display them. Those at the very peak of the socioeconomic pyramid, however, usually find it more fashionable *not* to be fashionable, and their use of clothing as a status symbol diminishes.

The majority of Americans in the middle class recognize that a "proper" appearance and "proper" dress are the keys to association with the "right crowd," which in turn opens the door to job advancement, increased income, success, and greater prestige. Thus, status for the members of middle-class society is more clearly dependent upon the symbols of dress than it is for either the upper or the lower classes. The worker attaches relatively little importance to the social significance of clothing,

---

[30]Solomon Poll, *The Hasidic Community of Williamsburg*, Free Press of Glencoe, New York, 1962.

even though the effects of mass production have made virtually all types of apparel available to him. In general, people tend to minimize the difference in dress standards between themselves and those in the next higher class, but clearly set themselves apart from those below.

Minority groups subconsciously may use clothing to compensate for lack of recognized status in other areas of activity. Because clothing is less expensive than other status symbols such as housing, furnishings, and automobiles, it is a common object of conspicuous consumption particularly among those of low income levels. A more conscious use of clothing by subcultural groups relates to the function of dress symbols in maintaining a style of life that will preserve the identity of a group which might otherwise be assimilated into the larger society.

Reference groups and clothing behavior

Objective descriptions of class and minority group characteristics cannot account for the sum total of group distinctions in dress that are discernible in modern society. It is conceivable, for example, that people of different status positions could develop a group feeling of belonging through common interests and goals that may be completely unrelated to the social system of stratification. In addition, a uniform pattern of behavior is largely dependent upon a conscious identification with a given group or class.

In Chapter 7, we saw how a person's behavior is shaped by his relationship to significant others. If we generalize "others" to the broader concept of the **reference group,** we will be able to understand the influence of group opinion in the determination of an individual's pattern of clothing behavior. A group functions as a frame of reference for an individual in one or both of two ways: (1) it may set and enforce standards for the person by giving recognition or withholding it; and (2) it may serve as the standard against which a person evaluates himself and others. In either case, the individual must recognize his relationship to the group in order to be motivated by it.

Class consciousness

Every individual seeks the security of knowing that he belongs to a particular social group, as well as the distinction within the mass society that such identification affords. Whether this identification is made within the large and diffuse status system of social class or within the context of a smaller, more intimate group depends on the person's orientation or point of reference. In terms of reference group theory, it would be a mistake to assign an individual to a given class solely on the basis of external criteria; i.e., he will be more strongly motivated to conform to the norms of the group to which he *feels* he belongs, or *should* belong, than the group to which he might be assigned by virtue of his income, occupation, lineage, or other status criteria.

The more extended knowledge an individual has regarding class distinctions in society, the more aware he becomes of his own position in the system. The wage earner, for example, tends to have a limited perspective of any social roles other than his own. He does not, through extensive reading or social participation, enlarge his view of society beyond his own immediate environment. In general, he thinks that people in the upper classes are there simply because they have more money. He sees only the gross similarities in styles of dress, and to him, one dark suit is just as good as another. His capacity for making differential evaluations of the more subtle differences in clothing is limited, and consequently he is insensitive to the symbols that distinguish him from anyone else. In short, he tends to have very little class-consciousness.

The increased access to a college education today, coupled with widespread communication through the mass media, brings a knowledge of "how the other half lives" to larger and larger segments of the population. In the process, the individual compares his own style of life with those of others in the social hierarchy, and the end result is a greater consciousness or awareness of his own class position.

A number of studies have demonstrated an increased awareness of dress as socioeconomic level rises. Bullock,[31] for example, found greater fashion awareness among girls who came from higher economic brackets than among those from lower brackets, and Bloxham found a similar relationship between an awareness of dress norms and socioeconomic status.[32]

It is this kind of sensitivity among members of the upwardly mobile middle class that stimulates their emulation of the fashions of the upper class and helps them to maintain their separateness from the lower stratum, out of which many have risen. Obviously, this produces a need for more rapid changing of styles among the upper-class fashion leaders, in order to maintain *their* separateness from the middle stratum.

Thus we see that increased class consciousness results in greater degrees of status seeking. As he establishes his identity, a person evaluates his own position against the standards of the group in which he desires membership.

Awareness of the subtle differences in dress is highly correlated to an individual's consciousness of class distinctions; people will try to conform to the norms of the group to which they feel they should belong.

---

[31]Marilyn Bullock, "Fashion Awareness of Students in Selected Rural and Urban Areas," Master's thesis, Texas Tech University, 1970.
[32]Thine Bloxham, "Adolescents' Awareness of Dress Norms," Washington State University, 1969.

Reference groups

In the early 1970's, a group of British teenagers known as the "Skinheads" plagued London police by their battles with the hippies. The "Skinheads" in turn were preyed upon by another group called the "Greasers," who were a kind of British version of the "Hell's Angels." Each of these gangs adopted a distinctive style of dress which was immediately identifiable. The uniform of the "Skinheads" consisted of heavy work-type overalls worn with suspenders and boots with steel-capped toes. Their heads were characteristically shaved as a counternorm against the long-haired hippies.

Membership in the group produced a feeling of confidence. In the words of one teenager, "Skinheads dress alike, think alike and act alike. When we take the streets in really big gangs, we feel proud."[33] The mere fact that such groups develop in society is not in itself a particularly newsworthy item. The "Mods" and the "Rockers" existed before the "Skinheads" and the "Greasers," and before them there were the "Teddy Boys" with their midnight-blue drape-shaped suits and pink shirts. New Zealand has had its share of "Bodgies," "Widgies," and "Milkbar Cowboys." In our own country we have gone through endless versions of "Zoot Suiters," "Rollers," "Ivy Leaguers," and a variety of "looks" too numerous to mention.

In attempting to explain how such group behavior develops, we might present a somewhat remote analogy. People in general have no particular affinity for others with the same color hair; we might say, for example, that they lack group consciousness. Those who have rather unusual hair coloring might be more conscious of it than others, and they would be even more aware of it if several of them with the same bright coloring got together and called themselves the "Ravishing Redheads." Their togetherness would be increased if they discovered that another group in town was called the "Blonde Bombshells." Now if someone started the rumor that gentlemen prefer blondes, the unity of outlook among the redheads might be so heightened that a challenge would ensue. Thus, we see that feelings of belongingness are greatly enhanced by intensifying the group identity. This may be accomplished by (1) giving each person a conspicuous emblem of membership, and (2) distinguishing the group by giving it a name.

Obviously, the importance that an individual attaches to clothing is influenced strongly by the values of the group with which he identifies. In the teenage culture, the conscious association between clothes and group belongingness is perhaps the most pronounced. Social factors other than age-status,

Figure 11-7. Group cohesiveness is greatly enhanced by wearing a conspicuous symbol of membership and giving the group a name. Like the Hell's Angels, this gang displays its insignia on the back of their jackets.

---

[33]Tom Cullen, "'Skinheads' Stalk Flower Folk," NEA news release, London, January 1970.

however, affect the prestige value assigned to clothing by particular reference groups. Patton compared college sorority girls with non-sorority girls, using a measure of prestige consciousness. Her findings revealed highly significant differences between the two groups: sorority women were much more aware of the status value of particular items of dress, and they recognized clothing as a way to "get in" with the popular students on campus. She also found a higher prestige consciousness among women of the upper and upper-middle classes than among those in the lower strata.[34]

In another comparison of female college students' opinions regarding "appropriate dress standards," there was far greater unanimity among sorority members than there was among independents who lived in the dorms.[35] Apparently those who bother to join fraternal organizations of this kind are more strongly motivated to conform to the patterns of a social reference group. The intensity of the need for belonging is directly related to the compulsion and avidity with which group norms are followed by the individual.

Clothing provides a conspicuous badge of group belonging.

SUMMARY *Reference groups and clothing behavior*

Every individual needs the security and distinction of knowing that he belongs to a particular group within the mass society. The extent to which he identifies with any group or class depends upon his own consciousness or awareness of the group's existence as well as a knowledge of his own relative status or position. People are more strongly motivated to conform to the standards of the group to which they feel they *should* belong, rather than the group or class to which they might be assigned on the basis of external criteria.

Feelings of group belonging are greatly enhanced by (1) giving its constituents an emblem of membership, (2) giving it a name, and (3) external threats to its existence. Clothing is probably the most conspicuous and the most visual of all possible badges of group belonging. Criticism of group standards of dress tends to increase group cohesiveness and the compulsion to conform to the established norms.

Social mobility and dress

Social mobility is the movement or shifting of membership that occurs between or within social classes. American society is marked by a relatively high degree of **vertical mobility**, i.e.,

[34]Elizabeth Patton, "An Analysis of the Prestige Factors in Clothing as Related to Selected Groups of Freshmen and Senior Sorority and Non-Sorority Women at the University of Alabama," Master's thesis, University of Alabama, 1964.
[35]Barbara Ross, "A Comparative Investigation of Conformity Patterns of Dress of Home Economics Students at the University of Nevada," Master's thesis, University of Nevada, 1970.

CLOTHING AND HUMAN BEHAVIOR

movement up and down the ladder of income and prestige. As we have seen, there is an extremely close relationship of clothing to class consciousness and status seeking, both of which have significant relevance to social mobility.

Movement within the mass

One of the favorite themes in American novels revolves around the struggles and disappointments of artless but wealthy prospectors whose wives seek access to high society: "Eventually they secured acceptance to such groups for their children by sending them to the 'correct' schools and dancing masters, outfitting them at the proper dressmakers and tailors, and providing them with the appropriate accouterments."[36]

A second theme, which presents the other side of the coin, describes the hardships of the once affluent upper-class family who strives to maintain its ancestral dignity in the light of economic adversity. The problems in both situations arise out of inconsistencies between class position and economic status, and both reflect the kind of social mobility that is characteristic of American society.

The greatest push, however, is not from the top down, but from the bottom up. Long before the government's poverty program got underway, great numbers of people were able to earn their way from the lower strata up to the ranks of the middle classes. Through the emulation of practices and values, through the attainment of higher educational levels, and through a "keeping up with the Joneses" made possible by increased purchasing power, individuals who were motivated to do so were able to improve their relative positions. Acceptance into this new way of life, however, was dependent upon outward conformity to middle-class standards—the right kind of house, the right model car, the right style of clothes and manners.

Empirical data appear to support this assumed relationship between clothes and mobility. Vener's findings indicate that a person's estimate of clothing importance is directly and significantly related to vertical social mobility; i.e., people seeking to improve their status positions place a higher value on clothes than those who regard themselves as socially stationary.[37]

The investigation of clothing habits of white-collar and manual workers by Form and Stone revealed that low-level white-collar workers had much more concern for styles of dress and appearance than manual workers of comparable income, and that they were much more likely to believe that their clothes affected their chances for social and occupational advancement.

The implication in all of these studies is that clothing is consciously recognized as a symbol which is capable of manipulation by those who seek to get ahead in the world. Knowledge of

[36]Ely Chinoy, *Society*, Random House, New York, 1962, p. 135.
[37]Vener, "Stratification Aspects of Clothing Importance."

Clothing, as an aspect of one's style of life, facilitates movement within the class structure of society.

the standards of dress required on the diverse levels of society will be a positive factor in one's attempt to achieve the social position he desires.

Barrier breakdown

Although many aspects of Veblen's theory of conspicuous consumption in dress still have validity in today's society, the clothing symbols that mark a man as a member of the leisure class are far less distinct than they were in the nineteenth century. Even fifty years ago, the professional man was still recognizable in his black frock coat and silk hat, while the worker or the farm laborer seldom exchanged his bulbous-toed shoes for any more refined style of footwear. Differences in income were accompanied by sharp differences in both the symbols of wealth and available leisure time. Mass production and mass marketing have blurred the distinctions in dress, and at the same time increased mechanization resulting in the shorter work week has provided leisure for all. The visible signs of stratification have become much more subtle, and both the upper and the lower categories have tended to converge toward a middle-class standard of living.

The big push for copies of high-fashion merchandise among the low-priced companies, has created an America with the best-dressed poverty the world has ever known:

> It is much easier in the United States to be decently dressed than it is to be decently housed, fed, or doctored. . . . There are tens of thousands of Americans in the big cities who are wearing shoes, perhaps even a stylishly cut suit or dress, and yet are hungry. . . . it almost seems as if the affluent society had given out costumes to the poor so that they would not offend the rest of society with the sight of rags.[38]

These examples are illustrative of two important phenomena. One is that technological developments contribute greatly to the weakening of class lines; the differences in dress that reflect one's mode of living are still there, but the shadings are more elusive and imprecise. The other—and perhaps the more significant of the two—is that clothes can "make the poor invisible"; if one *feels* equal in visual appearance and dress, many of the psychological barriers that divide the inferior from the superior are extraordinarily minimized. This simple fact explains the motivation which underlies much of our clothing behavior.

Clothing becomes a less reliable indicator of social class as similar styles in dress become increasingly available to all persons.

Diversity vs. discrimination

We have described in rather general terms some of the values and practices that appear to be characteristic of clothing

[38]Michael Harrington, *The Other America*, Macmillan Publishing Company, New York, 1962, p. 5.

behavior within each of the broad social classifications in American society. The bulk of the upper class possesses the refinement of taste that comes through exposure to the skill and craftsmanship of creative designers and tailors; its members have both the security and the social opportunity to exercise the kind of distinction in dress that can make them the fashion pace-setters for the rest of society.

At the middle level, individuality in dress is somewhat overshadowed by a widespread conformity to the "ideal" codes that are enforced by the opinion of the majority. People from the lower stratum may devalue the importance of dress, although those who are conscious of their positions often experience strong drives toward upward mobility. When such is the case, the functional value of clothing is often sacrificed for the outward, more ostentatious symbols that seem, at least to the wearer, to eliminate class distinctions in dress.

General statements such as these, however, present an oversimplification of a very complex organizational pattern. Elements of good and bad taste permeate all levels of society; dress, as a form of creative expression, is not necessarily limited to the upper classes, nor is conformity confined to middle-level living; a criss-crossing of clothing values and practices appears more obvious to the casual observer than strict adherence to any of the social class norms.

To expect, or even to assume, that any single standard of dress would be the most desirable for everyone in society would be to contradict the acceptance of diversity which is at the very core of the American cultural ideal. But conformity should not be interpreted only in the negative sense as an impediment to creative self-expression; it is a mechanism through which we are able to keep our society intact. To the individual who asks, "Who am I, and where do I belong?" conformity to a given set of norms can give a sense of identity and group belongingness. To place such a high value on clothing that it obscures all other worthwhile facets of living seems to be no more or less desirable than failing to recognize the significance of dress to the successful enactment of life roles. We may deplore the mass-produced tastes that our highly developed industrial system imposes upon us, but we can be grateful for a vastly improved standard of living that brings us closer each day to the elimination of widespread poverty.

The intelligent approach is to be fully apprised of the choices that are open to us, not only in terms of commodity availability, but in terms of the values by which we prefer to be known.

Diverse patterns in clothing behavior reflect differences in tastes and values that often overlap class lines; no single standard of dress can be best for all of society.

SUMMARY *Social mobility and dress*

American society is marked by a relatively high degree of vertical mobility. Upward movement is usually characterized by a consciousness of one's social position and greater emphasis on the importance of dress in affecting the transition. Mass production and mass marketing of apparel has greatly reduced class distinctions in dress by making a wide variety of commodities available to all.

FOR FURTHER READING

Anspach, Karlyne. "Clothing Selection and the Mobility Concept," *Journal of Home Economics* 53, June 1961, pp. 428–430.

Barber, B., and L. S. Lobel. "Fashion in Women's Clothes and the American Social System," *Social Forces* 31, 1952, pp. 124–131.

Bendix, R., and S. Lipset, eds. *Class, Status and Power.* New York: Free Press, 1966.

Rosencranz, Mary Lou. *Clothing Concepts.* New York: Macmillan Publishing Company, 1972. (Chapter 10, "Status," and Chapter 11, "Work and Leisure.")

Ryan, Mary S. *Clothing: A Study in Human Behavior.* New York: Holt, Rinehart & Winston, 1966, pp. 63–73.

Veblen, Thorstein. *The Theory of the Leisure Class.* New York: Modern Library, reprinted 1931. (Chapter 7, "Dress as an Expression of the Pecuniary Culture.")

DISCUSSION QUESTIONS

1. Explain Veblen's theory of the leisure class as it applies to clothing. Is it a valid theory for contemporary society? Why or why not?

2. How has modern technology affected class differentiations in dress?

3. Cite examples of clothing that are manifestations of social stratification in America. In what way may each of the following groups be labeled or identified: (a) lower working class; (b) middle class; (c) upper class?

4. In what ways may education increase class consciousness?

5. What is the function of a reference group? Describe some of the reference groups with which you are familiar. Can the members of any of these groups be identified through dress and appearance? How?

6. In previous chapters it has been suggested that a uniform type of dress would eliminate all forms of discrimination, including class distinctions in dress. Discuss the pros and cons of using clothing to maintain group identity (as opposed to the homogenization of society with few, if any, distinctions in dress).

PART THREE

Aesthetics and Dress

12

Artistic Perception, Expression, and Experience

ART MAY BE approached in any number of ways. We may see the flowing, graceful lines of a Japanese woodcut; feel the vast proportions of space inside a Gothic cathedral; contemplate the rounded contours of a Maillol sculpture; perceive the tactile richness of an elegant fabric; or respond to the clouds of color in a Kandinsky painting. Whatever the medium, the same plastic elements of line, space, form, texture, and color are the basis for all visual design. We may produce art, or we may merely look at it; we may enjoy it, appreciate it, or understand it.

Clothing is one means through which the components of art are illustrated, perceived, and experienced. Through clothing design, we can attune our eyes to subtle variations of line or of color, and this in turn helps to sensitize us to similar elements in other artistic forms. Whether we produce a complete design through garment construction, or whether our composition takes form by assembling the various parts of a costume, we are creating a "picture" for others to behold. A study of clothing design can contribute to the depth of our art understanding and increase appreciation of the visual richness of our environment.

Developing sensitivity

Just as chemical elements constitute the ingredients for all chemical compounds, all art is concerned with the combination or organization of the fundamental elements of line, space, form, texture, and color. These raw materials of design never appear in isolation, except in the abstract. In costume at least, every line and shape may have a character of its own, but such elements take on meaning only as they are seen within the context of the total appearance. In this chapter we shall study the plastic elements as discrete aspects of design to sharpen our recognition of their use in costume.

AESTHETICS AND DRESS

Line

Line often is used as the simplest form of representation. In all visual design, line functions to outline contour, to connect shapes, and to divide space within a shape. When line predominates in a design, it may provide a path of vision along which the eye may travel. The route may be straight and direct, or it may meander in devious ways. Even when line is broken, the eye tends to connect points in space to form a linear pattern (Figure 12-1).

Various types of lines differ in their expressive qualities. **Straight lines** tend to be stiff and severe: "To most people the straight line suggests rigidity and precision. It is positive, direct, tense, stiff, uncompromising, harsh, hard, unyielding."[1] Straight lines in themselves contradict the subtle curves of the human form by giving it an angular quality. In stiff fabrics that maintain a rigidity of line, straight seams and edges may obscure body contour; but in yielding, pliable textures, the line loses its stability and takes on the conformation of the curve beneath it.

Curved lines vary all the way from gentle undulation to full rounded convolution. A restrained curve is graceful, flowing, and gentle. The gradual transition in the change of direction imparts a slow but rhythmic quality to the line.

We see how straight line may take on aspects of the body contour; this effect is usually compounded in the case of curved line. A costume that appears to be restrained in line when worn by a slender person may seem to be excessively rounded on a fuller figure. The banded edge of the admiral's coat in Figure 12-5 exaggerates his corpulence in a wonderfully humorous manner.

Lines that are vigorously curved tend to be more active in character, and for this reason they can easily be overdone in costume. Wavy lines that constantly change their direction quickly become restless and aimless.

Zigzag line forces the eye to shift its direction abruptly and repeatedly, causing an erratic, jerky movement. Bold herringbones like the one in Figure 12-6 are at the same time both startling and tiring under prolonged observation.

The *direction* of line contributes as much to its quality as the type. Each direction—vertical, horizontal, diagonal—produces a different effect upon the beholder.

Vertical line predominates in the tall slender arches of Gothic interiors as well as in the architecture of our modern skyscrapers. Numerous examples of verticality in dress can be found throughout historical and contemporary periods (Figure 12-7).

---

[1]Maitland Graves, *The Art of Color and Design*, McGraw-Hill Book Company, New York, 1951, p. 202.

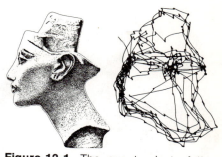

Figure 12-1. The eye tends to follow fairly regular pathways in the perception of objects within its field of vision. As a subject viewed the head of Queen Nefertiti (left), his eye movements (right) were recorded by Alfred L. Yarbus of the Institute for Problems of Information Transmission in Moscow.

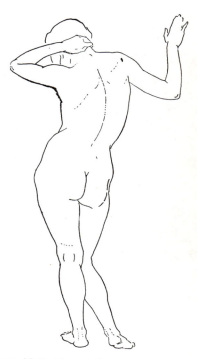

Figure 12-2. Line defines the contours of the human form.

Figure 12-3. Curved line may vary from gentle curves to more exaggerated roundness.

Figure 12-4. This illustrates the propensity of straight line to yield to the contours of the form beneath it. When parallel bands of light are projected onto a human figure, the light planes are broken by body curves, and the straight lines break into subtle undulations that highlight surface contour.

Figure 12-5. Curved lines predominate in this portrait of Admiral Keppel by Reynolds.

Figure 12-6. Zigzag lines can produce a startling effect but may become tiring under prolonged observation.

Figure 12-7. The exteme verticality of these elongated figures is expressive of the austere, straining effect that is so characteristic of the Gothic.

Horizontal lines suggest the pull of gravity and parallel objects in rest or repose, such as the surface of the earth, a quiet expanse of water, or a sleeping human figure. Line direction that causes the eye to travel along horizontal planes usually has the effect of increasing apparent width. A study of Figures 12-8 and 12-9 will draw attention to the use of horizontal line in dress.

Oblique or **diagonal line** gives an impression of greater movement or action than either vertical or horizontal line does. "When running or otherwise very active, the body assumes a diagonal position, head thrust forward, balance somewhat precarious, elbows and knees forming angles."[2] It is this association with movement that gives diagonal lines an active and somewhat unstable quality.

In addition to its type and direction, line is characterized still further by other factors such as strength versus fragility, tension as opposed to flexibility, or sharpness counter to blurred. Such qualities are expressed by the size and thickness of the line, its placement within the total composition, and the degree of contrast it enjoys with the other plastic elements.

Form

We have said that one function of line is to define contour or shape. The distinction between line and form is, therefore, quite arbitrary. While the term **form** also can be used in a broader sense to denote the visual arrangement and effect of all the plastic elements within the total design, we will use it here in the more restricted sense of being synonymous with shape or contour. We will recognize *line* as having only the single dimension of length.

In applying the concept of form to clothing, we are dealing with three basic shapes: the form of the human body itself, the external shape created by the costume silhouette, and the outline of individual parts within the silhouette. The beauty of any design is affected by the interrelationship among these three forms.

The human head, basically ovoid in shape, bears a unique mathematical relationship to all other parts of the body (Figure 12-11). The anatomy is essentially rectangular in its total configuration, always taller than it is wide, devoid of precise geometric shapes, and infinite in its subtle variation of contour.

Clothing has the particular advantages of being able to camouflage body contours that are less than ideal and to add graceful forms of its own. Every period in fashion history can be identified by the distinctive shapes that characterize its silhouette (Figure 12-12). There have been many design periods in

[2]Ray Faulkner and Edwin Ziegfeld, *Art Today*, Holt, Rinehart & Winston, New York, 1969, p. 304.

The expressiveness of line is determined by its function, type, direction, and quality.

Figure 12-8. Repeated horizontals form the basic theme of this mid-nineteenth-century ball dress. The puffs of the overskirt, as well as the bands and rosettes, diminish in size as they step up the figure, lending rhythmic progression to the total design.

Figure 12-9. In this painting of the Infanta Margarita by Velasquez, horizontal lines and forms predominate. The sweep of the peplum, the bertha, the accented bateau neckline, and the extended coiffure all accentuate the breadth of the composition. Even the length of outstretched arms does not exceed the extreme width of the silhouette.

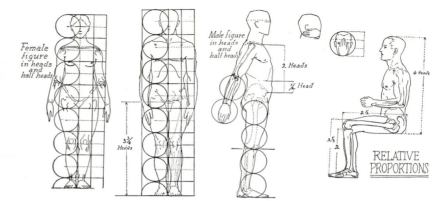

Figure 12-11. Relative proportions of the human form: each circle represents the length of a head from chin to crown.

Figure 12-10. The use of strong, unabashed line creates a forceful design.

Minoan
c. 1400 B.C.

Gothic
c. 1460

Renaissance
c. 1540

Baroque
c. 1630

Baroque
c. 1665

Louis XVI
1778

19th C.
1825

19th C.
1895

Figure 12-12. Shapes created by costume reflect the ideals of the era in which the design was created.

Figure 12-13. This painting of Anne of Cleves by Hans Holbein illustrates the quadrilateral form of Renaissance styles.

AESTHETICS AND DRESS

which geometric forms have been superimposed on the human body with little regard for the structure they adorned. Other silhouettes have retained a beauty over time by emphasizing the most pleasing proportions of the anatomy, while at the same time adding subtle areas of fullness that contribute to the over-all harmony of design.

Individual shapes within the silhouette may be seen in the outline of a collar, the contour of a sleeve, in lapels, pockets, and in shapes that form between seamlines and darts.

Form, like line, has an expressiveness that conveys feelings and emotions. The strained and elongated forms of the Gothic (Figures 12-7 and 12-12) are in sharp contrast to the stocky quadrilaterals of the Renaissance (Figures 12-12 and 12-13). In contemporary dress an infinite number of examples of forms can be found that have such distinctive characteristics.

In clothing, form is created by the body itself, by the silhouette of the costume, and by the individual shapes within the external contour.

Space

In visual design, space becomes the background against which forms or shapes are seen. In the perceptual process, one part of the design emerges as the "figure" or form, and the remainder becomes the "ground." "Moreover, perceptual experience never continues at a flat level; there is always a differentiation of the 'figure' which is central in awareness from the 'ground' which is perceived vaguely if at all."[3]

Far from being that which is "left over," space constitutes an important part of visual design, just as movements of silence are essential to the beauty of sound in music. Space provides relief from pattern, a kind of void against which decorative detail is highlighted.

A careful study of Figure 12-14 will reveal how the spacing of the pattern is calculated to accentuate the size and shape of the surface area that it covers. Through the bodice, the shapes and spaces are small in scale, dainty and feminine in effect. As the design descends to the hemline, the ears of wheat and leaves are separated by broader spaces, while at the same time the pattern increases in weight and movement.

Sensitivity to space is probably more difficult to develop because the observer is forced to reverse the figure-ground effect. The untrained observer usually pays no attention to the interstices between shapes and sees them only as meaningless parts of the background. Yet a subtle interplay between positive figures and negative spaces in a design contributes to the unity of the total composition.

Spatial voids in costume provide a unifying backdrop for decorative detail.

Texture

Texture is the plastic element most commonly associated with our sense of touch, although texture may be seen as well as

---

[3]M. D. Vernon, *A Further Study of Visual Perception*, The University Press, Cambridge, 1954, p. 41.

Figure 12-14. An early-nineteenth-century ball gown embroidered with rose blossoms and ears of wheat. The designs are formed by gilt wires, applied almost like pieces of jewelry.

Dull	Shiny
Rough	Smooth
Uneven	Flat
Grainy	Slippery
Coarse	Fine
Bulky	Gossamer
Heavy	Light
Compact	Porous
Bristly	Downy
Crisp	Limp
Stiff	Pliable
Hard	Soft
Rigid	Spongy
Inelastic	Stretchy
Warm	Cool
Scroopy	Waxy

felt. Every object in our environment has a surface quality that may be described in varying degrees of roughness or smoothness, hardness or softness. Most individuals would be able to identify articles with their eyes closed simply by running a finger over the surface—the cold polish of marble, the warm softness of a fleecy sweater, the slippery gloss of patent leather, the coarse-grained harshness of sandpaper. Such tactile sensations impart a character to objects—and to clothing fabrics in particular—that makes them suited to different purposes.

Not all tactile sensations can be translated precisely into visual experience. Two beige coats, for example, may appear similar from a distance of two or three feet, but a touch of the cloth immediately would reveal the difference between wool and cashmere. Trained fingers can easily detect the cool, crisp feel of linen from the softer fuzziness of cotton, or the liveliness of silk from the slipperiness of acetate. The oldest test of quality in fabric was to close the eyes and rub a piece between the fingers. For the experts at least, the test was surprisingly reliable.

Most of us learn to make certain associations between sensations of touch and sight. As Graves explains, "texture is perceived by our eyes as well as by our sense of touch, because wet or glossy surfaces reflect more light than dry, dull, or matt surfaces, and rough surfaces absorb light more unevenly and to a greater extent than smooth surfaces. Thus, by association of visual experiences with tactile experiences, things look, as well as feel, wet or dry, rough or smooth."[4]

This ability to *see* how a texture *feels* is thus made possible by the way in which fabrics absorb or reflect light. Those that are made from short staple fibers, or from yarns that are rough or tightly twisted, are usually dull-surfaced cloths that absorb the light, such as cotton hopsacking, wool challis or crepe, homespuns, and tweeds. Light-reflecting fabrics are either made from lustrous filament yarns (satin, lamé, taffeta), or they are given a glossy finish, like chintz, that deflects light rays from the surface. Many of the newer plastics fall into the light-reflecting category by virtue of the fact that they are not made from fiber at all but extruded into liquid smoothness.

Some fabrics both absorb and reflect light so that the edges appear almost white, while the folds are deeply absorbing and darker in color. Softly piled textures, velours, velveteens and short-haired furs have this characteristic.

Still another way of describing textures relates to their hang, or fall—a quality which is commonly referred to as **hand.** The weight, bulk, and flexibility of a fabric will determine the degree to which it follows body contour.

Some textures, by virtue of their own stiffness, create forms that are independent of the body. If such fabrics are opaque, they may camouflage or totally obscure the line of the figure.

[4]Graves, *Art of Color and Design*, p. 221.

Crisp fabrics, however, may also be transparent. From the tactile standpoint, they conceal the human form but visually reveal body contours if no backing or lining is used. Heavy satin, brocaded taffeta, peau de soie, piqué, and ottoman are illustrative of fabrics in the stiff, opaque category, while dimity, organdy, net, tulle, and organza are typical of the family of crisp sheers.

All sheers of course are not crisp. A totally different character is seen in the diaphanous softness of batiste, chiffon, and georgette. The weight of the fabric is also important; rayon marquisette—both soft and sheer—may hang in heavy folds, while silk chiffon literally floats in the air when the body is in motion (Figure 12-15).

Every texture has a unique character in the sense that it may combine any number of qualities. Similar to the kind of profiles that individuals score on interest and personality tests, textures could be rated somewhere along a continuum on the polar traits indicated in the margin of page 250.

Many textiles would not rate at either extreme but would probably show relative gradations nearer the center of the continuum. Textures that are neither rough nor smooth, coarse nor fine, of medium weight, thickness and luster, have a wide variety of uses as background materials, but they lack the strength of character to become the focal point of a design.

Textures used in combination can be most effective when they share a unity of idea or character and are suited to a similar purpose. The textural harmony in Figure 12-16 is achieved through a combination of consistent ideas. The lustrous folds of peau de soie, the luxurious softness of fur, the fichu ending in a floating bow of organza, the frivolous feather and curving lines, are entirely consistent and expressive of gay femininity.

Figure 12-15. When the body is in motion, silk chiffon literally floats through the air.

The character of texture is expressed through its visual appearance, feel, and hand.

Color

Sensitivity to color may be instinctive in some people, but most require the experience of direct observation before they can recognize and appreciate the infinite variation of color in our environment. The child learns at an early age to differentiate among the bright, intense hues, and learns the names of red, blue, green, and yellow. With increased exposure, he begins to note the difference between light colors and dark colors, bright colors and dull. To be knowledgeable in the use of color and articulate in matters concerning its use, we need to understand something about the color order system and develop a color vocabulary. Such learning experiences will also increase our enjoyment of color.

The white light coming from the sun contains all colors. We can actually see this when nature breaks down rays of sunlight into a rainbow, displaying all colors of the spectrum arranged in fixed order from red through orange, yellow, green, and blue

Figure 12-16. The costume of Mme. Mole-Raymond in this eighteenth-century portrait by Lebrun is an excellent example of textural harmony.

to violet. This unvarying order is explained by a difference in wave length or rate of energy, with red having the longest wave length, and violet at the other extreme having the shortest. This difference in wave length also accounts for the fact that red appears to carry greater distances than other colors.

When the source of light changes, color also changes. At dawn and at dusk the position of the sun is low in relation to the earth's surface, and its light rays therefore must penetrate more of the earth's surrounding atmosphere. Particles of dust and moisture in the atmosphere interrupt the shorter blue wave lengths and scatter them before they reach us. Consequently natural light at these times of the day is deficient in blue rays and therefore appears redder. Direct light from a clear sky on the other hand, permits a greater proportion of blue light rays to reach us. In the case of artificial light, incandescent bulbs emit more yellow rays, while fluorescent tubes vary from orange to blue. Mercury lamps used for highway illumination are deficient in red and proportionately high in blue and green. Colored lights make an excessive amount of light rays of a particular hue available for reflection.

Objects in our environment appear colored because they absorb some of these light rays and reflect others. A ripe tomato for example, absorbs all light rays except red, reflecting the red wave lengths back to the eye. The vine on which the tomato grows consumes most of the red, orange, and violet rays, reflecting equal amounts of blue and yellow, and most of the green, and therefore it appears green. The apparent color of an object then, depends upon its ability to absorb or delete certain wave lengths, with its visual color becoming a combination of the hues that remain in the beam of light which is reflected back to the eye.

Obviously the quantity of any hue that can be reflected by the surface of an object is dependent upon the proportion of that hue in the source of light. Under incandescent light which has an excess of yellow, the tomato will appear orange-red. In clear northern daylight it will seem nearer the blue side of red because more blue rays will reach its surface. Under a mercury lamp, extremely deficient in red, the poor tomato abstracts all the remaining hues from the light beam and ends up almost black. Costume colors are particularly affected by a change in the source of light. A lavender ball gown purchased in broad daylight may become a neutral gray under the yellow of artificial light.

All color systems are based upon a cross section of the rainbow, i.e., a series of hues arranged in fixed order, each blending easily into the next with no distinct demarcations between them. The basic difference among the various color systems is that each designates a slightly different set of primaries. The commonly used pigment system begins with red, yellow, and blue. The color printing process uses magenta, yellow, and cyan blue, while the primaries in colored television are red, green, and blue. We shall use the Munsell system in our study of color, because it provides a precise scale for defining color qualities. These qualities are discussed below in terms of the three dimensions of hue, value, and intensity.

Hue refers to the name of a family of colors, and is the term by which we identify reds, yellows, greens, blues, and purples. If we were to cut a cross sectional band of the rainbow and bend it into a circle, we would have the same arrangement of colors seen in the color wheel (Figure 12-17). In this position certain hues fall directly opposite other hues which have, in fact, opposite properties. Any two hues that oppose each other on the color circle are known as complements because together they reflect the full complement of the spectrum. If lights of complementary colors are mixed together, they will produce a neutral gray. If complements are not mixed but placed side by side, the eye experiencing extreme contrasts will see them as more intense than they really are. Thus, a bright turquoise sweater worn by a person with reddish brown hair will intensify the hair's red tinge. Viewed from a distance, however, small spots of complementary hues used in close proximity may mix in the eye and appear neutral. This is the reason that many tweeds and prints, vibrant with contrasting color when close at hand, seem to lose their life when seen from greater distances.

Hues that are adjacent to each other on the color circle such as blue, blue-green, and green are called analogous or related hues, because each family of colors is related through an intermediate offspring. The closer the interval between analogous hues, the more harmonious they will seem since there will be little contrast or conflict.

Hues may be distinguished further by their degree of warmth or coolness. Red, orange, and yellow have long been associated with the sources of heat—sun and fire; the blues, greens, and violets, on the other hand, are suggestive of cool waters, restful grass, shady trees, and distant hills. From a scientific point of view, the red end of the spectrum is actually warmer and the blue end cooler. Red, with its longer wave lengths, is an advancing hue and gives the sensation of warmth. Blue and violet, with short wave lengths, appear to recede and create a feeling of coolness. It is easy to see how this principle applies to dress; a figure or portion of a figure garbed in the warm hues will seem to advance into the foreground and appear larger, more important, while cool colors will cause it to recede into the distance and thereby seem smaller or less important.

The hue that is midway between the two extremes of red and violet is green, so that it usually marks the point of demarcation between the warm and cool ends of the spectrum. Greens that fall toward the yellow side, such as apple greens, are warmer greens than those on the blue side. All hues, however, are considered to have a warm or cool cast. Even blue may seem

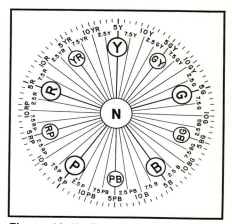

Figure 12-17. The Munsell Hue Circle.

Key:

R = red	BG = blue-green
YR = yellow-red	B = blue
Y = yellow	PB = purple-blue
GY = green-yellow	P = purple
G = green	RP = red-purple

The Munsell Hue Circle. The circle is divided into ten hue families, with each of the ten major hues having the notation of 5. Each family is subdivided into intermediate hues and designated by numbers 1 through 10. In the yellow family, for example, the yellows toward the red side of the color circle have low hue numbers (e.g., 1Y, 2Y, 3Y) and yellows on the green side have the higher notations (8Y, 9Y, 10Y). Further subdivisions may be made by using decimals (2.5Y, 7.5Y, etc.).

An almost infinite number of hue gradations are possible. The number and names of the principal hues have no special significance, except that they provide a simple way of dividing the color spectrum. Yellow-red could just as easily be called orange if it did not violate the system of color notation.

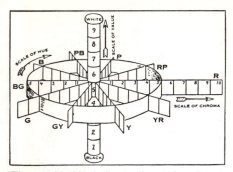

Figure 12-18. A three-dimensional projection of the attributes of color—hue, value, and intensity—in their relation to one another. The circular band represents the hues in their proper sequences. The upright center axis is the scale of value. The paths pointing outward from the center show the steps of chroma or intensity, increasing in strength as indicated by the numerals.

warmer with a touch of green if compared with a blue that contains a small amount of purple.

Value may be defined as the lightness or darkness of a color, and is determined by the total percentage of light rays absorbed or reflected. White objects may absorb less than 10 per cent of the light rays that reach them, in contrast to black objects which absorb over 95 per cent. No wonder black suits seem hot in the summer! Any fabric that is dark enough to absorb a high percentage of light energy will have an actual temperature higher than that of a pale fabric of similar construction.

Values are represented by a notation from 1/ to 9/ (see Figure 12-18), with near-black equal to 1/ and near-white at the upper extreme. An object that appears visually midway between black and white has a value notation of 5/. The lighter tints of a color are indicated by notations above 5/, while the darker shades will have numbers below 5/.

The home value level of a color is the step on the value scale at which the hue reaches its fullest intensity. The hues progress in a natural order of values from yellow (which is at full intensity at step 8/) in both directions until they reach the complement of yellow (purple-blue), which is the darkest. The home value level for green is 5/, red 4/, blue 4/, and purple 3/. These are the levels at which the greatest number of intensity variations will occur, i.e., the greatest number of yellows will be found at lighter levels, while the greatest number of purple-blues will be at darker value levels.

The natural order of values provides one of the fundamental principles of color harmony. When colors are combined, they are likely to be pleasing if they maintain their natural value relationship. For example, the combination of yellow, green-yellow, and green will result in greater harmony if the yellow is maintained as the lightest value in the scheme and green as the darkest. In some cases a reversal of this natural order of values will create a note of dissonance to produce unusual and exciting effects. A discord in color is analogous to its counterpart in music, in which a minor chord is introduced for brilliance or vibration. Value dissonance in costume can provide a touch of the unexpected, but unless it is done skillfully, it can be jarring and disturbing.

Value is the one dimension of color which can be seen independently from the other two (hue and intensity). The value pattern in a design is created by the distribution of light and dark areas into a pleasing arrangement:

A degree of value contrast is necessary to give structure to any design. It is difficult to see the boundaries between adjacent colors of the same value. Therefore, it is an important function of value contrast to define form and shape by making the boundaries between colors more visible. Similar values produce soft, vague boundaries, while sharp value differences cause hard, well-defined boundaries. Value contrasts also provide a welcome relief for our eyes from the monotony of seeing the same degree of lightness throughout a composition.[5]

The value key of a design may be predominantly light, medium, or dark, with value contrasts that are closely related or strongly contrasting. High-keyed designs in close value intervals achieve a delicate quality of femininity. Light values that are sharply accented by black are usually more forceful.

An intermediate or medium value key is illustrated in Figure 12-16. The light scarf is placed in close proximity to the skin tones, giving illumination to the face and making it the focal point of the composition. The patterning of low lights and high darks throughout the rest of the costume is created through the subtle contrast of highlight and shadow in the lustrous texture of hat and dress and the long-haired fur. A medium value also predominates in Figure 12-19, but the range in value is much greater. A black velvet ribbon is in sharp contrast against the silvery white wig in the same way that white stockinged legs are accented by black shoes. The suit, in medium value, lies halfway between the two extremes, with the richly embroidered design providing interesting gradations from light to dark and making a transition between the two areas of greatest contrast. Medium values with close intervals are somewhat subdued, but when accented forcefully with black and white they impart a rich, masculine quality.

Lack of value contrast in a design often leads to monotony. Some contrast is needed, and its location is of the utmost importance, for it is to this point that the eye will be drawn first. When we look at objects in the distance the contrast in value is slight, and their outlines are blurred and somewhat vague. The outlines of objects that are closer to the eye are sharp and in focus. For this reason, strong, sharp value contrasts appear as though they were in the foreground, and closely blended values seem further away. This principle has important application in costume for those who wish to increase or decrease apparent size. In like manner, the higher values, because they reflect more light, usually make objects and figures stand out and appear larger than objects of similar size in darker values. The latter phenomenon, however, is dependent upon the degree of contrast between the object and its background. An overweight skier will be more conspicuous against the snow-covered slopes in a black outfit than he would in camouflaging white.

It is clear that the degree of contrast in the lightness or darkness of colors helps to determine the predominant expression of the total appearance.

Intensity is the third dimension of color, and describes its brightness or dullness. Strong, brilliant, saturated colors are

Figure 12-19. Medium values accented by black and white impart a rich masculine quality.

---

[5]F. R. Quinn, A. Linn, and W. N. Hale, *Consumer Color Charts*, Munsell Color Company, Inc., Baltimore, Md., 1964, p. 11.

referred to as highly intense; weak, grayed, neutral colors are those that are low in intensity. In the Munsell system this attribute, which is termed **chroma,** is measured by the number of steps it departs from neutral gray. Starting with a neutral gray axis (see Figure 12-18), intensity steps are numbered outward from 1/ up to the strongest saturation obtainable for any given hue. The three-dimensional representation in Figure 12-18 shows the relationship of hue, value, and intensity, but only at value level 5/. These same relationships exist at all value levels.

The intensity of a hue is lowered by mixing it with its complement. Maximum saturation can be obtained only at the home value level for any given hue, and raising or lowering the value of a hue from that level automatically reduces its intensity. Hues with similar intensities usually combine to create a pleasing relationship, although weak or moderate hues are more harmonious than two or more different hues at maximum intensity. Vivid colors tend to produce strong, dramatic effects; grayed, subdued tones tend to be soft, subtle, and conservative.

Intensity, like the other dimensions of color, has its impact upon total appearance. Bright colors have much the same effect as warm hues; they tend to advance, attract attention, and thereby increase apparent size. Weak, subdued colors, like the cool hues, are receding, soothing, and less conspicuous.

Color illusions occur whenever two colors are juxtaposed. Since colors are rarely seen in isolation, it is important to understand how they affect each other when placed in close proximity. If we study the two reds in Plate II, we get the impression that they are different. When surrounded by yellow, red moves toward the violet side of the spectrum; when seen next to blue, red appears to be more orange. This simple phenomenon is known as the principle of **simultaneous contrast:** "Whenever two different colors come into direct contact, the differences between them will be intensified. They will tend to push apart. The change will be greater in proportion to the degree that they differ in value, hue, or chroma."[6]

The effect of hue contrast is readily demonstrated in Plate II. Contiguous hues force each other apart on the color spectrum. A bright yellow dress worn by a cool blonde will impart greenish tones to the hair. Turquoise next to green will appear blue, just as red will push purple toward blue.

In the case of value contrast, a middle value will appear lighter against dark colors, and lower in value against light colors. Again in Plate II the same red looks darker when surrounded by light yellow than it does when surrounded with a medium blue. This is why light colors seem more luminous when combined with black, and why dark colors appear brighter when contrasted against white.

---

[6]Quinn, *Consumer Color Charts,* p. 10.

The interaction between different intensities also alters the frame of reference in which we see color. A weak blue worn next to a saturated blue will turn into gray. Old rose will make a medium red more intense by comparison. A dull brown suit will intensify the color of rich brown hair.

Another phenomenon that affects the way we see color is commonly known as the **after-image.** If you gaze fixedly at the red circle in Plate III and then transfer your gaze to the white paper, you will see a pale blue-green spot of color, the complement of red. If you repeat this experiment with any other bright color you will find that a complementary after-image will appear. This occurs because the nerve endings in the human eye tire quickly of strong color; sensitivity to that color is reduced and the complementary receptors in the eye become dominant. In other words, the eye provides its own relief from strong color. When the eye shifts its gaze from a bright orange sweater down to neutral gray slacks, it will superimpose an after-image of blue, making the slacks appear bluish gray. A bright magenta worn next to white skin will impart a greenish tone to the skin.

When an intense hue is combined with the color from which it differs the most—its complement—a series of successive after-images are superimposed, increasing intensity to the point of vibration. This explains why it is difficult for the eye to look at strong complementary colors in close combination. The vibrating sensation is reduced when one or both complements are toned down or grayed. In costume, pleasing effects are difficult to achieve with intensifying opposites.

The **expressiveness** of color is evident in our common daily associations of color with mood or emotion. Even people who have a limited sensitivity to color talk about "feeling blue," being "in the pink" of condition, feeling "green with envy," or having a "rosy disposition." Individuals vary in their perception of color, and the meanings that they attach to specific hues are usually found to be dependent upon their past associations and experiences with color. There have been a number of experimental studies, however, that have identified some of the commonalities in the human reaction to color.[7]

One experiment for example, conducted in the pediatrics unit of the Teaching Hospital at the University of Florida, recorded the reactions of children between the ages of nine months and five years when approached first by a nurse in a white uniform, and then by a nurse wearing a softer pastel. The children were reported to be calmer, more relaxed, and amenable when nurses wore the tinted rather than the stark

[7]The research on color associations, attitudes, and preferences is too extensive to be summarized here. If the reader wishes to pursue this aspect of color further, reference to the *Psychological Abstracts* will yield a number of sources. Consult the subject index on color. A suggested text on the subject is C. W. Valentine, *The Experimental Psychology of Beauty*, Methuen & Company, London, 1962. See chapters 1 and 2 on "Colour and Colour Preferences," and "Attitudes to Colours and Combinations of Colours."

white uniforms. Similar studies indicate that wall colors have a decided effect upon the mental outlook of patients.

In general, studies have shown remarkable similarity in the characteristics attributed to particular colors by different individuals. The warm colors (yellow, orange, and red) are usually seen as cheerful, aggressive, stimulating, and exciting, while the cool hues are suggestive of quietness, aloofness, tranquility, or serenity.[8] It is important to keep the character of color in mind when judging or combining colors.

> For example, a sad brown might be enlivened by combination with a cheerful yellow, while a "strong, egotistical" purple overbears completely a "simpering, mild" blue. It is likely that this character aspect is inadequately grasped by many people in the combining of colours; and it would seem that some women in choosing dress colour schemes, whilst very sensitive to the clashing or blending of colours as such, ignore the more subtle beauty which is derived from a blending of this aesthetic character of the colours with their own characters and temperaments.[9]

Our sensitivity to color is sometimes conditioned by factors beyond our control. Some individuals, more prevalently men, are actually blind to one or more colors in the spectrum, while other rare individuals can "feel" differences in color with their eyes closed. Most people, however, can develop their sensitivity through a study of color attributes and gain an increased perception of color in their clothes and environment.

The expressive qualities of color are summarized in a charming yet movingly sensitive statement by Mary O'Neill:

> The Colors live
> Between black and white
> In a land that we
> Know best by sight.
> But knowing best
> Isn't everything,
> For colors dance
> And colors sing,
> And colors laugh
> And colors cry—
> Turn off the light
> And colors die,
> And they make you feel
> Every feeling there is
> From the grumpiest grump
> To the fizziest fizz.

---

[8]For the symbolic meanings usually associated with specific colors see Graves, *Art of Color and Design*, pp. 402–408, Morton, *Costume and Personal Appearance*, pp. 175–177, or Valentine, *Experimental Psychology of Beauty*, p. 57.
[9]Valentine, *Experimental Psychology of Beauty*, p. 62.

And you and you and I
Know well
Each has a taste
And each has a smell
And each has a wonderful
Story to tell. . . . [10]

SUMMARY *Developing sensitivity*

Clothing is at once so ubiquitous, so directly observable, and so personally relevant that it provides a common medium through which our sensitivity to the basic components of aesthetic expression can be developed. The five plastic elements have been defined as line, space, form, texture, and color. Variation in the qualities of each of these elements contributes to the overall effect of the total design. **Line** may vary in straightness, direction, and strength. **Space** varies in its relative size and shape. **Form** is a composite of the human figure itself, the silhouette of the costume, and the positive shapes within the boundaries of the silhouette. **Texture** may be described by its visual appearance, the tactile sensations it produces, and by its quality of "hand." **Color**, probably the most complex of all the elements yet at the same time the most stimulating, varies greatly in its three dimensions of hue, value, and intensity. In costume, none of the elements exists in isolation, and each one is affected by the other four in combination. The creative process requires a knowledge and understanding of the nature of these tools in order to use them effectively in dress.

Expressiveness in dress

We may approach the study of costume at the logical, objective, descriptive level; that is, we may consider separately the various aspects of line, form, space, texture, and color, and we may analyze their function in the total design. This level of human perception confines itself to intellectual observations and produces an awareness of design qualities, an understanding of their effects, and perhaps an appreciation of their aesthetic unity.

There are other phases of human perception, however, that are not objective observations but rather subjective reactions. Clothing has the power to arouse feelings and thoughts in the mind of the observer, emotions that are not easily described but keenly felt. The costume serves as a symbol—a kind of catalyst that evokes feelings which extend far beyond the costume

---

[10]"The colors live" from *Hailstones and Halibut Bones*, copyright © 1961 by Mary O'Neill. Reprinted by permission of Doubleday & Company, Inc. Written for children but more appreciated by adults, this delightful book is a series of rhythmic verbal images of the meaning and emotional qualities of color.

Figure 12-20. The tasteful flair of Douglas Fairbanks, Jr. is evident in this combination of a fitted, double-breasted camel coat, worn with contrasting muffler and velour snap-brim. His advice to would-be Beau Brummells: "It's better to be fitted than not."

Figure 12-21. Walt Frazier flamboyantly polishes his gleaming Rolls Royce with a $5,000 mink coat.

itself. If the wearing of a bowler hat and a tweedy suit conveys the essence of the "typical" Englishman, such symbols may conjure up associations of political sentiments, social formalities, moral sensibilities—none of which can be visualized, but all of which can be deeply felt or experienced.

A clothing symbol stands for something beyond itself. Symbolism in dress is often unconscious, but a symbol used consciously can be more powerful; that is, the designer or the wearer can—through careful manipulation—heighten the effect that he wishes to create. A dynamic, forceful personality can be emphasized by strong angular lines, or by forms that are large in scale and widely spaced. The effect may be compounded further through the use of coarse, heavy-handed textures, and bold colors in striking contrasts. Thus, through a knowledgeable use of symbols, the communicator draws the communicant more closely into the mood that is intended. A truly artistic experience is one that requires personal involvement, both at the level of creative expression and at the level of enjoyment, understanding, or appreciation. The creation of clothing, therefore, or the organization of dress, is a form of artistic expression through which feelings and ideas are communicated. This concept is embodied in the term **expressiveness.**

The creation of clothing

Every age has a distinctive flavor, just as every designer develops a characteristic style, and both these phenomena derive from expressiveness. "Style" is very closely allied to symbol making. Every buyer familiar with the products of the couture can spot the earmarks of a coat by Ungaro, a gown by Grés, or a suit by the tailors of Savile Row. In other words, the designer imparts his individual imprint to the product of his craft, and in doing so he reveals a part of his nature, his ideals, his thoughts, and his emotions. The product in turn evokes a similar or perhaps a widely different range of feelings and emotions in the observer.

Why is it that some designers see woman as something ethereal—beautiful, constrained, statuesque—while others see her as being quite logical—uncompromisingly modern and stripped for action? The answer of course is that all designers project themselves into their work. Courrèges began his career as an engineer. He was profoundly influenced by the ideas of LeCorbusier, the architect, and maintains almost as much interest in architecture as he does in the couture.

In his own words Courrèges explains: "Luxury in clothes to me has no meaning. It belongs to the past. My problem is not rich embroidery, useless lavishness—it is to harmoniously resolve function problems—just like the engineer who designs a plane, like the man who conceives a car."[11]

[11]"The Lord of the Space Ladies," *Life*, 21 May 1965, p. 57.

Some observers may find difficulty in perceiving in a design the same meanings that the creator himself intended to convey. Particularly if a designer is ahead of his time—as creative people often are—it is inevitable that many people will view his work in the light of their own experience rather than in the light in which the designer sees himself. The more we understand the goals of the artist, the more we will share in the expressiveness of his designs.

The organization of dress

Not everyone can express himself through the actual creation of clothing. Particularly in our world of mass-produced ready-to-wear wardrobes, the opportunity for self-expression often seems limited. Technology to some extent reduces individuality, yet at the same time it has made available a much greater variety of products to more people than ever before in history. The element of choice making becomes an increasingly complex problem. In this sense, every individual assumes the position of the artist; the extent to which the solution of a problem shows his personal influence is an indication of his expressiveness.

Long before Johnny Carson became involved in the apparel business, the clothes that he wore on the "Tonight" show had a powerful influence on the sartorial tastes of American men. For this reason, he thinks of himself as epitomizing the American man, and he shuns extremes of dress. "The average guy feels a little weird wearing costumes," he says. "Doc (Severinsen, the garishly attired bandleader) can carry it off. But people forget Doc is a musician, a personality."[12] Not all men, however, are so conservative. Some are elegantly flamboyant (Figure 12-21) and dramatic.

Expressiveness also can be reserved and dignified, as exemplified by the quiet grace of Pat Nixon. While she was consistently described as lacking a fashion image, her explanation was simple: "I want understandable clothes, clothes that appeal to the masses and don't get criticized."[13]

In contrast, the image that singer Chér projects through what she wears is anything but "reserved." Her clothes, which are as lithe and bone-pared as her figure, have made her a high-gloss sex symbol.

The expression of personality through the medium of dress comes about through the development of an individual style, a style that becomes the symbol of the person and gives the dominant external "tone" or expressive quality to his appearance. The symbol may not reveal all of one's traits, and in fact

The creation of clothing is a form of artistic expression through which feelings and ideas are conveyed.

Figure 12-22. This sultry dress with exposed midriff is typical of the bone-sleek styles that have made Chér Bono a fashion pacesetter.

Aesthetic expression of the self through clothing may lead to a deeper comprehension of one's most salient characteristics.

---

[12]Carson as quoted by Howard Kissel in "Johnny Carson: The Comedian as Clothier," *Gentlemen's Quarterly*, November 1971, p. 70.
[13]As quoted in *Women's Wear Daily*, 10 August 1972.

Figure 12-23. The expressive power of dress can transform one's character.

may even camouflage some. Yet a distinctive style gives a summarizing effect to personality, and offers a solution to an artistic problem that is unique to the individual.

SUMMARY   *Expressiveness in dress*

Clothing is an ideal medium through which man may fulfill his creative needs and express his individuality. The designer, as well as the person who selects and organizes the components of costume, may communicate moods, feelings, emotions, and ideas through the pervasive effects of art elements. Expressiveness in dress is that quality of appearance which is intensifying, unifying, and summarizing. It is the underlining of traits that facilitates a shared experience between communicator and communicant, and helps to create in the observer the same moods and emotions that were intended by the artist.

FOR FURTHER READING

Birren, Faber, ed. *A Grammar of Color: A Basic Treatise on the Color System of Albert H. Munsell.* New York: Van Nostrand Reinhold Company, 1969.

Faulkner, R. and E. Ziegfeld. *Art Today.* New York: Holt, Rinehart & Winston, 1969. (Chapter 11, "Form, Line, Texture, and Space," and Chapter 12, "Light and Color.")

Hoffman, R. M. "Measuring the Aesthetic Appeal of Textiles," *Textile Research Journal* 35, no. 5, May 1965, pp. 428–434.

Morton, Grace M. *The Arts of Costume and Personal Appearance.* New York: John Wiley & Sons, 1964.

O'Neill, Mary. *Hailstones and Halibut Bones.* Garden City, N.Y.: Doubleday & Company, 1961.

Valentine, C. W. *The Experimental Psychology of Beauty.* London: Methuen & Company, 1962. (Chapter 2, "Colour and Colour Preferences," Chapter 3, "Attitudes to Colours and Combinations of Colours," and Chapter 4, "Form: Lines, Shapes and Suggested Movement.")

DISCUSSION QUESTIONS

1. Bring to class a picture or magazine illustration of a garment or costume that you find particularly appealing.

   (a) What kinds of lines have been used in the design (e.g., straight, curved, vertical, oblique, thin, wide, contrasting, repeated, long, short, and so forth)? Is there a great variety of different kinds of lines, or does one type of line predominate?

   (b) What basic forms or shapes can you identify in the design (e.g., rectangles, circles, triangles or ovoids)? Do these shapes relate to or contrast with body contour?

(c) What do you see as the "background" of this design? What emerges as the "figure" or focal point?

(d) How would you describe the textures used? How would they rate with respect to the polar traits listed on page 250 in the text? Are they similar or strongly contrasting?

(e) If the illustration is in color, identify the hue of each color used according to the Munsell color chart. Do the same for value and intensity. Are the colors, in their three dimensions, related or contrasting? Does one color predominate? Which colors are subordinate? How would you describe the value key of this design?

(f) What qualities appear to be the most outstanding features of this design?

2. What is meant by "expressiveness" in dress?

3. How do people express themselves through dress?

4. What do you think are the "expressive qualities" of the design that you selected in question 1? Specifically, what kinds of feelings, ideas, or emotions are conveyed? Do other students in the class agree with your interpretation? If not, what may account for such differences in perception?

13

Standards of Taste and Beauty

WE HAVE SEEN that the effect of individual elements in a design may be compounded or intensified in their impact when combined with other elements of like qualities. Stimulating line may be reinforced by stimulating color in extreme contrasts of dark and light so that the total effect is quite shocking. On the other hand, the effects of such elements may also be tempered or even obscured when combined with dissimilar elements. Thus, we use straight lines to counteract the curves of a full rounded figure, and soft bulky tweeds to camouflage the hard and bony angularity of the beanpole.

By using art components in this way, we are able to alter the frame of reference in which we see the human form, and in doing so, we can create illusions or effects that would not be possible in any other way except through dress. Through the manipulation of art elements, dress may be organized into a satisfying and meaningful whole in such a way that the whole becomes more meaningful than its parts.

But what is the ultimate goal of such organization? The terms "more meaningful," "more effective," "more beautiful," imply that there are some universal standards by which we are to judge the value of the total design. How do we resolve the fact that lips distended with discs are considered "beautiful" by the Suyá Indians and "ugly" by most Americans? Why is it that a costume that was regarded as the ultimate in beauty ten years ago appears hideous to us today? Are the standards of beauty ever-changing—and often contradictory—from culture to culture, from era to era?

The evaluation of costume or dress can reflect all manner of criteria which may be only incidental to its aesthetic quality. We may judge it on the basis of the skill that was required to produce it. We may see it as valuable in one social context but not within another. We may place great weight upon its symbolic value, or on the power with which it communicates an idea. We may view it in terms of its cultural manifestations, that is, the extent to which it epitomizes the character of the times. Clearly, each of these approaches has some validity in determining the worth of a costume, and the ultimate judgment probably will involve them all.

If, however, we confine our judgments to those qualities that delight the eye, to the organization of elements that makes the design comfortable or pleasurable to behold, we are then dealing objectively with the aesthetic attributes of clothing.

What is beauty?

For centuries philosophers have argued the definition of beauty, a word that has such universal meaning, yet a concept that is difficult to express in objective terms. Reactions to aesthetic stimuli depend not so much upon association and experience as they do upon the psychological similarities in the minds of men. Beauty has come to be synonymous with the human desire for order: man is made restless by discord and confusion and thus seeks to systematize, organize, and categorize his experiences into something which is meaningful and satisfying to him.

Balance, for example, creates a feeling of rest or repose; it is a reassuring and stable quality. Lack of balance, on the other hand—or the fear of losing one's balance—becomes a disturbing factor and makes for insecurity. Simple action patterns, repeated over and over, become effortless when executed in time to rhythm or pattern. Rhythm means regularity—repetition on which one can depend—and like balance, gives a kind of psychological reassurance.

The human need for order and stability, however, is ramified by a corresponding need for interest and excitement. Thus, the principles of dominance and subordination, unity in variety, emphasis through contrast, all stem from man's attempt to maintain a pleasing relationship between order and diversity, between stability and new experience.

The organizing principles

Nature has a habit of combining elements in a way that is never absolute, seldom regular, yet always logical. In his search for beauty man attempts to simulate nature's way by tempering sameness with variation. There is often disagreement over the precise terminology that best describes this concept, but the semantic differences seem to be not so important as the overall agreement on intended meaning.

Beauty involves **order** (call it what you will—unity, compatibility, consistency, relatedness, integration, harmony), without which human sensations are troubled and confused; and its

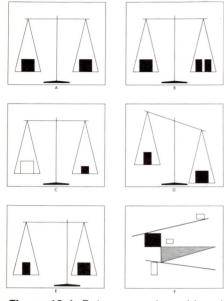

Figure 13-1. Balance can be achieved in a number of ways.

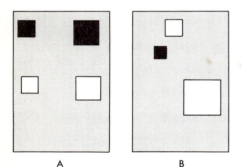

Figure 13-2. A design judgment problem in balance.

counterpart, **interest** (call it variety, contrast, conflict, difference), without which our sensations cannot be fully stimulated. In general, people are bored with the obvious, excited by the unexpected; yet they are uncomfortable in disorder and secure in regularity.

The problem is knowing how to achieve the proper balance between order and interest. Many years ago, Birkhoff developed a mathematical formula that would yield a precise quantity of aesthetic merit. It was based upon the theory that aesthetic measure (M) is equal to the order (O) divided by the complexity (C), or $M = O/C$. Thus, the value of M is increased if the complexity is diminished without altering the order, or if the order is increased without changing the complexity.[1]

In direct oppostion to such absolute standards is the theory that standards of any sort have no meaning for they impinge upon the individual's freedom to respond to art objects.

Somewhere between these two extremes lies a logical set of criteria that can guide us in the organization, interpretation, and evaluation of art experiences. The following principles may help the student in evaluating the organization of elements within a design.

Balance, the first organizing principle, is achieved through equal weights or forces on both sides of a central axis. If we observe the human figure in action, we will find that the head is always balanced over the center of gravity. Were this not true, the figure would fall over without some external means of support. Visual balance is much like our physical balance. Loss of equilibrium is an uncomfortable experience.

Balance may be accomplished in any one of several ways. The scales in Figure 13-1 are abstract representations of formal and informal balance. Scale A illustrates formal or bisymmetric balance, which is the most obvious and probably the easiest to achieve, because one side is the mirror image of the other. It presents a stately and dignified type of symmetry, but can easily become static and uninteresting if other aspects of the design are not handled skillfully. Scale B is a variation of formal balance, in which one shape is replaced by two smaller shapes having a combined equal weight. Another variation in Scale C uses a much larger object on the left, but because it is so much lighter in value it can still be placed at the same distance from the fulcrum. Obviously, all designs are not balanced designs. If unequal weights are used at equal distances from the center, equilibrium will be lost as it is in Scale D.

Informal or asymmetric balance brings unequal weights into equilibrium by arranging them at different distances from the axis, as is shown in Scales E and F. The latter is a more complex arrangement, and requires greater skill in identifying the visual weight of dissimilar elements. Usually the darker values,

---

[1]George D. Birkhoff, *Aesthetic Measure*, Harvard University Press, Cambridge, 1933.

the stronger intensities, and the warmer hues carry greater visual weight than light, dull, or cool elements of comparable size and shape. The heavier areas of a design, therefore, need to be reduced in size or placed nearer the center and bottom.

Balance affects the relationship between individual shapes and the background or field of a design. This is shown in a simplified way in Figure 13-2. The larger shapes in A are placed to the right of the axis and almost at the same distance as the smaller shapes on the left. In addition, the dark, heavy shapes are at the top, making the whole effect not only lopsided but top-heavy. The rearrangement in B eliminates the overpowering dark and increases the weight of the white square by enlarging it. The dark accent is small, high, and farther from the edge of the field. The design has been stabilized, and at the same time the forms have been brought into relationship with the ground.

A similar top-heaviness can be observed in Figure 13-3. But this also shows that merely transferring the weight to the bottom is not the answer, for a costume can easily become bottom-heavy. A reduction in size or area is usually required as well. It is this top-to-bottom balance that is often destroyed by a large bright hat, a dark blouse worn with a light skirt, or white shoes with a middle- or low-valued costume. Men's dress provides a standard formula for achieving balance: pocket handkerchief to the left, hat tilted slightly to the right.

Most types of informal balance provide greater interest than bisymmetric arrangements, but it must be remembered that asymmetry is not achieved merely by making two sides of a costume unalike.

Proportion is the principle of design that deals with relationships or ratios. When we talk about the proportions of a room, we are referring to its length in relation to its height and width. The spacial dimension of one measure is impossible to comprehend visually except in comparison with another. The human figure appears heavy or thin on the basis of its width/height ratio, which for the average person is 2:7.5.

There are two basic design problems that deal with proportion. One is the planning of shapes, sizes, spaces, or areas within the figure rectangle in such a way that each part bears a relationship to each other and to the whole. The second is the problem of creating the illusion of pleasing proportions with costume when the spacial dimensions of the body are not pleasing. The latter function of proportion will be discussed in Chapter 16, and we will concern ourselves here with an analysis of space division within the silhouette and the relationship of forms within the total design.

In Figure 13-4 we see that the body rectangle is subdivided into shapes, some of which are related to anatomy, and others that are dictated by fashion. Waistline placement and hem, jacket, and trouser lengths are the major horizontal divisions that fluctuate from year to year. An increase in hem width will

1931   1915

Figure 13-3. Top- and bottom-heaviness produce a lack of equilibrium in design.

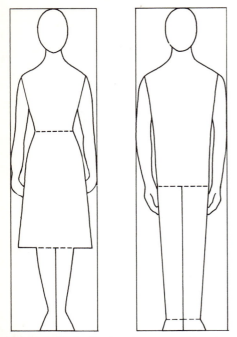

Figure 13-4. Basic shapes within the body rectangle.

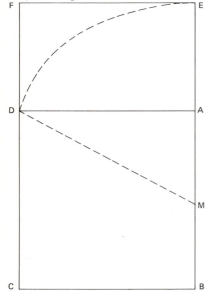

Figure 13-5 The Golden Mean Rectangle. (ABCD = perfect square; M = ½AB; MD = radius of arc to E.)

also alter the visual dimension of height, just as shoulder padding and wide trouser cuffs create different width/height ratios. It is important to identify the proportions of these basic shapes before going on to the more complex relationships.

Problems in proportion parallel those within the larger organization of interest in order. How can the figure be divided into shapes that give variety and at the same time maintain a relatedness to the whole? The Greek laws of proportion give us a clue that is embodied in the *Golden Mean*. The Golden Mean Rectangle has a width equal to the side of a square, and its length equal to half that measure plus the diagonal of half the square. This produces a ratio in which the smaller part (BC) is to the larger part (BE) as the larger part is to the whole (BC + BE). Rectangle ADFE will also be found to have the same proportions as the larger BCFE (see Figure 13-5).

In effect, this creates a relationship which is not too difficult for the eye to perceive, and yet not so obvious that the eye dismisses it without further exploration. The body rectangle itself does not conform to this proportion,[2] but many of the shapes within the silhouette take on a visual relationship that approximates it.

Of course *all* forms have proportions, whether they are pleasing or not. For this reason, it is probably more accurate to talk about **related proportions,** as opposed to equal and to unrelated proportions, than it is to use the term **proportion** alone as an organizing principle. If we were able to use as precise a measure as a scale, we might be able to say that a design either had balance or it was not in balance. Aesthetic judgments can never be that absolute, however, and the best that we can do is to say that design X is "more nearly balanced" or "less well-balanced" than design Y. Such judgments are always relative.

Another aspect of proportion is concerned with the sizes of different objects used in combination with the total costume. This is usually expressed by the more specific term **scale,** and refers to the size relationship between different parts of the costume and the wearer. A handbag that may in itself be designed with good proportions but scaled to a large figure can look like an outsized shopping bag when carried by a diminutive person. The sizes of hats, collars, pockets, and buttons all present problems in scale relationships. This also extends to surface patterns of fabrics. A small-scaled print that would be suitable and attractive on a petite woman often makes the large figure seem larger because of the heightened contrast in size. Details of costume and articles worn as accessories will appear to be more related if their sizes are scaled to the size of the wearer.

Rhythm is that quality of design that imparts a graceful, flowing movement throughout the costume. A dancer who lacks

---

[2]Body proportions are far more complex in both relatedness and variation. Refer to Figure 12-11.

AESTHETICS AND DRESS

rhythm is clumsy and awkward; music without rhythm is aimless and incoherent; a costume without rhythm is static and disjointed. Words become poetic when they are combined with a planned interval and a beat or accent. This same concept of orderly and related movement applies to visual design. Just as rhythm in music helps the ear to make an easy transition from one note to another, rhythm in costume leads the eye from line to line, from shape to shape, from color to color.

Rhythm, like balance, can be achieved in a number of ways, and it may vary from very simple to more complex forms. *Repetition* of lines or shapes, textures or colors, can produce a rhythmic pattern. Like the simple waltz, it has a regular beat, but without some variation it becomes incessantly repetitious and monotonous.

Greater interest can be generated by introducing some variety in the repeat. Note the increasing size of skirt puffs and rosettes in Figure 12-8 as the bustle cascades to the floor. The horizontals become wider and wider as they move down the figure, giving the silhouette the shape of a great cone, with the head of a woman at the apex. This type of gradual transition from the wide to the narrow, from the large to the small, is known as *gradation* or *progression*. Music that becomes progressively louder has a way of building up attention that is somewhat more dynamic than a composition which maintains the same resonance throughout. In like manner, progressions in the art elements can build greater interest by increasing or decreasing one or more quality. Colors may progress from hue to hue, from light to dark, from bright to grayed; textures may go from dull to shiny, rough to smooth.

Movement also can be created by the use of *continuous line* that may carry the eye throughout the design.

Emphasis is the fourth organizing principle. Emphasis helps to focus attention on the most important areas of a design, creating a center of interest through the dominance of a particular art element. The eye is disturbed and confused when confronted with equally strong conflicting ideas; the conflict cannot be resolved until one idea is allowed to dominate all others. Dominance of one kind of line, shape, texture, or color simplifies the appearance of an ensemble and helps to create an impression of unity.

Emphasis is illustrated in a simplified form in the comparison of the two designs in Figure 13-6. Design A has a dominant vertical direction; the repetition of the perpendicular can be seen in the background shape, in the lines and shapes having the longest dimension, and in the placement of elements within the total composition. Horizontals are used for contrast, but these are kept subordinate to the vertical and are grouped together to create the major focal point. The eye travels from there along the zigzag path to a secondary interest area of the five small

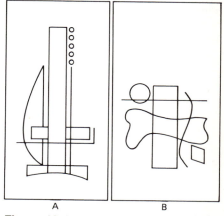

Figure 13-6. A design judgment problem in emphasis.

Figure 13-7. Here subordinate centers of emphasis are created by the buttons at the waist and sleeve.

Aesthetic integration in dress requires a satisfying balance between order (without which human sensations are confused) and interest (without which human awareness cannot be fully stimulated).

circles which contrast in shape with the predominantly straight lines and shapes. Their size and placement, however, do not alienate them from the other elements. Design B lacks a dominant form and direction. Verticals compete with horizontals, straight lines equal curved lines, diamond rivals disk; the same degree of contrast exists throughout the arrangement so that a center of interest is lost.

Men's costume provides a standard though somewhat static formula for the attainment of emphasis. The center of greatest contrast usually occurs near the face, with the tie making the transition to the dominant area of the suit. A less monotonous effect is achieved in Figure 13-7, where the value contrast at the neck is supported through repetition in subordinate centers created by the buttons at the waist and sleeve. At the same time, a pleasing rhythm is developed through the use of stitch-trimming on pockets and lapels, connecting major and minor centers of interest in their proper sequence of importance, and providing an easy path for the eye to follow.

Thus, emphasis can be achieved through strong contrasts in value, but the contrast can also come about through bright intensities of color, unusual shapes, the use of different textures, a boldness of size, or a juxtaposition of contrasting lines. Such contrasts create effective centers of interest only if they are seen against a background of dominant elements that give unity to the design. Too much contrast results in disorder; lack of contrast produces monotony.

When the art elements are combined according to the organizing principles of balance, proportion, rhythm, and emphasis, the overall effect is a unity of design that permits effortless enjoyment on the part of the beholder. A design must be evaluated with *all* of the principles in mind. An outstanding example of rhythm may be woefully lacking in balance; emphasis can often be achieved by sacrificing scale or good proportion. The final analysis will depend on our ability to integrate all of these ideas into a total pattern.

Organization in color

The fundamental principles underlying the aesthetic use of color in dress are the same as those which apply to the other art elements. Because color is somewhat more complex in its dimensions, however, it merits special consideration. There are three basic factors that control the effectiveness of costume colors.

Choice of the predominant hue

Unity in color organization begins with the selection of a hue that will be allowed to dominate in the design. Any color can be beautiful if combined skillfully, but in costume at least, the major hue will probably be more effective if it is related and flattering to the individual's skin tones, hair, and eyes. The predominant hue sets the mood or the feeling of the design. It may be warm or cool, subdued or striking, but whatever the choice, it will be the one color around which the harmony will be built.

The predominant hue may or may not occupy the largest area in the design. It will maintain ascendancy as long as the colors combined with it are shifted toward that hue from their normal position on the color circle. For example, if the major theme is to be yellow, reds that shift toward the orange side and blues that are on the greenish side, when used in combination, will produce an overall effect of yellow regardless of the amount or saturation of yellow actually used. In other words, if all hues take on a yellowish cast an impression of unity will be achieved.

A predominance of hue is thus made possible through the suppression of colors within the range of its complement. This does not mean that complementary hues can never be used together; a touch of red or orange is often needed to warm a predominantly cool color scheme, and the warm hues may require bits of blue or green for accent. If used in controlled amounts, opposite colors will not destroy the unity of a design.

Restricting the color range

In costume, a limited number of colors can be used together successfully. Most students will find that an organized plan provides a starting point for color harmony.

The simplest type of mechanical color scheme is the *monochromatic*, in which all colors in the scheme are value or intensity variations of the same hue. A monochromatic color scheme may be made entirely of greens (pale green, gray-green, forest green), or oranges (beige, apricot, brown), or any other single hue on the color circle.

Analogous hues are neighboring colors that have some basic hue in common. For example, blue-green, blue, and blue-violet all have blue in common. In general, the related color harmonies (monochromatic and analogous) produce quiet, restful combinations that are easy to wear.

Color chords based upon contrasting hues are at once more striking and more difficult to bring into harmony. *Complementary* color schemes are those which combine any two hues that are opposite each other on the color circle. Greater variety is introduced by including the two hues on either side of the complement, e.g., orange with blue-green and purple-blue. This type of color chord is termed the *split-complementary* because the complement is split into two components. A double complementary color scheme uses two adjacent hues with their respective complements.

Figure 13-8. Various types of color chords.

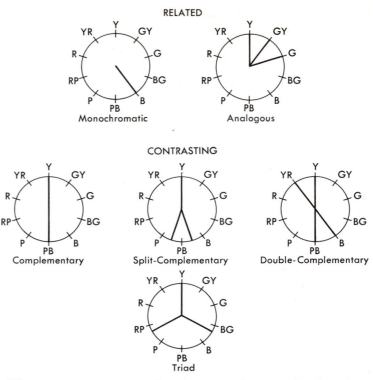

RELATED

Monochromatic

Analogous

CONTRASTING

Complementary

Split-Complementary

Double-Complementary

Triad

The greatest variety in hue is created in *triad* color plans which use any three colors that are equidistant on the color circle.

Almost any combination of hues can be made to seem pleasant or unpleasant if their values and intensities are carefully controlled. A close range of values will produce more harmonious combinations than strong contrasts. Increased unity also will be achieved if colors are combined in their natural order of value.

Restricting the range of hues, values, and intensities used together will provide a relatedness or unity in the color plan. Conversely, attraction is basically a matter of contrast, and contrast may be produced by any of the three color attributes. The degree of contrast that is desirable in any scheme is determined largely by the overall effect one wishes to achieve.

Unity in color organization can be achieved by allowing one hue to predominate, and by restricting the range of colors that are combined with it.

Determining the color areas

The use of equal amounts of different colors in a costume negates the principle of hue predominance. Another reason for avoiding equal areas of color is that some colors are visually "heavier" than others, and some more demanding in their attention-getting qualities.

AESTHETICS AND DRESS

Large areas of low-intensity colors are balanced by small areas of bright color. Research in color psychology seems to bear out the fact that most people prefer saturated colors in smaller quantities and larger areas of the less intense hues. As colors progress toward neutrality, their specific hue is less well defined. By increasing the size of the color area, a greater stimulating effect is produced and the uncertainty of its actual color is diminished. Stronger hues are less apt to lose their identity even when reduced in size. In some cases therefore, an extremely brilliant color can be used effectively with weaker ones, providing that its relative area is sufficiently restricted.

It is important to remember that all the qualities of color are relative, i.e., colors are relatively warm, relatively bright, relatively light in contrast with the other colors with which they are used. The greater the contrast in any of these dimensions, the greater the attraction. Closer intervals will produce a greater feeling of unity.

Coordination in dress

Every article of clothing is composed of lines, shapes, spaces, texture, and color. Harmony in costume begins with the ability to create or select a suit, a dress, a coat, or separates that are balanced designs with good proportions, rhythmically related parts, and pleasing emphasis. The beauty of a garment, however, can be destroyed completely if it is combined with accessories that either lack beauty in themselves or are incompatible with the basic garment. Each component of the costume may be a well-designed object in itself, but it is the complete ensemble that gives the total effect—including the form, coloring, and personality of the individual who wears it. The whole is therefore different from the sum of its parts because each component of dress has either an enhancing or a mitigating effect upon every other component.

The terms "overdressing" and "underdressing" relate in part to the suitability of a costume for a particular occasion, but they are also used to describe too much variety on the one hand, and plain monotony on the other.

Line coordination

Accessories chosen to complete the ensemble will enhance the major structural lines of a garment if they are similar in character. A broad-brimmed hat, for example, will reduce the perceptual stimulus of predominantly vertical lines in a suit or dress. Rhythm can be achieved through the repetition of line in various parts of the costume. Turn back to Figure 12-16 and observe the harmonious relationship that is achieved through the repetition of softly curved lines in hat, muff, fichu, and dress.

Figure 13-9. Changes in the line of the silhouette are accompanied by subtle changes in the lines of the accessories. (A) The curved line of the bicorne hat repeats the button-trimmed edge of the coat. (B) The slightly concaved line of the top hat flows gracefully into the S-shaped vertical that sweeps along the front edge of the frock coat and into the trouser stripe. (C) Crown lines straighten as the silhouette loses its curves. (D) The straight horizontals of the skirt are echoed in the banded hat. (E) The softly rounded curves give way to (F) deeper convolutions in hat and bell-shaped skirt.

Figure 13-10. Size and shape coordination in this "Portrait of a Man in Black" by Ter Borch is produced by a consistent repetition of pyramidal forms in different dimensions. (Collection, The National Gallery, London.)

In the organization of dress, the whole transcends the sum of the parts, for each component either reinforces or mitigates the effect of all others with which it is combined.

Remember that strong contrasts in line will capture the eye; competing centers of interest will detract from a major focal point if line detail in accessories creates attention-getting contrasts.

Size and shape coordination

The degree to which we consider an accessory large or small is influenced somewhat by fashion, but even if large hats are the current mode, a huge hat will appear incongruous on a small person. We are quick to note the inconsistency that exists between the large brawny man with a full face and a tiny hat with a pee-wee brim. Size ratios are also important in the selection of purse size, collar widths, and the scale of jewelry and prints. A distinct difference in shape can make an article seem completely unrelated to the rest of the costume. A box handbag, for example, geometric in form, will bear little relationship to the undulating shapes created by a softly draped silhouette. There is a consistent repetition of form in the "Portrait of a Man in Black" (Figure 13-10). The pyramidal shape of the cloak is echoed in the crown of the hat, the skirted breeches, and the fanning ruffles below the knee.

Texture coordination

Articles chosen to be worn together will appear more related if they have a common purpose and a unity of idea or character. A slippery-smooth satin tie will be incompatible with a roughly hewn tweed unless other elements such as line or color give them some relationship. Harmonizing textures are generally those which provide some degree of variation without extreme differences in surface quality. Review Chapter 12, pages 249 to 251, to reinforce your understanding of textural harmony.

SUMMARY *What is beauty?*

The evaluation of dress may reflect all manner of criteria in determining the ultimate worth of a garment, but if we confine our judgments to those qualities that please the eye we can identify certain universal responses to beauty that appear to be grounded in man's psychological make-up. The human mind is made restless by discord and confusion, and thus seeks order in its environment. The need for stability, however, is tempered by a craving for interest and excitement. Thus, the organizing principles of balance, rhythm, proportion, and emphasis develop out of the opposing forces of order and interest, unity and variety.

These same principles are employed in the organization of color. One method for achieving a unified color scheme consists of the selection of a predominant hue, a restriction of the range of colors that are used together, and a careful weighing of relative color areas.

Evaluation of dress is made not on the basis of the garment alone, but upon the combined effect of all articles that are worn with it. A further perceptual interaction occurs between the costume itself and the form, coloring, and personality of the individual who wears it. Since each component of dress affects all others with which it is combined, the whole of one's appearance takes on greater meaning than the sum of its parts.

What is taste?

Few people, if any, are willing to make their selections of dress solely on the basis of aesthetic criteria. Attitudes, feelings, emotions, and preferences determine to a large extent what we like and what we dislike, what we choose to wear and what we refuse to wear. Any attempt to attire oneself in a manner that is radically different from an immediate circle of friends, or from the majority of people in the society, is equivalent to alienating oneself from group values and the standards of the culture in which we live. Taste, simply defined, is what we like. It implies a preference among alternatives that have aesthetic implications, but may or may not be based upon objective aesthetic criteria. For the most part our tastes are shaped by the time and place in which we live, and yet each individual has a unique set of experiences that condition his personal preferences. Taste is both cultural and individualistic in nature.

Individual taste

We have seen that there are certain innate reactions to beauty in design. Infants and small children evidence sensitivity to balance, and the regularity of rhythm — particularly in sounds — produces a soothing, hypnotic effect. The extent to which individuals experience these "normal" reactions, however, depends upon their perceptual abilities. People possess varying degrees of sensitivity to rhythm, balance, order, and so forth. Some may be sensitive to certain colors and not to others; a number of people are wholly blind to color.

Individuals also differ in their perception of elements and wholes. Young children and untrained adults tend to become absorbed in the parts of design rather than in the effect of the total composition. One beautiful line in a dress that is otherwise ugly, or a beautiful color in a suit that lacks distinction in general, may often produce such a strong liking that it becomes the main factor in evaluating the costume as a whole. Sensitivity to the techniques of construction influences the skills-oriented person to become absorbed with the technical product rather than the beauty of the design.

Familiarity is another factor that shapes the individual taste. People tend to like the things to which they are accustomed. Studies have shown that the development of taste and judgment is highly correlated to exposure. After an object has been around for a while, one gets used to it. The initial exposure to a new art form is rarely accompanied by sufficient comprehension for full appreciation, but after repeated study the hidden meanings emerge and the beholder finds himself enjoying the more complex forms of art that at first appeared to have no significance or value.

Valentine explains the dichotomy of the soothing versus the stimulating qualities of art as follows: "If our attention is to be held for more than a few moments some complexity must be found. . . . Yet the unity and structure of the object must be such that apprehension is facilitated and not frustrated by undue difficulties. Here, as we have just seen, familiarity is a supreme help."[3]

The findings of Valentine's research indicate that training in art is linked to an increased liking of more complex figures. Judgments of design made on the basis of familiarity or upon the purely personal associations with selected parts of the design are found to be more common among children and adults with little aesthetic training. They also have less concern for overall unity, and make their evaluations on the basis of their own subjective feelings toward the art object rather than any objective analysis of its aesthetic excellence. It also has been shown that individuals with extended art experience and high levels of perceptual awareness tend to exhibit a greater tolerance of experimentation in dress than those with limited exposure and lower perceptual ability.[4]

Our tastes also are affected by the fact that matters of clothing and appearance (or beauty) are weighted differently in the unique value patterns of an individual. For example, there are studies that seem to show that women who place greater value on the aesthetic and economic factors in their environment tend to have greater interest in dress, while the women who place greater value on religious and theoretical factors are relatively disinterested in clothes. Disinterested or not, clothing still reflects the values of the wearer. One's tastes, therefore, become synonymous with a sensitivity to the kind of dress that is appropriate to one's outlook and personality. In this sense, the individual's approach to art and clothing becomes a form of his own self-expression.

The world is full of people with vastly different perceptual abilities, educational levels, value patterns, and cultural backgrounds. Individual taste is a product of all of these combined.

[3]Valentine, *Experimental Psychology of Beauty*, p. 420.
[4]Edith Pankowski, "Perception of Clothing and Selected Areas of Tolerance for a Group of College Males," Unpublished dissertation, Pennsylvania State University, 1969.

Within the broad range of resulting attitude and opinion, writers and philosophers have attempted to categorize various levels of aesthetic taste according to one's stated or manifest preferences. Lynes, for example, separates tastes into "highbrow," "middlebrow," and "lowbrow." Gerard writes humorously about "Borax," "Homey," "Safe," and "Mellow" tastes.[5] Yet beneath the facetious facade, we can discern gradations of at least three generalized patterns of response to art forms.

There are those people whose tastes remain untrained and uncultivated. Largely because they are insensitive to the elements of form, they have very little positive identification with art of any kind. As Lynes would say, culture leaves them cold. Their response to beauty is one of indifference, and clothes need not be beautiful anyway as long as they are comfortable.

At the opposite extreme are those who have a high degree of perceptual awareness of art in many forms, and experience a genuine enjoyment of beauty. Because they have been exposed to a wide range of aesthetic experiences, they are able to develop an intellectual and objective approach that enables them to appreciate the more subtle and complex creations. The vast majority of Americans fall somewhere between the two extremes, which of course is what makes "popular taste" popular. This is a taste that is conditioned by majority opinion; it is a taste based on the principle that when in Rome it is best to do as the Romans do.

Popular taste is something that can be determined by vote. In the mid 1960's for example, the Gallup Poll set out to determine if our country was experiencing a breakdown in good taste. The following is a sample of the kinds of questions that were asked and the replies received from the American public:

Which Do You Consider to Be in "Bad Taste"	Percentage of Men	Percentage of Women	Total Population
Wearing hair curlers in public?	62	65	63
Women wearing shorts in public?	53	67	60
Men who wear sports shirts in church?	46	48	47
Wearing stretch pants in public?	40	48	44
Men who do not wear coats in restaurants?	23	19	21
Men who work around the house in undershirts?	17	20	19

---

[5]Actually he distinguishes twelve categories of taste in all. See Sanford E. Gerard, *How Good is Your Taste?* Doubleday & Company, Garden City, N.Y., 1946.

One might conclude from this that it is not all right for women to wear curlers or shorts in public but that it is all right for men to eat in their shirtsleeves and wear an undershirt around the house. One might also conclude that these are just symptoms of a more casual age, and let it go at that. The point that should be clear by now is that popular opinions are rarely based on objective analysis, and in most cases they bear little relationship to aesthetic criteria. The tastes of aesthetically oriented people are more closely allied to standards of beauty; for them "taste" and "beauty" are more nearly synonymous.

Individual tastes are conditioned by one's perceptual abilities, education, value pattern, and cultural background.

The tastes of an era

Any form of art must be judged not only on the basis of aesthetic criteria, but in light of the culture and the era in which it is produced. "The ruins of antiquity were just as available in the twelfth century as in the fifteenth, and there were esthetically sensitive people at both times. The twelfth-century people remained much more aloof to the classical remains because they lacked the underlying affinity of outlook needed to make the classical forms seem vital, not because they were unexposed to the forms or lacked the esthetic capacity for their appreciation."[6]

Tastes are not only varied, but they are changing, and like the other forms of artistic expression, clothing reflects the cognitive, moral, and social aspects of the times. The immediate reaction to radically new fashions is usually one of dislike. Most women regarded the plunging neckline and thigh-high skirts as being in extremely poor taste. But as the eyes become accustomed to a new idea through its frequent appearance in fashion magazines and newspapers, as manufacturers pour hundreds of thousands of dollars into production, as fashion leaders are seen and photographed in the controversial style, and as more and more ready-to-wear garments appear on the market at prices that make them available to all, the once prevalent value of modesty becomes less and less important.

The revolution in male wardrobes that began in the 1960's reflected a changing social pattern that went far beyond the length of the hair and the cut of the suit. It reflected what some writers called "the spirit of the NOW." For the decade of the sixties, that spirit included:

. . . a whole generation with no memory of global war, an internationality that increases daily ("You can't," complains one sociologist, "tell American teenagers from European ones until they open their mouths"), the final shedding of prewar morality, freedom of movement in clothes as well as travel, affluence, vitality and a wholesale blossoming of idiosyncrasy in the face of big problems

[6]Frank Seiberling, *Looking Into Art.* Henry Holt & Company, New York, 1959, p. 242.

AESTHETICS AND DRESS

and bland governments. At no time since the 1930s have so many elements—books, dances, art, slang, movies, dress, everything—coalesced into the same mood.[7]

Out of that mood of the sixties grew the tastes of the seventies—in many ways a kind of blanket acceptance of anything that defied what had once been considered as the "canons of good taste." The term "funky" (originally something that was considered offensive) was applied to things that were really extreme and distasteful. One student described it as "old stuff that's new now; like wedgies, Jean Harlow satin dresses, ankle straps, and red nail polish." Even though it started out as a big joke, funky flowered into fashion, and tastes changed accordingly.

Changing tastes are all a part of the changing times. Fashion historian James Laver submits that the same costume will likely receive the following evaluations at different times throughout its fashion cycle:

Indecent	10 years before its time
Shameless	5 years before its time
Daring	1 year before its time
SMART	
Dowdy	1 year after its time
Hideous	10 years after its time
Ridiculous	20 years after its time
Amusing	30 years after its time
Quaint	50 years after its time
Charming	70 years after its time
Romantic	100 years after its time
Beautiful	150 years after its time[8]

A group at the University of Nevada set out to test the validity of Laver's theory.[9] A conceptual model was developed which depicted in graphic terms the relative levels of acceptance connoted by Laver's adjectives (see Figure 13-11). The most negative attitudes were represented by the terms "hideous" and "ridiculous," while the most positive reactions were assigned to the words "smart" (the current fashion) and "beautiful" (a 150-year-old style). Six dresses were chosen from an historic costume collection that epitomized the fashion of each of the following periods: 1960's, 1950's, 1940's, 1920's, 1900's, and 1870's. The costumes were worn by live models, photographed in color, and shown to a sample of female subjects.

---

[7]Gloria Steinem, "The Ins and Outs of Pop Culture," *Life*, 20 August 1965, p. 75.
[8]Laver, *Taste and Fashion*, p. 202. Laver is somewhat inconsistent in estimating how long it takes for a style to become "dowdy." In his 1969 publication *Modesty in Dress*, he states that the same dress is "dowdy *three* years after its time, hideous *twenty* years after its time." Since the acceptance of a well-established fashion is likely to span a period from five to seven years, and its total cycle from inception to obsolescence may take up to ten years or more, it is difficult to pinpoint exactly the year in which a style should be considered "after its time."
[9]M. J. Horn, M. Amis, and T. ZoBell, "Ecology and Fashion: A Test of Laver's Law," Unpublished manuscript, November 1973.

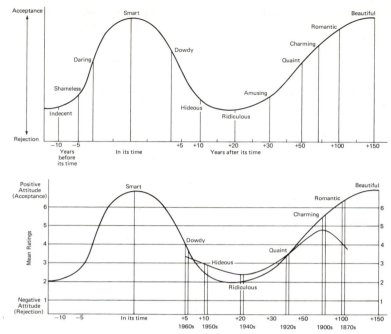

Figure 13-11. A theoretical model of Laver's Law.

Figure 13-12. Mean ratings of the six costumes plotted against Laver's Law.

Subjects were presented with Laver's list of adjectives and asked to select the word which they thought best described each of the six costumes. Each adjective was arbitrarily assigned a numerical value from one to six that was approximately equivalent to its position in the theoretical model of Laver's Law. In this way, it was possible to calculate mean ratings on a positive to negative continuum for each costume. These values were then plotted and superimposed on the theoretical model (Figure 13-12).

The most widely accepted style was the costume from the 1900's, a white cotton batiste accessorized with picture hat and parasol, and not unlike many of the "romantic" adaptations seen in the current retail market at the time. Almost half of all respondents chose the adjective "romantic" as most descriptive of this seventy-year-old fashion. Another 30 per cent thought it was "charming" or "quaint." Conversely, the style from the 1940's was considered to be either "hideous" or "ridiculous." Its broad padded shoulders and very tailored straight skirt was almost the antithesis of the 1900's costume with respect to design.

The astonishing "fit" of the two curves—the average ratings of the six costumes and the theoretical model—lends empirical support to Laver's Law. The greatest divergence from the model occurred in the evaluation of the 100-year-old style, a bustle-backed gown in purple taffeta. According to Laver's theory, it should have been considered at least "romantic" if not "beautiful," but it was more generally thought to be "quaint." Many writers today contend that the fashion cycle has been greatly accelerated. If we accept this proposition, it is not unreasonable to assume that the cyclical popularity of certain styles would be affected in a similar manner. In other words, the downward trend in appreciation after a hundred years may be indicative of a shortening of the fashion cycle itself.

In any case, it is clear that evaluations are made within a time perspective. The tastes of an era express a whole way of life. In whatever ways their manifestations may deviate from the accepted forms of beauty, the tastes of this era represent an outlook that typifies the here and the now. This relationship between the aesthetic character of clothing and the cultural forces that shape it will be discussed in greater detail in the next chapter.

Standards of taste are subjected to powerful cultural mutations and reflect the varied and changing spirit of the times.

SUMMARY *What is taste?*

Tastes are shaped by the time and place in which we live, and yet each individual's tastes are conditioned by his particular set of perceptual abilities, his education, and his values. Familiarity has a significant influence on our artistic preferences; most people know what they like, and they like what they know. Popular taste centers on art forms that are widely recognizable and preferred by the majority of people in a society regardless of aesthetic merit. Cultivated taste is developed through a broad exposure to many art forms coupled with a high degree of perceptual awareness.

Tastes vary not only with the individual, but with the changing times. The aesthetic values of dress must be judged in light of the culture and the era in which the clothing is produced. Attitudes, feelings, emotions, and preferences that dominate the tastes of a people at any given point in time coalesce into a spirit that reflects a total way of life, the flavor of an epoch.

FOR FURTHER READING

Beardsley, Monroe C. "Reasons in Aesthetic Judgments," in J. Hospers (ed.), *Introductory Readings in Aesthetics.* New York: Free Press, 1969.

Beitler, E. J., and B. C. Lockhart. *Design For You.* New York: John Wiley & Sons, 1969. (Chapter 2, "Guideposts for Organization.")

Birren, Faber. *Principles of Color.* New York: Van Nostrand Reinhold Company, 1969.

Gerard, Sanford E. *How Good Is Your Taste?* Garden City, N.Y.: Doubleday & Company, 1946.

Morton, Grace M. *The Arts of Costume and Personal Appearance.* New York: John Wiley & Sons, 1964. (Chapter 6,

"Principles of Composition," and Chapter 10, "The Art of Combining Colors.")

Seiberling, Frank. *Looking into Art*. New York: Henry Holt and Company, 1959. (Chapter 16, "The Question of Taste.")

DISCUSSION QUESTIONS

1. In what ways are the organizing principles derived from human experience?

2. What factors may affect the aesthetic tastes of an individual?

3. How does "popular taste" differ from aesthetic judgment?

4. Look through magazines from the 1950's and 1960's and select an illustration of a costume that you think would be considered beautiful today. Analyze the qualities of the design that seem to give it such timeless beauty.

5. How can you explain the fact that a costume which may have been considered beautiful a decade ago appears hideous to us today?

6. Philosophers have argued for centuries over the validity of aesthetic judgments. One school of thought suggests that there are absolute values in the form itself that establish its relative beauty. Another theorizes that it is only the meaning, or the ideas associated with the form, that can be evaluated. Our discussion of order and interest (or variety within unity), and the associated organizing principles lead us toward an interpretation of aesthetic experience dealing with the form or the object itself (in this case, clothing, or articles of clothing). Our discussion of expressiveness, on the other hand, leans toward the content or symbolic meaning of the form. How would you defend either of these positions? How do they relate to the concepts of "taste" and "beauty"?

14

Culture, Clothes, and Art

IN PART ONE of this book, culture was defined as the sum total of man's social inheritance, derived partly from the past and partly from contemporary innovations. Clothing was discussed in its relation to technical patterns, morals, customs, beliefs, values, and social structure. All of these factors contribute to the cultural climate in which art forms develop, and the forces that are exerted on the creators of dress are the same forces that influence architects, painters, sculptors, composers, writers, poets, and interior designers. The ascendant art forms of each period have a way of exaggerating the essential lines and elements that make it expressive of the needs and aspirations of the times. Even the aesthetic deficiencies of a style mirror the image that is favored by a society at any given point in time.

Clothing and other art forms

Neoclassicism

At the beginning of the nineteenth century the Western world was steeped in neoclassicism, a revival of the philosophy and styles of the ancient Greek and Roman cultures that existed some two thousand years before. The essence of that spirit is captured in painter David's portrait of Madame Récamier (Figure 14-1), a summary of the Directoire style in its purest form. David drew every detail of his pictures with the utmost precision in line, borrowing his forms exactly from the bits of painting and sculpture found in the excavated Roman cities of Pompeii and Herculaneum.

Figure 14-1. David's portrait of Madame Récamier shows the Directoire style in its purest form.

In this same period Josiah Wedgwood made exact reproductions of Roman glass and pottery to create the neoclassic dinnerware that is still highly prized by those with patrician tastes, and Robert Adam created his delicate furniture in forms copied directly from the wall paintings in Pompeii.

Women's fashions reached their peak of slenderness in 1800. The predominant character of the line was strictly classical, with a high waist in softly draped white muslin. Flat slippers or sandals replaced the high-heeled shoes of the Rococo period, and a draped shawl—reminiscent of the Roman *palla*—became an indispensable accessory. Even the hairstyles imitated the Greek coiffures. In short, costume was entirely in tune with the aesthetic philosophy that permeated all art forms of the day.

Refer to Chapter 5, pages 77–78, "Fashion in the Nineteenth Century," for a further description of the neoclassic period.

Figure 14-2. Costumes of the Romantic period c. 1821.

Romanticism

The spirit of the new century, however, was too strong to be held in check by the intellectual purity and sterile styles of the classical for very long and soon it gave way to nineteenth-century romanticism. The romantics dreamed of adventure in faraway places and exotic lands and drew upon all periods of the past as rich sources of inspiration. The German poet Schiller completed his work on *Maria Stuart* in 1800; soon after that the neck ruff in women's costume was revived, and dress designers went back to the second half of the sixteenth century for much of their inspiration. Even Goethe's *Faust* created a renewed excitement in the modes of the German Reformation.

In their emotional attraction toward all things antique, people were out to produce the picturesque. Architecture in church design returned to medievalism, and Queen Victoria commissioned the present Houses of Parliament to be built in the popular style of the perpendicular. In dress, the castellated edges of the Gothic, the neck ruff of the Renaissance, the full sleeves and wide, falling collars of the Baroque, even turbaned headdresses from the Orient were the popular vogue. The masculine silhouette took on an hour-glass shape, with widened shoulders and hips and a narrowed waist. No wonder George Sand could pass herself off for a gentleman in the curves of the masculine costume! Men also wore side curls that corresponded to the hair arrangement of the ladies with ringlets at the temples.

The Romantic period was an age of revivals. Never before had people been so style-conscious, and yet at the same time done so little to create a unique style of their own. In spite of this, the confusion and wide assortment of styles seemed to fuse into a character that was truly expressive of the romantic (see Figure 14-2).

Figure 14-3. The aesthetic unity in the art forms of an era can be seen in the similarity between the Gothic headdress and its architectural counterpart, the cathedral spire.

AESTHETICS AND DRESS

As the Industrial Revolution gained momentum at mid-century, clothes and furniture increasingly became the products of the factory rather than creations of the hand craftsman. Designs were dictated by the largely uneducated tastes of the majority, and a "rich, costly look" seemed to be the dominant criterion.

If one were forced to choose the most significant element of the Victorian period, it would probably be the consistent and recurring conflict between the ideals of tradition and reform. Popular tastes favored the revival of Grecian, Elizabethan, Rococo, and Gothic forms, but reformers were reacting against the shoddy vulgarity of commercial designs on the basis of aesthetic, moral, or rational criteria. William Morris was one of those who led the reform movement in furniture and architecture, believing that if the shape of an object were adapted to its purpose the object would be not only practical but beautiful as well. Oscar Wilde campaigned for the aesthetic movement in dress (Figure 6-13). But such literary and artistic philosophies that ran counter to the conventions of the age had limited acceptance, and the influence of men like Morris and Wilde was not felt until much later.

Eclecticism

By the last quarter of the nineteenth century, styles were hopelessly confused. There were Renaissance dining rooms, Oriental smoking rooms, leopard-covered divans, and drooping potted plants. The newly rich industrialists travelled all over Europe, bringing back bits of "culture" from every civilization known to man. The resulting hodge-podge of forms became known as "artistic broadmindedness." Basic structures were invariably covered up with superimposed ornamentation. The "architecture" of a building was usually "put on" after the structure was completed; the basic shapes of furniture were concealed under upholstery, drapery, tassels, and fringes, and costume followed the same general principle.

Figure 14-4. The slashed and bombasted breeches of the Renaissance found their match in the carved and bulbous supports of cupboards, table legs, and bed posts.

Art nouveau

By the end of the century, the styles had run their course, and the time for rebellion was ripe. The revolt was expressed in the Art Nouveau movement, which in many respects was clearer in terms of what was *not* acceptable than it was in regard to the development of a distinctly new style. However, some designers like the Belgian Henry van de Velde noted the relationship between the soaring curves of structural steel and the fluid lines of flowers and foliage. This treatment of line was reinforced by a growing penchant for Japanese art. The Oriental use of color and line was a revelation to the Art Nouveau designers, and the extreme simplicity of form and fluid ornamentation spread into costume, furniture, and architecture. The streamlining of

Figure 14-5. The same principles of prefabrication and steel construction were applied to both the architecture and the costume of the day. The famous Crystal Palace was created from an open web of metal girders covered with a skin of glass to produce a spacious and unencumbered interior. The framework of metal hoops used to create the dome-shaped skirts of the 1850's was a practical substitute for the intolerable weight of layers of petticoats. Both were practical solutions pushed to illogical extremes.

Figure 14-6. This lady's fashionable cape is not very different from its lampshade counterpart, both c. 1895.

Figure 14-7. The fluid lines of Japanese art provided much of the inspiration for Art Nouveau designers at the turn of the century.

Figure 14-8. The Japanese kimono was adapted in the styles of dresses, coats, and tunics. These two evening wraps are from 1912.

the feminine form was never more apparent than in the sway-backed figure of the first decade with its slender skirt swinging into spirals around the feet (Figure 14-9).

The leading fashion designer of the day was Paul Poiret. From the very beginning his creations showed an Oriental influence, but the effect was heightened by the success of the Russian Ballet in 1909. The settings in brilliant colors and Oriental splendor had a profound influence on the public taste. It led Poiret to introduce new violent hues in costume—purple, cerise, vermillion, and emerald green—and in doing so, he revitalized the textiles industry. Poiret's first theatrical production, *Minaret*, in 1913, proved to be a milestone in fashion history. The Minaret silhouette took on the lines of the Japanese kimono. Sleeves were no longer separate tubes set into an armscye, but were extensions of the garment body. The simplicity of cut made the corset obsolete, for the contours of the costume obscured the lines of the figure.

Figure 14-9. The soaring curves and fluid lines of L'Art Nouveau produced this "streamlined" lady of 1910. Here, a music stand of the same period.

Functionalism

Developments such as these foreshadowed the swing toward an extreme doctrine of functionalism. Architects and designers renounced all superfluous ornamentation, stripping their designs down to the most basic forms, and exposing the structure to view. Costume, furniture, architecture, even literature, coalesced into a style that was excessively simple and practical. Women's dresses were short and simply cut in the straightest lines possible; hair was severely cropped and worn uncurled. Deeply under the influence of cubism that sought a geometric purity of outline, interiors became arrangements of rectangles and cubes, extremely rigid in line and devoid of any softening curves. The steel furniture was unadorned and unrelieved by pattern or decoration.

Figure 14-10. The severely straight lines and rectangular shapes of functionalism dominated costumes, furniture, and buildings in the 1920's. Collection, The Museum of Modern Art, New York

287

Functionalism reached its peak near the end of the 1920's and gradually declined in popularity during the next decade. It was replaced by a style that once again accentuated the curves of body and form. Artistic movements and counter movements continue to supersede one another in search of the final victory of "good" over "bad." The twentieth century has moved through waves of expressionism, cubism, and abstract art, along with the counter-revolutions of surrealism and dada.

Pop art

More recently, pop art has been regarded as a significant reaction against the sterility of abstract expressionism. Even those who denounce it as a complete aesthetic failure are forced to recognize it as a movement that dominated the artistic world of the 1960's. Lichtenstein's adaptations of comic strip motifs and Warhol's now famous Campbell soup cans epitomize the pop approach to art. The latter, painted in endless sequence, has been hailed as an expression of the "archetypal 20th century nightmare": ". . . up and down narrow aisles between high walls of brand-name uniformity, with the lights glaring down and the canned music boring in, as we search desperately for one can of Cream of Mushroom where every label reads Tomato."[1]

The essence of pop is to create an illusion that either fools or confuses the observer into thinking that the fake beer can is a real one. Translated into costume, we find fabric prints with strands of realistic beads painted around the neckline, belt lines that are not belts at all, and conspicuous zippers gliding down the fronts of dresses that really open down the back.

Op art

The illusory aspect of pop art makes it a kin to op art which began to take ascendancy over the schools of pop and abstract expressionism in the late 1960's. Op (short for optical) art achieves eye-teasing three-dimensional effects by juxtaposing the simplest of lines, shapes, contrasting values, and pure spots of color in such a way that they create visual motion. Forms seem quite literally to pop, jump, quiver, wiggle, vibrate, and flicker in a manner that is so disturbing to the eye that it can "induce elementary hallucinations, bring on hypnotic spells, throw an epileptic into severe seizure and cause persons susceptible to motion sickness to reel from the room in spasms of nausea."[2] Almost the antithesis of the universal aesthetic principle, it creates chaos out of order.

Figure 14-11. The art movement of the early twentieth century was toward greater and greater abstraction. Pop art, its exact opposite, swung to literal realism by making the false, the ugly, and the deplorable even uglier than they really are. One argument extolled by the defenders of pop art is that it intensifies the cheapness and shoddiness of the man-made world to which we have become calloused through exposure. This example, "Soft Toilet" by Oldenburg, was created from a large piece of white vinyl.

---

[1]Calvin Tomkins, "Art or Not, It's Food for Thought," *Life*, 20 November 1964, p. 144.
[2]Tom Robbins, "'Op' Goes the Easel," *Seattle* 2, no. 16, 1965, p. 15.

Op art has developed out of a scientific age in which man is attempting to break down every element of his environment in search of increased understanding of the laws of nature. Op is an outgrowth of recent studies of visual experience which catalogue and analyze the infinite responses of the human eye to colors, lines, and shapes. It also suggests that art, like other mass-produced products of our age, may one day be scientifically determined and mechanically created. To many people it represents "a healthy departure from the meretriciousness and superficial existentialism of much Pop art and from the shabby technique of much abstract expressionism. It calls, above all, for a precision of technique, for meticulous execution."[3]

The movements that have been described here represent a limited sampling of the infinite number of ways man has approached art in the thousands of years of his aesthetic expression. The one point that should be clear is that fashion mirrors the aesthetic philosophy of a society; it is not a capricious invention that operates in isolation of the forces around it. Clothing and textiles are as much a part of art history as pottery, furniture, buildings, and wall paintings.

SUMMARY *Clothing and other art forms*

Clothing, like architecture, literature, music, painting, and sculpture, is an art form that derives from a particular set of cultural circumstances and reflects the needs and aspirations of the society for which it is created. Fashions in dress over the last one hundred and fifty years have mirrored the spirits of neoclassicism, romanticism, eclecticism, functionalism, cubism, expressionism, and abstraction. Even the more recent developments of pop art and op art have found immediate expression in the fashions of the day.

Clothing as a value model

Fashionable dress is more than a journal that records events after they occur. Clothing as an art image registers emotion, meanings, and social criticism, which in turn become value models for the members of society as a whole. Most people are convinced that the gradual evolution of fashion represents continual progress toward a style that is more versatile, more functional, more practical (and therefore more beautiful) than the fashions of the era which preceded it. Members of the younger generation, seeing pictures of parents in their heyday, roar with laughter at such ridiculous garb! The real joke, of course, is that in another twenty years their children will be laughing at them.

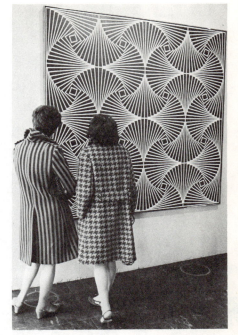

Figure 14-12. The eye-teasing effects of op art are even more striking when in contrast.

Clothing is a form of artistic expression that reflects the cognitive, moral, and social aspects of the period in which it is created.

---
[3]C. Lubell, "Op Art — The Responsive Eye," *American Fabrics*, Spring 1965, p. 83.

The delusion is not confined to youth. Any "up-to-date" individual with a deep-rooted concern and desire to be "with it" is susceptible to indoctrination in the values and virtues of the current mode and all that it stands for. Clothes are pieces of visual propaganda that shape our ideals of the good and the bad, the sensible and the stupid, the moral and the immoral, the right and the wrong.

Another Russian revolution

Little more than a decade ago it was considered unpatriotic for a citizen of the Soviet Union to indulge in the corrupt capitalistic extravagances of fashion (if indeed any citizen could afford them!). Clothing was strictly utilitarian and uniform in dark browns, dreary grays, and mournful blacks. Women's costume for the most part consisted of a long suit-jacket worn over a drab print dress, with coarse stockings, flat-heeled shoes, and the ubiquitous head scarf. It was not entirely a matter of poverty. The suppression of individuality in dress was a constant reminder that the worker was subservient to the state.

Then a number of changes took place. Gradually Russia began to emerge from its desperate economic straits. Communication with the Western world increased. In 1963, the Russian national newspaper *Izvestia* reported that a group of French designers had actually come to Moscow for inspiration in styling fashion boots for women. Nothing had given a greater boost to the Russian feminine ego since Valentina Tereshkova took off into outer space. Women began to notice their feet—and other parts of their anatomy as well. Today, in Moscow and Leningrad at least, one can see stylish skirts, ever-deepening décolletages, and beauty salons doing a thriving business. The GOUM department store is fairly well stocked with cosmetics and toiletries, most of them imported from East Germany. Of course, the store has always sold cosmetics of a sort, but "one must compare the old days with the new. Lipstick used to be like taffy, the powder like flour, and old timers recall when the only perfume in the entire Soviet Union was called Svetlana's Breath (after Stalin's daughter) and was powerful enough to restore consciousness to a dying man."[4]

Fashions have spread into male attire as well. Young men can be seen in fashionable trousers and shoes, with their hair combed in the latest mode. What, then, has happened to the communist philosophy? If fashion was a corrupt capitalistic influence a decade ago, why is it not corrupt today?

Clearly the old communism excluded individualism. The evolving communist doctrine, however, tolerates a wider range of ideas and allows for changing tastes, and clothing played a significant role in affecting the transition of attitudes.

Figure 14-13. Russia's recent transition from drab, utilitarian dress to fashionable attire and an interest in beauty, is evidence that evolving communist doctrine tolerates a wider range of ideas than did the dogmatism of earlier years.

[4]Geoffrey Bocca, "The Revolt of the Russian Women," *Family Weekly*, 30 May 1965, p. 5.

Consider the "revolutions" that have taken place in the last decade or two. There was "the nude look" that got underway in the sixties with Rudi Gernreich's topless bathing suit. Next to the topless, Ungaro's startling backless styles and Cardin's suggestive cutouts seemed pretty mild. By the time St. Laurent came out with his transparent chemise worn over a flesh-colored body stocking, the "nude look" was well on its way. By the 1970's, it was commonplace for women at the fashionable resorts to swim and sunbathe in their monokinis. Taste had absolutely nothing to do with modesty. Compared with exposed breasts in public, premarital cohabitation seemed not so bad after all. Clothing was part and parcel of the experimentation with new lifestyles and a new morality.

Revolution was by no means confined to women's wear. The gaudy styles that started on London's Carnaby Street spread to the United States with amazing rapidity. Young American males adopted the "rakish, thin-shanked, high-heel booted, broad-belted, narrow-hipped and epauleted variations of attire" that were the most brash change in men's clothes since the subtle Ivy League style invaded the fashion field. One Chicago retailer claimed that U.S. boys were spending up to $150 a month on new wardrobes. While this would be surprising even in feminine fashions, the phenomenon is all the more bewildering in the men's field "where change has always been measured in quarter-inches per decade."[5] The peacock revolution in men's wear threatened to wreck the whole he-man image of the American male.

Then there was the Women's Liberation movement. Its advocates objected to any differentiation made on the basis of sex, causing a rejection of clothes that highlighted sexual distinctions. The female's wholesale switch to bifurcates in the early 1970's was not merely the indecision over the proper length of hemlines. The growing trend toward unisex clothing could be observed in all articles of dress, including hairstyles.

The style changes in men's and women's fashions were mild compared with the changes advocated by the Gay Liberation movement, which brought homosexuals out of the closets and into the streets (Figure 14-14). Their deliberately contrived styles attempted to obliterate sex-role definitions of appropriate dress. Part of their platform was the freedom to dress as they pleased—as a male, as a female, or both. Even though such values may have been confined to the homosexual subculture, they helped to set the stage for the adoption of less restrictive dress codes on the part of heterosexuals.

The growing complexities of a highly industrialized society also contributed to the revolution in lifestyles. The establishment of agricultural communes, the popularity of folk music,

---

[5]"Face It! Revolution in Male Clothes," *Life,* 1966, pp. 82a–90.

Figure 14-14. These bearded and bizarrely dressed promenaders were members of the Gay Liberation Movement, demonstrating their direct confrontation with conventional society. They claimed that their garb, purposely intended to shock onlookers, would also liberate heterosexuals from sharply defined sex roles. The idea is that nothing else by comparison could seem quite so peculiar.

Figure 14-15. Can you tell the men's shoes from the women's shoes? This test was set up to demonstrate the growing trend toward unisex clothes.

and the adoption of a casual, homespun variety of clothing were among the more obvious manifestations of the search for the simple life. The association between casual clothes and country music has been described in terms of the development of a "looser attitude."

> First you wear the clothes, and then you find other things that make you comfortable. . . . The music fits the clothes, and the clothes fit the music. Both are simple and natural. For example, jeans and a checkered shirt are worn because they are comfortable, and they allow the wearer to be less uptight. . . . People that dress this way are geared to discover country music sooner or later.[6]

The one thing that all these examples have in common, and the thing that qualifies them for revolutionary status, is their flagrant disregard for anything that had been established as proper, fashionable, or tasteful. In this sense, we have witnessed a whole series of "revolutionary" movements in the anti-aesthetic philosophies. Pop art has already been described as a rebellion against the hyper-aestheticism of abstraction. Another kind of opposton to fashionable tastes came to be identified by the single word, **camp.** Camp was difficult to define because it could be anything as long as there was something grotesque about it. A typical camp comment would be: "Isn't it awful? I just love it!"

Camp always had something of a tongue-in-cheek air about it, and could be "a thing, a person or a fashion that is so bad that it is good . . . or so boring that it is entertaining . . . so banal that it is sophisticated."[7] It involved a kind of shared joke whenever the conventional was being upset. The term *camp* itself came from the tastes and attitudes of the homosexual subculture which has always considered itself the vanguard of forces against the standards of the bourgeois society. In the sixties the word came to mean a kind of exaggerated style that was anti-fashionable, anti-tasteful, and anti-aesthetic.

Funky was a kind of updated version of camp, except that it applied specifically to outmoded styles. Anything that was definitely *out* of fashion could not possibly be considered *in* fashion; hence it was an anti-fashion fashion. In this same category, the term **kitsch** has been used by the avant-garde to designate anything considered to be in bad taste.[8] Kitsch was defined as anything copied from a work of art but done in another medium, form, or setting. The Parthenon copied in plastic and a replica of Venus de Milo made into a cigarette lighter are examples of kitsch. The Mona Lisa's face printed on a sweatshirt is a pure example, but the term kitsch probably also would cover a $6,000 mink coat design made in authentic Orlon, or vinyl alligator shoes.

---

[6]"Country 'N Fashion," *Daily News Record*, 25 May 1973.
[7]"What Is Camp?" *Women's Wear Daily*, 12 August 1965.
[8]Gillo Dorfles, *Kitsch: The World of Bad Taste*, Universe Books, New York, 1969.

Oscar Wilde once said, "Fashion is that by which the fantastic becomes for a moment universal." At first, pop art was purchased just for fun by people who could afford to follow a funny fad. "Many a cocktail party that would otherwise have died a natural death has been saved by a piece of Pop art hanging on the wall (or lying on the floor, as much of it does)."[9] But gradually, pop art found some serious collectors, and in the process of changing American tastes, instead of looking "like comic strips or highway restaurant signs, highway restaurant signs and comic strips are now beginning to look like Pop art—which is an improvement of sorts."[10]

Anti-aesthetic movements such as these do not in the least negate the existence of an underlying set of aesthetic criteria. Quite to the contrary, if there were no standard to react against, there would be no purpose to the whole movement. If a beautiful object is to be "pleasing to the eye," or "easy to behold," then the psychedelic effects of clashing colors and visually baffling designs are anti-aesthetic. Needless to say, every revolution breeds reaction. Impressionism was revolutionary in its day, and reaction against it was strong. Reaction against a revolutionary fashion in dress is equally strong. However, once the eye becomes accustomed to such change and the mind begins to read meaning into the new forms, the innovations lose their revolutionary status and their attraction to the avant-garde as well.

The point that we cannot miss here is that clothing is a powerful tool of communication. As an art image, it registers attitudes and emotions; it manifests social criticism; it provokes reaction. Not only does it reflect and interpret the patterns of culture, but it establishes tangible and visual value models that can help to show the way the wind is blowing.

Clothing is a powerful social instrument in shaping the values of the multitude.

SUMMARY *Clothing as a value model*

Through its design and meaning, clothing creates a visual impression that is expressive of philosophical ideals and attitudes. Like other forms of artistic endeavor, fashion is subject to revolution and reaction. Changing aspects of the communist doctrine, for example, were facilitated and symbolized by the clothing image, and revolutions in men's wear and in women's fashions have mirrored the disregard for tradition that is characteristic of rebellion. Clothing as an art image registers attitudes and emotions, manifests social criticism, and provokes reaction.

[9]John Canaday, "Pop Art Sells On and On—Why?" in D. M. White (ed.), *Pop Culture in America*, Quadrangle Books, Chicago, 1970, p. 237.
[10]Canaday, "Pop Art Sells," pp. 239–240.

FOR FURTHER READING

Canaday, John. *Mainstreams of Modern Art*. New York: Simon & Schuster, 1959.

Dorfles, Gillo. *Kitsch: The World of Bad Taste*. New York: Universe Books, 1969.

Giedion, Sigfried. *Space, Time and Architecture*. Cambridge, Mass.: Harvard University Press, 1965.

Hayward, Helena, ed. *World Furniture*. New York: McGraw-Hill Book Company, 1965.

Janson, H. W. *History of Art*. Englewood Cliffs, N.J.: Prentice-Hall, 1963.

Laver, James. *Taste and Fashion*. London: George G. Harrap and Company, 1945.

White, David M., ed. *Pop Culture in America*. Chicago: Quadrangle Books, 1970.

DISCUSSION QUESTIONS

1. Describe at least three manifestations of the neoclassic period. How was this expressed in clothing?

2. In what way was romanticism a counter reaction to neoclassicism?

3. What impact did the Industrial Revolution have upon the cultural tastes of the late-nineteenth century? Give an example in dress.

4. How did the philosophy of the Art Nouveau movement provide the stimulus for the stark simplicity of the period which followed? Describe the basic changes that took place in dress between the 1910's and the 1920's.

5. Explain how pop art and op art evolved as counter-movements.

6. Give an example of a current style in dress that expresses an ideal or value emerging from the contemporary cultural climate.

PART FOUR

Clothing and the Physical Self

15

Clothing and Physical Comfort

SOME PEOPLE believe that man, by nature, is an unclothed creature, and that he would be better off both morally and physically to expose his skin to the sun and air and permit the regulatory processes of the body to make the adjustments necessary for thermal comfort. There is a wealth of anthropological data which attests to the fact that the human body is capable of adapting to a wide range of environmental conditions, often without the aid of protective clothing.

The actual need for clothing is dependent upon a number of factors, the most obvious of course being extremes in temperature; but the kind and amount of clothing required is affected by the physiological condition of the body, food intake, physical activity, and the duration of exposure. Beyond the factor of thermal comfort, however, we must consider the effects of clothing as it restricts or facilitates bodily movement, causes or prevents skin irritation, and protects or exposes the body to infection from pathogenic organisms. Although the exact limits of man's tolerance to any one or more of these factors has yet to be determined, our scientific knowledge has progressed beyond the point of mere conjecture. In this chapter we will consider the components of bodily comfort and the physical properties of fabrics and garments that contribute to our corporal well-being.

Factors affecting body comfort

Our physical comfort is affected by a number of variables that originate from within and outside the body. If we concern ourselves first with the matter of thermal comfort, we will see that man possesses an elaborate mechanism that attempts to keep his internal organs at a constant temperature in spite of the heat fluctuations in his immediate environment. The process calls for the production of heat at the same rate that heat is lost from the body. Such equilibrium can be achieved by either (1) consuming enough food and engaging in physical activity sufficient to produce the required amount of heat, or (2) preventing heat loss from the body through the use of clothing as a protective barrier. In order to utilize clothing as an effective means of heat insulation, it is necessary to understand the principles of heat exchange.

Principles of heat exchange

Optimal thermal conditions occur when the amount of heat produced by the body equals the loss of heat from body surfaces through radiation, convection, conduction, or evaporation. Just as we use oil, gas, or electricity to produce the units of energy that heat our environment, food serves as the fuel for heat production in the body. The 2,000 to 3,000 calories a day consumed by the average person are oxidized in the tissues, producing heat as a result of the internal and external work performed by the body. When the individual is at rest, 80 per cent or more of the total body heat is produced in the combined work of respiration, circulation, and activity in the brain, liver, and intestines.[1] If the individual engages in physical activity, more calories are expended in the muscle tissues, and a greater amount of heat is liberated. Muscles constitute about 45 per cent of the body, so that no other factor so powerfully influences the amount of energy liberated in the body as the activity of the skeletal muscles. A person lying in bed may generate from 70 to 75 calories per hour; in a sitting position, between 90 and 100 calories per hour. A slow walk will more than double the quantity, and a brisk walk uphill will triple it.

Heat thus generated is dissipated from the surface of the body through four major channels of heat loss: radiation, convection, conduction, and evaporation. **Radiation** is a transfer of heat or energy from a hot object to a cooler one by means of electromagnetic waves. The areas of the body which are exposed to the environment lose the most heat by radiation; the skin between the fingers, under the arms, between the legs, and under the chin merely radiate heat to adjacent skin areas and not into the environment. A person in a spread-eagle position will lose more heat through radiation than when curled up because the radiation area is increased.

The direction of heat flow, of course, may be negative instead of positive, i.e., from the environment to the body rather than from the body surface into the surrounding air. Radiation from the sun or from a red-hot stove may increase body temperature. The amount of radiated heat absorbed by the body depends

[1]H. C. Bazett, "The Regulation of Body Temperatures," in L. H. Newburgh, *Physiology of Heat Regulation and the Science of Clothing*, W. B. Saunders Company, Philadelphia, 1949.

upon its *emissivity*, the degree to which it emits radiant energy. As we know from our study of color, black objects absorb most of the rays which strike them. A perfect reflector, on the other hand, such as a highly polished metal, will reject the rays that strike it. Thus, surfaces which are good radiators are poor reflectors, and vice versa. The skin is a very poor reflector; white skin, for example, reflects about 30 to 40 per cent of the sun's radiation, while the dark skin of the Negro reflects less than 18 per cent.[2]

Most clothing will reflect appreciable amounts of environmental radiation. A nude man sitting in the sun gains an average of 143 calories per hour. White clothing, by reflecting the sun's radiant heat, will reduce that heat gain to about half.[3]

Heat transfer through **convection** occurs through the actual flow or spreading of warm molecules from a warm object to a cooler one. These currents, called convection currents, are stirred up by the slightest movement of the body, so that waving or swinging the arms and legs greatly increases the loss of heat by convection. Air movement or velocity determines the mass of air that comes in contact with the surface of the body, so that heat transfer is increased with an increase in air velocity.

Conduction refers to the flow of heat through a medium without the actual physical transfer of material. The molecules which make up all matter are always in a state of vibration. Adjacent molecules strike frequent blows upon each other, and in the process the fast-moving molecules transfer some of their energy to the slow-moving molecules, and these in turn carry it on to still other molecules, so that in time, molecules far removed from the source of heat will receive some of the transmitted energy through conduction. Heat is conducted in this manner from within the body, across the tissues, to the surface of the skin, and from the skin into any cooler object which may come into contact with the body.

Ordinarily, thermal conductivity is a slow process, although it is readily apparent that some objects conduct heat more quickly than others. Energy will spread rapidly through metals that have a high heat conductivity, as compared with still air, which transmits heat very slowly. Thermal conductivity values (representing calories per second per square centimeter per degree Centigrade per centimeter thickness) give some basis for comparing the relative insulating qualities of widely divergent substances:

Silver	0.99
Glass	0.0025
Human tissue	0.0005
Leather	0.0004
Paper	0.0003

[2]J. D. Hardy, "Heat Transfer," in Newburgh, *Physiology of Heat Regulation,* p. 85.
[3]Sid Robinson, "Physiological Adjustments to Heat," in Newburgh, *Physiology of Heat Regulation,* p. 195.

Wool felt	0.000125
Pure wool	0.000084
Still air	0.000057

Thus it can be seen that the muscle and fatty tissues of the body have relatively low thermal conductivities, as do many textile fibers. Wool and entrapped air are two of the poorest conductors, and hence two of the best insulators. The slow process of conduction is considerably hastened by convection in which air currents constantly remove the heated molecules and replace them with cold molecules.

Heat loss by **evaporation** is the only way of dissipating heat from the body when the environmental temperature is greater than the temperature of the skin. When the surrounding air is not cool enough to receive heat from the body through radiation, convection, or conduction, sweating becomes the chief protective mechanism against overheating. Liquid sweat is transformed into vapor at the skin surface, and passes into the environment to cool. The evaporation of moisture from the surface of the skin is tremendously effective in disposing of body heat because each gram of water thus evaporated carries away 578 small calories at skin temperature. Perspiration, therefore, is actually a cooling process, and brings a large measure of relief to the overheated body. Unlike the first three methods of heat transfer, evaporation is primarily a mechanism for disposing of body heat. Only under rare circumstances (such as steam burns) is heat acquired through the inverse process.[4]

Environmental factors

Obviously, the conditions existing in the immediate environment affect the physical comfort of the human body. Thermal comfort is influenced by air temperature, humidity, air movement, and radiation intensity.[5] **Air temperatures** with upper limits of 79°F. to 95°F. and lower limits of 64°F. to 73°F. (depending on humidity) provide the most desirable range for man's comfort. At higher temperatures increased evaporation from the skin surface occurs.

The amount of such evaporation also depends upon the vapor pressure of water on the skin and that in the air. A high **relative humidity**, i.e., a high percentage of water vapor in the atmosphere, will reduce the rate of moisture uptake by the air and limit the evaporative cooling process. In hot, humid atmospheres, the normal man perspires profusely, but because the air is already saturated with moisture, much of the sweat will be wasted as it drips unevaporated from the skin surface.

---

[4]W. H. Forbes, "Laboratory and Field Studies — General Principles," in Newburgh, *Physiology of Heat Regulation*, p. 321.
[5]P. Yaglou, "Thermometry," in Newburgh, *Physiology of Heat Regulation*, p. 70.

We have mentioned the effects of **air movement** in the discussion of convection. The displacement of large masses of air obviously increases the rate of heat transfer.

The effects of **radiation** depend not only on the temperature of the radiating body, but upon the temperature and emissivity of the surrounding areas. Indoors, for example, the radiation heat exchange is affected by the character of the walls, ceiling, floor, and other objects in the room having different emissivities. Outdoors, there are the factors of solar radiation, sky radiation, and reflection from the terrain. Human skin is an excellent radiator and a very poor reflector. If the body were placed in a large sphere made from highly reflecting materials, nearly all of the radiant heat emitted from the body would be reflected back to and reabsorbed by the skin. Even if the surface of the sphere were very cold, the body would lose little heat to it through radiation.[6]

Atmospheric pressure in itself has an effect on body comfort beyond its relationship to heat transfer. At high altitudes, man not only has less oxygen to breathe, but the rarefied atmosphere no longer provides enough counterpressure to balance the internal pressures of the body. At an altitude of 25,000 feet the air pressure is only a third of that at sea level, so that the body begins to swell. Airline companies have begun to furnish uniforms with self-expanding features for stewardesses. At altitudes of 5,000 feet and above, skirts with elasticized panels and button adjustments provide relief for swelling tummies.

Modern aircraft is pressurized, as are the suits of deep-sea divers and astronauts, but there is considerable variation in atmospheric pressure from sea-level towns to those at higher elevations. The normal individual readily adjusts to such changes in atmospheric pressure, but for those with abnormally high or low blood pressure, such change often brings discomfort. Some articles of clothing (elasticized stockings, for example) help to increase the external pressure on the body, and often are used to improve the circulation in low blood pressure cases. In a few rare instances a person's blood pressure may be so low that the simple act of rising from a prone to an erect position causes the blood to drain from the brain, and the individual faints immediately—a phenomenon comparable to a pilot's blacking out in steep climbs and dives. By wearing pressurized suits that squeeze the lower extremities and force blood upward through the body and head, fairly normal circulation may be restored.[7]

Beyond the atmospheric conditions relating to temperature and pressure, the environment may also produce various kinds of hazards or irritants that cause bodily discomfort. An infinite

---

[6]Hardy, "Heat Transfer," p. 83.
[7]"Medicine: New Garment Raises Blood Pressure by Squeezing," *Life*, 7 October 1966, pp. 73–74.

number of **mechanical agents** (e.g., sharp instruments, nails, thorns) cause abrasions, cuts, and wounds of the skin. Besides the effects of heat, cold, and solar radiation, other **physical and chemical agents** act on the skin in various ways, such as burns from electrical wires, or dermatoses from acids, alkalis, and other chemical irritants. **Biological agents,** which include bacteria, fungi, viri, and numerous parasites and insects, are capable of producing skin lesions and other harmful reactions. Many poisonous plants (Rhus toxicodendron, for example, more commonly known as poison ivy) produce dermatitis or other photosensitizing effects.

Properly designed protective clothing is one of the most effective means of reducing the danger from environmental hazards such as these. Closely woven cotton fabrics are often a sufficient barrier. Protection from solar radiation, on the earth's surface at least, is afforded by broad-brimmed hats and garments that cover the torso, arms, and legs. Impervious materials, such as rubber or synthetic films, give adequate protection against liquid irritants, while leather gloves and sturdy shoes are good safeguards against mechanical dangers. For the more extreme type of occupational hazards, there are air-proof suits fitted with mittens, boots, and helmet, and air conditioned for adequate ventilation.

Figure 15-1. Elaborate protective clothing is used against the more extreme types of occupational hazards.

Human adaptations to the environment

We have seen that climatic conditions, activity, a person's state of health, and clothing are all important modifying factors in regard to our physical comfort. Nature has endowed the human body with an excellent thermostat that automatically regulates the internal temperature. One of the adaptive responses that occurs almost immediately takes place in the **circulatory system.** When overheated, the blood vessels dilate, permitting an increased flow of blood and raising the skin temperature, which in turn increases the heat loss from the skin through radiation, convection, and evaporation. Following exposure to the cold, constriction of the blood vessels decreases heat transfer by decreasing the quantity of blood flowing through the skin and other surface tissues.

Two other nervous responses are **sweating,** which functions to speed up the heat loss by evaporation when the body is exposed to heat; and **shivering,** which consists of simultaneous contractions of small groups of muscles that greatly increase heat production in the body. Shivering is usually preceded by a pilomotor reaction of goose flesh that roughens up the surface of the skin and causes an erection of hairs, thereby diminishing air movement and consequently improving the layer of air insulation around the skin. This kind of insulation is considerably less for cylinders than for flat areas, which is why the skin temperature in the fingers, toes, hands, or feet serves as an effective thermostat in activating other physiologic responses to heat and to cold. At high environmental temperatures, much body heat is given off by evaporation via the hands and feet, and in moderately warm temperatures, mainly through convection.

Continued or prolonged exposure to extremes in temperature induces another phenomenon known as **acclimatization.** Englishmen, for example, appear to be particularly resistant to the cold, and become easily overheated in rooms that most Americans find comfortable, while the natives of tropical climates seem to be relatively unaffected by the extremes of heat. Chronic exposure to cold does in fact cause an elevation in basal metabolism and a resulting increase in heat production, enabling an individual to withstand low temperatures with less discomfort. Acclimatization to heat may also develop over a period of time in which the basal metabolic rate is lowered.

Some adjustments to the environment are learned human responses rather than reflex or motor mechanisms. Through **accustomization,** people gradually learn a multitude of techniques that increase the protective value of their clothing:

> No amount of reading will ever make a sourdough out of a tenderfoot upon first exposure to cold. The greenhorn in regions of extreme cold is apt to suffer unmercifully, whereas the experienced person has not only learned to tolerate the cold but is efficiently making adjustments in anticipation of his body heat needs. The tenderfoot opens his clothing after he has started to sweat. The sourdough never reaches the point of sweating if he can avoid it. The tenderfoot who has opened his clothing or taken off a garment rarely buttons up again until he is beginning to shiver. He seems to want to impress himself or others with the appearance of being "tough enough to take it." The sourdough puts his clothing on and closes up before he begins to get chilled, and he stays warmer much longer.[8]

SUMMARY   *Factors affecting body comfort*

Calories provided by our daily food intake are oxidized in the tissues to produce heat or energy, which in turn is dissipated from the body surface through the processes of radiation, convection, conduction, and evaporation. Clothing serves as a barrier to heat transfer in either direction, i.e., it reduces the amount of heat lost from the body to the atmosphere, and decreases the amount of heat absorbed by the body from the environment. Textile fibers and entrapped air, both poor conductors of heat, are excellent insulators.

Thermal comfort of the body is influenced by the environmental factors of air temperature, humidity, air movement, and radiation. Other environmental conditions that affect physical

When subjected to heat or cold, the human body vigorously opposes deviation of its internal temperature through a number of regulatory processes that attempt to keep heat production and heat loss in equilibrium.

---

[8]Paul A. Siple, "Clothing and Climate," in Newburgh, *Physiology of Heat Regulation*, p. 439.

comfort include atmospheric pressure and various kinds of hazards capable of producing bodily irritations.

In addition to the immediate nervous or motor responses made by the body to variations in temperature, the human body adjusts to prolonged exposure through a process of acclimatization over a period of time. Beyond this, the individual learns certain techniques of adjustment known as accustomization.

Clothes and physical well-being

The two major responses that man makes voluntarily to the stresses of cold are (1) increased food consumption which facilitates a greater energy output, and (2) adequate clothing. The two may be compared for relative efficiency in accomplishing the task because food can be measured precisely in terms of caloric value, and the insulative value of clothing can be determined by the unit of measurement called the **clo.** One clo is defined as the insulation necessary to maintain bodily comfort in a sitting-resting position, in a normally ventilated room where air movement is 20 feet per minute, temperature is 70°F. and humidity is less than 50 per cent.[9] The typical business suit has an insulation value of about one clo, but our requirements will vary from less than .5 clo in midsummer to 4 or 5 clo in the cold of winter.

The food requirements for the average man doing moderate work have been estimated at 2,880 calories per day if he is clothed, and at about 4,100 calories unclothed. In other words, if we did not wear clothing, our average food intake would need to be increased approximately 42 per cent.

Clothing also conserves body energy in warm climates. As early as 1937, studies confirmed the fact that men sitting in the sunshine fully clothed showed 130 to 180 grams per hour less sweating than when nearly nude.[10] A study of the physical properties of fibers and fabrics will help us to use clothing more effectively in achieving and maintaining thermal comfort. Beyond this, we will consider the uses and function of clothing in relation to physical health and efficiency.

Physical properties of fibers and fabrics

Much of the research relating to the functional properties of clothing was stimulated by the extreme demands of military service in which the supreme objective was a matter of survival rather than beauty. Although in most circumstances

---

[9]J. F. Hall and J. W. Polte, *Thermal Insulation of Air Force Clothing*, Wright Air Development Division Report 60-597, Wright-Patterson Air Force Base, Ohio, September 1960, p. 3.

[10]E. F. Adolph, "Heat Exchanges of Man in the Desert," *American Journal of Physiology* 123, 1938, pp. 486–499.

clothing is chosen on the basis of criteria relating to appearance and durability, some knowledge of the principles of physics and physiology as they relate to dress will improve one's ability to select appropriate clothing.

Our chief concern in the present discussion is with the structural properties of fabrics that affect the passage of air, heat, and water vapor between the body and its environment. The following characteristics of fibers, yarns, fabrics, and garments are pertinent to the thermal qualities of clothing:

Fiber—absorbency, resilience, density.
Yarn—smoothness, degree of twist.
Fabric—flexibility, porosity, recovery from compression, thickness, weight per unit area, finish, texture, color.
Garment—number of layers, design, fit.

Since still air is the poorest conductor of heat, the insulating value of any garment or fabric depends upon its capacity to entrap air. Even without clothing, the body is surrounded by a thin layer of relatively still air, as is each surface of cloth which envelopes the body, hence the more layers of clothing, the greater the insulation. For example, a suitable "layering" for extremely cold weather might include:

	Thermal Value in Clo
First Layer: Insulated underwear (T-shirt and pants), wool socks	.50
Second Layer: Wool shirt and trousers, shoes	1.15
Third Layer: Coveralls, wool knit gloves, wool helmet	1.30
Fourth Layer: Insulated parka with hood, mittens, fur-lined boots	1.80
Total clo	4.75

It is seldom feasible to wear more than 4 to 5 clo because the bulk of fabric hampers physical activity. Moreover, insulation has been found to stay essentially the same for nine-layer as for five-layer assemblages.[11] Besides, there is the problem of ventilation. Even at rest, the body exudes a certain amount of moisture through insensible perspiration. With increased activity, the individual may sweat considerably, getting the underlayers of his clothing wet, greatly reducing its insulating value. When fabric adheres to the skin, the layer of surrounding air is removed. The greatest disadvantage to sweating is that it stops when the activity stops. The body then produces little heat and

Figure 15-2. Too many layers of clothing will actually hamper physical activity.

"Mom, I'm home—peel me."

THE SATURDAY EVENING POST

[11]Deanna McCracken, "Thermal Insulative Values of Certain Layered Assemblages of Men's Wear," Master's thesis, Kansas State University, 1967.

needs to conserve all it has, but the wet clothing is a high heat conductor and goes on dissipating heat at great rate through evaporation. For this reason, it is best if clothing can be peeled off layer by layer as the level of activity is increased, or at least opened for ventilation to avoid sweating. The layers then can be put back on as needed when the activity lessens or stops.

For maximum insulation, garments should be so designed that the openings around the neck, wrists and ankles are close-fitting, but the garment itself should be loose enough to permit the easy formation of the air layer. Clothes that fit too tightly and cling to the skin reduce the effectiveness of the air surrounding the body. Conversely, garments for warm weather will be more comfortable if they are cut with large openings around the legs, arms, and neck so that heat can escape easily through the various apertures while at the same time the body is protected from radiation.

Thickness is probably the most reliable single indicator of a fabric's insulation value (see Table 15-1), but it is often difficult to produce a fabric that is both thick and lightweight. Quilted fabrics and foam laminates make possible much higher levels of insulation. The small pore size of the foam makes it more efficient than an equivalent thickness of fabric in immobilizing air.[12]

Still, a very thick fabric does not solve the ventilation problem and the need for adjusting the insulative capacity to varying levels of activity. Moreover, a fabric must maintain its thickness under the distortion of repeated crushing and bending. The ability to recover from compression is very important. A person wearing a very thick but easily compressible garment such as a down-filled parka will lose heat rapidly by conduction through the packed layers if the wearer leans against cold stone or ice. The flexibility of a fabric also influences its effective thickness and its relationship to the personal atmosphere of surrounding air. Stiff clothing that does not conform to the

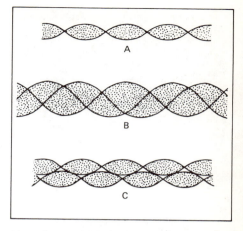

Figure 15-3. Three types of quilt constructions showing different thickness and layering effects. Stitching is necessary to hold the fill of insulation in place, but type A is the least effective because there is no insulation at the seams. Type B is better, not only because it is thicker, but because cold spots are eliminated. Type C has the additional value of built-in air pockets between the baffles.

TABLE 15-1 THERMAL RESISTANCE OF SELECTED FABRICS

Fabric	Weight in Oz. per Sq. Yd.	Thickness in Inches	Insulation Value in Clo
Cotton poplin	6.2	0.018	0.051
Herringbone twill	8.1	0.024	0.060
Wool serge	10.4	0.039	0.111
Wool fleece	14.0	0.127	0.285

Adapted from L. Fourt and M. Harris, "Physical Properties of Clothing Fabrics," in L. H. Newburgh, *Physiology of Heat Regulation and the Science of Clothing.*

---

[12] C. J. Monego, et al., "Insulating Values of Fabrics, Foams and Laminates," *American Dyestuff Reporter* 52, 7 January 1963, pp. 21–32.

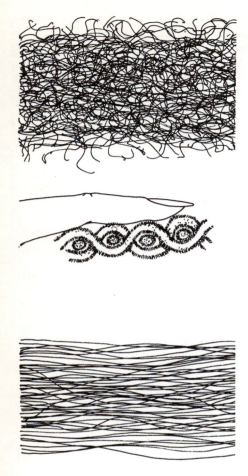

Figure 15-4. The type and spacing of the yarns in the weaving process are important factors in determining a fabric's insulation value.

shape of the body will contribute to heat loss through convection, pumping air out of the interlayer spaces during movement of the body. Limp fabrics are no better because they collapse onto the skin and air spaces between the clothing and the body are minimized.

Many of the new fabric constructions that were developed as part of the space program have now become available for consumer use. One of these is a lightweight nylon with aluminum on the reverse side and urethane used as a laminating agent. The fabric, reported to have the warmth of a quilted garment but weighing a mere ounce-and-a-half per square yard, is used chiefly for ski wear.[13] Bonding metallic particles to a fabric is done on the theory that they will reflect back to the body heat that would otherwise be lost through radiation. To be effective in this regard, the metal must be exposed, either to the skin or as the outer surface of clothing. If inserted as a lining between other layers of cloth, its function as a barrier to radiation is lost.

Dyes also differ appreciably with respect to absorption or radiation of heat from sunlight. As we have already seen, white garments are cooler in summer sunshine than dark or black ones. But white fabrics often require more shadow-proofing than black, and an added layer of cloth can easily offset the advantages of lighter colors.

Fabric **porosity** is an important consideration as wind velocity increases. A fabric could be thick but at the same time made with dense yarns that left wide-open spaces through which the air could pass quickly. A great deal of heat would be lost from the body through convection. Dense fabrics with tightly packed yarns afford good protection against the wind.

Finishes on fabrics sometimes fill the interstices between the yarns, rendering them less porous. Plastic coatings on the

TABLE 15-2 AIR PERMEABILITY OF SELECTED FABRICS

Fabric	Air Permeability in Cubic Feet per Min. per Sq. Foot
Mosquito netting	1700
Very open weave shirt	395
Cotton knit T-shirt	220
Broadcloth dress shirt	93
Tropical worsted suiting	42 to 60
Seersucker suiting	41 to 50
Army poplin, 6 oz.	6
Byrd cloth	3

Adapted from L. Fourt and M. Harris "Physical Properties of Clothing Fabrics," in L. H. Newburgh, *Physiology of Heat Regulation and the Science of Clothing.*

---

[13]Bob Spector, "Skylab Fabrics to Warm Skiers," *Daily News Record,* 7 June 1973.

surface of fabrics, for example, decrease the amount of heat lost through convection. Laundering also will affect air permeability of fabrics.[14] By removing some of the finish, washing may make a fabric more porous and thus more comfortable for summer wear.

The **texture** of a cloth is largely a matter of the type and spacing of the yarns in the weaving process. Smooth, tightly twisted yarns form a fabric with fewer air spaces surrounding the fibers and the surface of the cloth. Raising the ends of loose fibers through finishing processes of napping or brushing increases the number of free fiber ends capable of holding air films. Fuzzy yarns thus create an outer fur of projecting ends that entrap warm, still air. This also accounts for the fact that fuzzy fabrics, such as wool fleece, feel warmer to the touch than a sleek fabric like satin. Since most fabrics are at room temperature, which is almost always lower than that of the skin, heat passes from our skin to the fabric until the surface reaches skin temperature. In the smooth fabric, there is more surface in contact with the skin and hence more area to be warmed, while the skin touches only tiny sections or ends of fibers in the fuzzy fabric, and the fiber volume to be heated is minimal.

The structural factors of resiliency, weight, flexibility, texture, and so forth, also depend upon the choice of fiber. Continuous filaments such as silk, rayon, nylon, or any other man-made fiber produce more compact yarns, whereas those made from staple lengths or from texturized yarns impart a loftiness to fabrics without a great deal of weight. Wool is a fiber with particularly good insulating qualities because of its fine crimp (Figure 15-5), which has the effect of creating a fiber-to-fiber repellence, and assures the greatest amount of free fiber area within the yarns and fabric.[15] Wool also has a high degree of resilience that enables it to maintain its loft. Linen, on the other hand, with its long, straight fibers, tends to feel cooler than its fuzzier cotton counterpart.

Another property of fibers that is closely tied to their insulating value is their capacity for **moisture absorption.** If excess perspiration can be absorbed by the fiber without wetting the surface of the fabric, it will keep the cloth from sticking to the skin and help to prevent the clammy feel of a wet garment. It will be seen from Table 15-3 that wool has the highest moisture absorbency of any textile fiber. It can in fact hold almost 30 per cent of its weight in moisture without feeling wet to the touch. The low absorbency of nylon, Dacron, and the other hydrophobic fibers causes excess moisture to accumulate on the surface of the fabric rather than being taken up by the fiber.

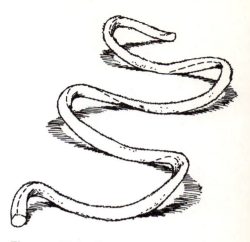

Figure 15-5. The three-dimensional crimp of the wool fiber.

[14]Sharon Frankenberry, "The Effects of Laundering and Layering on Air Permeability of Selected Cotton and Man-Made Fabrics," Master's thesis, Kansas State University, 1970.

[15]Giles E. Hopkins, *Wool as an Apparel Fiber*, Rinehart & Company, New York, 1953, p. 71.

TABLE 15-3 COMPARISON OF FIBER PROPERTIES

Fiber	Specific Gravity*	Moisture Absorbency at 95% r.h.	Elastic Recovery** @ 2% elong.	Recovery from Compression***
		(%)	(%)	(%)
Nylon	1.14	8	100	90
Acrilan acrylic	1.17	17	99	15
Orlon acrylic	1.14–1.17	2.5	97	17
Dynel	1.31	1.0	97	12
Wool	1.32	29	99	31
Acetate	1.32	14	94	11
Silk	1.34	25	70	
Dacron polyester	1.38	0.5	97	14
Linen	1.50		65	
Viscose rayon	1.52	27	82	8
Cotton	1.54	24–27	74	
Glass	2.54	0.3	100	

*Specific gravity indicates the density relative to that of water at 4°C.
**Elastic recovery is the per cent return from elongation toward the original length, while compressional recovery refers to the ability to return to original height following compression. Usually good elastic recovery correlates with good compressional recovery, although the percentage is considerably lower. The cellulose fibers (cotton, linen, viscose) tend to be similar in resilience or recovery.
***Values established by Kolb, Stanley, Busse and Billmeyer, *Textile Research Journal*, Vol. 23, 1953, p. 84.

In the case of absorbent fibers such as cotton and wool, water absorbed from the body or atmosphere and stored in the fiber also helps to discourage the accumulation of static charges that cause fabrics to cling tightly either to the skin or to adjacent layers of clothing. Cotton, rayon, and silk, although they have fairly high absorbency rates, lack the resilience that would give them an insulation value comparable to that of wool. Especially when sweating takes place, the fiber-to-skin repellence imparted by wool's crimp enables the fabric to stand away from the skin, creating that all-important air space; cotton, however, once it is saturated, will collapse on the skin.

Another way to keep fabric from collapsing on the skin is through the use of ventilating net underwear. The open square mesh construction permits insensible perspiration to evaporate, with the vapor-laden air then escaping out the neck or sleeve openings. Even in cold climates, this is an effective way to keep body moisture from entering the clothing.

Clothing for different climates

Heat loss from the body is not substantially affected by conventional clothing in moderate temperatures, but it may provide considerable protection beyond the range of the optimal comfort zone. When the air is below 77°F. skin temperature is higher than the surface temperature of our clothing, indicating that heat loss from the body has been retarded.[16]

[16]A. P. Gagge, C. Winslow, and L. Herrington, "The Influence of Clothing on the Physiological Reactions of the Human Body to Varying Environmental Temperatures," *American Journal of Physiology* 124, 1938, pp. 30–50.

When the temperature of the air is higher than that of the skin, it is important to use fabrics that are not only highly absorbent but relatively impermeable to air currents so that heat from the hot air is not transferred to the body by convection. The greatest protection in hot, dry climates is the insulation provided by clothing from solar radiation. As we have already indicated, white or light-colored garments are more effective than dark in reflecting the sun's rays. The Arab, accustomized to desert heat, wears a full covering of loose and flowing garments that are usually white in color. The robe is often made of wool, which not only offers protection against the hot wind, but provides insulation against the cold at night. Headgear that provides some shade for the face is extremely important.

When the atmosphere is both hot and moist as it is in the tropics, clothing should offer the very minimal resistance to evaporative cooling from the skin. Since evaporation from the skin is more efficient than evaporation from wet clothing, fabrics that will not absorb water vapor seriously hinder the cooling process. In humid high heat, an absolute minimum of clothing is desirable as long as the person can remain in a shaded area out of the sun's direct light. Natives of hot countries (including the ancient Egyptians and many of the peoples of South America and Africa) practiced the removal of body hair, either by shaving or plucking, permitting the sweat to run off or evaporate more easily from the surface of the skin. Sandals are better than an enclosed shoe for the same reason.

In cold regions, clothing must prevent body heat loss from exceeding the metabolic heat production. The biggest problem is the accumulation of moisture during periods of activity. Water then condenses in the intermediate layers of the clothing, and if the body vaporizes water faster than the outer layer of garments, the clothing becomes wet and insulation is reduced.

Maximum efficiency of insulation is built up rather quickly on the extremities, such as the hands, feet, and head. When feet are getting cold, it is far more effective to add additional insulation around the trunk of the body than to don additional footgear. The excess accumulation of heat thus produced in the torso will warm the blood sent to the extremities, and, as a consequence, they become heated. Waterproof material keeps out wind as well as external moisture, but it contributes to the problem of internal moisture accumulation. In areas of damp or wet cold, however, a moisture-proof exterior is essential.

For survival in cold weather, we can learn much from the Eskimo. His costume consists of two layers of animal skins and furs: (1) the outer one, a long and loose hooded parka, trousers, boots, and mittens that are worn with the hair side out, and (2) the inner layer, undershirt, drawers, and socks worn with the hair side in. Caribou and sealskin are the most widely used materials. Eskimo clothing is shaped to the body, but it actually fits very loosely. The undershirt and parka are worn outside the

Figure 15-6. One of the most difficult climatic conditions to control through clothing is wet cold. This uni-suit is made of foam neoprene, but water seepage is always a problem. Civilians may experience similar discomforts in cold weather when clothing is soaked through in the rain, or when feet get cold and wet. Waterproofing both the inner and outer layers of insulation becomes necessary.

trousers, gathered in at the waist with a belt when extra warmth is needed, and unbelted when activity increases. In order to avoid sweating, the Eskimo loosens his clothing when working, and begins to remove his clothing first by taking off the mittens, then throwing back the hood, and finally removing the outer parka. When indoors, he strips and sits almost naked because he knows that his clothing must be kept absolutely dry when not in actual use.[17]

Health and sanitation

Clothing is healthful to the extent that it aids in the heat regulation of the body, and protects the skin against insects, trauma, and environmental irritants. It may also be *un*healthful to the degree that it causes skin irritations, encourages bacterial growth, or restricts the body in such a way that deformation results.

Allergies

The incidence of dermatitis from wearing apparel is small, although occasional cases have been reported as due to sensitivity to certain fibers and fabrics.[18] Sensitivity to the protein fibers, such as silk, and fabrics made from wool and other animal hairs, may cause allergic dermatitis in a few rare individuals. Unprocessed vegetable fibers, such as cotton and linen, have never been known to cause allergies, and man-made fibers made from cellulose (e.g., acetate and rayon) as well as the true synthetics (nylon, Orlon, Dacron, and the others) are also non-allergenic. The only cases of irritation reported as being caused by fabrics made from these fibers have been caused by the finish or the dye and not by the fiber itself. The low absorbency of the synthetics is often responsible for the accumulation of moisture on the skin which is a source of discomfort to many people, but this cannot be construed as a sensitivity to the fiber itself. There have been some reports that nylon pantyhose cause irritations, but this again is attributable to the fact that nylon does not "breathe." The addition of a cotton crotch or cotton soles in stockings usually provides sufficient absorbency to eliminate the problem. The glass fiber, sometimes used for insulating purposes, may cause a mechanical irritation of the skin because of the sharp fiber ends, but it will not cause any irritation from allergy to the glass.

Items of wearing apparel made from rubber or synthetic rubber—girdles, dress shields, gloves, and so forth—all have been reported to cause dermatitis, but in all cases the cause of

---

[17]F. R. Wulsin, "Adaptations to Climate Among Non-European Peoples," in Newburgh, *Physiology of Heat Regulation*, pp. 9–10.

[18]L. Schwartz, L. Tulipan, and D. J. Birmingham, *Occupational Diseases of the Skin*, Lea & Febiger, Philadelphia, 1957, p. 370.

irritation has been the chemicals used in the processing of the material rather than the rubber itself. Resins and other finishes applied to fabrics or to leather are the chief causes of such irritation.

Bacterial growth

In general, clean textile fabrics—especially those that are laundered at high temperatures—can afford good protection to the skin. Soiled clothing, however, often contains large numbers of microbes, many of which may remain alive on fabrics for extended periods of time. Research studies of laundry hygiene have identified as many as five million bacteria per square inch in the underarm areas of a cotton T-shirt.[19] Many of these microorganisms are harmless, but some, such as *Staphylococcus aureus* and *Pseudomonas,* can cause skin lesions, pneumonia, or kidney infections, and paracolon bacteria may infect the intestines. Microbes, both harmless and infectious, may be transferred from the clothing to the skin or to other articles of clothing during laundering. Extremely hot wash temperatures provide one of the best ways of destroying these microorganisms. Unfortunately, the water in many home washing machines never goes above 130°F., which is considerably lower than the boiling temperature of 212°F. needed for sterilization. Outdoor drying in direct sunlight has a certain germicidal effect, but the only sure way to reduce the numbers of bacteria to a safe level is to add a disinfectant directly to the wash or rinse water.[20]

Although there are special anti-bacterial finishes that can be applied to cloth, their effectiveness tends to be diminished with repeated launderings. There is some evidence that a regular permanent press finish inhibits bacterial growth, and in this sense it may act concomitantly as an anti-bacterial finish.[21]

In cases where sanitation is of particular concern, disposable garments have much to offer. Disposable diapers and hospital gowns have been familiar items for many years, but the industry is now gearing up for a much larger market in disposable underwear.[22]

Restrictive clothing

Fashion history is replete with examples of clothing that must have been sheer torture to wear. Infants' heads have been

---

[19]Ethel McNeil, "Laundry Hygiene," *Consumers All,* The Yearbook of Agriculture, 1965, pp. 371–373.
[20]Chlorine (hypochlorite), phenolic, pine oil, and quaternary have been found to be effective for this purpose. See McNeil, "Laundry Hygiene," p. 372.
[21]Judith Redekopp, "Effect of Permanent Press Finish on Bacterial Growth," Master's thesis, San Fernando Valley State College, 1969.
[22]Becki Levine, "Sees a Future for Disposable Panties," *Women's Wear Daily,* 11 January 1973.

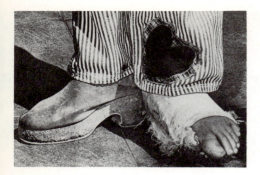

Figure 15-7. A broken foot resulted from the fatal combination of wide-cuffed pants and platform shoes. After the accident, the victim discarded the pants but continued to wear one shoe — because it balanced the cast on the other foot!

wrapped to conform to an elongated shape, feet have been bound, necks have been stretched, breasts have been depressed, and waists constricted. Few fashions have been fatal, but many have been the subject of much controversy. Doctors are still arguing the pros and cons of girdles and shoes. There is no doubt that many elasticized garments give healthful support to sagging muscles and tissues. However, any article of clothing that causes flesh to bulge above and/or below it can be said to be too tight. Round garters used to hold up stockings, for example, can have a tourniquet effect and restrict the flow of blood in the legs.

As far as feet are concerned, there is no disputing the fact that unshod primitive peoples are freer from foot troubles than "well-heeled" civilized folks who pound the city's pavement, often in ill-fitting shoes. The corn is strictly a product of cultivation caused by the pressure of a shoe against the counterpressure of the bony joint of a toe. To fit properly, the shape of the shoe should conform to the shape of the foot with sufficient width across the ball of the foot to allow for spread when the foot is in action. Low heels with a broad walking surface give the best support. But the woman's foot and ankle have long been regarded as erotic attractions more than a means of locomotion, and while her feet may be more comfortable in sensible shoes, her mind is not.

Safety

In spite of all the protection that clothing may provide, at times it can also be amazingly hazardous. Long, flowing garments such as full skirts and wide pant legs, can get caught in doors, escalators, and bicycle wheels, or they can trip the wearer on stairs and curbs. Besides all the rationalizing that went on about miniskirts in the early 1970's, there *were* a few safety factors in their favor. First of all, they never tripped the wearer; but beyond that, their shortness forced women to bend at the knees rather than at the hips (as so many do), thereby avoiding potential back injury.

Anything that dangles from the body—long scarves, ties, flowing sleeves, jewelry—is hazardous in the sense that it is apt to get caught on something (or *in* something, like the closing door of a bus). As well as causing foot problems and back problems, shoes also can be safety problems. Spike heels were notorious for getting stuck in floor cracks and street pavement, and they also caused many a turned ankle. But the "killer clogs," and the "perilous platforms" that replaced them were not much of an improvement from the standpoint of safety. A New York osteopath explained: "The new shoes elevate the feet and thereby elevate the center of gravity also. The higher the center of gravity, the less stable the victim. When you combine a high center of gravity with the almost nonexistent support these shoes give you and the fact that most of us have weak ankles anyway . . . what you get is an accident waiting to happen."[23]

Unfortunately, most textile fibers burn, and when they burn directly next to the skin, the damage is usually fatal. The most highly flammable fibers are pure cotton or other cellulosics such as rayon. Wool is a natural fiber that is inherently flame-retardant. Although synthetics may not burst into flames, they frequently melt into hot sticky globs that can cause severe burns. Fabrics with a brushed or pile surface are particular fire hazards because of the entrapped air between the fibers. In tests of flammability, untreated all-cotton plissé crepe has been shown to have one of the fastest burning rates, as do cotton flannelette and batiste.[24]

The **Flammable Fabrics Act** was first passed in 1953 following a number of fatalities resulting from the so-called "torch sweaters" made from brushed rayon. The standards were subsequently amended, and flame-retardant fabrics are now required for all children's sleepwear (see Chapter 17, p. 372). It may not be many more years before such standards are applied to all clothing. In the meantime, it will be wise to keep this potential danger in mind and to avoid highly flammable apparel items.

Utility and convenience

Sensible clothes should provide for freedom of action. From the standpoint of muscular activity, most clothing is hampering to a certain degree at least. The weight of clothing alone may add to the metabolic cost of walking and running. Regular street clothing would weigh about six or seven pounds more than a pair of running shorts and sneakers, while heavy arctic clothing would weigh about fifteen pounds more. In addition to the load imposed by this added weight, the hampering effects of heavy clothing on body movements could increase the work load about 10 per cent.[25] Under most conditions, however, the utility and convenience of clothing far outweigh these minor disadvantages.

The space suit

Probably no other garment is more essential to survival than the pressure suits which the astronauts wear into space. The basic suit consists of four layers: (1) a nylon comfort liner worn over specially ventilated cotton underwear, (2) a layer of neoprene-coated nylon which makes the suit airtight and maintains the air pressure surrounding the body, (3) a layer of link

[23]Dr. Richard Bachrach as quoted in "The High Heels Trip," *Moneysworth*, 30 April 1973, p. 1.
[24]Annette Johnson, "A Comparison of the Flammability of Three Types of Fabrics Used in Girls' Sleepwear," Master's thesis, Oklahoma State University, 1968.
[25]Newburgh, *Physiology of Heat Regulation*, p. 447.

Figure 15-8. This polyester and cotton eyelet nightgown was turned into a mass of flames when ignited with a match and was totally consumed within one minute (pictures were taken at 30-second intervals). Fire-resistant finishes now required by law on all children's sleepwear must withstand fifty washings. Such fabrics, however, cannot be washed with bleach or low-phosphate detergents or sent to a commercial laundry.

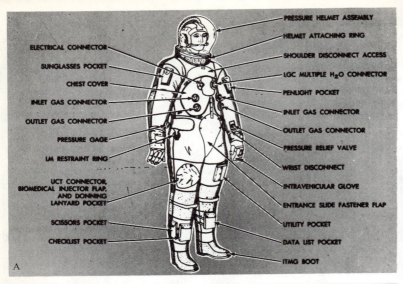

A

PRESSURE HELMET ASSEMBLY
HELMET ATTACHING RING
SHOULDER DISCONNECT ACCESS
LGC MULTIPLE H_2O CONNECTOR
PENLIGHT POCKET
INLET GAS CONNECTOR
OUTLET GAS CONNECTOR
PRESSURE RELIEF VALVE
WRIST DISCONNECT
INTRAVEHICULAR GLOVE
ENTRANCE SLIDE FASTENER FLAP
UTILITY POCKET
DATA LIST POCKET
ITMG BOOT

ELECTRICAL CONNECTOR
SUNGLASSES POCKET
CHEST COVER
INLET GAS CONNECTOR
OUTLET GAS CONNECTOR
PRESSURE GAGE
LM RESTRAINT RING
UCT CONNECTOR, BIOMEDICAL INJECTOR FLAP, AND DONNING LANYARD POCKET
SCISSORS POCKET
CHECKLIST POCKET

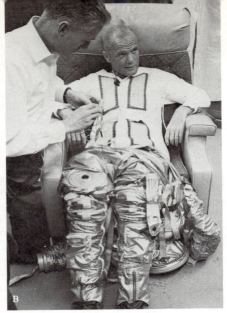

B

D

E

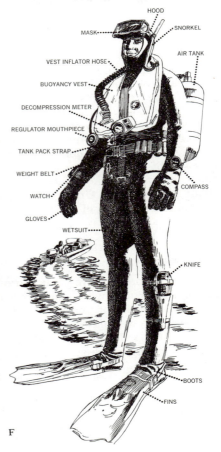

HOOD
MASK
SNORKEL
AIR TANK
VEST INFLATOR HOSE
BUOYANCY VEST
DECOMPRESSION METER
REGULATOR MOUTHPIECE
TANK PACK STRAP
WEIGHT BELT
WATCH
GLOVES
COMPASS
WETSUIT
KNIFE
BOOTS
FINS

F

Figure 15-9. (a) The space suit pressure garment assembly provides a total environment in which the astronaut is encased in pressurized oxygen.
(b) The astronaut's thermal underwear has ribbed sections that provide for circulation under the next layer of pressurized and rubberized nylon.
(c) Camouflage clothing helps man to blend with his environment and thereby reduce his visibility.
(d) The hockey player's clothing provides a lot of protection that is not even seen.
(e) Specialized clothing extends man's activities below water as well as above the earth's surface.
(f) The miner's hardhat and headlamp is another example of specialized occupational clothing designed for a specific function.

314

net nylon to prevent the suit from ballooning in the vacuum of space, and (4) an outer layer of aluminized nylon that can withstand temperatures up to 800°F. and which will reflect back most of the sun's radiation.

The suit itself is manufactured by a producer of women's girdles and brassieres—which is not so surprising in light of the fact that construction techniques for both types of garments have much in common. Perfect fit is essential:

> You cannot, of course, walk in and get a pressure suit off the rack. To fit it properly requires more alterations than a bridal gown. The first step is the creation of an individual body mold. This is made by dressing the Astronaut in cotton long john underwear and plastering him all over with wet strips of brown paper tape. After the tape dries, both it and the underwear are carefully cut away from his body, and the resultant mold is used . . . for manufacture of the suit itself.[26]

The underwear is cooled by water circulation, maintaining the inside of the suit at fairly constant temperatures, and the rubberized layer is inflated to exert five pounds of pressure per square inch against the body. The circulation system also furnishes a supply of oxygen to breathe, and carries away exhaled carbon dioxide as well as sweat and excess water vapor. Pressurizing has the effect of encasing the body in a rigid cylinder, making movement—particularly small finger movement—very difficult.

Many of the innovations that develop from space travel research will eventually be adapted to civilian use. It is predicted, for example, that temperature-controlled underwear may soon be available for popular consumption. Yarns with relatively high electrical conductivity may be knitted into fabric that will have a cooling or heating effect depending upon the environmental temperature. The power source may be either a microscopic transistorized unit, or even possibly solar radiation.

Sports clothes

Sports activity is one area of civilian life in which the individual is relatively uninhibited by the forces of fashion. Most sportsmen and athletes are willing to wear the most ludicrous attire if it improves their game or increases their prowess. There is still much of the fashion element in swimsuits, tennis shorts, ski wear, and golf clothes, but on the whole sportswear has encouraged the development of functional clothing more than almost any other area of human activity.

Occupational clothing

Unlike sportswear, work clothing is rarely influenced by the world of fashion, but it is another area in which function is often

[26]Walter Schirra, "A Suit Tailor-Made for Space," *Life*, 1 August 1960, p. 36.

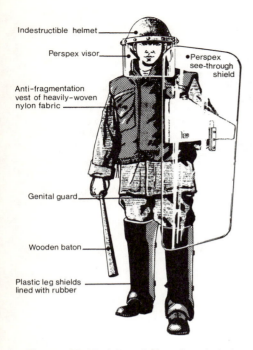

Indestructible helmet

Perspex visor

• Perspex see-through shield

Anti-fragmentation vest of heavily-woven nylon fabric

Genital guard

Wooden baton

Plastic leg shields lined with rubber

Figure 15-10. (above) Functional clothing for the riot policeman. With the increasing number of riots, the British Army's research unit developed this protective clothing assembly unit for its troops in Ireland.

Figure 15-11. Comfort, convenience, and utility can be built into clothing for the handicapped person to make him more independent. Here, a velcro front closure makes a wraparound dress easy to fasten.

Functionally designed clothing enables man to adapt to extremes in environmental conditions and contributes to his convenience in performing specialized tasks.

closely tied to design. The workman's overalls with their various hangers and pockets for tools, the hardhat of a construction worker, the mask and gloves of the welder, are all examples of clothing designed for a specific function.

Clothing for the physically handicapped

There are probably over 30 million people in the United States today who are physically handicapped. Dependency upon someone else for help with the daily task of dressing can become a demoralizing problem. Specially designed garments that fit more loosely than those worn by the physically normal can help to camouflage a deformity, and can provide ease in dressing that will contribute to the individual's feeling of independence. If a person is confined to a wheelchair, the clothing should be fitted to the figure in a sitting position. This means that for men, the trousers should be a few inches longer to provide for the bend in the knees, and jackets should be shorter to prevent bulking around the hips. Women's skirts are more comfortable if they are moderately full. If the person propels his own wheelchair, sleeves cannot be too long or too lose or they will be soiled by or caught in the wheels, and they should be cut with full armholes so that shoulder movements are unrestricted.

Front openings and easy fastenings facilitate dressing with a minimum amount of help. Roomy pockets set low in the garment to avoid spilling provide secure places for commonly needed articles, and often serve as an extra pair of hands when operating a wheelchair. Wrap-around garments, plackets and openings larger than usual, and tabs on the ends of zippers are all self-help features that simplify the task of dressing.

SUMMARY *Clothes and physical well-being*

Clothing functions to conserve body energy in the thermal regulation of physiological processes. The structural properties of fibers that relate to the thermal characteristics of clothing are fiber absorbency, resilience, and density. The smoothness or fuzziness of the yarns, in turn, contribute to the textural quality of the fabric. Other properties of the fabric that are pertinent to thermal behavior include flexibility, porosity, compressional recovery, thickness, weight, finish, and color. The design and fit of the garment as well as the number of layers also help to determine the insulating value of clothing, which is expressed in terms of the unit of measurement called the *clo*.

When the temperature of the air is higher than that of the skin, garments should be highly absorbent, light in color, and impermeable to air currents. If the atmosphere is both hot and humid, a minimum of clothing will permit a more efficient evaporation of perspiration from the skin. When temperatures are lower than that of the skin, the most effective barrier to heat loss from the body is a protective layer of still air. The ability of a garment to entrap air is the most reliable index of its potential warmth.

In most cases, clothing contributes to the health and comfort of the body, but it can also be the indirect cause of skin irritations, infections, or other physiological problems. Functionally designed clothing greatly increases man's versatility and enhances his performance in various kinds of activity.

FOR FURTHER READING

Fourt, L. and N. Hollies. *Clothing: Comfort and Function.* New York: Marcel Dekker, 1970. (Especially Chapter 1, "Factors Involved in the Study of Clothing.")

May, E. M., N. R. Waggoner, and E. B. Hotte. *Independent Living for the Handicapped and the Elderly.* Boston: Houghton Mifflin, 1974. (Chapter 7, "The Selection and Adaptation of Clothing to Suit Particular Needs for Men, Women, and Children;" Chapter 8, "Self-Help Clothing for Women and for Men," and Chapter 9, "Self-Help Clothing for Children.")

Newburgh, L. H., ed. *Physiology of Heat Regulation and the Science of Clothing.* New York: Stechert-Haffner, 1968.

Renbourn, E. T. "The Physiology and Hygiene of Clothing," *CIBA Review,* no. 4, 1964, pp. 26–36.

Renbourn, E. T. *Materials and Clothing in Health and Disease.* London: H. K. Lewis & Co., 1972.

Scott, C. L. *Clothes for the Physically Handicapped Homemaker.* Washington, D.C.: U.S.D.A. Home Economics Research Report No. 12, 1961.

Textile Handbook. Washington, D.C.: American Home Economics Association, 1970.

DISCUSSION QUESTIONS

1. In what ways cán equilibrium be maintained between heat production and heat loss from the human body?

2. Give an example of clothing (in terms of fiber, yarn, fabric, or garment design) that would prevent or inhibit heat loss from the body through each of the following types of energy transfers: (a) radiation, (b) convection, (c) conduction, (d) evaporation.

3. How may clothing facilitate adjustment to environmental conditions such as: (a) air temperatures above 95°F., (b) high relative humidity, (c) high wind velocity, (d) solar radiation, (e) high altitude?

4. What is the difference between acclimatization and accustomization?

5. Explain how clothing and food can be interchangeable factors in man's physical well-being.

6. List and define each of the physical properties or characteristics relevant to the insulative value of clothing for: (a) fiber, (b) yarn, (c) fabric, and (d) garment.

7. Describe a clothing assembly that you would recommend for (a) hot/dry, (b) hot/humid, (c) cold/dry, and (d) cold/wet climates.

8. Discuss ways in which clothing may be either protective or hazardous.

9. How may clothing extend man's versatility in performing various kinds of tasks or activities?

16

Clothing and Physical Appearance

SOME YEARS AGO, Loudon Wainwright gave an entertaining account of his experience in acquiring his first London-tailored suit. One needs to go back to the original story for the full flavor of Savile Row and particularly for the characterization of Mr. Perry, the courteous tailor; but suffice it to say here that Mr. Wainwright felt splendidly rejuvenated in his elegant suit which covered up what he called "a substantial secret." Before leaving the shop, he asked Mr. Perry if there had been any special problems in making the suit. Evasive at first, the tailor finally admitted after considerable prodding: "'Well, sir . . . you have rather a long body, and that's the thing we had to minimize. We had to lengthen your legs, so to speak, and shorten your body. Nothing serious, really, and it worked out quite well.' This was the first time I'd heard of this particular defect in my structure, and I took another look in the mirrors. Mr. Perry was right. It was impossible to tell now where my short legs ended and my long body began."[1]

Unfortunately, few individuals are endowed with perfect body proportions, and most people look better when their structural defects are camouflaged with clothing. Effective use of the art elements in costume can alter visual sizes and contours by modifying the frame of reference in which we perceive the human form. Attributes of the physical self can be maximized through an understanding of the cultural ideals to which we aspire, and a knowledge of the perceptual responses of the human eye. A skillful application of these principles to clothing can control the impressions that are picked up by the eye and subsequently interpreted by the brain.

The physical self

Contemporary figure ideals change with the times. Over the centuries the human body, amazing in its plasticity, has been

[1]Loudon Wainwright, "Disguising the Man," *Life,* 2 April 1965, p. 33.

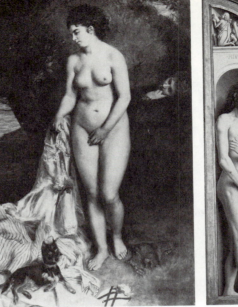

Figure 16-1. Changing ideals in women's body proportions.
Twentieth-century ideal, Raquel Welch.
Ideal of the 1870's, Renoir's "Bather with Griffin," Museu de Arte, São Paolo, Brazil.
Fifteenth-century ideal, "Eve," by Van Eyck, c. 1425. © A.C.L. Bruxelles.

Figure 16-2. Changing ideals in men's body proportions.

Figure 16-3. Differences in cultural ideals.
The prehistoric female figure was a fertility symbol.
The ideal Indian woman had broad shoulders, breasts set close together, and a slim waist.
Egyptian ideals of the male and female figures, c. 1350 B.C.

| 1600 BC | 1600 | 1640 | 1840 | 1860 | 1900 |

molded into an infinite variety of shapes, each of which in its day was considered to be the most desirable combination of proportions (see Figures 16-1, 2, 3). In addition to the manipulations possible through such devices as corsets, waist-cinchers, shoulder pads, and bust developers (men padded other parts of the anatomy in various periods of fashion history), certain physiological mutations take place over the years as a result of improved dietary habits and changes in physical activity. In general, Americans are slightly taller than they were a generation ago, have broader shoulders, narrower hips in relation to waistline circumference, and bigger feet.

It is difficult to present a tangible model of an ideal figure, even within the confines of a particular fashion era. For one thing, it depends on whether your tastes run toward the Raquel Welch or the Twiggy types. Furthermore, the actual tape measurements are not nearly as important as the visual proportion. Three figures with exactly the same bust, waist, and hip measurements can appear to be quite different in size if the length dimensions vary, or if the form is deep from front to back or wide from side to side (Figure 16-4). If we look to the international beauty contests, however, it would seem that the criteria for "ideal" proportions are becoming quite universal in nature. Beauty queen measurements seem to cluster around a height of five feet five or six inches, between 115 and 120 pounds, with bust, waist, and hip measurements in the vicinity of 36″, 24″, and 36″ respectively.

It is important to remember, however, that a figure of any stature can appear to be in good proportion. It is for this reason that we will concentrate here on relative proportions rather than upon actual measurements.[2]

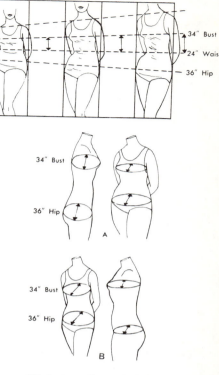

Figure 16-4. Length and depth variations in the human form.

Figure proportions

The unit of measurement used in Figures 16-5 and 16-6 is expressed as **head length,** the distance from the crown of the head to the bottom of the chin. The average figure, both male and female, is approximately seven-and-one-half heads high, with the fullest part of the hipline at wrist level dividing the total length exactly in half. The neck is about one-third the length of the head, and the shoulder line slopes a distance of a half head length from the level of the chin. The fullest part of the bust or chest is located two head lengths from the crown, and the smallest part of the waist (which coincides with the bend of the elbow) is two-and-two-thirds heads from the crown. Fingertip, knee, calf, and ankle positions are indicated on the figure charts.

---

[2]For a comparison of specific measurements according to height and weight, see Henry Dreyfuss, *The Measure of Man,* Whitney Publications, New York, 1959; and Morton, *Costume and Personal Appearance,* pp. 38–40.

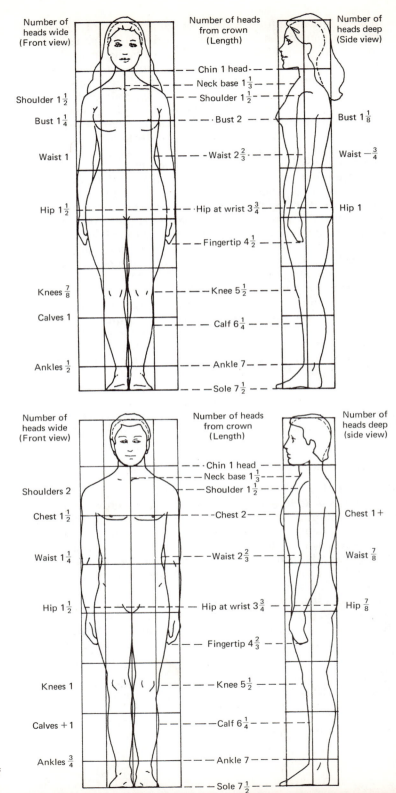

Figure 16-5. Average proportions of the female figure.

Number of heads wide (Front view)
- Shoulder $1\frac{1}{2}$
- Bust $1\frac{1}{4}$
- Waist 1
- Hip $1\frac{1}{2}$
- Knees $\frac{7}{8}$
- Calves 1
- Ankles $\frac{1}{2}$

Number of heads from crown (Length)
- Chin 1 head
- Neck base $1\frac{1}{3}$
- Shoulder $1\frac{1}{2}$
- Bust 2
- Waist $2\frac{2}{3}$
- Hip at wrist $3\frac{3}{4}$
- Fingertip $4\frac{1}{2}$
- Knee $5\frac{1}{2}$
- Calf $6\frac{1}{4}$
- Ankle 7
- Sole $7\frac{1}{2}$

Number of heads deep (Side view)
- Bust $1\frac{1}{8}$
- Waist $-\frac{3}{4}$
- Hip 1

Figure 16-6. Average proportions of the male figure.

Number of heads wide (Front view)
- Shoulders 2
- Chest $1\frac{1}{2}$
- Waist $1\frac{1}{4}$
- Hip $1\frac{1}{2}$
- Knees 1
- Calves +1
- Ankles $\frac{3}{4}$

Number of heads from crown (Length)
- Chin 1 head
- Neck base $1\frac{1}{3}$
- Shoulder $1\frac{1}{2}$
- Chest 2
- Waist $2\frac{2}{3}$
- Hip at wrist $3\frac{3}{4}$
- Fingertip $4\frac{2}{3}$
- Knee $5\frac{1}{2}$
- Calf $6\frac{1}{4}$
- Ankle 7
- Sole $7\frac{1}{2}$

Number of heads deep (side view)
- Chest 1+
- Waist $\frac{7}{8}$
- Hip $\frac{7}{8}$

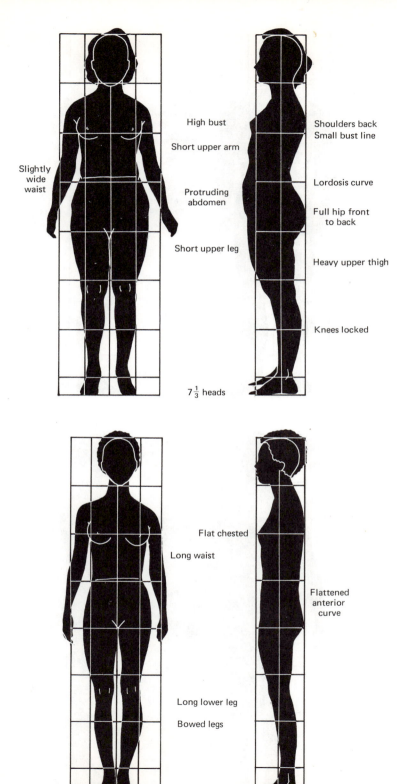

High bust

Short upper arm

Slightly
wide
waist

Protruding
abdomen

Short upper leg

Shoulders back
Small bust line

Lordosis curve

Full hip front
to back

Heavy upper thigh

Knees locked

$7\frac{1}{3}$ heads

Figure 16-7. This figure, less than 7½ head lengths, is visually shorter than average. Most of the length is lost in the upper leg since the torso is about a third of a head longer than the leg span. Shoulder line is more curved than usual; fleshy roll near waist, right hip irregular in contour. Legs meet from thigh to knee but do not touch at calves and ankles. In profile, body weight is forward with a lordosis curve caused by thrusting shoulders and buttocks back and stiffening knees.

Flat chested

Long waist

Flattened
anterior
curve

Long lower leg

Bowed legs

$+7\frac{3}{4}$ heads

Figure 16-8. This figure is taller and more slender than average, with body length equal to more than 7¾ heads. The torso is long-waisted but in proportion to the leg span. The lower leg is longer than average, legs slightly bowed. Right shoulder is higher than left with a correspondingly flatter hip on the right side. In profile, the body is in fair alignment but curves are flat and lack feminine contour.

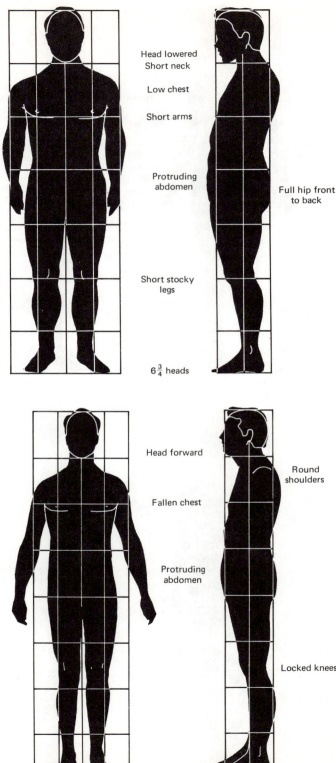

Figure 16-9. This figure, less than seven heads tall, gives a short, stocky appearance. The legs and arms are both quite short while the torso is average in proportion. Shoulders are fairly broad, the left one higher than the right, with a correspondingly flatter hipline on the right side. In profile, body weight is slumped forward, with chest fallen and abdomen protruding.

Head lowered
Short neck

Low chest

Short arms

Protruding abdomen

Full hip front to back

Short stocky legs

$6\frac{3}{4}$ heads

Figure 16-10. This is a tall, well-proportioned, eight-head figure with only slight variation in shoulder heights and hipline contours. In profile, body balance is destroyed; the head is held forward, shoulders rounded, chest fallen, abdomen relaxed, and knees locked.

Head forward

Round shoulders

Fallen chest

Protruding abdomen

Locked knees

8 heads

Male and female proportions differ only in circumference ratios. The female figure, front view, has a hipline that is visually equal to the width of the shoulders. While masculine hips are also one-and-one-half heads wide, they appear more slender because they are balanced by a broad shoulder line (two heads wide) and a thicker waist (one-and-a-quarter heads). There is also a greater difference in depth ratios from front to back in the female figure than there is in the male with respect to bust/waist and waist/hip relationships.

Body alignment is indicated by a perpendicular line falling from the ear lobe to the inside of the heel, and passing through the center of the shoulder and hipline and slightly to the front of the leg at knee level. The body weight at chest, waist, and hip levels is thus balanced on either side of the plumb line in profile view. Looking at the figure from the front, straight legs meet at upper thigh, knee, calf, and foot.

Few figures will correspond to these models in all respects, but the illustrations are useful for identifying major departures from the physical norm of individual physiques. Comparisons will be facilitated by dividing the figure into head-length squares, beginning with a plumb line down the centerfront, and marking the chin level with a horizontal line at right angles to it. The distance from the chin to the crown (not the top of the hair) can then be used as the unit of measure to grid the rest of the figure. Figures 16-7 through 16-10 show some common deviations from the norm.

The face and head

As we have seen, the size of the head is significant in establishing the visual height of the body. Large heads tend to dwarf the body, while small head sizes increase the apparent span even though the individual may not be very tall in actual inches. Again, male and female proportions of the face and head are surprisingly similar, except for the fact that male contours are usually more angular, and the neck is thicker.

Figure 16-11 illustrates the relative size and placement of the average facial features. Many faces that are considered beautiful or handsome do not conform to this ideal, but an understanding of average facial contours will help to identify the features that one may wish to emphasize through dress.

Composite coloring

Theoretically, the color of the skin could be identified anywhere on the body, but it is the most consistently exposed in hands and

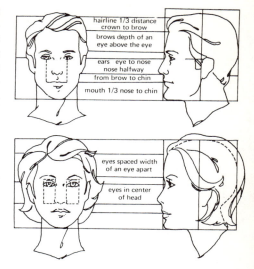

Figure 16-11. Average proportions of the human head.

Figure 16-12. The face on the left is long and narrow, and the head is shallow in the depth of the crown. Forehead and chin are slightly receding. Other features are average in proportion.

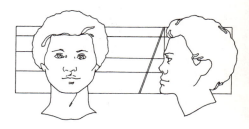

Figure 16-13. The full, round face left is almost as wide as it is long. Eyes are widely spaced. Nose and neck are both short; chin protrudes into a jutting jaw line.

face, and it is in the face that skin tones are in closest juxtaposition to the colors of the hair and eyes. We have already seen how contiguous colors affect each other. The three color areas should be studied carefully and given a color notation in order to determine the degree of contrast in the composite of individual coloring.

For example, there would be little hue contrast if a golden skin were combined with pale blonde hair and hazel eyes, while a blonde, blue-eyed person with predominantly pink skin would demonstrate a maximum contrast in hue. If the pale blonde with the golden skin had topaz eyes there would be little contrast either in hue or in value. Maximum value contrast would be found in the combination of near-white skin and raven hair.

Intensity patterns are also critical. Clear strong colors such as bright blue eyes or vivid Titian-red hair are more forceful determinants of costume colors than the neutralized smokey tones of drab blonde or brown hair, gray eyes or olive complexions.

In very general terms, individuals fall either into warm or cool types of composite coloring. The **warm type** has a predominance of red-orange or yellow-orange pigmentation, with brown, sometimes greenish shadows or overtones. Eyes are usually brown, black, or a little on the greenish side, and the hair may vary from red to dark brown. **Cool types** combine blue, violet, gray, or green eyes with skin tones of yellow-orange that lean toward the yellow side. Skin shadows are blue or red-violet, and hair may be blonde, black, or one of the cooler browns.

Texture should also be considered in the overall analysis of physical attributes. Skin may be smooth, clear, and transparent, or it may be rough and blemished. The textural quality of hair may vary anywhere from fine, straight and lustrous to the coarse and tightly curled. These characteristics may be masked or exaggerated through the choice of dress.

In visual appearance every individual is a unique combination of contours, proportions, textures, and colors.

Figure 16-14. This normal-sized actor seems Lilliputian in combination with the gargantuan scissors created for this set.

SUMMARY *The physical self*

Cultural ideals of the human form have been studied as a basis for identifying the unique attributes of individual physical conformations. Anthropometric data now available indicate that the relative proportions of the human face and figure are approximately the same for both sexes, varying only in circumference measurements and angularity of contour. Actual measurements are less significant in conveying a visual impression of size than the ratio of head size to other proportions of the body. Hue, value, and intensity patterns in the composite coloring of individuals establish a distinctive set of characteristics that influence the effect of costume colors that are combined with it. The textural qualities of skin and hair are additional aspects of the physical self that may be obscured or enhanced by the visual elements of dress.

Illusory responses of the human eye

Most people believe what they see. Scientific studies of visual perception, however, indicate that we do not always see things as they actually exist, for what we see is not merely a matter of visual images being picked up by the retina of the eye, as a camera receives images through its lens. Rather, the optical image is transmitted to the brain for an interpretation of its meaning. Seeing is combined with judgment, and the human organism looks for cues or clues in making discriminations regarding the size, color, and shape of objects.

If we were to see a figure floating in space, we would have no way of judging its approximate size. But if the figure is placed in connection with common objects of known dimensions (Figure 16-14), we are able at least to guess its relative size. Thus, our judgments of the visual shape, size, and color of objects are made in relation to the total perceptual field in which the objects are found.

Perhaps most important of all is the fact that the human brain seeks to establish some order or meaning among the visual stimuli that it receives. This tendency to organize our perceptual field into a meaningful whole is demonstrated in Figure 16-15. The shape represented in A combines nine straight lines in a configuration that we can easily recognize as a cubic rectangle. Even though the same form is contained within B, the simple figure of the cubic rectangle becomes imperceptible because the additional lines in the more complex figure change its meaning entirely.

This search for unity, or **sensory organization** as the Gestalt psychologists call it, also causes us to "see" illusions. If you cover the right illustration in Figure 16-16, you will perceive the solid black bar to be rather large. If you cover the left illustration, the dark bar looks short. In effect, we have organized the elements in each of these units, and made a visual judgment on the basis of size comparisons. In like manner, all of our visual discriminations are made in relation to the total field in which they are found. In order to see anything as "big" or "small," "straight" or "curved," "red" or "orange," we must have some basis for comparison. Illusions occur as a result of assimilation or contrast. **Assimilation illusions** are those which minimize or camouflage the deviant parts by increasing the similarity of relationship of the parts to the whole. **Contrast illusions** are those which exaggerate the deviant parts by placing them in juxtaposition with elements that are extremely dissimilar. In the following sections we will examine some of the ways in which optical illusions occur in line, shape, size, texture, and color.

Figure 16-15. Few people can distinguish the simple figure A in B, demonstrating that the parts are less meaningful than the unified whole.

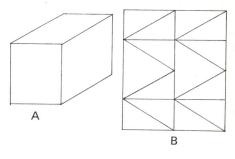

Figure 16-16. Sensory organization.

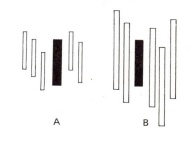

Figure 16-17. The Müller-Lyer illusion.

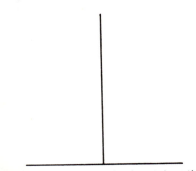

Figure 16-18. The horizontal-vertical illusion.

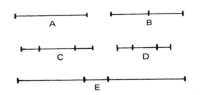

Figure 16-19. The effects of subdivision.

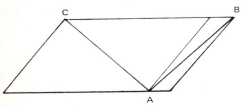

Figure 16-20. The Sander parallelogram.

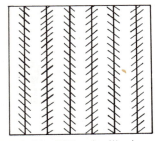

Figure 16-21. Zöllner's illusion of direction.

Line

Illusions in the apparent length, direction, or curvature of lines are quite common. The best known perhaps is the Müller-Lyer illusion in which a line is divided into two equal segments. Observers consistently see segment A as being shorter in length than B. One explanation is the tendency of the eye to follow along the path of a line. In segment B, the eye continues along a path that exceeds the actual length of the line, whereas in A, the eye is forced to reverse its direction abruptly at the ends and thus travels a seemingly shorter distance. The effect is compounded by the fact that the observer sees each segment as a whole, including the angles; as a unit, B is really longer than A and this impression carries over to the parts of the whole which the observer imagines himself to be judging.

Another illusion is that vertical lines are often perceived to be longer than horizontal lines of the same length. This has been explained by the theory that the eye moves more easily along a horizontal plane, and because it requires greater effort to ascend the vertical, the distance seems longer. In Figure 16-18, the horizontal is also bisected by the vertical. In terms of the eye movement theory, travel along the horizontal is interrupted before reaching the other end and diverted in an upward direction. The effects of line interruption are obvious in Figure 16-19. Naive subjects consistently take lines B and C to be shorter in length than A, and at the same time believe that the middle segment of line C is longer than either section of B. The same illusion occurs in D and E; the middle segment in D appears to be longer than the middle segment of E. Segments that are adjacent to long line lengths seem smaller by comparison, while segments adjacent to shorter lines appear longer.

Further error in the judgment of line length is caused by our tendency to read perspective into a figure. The parallelogram in Figure 16-20 is usually seen as a slanted surface, and because we "know" that the left parallelogram is larger than the right one, we assume its diagonal CA to be longer than the diagonal AB.

Adjacent lines and angles cause a distortion not only in the apparent length, but also in the direction and curvature of lines. The heavy black verticals in Figure 16-21, for example, appear not to be parallel. Cross lines slanting upward force the verticals to veer to the left, while diagonals that slant down to the right make the vertical shoot up to the right. The illusion is increased if the page is turned at about a 45 degree angle. Straight lines can also be made to bend in one direction or another. In Figure 16-22, the heavy black lines in A appear to bow out in the center, those in B appear slightly concave. Such illusions have been explained by the theory of figural after-effects that operate much like the phenomenon of the after-image in color. If the eye is fixed on a field that seems to converge in the center,

CLOTHING AND THE PHYSICAL SELF

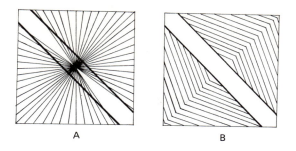

A B

Figure 16-22. Illusions of curvature.

the after-effect on the secondary figure is just the opposite, outward curvature. When the field bends outward from the center, as it does in B above, the after-effect is an opposing inward curvature. (It will also be noted that because the field of B tends to be seen in perspective, the enclosed border does not seem square.) Experiments in figural after-effects demonstrate that when a subject observes a slightly curved line in a vertical position for several minutes, a straight line shown next to it will appear to curve in the opposite direction. These same effects are observed when the hand follows a curved edge repeatedly and then shifts to a straight edge.

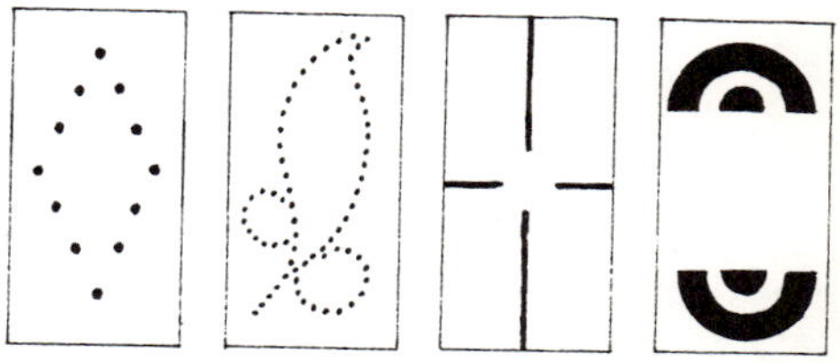

Shape

Illusions in shape or contour are just as numerous. In Chapter 12 we discussed the emergence of a "figure" as distinct from the background of a design. Usually we think of shape as something that is defined by an outline, but figures often emerge as a result of the eye connecting points in space. The four illustrations in Figure 16-23 demonstrate this phenomenon. This tendency to see continuous closed figures is called the **law of closure.**[3]

Shape is also affected by the element of shading which can give the impression of protuberances or indentations regardless of the outer contour of an object. The first illustration in Figure 16-24 appears as a flat disk, whereas the other two take on the third dimension of depth. It is this characteristic that accounts for the fact that lustrous fabrics with brilliant highlights have a wide range of gradients and thus emphasize body protuberances.

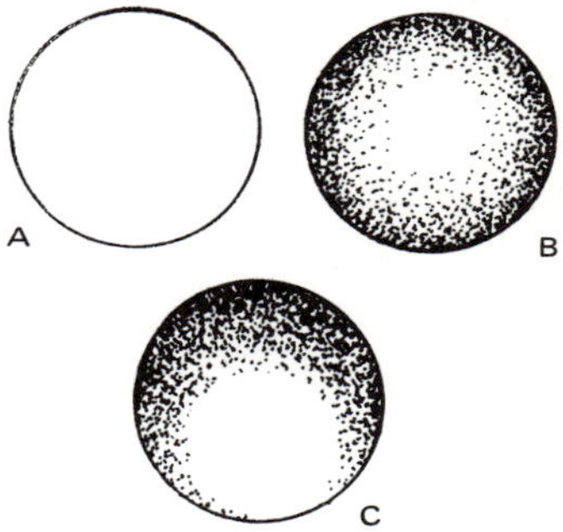

Contours that are parallel will be seen to reinforce one another in direct proportion to their nearness. In Figure 16-25 the oblique lines of the lower quadrilateral are closer together and reinforce the verticality of the shape. In the upper quadrilateral, the horizontals are closer together, and even though the sides are the same length in both, the upper figure emphasizes width rather than verticality. It is also difficult to see that the top horizontal lines of both shapes are equal in length, and that the width of the lower shape actually exceeds its height.

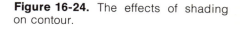

A B C D

Figure 16-23. The emergence of shape.

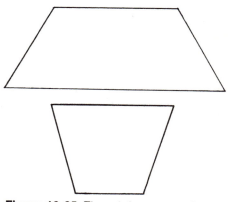

A B

C

Figure 16-24. The effects of shading on contour.

Figure 16-25. The reinforcement of parallel contours.

---

[3]K. Koffka, *Principles of Gestalt Psychology*, Kegan Paul, London, 1935.

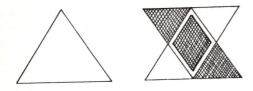

Figure 16-26. The masking of a figure.

Contours can be masked as well as reinforced. In Figure 16-15 we saw how simple figures may be included and at the same time obscured by more complex configurations. The transformation may be accomplished in a number of ways such as continuing lines beyond projecting corners of the simpler figure, concealing flat sides by placing other lines beyond them or dividing the interior space with contradictory lines. In short, the major characteristics of a shape may be concealed by the addition of new parts.[4]

The visual proportions of a shape are affected by the same comparisons and contrasts that affect the visual lengths of lines. Again in Figure 16-25 the upper quadrilateral appears as a wide shape and the lower one as a tall shape even though the heights of both are approximately the same. The oblique lines look short when juxtaposed to wider horizontals, and longer when adjacent to narrower horizontals.

Size or space

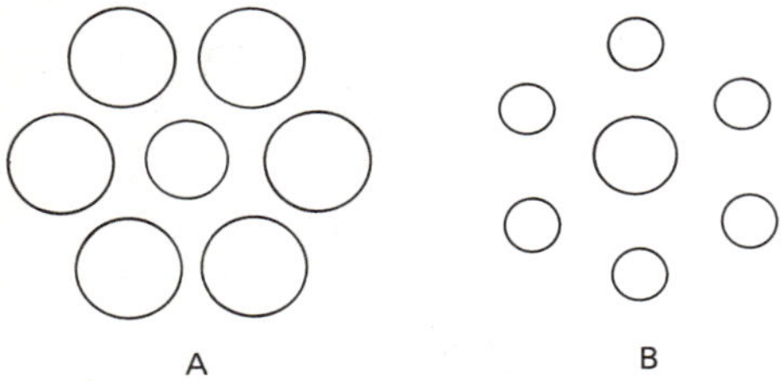

Difference in apparent sizes has already been demonstrated in Figure 16-16. The organization of similar elements of an object forces the dissimilar element further toward the extreme of its variant dimension. The center circles in Figure 16-27 appear to be different. Surrounded by larger shapes in A, the circle shrinks; next to smaller shapes in B, the circle swells.

In addition to such size comparisons, the dimensions of an object are altered by the well known illusions of "filled" and "unfilled" space. Generally the filled space appears greater in magnitude than the empty space, as illustrated in Figure 16-28. The series of dots in A seem to carry the eye a greater distance than the blank space between the two series. A similar illusion is perceived in B with the solid length of line appearing slightly longer than the same amount of unfilled space to the right. The effect is heightened in C, and most obvious in D. It becomes

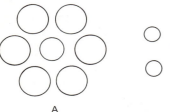

A   B

Figure 16-27. Illusions of size.

---

[4]R. S. Woodworth and H. Schlosberg, *Experimental Psychology*, Holt, Rinehart & Winston, New York, 1963, p. 416.

Figure 16-28. Illusions of filled and unfilled space.

CLOTHING AND THE PHYSICAL SELF

clear from these illustrations that the size of the interval between the verticals influences the extent of the illusion. The wider the interval the greater the illusion, i.e., as the space between the short verticals increases, subjects tend to increase their estimation of the horizontal distance traversed. The illusion is diminished as the spaces between the parts become so numerous that they are regarded as a whole rather than as individual lines.

An extension of this principle is illustrated in Figure 16-29. The "filled" square (A) that is divided vertically seems broader than it is high, while the square divided horizontally (B) increases in apparent height.[5] The addition of the perpendicular line in square C superimposes the horizontal-vertical illusion on the total area and compounds the effect of increased vertical dimension. Illustration C also demonstrates the opposing effects of the principle of space division versus the principle of filled space. In Figure 16-30 the effects of space division are obvious. Large, unbroken areas (A) seem more expansive than equal areas divided into smaller segments. When the division occurs vertically, the vertical illusion is increased (B), and when the division occurs horizontally (C), the horizontal illusion is increased. The effects of subdivision are the same for spaces as they are for lines (see Figure 16-19). The important point is that space divisions are seen as individual parts of the whole, while filled space is perceived more in terms of overall surface pattern.

As soon as we combine the element of a gradient with the effects of filled space, we complicate the illusion of size by introducing imagined perspective. In Figure 16-31, the straight verticals in A produce the same horizontal increase that they did in Figure 16-29, but in B, because the width gradient is reduced along the top level of the square, we see lines fading away in the distance and receive an impression of continuous depth. In D, the effect of horizontally filled space is compounded by the gradation of lines from the bottom to the top of the square, creating the illusion of continuous distance. In B, the gradient counteracts the effect of filled space, while in D the effect is exaggerated.

The tendency to read perspective into a figure accounts for many illusions of size and space, just as it does in judging the length of lines. The most familiar of these is illustrated in Figure 16-32. Because we tend to perceive converging lines as the vanishing point in linear perspective, we expect objects of the same size to be correspondingly smaller in "the distance." When their size does not diminish in proportion to the angle, the result is a distortion in our judgment of their actual dimensions.

[5]The extent of this illusion has been tested and reported in Lucy Stewart and Rose Padgett, "Interval Influence in Overestimation of Vertical and Horizontal Dimension," *Journal of Home Economics* 57, February 1965, pp. 133–137.

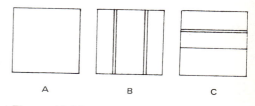

Figure 16-29. The effects of space division vs. filled space.

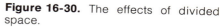

Figure 16-30. The effects of divided space.

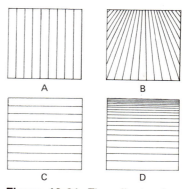

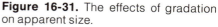

Figure 16-31. The effects of gradation on apparent size.

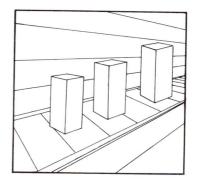

Figure 16-32. Size as determined by visual distance: the increasing size of the vertical blocks is illusory.

Texture

Textural contrasts create illusions in much the same way that filled space contrasts with unfilled space. Visual texture is, in fact, a kind of filled space. Visually, we might define texture as being composed of raised parts or projections, and depressions or areas between them. Large projections or wide gaps between them create deep, coarse textures, while perfectly flat surfaces with no projections or depressions result in smooth textures that are comparable to unfilled space.

Obtrusiveness of texture will tend to extend the size of the area which it covers. This principle also applies to the size of dots or the scale of figures in a printed fabric. The mere number or obtrusiveness of the parts will increase the apparent size of the whole. As the number of projections (or figures) in the filled space increases, the visual area will seem to increase until the parts become too numerous to be perceived separately.

Earlier we discussed the effects of gradients or shading on the visual impressions of contours (see page 329 and Figure 16-24). Textures having a close range of gradients, i.e., diffused or equal brightness from the edges to the folds, will produce soft, ill-defined contours that the eye will have difficulty in seeing. But if the protuberance contrasts sharply with the depression, with the gradient covering a wide range from light to dark, the contour will become more impressive and well-defined.

Textural comparisons or contrasts are much like size comparisons. Coarse textures seen against smooth textures will increase the effect of their difference. Smooth lustrous satin will make a porous skin appear grainy and pockmarked, while in comparison with rough-textured tweeds the same skin may look smooth and clear.

Color

Color illusions have been discussed to some extent in Chapter 12 but it will be helpful here to review the basic color principles that affect our perception of color and its subsequent influence on our visual impressions. Color perception involves the same kind of sensory organization that we discussed earlier, in which we recognize the similarity and dissimilarity among combined elements. Colors that are very similar in their dimensions of hue, value, and/or intensity will have their slight differences exaggerated when placed in close juxtaposition, while the contrasts between colors that are strikingly different will be emphasized still further.

The principle of **simultaneous contrast** describes the process whereby the eye adjusts itself to the predominant color of the field, accepting it as the norm and seeing all other colors as deviations from the norm in varying degrees. Try this experiment in simultaneous contrasts: cut out four identical figures from a blue-green color swatch that is medium in value and intensity. Place each one in the center of a larger field, one white, one black, and the other two of medium value and intensity but one yellow-green in hue, and the other, purple-blue. In the black field where the norm is darkness, the blue-green figure will appear lightest in value of all four figures. On the white field where the norm is lightness, it will appear darkest in value. Seen against the yellow-green field, the figure will take on a bluish cast, and against the purple-blue it will seem greener.

After-image is a response to a color stimulus so strong that satiation or fatigue overtakes the nerve endings in the eye. Strenuous activity on the part of one retinal area induces an opposing activity in an adjacent area—a kind of internal complementary chemical reaction. Effects of the after-image can be demonstrated in another experiment: cut out a figure from a bright green color swatch that is medium to light in value, and mount it on a larger field of black to enhance its intensity. Prepare four other fields the same size as the black mounting, one a neutral gray, another bright yellow, a third bright red, and the fourth light blue. Look fixedly at the mounted green figure for a minute or more and then shift the gaze to the center of the gray field and you will see a reflection of the figure's image in complementary magenta. Because the gray has no hue of its own, the complement is seen in its pure form. Repeat the experiment, transferring the gaze from the original green figure to each of the other three fields. On the yellow field, the magenta after-image will mix with the hue of the field and appear orange; on the other two surfaces a similar mixture will occur—the magenta after-image will mix with the red field to produce a darker, more intense red-purple figure, and with the blue field to create a purple figure.

Several other factors affecting our perception of color should be mentioned. Differences in light source, or the effects of colored illuminants were discussed briefly in Chapter 12. The eye readily adjusts itself to different levels of illumination after prolonged exposure. Everyone has had the experience of entering a darkened room after being in bright sunlight and suffering from momentary blindness. Gradually we begin to see differences between light and dark objects in the room and eventually we regain our "normal" vision in which all colors in the room take on their familiar relationship to each other. Standing in strong sunlight, we find it difficult to see clearly those objects that are in the shadows, but once in the shade the eye adapts to the reduced illumination and the overcast of shadow disappears, while at the same time objects out in the sunlight become too bright for us to see comfortably.

Very strong contrasts of color repeatedly juxtaposed in large or equal amounts will produce what is known as **flicker,** or chromatic vibration. Stark black and brilliant white, for example, combined into a large check or pattern will create a pulsating effect in which the figures seem to jump or quiver on the surface. Strong complements combined in similar fashion produce equally unstable images that the eye has difficulty bringing into focus. The illusion is reduced if the contrasting figures are separated by a neutral ground. The illusion is reversed if the figures are so small that the eye does not perceive them as individual units; contrasts then fuse to give an additive mixture that move toward neutral gray.

The "spreading" effect of colors that seem to "mix in the eye" results in the exact opposite of the principle of simultaneous contrast. Small spots of medium blue, for example, on a white ground will not appear darker and more intense as they would if they were seen as independent contrasts. Rather, the white will seem to mix with the blue and give a total impression of a lighter blue.

Experimental studies have also indicated that most subjects tend to perceive strong saturated colors and warm hues as being closer (and therefore larger), as opposed to the cool and/or grayed colors which seem farther in the distance (and therefore smaller). Perspective can be considerably distorted by reversing advancing and receding colors in the visual field.

The combined effects of color are complicated by the fact that we rarely have the opportunity to judge a color against a single contrast. In a normal situation, our field of vision includes many colors, all of which have an effect upon one another. In costume, it is not merely the garment color against skin, but skin against hair and eyes, and all of it together against a background. Regardless of the advancing or receding qualities of its color, any object will be less conspicuous if it is similar to its background in hue, value, and intensity. Objects that differ sharply from their backgrounds in any one of the color dimensions will stand out in greater contrast.

Moreover, the average observer cannot isolate his perception of hue from the other dimensions of lightness and brightness. It was indicated that neutrals will brighten colors by virtue of their intensity contrast; yet a dark neutral such as black will provide a minimum of contrast against a bright but dark blue because the values are so similar. At the opposite end of the scale, we might assume that black would intensify the pigmentation in the skin, but the greater contrast occurs in value rather than intensity; black makes the skin seem whiter by comparison, and as colors ascend the value scale they automatically decrease their intensity. Whenever two principles appear to be in competition, the one having the greater degree of contrast will usually take precedence.

The apparent size, shape, and color of an object are relative to the total situation in which they are found.

SUMMARY *Illusory responses of the human eye*

Illusion in the visual appearance of objects is largely a function of the sensory organization that takes place in the brain, through which we tend to perceive the similarities and the differences of juxtaposed elements in the visual field. Elements that are similar to one another, having a commonality of line, shape, size, texture, or color, tend to fall into a single configuration to which the law of closure is applied. Similarity or repetition of parts tends to reinforce or strengthen the total configuration. Conversely, single parts that are clearly differentiated from all the others that resemble one another will be conspicuous by their contrast.

Any abrupt change in line direction, contour, dimension, surface quality, or color will produce contrast. Illusions specifically related to line have been discussed in terms of the eye movement theory and the effects of bisection, perspective, and after-images. Shapes may be altered through masking or the use of gradients, and reinforced through concentric or parallel repetition. Size comparisons are affected by the principles of space division, and "filled" vs. "unfilled" space, and also by the tendency to read perspective into visual impressions. Textural contrasts contribute to illusory responses in much the same way as size and space comparisons. The principles of simultaneous contrast and the after-image account for the majority of illusions that are experienced in relation to color.

Figure 16-33. Carmichael makes an unsuccessful application of the principle of vertical illusion.

Illusion in dress

Application of the principles of illusion to dress can alter the frame of reference in which we perceive the human form. Physical aspects of the body that cannot otherwise be controlled through balanced diet, adequate exercise, and/or corrective posture can be manipulated in the direction of the desired proportion by a skillful use of the visual components of dress. By now we should be acutely aware of the importance of the organized whole. To concentrate on the sizes and shapes of individual parts of the body is to run the risk of camouflaging a minor problem with a solution that accentuates a major one. The most effective masking for a full, irregular hipline is a skirt that is full enough to obscure the contour completely. A widened hemline, however, also has the effect of diminishing apparent height, and unfortunately, broad hips and a short figure often go together. It may be helpful to demonstrate a systematic application of illusion principles to specific figure types.

The full figure

If we go back to the silhouette in Figure 16-7, we see a form with a totally unique combination of physical attributes.

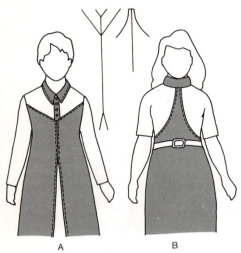

A   B

Figure 16-34. The full figure.

Assuming that the objective is to make the figure conform more closely to the visual proportions of the average model, we can then identify the illusions we wish to create. The major problem is that of organizing the whole into an illusion of increased height. Since the length of the waist is normal and the legs are slender and well-shaped below the knee, the alteration in visual length should be concentrated between the waist and knee. Other desirable illusions of secondary importance would be: (1) decreasing the width of the waist, (2) increasing bustline contour, (3) straightening the shoulder line, and (4) reducing the width of face and neck.

Each of the two designs in Figure 16-34 were developed from the contours of Figure 16-7. (Note: The drawings in Figures 16-33 through 16-36 are proportionate to the body silhouettes of Figures 16-7 through 16-10. Their proportions may be verified by comparing each drawing with the original figure. A comparison of the visual impressions made by each can be explained in terms of the optical illusions presented in the foregoing section. Application of the Müller-Lyer principle (Figure 16-17) is fairly obvious. In A, the eye travels along a vertical path that has no definite termination point. In B, the effects of the horizontal-vertical illusion (Figure 16-18) are totally obscured by the reinforcement of the waistline horizontal in contrasting value and extension into the cuff line. If the eye does in fact get started along the vertical path of the centerfront, it is quickly returned to the waistline via the downward angles of the arrow.

The effects of subdivision are utilized in A by dividing the figure vertically at the waist and continuing the line the full length of the figure (refer back to Figure 16-19, A and B). The outwardly slanting V of the bodice and the set-in sleeve help to mask the curve of the sloping shoulders.

The use of gradients also may be noted in comparing the effects of the two designs (Figure 16-31). The outward radiation of lines in A affords increased width to the shoulders, while the gradient in B gives width to the waist and reinforces the pyramidal shape of the total figure. Further, the reinforcement of parallel contours in the high rolled collar of design B increases the illusion of width through the face and neck (see Figure 16-25).

The hairstyle in A also reduces apparent head size, contributing to the overall impression of added height. In short, design A more nearly meets the objectives of illusion outlined in our preliminary analysis of body proportions.

The slender figure

Figure 16-8 exhibits body proportions that are probably closer to an ideal than to the average or normal configuration. In our culture at least, a long waist and long legs are not usually considered disadvantageous unless they shorten other body dimensions by comparison. The fashion model is typically an eight-head figure, very slender and often flat-chested. However, if we use the same average standard that we applied to the preceding example, we might state the major goal of visual organization in this particular case as softening body angularity and emphasizing the feminine contours of bust and hip.

The two designs in Figure 16-35 both employ horizontal lines as major constituents or elements. The total effects of the two are quite different, however, and illustrate the fundamental difference between the principle of space division and the principle of filled and unfilled space (Figures 16-28, 16-29, and 16-30).

Design A increases contour through bust and hipline by introducing added fullness in fabric and, at the same time, by increasing the contrast between bust and waist and waist and hip proportions (see Figures 16-25 and 16-27).

The horizontals in design B are used to fill space rather than to divide it (Figure 16-29). The figure appears cylindrical and lacking in contour, with little apparent difference in bust, waist, and hipline measurements.

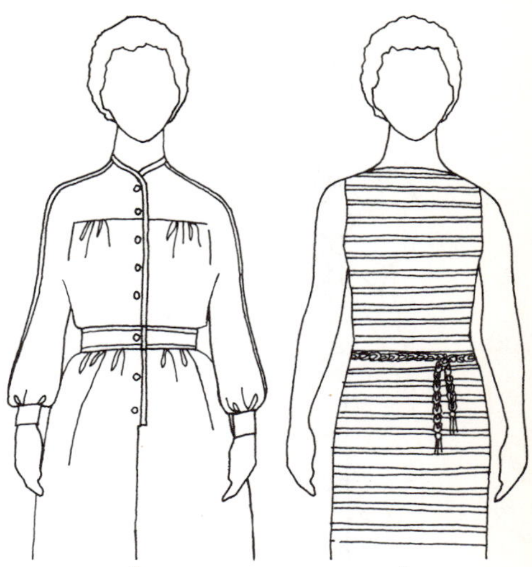

The short figure

Stockiness of build contributes to a dwarfing of the figure in 16-9. While the torso is average in proportion, the arms and legs are short. In Figure 16-36, design A avoids horizontal lines that will destroy any illusion of height. There is minimal contrast at the bottom of the coat, and the garment is cut a little on the short side to make the legs look as long as possible. The trousers are straight, pleatless, trimly fitted, and finished without a cuff, again to elongate the legs.

The double-breasted blazer in B is cut just full enough through the waist to give a broad, boxy look to the torso, which is accentuated by the squarish placement of buttons and the wide flap pockets that draw attention to the sides of the figure. Trouser legs are cut full enough to give a baggy effect, and width is again exaggerated by the double line of the cuff. Strong value contrast between the jacket and trousers emphasizes the horizontal space division and gives the figure a top-heavy appearance. Alternating values in dark tie and shirt, light blazer, dark pants, and light shoes create a spotty effect and, at the same time, present a series of rather powerful horizontal barriers. Design B is a prize example of contrast illusions, while A illustrates the effect of assimilation illusions.

The tall figure

The body build in Figure 16-10 conforms closely to average proportions, although it is eight heads in height. In terms of our

Figure 16-35. The slender figure.

Figure 16-36. The short figure.

A   B

Figure 16-37. The tall figure.

own cultural ideals, being tall is a decided advantage, particularly among males. The major "problem" in Figure 16-10 is largely a matter of posture, which could easily be corrected through practice and exercise. It is possible, however, to camouflage postural deficiencies with optical illusions in dress. Figure 16-37 shows two profile views which demonstrate the effects of the Zöllner illusion (Figure 16-21) on the alignment of the body. Oblique lines that contradict the perpendicular force the latter in the direction that will maintain its right-angle relationship to the crossbars. A figure that appears to be slumped forward, therefore, will counteract the slant by jacket lengths that are slightly shorter in back than in front, and pocket lines which repeat the angle, as in A. The slouch is exaggerated in B by pocket and jacket lines that slant downward from front to back, and also by over-fitting the back of the jacket. A round shoulder is improved by slanting the shoulder seam back from neck to armscye, and it is accentuated by a seam that shoots forward, as in B.

Textures and colors

It is important to remember that every texture has an independent effect upon body size and contour. Bulky, heavy fabrics, such as tweeds, shetlands, wide-waled corduroys, and thick bouclés add bulk to the figure and increase apparent size. They help to fill out a tall, slender figure and conceal its angularity. Stiff textures also increase size, but often mask irregular contours effectively by superimposing their own firm shape over parts of the silhouette. Textures that have luster call attention to body contours by virtue of their wide range of gradients (see Figure 16-24). Supple fabrics tend to emphasize the figure if allowed to cling to body curves. Transparent textures are also figure-revealing; if they are stiff in addition to transparent (e.g., organdy, tulle, net), they add their own bulk and at the same time reveal the contour of the figure beneath them. Medium-weight textures that are devoid of luster do the most to minimize the size of the figure by making it as inconspicuous as possible. Keeping in mind the principle of filled and unfilled space, it is important to select prints, plaids, and checks that are scaled to the size of the wearer.

In relating costume colors to personal coloring, the most related effects are achieved if the dominant hue of the costume enhances the color of the skin. Hair and eyes tend to be less important in determining which colors are most flattering, unless of course they are one of the individual's most outstanding attributes. Vivid red hair or luminous green eyes are certain to be noticed before skin tones. A healthy appearance, however, is largely dependent upon the clarity and color of the skin. In general, the cool skin types look better in cool, dark colors, and the warm types wear warm colors best. Usually costume colors

CLOTHING AND THE PHYSICAL SELF

that are slightly darker in value than the skin will improve its clearness. However, if one wishes to enhance a deep suntan, the lighter tints will do this best, particularly the hues in the blue-green range which provide a complementary contrast.

A florid complexion is minimized by warm colors that are low in saturation and dark enough in value to make the skin seem pale by comparison. Colors that are complementary to flesh tones (the blue-greens) will emphasize skin color and bring out the rosy tones in a pale face. Sallowness is exaggerated by hues in the blue-purple, purple, red-purple range, and reduced by yellow-greens. Individuals who lack strong contrasts in their personal coloring will find moderately bright intensities in the medium-light, medium-dark value range the most becoming. Strong, intense colors will weaken intermediate coloring, and drab neutrals in costume do not provide enough contrast to relieve the monotony.

Variation in the use of art components alters the frame of reference in which we see the human form.

SUMMARY *Illusion in dress*

A systematic application of the principles of illusion to dress has been demonstrated, using four different figure types as specific examples. In general, figure irregularities can be camouflaged by increasing similarity to adjacent components; other qualities can be emphasized by increasing the contrast. The danger in attempting to camouflage or accentuate isolated parts of the figure lies in the possibility of destroying the unified effect of the whole. The desired illusions must be clearly identified through a comparison of actual proportions with those of an ideal.

Areas of the body that are judged to be too large can be subdivided into smaller areas or counterbalanced by increasing the visual size of the surrounding elements. Body proportions that are considered too small may be masked or increased in size through the use of perspective and gradient techniques, or by minimizing the size of adjacent elements. Lines can lead the eye along pathways that travel in the desired direction, which is usually away from problem areas, and toward the attributes that one can afford to emphasize. Attention will be drawn to the points of greatest contrast. Some people may, in fact, choose to draw attention to their most deviant characteristics in order to emphasize their individuality.

FOR FURTHER READING

Luckiesh, M. *Visual Illusions: Their Causes, Characteristics and Applications.* New York: Dover Publications, 1965.

Mueller, C., M. Rudolph, and the Editors of *Time-Life* Books. *Light and Vision.* New York: Time-Life Books, 1969.

Mulvey, Frank. *Graphic Perception of Space.* New York: Reinhold Book Corp., 1969.

Patrick, Julia M. *Distinctive Dress*. New York: Charles Scribner's Sons, 1969.

Quinn, F., A. Linn, and W. Hale. *Consumer Color Charts*. Baltimore: Munsell Color Company, 1967.

Spears, Charleszine. *How to Wear Colors with Emphasis on Dark Skins*. Minneapolis: Burgess Publishing Company, 1965.

DISCUSSION QUESTIONS

1. What is the difference between a physical ideal and a physical norm?

2. Describe the average length proportions of the human form. How do male and female proportions differ in circumference ratios?

3. Given a specific figure, outline the ways in which it conforms to or varies from the physical norm.

4. Describe at least one optical illusion that is known to occur in line, shape, size, texture, and color, and explain how each applies to dress.

5. What is the difference between assimilation illusions and contrast illusions? How do they relate to the principles of simultaneous contrast and after-image?

6. Illustrate at least one type of illusion that will create an impression of (a) increased height, (b) a longer waist, (c) broader shoulders, (d) narrower hips. What is the danger in treating such isolated "figure problems" apart from the whole?

PART FIVE

Clothing in the Economy

17

The American Clothing Industry

IN OUR LAND of freedom and abundance, the individual consumer is apt to believe that what he buys (and wears) is nobody's business but his own. Very much to the contrary, however, the economic unit of the private household never operates in isolation from the economic system which surrounds it. The independent family—as well as the independent business firm—makes daily decisions regarding the use of its resources; these decisions, in turn, determine the character of local, national, and international markets. In this sense, the consumer is both the beginning and the end of all economic activity.

In the American enterprise system, the economy is based to a large extent on the private ownership of businesses with varying degrees of competition in the marketplace. As we shall see in the discussion that follows, however, the interests of all citizens are not alike, and some in fact are in serious conflict. When there is disagreement between or among various special interest groups, such as farmers, manufacturers, processors, retailers, importers, consumers, and the like, it becomes the government's job to make a decision that will benefit the largest number of people. Sometimes a government decision that benefits one group works to the detriment of another.

Most manufacturers will agree that the apparel business is indeed a highly uncertain one. Fashion requires a kind of hand-to-mouth buying and a speedy delivery of goods. Its demands are seasonal in nature, creating problems in the labor market. There is tremendous rivalry among the many small mills and manufacturing firms, as well as growing competition from foreign imports. As if these problems were not enough, the complexity of the industry creates an interdependence among its various segments all along the chain of production and distribution (see Figure 17-2).

In spite of the headaches, the production of textiles and clothing combined constitutes one of the five largest industries in the United States. American consumers spend over $69 billion annually for the purchase of clothing and shoes. Our purpose in Part Five is to show the impact that individual clothing choices have on the total economy. It will take the full span of the next three chapters to demonstrate this relationship between business and personal economic decision making. We will begin by taking a look at the significance of the apparel industry to the American economy in terms of our textile production, apparel manufacture, and retailing activities.

Some general economic concepts

Ideally, Western democracies strive for an economic climate that will make possible (1) *efficiency* in the use of the nation's resources; (2) *equity* in the distribution of goods and services among all members of society; (3) *growth* in the national output and elimination of short-term fluctuations in employment and production; and (4) as much *freedom* as possible for all members of society—consumers, laborers, businessmen—to make independent decisions within a framework that is consistent with social welfare. Needless to say, these goals have not been fully met, even though in America we come closer than most nations to achieving a mature economy.

Types of economic systems

All countries work out some economic system for the production, distribution, and consumption of goods and services. In the less economically developed countries of the world, **tradition** has long been the regulator of economic activity. Under a traditional system, production tasks are performed and goods are exchanged according to a pattern that changes little from generation to generation. Totalitarian societies, on the other hand, blow tradition to the wind in order to sweep their economy into industrial orbit. Under this kind of a **command** system, a central authority decides what shall be produced, and the individual consumer has very little influence over the nature of goods and services that are available to him.

A third type of economy is known as the **market system.** It differs from both the traditional and command systems in that it both fosters innovation and operates without superimposed authority or supervision. It is based upon the interplay of supply and demand, that is, a system in which the consumer determines what shall be produced by virtue of his behavior in the marketplace. In actual fact, each of the three economic systems has some elements of the other two. Even though the American economy comes closest to the market system, we have some mix of tradition and some elements of the command system through such regulatory devices as wage and price controls, quotas, tariffs, subsidies, and other artificial incentives or restrictions.

Success of the market system depends to a large extent upon the opportunity for open competition. This means that there

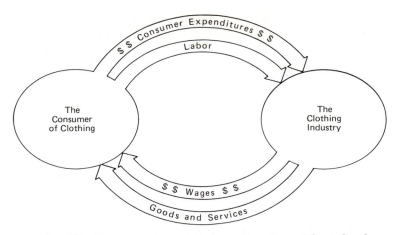

Figure 17-1. The circular flow in a market economy. The individual consumer or household and the individual firms that make up the clothing industry are linked together by a series of expenditures and receipts. The consumer buys goods from an individual firm. The consumer also sells his labor to the industry in exchange for wages, which enables him to buy more goods and services.

must be (1) a large number of firms competing with each other, (2) ease of entry and exit (it must be fairly easy to get into the business), and (3) no differentiation in products. In reality, there is no such thing as pure competition. For the most part, we operate in a market situation that is characterized by **imperfect competition.** As we shall see, various segments of the industry meet the conditions of the market system in different ways. In the apparel industry, there are many firms, all having relatively easy entrance and exit; but each firm tries to sell a product that is different from that of every other firm. The man-made fiber industry, on the other hand, is composed of relatively few companies. Access is limited by the demands for large capital investment, but the companies tend to manufacture undifferentiated products.

Economic indicators

It is important to keep in mind that the flow of money in the national economy is circular (see Figure 17-1). All persons are consumers of clothing and thus make some monetary input into the clothing industry. Obviously not everyone contributes labor and withdraws wages from the clothing industry per se, but as in other areas of production, the needs and wants of those who are themselves not producers must be provided for. The success of the clothing industry is vital to the economic health of the nation as a whole because of the supplies and services that it buys and the wages and taxes that it pays. The economic significance of the industry thus can be assessed in terms of such factors as the number of people employed, the level of wages and salaries that they receive, and the contribution the industry makes to our overall national income.

Textile production

Textile production has usually been one of the first steps taken by developing nations toward industrialization, and this was

CLOTHING IN THE ECONOMY

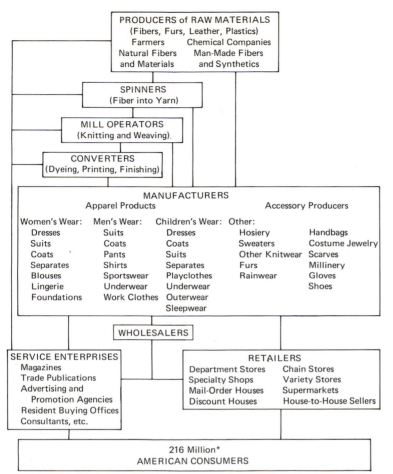

PRODUCERS of RAW MATERIALS
(Fibers, Furs, Leather, Plastics)
Farmers   Chemical Companies
Natural Fibers   Man-Made Fibers
and Materials   and Synthetics

SPINNERS
(Fiber into Yarn)

MILL OPERATORS
(Knitting and Weaving)

CONVERTERS
(Dyeing, Printing, Finishing)

MANUFACTURERS
Apparel Products   Accessory Producers

Women's Wear:	Men's Wear:	Children's Wear:	Other:	
Dresses	Suits	Dresses	Hosiery	Handbags
Suits	Coats	Coats	Sweaters	Costume Jewelry
Coats	Pants	Suits	Other Knitwear	Scarves
Separates	Shirts	Separates	Furs	Millinery
Blouses	Sportswear	Playclothes	Rainwear	Gloves
Lingerie	Underwear	Underwear		Shoes
Foundations	Work Clothes	Outerwear		
		Sleepwear		

WHOLESALERS

SERVICE ENTERPRISES
Magazines
Trade Publications
Advertising and
    Promotion Agencies
Resident Buying Offices
Consultants, etc.

RETAILERS
Department Stores   Chain Stores
Specialty Shops   Variety Stores
Mail-Order Houses   Supermarkets
Discount Houses   House-to-House Sellers

216 Million*
AMERICAN CONSUMERS

*Population estimate for 1975. A conservative projection for 1980 is 228 million.

Figure 17-2. The complexity of the clothing industry creates an interdependence among its segments throughout the chain of production and distribution.

certainly true in America. The production of cotton and wool fiber was an important segment of the early agricultural development in the colonies, and at his inauguration George Washington wore an American-made suit of homespun broadcloth to promote the young U.S. textile industry. The first textile mill began in Pawtucket, Rhode Island, in the year 1790, so the business of manufacturing textiles is one of our country's oldest industries.

Historically, there have always been many small operators who engaged in one or more of the major processes by which the raw material is produced and transformed into finished cloth: spinning the fibers into yarn, weaving or knitting the yarns into cloth, and finishing the fabric to impart color, pattern, or other desired characteristics. The flow chart in Figure 17-2 represents these operations as separate divisions of the industry, but many of the large firms integrate all processes.

Size and scope

The United States textile industry today is the largest in the world. Until recent years it was typified by small, family-owned type businesses and partnerships, generally set up by independent farmers, spinners, weavers, dyers, and finishers to cover single end use trades. There are still many small producers of the natural fibers (cotton and wool) who strive to get the best possible price for their product in the marketplace. Prior to the 1960's, cotton was by far the leading fiber percentagewise, but since the mid-sixties both cotton and wool comprise less and less of the end use consumption each year (see Figure 17-3). The 1973 figures, for example, showed cotton's share of the market as 29 per cent, compared with almost 70 per cent taken over by the man-made fibers. Wool constitutes less than 2 per cent of all fibers consumed, while silk and linen combined (neither of which is produced in the United States) probably account for less than 0.006 per cent.[1]

The tremendous growth in the man-made fiber field after World War II shifted the production focus from agriculture to the giant chemical corporations such as DuPont, Tennessee Eastman, Monsanto, Celanese, and others. Today there are probably not more than 75 companies operating about 125 plants throughout the country that make all of the man-made fiber produced in the United States. In 1971, this amounted to nearly six-and-one-half billion pounds of fiber.[2] Nearly one-third of these fiber-producing firms are listed among the 500 largest industrial corporations in the country.[3] In the early 1970's, there were almost 100,000 workers employed in man-made fiber producing plants. In the decade from 1960 to 1970, their gross annual payroll more than doubled, reaching an estimated $865 million in 1970.[4]

The primary producers of cotton and wool, on the other hand, still tend to be the small independent farmers and ranchers. Most of the cotton is grown in the southeastern part of the United States or in other states such as Arizona, California, New Mexico, Oklahoma, and Texas, where the climate is suitable. Most of the wool comes from the ranch areas of California, Colorado, Nevada, Texas, Utah, and Wyoming. Wool growers usually market their product through a cooperative association, although sometimes a mill representative will buy

[1]Source: Economic Research Service, U.S.D.A. These figures are for the domestic picture only. On a worldwide basis, cotton still holds a dominant position. In the early 1970's, the world production of cotton was 24.9 billions of pounds compared to 3.5 billions of pounds for wool, 7.6 for man-made cellulosics, and 10.9 for non-cellulosics. It will probably not be long before the spectacular growth rate of the man-made fibers will overtake cotton's present lead all over the world.
[2]*Textile Organon*, November 1972.
[3]"Fortune's Directory of the 500 Largest U.S. Industrial Corporations," *Fortune*, May 1972, pp. 188–224.
[4]1971 *Man-made Fiber Fact Book*, Man-Made Fiber Producers Association, Washington, D.C.

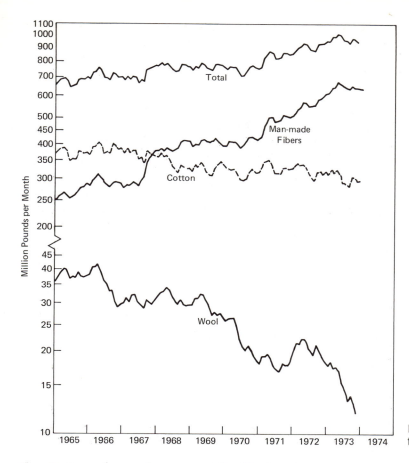

Figure 17-3. U.S. textile fiber consumption.

directly from the rancher, especially if he has developed a fiber with special qualities. Cotton growers often sell to wholesalers, who in turn do the bargaining with the mill representatives in a central market. In any case, before sale, both wool and cotton are graded as to quality and then sold to the highest bidder.

At one time, there was a high degree of specialization in the textile plant, but most mills today process more than one kind of fiber. Cotton mills combine synthetics in varying percentages; woolen mills blend cotton, rayon, silk, fur fiber, and man-mades into a wide variety of new fabrics. There is still considerable specialization in the industry. Some plants will process the raw fiber, spin it into yarn, and ship it on to another mill to be woven or knitted into cloth (see Figure 17-2). There are also a number of independent converters who buy unfinished goods, dye or print the fabric, and apply durable press, water or soil repellent, flame proofing, or other types of special finishes.

Figure 17-4. Raw materials. The cotton boll (left) represents a large portion of the farming economy and provides the fibers for nearly a third of all textile mill products. The man-made fiber (right) emerging from the spinneret is either twisted into yarn or blended with other fibers. It now constitutes almost 70 per cent of all fiber consumption and continues to provide an increasing share of total production.

Figure 17-5. Spinning fiber into yarn. Short fibers are drawn out and given a twist to form a fine, continuous length of yarn.

During the period of the 1950's, however, the American textile industry was faced with growing competition from foreign producers, many of whom built modern up-to-date plants after World War II. The U.S. mills began a series of mergers and acquisitions that eliminated many of the smaller plants and increased the size of many larger ones. What had been an industry that operated traditionally on small amounts of capital and huge amounts of labor gradually moved toward integrated operations that took over the spinning, weaving, dyeing, and finishing, as well as the control of the sale of the finished product. Private ownership gave way to corporations, and, as a result, the vertically integrated plants became the fastest growing companies in the country. Burlington Industries, for example, began in North Carolina in 1923 as a small mill. Gradually it acquired interests in a number of converting plants until today it comprises over thirty divisions that perform every operation from the conversion of raw fiber into yarn to the selling of the finished product. In 1972, with an annual sales record of $1.8 billion, Burlington was rated among the 100 largest industrials in the nation.[5] This period of rapid growth paralleled the growth of the chemical fiber companies.

The American fabric industry today consists of about 700 companies that operate approximately 7,000 textile manufacturing plants.[6] In the last two decades, many of the larger companies abandoned the small mills in the New England area and invested large amounts of capital in new plants and equipment, concentrating in the southeast where land and labor were readily available. This move created some serious economic problems in New England, which had for so long been the center of the American textile industry.

At first, the increased efficiency of the new plants reduced the total number of workers, but today, with vastly increased production requirements, the industry again employs nearly one million people. These textile employees, in turn, "play an important role in the national economy. Each year they earn $6 billion . . . pay $762 million in personal taxes . . . spend $1.4 billion for food, over $1 billion for housing and $550 million for transportation."[7] Sales from the goods that they produce amount to over $22 billion annually.

Most of the larger integrated firms not only produce fabric for apparel manufacture and home sewing, but they also loom carpeting and turn out a wide variety of finished consumer

---

[5]Next to Burlington, the five largest mills in terms of annual sales were: J. P. Stevens ($957 million), M. Lowenstein ($470 million), West Point Pepperell ($408 million), Springs ($399 million), and Cannon ($353 million). Source: *Daily News Record*, 5 March 1973.
[6]The impact of vertical integration can be seen in the gradual decline in the number of textile mills, which dropped from over 8,000 in the early 1950's to 7,500 in the mid 1960's.
[7]*A Profile of Textiles*, American Textile Manufacturers Institute, Inc., Charlotte, N.C., 1972.

CLOTHING IN THE ECONOMY

Figure 17-6. (left) A modern knitting machine. Cones of yarn arranged in circular fashion produce the knitted tubing visible at the bottom of the machine.

Figure 17-7. (above) Weaving and knitting yarn into fabric. This illustration shows a huge weaving room in a textile plant with looms producing "grey goods" or unfinished cloth.

products such as bedsheets and pillowcases, bedspreads, towels, curtains, blankets, and the like. Over 38 per cent of all goods manufactured goes into apparel. The home furnishings products run a fairly close second (31.1 per cent). The remaining third of the end use consumption goes into other consumer type items such as piece goods, shoes, slippers, and luggage, (10.5 per cent); industrial uses (17.3 per cent), and exports (2.8 per cent).[8]

Two other important economic indicators that reflect on the performance of an industry relate to prices and profits. In recent years the price of textiles at the wholesale level has been consistently below the average for all industrial commodities as a whole (see Figure 17-9). In 1970, for example, the wholesale price index for all textile mill products was 103.2, while the index for all other industrial commodities was 110. Since 1971, the price increases were due largely to the record increases in the raw agricultural fiber prices (as represented by the price index for cotton products). The industry's profits on sales also are generally below those for manufacturing in general (Figure 17-10). Profits for 1972, averaged 2.6 cents on the dollar for textile mill products as compared to 4.3 cents for all manufactures.

Activities of the textile industry

The small independent producers of natural fibers have little control over the end use products that utilize their raw materials. Whatever advertising is done to promote the use of cotton or wool is usually handled through a trade association such

Figure 17-8. Finishing processes. These include a number of chemical and mechanical treatments such as bleaching, dyeing, sanforizing, printing, embossing, and crease-resistant finishes. Here a plain fabric is imprinted with a colorful floral pattern. The design is engraved on copper cylinders, with a separate cylinder for each color.

[8]1972 figures were the latest summary statistics available at this writing. Source: *Textile Organon*, November 1973.

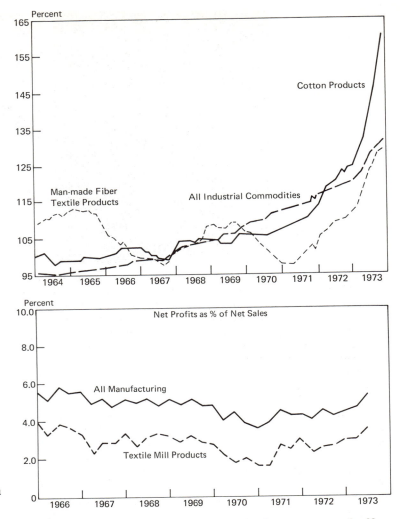

Figure 17-9. Wholesale price index (1967 = 100).

Figure 17-10. Corporate profit data (after Federal income taxes).

as Cotton, Inc., or the Wool Bureau. The large man-made fiber corporations, on the other hand, indulge heavily in competitive advertising in order to make the consumer conscious of their respective brand names or trademarks. Much of their promotional activity is done in cooperation with fabric and garment manufacturers, through whom they subsidize local and national advertising. In 1973, for example, Celanese paid $3 million just to sponsor the Johnny Carson show, and Hoechst invested $1.5 million in the Dr. Joyce Brothers Easy Living series.

Economists often view advertising as an economic waste, that is, an activity which creates market imperfections and reduces pure competition. However, effective advertising can

350   CLOTHING IN THE ECONOMY

serve to educate the consumer, and without advertising many new products would not find their way into the average household.

The trend among the textile mills toward big business has also put an emphasis on brand names, but the effects of consolidation have had other beneficial impacts as well. Larger amounts of money have been channeled into research and product development. As a result, new impetus has been given to technological changes and innovations, both in terms of greater efficiency of output and in terms of new fibers, fabrics, and finishes available to the consumer. The DuPont company, as an example, budgets more than $80 million a year for research and development.

Beyond this, the industry has stepped up its market research in order to gear its production more closely to consumer needs and desires. Several of the firms have employed home economists in their educational departments. More recently, companies have inititated consumer advisory groups to analyze consumer trends and to advise the industry on how it can respond most effectively to consumer needs and desires.

The fabric producers work so far in advance of the consumer market that they must be extremely adept at anticipating the trends in fashion. For this reason, most companies retain style specialists and market reporters who sound out leaders in the fashion field for hints of styles that are headed for popular acceptance in the season to come.

Fabric designers not only determine what will be available on the market next year, but they provide the inspiration for much of the design in the clothing or cutting-up trades. New developments in textiles greatly influence the construction of the garment. Laminates, stretch fabrics, and permanent press, for example, have forced a number of changes not only in the design of clothes but in production techniques as well. The long-range planning in the textile industry must be flexible enough to respond to quick changes in consumer demand, and at the same time must provide a wide variety in color, weight, thickness, texture, and finish to meet the needs of a diversified market.

Integration among firms and increased technological and market research have characterized the textile industry in recent years.

SUMMARY *Textile production*

The textile industry today is characterized by a decreasing number of smaller firms and an increasing diversification and efficiency of the larger companies. Firms utilizing large amounts of labor and little capital have found it increasingly difficult to compete with producers in other countries where the labor supply is more abundant. Larger firms have, therefore, attempted to improve their productive efficiency by investing in up-to-date machinery and by increasing their scale of operations.

Research has led to technological innovations in fiber, fabric, and finish that have increased the versatility and serviceability of fabrics that go into clothing. At the same time, market research reduces the errors in judging the market potential and helps the textile producer gauge his output more accurately in relation to consumer demand. This in turn reduces the inventory of unsold stock and passes price savings on to the consumer.

Because fabrics are often the source of inspiration for clothing designers, decisions made in the mill in regard to color, texture, and pattern influence the design of the garments that ultimately appear on the market.

Apparel production

The apparel industry—also known as the ready-to-wear industry, the garment makers, the cutting-up or needle trades, and sometimes as the "rag business"—is little more than a century old. As in the textile industry, some of the greatest changes have taken place within the last ten years. Traditionally a highly fragmented industry consisting of thousands of small, independent firms, the trend has been toward larger concerns, greater diversification of production, and from proprietorships or partnerships to corporations. These recent developments have taken place largely as a result of the increased competition from the growing industrialization abroad, and the challenge of new materials, new processes, and new markets.

Development of the industry

In Colonial days, practically every home was a factory, with its own spinning wheel and loom and the nimble fingers of family members to hand-stitch the homespun into wearable garments. It was not until the early 1800's that a small group of New England merchants conceived the idea of having ready-made trousers and shirts available for the sailors who had only a few days in port. By the 1840's the demand for ready-made garments was spurred by the rush to the west for gold. Inexpensive clothes were needed by laborers, plantation slaves, and the many bachelors who had no wives to sew for them. Still sewn by hand, the clothes were hurriedly made and ill-fitting.

The invention of the sewing machine and the Civil War gave further impetus to the ready-mades after the middle of the century. Women went to work in central places to make uniforms for the soldiers, and out of this concentrated effort a standardized system of sizing developed which was later adapted to civilian requirements. By 1880, the men's ready-to-wear business was well established.

The manufacture of women's clothing was first noted in about 1859, when the census figures reported a total of 5,739 workers engaged primarily in the production of cloaks, mantillas, and hoop skirts (see Figure 14-5). In the 1880's and 1890's, heavy immigration from Eastern Europe contributed a large number of eager workers to the clothing industry, many of whom had developed tailoring skills in their mother country. The 1890's was the era of the Gibson Girl, and the demand for women's shirtwaist blouses gave tremendous impetus to the ready-to-wear movement. By 1900, 2,070 manufacturers of women's clothing employed a total of 96,000 workers.[9]

The development of the clothing industry is significant from another standpoint in that it was one of the first enterprises to offer large-scale employment to women outside the home. Of the 5,739 workers reported in the 1859 census, 4,850 were women. Although men gradually took over the cutting operations, and the waves of immigrant tailors displaced many women, the apparel industry still employs a high concentration of female workers.

The earliest ready-mades were usually farmed out to women who sewed in their own homes. Some firms maintained their own factories, but working conditions in these "inside" shops were deplorable: "Unsanitary conditions, long hours, and low wages helped to give the sweat shop its unsavory name. Public opinion became aroused when epidemics broke out, and women objected to having their clothes made in tenement rooms, where people cooked, ate, and slept."[10]

It was in this atmosphere that the International Ladies' Garment Workers' Union was founded in 1900. From this time forward, the economic situation of the garment worker continued to improve. Today, the I.L.G.W.U. has a membership of over 442,000, of which 80 per cent are women. Garment workers in the men's wear industry are also highly unionized, organized under the Amalgamated Clothing Workers of America.

Location of the garment centers

New York City became the dominant manufacturing center early in the history of the garment trade. For one thing, the industry found a pool of skilled labor in the endless flow of immigrants that streamed into the New York harbor. For another, New York was strategically located between the southern cotton mills and the New England woolen mills. Once the industry was established there, the city attracted other related enterprises that established it as the mecca of trade for buyers from all over the country. So much of the business is concentrated in mid-town Manhattan that the term "Seventh Avenue" has come to represent women's fashionable ready-to-wear.

[9]*The Dress Industry,* Market Planning Service, National Credit Office, New York, March 1948.
[10]Florence S. Richards, *The Ready-To-Wear Industry 1900–1950,* Fairchild Publications, New York, 1951, p. 8.

New York still produces almost 60 per cent of all women's and children's wear sold in the United States, and over 40 per cent of the men's and boys' wear. Other cities, such as Boston, Philadelphia, Chicago, and St. Louis, have long been established as manufacturing centers, but none rival New York in terms of product diversity or volume. California is growing as a leading center for sportswear, with Los Angeles ranking second only to New York in apparel production. Almost every state plays some part in the clothing industry, but manufacture tends to concentrate in the urbanized industrial areas in or near large cities.[11]

Economic significance

In round figures, the apparel industry is comprised of about 20,000 clothing factories throughout the country.[12] Most of these enterprises are small establishments that employ on the average of fifty people each. There are a few large companies, but less than 1 per cent of them employ more than 500 people, and many have fewer than ten workers apiece. The size of plants producing men's and boys' apparel tends to be much larger than of those making women's clothing. In the last decade, as total employment in the United States was rising, the number employed in the textile and clothing industries represented a decreasing proportion of the total labor force (see Table 17-1).

TABLE 17-1 EMPLOYMENT IN THE TEXTILES AND CLOTHING INDUSTRIES (IN THOUSANDS)

	1960	1970	1971
Total U.S. Labor Force	72,104	85,903	86,929
Total employed in all manufacturing industries	16,796 (23.3%)	19,369 (22.5%)	18,608 (21.4%)
Number in textile mill products	924 (1.3%)	997 (1.1%)	962 (1.1%)
Apparel and related products	1,233 (1.7%)	1,372 (1.6%)	1,361 (1.5%)

Source: *Statistical Abstracts of the United States*, 1972.

While the apparel industry employs over 1.3 million workers, the weekly pay check of the apparel worker is considerably less than the average wage of all manufacturing production

[11]At the time of the last census, the only states with *no* commercial apparel production were Idaho, Montana, Nevada, North Dakota, and Wyoming.
[12]Over 12,000 of these firms were concentrated in the New York metropolitan area. The next largest area, Los Angeles, had about 1,800 at the time of the last census. Source: U.S. Department of Commerce 1967 Census of Manufacturers.

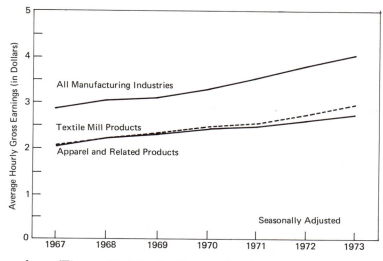

Figure 17-11. Production workers' hourly wages. Although hourly wages for apparel workers and textile workers are nearly comparable, weekly gross earnings of textile workers are generally higher because textile workers work over 40 hours a week compared to an average 36-hour work week for the apparel worker. Wages of both are significantly lower than wages of workers in all other manufacturing industries.

workers (Figure 17-11). Profit rates in the garment business are also lower than those in textiles production or in all manufacturing as a whole (see Table 17-2). The factors of low wages and low profits can be explained by intense competition within the ranks and the threat of the low-wage manufactures from abroad.[13]

Table 17-2 CORPORATE PROFIT DATA

| | Net Profits as % of net sales | | | | | |
	1967	1968	1969	1970	1971	1972
All manufactured nondurable goods	5.0	5.1	4.8	4.0	4.2	4.3
Textile mill products	2.9	3.1	2.9	1.9	2.4	2.6
Apparel and related products	2.3	2.4	2.3	1.9	2.3	2.3

Source: *Textile Hi-lights*, American Textile Manufacturers Institute, Inc., December 1973.

In addition to employment, wages, and profits, the economic significance of any business may be evaluated in terms of its contribution to the national income. The **national income** refers to the total earnings of our country as a whole. If we examine the national income figures over a period of time (Table 17-3), we can see that the textile and clothing industries combined contribute about $16 billion a year to the national income, although their proportionate share over the years has declined, as did the share of all manufacturing industries. The actual dollar amounts of income contributed by textiles and apparel have risen, but the wholesale price of clothing (see Table 17-4) has not increased at the same rate as other goods and services,

---

[13]The factor of foreign competition is so important that we have devoted the next chapter to a discussion of this topic.

and the proportion of national income derived from services (as opposed to the total value of goods) has gone up.

TABLE 17-3 NATIONAL INCOME
(in billions of dollars)

	1950	1960	1970
Total	241.1	414.5	795.9
All manufacturing	76.2	125.8	217.7
	(31.6%)	(30.3%)	(27.4%)
Textile products	4.4	4.5	7.3
	(1.8%)	(1.1%)	(0.9%)
Apparel	3.5	5.0	8.7
	(1.5%)	(1.2%)	(1.1%)

Source: *Statistical Abstracts of the United States, 1972.*

TABLE 17-4 WHOLESALE PRICE INDEX
(1967 = 100)

	1967	1968	1969	1970	1971	1972
All industrial commodities	100.0	102.5	106.0	110.0	114.0	117.9
Textile mill products	100.0	104.0	104.6	103.2	103.6	111.6
Apparel	100.0	103.2	107.2	111.0	112.9	114.8

Source: *Textile Hi-lights*, American Textile Manufacturers Institute, Inc., December 1973.

Trends

Garment makers have made a number of changes in their operations in an attempt to hold the domestic market. Although there are still many hundreds of small manufacturers, the really small firms have been disappearing, while the big companies have cornered an increasing share of the total apparel market. In the past decade, the number of establishments shrank by nearly 3,000. It is estimated that somewhere between 400 and 500 firms go out of business each year. The exact number is nebulous because the industry is characterized by a high degree of business turnover, and the same firm could be reported as entering and leaving the industry a couple of times in the same year.

Thus, many firms have simply gone out of business, but many more have been consolidated through mergers and acquisitions.[14] In addition, the traditional partnership arrangement is gradually giving way to the corporation. By expanding their operations, manufacturers have been able to reduce the unit cost of production through volume sales. Even so, in 1972 of the 20,000 or more firms, only sixty-five apparel manufacturers

Figure 17-12. Modern technological innovations like these speed up production and reduce labor costs, but they require large investments of capital and are generally applicable to standardized products. Many small operators, however, go into business with only a modest investment in a few sewing machines and a bit of work space.

[14]For example, General Mills, Inc., is a giant conglomerate whose fashion division includes David Crystal, Inc.; Kimberly Knitwear; Alligator outerwear; Knothe Pajamas and Belts; Siltex double-knit fabrics, and Monet costume jewelry. The subsidiaries retain their separate identities.

CLOTHING IN THE ECONOMY

and twenty shoe companies were listed on the national stock exchange markets.[15]

Despite this trend toward "bigness," the largest garment companies still cannot compare in size with the giant corporations that dominate other fields of manufacturing, or even with the larger textile mills. Jonathan Logan is probably the largest dress manufacturer with an annual sales of about $300 million. There are several larger apparel firms, but they tend to produce a more standardized product such as men's shirts, suits, and uniforms. The very nature of fashion behavior puts an automatic lid on the volume of any one design that a manufacturer can expect to sell. The woman who seeks individuality in dress is not going to buy a garment that hundreds of other women are wearing. In high fashion merchandise, the advantages of volume production are seriously curtailed.

Instead of producing more of the same kind of garment, therefore, the growing companies tend to diversify their output. For example, some men's wear firms have branched out into women's wear, blouse companies have started lingerie divisions, and dress concerns have expanded into sportswear. Some of the larger establishments have decentralized their sewing operations and have moved to less urbanized areas.

The manufacturer is caught in a fiercely competitive, low-wage, low-profit business. The only acceptable way for him to stay afloat is to capitalize on the consumers' desire for newness and tasteful clothes. More and more, he is attempting to do this through market research and promotion, developing increased communications with retailers and consumers through national advertising programs, and increased emphasis on brand names.

From textile to garment

Most apparel firms produce a new line of merchandise twice a year, although in the more fashionable categories such as women's dresses, there are often spring, summer, fall, holiday, and resort collections—five lines per year. The designer begins about six months before the garment is to appear on the racks of the retail store. For some firms, the "designing" means copying or adapting styles from higher priced merchandise, or updating the best sellers from the previous season. The designer's sketches are then translated into cloth garments, either muslin or finished fabric, and checked out against yardage requirements, ease of construction, and other production costs that will keep it within the firm's price range.

Designs that are approved "in the muslin" then go to the patternmaker and are made up in the sample size to be modeled at the "openings" when the line is shown during the market

---

[15]Source: *The Financial Weekly,* 1972. There were, of course, many more over-the-counter stocks available.

Figure 17-13. A modern clothing factory.

Figure 17-14. Racks of dresses are pushed along the street in New York's Seventh Avenue district. Adding to the congestion, delivery trucks are always double-parked so that the streets are virtually closed to traffic.

weeks to prospective retail buyers from all over the country. On the basis of orders received from the various buyers, manufacturers plan their production schedules. In most cases, almost a third of the line is eliminated because the number of orders are too few to warrant production. A garment that retails for $175 may not be put into production unless there are orders for a hundred or more. At higher prices, the manufacturer may go into production on several dozen of a particular style.

Once this decision has been made, the original pattern is graded and laid out for cutting. Garment pieces are then bundled according to size and moved on to the sewing operations. It is at this point that a firm may hire a contractor and send the bundles out to be sewn in an "outside" shop. If a manufacturer runs an "inside" shop, it means he produces the entire garment from start to finish. Technically, the manufacturer who contracts with "outside" shops is known as a jobber; he does everything but the sewing.

In higher-priced lines, a single operator may do all of the sewing on a garment, but in most cases, section work prevails in which each worker completes a single operation before passing the bundle on to the next station. Garments are usually returned to the manufacturer (if a contractor is involved) for final pressing, inspection, and shipment to the retail stores.

In either case, the industry is locked into a system of union wages, and even though apparel workers have a lower pay scale than those in other industries, the cost of labor is several times the cost of materials. A zipper may cost the manufacturer only seven or eight cents, but putting a zipper in the neck of a sweater can triple the labor costs.

Manufacturers depend heavily upon reorders for their profits, i.e., volume production on popular styles that continue to sell month after month. Known in the trade as "hot" items or "runners," styles that gain extensive consumer acceptance can be cut in quantity in a wide range of fabrics at a much lower unit cost. A great deal of the manufacturer's success is dependent upon the speed with which he is able to fill the reorders while consumer demand is at its peak.

The fashion creators

The most important person in the hectic business of fashion is the designer. No matter how well or how fast a garment is constructed, it will not sell if it has no style appeal.

The fashion creator in the United States has always been limited by the economics of mass production. Even those who have achieved fame in the design field—Bill Blass, James Galanos, Pauline Trigère and others—are not custom couturiers but ready-to-wear manufacturers. Their designs may be as creative and as expensive as anything that comes out of Paris, but they still sell at wholesale prices to retail stores rather than directly to the customer. Bill Blass, Ltd., one of the few designer-owned firms in the country, manufactures exclusive women's wear with prices that range anywhere from $200 to $2,000 an item. In addition to women's fashions, however, the company also licenses Blass' designs for the manufacture of men's clothing, swimsuits, rainwear, hosiery, scarves, watches, luggage, furs, sheets, and pillowcases. Early in the 1970's, Blass launched a line of men's cosmetics.

The name of a firm's designer used to be treated like something of a trade secret — never advertised in connection with the product. During World War II, however, when Paris fell to the Germans, the fashion scene shifted to the United States, and American designers gradually achieved recognition in their own right. Even after the war, when Paris regained its influence, the Americans remained leaders in the field of sportswear and casual clothes — a category of dress in which the French had little interest until recent years.

Unlike the French couturiers, however, who are subsidized by the government and protected by copyright laws, high-fashion designers in the United States are completely on their own. European houses are able to make their money by selling their designs to manufacturers for copying. American designers do not have this choice, since the most successful designs are copied anyway, and sometimes the cheaper imitations can be turned out faster than the originals.

But this also happens in the couture to some extent. A manufacturer with a keen eye and a good memory may buy a model or two at a Paris opening, but he comes home with enough ideas for a dozen or more "adaptations." A model may be copied at almost any price level, with certain modifications: complicated cuts are often simplified, construction details such as linings, interfacings, and hand workmanship may be eliminated, and yardage may be reduced. Style piracy in the fashion business is one of the facts of life.

This process of fashion imitation is the mechanism that keeps the fashion cycle moving and makes fashionable clothing available to those of limited means. Furthermore, the "knock-offs" stimulate consumer buying and this is good for business in the entire industry.

It used to be that the men's wear industry was relatively insulated from such rapid fashion fluctuations. A man could get far more quality in a $125 suit than a woman could in a dress of comparable price. That's because "men's suits are manufactured by grades or strictly set scales of labor. A grade-two men's suit that sells for $85 is a sound, machine-made product; a female equivalent might be an undistinguished $120 dress. A grade-five $185 suit may be made with fabric that costs the same as the $85 suit's, but it has a hand-set canvas and lining and hand-stitched buttonholes. Its female counterpart might be priced $400."[16]

---

[16]Marylin Bender, "Why Your Clothes Cost So Much," *McCall's*, May 1970, p. 94.

In a design field where standardized cuts and styles predominate, streamlined production methods can reduce unit costs tremendously. In the days before the peacock revolution, a man's white dress shirt was probably one of the most uniform products on the market. Volume was not only high, it was predictable. It was no accident that firms like Hart Schaffner & Marx (men's suits) and Cluett Peabody (shirts) had larger sales figures than the biggest dress manufacturer. But now high styling is penetrating the men's wear field as well. The sale of suits has gone down, and haberdashery items—shirts, slacks, belts, ties—have gone up. Some observers predict that in another decade or two men will not be wearing suits at all, but untailored clothing as light, casual, and varied as women's.[17]

While more and more women's wear designers (Blass, Beene, Cardin, et al.) are turning out lines for men, traditional men's wear companies (e.g., Levi Strauss) are branching into women's wear. In the past, traditional men's wear manufacturers presented only two lines of merchandise a year—spring and fall. Usually the order for piece goods would be made nine months in advance, and the actual construction of tailored garments would take about eight weeks. At the same time that many women's wear designers were eliminating their summer lines, a few innovators in the men's wear business were adding "holiday lines" and "cruise lines." Little by little, the men's wear industry is turning toward the women's wear concept of a quick turnover business to meet rapid fashion change. One begins to realize why the "rag business" is forced to operate on such slim margins, and why the ability to outguess your competitors is a necessary prerequisite to economic success.

A high degree of uncertainty is imposed upon the apparel producer by unpredictable consumer response to fashion change.

SUMMARY *Apparel production*

The ready-to-wear industry grew out of sweatshop working conditions of the late-nineteenth century. The stream of European immigrants to the United States provided a skillful, low-cost labor pool for the trades and helped to establish New York as the center of garment production. Now highly unionized, garment workers enjoy improved standards of work and wages, although their pay scale is still below that of many production workers in other manufacturing industries. Still, domestic labor costs are so high that we cannot compete with the low-wage countries on a world-wide basis.

While the general trend is toward larger, more diversified companies, the apparel industry as a whole is still characterized by many small, independent, and highly specialized firms. Most of these revise their line of merchandise twice a year, those that deal in more fashionable items, five times a year. The American economy is geared to volume production. Even the

---

[17]McQuade, "High Style," p. 71.

most influential designers are ready-to-wear manufacturers rather than hauts couturiers. Many firms resort to copying the styles that are doing well in the upper price lines.

The manufacturer who anticipates consumer acceptance accurately is rewarded for his risk taking through volume sales; those who guess wrongly suffer economic losses on unsold inventories and drastic markdowns on merchandise. The apparel industry remains an intensely competitive, low-profit business that can thrive only on the basis of fashion obsolescence and a constant flow of fresh ideas.

Retailing of clothing

In most cases, the distribution of clothing merchandise takes place as a direct transaction between the manufacturer and the retailer. In some of the staple lines, however, such as utility or work clothes, underwear, and pajamas, a wholesaler may work as a middleman between the garment maker and the independent retailer (see Figure 17-2). A few of the biggest apparel manufacturers have themselves moved into the retail business by buying out chains of independent retailers. Hart Schaffner & Marx, one of the largest suit makers, now owns about 250 retail outlets. Another example is Phillips-Van Heusen, operating some seventy-four stores throughout the country. In recent years, there have also been many mergers in the retail field just as there have been in the textile and apparel industries. Outwardly, the stores appear no different to the average consumer. They usually continue to operate under the same name, although they enjoy the advantages of pooled assets.

Types of retail stores

Taken as a whole, there are almost 1,800,000 retail stores of all kinds in the United States today. It is difficult to tell exactly how much of the retail business can be attributed to clothing or fashion, but we can understand some of the statistics better if we distinguish among the various types of retail outlets.

The **department store** evolved out of the old dry goods store of the early-nineteenth century. Its growth paralleled the growth of cities and the concentration of people in urbanized areas. A department store may be either independently owned or part of a chain, but characteristically it sells a line of home furnishings in addition to clothing, household textiles, and yardage. It also offers a number of customer services, which in addition to the sales personnel, includes such conveniences as charge accounts, mail and phone orders, delivery of merchandise, return privileges, and gift wrapping.

The **variety stores** sprang up around the department stores once the downtown area became established as a center for shopping. In the early days these were essentially discount stores, offering low unit-priced merchandise to customers who happened to be in the shopping area anyway. Today, variety stores such as Woolworth's and Grant's provide mass outlets for lower-priced ready-to-wear, and their price range has been broadened to include items considerably above the original "five and ten" cent categories.

The **chain store** title was applied whenever a group of variety or specialized stores became centrally owned. The Lerner Shops, for example, and the big chains of shoe stores have a tremendous sales volume with stores in almost every major city of the country. Department stores that may have several branches are not recognized as chains, although in many ways the difference is hardly perceptible to the consumer. Chains tend to be characterized by highly standardized merchandise, managed remotely from a central or regional office.

Mail-order companies grew out of the need to service isolated rural families who did not have access to convenient shopping areas. Everyone thought that the mail-order business would decline along with the decline of farm population, but as the automobile increased the mobility of the buying public, city and rural alike, mail-order houses opened chains of retail stores which in many cases, catered to the auto traffic. Usually located in a suburban area, they expanded into automobile tires and accessories, garden equipment, and home improvement supplies. Mail-order catalogs traditionally had featured the time-tested variety of housedresses and work clothes, but today buyers from stores like Sears can now be found at many European fashion openings, and the haute couture copies, manufactured especially for catalog sales, are now the most prominently featured items of merchandise. Today, Sears, Roebuck is the largest retailer in the world with an annual volume of business over $10 billion.

Discount stores appeared on the scene in increasing numbers during the 1950's, although many stores had been operating on a discount basis for a number of years. The phenomenal growth of the discounters may be attributed to a number of factors. One was the dispersion of the population into the suburbs. The discounter took the cue from those who had been successful with the "auto traffic" and built in outlying areas that provided plenty of parking space. Again, it assembled large assortments of merchandise under one roof, and the customer could make his selections supermarket style and check out his purchases in short order. Along with this, a large number of consumers were reacting against the retail methods of the conventional store, where the consumer was helping to pay for high rentals, salespeople, elaborate fixtures, credit, and other customer services, and not getting any more merchandise for the money. The discounter stepped in, started selling the goods right out of the packing boxes on a self-service basis, and reduced his overhead enough to sell below the prevailing price level.

Figure 17-15. Store fixtures and customer services are kept to a minimum in discount stores and department store basements, where customers help themselves to "bargain" merchandise.

CLOTHING IN THE ECONOMY

There is nothing new about discount stores from the standpoint of reducing services to increase volume. Stores such as Orbach's and Klein's, located in the most congested areas of New York City, have been selling fashion goods on a self-service, cut-rate basis for years. The idea of the discount, however, is still spreading.

There is a growing number of companies that specialize in what has been called "cut-rate haute couture." These stores have been able to buy the surplus stock from designer-manufacturers, cut out the labels to protect the producers, and sell the garments in piperack shops at rock-bottom prices. Of course, the customer has to be able to "read" the quality without the help of the label, and be willing to try on the garments in crowded community dressing rooms. It takes the spirit of the real bargain hunter to find the best buys.

Specialty stores, in terms of their definition, may vary all the way from the posh atmosphere of a Bergdorf Goodman or a Henri Bendel, to a modest little apparel store selling lingerie and blouses. Stores that specialize in related categories of merchandise (children's wear, men's furnishings, women's apparel, and so forth) may be independently owned or part of a chain. They may even be discounters, but they differ from the department store in that they do not sell home furnishings or hard goods.

There are, of course, many other types of retail outlets for clothing merchandise. Many supermarkets today carry standardized lines of children's play clothes, hosiery, and underwear, and some have expanded into work clothes, shorts, slacks, and blouses, and even drug stores carry some items of apparel. Beyond this, the number of **second-hand clothing stores** is on the increase. Nearly everyone is familiar with the typical Goodwill thrift store, but not many people are aware of the shops that deal in high fashion. "Encore," for example, is a three-story shop in New York, with another operation in Washington, D.C., where the designer clothes of the rich are resold to the less rich at about one-third of the original retail price. The proprietor may resell a $1,000 de la Renta for $333 and split that with the original owner of the dress. This procedure gives a better incentive for disposing of worn-once clothes than does a tax deduction for contributions of clothing to the Salvation Army.

Figure 17-16. Specialty shops give individual attention to each customer and often establish themselves as the local authorities on incoming fashion trends.

Economic significance

Without counting the local supermarkets, drug stores, and second-hand shops, there are probably close to 180,000 retail outlets for fashion merchandise in the United States today. The largest number of these are the specialized apparel and accessory stores, although the big general merchandise companies have a greater number of employees by far. In the early 1970's, there were over 2.3 million people on the payrolls of department and variety stores and the large chains, while only 733,000 were working in specialty shops.[18] Together, they earn over $8 billion a year in wages and salaries.

Obviously, the general merchandise stores (the chains, department, and discount stores) also have the largest volume of retail sales. Early in the 1960's, the apparel trade was almost evenly divided (55 per cent general merchandise, 45 per cent specialty shops and other). A decade later, the chains, department stores, and discount houses were doing 62 per cent of the business with an annual sale of apparel merchandise of $25 billion as compared to the $11 billion's worth of goods sold in apparel and accessory stores (see Table 17-5). Growth rate was highest among the four big chains. In 1963, Sears, Penney, Grant, and Ward accounted for $3.1 billion in apparel sales. A decade later, their sales were more than doubled ($8.0 billion in 1973).

Prices and profits

Price lines and merchandise markups clearly vary with the type of store. The average markup on goods may vary anywhere from 17 per cent over wholesale in the discount houses, to 70 per cent for a high-priced designer dress sold in a fashionable specialty store. This does not necessarily mean that the specialty shop is making a bigger profit. In a typical department store, the markup is usually between 35 and 40 per cent of retail. Even at that, the average profit on sales rarely amounts to more than 2 or 3 per cent. Let us say that a store does a million dollars worth of business a year. It costs the store about three cents to make every transaction, and if a customer returns a piece of merchandise, it costs another three cents to remove the sale from the books. Obviously, these kinds of costs must be absorbed in the sales price. So from the gross sales of $1,000,000, the store must deduct about $100,000 for returns and other allowances plus the wholesale cost of the goods (which would be close to $600,000), leaving the merchant with a gross margin of $300,000. Out of this he must pay the wages and salaries of his employees, rent, and other operating expenses which amount to 25 per cent or more of the gross sales, or $250,000, leaving a net profit of $50,000, on which the retailer must still pay taxes. If he is lucky, he may end up with three cents on the dollar of gross sales.

The small retailer today faces a serious threat from the mass merchandisers and factory outlet operations. The big chains like Sears and Penney have upgraded their fashion image in recent years, and for volume-produced clothes their retail prices are hard to match. It is difficult for them, however, to offer a high degree of style differentiation. The top of their lines may be a $40 sportcoat or $35 dress, and clothes that retail at $200, let us say, are simply not available in the chains. The

---

[18]*Statistical Abstract of the United States*, 1972.

specialty store can offer the type of service and merchandise that some consumers demand. "The business executive who wants to buy expensive, well-tailored clothing, for instance, wants a certain amount of service and expertise to go along with the product. He wants to be called by name when he walks into a store; he wants a professional clothier to wait on him—not a clerk."[19] In short, there are a number of consumers who are willing to pay for service and a pleasant shopping environment.

TABLE 17-5 APPAREL SALES BY RETAIL OUTLET*
(in billions of dollars)

	1963	1967	1972	1973 (est.)
Chain stores (Sears, Penney, Grant, and Ward)	$3.1 (15.5%)	$5.1 (17.5%)	$7.3 (18%)	$8.0 (19%)
Department stores	6.3 (31.5%)	9.4 (32.4%)	13.2 (33%)	14.2 (33%)
Discount stores	1.6 (8.0%)	2.8 (9.6%)	4.5 (11%)	4.8 (11%)
Specialty shops	7.8 (39.0%)	9.5 (32.7%)	11.1 (28%)	11.5 (27%)
Other	1.2 (6.0%)	2.2 (7.5%)	3.9 (10%)	4.3 (10%)
TOTAL	$20.	$29.	$40.	$42.8

*Figures do not include shoes or jewelry.
Source: *Profile of Apparel/Retail Market*, American Apparel Manufacturers Association, November 1972.

All stores, however, have certain fixed overhead expenses. Obviously, retailers in low-rent districts who hire inexperienced sales personnel at minimum wages will have lower operating costs than those who have higher maintenance expenses, pay higher salaries, and offer more services. The type of merchandise also influences the profit potential. If a cocktail dress has to be marked down from $60 to $40 at the end of a season, the retailer is just barely meeting his costs. On clothing that is marked off 50 per cent or more, the store is actually taking a loss.

The retail price of clothing has gone up in recent years, although it has not increased at the same rate as other commodities (see Table 17-6). There is, nevertheless, a greater difference between wholesale and retail prices than there used to be. Stores have had to raise their markups because they have to pay more today for office and sales help, delivery services, advertising, and window displays. Another phenomenon contributing to higher price tags is the increase in stock

[19]Sanford Josephson, "Challenges Beset Smaller Retailers," *Daily News Record*, 14 February 1973.

Figure 17-17. Some retailers are investing in elaborate surveillance systems, such as the one above, to monitor shoppers throughout the store. It is not uncommon for storewide television monitors plus security agents, to cost the store as much as $80,000 to $100,000 a year.

shortages—otherwise known as shoplifting. According to a nationwide survey, the incidence of shoplifting increased nearly 70 per cent in 1971 over what it had been in 1970.[20] One discount store reported stock shrinkage amounting to half a million dollars.[21] Unfortunately, the loss must be passed on to all consumers.

TABLE 17-6 COMPARISON OF WHOLESALE AND CONSUMER PRICE INDICES
(1967 = 100)

	1960		1967		1970		1971	
	WPI	CPI	WPI	CPI	WPI	CPI	WPI	CPI
All commodities	94.9	88.7	100		110.4	116.3	113.9	121.3
Apparel and upkeep	94.9	89.6	100		111.0	116.1	112.9	119.8
Footwear	87.6	85.1	100		113.0	117.7	116.8	121.5

Source: U.S. Bureau of Labor Statistics, *Monthly Labor Review.*

Figure 17-18. Many modern shopping malls now offer luxurious atmosphere along with the convenience of many stores under one roof.

Trends in retailing

The trends in retailing have followed the trends in social structure and organization throughout the country. The dispersion of the population into the suburbs, coupled with the universal dependence upon the automobile, gave tremendous impetus to the growth of shopping plazas. As many of the large chains built modern facilities in the outlying population centers with plenty of parking space, other stores moved out to join them. Parent stores opened branches, and specialty shops improved their locations. In some cases, severe losses from this mass migration were suffered by the downtown stores, many of whom had large capital investments and/or long-term leases that prevented them from moving out into space. Those with sufficient capital are now modernizing their structures to include built-in parking facilities, but the trend toward decentralization continues.

Congestion in the cities is also probably the reason that mail-order buying has increased. Sears, for example, can do business anywhere without having to worry about plant location, and without the consumer having to worry about parking.

Consumer shopping habits have influenced retailers in another respect, and that relates to the peak shopping times. With more women working during the day, families often go shopping together in the evening. Many stores have found it necessary to remain open several nights a week as well as on Sundays to meet the competition.

Installment buying, prevalent for many years in the automobile, furniture, and large appliance lines, is now widely used

[20]William Moore, "The Shoplifting Epidemic," *San Francisco Chronicle,* 14 February 1972.
[21]Beverly Stephen, "Shoplifters Star on Store's TV Cameras," *San Francisco Chronicle,* 26 July 1972.

for the purchase of clothing. The majority of department, specialty, and chain stores have developed some plan of extending credit to their customers. For many retailers, the charges made for credit service constitute a substantial proportion of their net profits. Stores which do not have the financial assets to carry credit accounts are losing much of their business to the larger firms that have such resources. The same trend toward "bigness" that was observed in the textiles and the apparel industries also is evident in the retail establishments.

Thus, mergers and acquisitions are on the increase. The independent, family-owned store is gradually being bought out by larger establishments. Even the larger department stores have consolidated. The May Company, for example, owns the May's stores in Cleveland, Denver, Los Angeles, and San Diego, but it also owns the Hecht Department Stores in Washington and Baltimore, Kaufmann's in Pittsburgh, Meier & Frank in Portland, Strouss-Hirschberg in Youngstown, Ohio, and Famous-Barr in St. Louis.

Actually, the trend has been going on for more than thirty years, but the impact can be observed on a much shorter-term basis. In the four years from 1963 to 1967, for instance, the number of establishments in the department store and chain categories increased from 62,000 to 67,000, while the apparel and accessory stores declined from 116,000 to 110,000 in the same period (Table 17-7).

TABLE 17-7 RETAIL TRADE: NUMBER OF ESTABLISHMENTS AND NUMBER OF EMPLOYEES

	Number of stores (in thousands)		Number of employees (in thousands)	
	1963	1967	1963	1967
TOTAL RETAIL TRADE	1,707.9	1,763.3	8,410.1	9,380.6
*General merchandise stores	62.0	67.3	1,468.4	1,646.5
Apparel and accessory stores	116.2	110.1	630.2	658.6

*Includes department stores, variety stores, mail order (department store merchandise). Source: Statistical Abstracts of the United States, 1972.

The central buying operations that are made possible through large volume sales make fashion merchandise more quickly available to consumers in all parts of the country. By the same token, many people view the clothing market as one having less and less product differentiation each year. The same knitted pantsuit can be found in stores from Washington, D.C. to San Francisco, with not more than a two-dollar variation in retail price. Many of the larger stores today have electronic computers that evaluate retail activites on a day-to-day basis. A daily analysis of store sales provides a fashion profile of the sizes, fabric textures, silhouettes, color preferences, and other style features that are favored on the local market. Through the customer's purchases, requests for merchandise, complaints, and returns, the retailer can draw many conclusions about consumer acceptance at the local level. In this sense, the customer's behavior in the marketplace is quickly assessed, and becomes a useful guide to the retailer in gearing the store's merchandise to the requirements of consumer demand.

Related activities

In addition to his merchandising function, the retailer contributes taxes to local, state, and federal governments, and through advertising he contributes to the cost of newspapers and other advertising media. Besides the textile producers, the apparel manufacturers, and the retailers, there are many, many people engaged in fashion-related activities that also figure in the overall economics of the clothing business. There are fashion advisory services and resident buying offices that operate as intermediaries between the manufacturer and the retailer. Fashion publications are also a big business. In the early 1970's, more than $22 million was expended in newspapers for national advertising of wearing apparel, $47 million for magazine advertising, and $71 million for television.[22]

There are also advertising and public relations firms whose job it is to prepare the ads for newspapers and magazines, to plan large-scale promotional campaigns, and often to conduct the marketing research on consumer preferences and shopping habits. In short, there are probably more than 15 million persons in the United States whose livelihoods are dependent in one way or another upon the clothing industry.

The successful retailer must make rapid adjustments in his business practices to meet consumer demands and preferences.

SUMMARY *Retailing clothing merchandise*

The retailer is the last link in the clothing chain from the fiber producer to the ultimate consumer. The retailer has the responsibility of stocking the combination of styles, textures, colors, sizes, and prices that the customer will demand. The retailer's purchases, in turn, constitute a feedback to the manufacturer concerning the consumer's acceptance of his products.

The consumer who knows the retail market is better prepared for selective shopping. Department stores and specialty shops offer a variety of customer services along with a wide

---

[22]*Statistical Abstract of the United States, 1972.*

range of merchandise. Discount stores can offer clothing items for sale on a self-service basis at a much lower markup. Mail-order houses offer the convenience of shopping at home, and these—along with many apparel chains—are now getting into more fashionable merchandise. The individual consumer must weigh the relative value of each of these advantages, including the quality of the merchandise offered for sale, the privileges of return on unsatisfactory purchases, the willingness of the merchant to stand behind his goods, and the convenience of shopping itself. A knowledge of the retail stores in your community and how they operate will increase your competence and satisfaction as a purchaser of clothing.

Industry responsibility

Most firms count on the repeat sales that will occur if a customer is satisfied with the merchandise. It goes without saying that all manufacturers and retailers are in business to make money. There are, no doubt, some businessmen who will sell an inferior product for as long as they can get away with it, but they usually do not stay in business very long. Not more than twenty years ago, the average American consumer had to be content with shirts that wrinkled, dresses that shrank, colors that faded, and many fabrics that could be cleaned only once, if at all. Today, the consumer not only gets an improved product, but he expects satisfactory performance as a kind of legal right.

For many years the clothing industry has engaged in research for the development of better products and has regulated its output through a system of quality control. When such voluntary controls proved to be inadequate, or in cases where business practices were fraudulent or harmful to the consumer, the government usually stepped in to regulate the industry through legal processes.

Voluntary standards

Many instances could be cited in which various segments of the clothing industry have demonstrated their social responsibility. Many manufacturers maintain their own quality control on textile and apparel products through testing and research in company-owned laboratories. For years, men's suits and coats have been graded on a numerical scale according to the quality of the material and the tailoring that goes into each garment.[23] Retail companies, as well, operate their own laboratories for the purpose of keeping their merchandise up to certain minimum standards.

[23]Today, with the scarcity of wool and the high cost of labor, these quality standards have become economically unfeasible for all but the top of most manufacturers' lines. The mass merchandisers, for example, have quit handling men's business suits altogether.

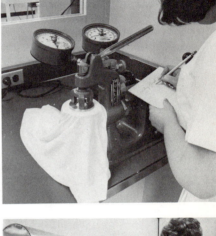

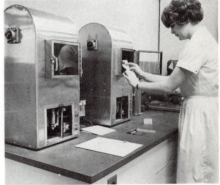

Figure 17-19. Many retail stores maintain their own test laboratories for purposes of quality control. Durability of fabric is tested by a hydraulic machine; colors, treated specifically to resist fading from air pollution are tested.

As early as 1956, the American Standards Association, under the sponsorship of the National Retail Merchants Association (NRMA), led the way in establishing a set of performance standards for wearing apparel and home furnishings. The American Apparel Manufacturers Association (AAMA) has also worked toward the establishment of voluntary standards for apparel within the industry itself.

Government regulations

One of the earliest pieces of legislation which attempted to insure a competitive market for American consumers was the **Sherman Antitrust Act of 1890.** Essentially, the goal of the Act and its subsequent amendments was to protect the market from monopolistic price fixing by a few large firms. Even though the clothing industry is generally characterized by a high degree of competition, there have been a few cases of antitrust violations. In 1972, for example, the Federal Trade Commission opposed the purchase of New York's Bergdorf Goodman by the Broadway-Hale Stores. Broadway-Hale had previously merged with Emporium Capwell and already operated forty-eight department stores in the southwest, plus four Neiman-Marcus stores in Texas. The FTC maintained that the California firm would have an unfair competitive advantage over other New York retailers.[24]

Although the antitrust laws forbid the manufacturer or retailer to fix prices, the **Miller-Tydings Act of 1937** and state fair-trade laws enabled the manufacturers of "name-brand" goods to stipulate the retail price for their products. Such fair-trade laws are clearly incompatible with a market economy. Many discount stores have ignored the fair-trade prices, and lawsuits have ensued. Nevertheless, collusion among enterprises for the purpose of controlling prices is prohibited. On these grounds, four swimsuit manufacturers were indicted a few years ago for attempting to force retailers to adhere to the prices set by the manufacturers. The Justice Department claimed that competition had been eliminated by fixing prices at artificial levels, and that retailers had lost their freedom to set their own retail prices.

The Wheeler-Lea Act of 1938 is directed against false or misleading advertising. A garment must live up to claims made on the label; also, the failure to reveal facts about the product is considered "false advertising." In other words, if the advertising is written in such a way that the consumer is led to believe that a fabric will behave in a certain manner when actually it does not, the practice is considered deceptive.

---

[24]The sale was subsequently approved, however, on the grounds that Bergdorf's was a unique situation in that the store would have gone out of business had it not been sold.

The Wool Products Labeling Act of 1939 requires that a product containing any amount of wool—virgin wool, reprocessed, or reused wool—must be labeled to show the fiber content by percentages. Before the enactment of this statute, manufacturers had been able to pass off as "virgin wool" or "pure wool" products that were made from shoddy, reclaimed wool, or even products that were not made from wool. Textile mills are now required to keep such records that will enable them to identify the particular lot of yarn and fibers that went into each piece of cloth. You will find a lot number label sewn into most of your wool garments that will connect up with a manufacturer's cutting ticket that can be traced back through the weaving, spinning, and blending records to the original raw stock.

The Fur Products Labeling Act of 1951 prohibited the use of such names as Hudson seal, Mendoza beaver, mink-dyed muskrat, mountain sable, and a host of others, all of which were deceptive titles for various grades of opossum, muskrat, and rabbit. The fur act requires that every article bear a label which includes (1) the true name of the animal from which the skin was taken, (2) the country of origin, (3) whether the fur is natural, dyed, or otherwise artificially colored, and (4) an identifying mark by which the fur product can be traced back to its source. Many retailers as well as consumers are thus protected from deceptive practices on the part of manufacturers or wholesalers.

The Textile Fiber Products Identification Act of 1958 is the third "truth-in-fabrics" statute to be passed by Congress. This act covers the labeling of all apparel textiles that were not covered by the Wool Act. The Textile Act requires that all products be labeled as to fiber content by percentage, in the order of predominance by the weight of each fiber in the fabric. Prior to this legislation, a product could have been falsely advertised as "silk," when it may have contained only 3 or 4 per cent silk and 96 or 97 per cent rayon. In order to avoid the confusion of a proliferation of new man-made fibers sold under a wide variety of trade names, the Federal Trade Commission adopted a set of generic classifications that designate man-made fibers according to their chemical characteristics.[25] These may be used along with the names of the natural fibers, such as cotton, wool, and silk.

Many of these generic names, however, proved to have little meaning to the average consumer. For a number of years the apparel industry had been working voluntarily toward a program of care labeling. The Federal Trade Commission held discussions with members of the industry and with consumers,

---

[25]These are: acetate, acrylic, anidex, azlon, glass, lastrile, metallic, modacrylic, nylon, nytril, olefin, polyester, rayon, rubber, saran, spandex, triacetate, vinal, and vinyon. Azlon and vinal are not currently produced in the United States, nytril is not currently produced in the world, and lastrile has never been produced commercially.

and the **Trade Regulation Rule** on permanent care labeling went into effect in 1972. The Rule requires all textile apparel products[26] and piece goods to have a permanently legible care label affixed to the product for its useful life. (See examples of labels Figure 17-20.) This represented a big step for the textile industry. "It will not only cost the manufacturer anywhere from $2.50 to $35 a thousand to print the labels, but up to 2½ cents to sew them in. One big apparel maker estimates this cost at about a half million dollars a year."[27]

The Flammable Fabrics Act was originally passed in 1953, and amended in 1967 and 1972. The act prohibited the manufacture or sale of wearing apparel made from fibers or fabrics that were dangerously flammable. The 1972 amendment was essentially a flammability standard involving children's sleepwear (sizes 0-6X) which required that five specimens of every item of sleepwear be selected for testing. In effect, this meant that the industry had to produce fire-retardant sleepwear whether it wanted to or not, since all merchandise that did not meet the standard would be banned from the market. Some estimated that the cost of testing plus the application of the finish would add as much as 50 per cent to the cost of the article, and reduce the wear life of the garment by as much as 50 per cent. Inability to retool to meet the stringent requirements forced some of the smaller manufacturers out of the market completely.

The consumer is protected from fraudulent business practices and products by a number of voluntary controls within the industry itself, as well as by federal legislation.

Here are the 9 care labels which are the basis of the
"Triangle Care Labeling Plan"

METHOD 1
Machine wash, warm

METHOD 2
Machine wash, warm;
line dry

METHOD 3
Machine wash, warm;
tumble dry;
remove promptly

METHOD 4
Machine wash, warm;
delicate cycle; tumble dry,
low; use cool iron

METHOD 5
Machine wash, warm;
do not dry clean

METHOD 6
Hand wash separately;
use cool iron

METHOD 7
Dry clean only

METHOD 8
Dry clean; pile fabric
method only

METHOD 9
Wipe with damp
cloth only

Figure 17-20. Coded labels developed by the Textile Distributors Association for use with retail fabrics.

SUMMARY *Industry responsibility*

The Federal Trade Commission administers a number of acts designed to protect the consumer from deceptive practices by unscrupulous manufacturers or merchandisers. Most reliable firms willingly comply with the statutes because they seek the repeat sale that comes with customer satisfaction, and because they find that labels are a good way to promote their trade name. In many cases, compliance to federal regulations means additional expense, which is passed on to the consumer in the form of a higher retail price.

FOR FURTHER READING

Bender, Marylin. "Why Your Clothes Cost So Much," *McCall's*, May 1970, p. 94.
Gregory, P.M. "An Economic Interpretation of Women's Fashions," *Southern Economic Journal* 14, no. 2, October 1947, pp. 148–162.
McQuade, Walter. "High Style Disrupts the Men's Wear Industry," *Fortune*, February 1971, p. 70.

[26]Products *not* covered are hosiery, hats, gloves, footwear, fur, leather, remnants, disposables, see-through items, and garments that retail for three dollars or less.
[27]"Message from the FTC: We Always Knew You Cared," *American Fabrics*, Summer 1972, p.64.

Troxell, M. D. and B. Judelle. *Fashion Merchandising.* New York: Gregg Division/McGraw-Hill Book Company, 1971. (Part 2, "Marketers of Fashion.")

Economic data change constantly; the following publications offer current information on the clothing industry:

Business Week (published weekly).

Daily News Record (daily newspaper published by Fairchild).

Statistical Abstract of the United States (published annually by the U.S. Department of Commerce).

Stores (monthly publication of the National Retail Merchants Association).

Survey of Current Business (published weekly by the U.S. Department of Commerce).

Textile Hi-Lights (quarterly publication of the American Textile Manufacturers Institute).

Textile Organon (published monthly by the Textile Economics Bureau).

Women's Wear Daily (daily newspaper published by Fairchild).

DISCUSSION QUESTIONS

1. What is meant by a market economy?

2. Compare or contrast the operations of fiber and fabric producers with apparel manufacturers by: (a) number of firms, (b) ease of entry and exit (e.g., capital investment required, business turnover), (c) product differentiation.

3. What factors gave impetus to the development of the ready-to-wear industry in the United States?

4. What are some of the reasons that may account for the low profits in the clothing industry?

5. Why are the advantages of volume production seriously curtailed with respect to fashion merchandise?

6. Discuss some of the social changes affecting consumer shopping behavior that have influenced retailing trends and practices.

7. Why are fair-trade laws in conflict with a market system?

8. In what ways may protective legislation make the consumer pay more for apparel products?

9. A market system is based on the concept of consumer sovereignty (i.e., power vested in the collective hands of the consumers who constitute the source of demand). What factors in business, labor, and government have greatly reduced consumer sovereignty?

18

Clothing and the International Market

THE INTERPLAY among the factors of market supply, consumer demand, and purchasing power is by no means confined to the domestic production, distribution, and consumption of textiles and clothing. From a global standpoint, the attempt to achieve a balance of interests becomes even more complicated. International trade is highly desirable because it enables us to enjoy commodities not otherwise available, it fosters competition and greater efficiency within the industry, and it advances our cultural and political relations with other nations.

On the other hand, it is important to prevent the deterioration of our own national wealth. We seek to maintain a high level of employment, protect our home industries, and retain our self-sufficiency. It soon becomes apparent that our economic security and prosperity is affected by conditions that exist in other countries as well as in our own. The United States has the highest per capita income in the world, and by far the greatest consumption of textile fibers per person. In many other countries, particularly in the developing nations, the availability of raw materials as well as the power to purchase them are far below the need. The disparity that exists between human wants and the means for satisfying them constitutes the major problem in all economic activity. In this chapter we will consider the role that textiles and clothing play in the international market.

International trade

The United States is both the largest producer and the largest consumer of textiles and clothing in the world market. Strange as it may seem, some of the same ships and planes that bring foreign-made fibers, fabrics, and garments to our shores carry U.S. textile products to other countries. In 1972 we shipped about $993 million worth of textiles and clothing abroad, and at the same time imported over $3.4 billion in goods from other nations.

CLOTHING IN THE ECONOMY

Increased variety of goods

Foreign imports greatly extend the variety of merchandise on the local market from which we may choose. Through a combination of native skills and availability of raw materials, many national products have a unique quality that cannot be duplicated in other parts of the world. Oriental designs from Hong Kong, batiks from Indonesia, bleeding Madras from India, Belgian lace, and Italian knits are but a few examples of the many textile and apparel items that are easily identified with their place of origin.

There is a certain status appeal to American consumers of labels that read "100% imported cashmere" or "pure Irish linen," and by the same token the United States sells large quantities of American goods abroad because the "Made in U.S.A." label enjoys a prestige on many foreign markets. In some cases the "snob appeal" is accompanied by increased quality. The well-known Harris tweed is a good illustration. The Highland Blackface sheep that are raised on the island of Harris in the Outer Hebrides yield a long staple wool that is characteristically rough, tough, hairy, and durable. This, coupled with the unique fabricating techniques of the crofter-weavers, produces a distinctive fabric that offers superb protection against the elements.

Sometimes the added value lies in the quality of design. Marimekko fashions from Finland are status symbols for intellectual young American women, but they also have a sophisticated simplicity that accounts for much of their popularity. Benjamin Thompson of Design Research explains:

> There is a demand for unusual things, whether they come from Italy or Albany. . . . In the U.S. we are heavily industrialized, while Europe retains some handicraft traditions which sometimes result in one-of-a-kind products. As time passes and the world develops fewer artisans, certain handicraft items will take on even greater value. The link with the past is appreciated, particularly those things which have retained a folk-way shape, material and use for thousands of years.[1]

In addition, there is a limited extent to which one textile fiber will substitute for another. No fabric has quite the degree of warmth, resilience, or tailoring qualities as wool; none has aesthetic crispness that compares to that of linen; none is as versatile and as cool as cotton; none has a more beautiful luster than silk. Because fiber production is limited to certain geographical areas of the world, trade becomes necessary if we are to enjoy the benefits of diverse qualities.

Figure 18-1. Shirt from Pakistan.

Figure 18-2. The demand for American-made blue jeans on a worldwide basis has made it impossible to keep up with the demand. Here a French dealer at Paris' Flea Market proudly advertises the real thing—"le vrai Levi's."

---

[1]Cecil Lubell, "Marimekko, Fashion's Status Symbol for the Intellectual," *American Fabrics*, Fall and Winter 1963, p. 50.

Specialization in production

Technological advances have greatly increased the production of fibers, fabrics, and wearing apparel throughout the world. Still, there are geographic and economic conditions in all countries that create an excess of some products and a scarcity of others. The United States produces millions of bales of cotton for export to other countries, but at the same time produces no silk and virtually no linen. Japan and India, on the other hand, have both the supply of mulberry leaves and cheap labor that make the cultivation of silk worms feasible, while Ireland and certain parts of Russia have ideal climates for the production of flax. Wool requires suitable pasture land for sheep, and the cotton plant thrives only in restricted climatic regions. Even man-made fibers for the most part are created from raw materials that have an agricultural base.

As a result of differences in natural resources as well as the availability of labor and machinery, over 60 per cent of all the cotton consumed throughout the world is grown in only four countries — the United States, China, Russia, and India. Japan, India, and Italy furnish 70 per cent of the world's supply of silk, and the principal wool producers are the countries of New Zealand, Australia, and Argentina.

Even though a country could produce a variety of textiles and clothing, it may pay to concentrate on one or a few and buy the others from foreign countries. In the case of some products, a country may have what is known as an **absolute advantage,** meaning that it can produce something at a lower cost than another country. At the same time, it may have a **comparative advantage** in the production of one or two particular items. Let us suppose that China could produce both cotton and wool clothing more cheaply than the United States. It might pay to concentrate on the production of cotton goods and let the United States concentrate on the production of wool, if China's comparative advantage in cotton were greater than in wool. To state it another way, the United States would have the **least disadvantage** in producing wool.

There are any number of reasons why, in a particular country, specialization in production may be more economical than diversification. In addition to the difference in natural resources, there may be considerable difference in the productivity or wage rates of labor. If low wage rates merely reflect a low productivity on the part of labor, it may not give a country any competitive advantage in foreign markets; but if low wages are accompanied by high productivity, such producers have the advantage in selling to other countries. Besides this, there may be differences in the amount and quality of capital equipment available, or certain advantages in terms of the competence of business management.

With the exception of silk, flax, and a few specialty fibers, the United States could be relatively self-sufficient with respect to raw materials. Production does not stop with the fibers, however. Japan is our biggest purchaser of raw cotton, and we in turn provide the largest outlet for Japan's manufactured textiles. The extremely low labor costs in the Far East make it more economical for us to ship the raw material to Japan for fabrication and then buy it back, than to produce the goods here at home. With its high concentration of population and limited natural resources, Japan is forced to export large quantities of merchandise manufactured by its low-cost industries in order to sustain its economy. Holland is another country that is heavily dependent upon foreign sources for its supply of raw materials and, like Japan, must export great volumes of manufactured goods to maintain an even balance of trade. Large quantities of low-cost cottons from the Far East are finished in the Netherlands and then reexported to countries outside the Western European community.

In sharp contrast, a country like France, which is highly self-sufficient in textile production, exports very little in the way of yardgoods and protects its home market from outside competition through a system of high tariffs and trade restrictions. When it comes to the French haute couture, however, it is a different story—one which we will come to shortly—but it is important to realize that when nations close their doors to low-cost suppliers like Japan, there is increased pressure on the relatively open United States market to buy the goods that cannot be sold elsewhere.

International relations

The United States government recognizes the importance of foreign trade not only to our national economy, but to our foreign relations as well. Increased international trade promises a rising level of consumption in all parts of the globe. The United States has long been committed to a policy of liberal trade. Since 1934, for example, import duties have gradually been reduced, while, at the same time imported goods have become a larger percentage of our total domestic consumption.

The **Trade Expansion Act of 1962** gave the President unprecedented tariff-cutting powers in an attempt to enlarge our foreign markets and strengthen our economic and political relations with foreign countries. Obviously, the United States is placed in a less advantageous competitive position if the tariff differential is high. International trade is essential to the U.S. economy, not only because it provides an outlet for our own products, but also because imported products enable us to maintain a high standard of living. Beyond this, the sharing of cultural traditions fosters both individual and international friendships, which hopefully help to avoid world conflict.

Balance of trade

Most people favor the importation of goods that are not readily available in our own country, but there is considerable disagreement surrounding imports that sell for less than our own competitive products. Whenever we import foreign-made textiles and apparel, essentially we are providing work for labor in countries other than our own. There are many groups, such as the International Ladies' Garment Workers' Union, who have held out consistently against imports of ready-to-wear clothing because they pose a threat to our own domestic apparel industry. Many American textile mills have had to reduce their production or close down completely in the face of competition from abroad. In many of the emerging nations of Asia, Africa, and South America, one of the first steps taken toward industrialization is the processing of textiles. For example, in Nigeria, South Africa, and the Sudan—countries that have always been big importers of cotton fabrics—there have sprung up local industries that produce millions of yards of cotton goods annually. The biggest competition comes from Korea, Hong Kong, Taiwan, and Japan.

While foreign trade is necessary for a balanced world economy, the United States government is also mindful that a prosperous domestic textiles and clothing industry contributes to the maintenance of a technically balanced national economy. Essentially there are three ways to control international trade. One is to place a **tariff** or import tax on goods brought into the country. The second is to place limits or **quotas** on the total volume or value of goods that may be imported in a given

TABLE 18-1 COMPARISON OF WORKERS' PAY SCALES
IN THE UNITED STATES
AND COMPETITIVE COUNTRIES

	Average Hourly Wage	
	*Textile Workers	†Apparel Workers
United States	$2.56	$2.31
Japan***	.54	.55 to .65
Hong Kong	.31	.35 to .40
Taiwan	.11	.15 to .20
South Korea	.14	.12 to .15

Source: *Figures as of July 1, 1971, "Profile of Textiles," ATMI, 1971
†Report of the Technical Advisory Committee, AAMA, 1972
***Keep in mind that these are 1971 figures. Japan's growing affluence is producing rapid changes in wages and prices. Even at the time of this writing, the Japanese economy was shifting from textiles and other labor-intensive industries to the advanced technology industries such as computers, electric automobiles, and industrial robots.

Although comparable figures were not available for Red China, it is reported that mill workers in Peking work eight-hour shifts six days a week for wages that average about $27 a month. This would make their wages comparable to workers in Taiwan.

CLOTHING IN THE ECONOMY

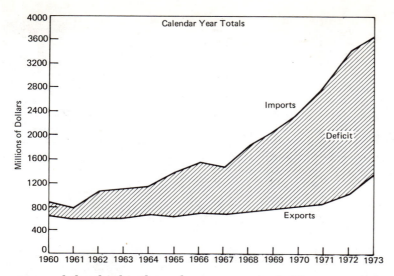

Figure 18-3. U.S. textile trade. By the early 1970's, the value of U.S. textile imports reached over $3.2 billion, while exports were less than $1 billion, leaving a deficit in the U.S. textile trade balance of over $2 billion. Trade in articles of man-made fiber accounted for approximately 56 per cent of the total trade deficit. By 1972, textile imports from Japan, Hong Kong, Taiwan, and South Korea had been brought under control, but imports from the uncontrolled countries increased significantly.

year; and the third is through **government subsidy** payments to the home industry, thereby making it possible to sell domestic products at lower comparative prices both at home and abroad.

TABLE 18-2 COMPARATIVE COSTS OF MANUFACTURING
A MAN'S SHIRT IN A TYPICAL U.S. PLANT
AND A COMPOSITE FAR EASTERN PLANT

	Dollar Cost per Dozen		
	Typical U.S. Plant	Composite Far Eastern Plant	Dollar Gap
Direct labor and fringe benefits	$11.60	$ 3.40	$8.20
Fabric and trim	17.80	14.20	3.60
Plant management and overhead	6.55	1.70	4.85
Importing cost	——	9.65	(9.65)
TOTAL COST	$35.95	$28.95	$7.00

Source: Report of the Technical Advisory Committee, AAMA, 1972.

Protective tariffs help to reduce the flow of foreign merchandise on the American market, but even when calculated at 50 per cent of cost in low-wage countries (see Table 18-2), the American-made product is often still at a disadvantage. In addition, our tariffs are fairly low in comparison with the tariffs imposed by European countries on American-made goods. As a result of trade negotiations concluded in 1967 under the **General Agreement on Tariffs and Trade (GATT)**, the United States agreed to cut tariffs on a broad range of textile products from abroad. This action led to a flood of textile imports from

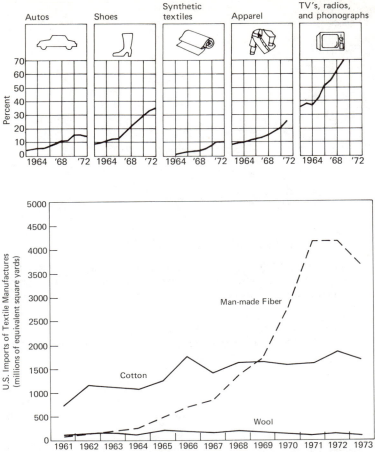

Figure 18-4. Growth of imports to the U.S. market. Imports hit the United States the hardest in labor-intensive industries. Domestic producers of textiles and clothing are generally worse off than the steel and auto industries, but not as bad as manufacturers of TV's, radios, and phonographs.

Figure 18-5. U.S. imports of textile manufactures, 1961–1973. Import quotas are set in terms of yardage, even though the figures here refer to finished products. The Long Term Cotton Textile Arrangement kept the lid on cotton imports, but uncontrolled imports of apparel made from man-made fibers continued to soar in the early 1970's, and disrupted the U.S. apparel market. Bilateral agreements were subsequently made with the four major Far Eastern exporters to limit man-made fiber and wool imports as well. (Source: American Textile Manufacturers Institute, Inc.)

other countries (see Figure 18-3) and displaced over 100,000 American textile and apparel workers.

Leaders from the American textiles and clothing industries pressured for government restraints on the soaring growth of textile imports. This resulted in bilateral agreements with the low-wage countries of the Far East to establish, on a country-by-country basis, import quotas on textiles, shoes, and apparel (see Figure 18-6). The biggest squeeze, of course, is in terms of manufactured products. When it comes to natural resources, Americans fear depletion rather than inundation. Raw materials for leather shoes are a good example. When Argentina, one of the world's largest producers of cattlehides, put an embargo on its entire production, the world buyers came flocking to the United States for leather. The biggest buyers were the giant Japanese firms, who bid up the price of hides and brought leather to a premium level. Not only did this mean increased costs to the footwear industry, but the American consumer had

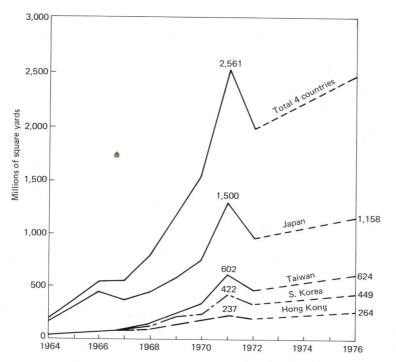

Figure 18-6. Effect of bilateral quota agreements. In 1971 the United States entered into an agreement with Japan, Taiwan, South Korea, and Hong Kong to limit their exports of wool and man-made fibers to the United States.

to pay between 8 and 15 per cent more for shoes. Thus, the footwear and leather industries asked for government controls on the export of cattlehides to guarantee an adequate supply for the home market.

Another way to encourage domestic production of raw materials is to guarantee minimum prices. **The National Wool Act,** for instance, encourages the production of wool by making incentive payments to sheep raisers. At the end of each year, when the average price of wool sold during the marketing year is known, payments are made by the government to bring up to the incentive level the national average received by all growers. Such payments are made from the customs duties collected on wool and wool products. American cotton growers are subsidized through a similar kind of support program.

Many economists maintain that restrictions on free trade, such as tariffs and quota systems, are wrong from both the standpoint of the national economy and that of the ultimate consumer. They argue that the consumer should have the benefit of price advantages that open competition from foreign goods would provide, and that through government subsidy of home products and industries, we price ourselves out of the world market. There is no question that protective programs such as those described above mean higher prices to the consumer. We must realize, however, that the United States has by

Figure 18-7. Workers in a Hong Kong shirt factory inspect, press, and fold about 15,000 shirts and pajamas a day, about one-third for export to the United States.

CLOTHING AND THE INTERNATIONAL MARKET

far the highest per capita income and the highest level of consumption of any nation in the world. By way of comparison, the per capita fiber consumption is now at about 7.4 pounds in the developing countries, compared to 19.8 pounds in the socialist countries of Eastern Europe and 34.1 pounds in the industrialized nations as a whole. The level of fiber consumption in the United States is about 47 pounds per person.

Consider also the fact that textiles and clothing account for nearly one-third of the total U.S. trade deficit. One reason for this, in addition to the tremendous inequity in labor, is the fact that foreign industries in rapidly growing countries like Japan are more vertically integrated than those in America. There are fifteen giant Japanese firms, for example, with more than 10,000 workers apiece, that do 70 per cent of all the textile business.[2] In overseas plants, the ownership often includes cotton plantations, forests for rayon pulp, and chemical factories, and the textile mill often extends into apparel manufacturing and distribution. In spite of the few big companies in America, the industry here remains split into comparatively small companies. While the general trend in American business is toward acquisitions and mergers, the Federal Trade Commission prohibits any merger that would result in a company exceeding $300 million in annual sales. Such a proviso encourages fair competition among domestic firms, but it cripples the industry on a worldwide basis.

Another important aspect of our international economic relations involves the **European Economic Community** (EEC), better known as the Common Market. Created in 1957 with six member countries (Belgium, France, West German, Italy, the Netherlands, and Luxembourg), it admitted the United Kingdom in 1973. Essentially, the aim of the Common Market is to engage in economic disarmament which eliminates tariff barriers and provides for the free movement of goods, capital, labor, and services among the cooperating countries. At the same time, the EEC applies uniform external tariffs on imports from non-member nations. This tremendous consolidation of interests represents the largest single economic unit in the world, with a staggering bargaining power.

The EEC further has less restrictive trade agreements with the countries of the **European Free Trade Association** (EFTA).[3] Economically, the EFTA is less powerful than the EEC, but the tariff reductions on EFTA goods make the U.S. exports less competitive in the EEC markets.

Recent trends indicate that the quantity of imports will con-

Figure 18-8. Looms in a South Carolina textile plant are left to rust beneath plastic dustcovers. Many mills and clothing plants in the southeast were forced to close down in the face of Asia's competitive advantage in the labor market.

[2]John M. Mecklin, "Asia's Great Leap in Textiles," *Fortune*, October 1970.
[3]The EFTA includes Austria, Denmark, Norway, Portugal, Sweden, and Switzerland. Thus, the only Western European countries outside EEC and EFTA are Finland, Greece, Ireland, Spain, and Turkey.

CLOTHING IN THE ECONOMY

tinue to increase. One thing is clear: no country can live in economic isolation from the rest of the world. Economic decisions made in Tokyo and Paris become the concerns of businessmen in San Francisco and New York. The clothing and textile industries are enmeshed not only in the foreign trade policies of the United States, but in the welfare of peoples in all corners of our shrinking world.

SUMMARY *International trade*

The trading of goods and services between and among the nations of the world is desirable for three basic reasons: (1) it gives the consumer a wider range of choice and often provides unique commodities that cannot be produced in a highly industrialized economy; (2) differences in climate, natural resources, native talents, the cost of labor and availability of machinery result in the excess production of some commodities in most countries, while at the same time a scarcity exists in others, so that some goods may be acquired at a lower price abroad than they can be produced domestically; and (3) liberal trade policies make for improved foreign relations and promise a rising level of consumption in all parts of the world.

It is necessary to maintain a favorable balance of trade, however, if we want to protect our national income and maintain a high level of consumption. The American clothing industry must find ways to reduce costs to meet the foreign competition, or it must face eventual adjustment to other types of production and employment. Limitations on free trade through the operation of tariffs, quotas, and subsidies tend to penalize the consumer by generating higher prices. On the other hand, they protect our domestic industry, which in turn contributes to a technically balanced national economy.

The international couture and ready-to-wear

Since the dawn of history, fibers and fabrics have been used as important items for barter, first between neighbors within a community, and gradually extending to include wide areas of trade. Over two thousand years ago, Phoenician merchants sold fine-textured woolens and linen along the trade routes of the Mediterranean, and it is probable that weavers' guilds existed as long ago as the ancient Babylonians. With the rise of the factory system and vast improvements in transportation, the exchange of textiles and clothing among the nations of the world has become a common and daily occurrence.

All countries have a history of clothing production, even though it may be limited to those people who grow, spin, and weave fibers into cloth in their own homes. The development of fashionable clothing as we know it today has a related but

The complex interaction of the clothing industries in a global economy affects the variety, cost, and quality of goods available to consumers in all parts of the world.

somewhat different background. Prior to the French Revolution, the extravagances of fashion were confined to that small segment of the population having extreme wealth. The large masses of the common people had no part in fashion; their garments were simple in design, made from coarse homespun fabric, with men often wearing leather breeches that lasted for much of their lifetime.

Wealthy American colonists sent to London for their suits where their measurements were kept on file in the English tailor shops. The ladies kept in touch with fashions via *les fameuses poupées*, the French costume dolls that were dressed in the latest designs. They were sent from Paris to London every month, and from there to friends in America, where a local seamstress would be employed to copy the style.

Throughout the course of the Industrial Revolution, home production of clothing was gradually replaced by mass-produced apparel which made the luxury of fashion available to the great masses of people who had once enjoyed little more than bare subsistence. The factory system, coupled with the unprecedented opportunities for economic advancement during the nineteenth century, gave tremendous impetus to the growing market for fashionable merchandise.

Today, even the French couture—center of the fashion world for more than a century—is threatened by the economic competition of the ready-to-wear industry. American apparel manufacturers are currently researching the style preferences of European consumers, and many have established European sales offices as well as foreign factories in England, France, Holland, Belgium, Northern Ireland, and Italy. At the same time, European manufacturers are studying U.S. production methods, and many are retaining American consultants to promote their sales on this side of the Atlantic.

France

Paris had been a world center of fashion since the days of Louis XIV, but the modern couture began about the middle of the last century with a designer named Charles Frederick Worth, an Englishman by birth, who was the first dressmaker to show made-up samples on living models. Worth's business acumen, coupled with the perfection of the sewing machine in the 1850's, led to the development of a large-scale dressmaking establishment and the initiation of wholesale relationships with foreign trade buyers.[4]

Paris designers have held an enviable position of fashion leadership ever since. Their enduring influence may be attributed to a combination of factors, not the least of which is the continued support of the French government, which subsidizes

---

[4]Before the days of Worth, dressmakers would suggest a design through a sketch or fashion doll. The garment would then be cut to the measurements of the individual client with no intention of making more than one of a kind.

the couture houses on an annual basis. Beyond this, the French tradition of perfection is a matter of national prestige. The teaching of sewing skills begins at an early age, so that a great number of skilled seamstresses are available for work in the ateliers of the couture. The related industries, such as the makers of French textiles, accessories, buttons, and other findings, cater to the requests of the creative designer. The couture itself is highly organized under the *Chambre Syndicale de la Couture Parisienne,* a trade association that deals with various labor and administrative problems in all segments of the industry. In addition, the Chambre registers the designs of its members to insure against fashion piracy; unauthorized producers of registered designs are prosecuted under French law.

In spite of its financial difficulties in recent years, the couture still brings in over a billion dollars a year in retail turnover, although this figure now covers the sale of everything that bears the couturier's name—including perfume, scarves, hosiery, ready-to-wear, and other boutique items. There are probably not more than twenty or twenty-two successful couture houses in Paris today. Each of these shows a sample collection twice a year to clothing manufacturers and retail store buyers, who in turn purchase models to reproduce in their own countries. Following the openings, designers cater to individual customers, for whom they make custom copies of any model in the season's collection.

The commercial buyers pay an entrance fee or **caution** in order to view the collection, which may be applied toward the purchase of a model. In 1972, for example, the caution was $1,800 per person at Ungaro, $1,100 for one model at Ricci, $1,500 for two models at Lanvin. In the popular houses, a dress, suit, or coat is likely to sell for $1,500, while an elaborate evening gown may be twice that much. Individual customers pay somewhat lower prices, since they do not buy the copying privilege, but still the houses could never survive financially on the custom business alone. A dress usually requires three fittings on the customer and up to ninety hours of labor. On a $1,000 dress, the designer probably has to pay $200 for the materials, $330 for labor, $240 in taxes and sales commissions, and nearly $190 for overhead. This leaves a profit of about 4 per cent if the house is lucky enough to sell thirty or forty copies of the same design. If a number is reproduced only three or four times, the house ends up in the red.

Most couture houses maintain their custom salons for the international prestige it brings to the name of the designer, but almost all of them are forced to seek other sources of income to remain financially solvent. In addition to the government subsidies, some houses are backed by various textile firms, but more often they sell other commodities—notably perfumes— which reap a sizable profit. In recent years, nearly all the successful houses have launched ready-to-wear lines. The luxury

Figure 18-9. Givenchy's salon is one of the largest of the couture houses in Paris. Here, the designer is photographed in his atelier.

trade of the haute couture is gradually losing out to mass production. With the revolution in masculine fashions, some of the designers have gone into men's apparel lines. Pierre Cardin was one of the first of the couture group to venture into a complete collection for male clientèle. He was so successful that he is now distributing his men's wear and accessories not only in Europe and the United States, but in South America, Asia, Africa, the Near, Middle, and Far East as well. His men's wear line has grown into a $23 million business, while his women's fashions, both couture and rtw account for only $12 million a year.

Other houses report similar transitions in terms of their source of sales. In the early seventies, Dior did a $60 million business, exclusive of perfume, with only $2.5 million coming from the couture. Givenchy's couture sales were about $3 million, but his perfume sales reached almost $70 million. At St. Laurent, the annual turnover was about a million dollars in sales to private couture customers, $700,000 in couture sales to buyers, and more than twice those figures in ready-to-wear.[5]

More than 30 per cent of the couture's private clientèle comes from the United States. As one American customer explained: "In America, you see the same things all over. Halston does marvelous clothes, but everyone is wearing them. . . . In Washington at a big ball, it is possible for ten women to turn up in the same de la Renta or Blass dress. It isn't likely to happen with a Givenchy or a Dior. . . . French couture clothes never wear out, never lose their shape."[6]

Nevertheless, in the last ten years, couture customers have dropped nearly one-third in number. There are probably not more than 300 women who still buy couture, and only twenty-five to thirty really "big customers" left in the entire world.[7] There are fewer big spenders, and even the big spenders are spending less on clothes. In today's economic world, extravagant consumption seems as out of place as a Baroque chariot on a California freeway. While the most creative talent still may be going into the couture, businesswise the big emphasis now is on ready-to-wear.

Separate from the couturiers, there is, of course, a growing French ready-to-wear industry. The rtw designers show their collections twice a year at the Porte de Versailles exhibition hall in Paris. In spite of its growth, which has more than doubled in the last decade, the French ready-to-wear industry still has some production problems. Many of the firms are too small to turn out big orders, and U.S. retailers find their delivery schedules unreliable.

In spite of poor delivery, names like Sonia Rykiel, Kenzo, Cacharel, Dorothée Bis, Georges Rech, and Christian Aujard

[5]G. Y. Dryansky, "The Couture—Not What It Was but Still a Power," *Women's Wear Daily,* 26 January 1973.
[6]Deeda Blair as quoted in *W,* 9 February 1973.
[7]Dryansky, "The Couture."

CLOTHING IN THE ECONOMY

are already familiar to many Americans because American manufacturers are so adept at copying their styles. "As a result, the French ready-to-wear industry is big in influence but relatively small in dollar volume. That's partly because French production is fairly small-scale, but the French also have a right to blame it on the American stores and manufacturers who prefer to steal ideas rather than buy French merchandise."[8]

The French *prêt-à-porter* firms are laying the groundwork for expansion into the American market. The French Apparel Center, Inc. has encouraged them to establish New York showrooms, and many of them already do a million-dollar business in the United States. Gradually the men's wear industry is organizing itself along lines similar to its feminine counterpart. Independent designers like Cardin have their own men's wear showings, while other manufacturers from all over Europe show their collections together at the *Salon European de L'Habillement Masculin* in Paris.

Italy

Following World War II, Italy set out to rebuild its shattered economy. Emilio Pucci, who scored a hit with American consumers with his new look in sportswear, was one of the many Italian noblemen and women who turned their refined tastes and creative talents into the fashion field. In the early 1950's, G. B. Giorgini, an Italian merchant dealing in antiques and handcrafts, organized a group of nine couturiers and invited American buyers to his home to view their collections. From this beginning, the Italian couture developed into an industry that now rivals the French in terms of its export trade. Three national organizations receive government support in the promotion of Italian fashions,[9] and the couturiers, like those in France, are subsidized with state monies.

By 1970, there were more than forty haute couture designers who showed their collections every January and July in Rome. Buyers and reporters battled for seats to view the openings. Business was so good that top designer Valentino could afford to toss out half-a-dozen representatives from the largest newspapers in the EEC and the U.S.A. because he disliked their copy on the previous season's line. But the couture in Italy, as in France, proved to be just too costly. Many designers began to cut their collections to fewer and fewer models. Some closed shop completely, and others continued only their ready-to-wear lines. The houses that continue to present regular collections do so with financial aid from the government.

The high fashion rtw collections are shown twice yearly in Florence along with knitwear, leather goods, and furs. The

---

[8]Joan Chatfield-Taylor, "The Great Idea Ripoff in Paris," *San Francisco Chronicle*, 13 April 1973.
[9]The Centro di Firenze per la Moda Italiana in Florence, and the Camera Nazionale della Moda Italiana and the Italian Institute for Foreign Trade in Rome.

Italian government provides the historically famous Pitti and Strozzi Palaces for showrooms and trade center. Italy has always been famous for its knitwear and leather. Names like Missoni (knits), Gucci, and Ferragamo (shoes) are popular in American stores. Leather gloves, handbags, and other accessories are all a part of the industry which has become one of Italy's most important national assets.

Of special interest is the fact that the Italian showings include both men's and women's fashions. Men's wear collections are scheduled right along with the others. American males also find Rome a good place for custom-made suits, especially in the summer weights of Italian silk. The average cost of a completely hand-tailored suit is under $300, and it takes about five days to make one up.

The fashion industry (textiles, apparel, and accessories) is second in Italian export trade and brings into Italy's coffers over $1 billion a year in foreign exchange. It is Europe's biggest exporter to the American market (see Table 18-3).

United Kingdom

Britain ranks second to Italy in terms of the volume of European exports shipped to the United States market. The British couture designers operate much like those in France and Italy, showing their collections regularly to American and other foreign buyers, and then existing as a custom salon for private customers. The couture is considerably smaller in England than in France or Italy, and the models are considerably less expensive. English designer Hardy Amies—like France's Cardin—came out with a men's ready-to-wear line which he distributed in retail stores throughout the United States.

The London tailors of Savile Row, however, are to the well-heeled fashionable gentleman what the Parisian couturiers are to the international feminine socialite. The quality workmanship, superb fit, and individual attention given each customer draws prominent men from all over the world to Savile Row.

British tweeds and woolens have been traditional import items on the American market for generations, but the ready-to-wear industry is a relative newcomer to the export field (as is true all over Europe). The wholesale manufacturers got their greatest boost during World War II, when the British Board of Trade ordered drastic cuts in the consumption of yardgoods. Up until that time, ready-made clothing was poorly designed and lacking in quality, but the government commissioned the leading designers of the country to come up with simple, tasteful styles that could be mass-produced.

Gradually, the British learned to tailor their lines to American tastes, using lighter weight fabrics and improving the sizing, and as a result, the United States has become Britain's biggest ready-to-wear customer. The competition from English goods is still in the upper price bracket, just as it is with French rtw. Usually the workmanship is superior and the prices are lower than the highest priced American rtw. The reason is simple: labor costs are roughly one-third those of the average worker in the United States.

The biggest fashion revolution of the sixties started with the youthful English designers who launched the "mod" look among the newly affluent British teenagers. In 1960, John Stephen opened a small shop on Carnaby Street and became an overnight success selling tight, hip-slung pants and turtleneck sweaters. Mary Quant, who later became known as the "Mother of the Mini," had a boutique in Chelsea as early as 1954. But it was not until 1962, when she turned out a collection for the J. C. Penney Company, that her designs gained impetus in the United States. Another trendy designer, Tommy Roberts, is credited with the introduction of hot pants. The American teen-age market continues to be influenced by British styles, and this helps to swell the volume of imports from the British Isles.

Israel

In the early 1960's, Israel's Ministry of Commerce invested many millions of dollars in the construction of textile plants, particularly in the outlying development areas of the country where manpower was plentiful. Today there are over 65,000 textile workers in Israel, and in many of the outlying areas, half of all industrial jobs are in textiles. More recently, Israeli manufacturers have been concentrating on fashion goods, where profits are higher.

Israeli textile exports reached $130 million in 1972, with apparel exports accounting for $87 million. That represented an increase of $77 million over 1961, when fashion exports totaled only $10 million. Well over half of Israel's apparel exports go to the United States and Canada. This has been facilitated by and large by ATID (American Trade and Industrial Development with Israel, Inc.), a non-profit organization based in New York that works as a liaison between Israeli manufacturers and American stores. It sponsors a semi-annual trade show of Israeli fashions in New York, and it also establishes working arrangements with U.S. manufacturers to have their lines produced in Israel where labor is cheaper. Another plus factor is that the Export Institute has established a quality control system to insure that all exported goods meet the standards of comparable merchandise produced in American factories.

Israeli fashion apparel is geared to a moderate-priced market. Israeli knitwear sells for less than Italy's, although it still cannot compete with the Far East price-wise. It is reported that Israeli fashions retail in the United States at three times the

Figure 18-10. Israel's biggest apparel exports are knitwear, leather coats, swimsuits, lingerie, and children's knitwear. Leather pantsuits, like the one above, and traditional Middle Eastern caftans are typical.

price paid to the manufacturer. The United States is not Israel's only customer, however. The country has made a concentrated push to get its products into the world market. Manufacturers have developed special-sized clothing for sale in Japan, for example, where they have been holding fashion exhibitions for the promotion of their products. Because of the export dollars that clothing brings into the country, apparel manufacturers are now subsidized at the rate of about twenty cents on every dollar that they earn outside of Israel.[10]

Other European markets

A number of other European countries are rapidly developing their talents in terms of both designing and marketing in the fashion field. In addition to their exports of Irish crochet lace, linens, and tweeds, Ireland has a growing rtw industry, particularly in men's wear. The Spanish capitalize on up-to-date versions of their traditional beadwork, laces, and leather craft, and their designs sell well in the more exclusive American specialty shops. Sweden does a good export business to the United States in coats, jackets, and sportswear. Wool sports sweaters are a specialty of the top Swiss knitwear firms.

Although many of the European manufacturers already have sales outlets in the United States, representatives from Austria, Sweden, West Germany, Switzerland, France, and Finland display their wares to American buyers twice a year at the European Fashion Fair in New York. As a kind of return favor, in 1973 American manufacturers were invited for the first time to participate in the Overseas Import Fair held in West Berlin. They were encouraged to display a sample of their lines to test the market for U.S. products in Germany.

The early 1970's also saw the beginning of trade negotiations with some of the socialist countries of Europe. After the Nixons' visit to Russia in 1972, Americans took the initiative in seeking out fashions produced in the U.S.S.R. One department store in Pennsylvania was the first to purchase four evening outfits that were made in Moscow. If an American woman wanted to buy one, the price tag was $900, but the store was not particularly interested in selling the clothes — they were purchased more or less as Russian "showpieces."[11]

For many years the typical pattern in Europe was for most of the retail shops to sell fabric, and the consumer then made the clothes at home or had them made at a local tailor shop. Now, almost all countries are getting into ready-to-wear production of some kind.

---

[10]"Israeli Rtw: Diversification Is the Game," *Women's Wear Daily,* 21 February 1973.
[11]Nina S. Hyde, "Peekaboo—From Russia, With Love," *Washington Post* News Service, 8 March 1973.

Japan and the Far East

Of all the countries in the world, the United States imports more clothing and textiles from Japan than from any other nation. Table 18-3 compares our imports from the Far East with those from Italy, the biggest European exporter to the United States, and it can easily be seen that our trade with Japan is ten times that of our trade with Italy. Just a few short years ago, our exchange was mainly in silk and in made-up cotton blouses. It was not until the 1930's, for example, that the Japanese began to wear any Western-styled clothing at all. Their phenomenal growth in fashion is explained by a Japanese in his own words:

> Tie-ups with overseas makers have helped Japanese clothes manufacturers to catch up with overseas makers, who are advanced in fashion, thus enabling Japan, once backward in fashion, to attain the international level in fashion. Everything from designs and patterns to technical know-how imported from overseas, therefore, served as textbooks for Japanese fashion designers and prêt-à-porter makers. The Japanese were extremely diligent and brilliant in learning and mastering the textbooks they had bought from foreign countries. Tokyo and Osaka, as a result, have grown into big fashion-consuming centers comparable to New York, Los Angeles, London and Paris.[12]

Figure 18-11 Japanese designer, Shiro Makita models her award-winning coat, the design of which was inspired by traditional Japanese calligraphy.

TABLE 18-3 COTTON, WOOL, AND MAN-MADE
FIBER APPAREL IMPORTS
(in millions of square yards equivalent)

Exporting Country	1967	1970
Japan	279.5	396.8
Hong Kong	246.0	380.7
Taiwan	85.7	335.0
South Korea	68.1	256.8
Philippines	44.2	51.9
Italy	29.6	35.2
TOTAL	753.1	1,456.4

Source: AAMA Apparel Imports: The Challenge of the 70's.
The six countries above were the leading exporters to the United States in the early 1970's. Apparel imports from these countries constituted 86 per cent of all clothing exports to the United States.

At the same time that the creations of Japanese designers like Issei Miyake, Mori Hanae, and Kansai Yamamoto are being marketed in American and European retail stores, most of the leading department stores in Japan have marketing arrangements with overseas suppliers. You can buy Pierre Cardin in the Takashimaya Department Store, St. Laurent and Louis Feraud at Seibu's, and Oleg Cassini designs at Mitsukoshi. It is

---

[12]Makoto Urabe, "Internationalized Japanese Fashion," *Japan Illustrated*, Autumn 1972, p. 7.

reported that many of the French rtw designers have lucrative contracts to have their lines adapted, manufactured, and sold in Japan. There are over 200 Japanese apparel manufacturers today who contract with overseas companies. Jantzen and Catalina swimsuits, Munsingwear, and Big John blue jeans are just a few of the name brands that are adapted to Japanese sizing and produced in Japan.

Second only to Japan, Hong Kong has a growing fashion industry that exports millions of dollars worth of clothing to the United States annually. The Dynasty line, for example, employs a New York designer and manufactures dresses and loungewear that retail in the States for as much as $300. Hong Kong's biggest asset fashionwise is an army of skilled workers available at unbelievably low wages. American merchants can buy silk in Thailand and have it converted by Chinese dressmakers into styles that were purchased from the Paris couture. The more handwork required in constructing the garment, the greater the advantage of the Hong Kong manufacturer. Hong Kong is, of course, the mecca of American tourists for custom-made suits, shirts, and shoes of all kinds. Thousands of custom tailors measure clients, both male and female, day and night, and produce replicas of almost any design. A good quality tailor-made suit can be had for as little as $70 to $80, and in most cases the customer has the pick of the world's fabrics: English worsteds, Irish tweeds, and Italian silks. Custom-made shirts sell for about $8 in such rare materials as Sea Island cotton and English broadcloth. Bespoke shoes are available from $20 to $40, depending upon the kind of leather. As one American visitor explained, "A guy could go broke taking advantage of all the bargains."

A plentiful supply of skilled labor, low wages, and high productivity, give the Far Eastern countries a tremendous competitive advantage in the international market.

SUMMARY *The international couture and ready-to-wear*

In terms of the economics of clothing production, societies of the world pass through successive stages of producing all of the family clothing in the home; of high-fashion luxury goods being available only to the wealthy few; of a growing ready-to-wear market; and ultimately of a wide range of fashionable, good quality merchandise available for all.

Competition in the apparel markets of the United States has come not so much from the fashion rivalry of European goods as from the lower-cost products of Japan and other low-wage countries of the Far East. The European couture serves mainly as a source of ideas and is a stimulus to American fashion.

The same problems plague apparel manufacturers the world over: lack of skilled labor, ever-increasing wages, and sky-rocketing costs of cotton, wool, and other natural raw materials.

The United States abroad

All together, United States imports of foreign-made apparel account for a relatively small percentage of the total consumer expenditures for clothing and accessories made by the American public, in spite of the varied markets in which we trade. Nevertheless, imports are rising steadily each year in millions of dollars, and more important perhaps is the fact that our apparel imports greatly exceed our exports (see Figure 18-3).

U.S. imports

Strangely enough, the European couture, rather than posing a threat, actually serves to boost our domestic apparel production. We really have no American couture as such, and a designer-owned firm in the United States is the exception rather than the rule. Most of our leading creative artists are in high-priced ready-to-wear, not in custom production.

The business of reproducing "line-for-line" copies of Paris is a powerful asset to American retailers and manufacturers. Twice a year buyers from America's leading retail stores attend the European couture openings to buy the models they think will appeal most to American women. Twice a year a jet airliner carries more than half-a-million dollars worth of Paris originals into the United States, delivering the precious cargo to its respective purchasers. In the weeks that follow, there is a frenzied duplication of each model that varies all the way from exact replications to cheap adaptations. The biggest buyers are stores like Orbach's, Macy's, and Alexander's, who maintain a worldwide reputation for their couture copies. Orbach's, for example, contracts with about thirty New York manufacturers to produce a volume of copies between the time the models arrive (in winter, it is the last week in February) and the second week in March when the copies go on sale. The processing is so amazingly fast that some of the cheaper, less complicated mass-produced models are ready in a matter of days.

In most cases, the copies sell at a fraction of the original cost. The counterpart of a St. Laurent gown purchased in Paris for $1,250 can often be found at Orbach's for $79.99. The answer, of course, is in volume sales. At one store, all 200 copies of a Chanel suit were sold before the end of the first day of sales. Nevertheless, the margin of profit is extremely small. If a retailer sells a hundred copies of a dress at $50 each, he must deduct from $700 to $1,200 paid for the original, the expense of a trip to Paris, as well as the cost of manufacture from the $5,000 in sales.

Not all couture originals are produced in volume, of course. Copies that reproduce the exact model with all the fine details of workmanship were once available in the custom salons of the exclusive American specialty stores. Today, I. Magnin in San Francisco is the only store left in the United States that still makes custom copies of European haute couture. Because custom work is done to individual measurements and labor costs are high, a copy made in San Francisco could easily be higher in price than the original bought in Paris.

The European models, incidentally, are brought into the country "in bond," which means that the buyer does not pay duty (which may be as high as 60 per cent of the cost) if he does not resell the garment in the United States. Within a year, therefore, the models are shipped off to Canadian and Latin American stores that specialize in "second-hand" couture, where a $1,200 St. Laurent gown may be sold at the bargain basement price of $250. In other words, the American store or manufacturer who buys in the European salons is really paying for the privilege of copying a design rather than purchasing resaleable merchandise.

The amount of goods that we import from Europe, however, is a drop in the bucket compared to the volume of imports from Asia. Particularly in the low-priced field, by far the largest percentage of all apparel imports come from Japan, Hong Kong, Taiwan, and Korea. The recent quota regulations have had a curious effect on the quality of the goods brought into this country. Since the quotas are based on units rather than dollars, manufacturers want to make the most out of their dozens, and hence they have turned to producing better quality garments.

As yet, goods from the socialist countries — Russia, Rumania, China — have been considerably lower in quality than those from the Asian countries, and importers have to pay a double duty on their shipments. It may be some time before they will be able to make a significant input into the American market.

U.S. exports

It has been said that the French design while the Americans make fashion. In short, the French have the Americans to thank for popularizing their styles. But if Paris designs are coveted by Americans, the quality of United States ready-to-wear is treasured by Europeans. Many American lines, such as designs by Lanz of California and Jonathan Logan, sell like hotcakes in Europe, where it is a rarity to find well-made and well-fitting clothes available off the rack.

This unusual exchange of talents between Europeans and Americans has stimulated some of the most intensive market research in years. United States apparel manufacturers have set out to investigate the style and fabric preferences of the European consumers as well as the modifications in sizing required by the difference in national body types. In the 1960's, less than 0.5 per cent of all male apparel produced in the United

CLOTHING IN THE ECONOMY

States was sold abroad. American manufacturers discovered a growing interest among European men for lighter-weight suits and colorful sportswear, and no other market can compete with American products in these categories.

It is anticipated that the European consumer will have increasing amounts of disposable income, and that he will pay increasing attention to fashion in the purchase of items heretofore considered as luxuries.

Gradually the barriers between countries are being broken down by international trade. Physical distances are reduced by the speed of jets and the power of mass communication. The American market is rapidly becoming a world market.

Multi-national trends

Corporations that maintain a base of operations in more than one country are commonly known as **multi-national companies.** In the past twenty years there has been an amazing growth in the number of American firms that have extended themselves into foreign lands. The British, of course, have been doing this since the early 1900's, but American expansion has been relatively recent. The big retail chains were among the first to establish overseas outlets. Sears, for example, opened stores in Havana and Mexico City in the forties, and it has since spread to a number of other countries. Joseph Magnin opened a chain of stores in Japan in 1973, with some of the same merchandise available in the Western JM shops. Italians can buy some of the same clothes from J.C. Penney in Milan as Americans can buy in Los Angeles.

As indicated earlier, there are a number of American apparel firms who contract with manufacturers in Japan and Hong Kong to have their brand name merchandise produced where labor costs are low. But the idea is spreading to American designers and manufacturers who plan to market their products abroad: Anne Klein, for instance, opened a shop in Paris, and Jerry Silverman has a boutique in London.

At the moment, the biggest push toward multi-national organization is coming from the textile producers. The giant fiber producers are already well ensconced overseas. DuPont, for example, has plants in Brazil, Canada, Germany, the Netherlands, and the United Kingdom; Celanese is also in Brazil and Canada, and in Colombia, Mexico, Peru, and Venezuela as well. Many of the weaving mills have made similar kinds of overseas investments.

In most cases the American company makes a direct capital investment in the multi-national corporation abroad, thereby creating an entirely new operation. There are a number of reasons why manufacturers seek to make such an investment. First of all they do so in order to secure new resources of raw materials. America is rapidly becoming resource poor, and plants are usually opened in areas with high resource potential. Another reason is that manufacturers seek low-cost labor as a means of producing more economically. In addition, they capture the existing market of the country in which the goods are produced. Beyond this, however, the national company can give to the developing foreign nation the benefits of technical expertise and an opportunity to learn modern management controls.

There are many individuals and groups – notably the American labor unions – who see this kind of investment as a threat to the American economy. They believe that we are exporting both capital and technology, and by setting up operations overseas we are shutting down American industries and creating unemployment here at home. In addition, they argue that "huge investments in foreign countries enable multinationals to expand foreign holdings and avoid paying U.S. taxes on foreign earned profits."[13]

In the face of growing competition from abroad, however, the multi-national trend seems inevitable. Quite aside from the promise of lower labor costs and more efficient production, it also helps to overcome hidden international trade barriers. It suggests that we may indeed be looking forward to a division of labor on a worldwide basis between the advanced and the developing nations. The biggest explosion of the world's population has taken place in Asia, pointing to an abundant supply of labor. High-wage countries like the United States may be forced to discontinue their non-competitive manufacturing operations and transfer them to low-wage areas. Thus, the rich, industrialized countries may tend to concentrate on capital-intensive production, research, and product development, while the developing countries may make their greatest contribution in the labor-intensive areas.

The demand for textiles will continue to increase as long as the world population increases. The changes that have come about in the textiles and clothing industry in the last century have been the result of continued growth and expansion based upon consumer demands. It may well be that in the coming years the problems of expansion will give way to the problems of maintaining an ecological balance on our planet.

A rising level of consumption in all parts of the world creates new outlets for U.S. goods abroad, and new sources of supply for American consumers.

SUMMARY *The United States abroad*

Domestic producers are affected differently by competition from foreign markets. In the developing countries, textile plants are the least expensive to equip, and they can absorb a great deal of relatively unskilled labor. Consequently, the squeeze of competition is felt first among the small domestic

---

[13]Penny Girard, "Multinational Firms Hurt Economy, Society: AFL-CIO," *Daily News Record*, 7 March 1973.

textile firms. On the other hand, with increased wealth, foreign nations become better customers for United States merchandise, particularly in areas where they cannot compete with American technology.

Because of the efficiency and volume of the American ready-to-wear industry, its fashion products are in demand not only by our citizens here at home, but by an increasing number of people in all parts of the world. It may be, however, that workers in the highly competitive industries face eventual adjustment to other types of employment. The trend toward multi-national corporations has the potential of eliminating many of our current trade barriers, and of tying nations closer together through cooperative production and international trade.

FOR FURTHER READING

Bosworth, Patricia. "Who Killed High Fashion?" *Esquire*, May 1973, pp. 124–127 and 214–218.
Dorsey, Hebe. "Prêt à Porter v Couture," in R. Lynam (ed.), *Couture*. Garden City, N. Y.: Doubleday & Company, 1972.
Loving, Rush. "What the U.S. Textile Industry Really Needs," *Fortune*, October 1970, pp. 84–87 and 161–163.
Mecklin, J. M. "Asia's Great Leap in Textiles," *Fortune*, October 1970, pp. 77–83 and 138.
"Towards the Multi-National Textile Company," *American Fabrics*, Summer 1972, pp. 59–61. (Two short articles: "An American View," by C. F. Myers, Jr.; and "A Japanese View," by Junji Itoh.)

DISCUSSION QUESTIONS

1. Why is international trade important to the United States?

2. What are the three basic ways a country is able to maintain control over its imports and exports? What are the advantages and disadvantages of each?

3. What would be the immediate effects on the American clothing industry if all countries agreed to eliminate tariffs and quotas? What would be the long-term effects?

4. Many U.S. firms are making substantial investments in establishing overseas subsidiaries, and this results in an outflow of U.S. capital abroad. What do you see as the ultimate outcome of such a trend?

5. What factors are contributing to the demise of the couture as a business enterprise?

19

Clothing Consumption Patterns

EVERY BUSINESS is guided by the consumer demand for its products. The fiber and apparel producers as well as the clothing retailers make continual adjustments in their operations in light of the spending patterns, tastes, and preferences of American consumers. The quantity or quality of clothing that the individual stands ready to buy is determined by a number of factors, including his personal income, his changing needs and desires, the price of the commodity, as well as the prices of substitute goods or services. In this chapter we will examine some of the trends in clothing expenditures, the social and economic changes that may influence how much we spend for clothing in the future, and the power of the consumer in forcing changes in the clothing industry.

Where the money goes

The performance and growth of an economy can be measured in terms of its **gross national product,** which represents the total output of goods and services of a country for any given year. In 1970, the GNP of the United States reached $974 billion. In the process of this production, capital goods wear out, so if we deduct the allowance for capital depreciation and other indirect business taxes, we arrive at a figure described as our **national income** (see Table 19-1). By subtracting corporate profits and contributions made for social insurance, and adding money earned through interest, dividends, and other transfer payments, we then have the total **personal income** for the population of the United States as a whole.

Disposable personal income is the amount left after the payments of personal taxes are deducted, and it refers to the money that consumers are free to dispose of as they wish. In the decade from 1960 to 1970, our disposable personal income rose from $350 billion to $687.8 billion, an increase of almost 97 per cent. During this same interval, the American population jumped from 180 million to 203.8 million people, so that the

per capita income increased from $2,699 to $3,516, or about 41 per cent.

TABLE 19-1 RELATION OF GROSS NATIONAL PRODUCT,
NATIONAL INCOME, PERSONAL INCOME,
AND SAVINGS

	For the year 1970 (In billions of dollars)
Gross National Product (GNP)	$974.1
Less: capital depreciation	− 87.6
Equals: Net National Product	= 886.5
Less: indirect business taxes	− 90.6
Equals: *National Income* (NI)	= 795.9
Less: corporate profits and social security payments	− 128.4
Plus: interest and dividends	+ 136.2
Equals: *Personal Income* (PI)	= 803.6
Less: personal taxes	− 115.9
Equals: *Disposable Personal Income* (DPI)	= 687.8
Less: personal consumption expenditures	− 633.7
Equals: personal saving	= 54.1

Source of figures: *Statistical Abstract of the United States, 1972.*

One factor that influences our **purchasing power** is the price we have to pay for goods and services. Prices also went up in this period, so that the dollar in 1970 did not buy as much as it did in 1960. The rise in the average cost of living can be measured by the **consumer price index,** which in 1960 was 88.7, and 116.3 in 1970 for all items (1967 = 100). In other words, higher prices reduced the purchasing power of the dollar in 1970 by 27.6 per cent, compared with the value of the dollar in 1960.

In spite of inflationary prices, however, our real income continues to rise, and the national economy has been characterized by a relatively high degree of prosperity. Our total income is not evenly distributed, of course, and many groups in our society continue to suffer economic hardships. But as a total population we enjoy a higher consumption level than ever before in our history, and we are better off economically than most of the other nations of the world (see Table 19-2).

Clothing expenditures

In 1973, consumers spent over $69 billion to buy clothing and shoes. This represents an increase of almost $8 billion over the previous year's allocation to the nation's clothing budget. But despite the fact that our per capita expenditures for apparel are the highest that they have ever been, consumer clothing expenditures in the last decade have consistently represented between 7.5 and 7.9 per cent of our total disposable income

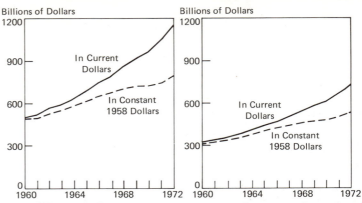

Gross National Product   Personal Consumption Expenditures

Figure 19-1. Gross national product and personal consumption expenditures.

(see Table 19-3). By comparison, twenty years ago the average American family spent over 12 per cent of its income on clothes. While the share of the total income absorbed by clothing today remains at less than 8 per cent, our annual expenditures for services, medical care, and recreation have risen at a much faster rate than personal consumption expenditures (Figure 19-2).

TABLE 19-2 COMPARISONS OF PER CAPITA INCOME AND PER CAPITA FIBER CONSUMPTION

	Per Capita Income		Per Capita Fiber Consumption	
	1960	1969	1960	1969
United States	$2,699	$3,577	35.6 lbs.	48.6 lbs.
Industrialized countries	1,750	2,487	24.8	34.1
Socialist countries	741	1,201	14.7	19.8
Developing countries	154	192	6.1	7.4

Source: *American Fabrics,* Summer 1972.

A number of factors may account for clothing's declining share of the consumer dollar. For one thing, the population growth has been largely at the two extremes of the age scale, in the groups under 18 and over 65, and the clothing needs of the very young and the very old are considerably less than those of the young adult or the wage-earner. Since the end of World War II, moreover, there has been a significant trend toward casual dress, with a corresponding expansion of "separate" items in the wardrobe (e.g., skirts, blouses, sweaters, slacks, sports jackets, and the like), and casual clothing in general is less expensive than more formal wear.

The parallel development of synthetic fibers has made clothing lighter in weight, easier to care for, and longer wearing. Only a small percentage of our clothing today has to be replaced because it wears out.

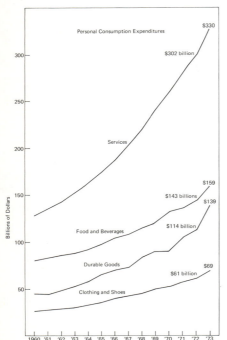

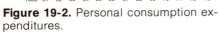

Figure 19-2. Personal consumption expenditures.

TABLE 19-3 PERSONAL INCOME DISPOSITION
(in billions of dollars)

Period	Disposable Personal Income	Personal Saving	Services	Personal Consumption Expenditures			
				Food and Beverages	Durable Goods	Clothing and Shoes	Per cent of Income
1960	$350.0	$17.0	$128.7	$80.5	$45.3	$27.3	(7.8)
1961	364.4	21.2	135.1	82.9	44.2	27.9	(7.6)
1962	385.3	21.6	143.0	85.7	49.5	29.6	(7.6)
1963	404.6	19.9	152.4	88.2	53.9	30.6	(7.6)
1964	438.1	26.2	163.6	92.9	59.2	33.5	(7.6)
1965	473.2	28.4	175.5	98.8	66.3	35.9	(7.6)
1966	511.9	32.5	188.6	105.8	70.8	40.3	(7.9)
1967	546.3	40.4	204.0	108.5	73.1	42.3	(7.7)
1968	591.0	39.8	221.3	115.3	84.0	46.3	(7.8)
1969	634.4	38.2	242.7	120.6	90.8	50.2	(7.9)
1970	687.8	54.9	261.8	132.1	90.5	52.0	(7.5)

Source: U.S. Department of Commerce; Council of Economic Advisers.

In general, the percentage of a family's income spent for clothing increases as the income goes up (Table 19-4). However, in successively higher income brackets over $15,000 clothing constitutes a diminishing proportion of total expenditures.

TABLE 19-4 COMPARISON OF EXPENDITURES FOR CLOTHING, CLOTHING MATERIALS, AND CLOTHING SERVICES BY NON-FARM FAMILIES AND SINGLE CONSUMERS IN THE UNITED STATES, 1960–1961

Money Income (before taxes)	Dollars Spent	Per cent of Income
Under $3,000	$145	(7.1)
$3,000 to $4,999	348	(9.0)
$5,000 to $7,499	528	(9.9)
$7,500 to $9,999	720	(10.6)
$10,000 to $14,999	1,001	(11.5)
$15,000 and over	1,550	(12.2)
TOTAL	525	*(10.2)

*These figures include not only clothing and shoes, but also jewelry, jewelry repair, drycleaning, and other costs of upkeep. The per cent of income is therefore higher than the percentages listed in Table 19-3.

Source: *Consumer Expenditures and Income: Survey guidelines*, Bulletin 1684, U.S. Department of Labor, 1971.

Clothing prices

In 1972, the per capita expenditure for clothing and shoes was approximately $296, which represented an increase of 7.6 per cent over the previous year. The actual dollars spent for clothing, however, must be viewed against the inflationary prices that were characteristic of the economy in general. Except for the years 1968 and 1969, the consumer price index for all apparel and upkeep was generally lower than for all items (see

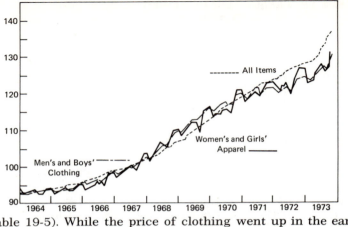

140
130
120
110
100
90

- - - - All Items

Women's and Girls'
Apparel ————

Men's and Boys'
Clothing

1964 1965 1966 1967 1968 1969 1970 1971 1972 1973

Figure 19-3. Consumer price index for clothing. (1967 = 100)

Table 19-5). While the price of clothing went up in the early seventies, it did not increase as sharply as many of the other commodities and services.

TABLE 19-5 CONSUMER PRICE INDEX FOR SELECTED COMMODITIES AND SERVICES (1967 = 100)

Period	All Items	Food	Housing	Clothing			
				All Apparel and Upkeep	Apparel less Footwear	Men's and Boys' Clothing	Women's and Girls' Clothing
1965	94.5	94.4	94.9	93.7	94.5	94.0	93.8
1966	97.2	99.1	97.2	96.1	96.2	96.5	95.6
1967	100.0	100.0	100.0	100.0	100.0	100.0	100.0
1968	104.2	103.6	104.2	105.4	105.7	105.7	105.9
1969	109.8	108.9	110.8	111.5	111.9	112.4	111.7
1970	116.3	114.9	118.9	116.1	116.3	117.1	116.0
1971	121.3	118.4	124.3	119.8	119.9	120.3	120.1
1972	125.3	123.5	129.2	122.3	122.3	121.9	123.0

SOURCE: U.S. Department of Labor

One reason for this is that, unlike certain other industries in which a few large firms tend to control a sizeable percentage of the total output, the apparel industry is one in which a large number of firms has created a highly competitive market situation; this is reflected, in part, in considerable price flexibility. Price inflation was generally stronger at the retail level than at the wholesale level (refer back to Table 17-6). The difference in the rate of increase in consumer prices is due mainly to the marked increase in the costs of retailing (see Chapter 17).

Another important factor which affects our consumption of clothing is the price of other services and commodities which compete for the consumer's disposable income. In the 1970's, for example, housing costs went up at a faster rate than costs for either food or clothing. Early in 1973, however, food prices skyrocketed, while clothing prices actually went down.

Most importantly, the price of clothing is affected by the forces of supply and demand. When supplies go down, prices go up. In 1972, the supply of raw cotton was extremely tight because of a poor crop in 1971. As a result, 1972 cotton prices went up 10 per cent, compared to man-made fiber textiles which rose only 7 per cent, and wool goods which increased 6 per cent. The 1972 cotton crop was almost one-third larger than that of 1971, but this increase was partially offset by the fact that Japan bought up a large chunk of the supply. On the other hand, wool production in the United States declined in 1973, and we were forced to make larger imports of raw apparel wool to meet the demand—of course at higher prices. Similarly, the price of leather goods went up in the early 1970's because of the scarcity of hides on a worldwide basis. In 1970, for instance, we exported nearly one-third of our entire production in cattle hides. By 1973, as the demand for beef reached its peak and more stock went to market, the supply of leather was increased.

This highlights another advantage of the man-made fibers in the apparel market. The producing capacity for man-made fibers is considerably higher than our actual production. Domestic production, moreover, is concentrated in a few firms who sell directly to the textile mills. They can gear their production schedules precisely to mill demands and thereby maintain a relatively stable and predictable price.

As we saw in the two preceding chapters, clothing prices have been kept down in relation to other commodities by the competition of the low-wage countries abroad. In order to meet the competition, clothing and textile workers in America are generally paid less than workers in other industries. In effect, then, the textiles and clothing industry is more or less subsidizing the rest of the economy.

Categories of apparel

Apportionment of the family clothing dollar has changed gradually over the years with respect to the relative amounts spent for various types of clothing. One of the most notable changes has been the steady increase in the outlays for women's and children's wear as compared with men's and boys' clothing. Half a century ago clothing expenditures for the man of the household exceeded those for his wife by almost a third. After World War I, the woman's wardrobe began to expand until early in the 1930's clothing expenditures for women and girls surpassed those for men and boys. By the 1960's, one out of every three workers in the labor force was a woman, compared to only one out of four in the 1940's. The woman who works requires a larger wardrobe than the woman who stays at home, and as her earnings increase, more of her money goes toward clothing.

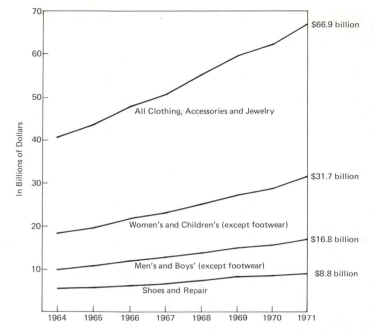

Figure 19-4. Personal consumption expenditures for clothing by category, 1964–1971.

The largest expenditures for clothing occur in families having older children, or among the young married groups with no children. Unmarried consumers below the age of 35 spend more on clothes than do consumers who are married with families. In general, proportionate amounts spent for apparel decrease with advancing age.

Men's and boys' clothing, excluding footwear, took $16.8 billion of the consumers' income in 1971, as compared with only $9.9 billion in 1964 (Figure 19-4). In the last decade, however, this consistently represented about 25 per cent of the total expenditures made for all clothing, accessories, and jewelry. Men's wear is following the same general trend toward more casual dress that is shown by clothing in general, moving away from formal wear and business suits to the more informal slacks, sweaters, and sport coats. In 1970 the sale of men's suits went down 13 per cent below the 1962 figures, while in the same eight-year period the sale of jeans and dungarees went up 201 per cent![1] The average man today buys a new suit about once every three or four years (if at all); twenty years ago, he bought one every other year. The suits that he does buy are lighter in weight, with an increasing proportion of fabrics that are blended with man-made fibers. Men's expenditures in the early 1970's were way up on haberdashery items and furnishings, such as shirts, slacks, belts, and neckties. In spite of the

[1]*Focus: Economic Profile of the Apparel Industry,* American Apparel Manufacturers Association, Arlington, Va., 1972.

fact that the male population has increased by several millions during the last decade, the consumption of socks remains about the same—another illustration of the effects of longer wear imparted by such features as nylon-reinforced heels and toes. The fact that modern man does most of his travelling by automobile rather than on foot is reflected in the falling number of raincoats, overcoats, rubbers, and other types of protective clothing in his wardrobe. The number of hats purchased by men has also decreased appreciably, while items in the underwear and pajama categories are on the upswing. Underwear, incidentally, shows an unusual relationship to technological innovation; prior to 1920, all men wore heavy union suits, but in the atmosphere of today's heated buildings and cars, long drawers are virtually extinct. Cotton undershorts, on the other hand, practically unheard of fifty years ago, have taken over the underwear market almost completely.

Women's and children's clothing accounts for about 46 per cent of all the money spent by American consumers for items of apparel, shoes, jewelry, and accessories. As family incomes increased over the years, larger proportions of money went for women's clothes. In the past decade, the purchase of blouses, pants, and sweaters skyrocketed at the expense of dresses and suits. Today, leisure wear and sports clothes account for a large portion of the modern woman's wardrobe.

Per capita production of dresses has dropped drastically. Throughout the first half of the twentieth century, dresses were the mainstay of a woman's wardrobe. Today, she buys fewer dresses in proportion to separates, and fewer house dresses in proportion to street dresses. Women's wear parallels men's wear with respect to a sharp decrease in the purchase of hats and heavy coats. The fact that fewer women wear hats today is another indication of the trend toward casual dress. Again, in our protected winter atmosphere, lighter weight, all-purpose coats have replaced the heavier, interlined variety.

College students' wardrobes provide an interesting area of study from the standpoint of clothing expenditures. More homogeneous than the total male or female populations, college students also represent an age group which not only demands greater variety, but is the most sensitive of all population groups to style obsolescence. In recent years there has been a tremendous increase in the buying power of consumers between the ages of 18 and 21. The growing affluence of young adults in today's society is clearly and tangibly reflected in their clothing purchases.

Expenditures for clothing have kept pace with the rise in total consumption expenditures, in spite of the fact that the general trend has been toward more casual dress.

SUMMARY *Where the money goes*

In the last quarter of a century, annual expenditures for clothing have declined in relation to the sharp gains in disposable income for the population as a whole. For the last decade, however, American consumers have rather consistently spent about

10 per cent of all personal consumption expenditures for clothing, accessories, and jewelry. While dollar amounts spent for clothing have increased each year, prices in general have been inflationary, and although apparel prices have gone up, they have not increased as sharply as those of many other commodities.

Women's and children's wear accounts for a larger share of total expenditures for clothing than men's and boys'. The wardrobes of both men and women show the trend toward lighter-weight clothing, casual wear, and an increase in the "separate" items of apparel over the suits, coats, and dresses (especially the dressy or formal type). The textile and fashion trades catering to the young adult have expanded enormously.

Factors affecting demand

How much money consumers are able and willing to spend on clothing depends not only on prices and income, but also upon a number of factors outside the economy which have their origin in political, social, and cultural forces. The reader may find it helpful at this point to review quickly the summaries in Chapter 6 that deal with the relationship between sociocultural trends and fashion change, because some of those same trends have particular relevance to the current economic situation.

Diffusion of income

One important factor that influences our expenditures for apparel is the amount of money that we have available. The unprecedented increase in personal and family income in the last thirty years has resulted in a tremendous growth of the middle-income class of Americans. In 1950, less than a quarter of all families in the United States earned more than $5,000 a year. Today, more than 80 per cent have incomes at or above this level, and almost 50 per cent earn $10,000 or more (Table 19-6). Obviously much of this increase in income level has been purely inflationary, but there is considerable evidence that America's wealth is also becoming more equally distributed. Before the 1940's, the 1 per cent of the population at the very top of the economic bracket possessed almost 20 per cent of the nation's wealth; today, their share is less than 8 per cent.[2]

Another pattern these days that tends to equalize the money income is that young people tend to break away from the family and set up separate households. Formerly, most families had to pool their incomes to make ends meet. This shows up in the

---

[2]The inequality in income distribution was reduced markedly during the 1940's. The trend toward greater equality has continued, but at a slower rate. For a more thorough analysis of the dispersion of personal income, see Sanford Rose, "The Truth About Income Inequality in the U.S." *Fortune*, December 1972, p. 90.

census data as an increase in the number of households at the low end of the income spectrum, when actually these single-person households are not really as poor as their incomes would indicate. As indicated earlier, there is also a growing number of women in the work force, and the American working girl — married or single — spends about a quarter of her income on clothes. In short, the mass market has shifted upward from the bottom of the economic scale to the middle; the exclusive market, once reserved for the economically and socially elite, has trickled downward. American secretaries are probably better dressed than most of Europe's upper crust.

TABLE 19-6 PER CENT DISTRIBUTION OF MONEY INCOME
BY INCOME CATEGORIES, 1950–1970

Money Income	Percentage of All Families		
	1950	1960	1970
Under $3,000	42.5%	21.7%	8.9%
$3,000 to $4,999	34.3	20.3	10.4
$5,000 to $9,999	20.0	43.7	31.7
$10,000 to $14,999	} 3.3	10.6	26.8
$15,000 and over		3.7	22.3

Source: *Statistical Abstract of the United States*, 1972.

Closely linked to the dispersion of wealth and high employment is the trend toward shorter working hours and paid vacations. This has contributed immeasurably to an increased taste for travel, a growing participation in sports, and the switch to more casual dress.

For the largest segment of the American population, the dispersion of wealth has lead to the gradual elimination of dress differences between adjacent socioeconomic groups. Strictly speaking, the families at either end of the economic scale may be considered minority groups in the sense that they represent increasingly smaller segments of the population. The discussion of our rising level of consumption may seem to obscure the fact that we still have sizeable numbers of people who cannot afford mink coats and $500 dresses. There are some in the low-income bracket who cannot afford the purchase of any new clothing. There is, however, an important source of apparel other than that found on the racks and shelves of the typical retail store, and this relates to the acquisition of second-hand merchandise. In a society such as ours where the average income is high, many articles of clothing are discarded by the original owners before they are worn out, and subsequently acquired by other individuals. This process of filtering is widely recognized in the housing field. When upper-income families trade up or move to more modern facilities, their vacated unit becomes available to someone else. Second-hand automobiles are also commonly accepted as reusable items.

There seems to be considerable evidence that used-clothing sales are rapidly growing in number. Rummage sales and clothesline sales are fairly common throughout the cities of the United States. Not all purchases of used clothing are made by low-income families either. There are thrift houses in some of the larger cities that sell second-hand ball gowns and mink coats.

The expanded use of consumer credit also makes clothing accessible to those who do not have the ready cash, and in part accounts for the fact that America has the "best-dressed poverty" in the world.

Population shifts

We have already noted the rapid gains in the total population of the United States. Obviously, as the number of people increases, the need for clothing also increases. But just as important as the per capita figures are those statistics which relate to composition of the population. The baby boom of the late 1940's and 1950's created a population bulge at the lower end of the age scale. As these babies grew to maturity during the sixties and seventies, the clothing market expanded accordingly, since this is the age group that represents the most clothes-buying, style-conscious segment of society. The proportion of 15- to 24-year-olds will peak in the decade of the seventies, while the groups that feed into this prime market will actually decrease as a result of the declining birth rate.

By 1980, the "boom babies" will be in their early thirties, and by 1990, in their forties. Thus, the age group from 25 to 34 will show the greatest increase of all population shifts in 1980 (3.8 per cent). The youth market is expected to decrease proportionately (see Figure 19-5).

The youth market of the 1960's and 1970's had a tremendous impact on the clothing market as a whole. Young people had money to spend, and their tastes influenced all other segments of the market—young adults, parents, and older people. Recent studies seem to indicate that stage in the life cycle may be an even more important determinant of consumer behavior than social class distinctions.[3] The young shoppers of the last decade have turned into the young marrieds with small children, and they currently provide the bulk of the business in the large chains and discount stores. Shoppers over age 40, especially those with no children, tend to prefer the department store for many of their clothing purchases.

Another factor that will continue to influence future expenditures for clothing is the decreasing family size. Families with fewer children and higher incomes have more money available for discretionary areas of spending. The rural population is also diminishing. In the 1940's, clothing purchases made by farm families were about half as great as those of city families. Today, even those who live in isolated areas are familiar with

---

[3]S. U. Rich and S. C. Jain, "Social Class and Life Cycle as Predictors of Shopping Behavior," in A. P. Govoni, *Contemporary Marketing Research*, General Learning Corporation, Morristown, N.J., 1972.

Ages 14 and under

Ages 15-19

Ages 20-24

Ages 25-34

Ages 35-64

Ages 65+

Percent of Total Population

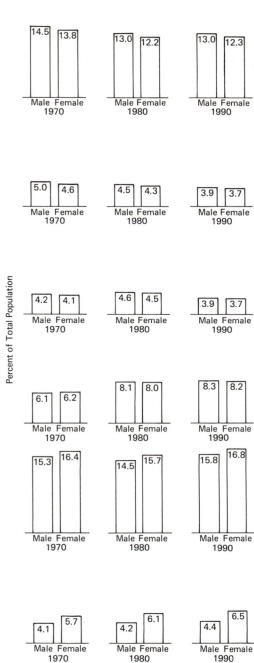

	1970	1980	1990
	Male 14.5 Female 13.8	Male 13.0 Female 12.2	Male 13.0 Female 12.3
	Male 5.0 Female 4.6	Male 4.5 Female 4.3	Male 3.9 Female 3.7
	Male 4.2 Female 4.1	Male 4.6 Female 4.5	Male 3.9 Female 3.7
	Male 6.1 Female 6.2	Male 8.1 Female 8.0	Male 8.3 Female 8.2
	Male 15.3 Female 16.4	Male 14.5 Female 15.7	Male 15.8 Female 16.8
	Male 4.1 Female 5.7	Male 4.2 Female 6.1	Male 4.4 Female 6.5

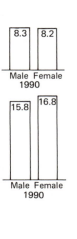

Figure 19-5. Population distribution by age and sex, 1970, 1980, 1990.

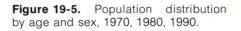

urban tastes and habits, and the characteristic differences between urban and rural groups is fast disappearing.

Exogenous forces

Changes in income and population statistics have a rather obvious relationship to economic activity, but clothing consumption patterns are also affected by a variety of non-economic trends, such as education, lifestyle, the consumers' general mood, and changing values. In a study of demographic variables related to family clothing expenditures, Daub[4] found that education of the family head had the greatest relative importance to the proportion of family income spent for clothing. The dispersion of wealth combined with an increasing level of education gradually results in a cultural sophistication that makes a more discriminating shopper out of the average consumer. This often means upgraded tastes and a greater demand for individuality in design.

Many observers of the social scene believe that the demand for individuality is at the root of the current revival of handcrafts in this, the world's most industrialized nation. The resurgence of home sewing and needlecrafts has been phenomenal. Retail sales of fabric, notions, patterns, and sewing machines jumped from $1,950 million to $3,250 million in the short period from 1969 to 1972. While a few people will tell you they sew to save money, it is clear that these sales have enhanced rather than diminished the volume of business in the textiles and clothing industry as a whole.

The degree of confidence that consumers feel about their economic situation is quickly reflected in their buying habits. Experienced retailers know that in periods of recession one of the earliest bellwethers is a drop in the sale of dresses. "A healthy dress business," says one store owner, "means that women expect their husbands to take them out more."[5] If clothes on the racks in second-hand stores are more than five years old, it is usually a sign that people are hanging on to their clothing rather than getting rid of old fashions and buying new ones. Many will claim this is a sure sign of hard times.

In earlier chapters we discussed how shifts in values alter lifestyles, and these same trends affect the relative importance we place on certain economic factors, such as the price and the desirability of other goods, goals, and services that compete for the clothing dollar. Another example of how social values can influence economic decisions relates to our growing preoccupation with the quality of our physical environment. The textiles industry is particularly affected by the demands to control the pollution of lakes and streams into which their effluent flows.

---

[4]K. E. Daub, "Demographic Variables and Family Clothing Expenditures," Master's thesis, Purdue University, 1968.
[5]"Indicators: Forecasting Self-Taught," *Time*, 3 April 1972, p. 23.

But such control is extremely costly. Some industries will be able to pass the cost of pollution control on to the consumer by raising prices, but others in highly competitive areas (especially those affected by imports) will be forced to absorb much of these "social costs" by reducing capital investments and profits. These new concerns with the environment could ultimately lead to a renunciation of economic growth as a national goal.[6] Consumers will have the inherent ability to decide whether the benefits derived from these kinds of controls are worth it. Just as we might ask if Americans would give up the automobile in exchange for cleaner air, we could ask if Americans would give up clothes in return for cleaner water.

Changes in consumer values, tastes, and living habits force continual adjustments in the clothing industry.

SUMMARY *Factors affecting demand*

In addition to the price/cost relationships discussed in the previous sections, socioeconomic trends that influence consumer expenditures for clothing include (1) the unprecedented increase in personal income coupled with a greater dispersion of wealth throughout the various segments of the population; (2) the overall growth in population which increases needs, plus the changes in age mix and family size; and (3) the exogenous forces of the consumer's education, lifestyle, and changing values. All of these factors require constant adjustments on the part of fabric producers, apparel manufacturers, and fashion retailers to match changing consumer demands.

Consumer sovereignty and responsibility

Unconscious and irrational though it may be, the motivation underlying most of our fashion purchases cannot be explained in terms of dictates by the fashion industry and helplessness on the part of the consumer. Fashion history is replete with styles promoted by designers and publicists that never got to first base on the consumer's popularity list. Whether we realize it or not, our behavior in the marketplace contributes to an economic decision that is reached by the multiple choices of millions of individual consumers acting independently. The choices we make as consumers thus affect not only our own welfare, but the welfare of our neighbors as well; they also help to shape the character of our economy on a local, national, and worldwide basis.

The collective aspects of consumption

The individual consumer casts a ballot in the marketplace every time he makes a clothing purchase. The records of daily and weekly sales kept by the local retail store constitute the election

---

[6]G. Bylinsky, "The Mounting Bill for Pollution Control," *Fortune*, July 1971, p. 86.

returns from one precinct. Let us say that the local merchant has stocked a small quantity of velour stretch knits, and suddenly he finds they are selling like hotcakes in men's sweater-shirts and women's sportswear. The retailer goes back to the apparel manufacturer and orders more. The phenomenon is seldom restricted to one store, and if you multiply the reorders by the hundreds of retailers that may buy from one manufacturer, you get some idea of the volume of information that is channeled back to the maker in regard to consumer acceptance of his product. If a style has no reorders, chances are it will be found on the markdown racks in a number of stores, and both the producer and the retailer will have learned their lesson. The flow of information goes further than the garment maker. If the manufacturers order more stretch velour from the knitting mills, the fabric producers will have to order more nylon and cotton yarns, and so on all the way back to the fiber producers.

It is through this process that the collective power of the consumer is felt throughout the industry. The articles that we purchase (as well as those that we refuse to buy) give tangible evidence of our acceptance or rejection of style, quality, color, fabric, fit, and/or price. The final result, though not immediate and direct, is that the collective behavior of individual consumers has a tremendous influence on the character of the merchandise that will appear on the market the following season. In most cases, the consumer's reaction is automatic and unconscious. Sometimes, however, he is asked for a direct opinion. Much of the early research conducted by home economists in the area of textiles and clothing related to consumer preference studies, and this continues to be an important area of investigation. One such study surveyed over 400 men in regard to their favorite and least-liked shirts. Women were also interviewed about their favorite garments, and subjects in each case were asked to explain their preferences. Women rated appearance over comfort, and said that the most important reason for dressing attractively was to boost their morale. The majority of the men, however, referred most frequently to the temperature and absorbency features of the fabric.[7]

These kinds of findings have rather obvious implications for the fabric and apparel producers. In the case of shirt fabrics, for example, the textiles people went to work trying to find the right blend of fibers and fabric construction that would yield a maximum of comfort with good wash-and-wear characteristics. The very core of motivational research is to find out what consumers want, and then to design a product that will meet their desires.

_____

[7]_Consumer Satisfaction with Men's Shirts and with Women's Slips and Casual Street Dresses_, Bulletin #984, Cornell University Agricultural Experiment Station, New York State College of Home Economics, Ithaca, N.Y., July 1963.

Today, even retailers seek the opinions of their customers. Many stores sponsor high-school or college fashion boards that bring in young people to react to new styles and predicted trends, and the manufacturers and retailers who are really on their toes actually encourage consumer complaints. It pays them to find out what is wrong with their merchandise. All too often consumer dissatisfaction is politely ignored by the consumer himself, and the real cause is never identified.

Consumer rights and responsibility

In Chapter 17 we talked about industry responsibility; here we shall discuss consumer responsibility. In the past few years, interest in consumer welfare has become a growing concern for both business and government. Consumer "rights" have been described as the right to safety, the right to be informed, the right to choose, and the right to be heard. The implementation of such a philosophy calls for effective communication between consumers in general and the industry.

Bona fide complaints should be made to the store, to the manufacturer, or to other appropriate groups when the merchandise does not give satisfactory service. Otherwise, the manufacturer may never know that his product is not meeting consumer expectations. It is also helpful to praise businessmen when they improve their products or their services so that they may know what it is that pleases you. Let him know, too, if there are things you want that he does not carry. He may be happy to stock them if he is aware of the demand.

The most effective way to register consumer opinion about clothing merchandise (or any other type of merchandise for that matter) is to write to the consumer relations department of the store in which the garment was purchased (a typed letter usually receives more attention than a handwritten one). State the facts clearly, without exaggeration or sarcasm, and explain exactly what is wrong with the article. If the store is a small, independently-owned specialty shop, address your complaint to the owner. If there is a manufacturer's label in the garment, write to him directly and send a carbon copy to the retailer. Voicing consumer opinion is just as important as going to the polls to vote.

The old business motto, "The customer is always right," has been used so often that even the customer has come to believe it. It is easy to assume that when a consumer is dissatisfied, the culprit must be either the manufacturer or the retailer. Certainly the seller is at fault if he misrepresented his goods, either by practicing deliberate deception, taking advantage of the buyer's ignorance, or being ignorant himself about the quality of his product. The buyer, however, also may be at fault by failing to state his needs accurately, failing to ask questions, not really knowing what he is looking for, or neglecting to follow the manufacturer's directions for use and care. The woman who demands an adjustment on a cashmere sweater because it shrank out of fit is abusing her privilege if she washed the sweater in hot water and tumble-dried it in the machine.

Comparison shopping should be done before you make a purchase, not after. If you buy a blouse and then find another down the street that you like better, you have no reason to expect the retailer to refund your money cheerfully. Remember, too, that the attitude with which you approach the salesperson will determine to a large extent the treatment that you will receive. State your wishes in a pleasant manner, and be conscious of your mood when shopping.

As a consumer, you should also be aware of market conditions and problems. When particular commodities are scarce, stockpiling goods will only help to bring about inflationary prices. Buying according to your normal needs will work to the benefit of the largest number of people.

There is a dual approach to good citizenship in the market economy of our nation. One is to educate ourselves not only to be discriminating shoppers, but to have a broad social intelligence about economic problems. The other is to develop an interest in the affairs of the consumer and take an active role in organized movements that work toward the betterment of consumer welfare. Participation in consumer cooperatives, credit unions, and buying clubs not only helps us to get more for our money, but helps us to understand what is going on in business. The government has already taken action on the needs of the consumer. In 1962, a National Consumer Advisory Council was established by the President. This was followed by the appointment of a President's Committee on Consumer Interests and a Special Assistant to the President on Consumer Affairs. The consumer will find it advantageous to keep informed of their activities, and cooperate with government and business in finding better solutions to common problems.

Improved choice making

It is estimated that seven out of ten buyers are habit shoppers, that is, they buy in the same manner, over and over again without much conscious attention to how they are doing it. The production and marketing of quality merchandise at fair prices becomes the responsibility of manufacturers and retailers, but both will supply what the consumer demands.

A satisfactory wardrobe is dependent not so much upon the amount of money that is spent as it is upon careful planning. The basic assumption underlying intelligent decision making is that the individual knows what he wants or needs. The teenager who claims she "needs" a new sweater, when she already has seventeen in her wardrobe, appears on the surface at least not to be able to recognize the difference between a "need" and a "desire." A rational choice of clothing is predicated upon an honest evaluation of why we want the things that we do. The basic difference between *needs* and *desires* may be illustrated by our physiological need for protection against the cold. People satisfy this need in a variety of ways. The Eskimo keeps warm by wearing an undershirt of caribou skin. The Mongol wears a long sheepskin gown that covers the hands, and boots several sizes too large to permit the use of fur socks in winter. The Englishman is apt to wrap a long wool muffler around his neck and increase his activity by a brisk walk. Thick woolen stockings and warm boots are efficient insulators for the legs and feet in winter climates, but the majority of American women prefer to shiver in sheer nylon hose and thin pumps. Most people prefer the things to which they have become accustomed.

Our needs, of course, are not limited to the physiological. We have a variety of social and emotional needs that must also be satisfied in some way. For some people, clothing satisfies the need for creative self-expression. For others, it provides social status and prestige. Still others value the social approval and the feeling of belonging that can be achieved through dress.

Our desires increase as we are exposed to a greater variety of goods. Eskimos who know nothing but animal skins as a medium for clothing usually want nothing else, but through increasing contact with the white man's culture, many are coming to prefer jackets made from synthetics, or rubber boots, even though such clothing may be decidedly inferior to their traditional parkas and mukluks. Most Americans today are familiar with a wide variety of styles and materials, and the mere knowledge of such products tends to expand our desire for greater variety in our wardrobes.

The fact that our wants change over a period of time sometimes causes us to be dissatisfied with the clothes that we already have in our wardrobes, even though when purchased, they may have fulfilled the same basic needs. Desires, moreover, are not usually equal in importance. Everyone — to some extent at least — wants clothing to do a number of things: keep them warm, make them more attractive, help them to feel part of a group, give them individuality, provide aesthetic satisfaction. Not all of these wants have the same value to the individual, and some of them may even be in conflict. Some wants must be satisfied immediately, others can be postponed for the future. It may be very important to be warm now and attractive later.

For all of these reasons, desires are often not very clearly defined, and people frequently have little understanding of what it is they really want. Everyone needs some experience in verbalizing his desires and consciously evaluating them in order to make rational choices in the selection of clothing. While our needs may be satisfied in a number of alternate ways, it is rarely possible to achieve all of our desires.

Our clothing needs and desires are determined by the kind of life we choose to lead. There is really no average individual, because each person has a unique set of requirements that are bound to influence his clothing purchases. Income, occupation, social participation, the climate in which we live, the way we spend our leisure time, our style of living—all of these factors affect the logic of a clothing decision for a particular individual.

The term **standard of living** usually is used to designate the way people believe they should live or want to live. It includes all of the goods and services that an individual or family considers important, along with some beliefs about the way in which the goods should be used. For some families, this might involve a comfortable home, abundant food, practical and suitable clothing, a new car, camping gear, a yearly vacation, adequate medical care, protective insurance, and a number of other wants that individuals in the family may have. Through the use of such goods, people may hope to achieve the ultimate satisfactions of physical health and comfort, happiness, leisure, beauty, order, prestige, success—in short, the goals they regard as worth striving for.

It is not just the possession of certain kinds of goods that people desire, but the way in which they would like to use them that also determines the standard of living. Some people, for example, eat dinner in the same clothes that they have been wearing all day. Others look forward to getting out of their work or business dress and putting on something comfortable. Still others believe in bathing and changing into dinner suits and dresses. One person may think a garment should be worn until it develops a hole or a tear and should then be tossed out. Someone else may take the time and the effort to repair or mend clothing and continue to enjoy its use.

Few people have the resources to achieve all of their wants. Their **level of living** is different from their standard of living in the same way that what we want is different from what we actually have. As we make progress toward our goals, our level of living gets closer and closer to our standard of living, although by the time the standard is approached, we have usually learned about other things that we want, so that the standard continually moves ahead of the level.

Level of consumption is still another term used to describe people's living conditions, but it refers only to the actual consumption of goods rather than the way people feel about what they use. Frequently we talk about a family or a society as having a "high standard of living," when actually all that we can observe is their level of consumption. A standard of living cannot be accurately defined by anyone outside the group itself, because outsiders do not really know how the individual or the family regards its possessions. We may think that a person has a low standard of living because he wears shabby clothes and drives an old car, but such an evaluation is more a reflection of our own standards than the standards of the individual we are observing.

This discussion of standards is pertinent here because standards greatly influence the clothes that we choose. Standards probably first develop from the family in which we grow up, where we learn how children "ought" to dress for school, and how people "should" dress when they go to church, or to the grocery store, or out to play. Beyond this, standards evolve from actual use of goods. For instance, if we have had a sad experience with nylon shirts that were uncomfortable to wear and became gray and dingy with washing, we would probably not want to buy another nylon shirt. But if we received many flattering comments while wearing the blue sweater, we might tend to select other blue garments, and our partiality to blue may even extend to items besides clothes.

A rational approach to choice making is suggested in this section. It is not intended to imply that wearing apparel should always be chosen on the basis of its quality or durability. These factors have a place of relative importance among the other criteria of comfort, appearance, fashion value, maintenance requirements, status or social significance, and price. Some of these factors will always rate higher than others in the value patterns of individual consumers. For most people, however, the weighing of criteria will be slightly different in every situation. Few brides would choose their wedding gowns with comfort, durability, and ease of care as the prime considerations. And it would take a vain person indeed to choose all of his clothing solely on the basis of appearance.

The purpose is not to dictate what values the consumer should have, but to replace haphazard, impulsive buying with conscious, intelligent, and informed behavior. Throughout our discussion we have referred to numerous agencies, groups, and laws intended to protect the consumer from fraudulent practices and inferior merchandise, but no one else can make our decisions for us, and no amount of legislation will ever replace the perceptive consumer. If the customer is sure of what he wants, if he is reasonably well informed, if he asks intelligent questions, and if he makes the best judgment he knows how to make, his satisfactions as a consumer of clothing will be greatly increased. Above all, he must be cognizant of how his actions and decisions affect the total economy.

Consumer behavior is a controlling factor in determining the character of goods that appear on the market. A rational approach to clothing needs and expenditures makes the consumer a more effective participant in the entire market economy.

SUMMARY *Consumer sovereignty and responsibility*

The feedback from individual consumers to all segments of the clothing industry takes place through the retailer and his daily record of sales and reorders. Every clothing purchase that we make is a ballot cast for the continued production of similar kinds of merchandise. Learning to voice individual opinion in an effective manner is an important contribution that the consumer can make to the clothing industry as a whole.

FOR FURTHER READING

Anspach, Karlyne. *The Why of Fashion*. Ames, Iowa: The Iowa State University Press, 1967. (Chapter 8, "A Uniform Package.")

Britt, Steuart H. *Consumer Behavior and the Behavioral Sciences: Theories and Applications*. New York: John Wiley & Sons, 1966.

Gaedeke, R. M. and W. W. Etcheson. *Consumerism—Viewpoints from Business, Government, and the Public Interest*. San Francisco: Canfield Press, 1972.

Ryan, Mary S. *Clothing: A Study in Human Behavior*. New York: Holt, Rinehart & Winston, 1966. (Part Two, "Social-Psychological Aspects of the Individual as a Consumer of Textiles and Clothing.")

Troelstrup, Arch W. *The Consumer in American Society*. New York: McGraw-Hill Book Company, 1970.

DISCUSSION QUESTIONS

1. American consumers spend more total dollars every year for apparel and upkeep, yet they spend less proportionately for clothes than they did twenty years ago. How can you account for this?

2. In what ways do population shifts affect the clothing market?

3. What is meant by "exogenous forces" in the economy? Give two or three examples and explain their effect on consumer demand for clothing.

4. Explain how a shortage of raw materials influences the price of clothing. Give examples.

5. Compare the responsibilities of industry (from Chapter 17) with the responsibilities of the consumer. In what ways has the government picked up a share of the consumer's responsibility?

6. How can an independent clothing choice on the part of one consumer influence the character of goods that appear on the apparel market?

7. Give a hypothetical example of how each of the following factors may affect our pattern of clothing consumption: (a) needs, (b) desires, (c) standard of living, and (d) level of living.

PART SIX

Acquisition and Use of Clothing

20

The Informed Consumer

INTELLIGENT consumer choice is a fundamental problem for people in almost all modern societies, but it becomes an even more complex process in a country such as ours where goods are abundant and the number of alternatives increases each year. The quality of living achieved by any society as a whole is dependent largely upon the way in which the individual consumer casts his ballot in the marketplace. Clothing is but one of the many goods and services that must be provided for in the average household, but through its study we can clarify our wants and needs to become more effective managers of our personal and family incomes and more intelligent users of our nation's resources.

Planning clothing expenditures

Analysis of clothing requirements

One tangible way to get started on the analysis of clothing requirements is to list the kinds of activities in which we engage on a daily or weekly basis, and then those in which we participate less frequently. A listing such as this helps people to see the type of clothing that is worn most often. Most people find greater rewards in spending the bulk of their clothing budget for garments that are used regularly, and less on the items that are seldom worn.

Once our clothing needs are identified, we can then evaluate the articles of clothing already on hand that are suitable for the activities listed. One way of doing this is to list all items of clothing owned currently, along with an estimate of the need for yearly replacement (see Appendices A, B, C, D, and E). A wardrobe inventory is a practical exercise for a number of reasons. It is not only a logical step in planning future clothing purchases, but it forces the individual to weed out and discard items that are never worn, or no longer suitable. It also shows what proportion of the total family income goes for apparel and upkeep.

The wardrobe can then be checked against the activity list. Many items will be suitable for a number of occasions, particularly if they are basic in design. Some activities, however, will require specialized clothing. A uniform may be required for work, and participation in sports such as skiing, swimming, riding, and so forth, may call for garb that is more or less restricted in its use.

Annual additions or replacements of clothing can be determined by the difference between clothing requirements and clothing already on hand. In addition to needed replacements, the inventory will show those items that tend to be overstocked. Further investment in categories of clothing that are already in full supply is a questionable practice. The cost of each new article that is desired should be estimated as closely as possible so that an overall plan may be developed in which the total cost of all items is anticipated. Unsatisfactory purchases are often made because we see something at a bargain and buy impulsively. A bargain is never a bargain, whatever the cost, unless the garment has a purpose and fits into an overall plan. Impulse buying is a threat toward overspending and a poorly coordinated wardrobe. Few people are in a position to buy a completely new wardrobe at one time, but planning ahead will enable a person to take advantage of the sales when they come along, and still buy the things that are needed.

How much to spend

The percentage of the total family income spent on clothing varies considerably, although families in general spend an increasing proportion for apparel as incomes progress from low- to middle-income levels (see Table 19-4). American families as a whole spend about 10 per cent of their disposable incomes on clothing, accessories, and jewelry, and almost another 2 per cent on personal care (see Table 20-1).

Looking at it another way, we might consider the average expenditure for clothing per capita and the proportion of one's total personal consumption that it represents (see Table 20-2).

Most college students spend a higher percentage of their income for clothing than the average figure indicated in Table 20-2. Knowing how much you have to spend, regardless of the actual amount, will result in a better wardrobe plan. If the list of wants greatly exceeds the purchasing power available, the wants must be reevaluated in light of the most urgently needed items. Sometimes a basic design will serve more than one purpose and thus extend the wardrobe at little additional cost. If one's purchasing power actually exceeds the list of wants, it

TABLE 20-1 CONSUMER EXPENDITURES

	Percentage of Total Expenditures		
	1950	1960	1970
Food, beverages, tobacco	30.4	26.9	23.2
Household operations	15.4	14.4	13.9
Housing	11.1	14.2	14.8
Transportation	12.9	13.3	12.6
Clothing, accessories, and jewelry	12.4	10.2	10.1
Medical care	4.6	5.9	7.7
Personal business	3.6	4.6	5.8
Recreation	5.8	5.6	6.3
Personal care	1.3	1.6	1.6
Education and research	0.8	1.1	1.7
Religion and welfare	1.2	1.5	1.4
Foreign travel	0.3	0.7	0.8

Source: *Statistical Abstract of the United States, 1972.*

TABLE 20-2 AVERAGE EXPENDITURES FOR CLOTHING, ACCESSORIES, AND JEWELRY

Year	Expenditures Per Capita in Dollars	Per cent of Personal Consumption Expenditures
1950	$188	12.4
1960	178	10.2
1970	235	10.1

Source: *Statistical Abstract of the United States, 1972.*

may be possible to trade up in quality on some of the planned purchases. Investment in a better grade of merchandise often extends the wear life of a garment, and it can add immeasurably to the distinctiveness of the wardrobe.

Sources of clothing

People sometimes forget that the outright purchase of new ready-to-wear items on the retail market is not the only way that clothing may be provided. Many usable garments are passed on in good condition from one member of a family to another, or from one family to another. In some cases such clothing is actually of a better quality than the individual might be able to purchase for himself, and with minor adjustments in fit or design, may be suitably adapted to the needs of the new owner. Gifts are also an important source of new clothing, although like the passed-on items, they may not always fit perfectly into the wardrobe plan.

The purchase of used clothing can be a very satisfactory way to obtain garments for a particular purpose without investing a great deal of money. Children's clothes that are quickly outgrown are common items on the used-clothing market, and many good values can be found. Those people with creative sewing talents can often find garments of excellent quality that can be updated to conform to the current fashion through simple renovation. Some shops in particular receive clothing from individuals with large expensive wardrobes who dispose of garments after very little wear.

Home sewing, of course, continues to be an important source of clothing for many individuals and families. In 1973, Americans spent over $3 billion on fabric, patterns, notions, and sewing machines.[1] The desire to save money is probably an important incentive to home sewing. A study of costs made a number of years ago indicated that even inexpensive daytime dresses and children's wear could be made at home at about half the cost of comparable garments sold at retail.[2] The real question, however, is whether or not the time spent in home sewing could be used more lucratively in other endeavors. An analysis of the wardrobe inventories of a group of college girls revealed that those who made most of their clothing at home had much greater variety in their wardrobes, but they did not spend less money. As a matter of fact, annual expenditures of students who made their own clothes were in many cases considerably higher than the average expenditures for the class as a whole.

Some families may pay a local seamstress or tailor to make their clothes. For those with special fitting problems or unique tastes, custom work or home sewing may provide the only satisfactory means of obtaining the desired clothing. When the cost of labor is added to the cost of materials, however, this usually turns out to be an expensive method of obtaining new articles. Especially when the clothing budget is limited, all sources of clothing should be considered for their relative value in meeting needs and desires.

Where to buy

Even if the decision is to buy ready-to-wear clothing in the retail store, the consumer is still faced with a number of alternatives. As we noted in Chapter 17, department stores, specialty shops, variety and chain stores, discount and mail-order houses all offer the customer different shopping advantages. Through the process of comparison shopping, the customer should be

---

[1]"Report from the Home-Sewing Front," *American Fabrics*, Spring/Summer 1973, p. 56.
[2]Margaret L. Brew and Carol M. Jaeger, *Exploratory Studies of Measuring Money Savings and Time Costs of Homemade Clothing*, U.S. Department of Agriculture, Washington, D.C. (ARS 62-8), August 1958.

able to find the store (or stores) at which he can find the type of merchandise that he wants at a price that he is willing to pay. The buyer should be conscious of several factors in the selection of a clothing store.

The **range of merchandise** offered for sale is one important consideration. A store may sell suits beginning at $75 and ranging upward, while another retailer may not carry any item priced higher than $50. A customer can lose a good deal of time looking through merchandise that is not within his price range. Some stores also specialize in a restricted line of styles and sizes.

The **types of service** provided by a store should also be evaluated. Efficient and courteous salespeople, delivery service, charge accounts, gift wrapping, and return privileges are all beneficial to the customer, but they add to the cost of actual purchases. Some people prefer to shop in a store that has a pleasant atmosphere and attractive surroundings. To them, the shopping environment itself constitutes an added value for which they are willing to pay.

Convenience in shopping is a significant factor if the shopper considers his time to be valuable. One's ability or willingness to travel distances in order to buy at a particular store depends not only on the time available, but upon the cost of transportation. Mail-order houses offer the convenience of shopping at home, which in effect saves both travel time and cost.

The **business practices** of the store or retailer should also be studied carefully. One can learn a great deal by checking merchandise against a store's advertising to see if information has been presented honestly and accurately. An intelligent consumer who knows how to judge quality usually can tell if salespeople are truthful and competent in the presentation of their merchandise. A retailer who is willing to stand behind his goods is the best protection a consumer can find against tricky or unfair dealings.

The consumer must always remember that by patronizing a particular kind of store, he is giving his vote to one group of merchants over another. By giving your business to unprincipled competitors, you make it more difficult for the reliable merchants to survive.

When to buy

Another advantage of a wardrobe plan is that it enables the consumer to shop the sales. If one can anticipate the year's clothing needs, garments can often be purchased at the end of a season at considerable savings. The percentage of the markdown should always be considered in light of the store's profit margin. Higher-priced stores may have an original markup anywhere from 35 to 50 per cent. Obviously, "one-third off" sales in this type of store would not be as much of a bargain as

a 20-per-cent reduction in a store that operated on a 20- to 25-per cent margin.

Clearance sales usually offer the biggest price reductions, and are held to get rid of the fashion items that have not moved. Clearance sales in men's and boys' wear are commonly held in January, and February is a good month for women's fashions, but end-of-season selling may take place any time after the demand has fallen off. Swimsuits, for example, can often be found at half price near the end of the summer. If one buys basic styles, or is familiar enough with the fashion cycle to gamble on styles that may be halfway through their fashion life, clearance sales offer good savings.

Annual sales generally do not afford the drastic reductions that are found in clearance sales, but they are considered more reliable because goods from regular stock go on sale for a short period of time. The purpose here is not so much to get rid of the merchandise as to attract customers to the store during a slack selling season. It is wise economy to wait for the annual sales to buy the staple items of dress, such as hosiery, underwear, men's white shirts, pajamas, and the like. Buying hosiery by the box instead of by the pair is always more economical because a sock will always have a mate until you get down to the last one.

Special purchase sales come about as the result of a special price reduction in the wholesale market for large lots of a particular item. The price reduction is usually better than the markdown in annual sales, but not as great as in clearance sales. The customer needs to be wary of some slight imperfection in special purchase merchandise that may detract from the value of the sale price.

Anniversary sales are most often storewide sales in which each department marks down a few items. Like annual sales, the anniversary sale is intended to stimulate business during the slack periods.

Obviously, no one can fill all their clothing needs through sale purchases, but if one plans ahead, considerable savings can be effected.

How to pay

The decision concerning when to buy is closely tied to the method of payment. Those who believe in the cash and carry system will buy only when the money is available, while others may use some type of credit plan either to take advantage of sales or to have the clothing on hand when it is the most useful. Since clothing is a commodity that earns no money for the buyer and is generally non-durable in nature, it is wiser to pay cash whenever possible.

Credit plans include the familiar **charge account**. Usually there is no service charge for open accounts that are billed at the end of the month. Some banks now issue credit cards that may be used in a number of stores, and the customer is billed once a month for all purchases. This type of credit is a convenience because it eliminates the necessity of carrying large amounts of cash, and the monthly statements provide a valuable record of purchases. As long as the charge account is used in such a way that it does not encourage overspending, it has certain decided advantages. **Revolving credit accounts** and **lay-away plans** are slightly different in that they usually involve a service charge. Revolving plans establish a maximum credit level, and the customer has from six months to a year to pay for his purchases. In using the lay-away plan, the buyer makes a small deposit to hold the merchandise until he has the full purchase price of the article.

Installment buying differs from the various types of charge accounts by making a small down payment at the time of the initial purchase and agreeing to make regular payments until the balance is cleared. The customer has the use of the merchandise while he is paying for it, but the failure to meet one installment often means that the merchandise is repossessed by the store, and the consumer loses all of his investment. Whenever it seems necessary to purchase clothing on an installment basis, the individual should be thoroughly aware of how much extra he is paying for the privilege of deferring payment, as well as what will happen if payments are not made promptly. Installment buying is usually very expensive in terms of the interest rates that are paid, and it should be avoided if possible. Clothing may very easily be worn out before it is paid for, and the individual finds himself in debt for something he can no longer use.

Preparation for shopping

Learning to recognize quality and good workmanship in clothing is an essential part of the consumer's education. A buyer should be well informed before going into the market if he expects to get full value for his clothing dollar. Strange as it may seem, the people who shop the market, compare values, and look for the best buys are usually those with a fairly high standard of living. Studies have shown that low-income families tend to restrict their shopping to one store, and favor the well-known brand names that are often priced at the high end of the line. Susceptibility to over-selling on the part of salespeople is greatly reduced when the customer is fortified with facts.

Recognizing quality

Assuming that a garment meets the needs of the shopper in terms of its style, color, and fashion appeal, and fits into the wardrobe plan, a further examination of its true value should be made before buying. The following five points should be checked in judging the serviceability of a fabric.

Fiber content

A knowledge of the fiber content will help the consumer anticipate the care that will be required and help to determine whether the garment will be suited to its end use. This implies that the individual is sufficiently informed to be able to relate the generic name of a fiber to a particular set of fiber properties or characteristics. Nylon, for example, is a very strong, long-wearing fiber with high elasticity and low absorbency. It washes easily, dries quickly, and requires little pressing. Socks made from nylon will hold their shape and resist holing. Because of their low absorbency, however, they may not be particularly comfortable to wear in warm weather. Cotton may be a better choice for summer, and wool would be warmer in winter.

Learning fiber properties is not difficult if one knows how to group them properly. Cellulose fibers (cotton, linen, rayon), for instance, have many characteristics in common; they tend to be highly absorbent, wrinkle easily unless chemically treated, and are subject to attack by mildew. Thermoplastic fibers on the other hand do not absorb moisture and tend to build up static electricity; but they are sturdy and light-weight, resist wrinkling, are usually dimensionally stable, and are resistant to moths and mildew. When the customer is unsure of fiber terminology, he must rely on the manufacturer's label to supply information relating to performance and directions for use and care.

Yarn construction

Sometimes yarn construction limits the fabric's serviceability and dictates its care. Very loosely twisted yarns may pick up soil more readily and fuzz or pill on the surface. Highly twisted yarns such as those used in crepe fabrics, are subject to excessive shrinkage.

Fabric construction

Whether the fabric is woven or knitted, laminated or bonded, further determines its wearing qualities. Open-weave fabrics in which the yarns are widely spaced usually snag easily and do not hold their shape as well as those with a higher thread count. Loose weaves often fray badly in the seams and pull out around buttonholes. Knitted fabrics have greater elasticity than woven fabrics and conform to the shape of the body, but, by the same token, they have less dimensional stability and may bag, sag, or stretch. Pliable fabrics are sometimes bonded to a lining fabric or laminated to urethane foam. Their shape-retaining qualities are then about as good as the backing material.

Colorfastness

The label should carry some assurance that the color will hold up under light, washing, or dry cleaning. In certain types of garments, colorfastness to perspiration and to crocking (a rubbing off of color) should also be demanded.

Finish

Almost all fabrics today are finished in some way to improve their sales appeal or to impart certain functional features that increase the wearing qualities of the fabric. Most common perhaps are the wrinkle-resistant finishes that cut down on the maintenance required. There should be some guarantee that the fabric has been sufficiently relaxed in finishing that residual shrinkage is minimal (Sanforized fabrics, for example, are guaranteed to shrink less than 1 per cent). Water repellency, flame retardation, and a variety of aesthetic finishes (glazing, embossing, and others) are among the many treatments given fabrics to improve their serviceability or appearance. Such finishes should be durable enough to last the wear life of the garment.

Checking workmanship

Quality of construction is equally as important as the quality of the fabric. Good workmanship contributes to the durability of the garment and at the same time enhances its aesthetic appeal.

Cut

Pattern pieces should be cut from the fabric so that they hang grain-perfect on the figure. In most cases this means that the lengthwise threads are perpendicular, and crosswise threads parallel, to the floor. Fabric patterns, such as a stripe or plaid, should be carefully matched along the seam lines and pockets, and the pattern should be balanced on both sides of the figure.

Seams and stitching

Width of the seam allowances is another mark of quality. Skimpy seams usually mean that corners have been cut in other areas of construction as well. Wide seam allowances will lie flat, and allow for alterations if necessary. Machine stitching should be straight, with stitches small enough (about 12 to 15 to the inch) to prevent the seam from splitting open. On fabrics that fray badly, a seam finish more durable than pinking is desirable. Narrow seams on knit constructions should be pliable, and the raw edges should be overcast.

Buttonholes and fasteners

In women's wear, the better garments usually have bound buttonholes. These should be even in width and carefully finished on the side of the facing. In wash dresses and blouses, men's suits and shirts, buttonholes are worked or machine-made. Stitches should be close together and deep enough to keep them from pulling out. Buttons should be smooth so they will not abrade the edges of the buttonhole, and washable if the garment is washable. The quality of snaps, hooks and eyes, zippers, or other fasteners should be examined carefully.

Interfacings and linings

Interfacings are a means of giving body and shape retention through such areas as the collar and lapels, cuffs, and center-front closings. The material used should not be sleazy, and should be finished or tacked along the edges to prevent fraying or curling. Linings should be made with a firm weave, and be smooth enough to slide easily over other fabrics. Skirt linings are intended to take the strain from the outer fabric and should fit more closely than the outer layer. Linings cut fuller than the skirt merely add bulk or wrinkles.

Hems and other detail

A generous hem also allows for alterations and usually hangs better than a narrow one. Hems should be even in width and stitched inconspicuously to the garment. Other details such as reinforcements in the corners of pockets, even top-stitching, facings that lie flat, collars that cover the neckline seam, and edges that roll to conceal the facings are all indices of careful workmanship in a garment.

Analyzing the fit

A properly fitted garment will have adequate ease for movement, but it will hang free of wrinkles. It will not restrict or bind the figure, and in general it will be comfortable to wear. If a person has a figure that is difficult to fit, the cost of alterations should be figured into the total cost of the garment.

Making sound judgments

The intelligent consumer collects as much information as he can about the article he plans to buy in order to make the final choice as objectively as possible. There are a number of sources from which a clothing buyer may obtain such information.

Informative labels may state the performance characteristics of the garment (e.g., crease or stain resistant, Sanforized, and so forth) and give instructions for its care (machine wash, dry clean, drip dry). We may know from experience what to look for in fabric construction and workmanship, but neither the eye nor the fingers can tell us much about the quality of the finish, or how it will wash. Since manufacturers are now required by law to affix permanent care labels to all textile apparel products (refer back to Chapter 17, page 372), it becomes a relatively simple matter for the consumer to estimate the maintenance demands of a given article.

Brand names alone tell the customer very little about the performance he may expect from a garment. They do, however, help to identify a product which, through past experience, has proven to be a satisfactory article. Ranch hands and cowboys, for example, may find that Levis last longer than any other heavy denims or jeans, and it becomes easier to purchase by brand name than to make a judgment about quality when one is not sure whether the unfamiliar product will be as good. Manufacturers who sell under brand names or registered trademarks usually make an effort to keep the quality of their products fairly uniform and try to maintain a given standard.

Standards have been established by various groups to describe the minimum expectations desired in a textile or garment. The American Standards Association is one voluntary organization that has attempted to define the minimum performance requirements of textile fabrics for specific end uses, along with the designation of test methods to be used in the evaluation. Adherence to such standards is entirely voluntary, but manufacturers who do comply usually label their products with the test results and provide information relative to proper care and maintenance. The consumer may purchase products bearing the L-22 label (American Standards Performance Requirements for Textile Fabrics)[3] in the knowledge that they will give the service indicated.

Standardization for pattern sizes has also come about through the joint efforts of industry and the Departments of Commerce and Agriculture. Years ago getting a good fit was a serious problem because each manufacturer used his own system of sizing. Research on body measurements has resulted in a set of commercial standards for infants', children's, and girls' wear, boys' apparel, and four different categories of women's

---

[3]*American Standard L-22, Performance Requirements for Textile Fabrics, American Standards Association, New York, 1960.*

sizes (misses', women's, half-sizes, and juniors').[4] Use of the standards is still not mandatory, but many manufacturers, and mail-order companies in particular, have adopted the sizing system enthusiastically.

Advertising is another medium through which the customer can size up the integrity of the seller. A seller advertises in order to inform the public about his merchandise and to create an interest in buying it, but the information he presents should be accurate. The consumer must educate himself in recognizing misleading statements and false claims. Selling gimmicks such as "savings up to one-half," "made to sell for," "valued at twice the cost," or "priced elsewhere" are not accurate guides to the true value of the article. The terms "original price," which refers to the first price at which the garment sold, or "regular price," meaning the price before the current sale, are more helpful in determining the value of the buy being offered. Consumers should be wary of any emotional appeals in advertising that play on the ignorance of the less well-educated audiences. Again, it is the consumer's responsibility to check the accuracy of the seller's advertising, and refrain from patronizing those stores that engage in questionable practices.

Other sources of consumer information about clothing and textiles products include the American Home Economics Association; Consumers Research, Inc.; Consumers Union of the United States; the International Fabricare Institute, Inc.; the National Better Business Bureau; the National Retail Merchants' Association. Not to be overlooked are the many educational materials distributed by reputable commercial concerns, as well as U.S.D.A. publications and the many state and county extension bulletins that are available through your local Cooperative Extension office. It pays to remember that the consumer's judgment is no better than the information which he possesses.

Clothing maintenance

Consumer dissatisfaction is not always the result of defective or inferior merchandise. The wear life of a garment is dependent to a large extent upon the care that it receives. The proper care of clothing can actually mean a considerable savings in time and money.

General care

Garments will retain their shape longer if they are put on a hanger immediately after wearing and hung in a well-ventilated

---

[4]*Commercial Body Measurement Standards*, Office of Engineering Standards, Institute of Applied Technology, National Bureau of Standards, Washington, D.C.

place to air before storing. Closing zippers and buttoning front openings will help to hold the garment on the hanger and improve the shape retention. The accumulation of the day's dust and lint should be removed with a soft-bristled brush. Wooden or plastic hangers are usually better designed to conform to the shape of the shoulders than wire hangers from the cleaning plant. The latter sag under heavy garments and sometimes leave crease marks along the shoulder. Knitted articles should be stretched out flat to air or hung over the back of a chair before putting away in a drawer. Wear wrinkles can usually be removed from clothes by hanging them in a closed bathroom while running a hot shower or tub. This is preferable to pressing with an iron because overpressing may cause fabrics to glaze or shine. Just be sure there is ample time for the fabric to dry thoroughly before returning to the closet.

Since perspiration causes a breakdown in shoes, their wear life will be greatly extended if the feet are bathed daily, thoroughly dried, and protected with a clean pair of hose. Resting shoes between wearings will give them a chance to air out and dry completely. Needless to say, shoes should be protected with rubbers or overshoes in wet weather. Run-down heels also shorten shoe life because they distort the shape and cause a breakdown in other parts besides the heel.

Clothing will last longer if you strengthen the weak spots before they break into tears or holes. Garments should be checked after each wearing for needed repairs. Dangling buttons, popped seams, loose threads, or hems should be taken care of immediately.

Renovation methods

Not all fabrics are washable, and not all garments made from washable fabrics can be laundered successfully because of the possible limitations of trim, construction, or lining. The Care Guide in Figure 20-1 was developed by the Consumer Affairs Committee of the American Apparel Manufacturers Association, and it is intended to amplify the brief care instructions found on the permanent labels sewn into garments. Renovation methods for specific types of garments are given in Appendices C, D, and E.

Garments should be checked for rips or needed repairs before laundering, not after, and pockets should be emptied and turned inside out if possible. Heavily soiled areas should be pretreated, and spots and stains should be removed. Since many spots are set permanently by the use of the wrong solvent (even plain water can set some stains), a reliable guide to spot and stain removal should be kept in the laundry area. Fresh stains are usually easier to remove than those which have been allowed to harden because some deposits form chemical bonds with the fiber that become insoluble upon drying.

CONSUMER CARE GUIDE FOR APPAREL

	WHEN LABEL READS:	IT MEANS:
MACHINE WASHABLE	Machine wash	Wash, bleach, dry and press by any customary method including commercial laundering and dry cleaning
	Home launder only	Same as above but do not use commerical laundering
	No Chlorine Bleach	Do not use chlorine bleach. Oxygen bleach may be used
	No bleach	Do not use any type of bleach
	Cold wash Cold rinse	Use cold water from tap or cold washing machine setting
	Warm wash Warm rinse	Use warm water or warm washing machine setting
	Hot wash	Use hot water or hot washing machine setting
	No spin	Remove wash load before final machine spin cycle
	Delicate cycle Gentle cycle	Use appropriate machine setting; otherwise wash by hand
	Durable press cycle Permanent press cycle	Use appropriate machine setting; otherwise use warm wash, cold rinse and short spin cycle
	Wash separately	Wash alone or with like colors

	WHEN LABEL READS:	IT MEANS:
NON-MACHINE WASHING	Hand wash	Launder only by hand in luke warm (hand comfortable) water. May be bleached. May be drycleaned
	Hand wash only	Same as above, but do not dryclean
	Hand wash separately	Hand wash alone or with like colors
	No bleach	Do not use bleach
	Damp wipe	Surface clean with damp cloth or sponge
HOME DRYING	Tumble dry	Dry in tumble dryer at specified setting — high, medium, low or no heat
	Tumble dry Remove promptly	Same as above, but in absence of cool-down cycle remove at once when tumbling stops
	Drip dry	Hang wet and allow to dry with hand shaping only
	Line dry	Hang damp and allow to dry
	No wring No twist	Hang dry, drip dry or dry flat only. Handle to prevent wrinkles and distortion
	Dry flat	Lay garment on flat surface
	Block to dry	Maintain original size and shape while drying
IRONING OR PRESSING	Cool iron	Set iron at lowest setting
	Warm iron	Set iron at medium setting
	Hot iron	Set iron at hot setting
	Do not iron	Do not iron or press with heat
	Steam iron	Iron or press with steam
	Iron damp	Dampen garment before ironing
MISCELLANEOUS	Dryclean only	Garment should be drycleaned only, including self-service
	Professionally dry clean only	Do not use self-service drycleaning
	No dryclean	Use recommended care instructions. No drycleaning materials to be used.

This care Guide was produced by the Consumer Affairs Committee, American Apparel Manufacturers Association and is based on the Voluntary Guide of the Textile Industry Advisory Committee for Consumer Interests.
The American Apparel Manufacturers Association, Inc.

7/72

Figure 20-1. Consumer care guide for apparel.

If there is any doubt about the nature of a stain or how to remove it, the garment should be taken to a professional cleaner as soon as possible. A cleaner will have spotting reagents and techniques that the average consumer would not have. Drycleaning itself may remove many types of soil that cannot be removed by washing. Many garments that are washable are also drycleanable, but not all. Olefin fibers (polyethylene and polypropylene) are degraded by drycleaning solvents, and other articles, such as washable leather gloves, will lose their washability once they have been drycleaned. However, garments will shrink less in cleaning than in washing, and colors usually hold up better. The biggest advantage of drycleaning, of course, is that the tailoring details are preserved intact.

The consumer may choose to use a self-service coin-machine cleaner, and many people obtain very satisfactory results. In professional cleaning, garments are sorted according to color and fabric type; they are spot cleaned, steamed to remove wrinkles, and pressed to restore shape. Most reliable cleaners also make minor repairs, such as sewing on buttons, replacing trim, or catching a loose hem. Research studies have shown that the two major causes of fabric breakdown are abrasion from actual wear, and the accumulation of dirt and soil. Frequent drycleaning will extend the wear life of clothing by removing damaging soil.

The Director of Consumer Relations of the International Fabricare Institute suggests that you check the following points when items are returned from cleaning:

- There is no odor of drycleaning solvent.
- Clothes are clean and lint-free.
- Entire garment is free from pocket, seam, fastener, and button impressions.
- There is no fastener damage.
- Spots and stains have been removed, where it was safe to do so.
- Colors are bright and true.
- Creases are straight and sharp. There are no wrinkles.
- Pleats are straight, and hemlines even.
- Bows, ornaments, and buttons, if removed in cleaning, are replaced.
- Lapels and sleeves are rolled, unless creases were specified.
- Collars, shoulders, and necklines are remolded to original fit.
- You are notified should problem circumstances have arisen.[5]

If the customer is dissatisfied in any way, the garment should be returned and the cleaner asked to correct any details that may have been overlooked. The customer should never have a soiled article pressed without cleaning, nor should a garment continue to be worn until it becomes excessively soiled. Both

---

[5]Dorothy S. Lyle, *The Clothes We Wear,* Department of Home Economics, National Education Association, 1966, p. 21.

practices will set stains and odors and the chances for thorough cleaning later are very slim.

Storage

Seasonal storage of clothing can be damaging unless a few precautions are taken. The most important thing is to be sure that garments are clean before they are put away for any period of time. Even though man-made fibers do not attract moths and carpet beetles, insects will eat through these fibers in order to get at certain types of soil or food stains. Summer clothes should be washed, left unstarched (starch may attract silverfish), and stored in a box unironed. In damp climates, it becomes necessary to get adequate air circulation in the closet in order to prevent mildew. This can be accomplished by taking clothes out to air several times during the storage period, or running an electric fan in the closet occasionally to move out dead air.

For storage of winter clothes, any items that do not need washing or cleaning should be aired and brushed thoroughly with collars up, cuffs down, and pockets inside out. All knitwear should be stored flat, but other items may be hung in garment bags. Belts should be removed from their carriers and hung straight to prevent the backing from cracking. Paradichlorobenzene crystals or naphthalene balls or flakes are effective in discouraging insects if the storage containers are well sealed. Since their vapors are heavier than air, they should be placed high in the closet or garment bag. Clothes may also be wrapped in heavy paper, sprinkled with a moth repellent, and sealed tightly with masking tape. Ideally, the storage area should be dry and fairly cool. If temperatures are likely to be high, never use plastic hangers in a closed garment bag with paradichlorobenzene. The plastic is apt to soften and fuse into the fabric. Plastic buttons, plastic containers, even coatings on wire hangers are affected by paradichlorobenzene vapors.

Furs should also be cleaned and stored. Department stores in large cities and local furriers usually have storage vaults with controlled temperature and humidity. If you do not have suitable storage space at home, even for regular cloth garments, many drycleaners will provide seasonal storage for a nominal fee.

Consumer satisfaction

Over the years, the textiles and clothing industry—fiber producers, fabric makers, garment manufacturers, and retailers—have come to realize that quality control in merchandise is as important to the consumer as price. Many have learned through experience that when they lower their standards, disappointed customers stay away from the product in droves.

As we learned in Chapter 17, there is an increasing number of government controls over industry that are designed to guarantee consumer satisfaction. Many people argue, however, that consumers themselves, and not government bureaucrats, are the best judges of what they want.[6] One industry spokesman reasoned: "Acceptance of our products should depend primarily on how well business, education and government do their jobs of communicating with consumers and determining what consumers want and need. That will require much more careful research and interpretation than has been evident in the current emotional binge of consumer protection."[7]

Most reliable firms attempt to establish this kind of communication with their customers, but at the same time there are many other companies that will offer the minimum in quality for the biggest price that they can get. Even if they go out of business, there are the thousands of consumers who are stuck with inferior merchandise before the sales are curtailed. Consumers can discourage deceptive business practices either by (1) refusing to buy a garment that does not bear an informative label with the manufacturer's name and address, or (2) returning inferior goods to the place of purchase as soon as the defect is noted.

If the consumer has a justifiable complaint, the majority of retailers and manufacturers seek to generate the goodwill of their customers through a generous refund or replacement policy. Unfortunately, the customer is not always right.

Consumer expectations

Some consumers expect the impossible. It might be desirable to buy a suit for $39.95 that looks like a million, wears like iron, never needs pressing, and does not soil. But the fact is that our present state of technology simply does not offer that kind of a product. There are many instances of consumer complaints in which the performance expected from a product is clearly beyond the limits of reasonable usage. One example is the case of the mother who expected the store to replace a pair of jeans she had purchased for her son. The pants were torn when the boy slid down a board and caught them on a protruding nail. The mother honestly thought that jeans should be able to withstand that kind of wear. Another man asked for a refund on a shirt that had worn through at the elbows. The shirt was ten years old.

---

[6]For a summary of the industry's stand on consumerism, see "Consumerism: Challenge of the 70's," *Women's Wear Daily*, 28 June 1972.
[7]H. W. Close, Chairman of Springs Mills, Inc., and past Chairman of ATMI, speaking at the 1973 Annual Meeting of the American Home Economics Association.

In order to provide the consumer (as well as manufacturers, retailers, cleaners, and insurance and claims adjusters) with a reasonable estimate of the life expectancies and serviceability of textile products, a set of guidelines was developed under the sponsorship of the National Institute of Drycleaning;[8] The guide now is published by the International Fabricare Institute, which is the successor to the American Institute of Laundering and the National Institute of Drycleaning. Life expectancy rates for specific categories of clothing are given for men's and boys' wear, women's and girls' wear, and children's wear (see Appendices C, D, and E).

In addition, the guidelines state that a textile product shall afford reasonable service in use, and that failure to wear or clean satisfactorily constitutes a justifiable cause for complaint. If care instructions on the label are followed, a garment is expected *not* to:

- Shrink or stretch out of size or shape
- Become yellow, gray or otherwise discolored or changed physically in appearance
- Lose or change color, or stain other materials
- Become stiff, limp or otherwise changed in feel or touch[9]

It should be remembered that the manufacturer or retailer *is not responsible* if a garment fails beyond its life expectancy, or if the damage is due to acts of carelessness or incompetence on the part of the consumer.

Fraud by consumers

Retail stores have considerable evidence that many consumers deliberately set out to deceive or take advantage of the retailer's merchandise return policy. Stores lose a considerable amount of money each year through unreasonable and/or deceptive refund demands. Zabriskie cites a number of such cases, including this one:

> In the month of June there are a lot of graduation dances and balls. A few young women bought gowns the week before the dance and returned them for credit early the next week claiming they didn't fit. The gowns had make-up, perspiration, and lipsticks stains that indicated they had been used and therefore could not be returned.[10]

There are also consumers who shoplift from one store and take the merchandise to another store for a refund. Clearly, as

[8]The guidelines were developed in cooperation with: the Association of Better Business Bureaus, Association of Home Appliance Manufacturers, American Institute of Laundering, National Retail Merchants Association, American Home Economics Association, Menswear Retailers of America, a national insurance adjusting organization, a mail-order firm, a textile licensing company, a fiber producer, and NID's Textile Analysis Advisory Committee. See *International Fair Claims Guide for Consumer Textile Products*, International Fabricare Institute, Inc., Joliet, Illinois, 1973.
[9]*Fair Claims Guide*, p. 4.
[10]Noel Zabriskie, "Fraud by Consumers," *Journal of Retailing*, Winter 1972–1973, p. 26.

Consumers protect their own interests by making informed and intelligent decisions in the marketplace.

Zabriskie points out, "honest customers pay higher prices to compensate for the activities of the dishonest, shady, and unscrupulous."

SUMMARY *The informed consumer*

The responsible consumer is one who manages his personal and family income effectively by (1) taking a rational and objective approach to his clothing needs and requirements, (2) planning expenditures in order of priority, (3) seeking out all sources of information about the articles he intends to buy, (4) comparing values and product quality at a variety of merchandise sources, (5) making intelligent decisions regarding where and when to buy, and (6) caring for the merchandise properly once it has been purchased.

The consumer may assume his responsibilities in the marketplace by (1) educating himself to be a discriminating shopper, (2) not patronizing stores that engage in questionable business practices, (3) informing the merchant or manufacturer when a garment does not live up to expectations, (4) letting the businessman know when you appreciate his services or products, (5) reporting all cases of dishonesty, fraud, or violation of the law to the proper agency, (6) not abusing customer privileges, and (7) keeping abreast of consumer action programs.

FOR FURTHER READING

Chambers, H., and V. Moulton. *Clothing Selection.* Philadelphia: J. B. Lippincott Company, 1969.

International Fair Claims Guide For Consumer Textile Products. Joliet, Illinois: International Fabricare Institute, 1973.

Kefgen, M., and P. Touchie-Specht. *Individuality in Clothing Selection and Personal Appearance.* New York: Macmillan Publishing Company, 1971. (Chapters 15 through 19.)

Textile Handbook. Washington, D.C.: American Home Economics Association, 1970.

Tolman, Ruth. *Guide to Fashion Merchandise Knowledge.* Bronx, New York: Milady Publishing Corporation, 1973. (Sections on "Textiles," and "Accessories.")

Troelstrup, Arch W. *The Consumer in American Society.* New York: McGraw-Hill Book Company, 1970.

DISCUSSION QUESTIONS

1. What is the purpose of a wardrobe inventory? How can it help the consumer make informed and intelligent clothing decisions?

ACQUISITION AND USE OF CLOTHING

2. What factors must be considered in planning clothing expenditures?

3. Outline some of the signposts of quality that will guide the consumer in the selection of apparel merchandise.

4. In what ways can consumers make their clothing needs and desires known to retailers and manufacturers?

5. Give several examples of legitimate reasons for returning merchandise to the store. When are returns or exchanges *not* justified?

6. How does advertising serve the consumer?

7. In what ways can you tell reputable sellers from unfair or dishonest sellers?

21

Toward a Philosophy of Clothing

IN THE PRECEDING chapters we have attempted to place the study of clothing within the totality of its cultural, social-psychological, aesthetic, physical, and economic setting. The study of one aspect of dress to the exclusion of the others often leads to faulty conclusions. Taken out of context to the whole, any analysis of clothing confined to a single viewpoint is not only incomplete, but hazardous as well. If we evaluate clothing solely in terms of its economic worth, we may deny the individual the psychological security that a seemingly "worthless" garment may provide. Yet if we restrict our decision making to psychological considerations, we may risk some of the values important to the welfare of society as a whole. The analysis of dress so often made in terms of its sexual symbolism overemphasizes the erotic in ignorance of the forces of fashion and the natural evolution of styles. It is possible to build a most convincing argument (as many writers have tried to do) to support the contention that clothing fashions derive primarily from subconscious drives to intensify the sexual characteristics of the body. Almost without exception, a far more plausible explanation for the same phenomena of dress may be found within the framework of a totally different discipline. The psychoanalyst, for example, may see the hobble skirt as a manifestation of man's suppressed desire to immobilize the woman, but to the fashion historian it suggests the swing of the fashion pendulum from excessive amplitude to the opposite extreme of slenderness.

To deny that clothing is used as a means of sexual attractiveness, however, is equally fallacious. The limits of our knowledge may be held responsible for the biases that shape our attitudes and values. It is perhaps a human tendency to dismiss as unimportant the things we know the least about. The purpose here has been to achieve some balance in the weighing of factors that affect clothing decisions. Two final

ACQUISITION AND USE OF CLOTHING

questions present themselves in this concluding chapter: (1) how do we evaluate the currents of our times, and (2) what significance do these concepts have to the individual as he attempts to solve his own clothing problems?

Gaining perspective

Probably one of the most common assumptions regarding the origin and purpose of clothing is that man chooses to cover his body for reasons of modesty. In our study of dress, however, we have seen that feelings of shame associated with the exposure of various parts of the anatomy vary widely from culture to culture. Clothing has, moreover, been used not so much to cover as to attract attention to one's physical attributes. We also know that once the eyes have become accustomed to the sight of the human form, the importance attached to sex differentiations soon disappears.

This leads us to the acceptance of the theory that the primary motive underlying the origin of clothes is man's basic drive to render the body more beautiful than nature made it (as "beauty" is conceived in his particular cultural setting). There are few people, if any, who do not embellish or mold the body in some way in order to appear more attractive, and many will submit to extreme pain in order to accomplish their purpose.

Standards of beauty, however, are subject to rather powerful cultural mutations. A person usually follows certain accepted patterns of dress not because they enhance the body, but because they represent the customs or the cultural habits of a society in which the individual desires membership. Conformity to a normative pattern of dress thus provides a sense of belonging to the individual who seeks to establish his identification with a particular group of people.

By the same token, clothing also provides a vehicle through which man is able to distinguish himself from others. The status differentiations that are possible through the use of a wide variety of clothing symbols afford the individual a means of obtaining recognition and prestige, especially among those whose opinions are held to be important.

Still another theory which figures in the analysis of the functions of dress embodies the concept of clothing as an extension of the self. In this sense, clothing functions to extend the feelings of self beyond the physical boundaries of the body, and provides an expansiveness to the wearer's attitudes and emotions.

Certainly we cannot overlook the important function of clothing as it relates to protection and utility. Clothing serves as a buffer between man and his environment, shielding him from harmful elements, both physical and psychological. It must be admitted that in many instances man has used clothing in a most minimal way when adapting to his environment. Many articles of dress, even in so-called civilized societies, not only lack this protective function but actually defy it. Women's sheer hosiery does precious little to warm the legs in winter, and the collars of men's shirts do not contribute much to their comfort in summer. Clothing does, nevertheless, extend man's performance in many areas of activity in which he would otherwise be hampered or helpless.

Clothing is, in fact, a product of *all* of these motives and functions. The incidence of conscious purpose in dress is slight, and many of a person's reasons for wearing clothes are not known even to the individual himself.

The many intrinsic values of clothing are often overlooked by virtue of its close association with the phenomenon of fashion. Fashion has been declaimed by many critics, both historical and contemporary, as contributing to immorality and snobbery, perpetuating class discrimination, forcing slavish imitation, encouraging waste – both in production and consumption – creating market imperfections, and in some cases even endangering the health of its followers. Yet, fashion is not confined to clothes; it exists in almost every field of human activity. Contrary to popular opinion, fashion is not definable in terms of its style features, but rather in terms of its fluctuation and the status of the groups who follow it. Even those who do not follow fashion usually conform to some type of normative clothing behavior.

Alternatives to fashion include nudity, the uniform, or some form of traditional dress, all of which are not without their own shortcomings. Probably the most tangible value of fashion may be stated in terms of dollars and cents. It is estimated that American families spend nearly $70 billion yearly on clothing items, and almost half of that dollar value may be positively assigned to fashionable garments. Fashion is responsible for one of the largest industries in the United States, giving employment to millions of Americans as well as stimulating international trade.

From the scholar's point of view, fashion represents a unique phenomenon that facilitates a kind of social analysis that is not possible when one deals with less tangible manifestations of human behavior. Fashions can be rather precisely dated, skirt lengths and other proportions may be measured, the number of people wearing the fashion can be counted, and the beginning and end of the fashion cycle can usually be determined fairly accurately.

But perhaps the most important "good" of fashion is the value it imparts to the individual who wears it. If fashion can provide a sense of psychological security, a renewed interest in and appreciation of the self, a "lift" from the doldrums of depression, and enrichment of personal experience, it has much that can be said in its favor. Moreover, the acceptance of fashion is

ACQUISITION AND USE OF CLOTHING

not compulsory; each individual is free to weigh the values of fashion against its evils, in accordance with his own beliefs.

The philosophy of a number of writers in regard to fashion was admirably expressed by Lawrence Langner:

> If there is to be a new goal for humanity, the uniform man or robot, then by all means do away with fashion, for it is the enemy of the stereotyped individual, the mass-produced mind and the unthinking human product of the propaganda machine. But since the world progresses by the progress of its individuals, as well as by its masses, there is reason for optimism in believing that fashion, which is the product of individual taste, exercised without compulsion, will continue to exist as it has in the past as a constructive force in the world of the future.[1]

If we were to draw a single conclusion from our study of fashion, it would have to be that fashion is change and change is inevitable. We can look back in history and pick out the most significant themes that characterized each of the periods, and yet as we view the wide range of values, including those in our contemporary setting, none seem so sensible, so practical, so right, as those which we currently hold for ourselves. The present, the familiar, is always more comfortable. But what of tomorrow? Will the styles of the younger generation seem as ugly, as idiotic, and as vulgar ten years from now as they seem to us today?

It is difficult for us to accept the idea that there are no unchanging standards of taste, and even more difficult to acknowledge that our own standards and beliefs are subject to change. We look with amused superiority upon statements made little more than fifty years ago, such as Veblen's comment on the practice of shaving the face: "There has of late years been some slight recrudescence of the shaven face in polite society, but this is probably a transient and unadvised mimicry of the fashion imposed upon body servants, and it may fairly be expected to go the way of the powdered wig of our grandfathers."[2]

We can laugh now at a law that required all cycle riders to wear "baggy continuations" that covered the legs to the heels, but can we laugh when contemporary clergymen insist that "the right length for hemlines is just below the kneecap," or that "untidy dress is an outward sign of an untidy mind." How can we evaluate the emerging trends without the perspective of time? What rational approach can be taken to elements of dress that seem entirely alien to our habits and tastes? Is it possible for anyone to be completely free from his emotions and biases in reacting to anything as intimately personal as a second skin—the clothing he wears? Perhaps not. But if we were to try, we would probably need some set of objective criteria

---

[1]Langner, *Importance of Wearing Clothes,* p. 299.
[2]Veblen, *Theory of Leisure Class,* p. 186.

against which to check our observations. The concepts presented in the preceding chapters give some suggestion as to what such criteria might be. We might ask ourselves, for example:

(1) Does the costume make effective use of new materials, tools, and processes that result from our rapidly developing technology?

(2) Does it reflect the dominant characteristics of the culture in which it was created?

(3) Is it consistent with the moral values that typify the times?

(4) Does it represent a value model expressive of the dominant themes in contemporary life?

(5) Does it accurately represent the values of the individual wearing it?

(6) Does it help the wearer to establish his identity, or to make him more effective in the performance of his social roles?

(7) Is it compatible with the wearer's body type, self-image, and style of life?

(8) Does it contribute to one's feelings of self-acceptance, self-respect, and self-esteem?

(9) Is it an effective cue in setting the stage for positive social interaction?

(10) Does it enable the wearer to increase his identification with the group to which he aspires to belong?

(11) Does it provide an outlet for the wearer's creative talents?

(12) Is it an integrated design with a pleasing relationship of parts?

(13) Does it have an aesthetic unity with other contemporary art forms?

(14) Is it practical from the standpoint of the wearer's comfort and physical well-being?

(15) Is it easy to maintain?

(16) Is it functionally designed to make the wearer more efficient in the performance of his specialized tasks or activities?

(17) Does it enable the wearer to conform more closely to his physical ideal by masking those aspects of physique or physiognomy which he considers to be undesirable or unattractive?

(18) Is the cost of the costume reasonable within the limitations of one's income and other financial obligations?

(19) Is the quality and workmanship consistent with the costume's anticipated fashion life?

(20) Does its acceptance contribute to a demand that is beneficial to the economy?

No costume or item of clothing will ever meet all of these criteria, and yet it is hard to imagine a garment that would meet none of them. It would be an interesting exercise to evaluate some of the items in our current wardrobes on the basis of such a list, and to make a similar analysis of clothing which is not now suitable to our tastes. It might, in fact, help to resolve some of the conflict in values that appears to exist today between the teenage world and the parent world. Distraught mothers and fathers vainly attempt to instill the traditional standards of dress in their youngsters, and the offspring respond with what seems to be a complete rejection of the aesthetic and moral values of their seniors.

Today's youth are years ahead of currently accepted adult values in their design preferences. In their extremes of dress, they influence the fashions that will gain ultimate acceptance in the future. The impact of consumer change in tastes will be felt more keenly as today's teenager becomes tomorrow's adult, and his value-judgments shape the clothing practices of the next generation.

The decision-making process

By now it should be clear that the clothing needs and desires of the individual and of families are influenced by a multitude of circumstances. Buying motives are seldom simple, and rarely is the final selection made on completely rational terms.

There is no simple formula for combining these factors into a blueprint for decision making. Every day the individual is faced with a number of choices regarding the selection of his apparel. Many of our daily decisions become so routine that the choice is made almost automatically, yet there are numerous situations that demand a conscious effort to choose among alternatives, and even our routine decisions ought to be examined from time to time in light of the perspective we gain through experience, and the changes that come about in the circumstances of our living.

Ignorance of the choice-making process does not relieve the individual of the responsibility of his decision. Choices are made, consciously or unconsciously. The question is not whether to decide, but how the decision can be made so that the choice of what we wear will yield the maximum benefits to ourselves, to our families, and to society as a whole. A knowledge of the decision-making process will help us to be more aware of the alternatives and hopefully more satisfied with the results of our actions.

Clarification of the goal

There is a reasonable agreement that the process of decision making has five basic components. The first of these involves a **clarification of the choice to be made**. Many a person has gone to the closet or to the market without really knowing the kind of decision that needs to be made. Mary may recognize that she needs a new winter coat to wear to school. This is a fairly straightforward problem, particularly if Mary has enough money in her clothing budget to make the purchase. The problem is less well defined, however, if Mary needs new clothes for school. The question then becomes "What kind of clothes? What categories of apparel?" But maybe Mary wants a car more than she wants new clothes. A conscious recognition of the precise limitations of the choice-making situation is essential at the outset.

Considering alternatives

The **recognition of possible alternatives** is the second step toward the solution of the problem. If the choice is defined as the selection of a new coat for school, one then seeks alternatives in the retail market by shopping the stores, trying on different styles, and comparing values. Theoretically, one should have a complete knowledge of the market to make the best possible decision, but this is not always feasible. Particularly for those who have limited skill in decision making, too many alternatives may confuse the issue. Young people will have a difficult time making a selection if confronted with too many choices.

Evaluating alternatives

Weighing advantages of the alternatives is perhaps a more difficult step than either of the other two because it requires the ability to foresee the consequences of each course of action. Obviously, the more knowledge and experience the individual has, the more competent he will be in predicting the possible outcome. Let us assume that Mary has found two coats that would fit into her wardrobe plan: one is a brown fleece, and the other an orange broadcloth. Both fit equally well and have style lines becoming to her figure type. From experience she knows that the fleece will be warmer than the broadcloth, especially since the brown coat has long, close-fitting sleeves, while the orange has a wide cuff. At present, the orange color will go with most of her other color choices, but she recognizes that it may not be as versatile as the brown in terms of the future purchases she may make. The brown coat is classic in line and will probably have a longer fashion life than the orange broadcloth which is somewhat "modish" in design. The latter will obviously require more frequent cleaning, but it has a bright, cheerful look, and no one else she knows owns an orange coat. It will be admired by the other girls, and give a lift to her spirits. Still, the brown fleece has a soft, pleasant feel, and she may tire of it less easily. The bright orange may, in fact, be just a little too conspicuous on a conservative campus such as theirs.

Choosing among alternatives

Choosing one of the alternatives is the step that many people see as the entire decision-making process. Actually the success of the choice depends upon the mental considerations that went on beforehand. The decision-maker is guided not only by the predictions of outcome made in step three, but by his personal value system that determines which of the advantages are more important to him. The mental process might be represented somewhat as follows:

Alternative	Advantages	Underlying Value
Brown fleece	Warmer	Physical comfort
	Shows less soil	Economic-cost of upkeep
	Versatile, basic in color and line	Economic-serves many purposes and will not require early replacement
	Not too conspicuous	Conforms to campus customs and group expectations
Orange broadcloth	Fashionable, chic	Social status, prestige
	Bright, cheerful	Psychological lift
	Different	Personality expression, individuality
	Beautiful	Aesthetic satisfaction

Obviously, the underlying values will be weighted differently by different individuals. For those on limited incomes, the alternative yielding the greatest economic value would be the most expedient choice. For others, the social and psychological values may be far more important.

Accepting the consequences

Accepting the consequences of one's decision is also a fundamental part of the process. The decision-maker must be willing to assume the responsibility for his action. If Mary chooses the orange coat, for example, with the prior knowledge that it would soil more easily, she must be willing to assume the burden of added cleaning costs. Moreover, if her budget will not permit the purchase of another new coat for three years, she may have to continue to wear one that in another year or so will have lost much of its fashion appeal. Her other wardrobe additions will also be restricted to a limited color range. This subsequent dissatisfaction with her choice should contribute to her knowledge and experience in making future clothing decisions.

The optimal value pattern

Clothing is probably one of the most tangible expressions of an individual's unique value system. Values, taken together with one's set of beliefs, may be thought of as the individual's philosophy about life in general, and about clothing in particular. Clothing represents but a part of one's total philosophy and way of life and cannot be divorced from the whole of existence.

Because we are continually exposed to new items, and because our own needs and interests change, goals seldom remain fixed. Our material goals are usually recognized more readily than our intangible goals, which are expressed in terms of values rather than actual goods or services. The recognition that we want a new suit, or a fur coat, or a cashmere sweater represents a conscious awareness of our desire for material goods. We are less apt to verbalize *why* we want the clothes that we do, but even if we are not conscious of our values, they still influence the choices that we make.

A conscious ordering of values on the part of the individual is a far more effective way of achieving the ultimate goals that he seeks than making a list of clothing items that he wants. If a person recognizes and accepts the fact that he values his status and prestige in the group as more important than his physical comfort or his individuality, his choice of clothing is not only simplified, but it is more likely to carry him in the direction of his long-range goal.

A philosophy of clothing, then, is a part of one's philosophy of life. It determines our choices, it guides our actions, and it conditions our satisfaction. The clothes we wear help us become the kind of person we wish to be.

As we have seen throughout the pages of this book, clothing relates in some way to virtually every sphere of human activity. If we could predict with any reasonable degree of accuracy what will take place within the next ten, fifty, or even one hundred years of man's existence in terms of technological advances, international relations, progress in the social sciences, and worldwide economic development, it would be a relatively simple matter to define the future of clothes. It has already been demonstrated that clothing will function to help man in his conquest of outer space, and it may also be a tool in his conquest of poverty and dissension among nations. Already the diffusion of Western culture can be observed to a marked degree through the clothing of people in many parts of Africa, in India, Japan, the Middle Eastern countries, and to a growing extent in Russia. It is reasonable to assume that as the resources of the world become available to all of earth's inhabitants and the inter-mingling of cultural elements is complete, the symbols of national differentiation and class distinction inevitably will be obliterated.

In such an atmosphere one might expect that the design of clothes would not only follow the dictates of efficiency and individual need, but would be based on the true aesthetic principles that are universal in mankind. But such a utopia, in which man exists in perfect harmony with his environment, is not likely to materialize tomorrow. In the time which intervenes, the sensible person will examine the reality of his present environment and utilize his clothing in positive ways to achieve his personal goals.

Appendices

APPENDIX A. MAN'S WARDROBE INVENTORY

Item	Number on Hand	Average Unit Price	Annual Replacement	Annual Cost
Coats				
Overcoats	⸻	⸻	⸻	⸻
Car coats	⸻	⸻	⸻	⸻
Raincoats	(example)	$30.00	⅓	$10.00
Suits				
Business	⸻	⸻	⸻	⸻
Evening or formal	⸻	⸻	⸻	⸻
Separates				
Jackets	⸻	⸻	⸻	⸻
Slacks	⸻	⸻	⸻	⸻
Walking shorts	⸻	⸻	⸻	⸻
Sweaters	⸻	⸻	⸻	⸻
Dress shirts	⸻	⸻	⸻	⸻
Sports shirts	⸻	⸻	⸻	⸻
Evening shirts	⸻	⸻	⸻	⸻
Swim Trunks	(example)	$7.00	½	$ 3.50
Underwear				
Undershirts	⸻	⸻	⸻	⸻
Shorts	⸻	⸻	⸻	⸻
Leisure Wear				
Pajamas	⸻	⸻	⸻	⸻
Bathrobes	⸻	⸻	⸻	⸻
Smoking jackets	⸻	⸻	⸻	⸻
Shoes and Footwear				
Sport shoes	⸻	⸻	⸻	⸻
Work shoes	⸻	⸻	⸻	⸻
Business shoes	⸻	⸻	⸻	⸻
Dress shoes	⸻	⸻	⸻	⸻
Slippers	⸻	⸻	⸻	⸻
Socks	(example)	$1.00	1	$ 1.00
Accessories				
Hats	⸻	⸻	⸻	⸻
Gloves	⸻	⸻	⸻	⸻
Mufflers	⸻	⸻	⸻	⸻
Ties	⸻	⸻	⸻	⸻
Garters, braces	⸻	⸻	⸻	⸻
Handkerchiefs	⸻	⸻	⸻	⸻
Annual Upkeep				
Cleaning and pressing				⸻
Blocking hats				⸻
Shoe repair				⸻

Total Annual Replacement Cost $⸻

Total Wardrobe Cost: $⸻

APPENDIX B. WOMAN'S WARDROBE INVENTORY

Item	Number on Hand	Average Unit Price	Annual Replacement	Annual Cost
Coats				
Fur	_____	_____	_____	_____
Cloth	(example)	$75.00	¼	$18.75
Car coats	_____	_____	_____	_____
Suits, pantsuits				
Summer	_____	_____	_____	_____
Winter	_____	_____	_____	_____
Dresses				
Casual	_____	_____	_____	_____
Dressy	_____	_____	_____	_____
Formal	_____	_____	_____	_____
Separates				
Blouses	_____	_____	_____	_____
Skirts	_____	_____	_____	_____
Sweaters	_____	_____	_____	_____
Shorts	_____	_____	_____	_____
Slacks, jeans, etc.	_____	_____	_____	_____
Jackets	_____	_____	_____	_____
Bathing suits	_____	_____	_____	_____
Underwear				
Slips	_____	_____	_____	_____
Bras	_____	_____	_____	_____
Panties	_____	_____	_____	_____
Foundations	(example)	$ 9.00	1	$ 9.00
Leisure Wear				
Nightgowns, pajamas	_____	_____	_____	_____
Housecoats	_____	_____	_____	_____
Bathrobes	_____	_____	_____	_____
Shoes and Footwear				
Sport shoes	_____	_____	_____	_____
Dress shoes	_____	_____	_____	_____
Evening shoes	_____	_____	_____	_____
Slippers	_____	_____	_____	_____
Galoshes or boots	_____	_____	_____	_____
Stockings, pantyhose	(example)	$1.25	10	$12.50
Socks	_____	_____	_____	_____
Accessories				
Hats	_____	_____	_____	_____
Gloves	_____	_____	_____	_____
Scarves	_____	_____	_____	_____
Handbags	_____	_____	_____	_____
Miscellaneous	_____	_____	_____	_____
Annual Upkeep				
Cleaning and pressing				_____
Shoe Repair				_____

Total Annual Replacement Cost $_____

Total Wardrobe Cost: $_____

Item	Renovation Method	Rate (yrs.)
1. Bathing suits	Hand wash	2
2. Coats and jackets		4
Cloth, dress	Dryclean	
Cloth, sport	(See #20)	
Pile (Imitation fur)	Dryclean. Cold tumble only. No steam.	
Fur	Fur Clean	10
Leather & Suede	(See #7)	
Plastic	(See #10)	
3. Formal wear	Dryclean	5
4. Gloves		
Fabric	Med. wash; dryclean	1
Leather	Leather Clean only	2
5. Hats		
Felt and straw	Clean by hat renovation specialists only. Water resist.	2
Fur	Fur Clean	5
6. Jackets	(see #2 or #11)	
7. Leather jackets and coats		5
Suede and grain leather products require special care in cleaning. Colors normally subject to fading and some loss in cleaning. Suedes and most grain leathers restorable by application of color and finishing products.		
8. Neckties	Dryclean	1
9. Sleepwear		2
White goods	Hot wash	
Colored goods	Med. wash	
10. Plastic apparel	(See #11)	3
Imitation leather and suede	Hand wash; no press	
11. Rainwear		
Film and plastic coated fabrics	Hand wash; no press	2
Fabric		
Unlined	Med. wash, dryclean	3
Lined and quilted	Dryclean	
Rubber	Wipe down with damp cloth; no press	3
12. Robes		
Silk or wool	Dryclean	3
Other:		2
Unlined	Med. wash; dryclean	
Lined	Dryclean	

Item	Renovation Method	Rate (yrs.)
13. Shoes		
Can be cleaned and polished, resoled, heeled. Thread in uppers holds sections securely for normal service life without undue breakage.		
Men's		3
Boys'		1
14. Shirts		
Dress and plain sports		2
White and partly colored	Hot wash	
Colored	Hot wash; no bleach	
Sports (Fancy)		
Cotton and blends	Med. wash; dryclean	3
Wool or Silk	Dryclean; hand wash	2
15. Shorts	(See #17)	
16. Ski jackets	(See #11)	
17. Slacks and shorts	(including matching sets)	
Wool or wool blends	Dryclean	4
Cotton	Med. wash; dryclean	2
Synthetics	Dryclean	2
18. Sneakers	Med. wash; bleach; air or tumble dry.	0
19. Socks		
Wool	Hand wash	
Other	Med. wash	
20. Sport coats		
Wool and wool blends	Dryclean	4
Cotton and synthetics	Dryclean	2
21. Suits		
Summer Weight:		
Wool or wool blends	Dryclean	3
Cotton and synthetics	Dryclean	2
Winter weight	Dryclean	4
Wash suits	Med. wash; dryclean	2
22. Sweaters		3
Wool and synthetics	Hand wash; dry flat only; dryclean; wetclean	
23. Underwear		2
White	Hot wash	
Colored	Med. wash	
24. Uniforms		1
Unlined and work types	Med. wash; dryclean	
Lined and dressy	Dryclean	
25. Vests		2
Fancy and regular	Dryclean	

Item	Renovation Method	Rate (yrs.)
26. Windbreakers	(See #11)	
27. Work clothing Customarily shows noticeable signs of wear to greater or lesser degree depending on amount of use. Color may be expected to appear rubbed off in areas. Fabric has strength to withstand strains of use and laundering at 160°F. with heavy duty soap.		

APPENDIX D. IMPLIED SERVICEABILITY DESIGNATIONS AND LIFE EXPECTANCY RATES FOR WOMEN'S AND GIRLS' WEAR

Item	Renovation Method	Rate (yrs.)
1. Aprons		
Regular	Med. wash; bleach white only.	1
Fancy	Hand wash; dryclean	4
2. Blouses		
Dress & Sports		
White cotton	Hot wash; dryclean	3
White synthetics and all colored.	Med. wash; dryclean	2
3. Coats and jackets	(See men's #2)	
4. Dresses		
House and sports	Med. wash; dryclean	1
Afternoon	Dryclean	3
Street	Dryclean	2
Evening or cocktail:		
High Fashion	Dryclean; special handling of delicate and decorated styles.	3
Basic	Dryclean	5
5. Gloves		
Fabric	Med. wash separate; dryclean.	1
Leather	Leather Clean	2
6. Hats		
Felt	Clean by special hat renovation methods.	1
Straw	Same unless trim detail precludes cleaning.	2

Item	Renovation Method	Rate (yrs.)
Fur	Fur Clean	5
7. Housecoats and robes		
Lightweight cottons and synthetics	Mild wash; dryclean	1
Quilted and heavy	Dryclean	3
8. Jackets	(See men's #2 or #11)	
9. Negligee		
Cotton and nylon types	Med. wash	2
10. Sleepwear		2
White goods	Hot wash	
Colored goods	Med. wash	
11. Rainwear	(See men's #11)	
12. Robes	(See #7)	
13. Scarves		2
Wool	Dryclean	
Other	Mild wash; dryclean	
Fur	Fur clean	5
14. Shoes		
Dress and walking	(See men's #13)	2
Work		1
Evening, formal		5
15. Shorts	(See #17)	
16. Skirts		2
Winter and fall	Dryclean-wetclean	
Resort and summer	Med. wash; dryclean	
17. Slacks and shorts		
Lounging and tailored	Dryclean	2
Active Sport	Hand wash; dryclean	2
Dress	Dryclean	3
18. Sneakers	(See men's #18)	
19. Socks	(See men's #19)	
20. Sport coats	(See men's #2)	
21. Suits		
Basic	Dryclean	4
High Fashion	Dryclean. Special handling on delicate and decorated styles.	3
22. Sweaters	(See men's #22)	
23. Swimwear	Hand wash	2
24. Underwear		
Slips	Mild wash; bleach white cottons	2
Foundation garments	Med. wash	1
Panties	Med. wash; bleach white cottons	1
25. Uniforms		1
Unlined and work types	Med. wash; dryclean	
Lined and dressy	Dryclean	
26. Wedding gowns	Dryclean	Indefinite
27. Windbreakers	(See men's #11)	
28. Work clothing	(See men's #27)	

APPENDIX E. IMPLIED SERVICEABILITY DESIGNATIONS
AND LIFE EXPECTANCY RATES
FOR CHILDREN'S WEAR

Item	Renovation method	Rate (yrs.)
1. Coats	Dryclean	2
2. Coat sets	Dryclean	2
3. Dresses	Med. wash; dryclean	2
4. Hats, Bonnets	Dryclean	1
5. Playclothes	Med. wash	1
6. Snowsuits		2
Wool and wool blends	Dryclean	
Cotton and synthetics	Med. wash; dryclean	
7. Suits	Dryclean	2
8. Undergarments		1
White goods	Hot wash	
Colored	Med. wash	

AUTHOR INDEX

SUBJECT INDEX

Value(s): aesthetic, 87–88, 276; "anti-materialistic," 86, 227–228; and Chinese dress, 75–77, 81; color, 254–255; conflict in, 89–91, 94, 415, 445; and cultural change, 91–94; explicit vs. implicit, 82–84; of the family, 74, 81–82, 90–91; male vs. female, 84–85; mass media and, 81, 94; patterns (interrelation). 88–91. 276. 448; politics and, 74, 77, 86; traditional, 88–89, 98; of youth, 91–92. *See also* Conformity

"Vamp" era, 117
Van de Velde, Henry, 285
Variety stores, 361–362, 364
Vatican, clothing restrictions in, 68
Victoria, Queen, and Victorian era, 3, 206, 284–285; and clothing, 21–22, 64, 79, 108
Vietnam war, 107

Warhol, Andy, 288
Washington, George, 345
Wealth: clothing as symbol of, 15, 44, 47, 79, 97–98, 102, 226; and clothing expenditures, 86, 227–228, 386; shift in, 230, 406–408, 411

Weaving, 17, 19, 20, 33–34, 37, 49–43, 46, 48, 51
Wedding clothes, 58, 98, 188, 190–191, 417
Wedgwood, Josiah, 285
Weitz, John, 106
Western world and influence, 23, 25–27, 75–77, 105, 202, 395, 448
White-collar workers, 1–2, 135, 186, 198, 207, 208, 227, 230, 239, 240
Wilde, Oscar, 112, 285; quoted, 293
Women and clothing: awareness of, 1, 84–85, 194, 202, 236, 276; body types, 129, 321–322; and conformity, 82–83, 87, 165, 204, 206, 238; cultural/national costume of, 40, 41, 44, 47, 48, 60, 64, 75–77, 81, 108, 204n; expectations, 135–136, 205–206, 209–210, 214, 216, 217, 412; expenditures, 233, 359, 403–405, 406, 407; feminism and liberation, 65, 79–80, 86, 107–109, 111, 123, 202–204, 205, 213, 217, 221, 291, 352–353, 407; functionalism vs. restrictive clothing, 50, 56, 80, 154, 203–204, 287, 440; and neoclassicism, 78, 111, 283–284; and status, 47, 79, 107–109, 189, 210, 224, 227–229, 233; and values,

66, 82–89, 131–133, 224, 276; wedding dress, 58, 98, 188, 190–191, 417
Wool, 17, 21, 40, 42, 226, 375; legislation and, 371, 381; production and advertising, 346–347, 349–350, 369n, 376, 403; properties of, 30, 304, 305, 307, 308, 309, 313, 374, 427
Working class, defined, 231. *See also* Blue-collar (manual) workers; White-collar workers
Work week, 102, 240
World's Fairs and Expositions, 116
World War II, 99, 107, 162–163, 359, 388
Worth, Charles Frederick, 384

Yang and *yin*, 183–184
Yarn, 33, 37, 40, 315, 317; characteristics of, 304, 306–307, 427. *See also* Fibers; Spinning
Youth: affluence of, 405–408; "antimaterialism" of, 86, 227; emphasis on, 80, 106, 205; values of, 91–92, 227–228, 445. *See also* Adolescents

Zeitgeist, 118, 162
Zipper(s), 22, 109, 358, 429

PICTURE CREDITS

Illustrations by Mulvey-Crump on the following pages: 17, 19, 25, 26, 30, 38, 43, 44, 45, 76, 78, 111, 114, 128, 152–153, 154, 189, 267, 268, 284, 285, 306, 307, 322, 323, 324, 325, 336, 337, 338.

Illustrations by Anco Technical Services on the following pages: 150, 151, 155, 250, 268, 269, 280, 305, 328 (top), 330 (center and bottom), 344, 345, 347, 350, 355, 379, 380 (Top: based on material originally appearing in Fortune Magazine; Fortune Art Department/Parrios Studios), 381, 400, 402, 404, 409.

Chapter 1

p. 8 (top left) Philip Jon Bailey; (center and right) Louise E. Jefferson; (bottom left) Cyril Maitland, Camera 5; (center and right) C. Zagourski, from the postcard series "L'Afrique que disparait," photo courtesy J. Bucquoi and the Museum of Modern Art. p. 9 (top, left to right) Courtesy the Gillette Company; Fred W. McDarrah; Dancer Fitzgerald Sample, Inc. (bottom) Carole McCole.

Chapter 2

p. 13 FAO Photo; p. 16 Courtesy of the American Museum of Natural History; p. 17 Hakim; p. 18 (left to right) Louise E. Jefferson; Irwin from Monkmeyer Press Photo Service; Frank Siteman; p. 19 National Museet, Copenhagen; p. 21 Alison Frantz; p. 23 (left to right) *Paris Match/Picherie*; Wide World; p. 26 Wide World; p. 27 Wide World.

Chapter 3

p. 31 Margaret M. Wheat, from *Survival Arts of the Primitive Paiutes*, © 1967 by University of Nevada Press; p. 32 (top) The Irish Linen Guild; (bottom) Courtesy of the American Museum of Natural History; p. 33 Margaret M. Wheat, from *Survival Arts of the Primitive Paiutes*, © 1967 by University of Nevada Press; p. 34 Fur Information and Fashion Guild; p. 35 (bottom) Smithsonian Institution; p. 36 Merrimack Valley Textile Museum; John Ross from Photo Researchers; Merrimack Valley Textile Museum; Merrimack Valley Textile Museum; Whitin Machine Works; p. 37 Merrimack Valley Textile Museum; Draper Division, Rockwell International; p. 40 George Hight, photograph courtesy of Museum of the American Indian, Heye Foundation; p. 41 Ilka Hartmann, Courtesy Jeroboam; p. 46 Japan Travel Bureau, Inc.; p. 47 (top) Japan Travel Bureau, Inc.; (bottom) Photo courtesy Central Office of Information, London; p. 48 (top, left to right) The Cleveland Museum of Art, Delia and L. E. Holden Funds; The Bettmann Archive, Inc.; (bottom) The Metropolitan Museum of Art, The Cloisters Collection, Gift of John D. Rockefeller Jr., 1937; p. 49 (left to right) The Metropolitan Museum of Art, Rogers Fund, 1904; The Metropolitan Museum of Art, The Bashford Dean Memorial Collection, Gift of Helen Fahnestock Hubbard, 1929, in memory of her father, Harris C. Fahnestock; p. 50 (top) Bob Hanson, courtesy the American Crafts Council, Museum of Contemporary Crafts, "Body Covering" Exhibit, 1968; (bottom) Monkmeyer Press Photo Service.

Chapter 4

p. 56 (left to right) Mauritius, Black Star; John Lanois, Black Star; p. 57 (left to right) Tom Hollyman, Photo Researchers; Greek National Tourist Office; Diane Rawson, Photo Researcher; p. 58 Reprinted by permission of Newspaper Enterprise Association; p. 60 (top) French Embassy Press, Collection Louise E. Jefferson; (bottom) FAO Photo; p. 61 (top left) Emil Schulthess, Black Star; (right) Marburg-Art Reference Bureau; (bottom) The Metropolitan Museum of Art; p. 62 (left to right) Elizabeth Wilcox; photo courtesy of Sony; p. 63 (top) Black Star; Photo Trends; (bottom) Copyright The Frick Collection, New York; p. 65 Wide World; p. 68 (left to right) COMPIX; Wide World; p. 70 (left to right) COMPIX; Owen Franken, Stock Boston.

Chapter 5

p. 76 COMPIX; p. 79 James Laver, *Taste and Fashion,* George C. Harrap and Co., London; p. 80 By permission of Mrs. John Held, Jr.; p. 86 (top) Daniel S. Brody, Stock Boston; (bottom) Reprinted by permission of Newspaper Enterprise Association; p. 87 Engleman in *The Christian Science Monitor,* © 1969. TCSPS; p. 88 COMPIX; p. 90 Wide World; p. 93 Bonnie Freer, Photo Trends.

Chapter 6

p. 102 James Laver, *Dress,* John Murray Ltd., London; p. 103 (all photos but lower right) Brown Brothers; (lower right) Russell and Sons, Wimbledon, from the collection of John Murray Ltd., London; p. 105 (top, left to right) Steve McCutcheon, Alaska Pictorial Service; Genzo Sugino, courtesy Tom Stack and Associates; (bottom) Georg Gerster, Rapho Guillumette Pictures; p. 107 J. C. Allen and Son; p. 108 (top to bottom) T. A. Rothschild, Stock Boston; Levi Strauss & Co.; Christopher W. Morrow, Stock Boston; p. 109 I.L.G.W.U.; p. 110 The Bettmann Archive, Inc.; p. 111 From the collection of John Murray Ltd., London; Lawrence Langner, *The Importance of Wearing Clothes,* Hastings House, New York, 1959; p. 112 Fred W. McDarrah; p. 114 James Laver, *Dress,* John Murray Ltd., London; p. 115 (left to right) Reproduced by permission of PUNCH; Fred W. McDarrah; Hakim; p. 116 Louise E. Jefferson; p. 117 (top) The Museum of Modern Art/Film Stills Library; (bottom) Hakim.

Chapter 7

p. 119 Frank Siteman; p. 121 Elizabeth Wilcox; p. 121 Rosemary Winckley for Alvin Ailey Dance Theater; p. 122 James Laver, *Costume Through the Ages,* Thames and Hudson, London, 1963; p. 123 Reprinted by permission of Newspaper Enterprise Association; p. 126 Wayne Miller, Magnum; p. 127 (left to right) Fred W. McDarrah; Hakim; Hakim; p. 132 (left to right) Fred W. McDarrah; Nestor from Monkmeyer Press Photo Service; Irene Bayer from Monkmeyer Press Photo Service; p. 141 Erwitt, Magnum.

Chapter 8

p. 147 (top) Wide World; (bottom) Wide World; p. 148 Photo Trends; p. 149 (left to right) T. Lowell, Black Star; Wide World; p. 152 Joe Covello, Black Star; p. 153 Joseph Farris, reprinted from Saturday

Review, January 9, 1971; p. 156 (top) Mimi Forsyth from Monkmeyer Press Photo Service; Tim Carlson, Stock Boston; Black Star; p. 158 (bottom) Jerry Keith; p. 159 (left to right) Fred W. McDarrah; Camera 5; p. 160 Reprinted by permission of Newspaper Enterprise Association; p. 162 (top to bottom) AGIP, Black Star; Wide World; p. 164 Reprinted by permission of Newspaper Enterprise Association; p. 167 (left to right) COMPIX; Wide World; Wide World; p. 168 (left to right) Fred W. McDarrah; Wide World; p. 173 John Ruge, reprinted from Saturday Review March 5, 1966; p. 176 Wide World; p. 177 COMPIX.

Chapter 9

p. 180 Reprinted by permission of Newspaper Enterprise Association; p. 181 (top) A. Devaney, Inc.; (bottom) Josef Muench; p. 187 PARIS MATCH; p. 188 (top) Central Office of Information, London; (bottom) Maxwell Coplan; p. 190 (top) Bill Samaras; (bottom) Paul Conklin, from Monkmeyer Press Photo Service; p. 191 Frank Siteman; p. 192 Michigan State University photo; p. 198 Fred W. McDarrah, sculpture by Dwane Hansen.

Chapter 10

p. 202 James Laver, *Seventeenth and Eighteenth Century Costume,* The Victoria and Albert Museum; p. 203 Reform-Moden-Album, 1904; p. 204 Optic Nerve, courtesy Jeroboam; Kellogg's; p. 205 (top to bottom) Anna Kaufman Moon, Stock Boston; Philip Bennett; Mimi Forsyth from Monkmeyer Press Photo Service; p. 206 from *Body and Clothes* by R. Broby-Johansen. © 1968 by Litton Educational Publishing, Inc. Reprinted by permission of Van Nostrand Reinhold Company; p. 207 Japan Air Lines; p. 208 Frank Siteman; p. 209 (top to bottom) Frank Siteman; Frank Siteman; Margie Spence photo from *Horseman* Magazine; p. 213 Joe Clark; p. 214 Copyright Los Angeles Times. Reprinted with permission; p. 215 Frank Siteman; p. 221 COMPIX.

Chapter 11

p. 227 Roger Lubin, Jeroboam; p. 229 (top) COMPIX; (bottom) Courtesy Saks Fifth Avenue; p. 232 Courtesy of Sony; p. 238 David S. Strickler from Monkmeyer Press Photo Service.

Chapter 12

p. 243 Charles Moore, Black Star; p. 245 (top) From "Eye Movements and Visual Perception" by David Noton and Lawrence Stark Copyright © 1967 by Scientific American Inc. All rights reserved; (bottom) Victor Perard, Anatomy and Drawing, Pitman Publishing Corporation; p. 246 (top, left to right) Rosenborg Palace, Copenhagen; Collection Blanche Payne; Elvin Powell; (bottom) National Portrait Gallery, London; Courtesy National Cotton Council of America; Marburg-Art Reference Bureau; p. 247 (top) Museum of Fine Arts, Boston, Gift of Mrs. Robert Homans; (bottom) The Prado, Madrid; p. 248 (left) Reprinted from *Vogue,* © 1966 by the Condé Nast Publications, Inc. (right, top) Victor Perard, Anatomy and Drawing, Pitman Publishing Corporation; (bottom) The Louvre, Paris; p. 250 Museum of Fine Arts, Boston, The Elizabeth Day McCormich Collection; p. 251 (top) Hakim; (bottom) The Louvre, Paris; p. 252 (top) Munsell Color; p. 253 Munsell Color;

p. 255 Museum of Fine Arts, Boston, The Elizabeth Day McCormick Collection; p. 260 (top) R. T. Kahn; (bottom) COMPIX; p 261 Peter Borsari, Camera 5; p. 262 (top and bottom) Hakim; Color plates: Munsell Color.

Chapter 13

p. 266 (top) E. J. Beitler and B. Lockhart, *Design for You*, John Wiley and Sons, Inc., New York; (bottom) Maitland Graves; p. 270 Frank Brothers, Fenn-Feinstein for *Gentlemen's Quarterly*; p. 273 From the book *Costumes and Styles* by Henny Harald Hansen. Copyright © 1956 by E. P. Dutton and Co., Inc., publishers, and used with their permission; p. 274 Reproduced by courtesy of the Trustees, The National Gallery, London.

Chapter 14

p. 283 The Louvre, Paris; p. 284 (top) Collection Marilyn Horn; (bottom) French Government Tourist Office; p. 285 Kunsthistorisches Museum, Vienna; p. 286 (top) The Victoria and Albert Museum; The Bettmann Archive, Inc.; (center) James Laver, *Costume Through the Ages*, Thames & Hudson, London; James Laver, *Taste and Fashion*; George G. Harrap, London; (bottom) The Metropolitan Museum of Art, Harris Brisbane Dick Fund, 1949; From the book *Costumes and Styles* by Henny Harald Hansen. Copyright © 1956 by E. P. Dutton & Co., Inc., Publishers, and used with their permission; p. 287 (top) James Laver, *Dress*, John Murray Ltd., London; Musee des Arts Decoratif, Paris; (bottom, left to right) James Laver; New York Daily News photo; Le Corbusier (Charles-Edouard Jenneret), Armchair with Adjustable Back, 1929, The Museum of Modern Art, New York, gift of Thonet Industries, Inc.; p. 288 Geoffrey Clements from the collection of Mr. and Mrs. Victor W. Ganz; p. 289 Patricia Hollander Gross, Stock Boston; p. 290 *Tass* from Sovfoto; p. 291 (top to bottom) Michael Abramson, Black Star; Hakim.

Chapter 15

p. 295 T. D. Lovering, Stock Boston; p. 301 (top) Reprinted from Motor-land by courtesy of the California State Automobile Association, copyright owner; p. 302 Dave Hirsch, Reprinted with permission from *The Saturday Evening Post* © 1960 The Curtis Publishing Company; p. 3–9 Vincent Maggiora, Reprinted by permission of the San Francisco Chronicle; p. 312 Clem Albers, reprinted by permission of the San Francisco Chronicle; p. 313 Greg Peterson, reprinted by permission of the San Francisco Chronicle; p. 314 (a) COMPIX; (b) NASA; (c) U.S. Army photograph; (d) Louis L. Okmin; (e) Reprinted from Motorland by courtesy of the California Automobile Association, copyright owner; (f) National Coal Association; p. 316 (left to right) Gemini News Service; Photo courtesy Vocational Guidance and Rehabilitation Services.

Chapter 16

p. 320 (top) Photo Trends, Museu de Arte de São Paulo; Copyright A.C.L. Bruxelles; (bottom left to right) Prähistorische Abteilung, Naturhistor-isches Museum, Vienna; Fogg Art Museum; Staatsbibliothek Bildarchiv, Berlin; p. 327 From the film "The Incredible Shrinking Man" courtesy Universal Pictures; p. 335 Carmichael © 1964 *Los Angeles Times*.

Chapter 17

p. 341 Patricia Hollander Gross, Stock Boston; p. 348 American Textile Manufacturers Institute Inc.; p. 349 American Textile Manufacturers Institute Inc.; p. 350 Graphs reprinted with the permission of the American Textile Manufacturers Institute Inc.; p. 355; p. 356 Photo courtesy Hughes Aircraft Co. Industrial Products Division; p. 358 (top) I.L.G.W.U.; (bottom) Courtesy of YKK Zipper Inc. Photograph by Streisand, Zuch and Freedman Advertising, New York; p. 362 Courtesy Filene's; p. 363 Philip Jon Bailey; p. 365 Patricia Hollander Gross, Stock Boston; p. 366 Lawrence S. Williams Inc., photo courtesy Armstrong Cork Co.; p. 369 J. C. Penney; p. 372 Textile Distributors Association.

Chapter 18

p. 375 (top) Bruce Anspach/EPA Newsphoto; (bottom) Steve Ettlinger; p. 382 Chuck Rogers, Black Star; p. 386 Claus Ohm; p. 389 Dave Randolph, reprinted by permission of the San Francisco Chronicle; p. 391 PANA, Black Star.

Chapter 19

p. 400 Data from US Council of Economic Advisers, courtesy US Bureau of Census; p. 409 Data courtesy US Census Projection.

Chapter 20

p. 419 Ellis Herwig, Stock Boston; p. 433 Apparel Manufacturers Association, Inc.